ELITES

in the PEOPLE'S

REPUBLIC

of CHINA

Washington Paperbacks on Russia and Asia   W PRA-11

ed with an Introduction by

ROBERT A. SCALAPINO

$4.95

Elites in the People's Republic of China

Studies in
Chinese Government and Politics

1. CHINESE COMMUNIST POLITICS IN ACTION
Edited by A. Doak Barnett

2. CHINA: MANAGEMENT OF A REVOLUTIONARY SOCIETY
Edited by John M. H. Lindbeck

3. ELITES IN THE PEOPLE'S REPUBLIC OF CHINA
Edited by Robert A. Scalapino

Sponsored by the Subcommittee on
Chinese Government and Politics
of the Joint Committee
on Contemporary China of the
American Council of Learned Societies
and the Social Science Research Council

Elites in the People's Republic of China

EDITED BY ROBERT A. SCALAPINO

~P 21

CONTRIBUTORS

GORDON A. BENNETT

WILLIAM W. WHITSON

DEREK J. WALLER

JUNE DREYER

ROBERT A. SCALAPINO

SIDNEY LEONARD GREENBLATT

THOMAS W. ROBINSON

PARRIS H. CHANG

VICTOR C. FALKENHEIM

RICHARD BAUM

HEATH B. CHAMBERLAIN

RONALD N. MONTAPERTO

LYNN T. WHITE III

DONALD W. KLEIN

UNIVERSITY OF WASHINGTON PRESS
SEATTLE & LONDON

Library of Congress Cataloging in Publication Data
Main entry under title:

Elites in the People's Republic of China.

   (Studies in Chinese government and politics, 3)
   Includes bibliographical references.
   1. China (People's Republic of China, 1949–   )
—Politics and government—Addresses, essays, lectures.
2. Elite (Social services)—Addresses, essays, lectures.
I. Scalapino, Robert A., ed. II. Bennett, Gordon A.
III. Series.
DS777.55.E44   320.9'51'04   72-3734
ISBN 0-295-95230-X

ROBERT A SCALAPINO

Introduction

The disciplines involved in the study of politics have long wrestled with two seemingly antithetical concepts: *the political system,* with its strong implications of symmetry, an organic structure, and permanence, versus *conflict,* with its ingredients of irregularity, dysfunctionalism, and impermanence. As yet, no model or theory has fully met the challenge of interrelating these two concepts in a manner that is at once precise and dynamic, susceptible both to measurement and to constant readjustment, hence to prediction. Even those general theories advanced recently which define the political system as interrelated sets of stimuli and responses, with inputs and outputs made dynamic by means of the feedback mechanism, remain essentially organistic, rational models, troubled by the distortions to which such models are susceptible.

There is no intention to claim that elite studies can accomplish what has thus far been denied to general theory. To study elites—more precisely, political elites—is to cut into the political system from a particular vantage point, taking merely one element of that system, or if one prefers, one element of the struggle to secure and hold political power. Like all "partial" studies, elite studies are subject to abuse, especially if they are undertaken in isolation from the total environment which surrounds the political actors. It does not follow, however, that meaningful theory—even general theory—can flow only from studies of a total system. In any case, in political science we require much more middle-level theory and hypotheses of intermediate scope at this point if we are to make further progress. Attention cannot be focused singularly upon the cosmic scene. The most relevant questions are: Do elite studies provide us with opportunities to advance middle-level theory? Do they offer the potentiality for amending certain conceptual frameworks of the past and structuring new ones?

Certainly, such studies have one potential advantage. They force a concentration upon the essence of the political process. Despite all of the emendations of recent decades, we continue to define the study of politics essentially as the study of power: its acquisition and loss; its allocation and interconnections; the manner in which it is exercised, including the institutions, formal and informal, through which it is channeled; its goals and the value structure that underlies these goals; and its results in terms of the policies, programs, and attitudes that flow from its application.

Elite studies are concerned with those who manipulate power, whether at some level within the political system or within another branch of society. An elite may be defined broadly as a group within the society differentiated from others on the basis of the authority which it commands, hence, the power which it can wield. An elite is a collectivity, not an individual; moreover, it is a collectivity having a separate identity, internal structure, and elevated status based upon its special role in the decision-making and enforcing process. Elites, however, are not confined to the dominant, controlling institutions: they encompass every organized aspect of a society, including those portions denominated "revolutionary" or "counterculture." Indeed, in the particular collection of studies presented here, we are dealing primarily with men who were "subversives" struggling, as a part of the Communist elite, against the government in power throughout the greater part of their lives.

These general definitions, however, provide little guidance in meeting some of the more intricate yet crucial problems involved in elite analysis. We may commence with questions relating to the recruitment of elites, questions that possibly present the fewest difficulties, but even here a considerable amount of new conceptualization is required. For example, old socioeconomic categories of elite identification are inadequate, and past methods of typologizing career patterns are relatively primitive. If we are concerned about the degree to which elite changes occur at certain points in the development of a given unit, previous descriptions and categories relating to class and status, education, and life experience should be thoroughly re-examined.

And there are more basic issues to be raised. In the case of the Chinese People's Republic (CPR), we are dealing with a relatively complex recruitment process, contrary to first impressions. Despite the formal electoral process, the political elite are recruited from above with few exceptions, the exceptions being generally at the lowest levels. In the recruitment, the organization bureaus of the Party at various levels normally play a key role, although insights into the precise method of operations are still scanty. In recent times, however, the process has been complicated by the apparent need to balance separate, partially competitive organizations and groups. The effort to form "three-way alliances" among the military, Party, and "mass representatives" in establishing the revolutionary committees, and the effort to represent both major occupational and generational groups in the reconstructed Party constitute evidence of this fact. The length of time consumed in the latter process, moreover, together with recurrent evidences of political instability, suggest the difficulties involved.

Indeed, the recruitment process, studied carefully, reveals that this particular Communist system has had, and will probably continue to have, complicated center-regional relations, in a manner dissimilar to many other Communist states. At the center itself, however, questions familiar to students of communism are in order. For example, has Mao Tse-tung recently had absolute power over Politburo selection, in the sense of being able to intervene successfully in any case, whether in support or in opposition? And even if this is theoretically true, are there any significant practical constraints upon such intervention from case to case?

Whatever the answers to these and similar questions (presumably no answers are wholly valid without relation to time), recruitment in the CPR has clearly involved ascriptive elements as well as efforts at measuring and rewarding loyalty, seniority, ability, and training. Familial ties, both formal and informal, have played a not insignificant role in recruitment, in part because they bear a relationship to loyalty, which is a highly critical consideration at this stage in the evolution of the Party and state. In a broader sense, moreover, the emergence of certain status groups (such as the Long March veterans) connected with the earlier history of the Communist movement and the preferential treatment given certain classes constitute additional examples of ascriptive principles in operation.

The task of combining these principles with tests of loyalty, doctrinal orthodoxy, experience, and job performance has proven to be a formidable one thus far, and the relative weight to be given to each of these criteria has been a subject of much concern. Various patterns have emerged, and some of the essays in this volume represent pioneer efforts to discern and analyze them.

The dependence of recruitment upon availability raises additional issues of interest and importance. Apart from the ascriptive principles noted above, are there other factors affecting the pool from which the various elites are drawn? Confining our discussion essentially to the political and military elites, the rewards of such status in the CPR have generally been sufficient to induce intensive competition for positions. Even at the lower echelons, the prestige and power of the cadre are substantial under "normal" circumstances. Having made this generalization, however, we are compelled to examine the contradictory evidence. The punishments involved in being a member of the political-military elite can also be substantial, providing a recurrent problem for the Party and the State. The political elite of this society are not only expected to outperform "ordinary citizens," but must work under stern injunctions from above and thus under conditions of more or less continuous tension. Recurrent criticism, including self-criticism, has been built into the system. Periodically, moreover, when "rectification campaigns" sweep the Party, careers are abruptly terminated and many figures are subject to fierce condemnation. In recent years, a number of veteran Party cadres have been "rehabilitated" after having been attacked and removed from office previously. At least an equal number, however, remain in oblivion, including men formerly of the highest status and others of relatively lowly positions.

Thus, at times the risks of elite status may appear to outweigh the benefits. After the Great Leap Forward fiasco, when local and provincial cadres were being rigorously criticized for diverse acts of "commandism" (exhibiting authoritarian tendencies) and "tailism" (following the masses "blindly"), it was not uncommon to hear the abused officials lament that being a Party cadre was the most unhappy and unprofitable experience one could endure. For a time at least, the balance of rewards and punishments was so tilted that recruitment in some locales was rendered quite difficult. However, we are dealing here with a dynamic situation; the intensity of risk, the extent of punishment and strain go up and down, depending upon shifts in the overall environment. There is no evidence that recruitment is permanently or uniformly depressed by those negative elements which rise from time to time, and are always present in considerable degree.

Elite availability is not the only factor influenced by the reward-punishment pattern. Elite circulation is also affected. But many other conditions have influenced circulation: the historical evolution of the Chinese Communist movement, and the generational divisions that have come out of this evolution; the dramatic expansion in the depth and scope of Party responsibility that followed victory in the civil war, an expansion now slowing even as new generations come forward; the pace of economic development, and the correlative elite requirements. Some data and interpretations are provided on these issues in the essays that follow.

In general, a combination of factors has made possible—indeed, demanded—a fairly intense circulation of political and military elites at all levels. On the other hand, once again we must accommodate major exceptions to this general rule. The relative stability of the top Communist political and military leadership at all levels, including military regions, provinces, and localities, was a supremely important fact for a protracted period after the early 1950's. Indeed, many students of the CCP regarded that Party as one of the most stable in the world. It was not until later, when serious trouble erupted at the center, that the adverse implications of regional stability came to be realized: the existence of potentially threatening regional power centers and closely knit personal coteries, strongly integrated and highly resistant to external penetration.

Thus, careful analyses of elite circulation, as well as elite composition, in the CPR at various levels are essential to establishing a more accurate picture of the allocation of power in this society, under this system, at this time. Such a picture, in turn, will enable us to compare and contrast the CPR with other Communist and/or "emerging" states, thereby working toward certain general theories of elite recruitment, circulation, and structure under varying political conditions.

The latter concern, namely, the character of the elite structure, must be given a high priority if we are to probe more deeply the basic nature of the current Chinese political system. Two different sets of problems present themselves. First, there are the issues pertaining to the internal structure of a given elite, for example, the Party elite. How steep is the hierarchical pattern, or conversely, how egalitarian are the relationships from one level within the Party to the next? What are the channels of communication, and how widely are they available, or conversely, how narrowly are they controlled? Many of the essays present some very interesting data on these matters. Despite some surface evidence of a highly egalitarian structure (the abolition of ranks within the PLA, for example, and the humbling of senior cadres at the hands of Red Guard youth at the climax of the Cultural Revolution), the overall pattern appears to be one of a steeply graded hierarchy, with intraline communications limited, especially between the center and the provincial and local levels. Few of the Red Guard leaders at local levels knew anything about the power struggle at the center, and as several of our papers show, even provincial leaders suffered from not knowing how to interpret the instructions that came during periods of crisis, possibly because in the Great Proletarian Cultural Revolution (GPCR) era, top leadership itself was frequently divided and imprecise. It must be emphasized, of course, that this era was "abnormal." Yet a steeply graded hierarchy and constricted communications appear to exist under "normal" conditions as well.

We must also be concerned about relations among elites. For example, there is the central issue of military-civil relations, and in addition, the question of the roles of intellectuals, technicians, and other elites operating within the system. On this general subject, we are greatly hampered by a paucity of hard data and also the problem of establishing appropriate and distinctive categories. Naturally, the Chinese military man today is highly politicized and cannot be equated—at least automatically—with his counterpart in non-Communist "emerging" societies. There are distinctions, however, among Communist military men. Some have long been extremely active in political affairs, occupying high posts within the Party, including the Politburo. Others, while being Party men and continuously involved in "political training," have spent their careers primarily as professional soldiers, and only entered high Party service at some point of crisis, such as the GPCR, if at all. Surely it is important in the evolution of Party and state which type of military men gains general political and/or military predominance. The Communists themselves have long been aware of the issue, and once again, in the aftermath of the Cultural Revolution, it has emerged as a major issue. Does the Party control the gun, or the gun, the Party?

An equally fascinating issue relates to the role, or roles, of the intellectual in the Party and state. Once again, the issue of definitions is a critical one. If we define as "intellectuals" the individuals who have had a higher education, we are discussing a wide range of types: literati, scientists, teachers, artists, and professional men, among others. In general terms, the intellectual has fared badly; perhaps he has even suffered a greater deterioration as a class than almost any other group. Socialist realism has made true creativity in the arts difficult, if not impossible. In many branches of higher learning, intellectualism is neither permitted nor desired at present, at least as that term would be understood in open societies. In the ideological realm particularly, creativity in the presence of Mao could only be regarded as lese majesty.

Once again, however, one must take into account contradictory or paradoxical features of the system. Clearly, the Party needs a scientific-technological elite, and this elite has generally been rewarded amply for its services. Moreover, for those artists who throw themselves into the tasks of socialist realism—which in one of its forms can be found in the New Peking Opera—the rewards can also be substantial. The CPR talks incessantly about creating a new intelligentsia, drawn from the "proletariat" and "peasant" classes, shorn of "bourgeois" individualism and a "feudal" superiority complex. The nature of the new intelligentsia, its relation to the "old" intellectuals, and the changing role of the intellectuals as a class provide subjects for substantial research in the future. Such concerns, moreover, lead to broader issues: will "generalists" continue to dominate the political decision-making process in Party and state after the first-generation revolutionary leadership has faded from the scene, or will we witness the advent of some of these "new" intellectuals at the top in the form of technicians and scientists? Has intellectualism itself become passé or moribund in certain fields (the ideological realm, for example) and dynamic in others (science, technology, administration)?

Recruitment, circulation, and role-playing are thus aspects of elite studies that can shed light upon the most fundamental issues involving a given political culture. Mention should also be made of elite socialization, because for the Chinese Communists this has been a vital and continuing program. Entry into elite status represents to the "good" Communist the beginning, not the end, of an educational-socialization process. The cadre, junior or senior, is expected to engage in a work-study program throughout his life. He is supposed to re-examine constantly his actions and experiences, his relations to the Party and to the masses, and reflect upon his own attitudes and those of comrades working above and below him.

Out of such reflection and "self-criticism" is to come the New Socialist Man, or in this case, the New Socialist Official. Rhetoric aside, the social scientist/observer faces the difficult task of relating these efforts to actual elitist behavior, elite-mass relations, and to the more concrete, specific questions of how decisions are made and then how they are executed. The field of comparative administration will be greatly enriched when we can speak with assurance upon some of these matters, discerning the various psychological, ideological, political, and organizational ingredients that go into the actual decision-making and enforcing process in a state like the Chinese People's Republic.

Finally, we come to the most complex problem of all, namely, the correlation, if any, between given elites on the one hand and given policies, values, and political styles on the other. Let us assume that one can demonstrate conclusively that with the advent of Communist rule in China, primary power gravitated into the hands of men who can be characterized broadly as coming from the middle peasant, upper peasant, and urban lower-middle classes, from the interior of South-Central China, and frequently from rural areas adjacent to urban regions; that they were men who had modest to fairly good educations, being petty-intellectuals possessing few sustained contacts with China's historic centers of advanced learning; and finally, that they were men of limited acquaintanceship with the external world, albeit men who stood as self-proclaimed adherents of a cosmopolitan ideology, Marxism-Leninism. Can we draw any conclusions from such data with respect to policies, values, and style?

Initially, to be sure, this elite appeared to accept the Soviet model of modernization, with its strong emphasis upon heavy industrial priorities and urbanization. Nor has that emphasis been totally abandoned. Nevertheless, the great struggle that commenced in the mid-1950's over modernization techniques reflected in some measure the background and values of many of the key political actors on the Chinese scene. Like their Japanese counterparts of the Meiji era, the first-generation Chinese Communist leaders of the post-1949 era were drawn toward an indigenous modernization program that placed the agrarian sector in a role of critical importance. A Po I-po or even a Liu Shao-ch'i may have opposed critical aspects of the sinicization campaign—although the evidence on this score is far from conclusive. In any case, the major trends reflect group value judgments as well as group performance estimates, and hence they pertain directly to the dominant subcultural traits of the governing elite.

Naturally, we are on safer ground if we speak of proclivities rather than to insist upon a rigid deterministic approach in relating the dominant subcultural traits of the elite to the complex of policies and values that have ensued, or the characteristic political styles employed. An important relationship, however, can be established, and one current challenge is to seek greater precision in identifying the precise connections.

In the main, we have been speaking of the macropolitical scene thus far. Yet many of the studies in this volume deal with microlevel groups, and in at least one case, a group outside the strictly political sphere. It is entirely possible that some of our most useful future theory will evolve from studies at this level. Microstudies can take into account more detailed variables, relating to such aspects as career patterns, interelite relations, responses to crisis situations, or decision-making processes. At this level, moreover, it is easier to discern the true complexities, the elements of cooperation, conflict, and coexistence of plural elites. However clear may be the organizational and jurisdictional boundaries on paper, the Party and state in the CPR are plagued with extensive duplication and conflict of authority, quite apart from whatever ideological, policy, or personal differences may exist among and within elites. Studies at this level will help dispel the lingering myth of complete monolithism still strongly associated with studies of Communist societies.

Ultimately, the greatest benefit is likely to be derived from comparative elite studies, rather than from in-depth studies of a single unit, although we should not deprecate the potential contribution of this type of work. Comparative studies, however, can come in a variety of forms: linkage studies which center upon a given complex of units within a single basic system; parallel studies whereby the same type of unit is studied in multiple systems, or even within a given system; time studies in which the same unit is studied over time; and systemic studies in which the full range of elites within comparable systems is examined. To the extent that the studies included in this volume are comparative in nature, they are generally of the first, second, and third types; we are scarcely ready to undertake the elaborate study involved in our fourth category.

An introduction is a place to suggest the primary issues and signal the basic problems, not to discourse at length upon the conclusions of our various authors. It might not be amiss, however, to call attention briefly to the central thrust of each study and its interrelation with other essays in this volume. I do not find it necessary, incidentally, to assert that every research piece included herein is closely integrated with all others. Each of the studies deals with the central subject of Chinese elites under communism, although the opening and closing essays serve special purposes. It will be seen, moreover, that we have grouped those studies together which most closely complement each other, so that the data and analyses can be used and compared conveniently.

In the opening essay, Gordon A. Bennett sets forth both the broad trends and the unsolved problems in connection with elite studies. He asserts that the new direction of such studies is and should be toward using elite data instrumentally, to shed light on various political outcomes. Our ultimate quest, according to Bennett, ought to be to determine what difference a given elite makes in terms of policies and values. He then proceeds to suggest the key definitions, categories of analysis, and conceptual framework that might be conducive to this crucial task. Thus, his work serves as a valuable introduction to the substantive contributions which follow, a thoughtful analysis of the "state of the art" which should provoke further consideration of both the conceptualization and the methodology required to advance elite studies.

The section that follows includes three essays dealing with the Chinese Communist political elite at the national level. The first two essays, those by Derek J. Waller and the editor, are studies of the national Party elite over time. Waller takes as his two primary reference points the Kiangsi Soviet era (1930–34), when the Party was first establishing itself as a guerrilla movement operating from a base in South-Central China, and the period of the Eighth National Congress, September, 1956, when the Eighth Central Committee was elected in the midst of the high tide of optimism that followed seven years of Mainland rule. A central conclusion drawn by the author is that during this lengthy period of approximately one-quarter of a century, one dominant characteristic of top Chinese Communist Party (CCP) leadership was its essential continuity. And among the various reasons for this trend, in Waller's view, one factor stands out: the existence of a solid phalanx of revolutionary veterans, mostly recruited in the 1920's and gradually welded into a unified group, who blocked the upward mobility of later Communist generations into the topmost Party positions in the opening years of Communist rule.

The editor's study concentrates upon the era immediately thereafter, the period between the 1956 Eighth Party Congress and the Ninth Party Congress of 1969. As is well known, this extraordinary period of thirteen years was marked by recurrent crisis and conflict within the Party. The author initially sets forth certain new or refined definitions, categories, and methods of measurement in an effort to sharpen distinctions and similarities among the political-military elite and to delineate significant trends. As might be expected, he finds important changes within the top elite between 1956 and 1969, not merely in terms of specific individuals but also in terms of general types. In the Ninth Central Committee as fashioned in the spring of 1969, the trend was toward greater heterogeneity, whether with respect to socioeconomic backgrounds, generation, or career patterns. The transition away from the first-generation revolutionary leaders of the past was now underway. In its initial stages, one pronounced trend was the emergence in greater force of the veteran peasant-soldier, coming out of a rural or quasirural background, and not infrequently having had lengthy experience in one or several regions rather than having been always attached to the center. This, together with other, equally important trends, suggests that whatever the subsequent stages of top elite formation, political stability in the Chinese People's Republic may hinge in the immediate future principally upon two critical factors: the character of center-regional relations and the unity of the military.

Thomas W. Robinson completes this section by presenting us with a timely, thoroughly researched study of Lin Piao, one of the central yet enigmatic figures among the top political-military elite. Lin, once heir-apparent and now in eclipse, had a career pattern not differing significantly from the aggregate pattern of others in his bracket; but, as the author makes clear, his was also a life closely interwoven at all points with the life—and hence the moods—of Mao Tse-tung. In political style, moreover, Lin differed considerably from his peers; while health and personality combined to make him one of the least visible individuals among the top hierarchy, in addition the man totally lacked charisma, at least as that term is currently used. Nor did his individual development, in terms of ideological commitment and policies, necessarily accord with the Party's development. It is yet too early to be certain of the mix and relative weight of the factors involved in Lin's demise, but this study suggests both the strengths and the vulnerabilities of a man who nearly reached the top, as well as pointing to the relation between that man and his times.

We turn next to a series of studies of subnational elites, beginning with Victor C. Falkenheim's analysis of Fukien provincial leadership during the period from Communist victory through the Cultural Revolution. In it, we are given a fascinating insight into the problems of integrating Communist leaders drawn from decidedly different career patterns and also of sharing the available elite between province and center in a period when administrative/political responsibilities were so drastically expanding. Despite the challenges, a basic stability prevailed in Fukien up to the Cultural Revolution which, as Falkenheim's research makes clear, struck Fukien hard, as it did almost every province. Perhaps its basic impact was to break the dominance within the province of the old native guerrilla leaders, bringing "outsiders" to the fore. It is the author's view, moreover, that although regional leaders in the aftermath of the GPCR can and do adjust the timing and substance of central policy within narrow limits, they possess no truly autonomous power. While often caught in a cross fire of pressures, they cannot use these countervailing pressures to create any meaningful measure of independence, primarily because the controlling pressures are from the top.

The following studies by Heath B. Chamberlain and Lynn T. White III complement the work of Falkenheim very well. Chamberlain's research deals with political leadership and organization in three important urban centers (Tientsin, Shanghai, and Canton) in the years immediately following Communist victory in the Civil War. He is interested in relating initial developments in several major metropolitan areas to basic Communist concerns both in the ideological and political fields. For the Communists, "integration" involved unity *and* struggle: it represented an aspect of the omnipresent contradictions involving political society, and hence was reflected in a dialectical, unending process. In the period immediately after 1949, as Chamberlain indicates, the Communists had to concentrate upon the problems of transition and, notably, upon how the region was to be related to the center, a problem that has always confronted Chinese rulers. The author indicates the methods used in tackling this problem, the functions and interrelations among the various elements of the local elite, and the linkage established between municipality and higher levels. In so doing, he develops some highly useful leadership typologies and analytic concepts.

White's research deals with the leaders of a single municipality, Shanghai, for the period from 1956 to 1969, the crucial thirteen years between the Eighth and Ninth Party Congresses. He sheds extensive light upon the complex nature of intraelite conflict at the local level during this period. Shanghai, as White illustrates, had a wide range of disputes between and among its political elite, even in periods of relative tranquillity. Some of these disputes engulfed the entire political leadership; others were confined to various individuals or functional units. The causes of intraelite conflict were equally diverse, ranging from issues of personality conflict and power rivalry to basic differences over substantive policies. Often the latter differences were exacerbated or even initiated by policy shifts at the center, indicating once again the crucial and constantly shifting relation between center and region.

The next three essays deal with special elites within the Chinese People's Republic, elites having functions of great importance to the Party and government. William W. Whitson focuses upon the military elite and, more precisely, upon the relation between the major groupings within the People's Liberation Army and various organizational interests, values, attitudes, and goals. Building upon his earlier work, Whitson outlines those informal and formal groups within the PLA, starting with the diverse "military generations" which could be expected to produce different viewpoints concerning critical questions of military tactics and strategy. To this he adds the key administrative-geographic units into which the Communist military were divided in recent decades, seeking to probe the relative importance of local versus national considerations. Finally, he analyzes the various career channels through which military men might pass, seeking to assess the impact that various functions and branch affiliations might have upon an individual's priorities of tactics and strategy. The author's conclusions are that Chinese strategic doctrine is likely to shift continuously during the 1970's, but that it will remain multiple in purpose: concerned with attaining greater security against sophisticated external opponents, continuing aid to "liberation" movements, and providing internal security in an era when recurrent domestic threats are possible.

June Dreyer directs our attention to the highly sensitive area of the elites involved in minority work, where both Han Chinese leaders and leaders from the minorities themselves have played important roles in the Party or governmental structure. She is concerned with the full range of problems that have confronted the Chinese Communists in connection with minorities: reliance upon traditional elites from the minority community; elite recruitment methods; career patterns of Han Chinese specializing in minority work; the mix of Han and non-Han leaders in this field; relations between coopted minority

leaders and their own people; the results of various Communist programs, particularly as they relate to loyalty patterns; and the impact of such upheavals as the GPCR. Among the conclusions to which
her data lead her is the thesis that the Cultural Revolution, though
falling short of its intended goals, was a major milestone in the elimination of the power and cohesiveness of minority elites as especially
designated spokesmen for their people, and the further integration of
minorities into Han-Chinese Communist society.

Sidney Leonard Greenblatt has selected the intellectual elite, specifically, the faculty of Peking University, as a case study in organizational structure and behavior in a Communist setting. Drawing upon
the earlier work of Etzioni and Skinner, he seeks to advance middle-
range theory in this vitally important area. He uses such dimensions
as recruitment, forms of socialization, role styles, and locations of
charisma to seek an answer to such strategic questions as who has
access to what powers in which locations of the organizational structure, in which stages of the organization's life, and over whom. The
authority structure of the Peita faculty becomes the focal point of
this significant piece of research.

We turn next to three studies of elites under conditions of strain
and crisis. Parris H. Chang provides an analysis of the responses of
provincial Party leaders to the Cultural Revolution, a political movement that seriously threatened them. His is a fascinating study of the
intricate defense mechanisms utilized by skilled, veteran politicians in
an effort—generally futile in the end—to protect themselves. Here we
get an insight not only into the successive strategies adopted but also
into the manner in which the key provincial elite perceived events at
the center from one stage to another, and the nature of interelite communications in a highly fluid, extremely dangerous era.

Richard Baum's paper deals with the same basic issue, concentrating upon the period of the most intensive Red Guard assault upon the
official Party establishment, 1966–67. He advances the interesting
thesis that as this type of conflict is progressively diffused, those
actors who perceive themselves in imminent danger of defeat in what
is essentially a struggle for survival are compelled sequentially to
enlarge the scope of the conflict, in an effort to secure a more favorable
balance of forces. Thus, in the autumn of 1966, the Cultural Revolution conflict was purposely enlarged to encompass sizable portions of
the rural areas in China, and the resulting rural turmoil was brought
under control only after a series of palliative measures *and* the inter-

vention of the regular military forces. Baum also surveys in a most interesting fashion the legacy of bitter antagonism, cadre wariness of assuming responsibility, and institutional decay that collectively served as complications in the re-establishment of authority in general, and the Party specifically, in the aftermath of the GPCR upheaval. He concludes that among the "power-holders," self-interest remained an extremely formidable consideration in elitist behavior during this entire era, Maoist injunctions to give priority to the public interest notwithstanding.

Ronald N. Montaperto adds to the picture of elitist behavior under stress by presenting us with a revealing account of a single student leader's perceptions of events during the early period of the Cultural Revolution, and his responses to these events. His respondent had access to the type of information generally available to local-level Party leaders—which was relatively limited in character. As the author indicates, the decisive element injected into the political situation by the center affecting political attitudes and behavior at the local level was a changed perception of the Communist Party itself. By the time of the first Red Guard rally in Peking in mid-August, 1966, the Party was seen not as an institution epitomizing supreme, unchallengeable authority and permanent values, but as a collection of personalities engaged in a particular style of action and as an association in conflict, indeed, in mortal danger of losing its soul. Thus, one could attack local Party units and still proclaim oneself fully loyal to the Party. Nevertheless, the student participants in the Cultural Revolution never lost sight of personal concerns, including the potential benefits and dangers of involvement. Thus, political idealism and self-serving ambition were joined in fashioning the character of student participation in this major political event.

This volume concludes with a critical analysis of the sources for elite studies by Donald W. Klein, a scholar who has contributed mightily to making available for all of us essential biographical materials on Chinese Communist elites. Klein's essay provides not only a valuable guide to the existing source materials, but also indicates the methods of classification that can and should be employed to make the available data more meaningful. In addition, he suggests some of the pitfalls in using biographic materials uncritically and without an awareness of certain built-in biases and deficiencies. Finally, he provides us with specific information on the relative wealth or paucity of data on the most critical hierarchies or elite groups within contemporary Chinese society, including the governmental, Party, intellectual, and military communities.

This volume would not have been possible without the support of the Joint Committee on Contemporary China of the Social Science Research Council and the American Council of Learned Societies. Each of us owes a special debt of gratitude to Bryce Wood as the individual at the Social Science Research Council whose long-sustained interest in modern Chinese studies was of such benefit to the entire field. We are also indebted to the late John M. H. Lindbeck who headed the joint committee for many years and devoted himself selflessly to advancing the field of Chinese scholarship.

Contents

ABBREVIATIONS USED IN NOTES

CB	*Current Background*
CFJP	*Chieh-fang jih-pao* (Liberation Daily)
CKCN	*Chung-kuo ch'ing-nien* (Chinese Youth)
CKCNP	*Chung-kuo ch'ing-nien pao* (Chinese Youth News)
CQ	*The China Quarterly*
JMJP	*Jen-min jih-pao* (People's Daily)
JPRS	*Joint Publications Research Service*
NFJP	*Nan-fang jih-pao* (Southern Daily)
NCNA	New China News Agency
SCMM	*Selections from China Mainland Magazines*
SCMP	*Survey of the China Mainland Press*
TKP	*Ta kung pao* (Impartial Daily)
URI	Union Research Institute

PART I

On Elite Research

GORDON A. BENNETT

Elite and Society in China: A Summary of Research and Interpretation

Elite studies currently are experiencing a subtle shift in emphasis. The new direction is away from taking either elites or "the elite" as an object of analysis *per se*—in the tradition of Plato, Robert Michels, Vilfredo Pareto, C. Wright Mills, Harold Lasswell, Edward Shils, and William Kornhauser—toward using elite data instrumentally to shed light on various political "outcomes." At first glance such contemporary work as that of Seymour Martin Lipset, Carl Beck, Frederic Fleron, Frederick Frey, Robert A. Scalapino, and G. William Domhoff, which focuses upon specific national elites, would seem to deny the trend; careful inspection, however, will reveal that these studies tend rather to affirm it. The participants at the Conference on Theory and Method in Comparative Elite Analysis held at Columbia University in April, 1969, displayed an air of mild desperation about the present state of elite sociology.[1] Just as significantly, the Social Science Research Council's Committee on Comparative Politics did not see fit to include a study of elites and political development in their widely heralded series on political modernization. As illustrated by the wide diversity of research reported in this volume, the shift is readily apparent in the China field as well.

In 1970 the "elite" concept still remains uncomfortably imprecise,

[1] A transcript is available from Columbia University's Bureau of Applied Social Research, European Institute, or School of International Affairs, which jointly sponsored the conference.

a fact which contributes heavily to the widespread scholarly desertion of its sociology. But at the present stage of the quest for theoretical generalizations relating elites and societies (and this is the principal point I wish to argue here), the new wind might be favorable. Only one important condition need be met: the newly employed concepts must help pinpoint important political "outcomes" directly traceable to differences among elites. This development in turn should facilitate identification of various dimensions of the elite concept itself. Below I will borrow examples from existing monographic literature on China to illustrate concepts which I feel could fulfill this necessary condition.

Regarding scientific method, I prefer the deductive approach of skeptically matching alternative theoretical paradigms against available evidence. The inductive "building block" approach, despite its many strong points, provides no systematic way to identify gaps in existing knowledge. A decade ago Daniel Bell was acutely conscious of this very problem when he proposed: "Given all these problems and pitfalls, it would be a forward step in the social sciences if a group of Soviet experts were, at regular intervals, to make predictions, at different levels, of probable Soviet developments and state the reasons for their inference. . . . By systematic review of the predictions, the successes and failures, one could probably obtain a more viable operational model of Soviet behavior."[2] To readers who object that by working deductively I am stubbornly slighting well-known data limitations in China studies, I hasten to emphasize that the scientific value of continually comparing bold hypotheses with sketchy, incomplete data is in no way affected by the absolute amount of factual material at hand.

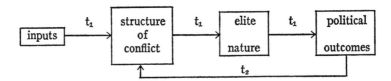

For the purpose of imposing a unifying theme upon the discussion, let me begin by describing an hypothetical causal chain composed of four "variable groups." Similar to "factors" in factor analysis, each will represent collectively several operational distinctions. My approach will be to discuss each of these variable groups separately, first reviewing relevant pieces of general and comparative literature on

2 *The End of Ideology* (2nd rev. ed.; New York: Collier Books, 1962), p. 348.

elites and then showing some interesting applications already made to the China case. My ultimate purposes are to suggest additional applications as well as to encourage experimentation with them.

One pervasive and intractable problem that must be faced from the outset is how to define "elites," or harder yet, "the elite." Several ways exist to stratify societies and thereby to mark off particular elite segments; each has its own analytical strengths and weaknesses depending on the object of analysis.[3] Thus one promising approach to the difficulty would be as follows: (1) enumerate alternative stratifications; (2) select the most useful ones for immediate purposes; and (3) show how those stratifications relate to the others. For example, if a society's military elite overlaps its social, academic, business, and/or foreign policy elites, then more than simply a military elite is under examination.

Moreover, writers wishing to devote special attention to a unitary political "stratification" and its attendant political "elite" must be prepared to define in addition what constitutes "political influence." Since influence can be wielded at many levels, the most promising approach to this difficulty might be to specify the range of issues to be dealt with in the study and then compare that range with the full spectrum of potential issues in the subject society's politics. More specifically, should "influentials" be thought of as those who determine a community's general values, such as faith in free-enterprise capitalism or suspicion of mass democracy (for example, the bourgeoisie)? Should they be thought of as those who monopolize traditional political resources in a community, like wealth, social status, organizational membership, or access to the media (such as the Pyongyang regime)? Or should they be thought of as those who, while their control over the raising and deciding of issues is more effective in some policy areas than in others, can nevertheless impose their will over a greater range of issues, can exercise power of greater scope, than can other members of the community (for example, New Haven's governors)?

In other words, it is essential to distinguish whether the object level of influence is to be values, resources, or decisions, and whether the spectrum of "influentials" determinant in each case is wide or narrow, before concrete hypotheses can be framed about the composition of the elite, its source of recruitment, its base of authority, its representa-

[3] Gerhard E. Lenski, *Power and Privilege: A Theory of Social Stratification* (New York: McGraw-Hill, 1966), pp. 73 ff.

tiveness, or its adaptability. And only then can evaluations be made of its ability to make good policy, undertake economic planning, uphold moral preferences of the community-at-large, handle conflict, or perform other functions. Elite literature unfortunately is often unclear on these points.

With these initial assumptions stated, however briefly, we can now proceed to review the first variable group.

INPUTS

In dynamic causal analysis, independent variables can fall into widely different time patterns. Since these different inputs, or starting points for analysis, are rarely compared with one another in scholarly literature, it will be helpful for our purposes to make four such time patterns explicit. (1) Random factors are unique events which occur unpredictably, such as famines, migrations, and technological breakthroughs.[4] (2) Cyclical factors are patterned events which repeat themselves at roughly predictable intervals, such as economic recessions, new generational perspectives, and organizational experience with bureaucratization and innovation. (3) Trend factors are developments which move continually in the same direction over a long period of time, such as population growth, urbanization, and increased media penetration.[5] (4) Parametric factors are conditions that remain constant (at least for the period covered by the analysis), such as geographic location, economic factor endowments, or intellectual traditions.

We can easily find examples of each kind of input in the China

[4] One example of a random factor is found in Harold D. Lasswell, Daniel Lerner, and C. Easton Rothwell, *The Comparative Study of Elites: An Introduction and Bibliography* ("Hoover Institute Studies, Series B: Elites, No. 1" [Stanford, Calif.: Stanford University Press, 1952]), p. 35. "[The] plebeian character of the Nazi elite led to an important conflict in the later phase of Nazi history. This was the conflict between the Nazi specialists on coercion and the traditional class of professional soldiers (the so-called *Junkers*). The roots of the conflict lay deep in the structure of German society but came eventually to the surface when, after two decades of playing along with each other (1923–43), the payoff point was reached. The *Putsch* of July 1944, the widespread conspiracy led by professional soldiers to assassinate Hitler and take over the regime, was the final indication that the cleavage between the Nazis and the soldiers had not been bridged. The goal of the soldiers was to preserve German independence and military power, whether World War II was won or lost; the Nazi goal was to win the war and maintain their regime, whether or not Germany was destroyed and vassalized in the defeat of this effort. By 1943–1944 these goals had become incompatible and the military policies they entailed had become irreconcilable. At that point the cleavage widened into a fatal chasm."

[5] Lasswell's "broad expectation that bureaucratic state systems are succeeding pluralistic (mixed) state systems" would fall under this category. *Ibid.*, p. 16.

literature. As an illustration of random factors, Robert Dernberger has stated that after the Great Leap Forward, "almost by default, the technologists were provided an opportunity to implement their economic policies when they were given responsibility for reviving the economy." For cyclical factors, G. William Skinner and Edwin A. Winckler have described how goal, power, and involvement cycles result in predictable compliance and policy cycles. James R. Townsend has detailed a trend factor:

[Party] members of peasant origin fell from 80 per cent of the CCP in 1949 to 66 per cent in 1961; the percentage of industrial workers as members rose from near zero to 15 per cent in the same period, while intellectual members rose from about 5 percent to 15 per cent. In 1956, approximately one-third of all intellectuals, about 18 per cent of the workers and only 1.4 per cent of the peasants were members; the path of entrance into Party was plainly shifting toward urban strata. . . . These scattered figures outline a fundamental change in the meaning and demands of Party membership.

And parametric factors are illustrated in Lucian Pye's statement that "Chinese political culture," as "a distinctive Chinese approach to politics," helps to explain the particularities of China's response to its "transitional" phase.[6]

Even though we all recognize that Chinese society under Communist rule still conforms to some traditional ideas and structures while deviating from others, the comparative importance of each kind of input for different explanatory purposes has not been considered in depth. For example, what relative weight should be given to China's "tradition of a strong political-ideological center . . . this tradition which probably created the continuous predisposition to and expectation of reestablishing such centers and tended to deny legitimation to any regime which was not successful in this respect" (desire to unify China—parametric)? Alternatively, what relative weight should be given to the changing outlooks of successive "military generations" defined by "political crisis" and "military ethic and style" (qualifications sometimes giving rise to a regional outlook—cyclical and random)? What

[6] Dernberger, "Economic Realities and China's Political Economics," *Bulletin of Atomic Scientists*, XXV, No. 2 (February, 1969), 41. Skinner and Winckler, "Compliance Succession in Rural Communist China: A Cyclical Theory," in Amitai Etzioni (ed.), *Complex Organizations: A Sociological Reader* (2nd ed.; New York: Holt, Rinehart and Winston, 1969), pp. 414 ff. Townsend, "Intra-Party Conflict in China: Disintegration in an Established One-Party System," in Samuel P. Huntington and Clement H. Moore (eds.), *Authoritarian Politics in Modern Society* (New York: Basic Books, 1970), p. 303. Pye, *The Spirit of Chinese Politics: A Psychocultural Study of the Authority Crisis in Political Development* (Cambridge, Mass.: M.I.T. Press, 1968), pp. xv–xvi and 40–42.

independent effects should be attributed to the single random input variable "Communist government"? Should not the Skinner-Winckler analysis be faulted for failing to relate its cyclical fluctuations to developmental trends? [7]

Having now stated these necessary caveats about dissimilar causal effects of input variables which follow dissimilar time patterns, we can proceed to the next step, analyzing the conflict basis of politics.

STRUCTURE OF CONFLICT

Every society displays numerous "cleavages" or lines of potentially open conflict among subgroups within it. Among possible categories of political cleavage are class or status, region or communal group, economic sector, functional bureaucracy, party or faction, and belief system or analytical policy preference. They tend to be quite stable over time, as evidenced by experimental small-group research undertaken by psychologists.[8] Some cleavages divide entire communities, elites and nonelites alike; some of them divide only nonelites; others horizontally divide elites from nonelites. Especially with regard to the question of ideology or "political myth," research into single communities has commonly discovered a lesser degree of cleavage (or stronger

[7] See S. N. Eisenstadt, "Tradition, Change, and Modernity: Reflections on the Chinese Experience," in Ping-ti Ho and Tang Tsou (eds.), *China in Crisis* (Chicago: University of Chicago Press, 1968), I, Bk. 2, 771; William W. Whitson, "The Concept of Military Generation: The Chinese Communist Case," *Asian Survey*, VIII, No. 11 (November, 1968). Chalmers Johnson, "Building a Communist Nation in China," in Robert A. Scalapino (ed.), *The Communist Revolution in Asia* (2nd ed.; Englewood Cliffs, N.J.: Prentice-Hall, 1969), p. 70. Richard M. Pfeffer, "Revolution and Rule: Where Do We Go from Here?" *Bulletin of Concerned Asian Scholars* (April–July, 1970), pp. 93–94.

[8] Michael Taylor and Douglas Rae in "An Analysis of Crosscutting between Political Cleavages," *Comparative Politics*, I, No. 4 (July, 1969), 536, define cleavage as "the division of a collection of individuals into two or more nominal groups. We might discern three types of cleavages: opinion cleavages—such as a preferred political party or a preferred policy position; trait cleavages—such as social class, religion, region, or language group; and behavioral cleavages—such as 'party actually voted for.'"

. . . Herbert Shepard described the results of his small-group research in "Responses to Situations of Competition and Conflict," in *Conflict Management in Organizations* (Ann Arbor, Mich.: Foundation for Research on Human Behavior, 1961): ". . . we might say that the losers know they have internal problems, and that they must work on them. The winners are trapped in the rigid structure *which won for them*, and hence are less able to engage in problem-solving behavior. Questioning of the structure that produced victory is psychologically impossible. The Win-Lose Trap continues to exist after victory and defeat have occurred. The feeling of conflict has not been resolved, and it is very difficult to establish any relationship between the two groups besides that of winner and loser. There is a complete absence of empathy between them. After the experiment has been performed, it takes many hours of intensive work with both groups in joint session to get them out of that trap, and back on the road to creative problem-solving" (p. 39).

consensus) among the elite than among the community-at-large.[9] Kalman Silvert provides one example from his analysis of "National Political Change in Latin America":

> In contemporary Latin America . . . common aspirations and a common dependence on a common world buttress the fraternal feelings of the commonwealth notion.
> A factor weakening feelings of hemispheric identification, however, is that these sentiments are restricted largely to elite leadership groups whose ideas are projected against much political divergence and large sectors of non-participant persons alienated for one or another reason from the mainstream of the nation.[10]

Intensive, detailed concern for intraelite conflict is an enduring hallmark of the so-called pluralist school of writers on elites. Raymond Aron seems to have set the pace with his 1950 analysis of the "transformation in the structure of the [French] elite, by which company directors are replaced by managers, trade union leaders are introduced into the councils of the government and public affairs, the political power of the capitalist economic leaders is reduced and that of the leaders of the masses is increased. . . ." Suzanne Keller, for another, overoptimistically asserts that Aron has made "a significant contribution to the analysis of elites, one that should discourage, if not prevent, the equation of political and economic hierarchies in industrial societies." But in essence the formulations of Aron and subsequent writers on the subject were all specific variations on the general theme enunciated by Carl Friedrich in his essay (1942), *The New Belief in the Common Man:* "In the light of the continuous *changes* in the composition of the majority, it is not possible to say, under conditions such as prevail in a functioning democracy, that those who play some considerable part in government constitute a cohesive group." [11]

Unfortunately, at this early and less empirical stage of elite analysis,

[9] Samuel Stouffer, *Communism, Conformity, and Civil Liberties: A Cross-Section of the Nation Speaks Its Mind* (Gloucester, Mass.: P. Smith, 1955).

[10] *The Conflict Society* (rev. ed.; New York: Harper Colophon Books, 1968), p. 13.

[11] Aron, "Social Structure and the Ruling Class," *British Journal of Sociology* (1950); the quotation here is from selections of the article reprinted in Reinhard Bendix and Seymour Martin Lipset (eds.), *Class, Status and Power: A Reader in Social Stratification* (Glencoe, Ill.: Free Press, 1953), p. 576. Aron continues: "The composition of the governing elite may be progressively altered, the relative importance of the various groups in the elite may be changed, but a society can only survive and prosper if there is true collaboration between those groups. In one way or another there must be unity of opinion and action on essential points in the elite." Keller, *Beyond the Ruling Class: Strategic Elites in Modern Society* (New York: Random House, 1963), pp. 17–18. Friedrich, *The New Belief in the Common Man* (Boston: Little, Brown, 1942), pp. 259–60.

scholars writing at a high level of generality could come to nearly opposite conclusions with equal plausibility. Raymond Aron once asserted that "we see [in the French case] that the *structure of the elite* is not merely a reflection of the *structure of society*. The extent to which the social groups are consciously organized and the nature of their ideologies are far from being completely determined by the economic sub-structure." Not long afterward, however, his German colleague Ralf Dahrendorf contended precisely to the contrary, that "the governments of Western societies are often mere switchboards of authority; decisions are made not by them but through them. In this respect, the political parties from which the personnel of governmental elites is recruited do not differ very greatly from these elites." [12]

As research on the American elite has become gradually more empirical, divergencies rooted in conceptual vagueness have begun correspondingly to decline. Divergencies are still present, of course, but now that scholars will measure concepts instead of just defining them, even clarifying the issues which separate opposing camps of "pluralists" and "power elitists" has become simpler if not indeed possible for the first time. Nevertheless, it is interesting to note that neither side yet specifies systematically what I referred to above as the "object level of influence." The pluralists generally point to legislation in which "interested economic elite pressure groups were mostly defeated" (Arnold M. Rose) or to "key political choices" (Robert A. Dahl) to see whose interests were served.[13] The power elitists prefer instead to emphasize membership in "the controlling institutions and key decision-making groups" in the country (G. William Domhoff).[14]

[12] Aron, "Social Structure and the Ruling Class," p. 577. Dahrendorf, *Class and Class Conflict in Industrial Society* (Stanford, Calif.: Stanford University Press, 1959), p. 306.

[13] Rose, *The Power Structure: Political Process in American Society* (New York: Oxford University Press, 1967), pp. 483–94. Dahl, "A Critique of the Ruling Elite Model," *American Political Science Review,* LII (June, 1958); reprinted in Norman L. Crockett, *The Power Elite in America* (Lexington, Mass.: D. C. Heath and Co., 1970). Dahl writes: ". . . I do not see how anyone can suppose that he has established the dominance of a specific group in a community or a nation without basing his analysis on a careful examination of a series of concrete decisions. . . . To sum up: The hypothesis of the existence of a ruling elite can be strictly tested only if: (1) The hypothetical ruling elite is a well-defined group. (2) There is a fair sample of cases involving key political decisions in which the preferences of the hypothetical ruling elite run counter to those of any other likely group that might be suggested. (3) In such cases, the preferences of the elite regularly prevail" (pp. 40–41). An interesting criticism of Dahl's test can be found in Peter Bachrach and Morton S. Baratz, "Two Faces of Power," *American Political Science Review,* LVI (December, 1962), 947–52.

[14] Domhoff, *Who Rules America?* (Englewood Cliffs, N.J.: Prentice-Hall, 1967), p. 142. In a later section subtitled "So What?" Domhoff faces the issue squarely if not explicitly: "So what if the upper class controls a disproportionate amount of the wealth,

Theodore Lowi makes an important contribution to the solution of this problem by distinguishing broad types of issues (distributive, regulative, redistributive) and then arguing that "for every type of policy there is likely to be a distinctive type of political relationship." [15] In particular, Lowi finds that regulative issues engender pluralist politics while redistributive issues usually lead to more elitist behavior.

Yet in any society it is ordinarily "radical" critics who are most attentive to fundamental values which, when questioned, induce consensus among the established "elite" and cause them to rally politically. A psychologist collaborated with a founder of the Students for a Democratic Society to provide such an analysis of American politics:

> The tendency in social science has been to study decision-making in order to study group differences; we need to study decision-making also to understand group commonalities.
>
> Were such studies done, our hypothesis would be that certain "core beliefs" are continuously unquestioned. . . .
>
> Demonstrating the absence of a discussion of the shared premises, among the most potent sectors of society, would go far in highlighting the area of forced or acquiescent consensus. . . . The "core beliefs" which we listed as unchallenged by any potent locus of institutionalized power are: (a) Efficacy is preferable to principle in foreign affairs (thus military means are chosen over non-violent means); (b) Private property is preferable to public property; and (c) Limited parliamentary democracy is preferable to any other system of government. . . .
>
> We have been arguing that the transition to peace is a process of redistributive decision.[16]

This hypothesis is obviously subject to considerable refinement to account for cases where the radical argument is presented in such a way as to appeal to a portion of the elite; then forceful pressing of the radical cause can contrarily induce division among the elite. Neverthe-

---

and controls the corporations and the federal government? The important thing is whether or not their decisions are in the interests of the country as a whole. Would members of other classes make similar decisions on key issues? The answer to this question, above and beyond the special interests that are implied by disproportionate income and wealth, is that it is not really pertinent. This book has not tried to show that the rule of the American upper class has been a benevolent one or a malevolent one. Rather, it is concerned with the existence and the mechanics of the national upper class, not with an interpretation of the impact of its rule on American civilization for better or for worse" (pp. 150–51). Domhoff also gives some interesting criticisms of Dahl's test for a "ruling elite" from the power elitist point of view.

[15] "American Business, Public Policy, Case Studies and Political Theory," *World Politics,* XVI (July, 1964); selections reprinted in Crockett, *Power Elite in America.* Quotation is on p. 83.

[16] Marc Pilisuk and Thomas Hayden, "Is There a Military-Industrial Complex Which Prevents Peace: Consensus and Countervailing Power in Pluralistic Systems," *The Journal of Social Issues,* XXI (July, 1965), 67–117; selections reprinted in Crockett, *Power Elite in America,* pp. 106–14.

less, it does help make the point that speaking solely of control or domination without naming the object level of influence (for example, core beliefs or key decisions) can effectively disguise the boundaries where conflict ends and consensus begins.

With this difficulty overcome, the empirical problem of greatest interest to analysts of conflict structure is that of "crosscutting cleavages" which produce the politically relevant effect of "cross-pressuring." As Lipset describes it, "multiple and potentially inconsistent affiliations, loyalties, and stimuli reduce the emotion and aggressiveness of political choice." [17] An example of the converse, polarizing effect is hypothesized by Keller: "In times of rapid social change, the youth . . . experience these changes not as changes but as absolutes. And disagreement between the generations, if not conflict, is usually the result." Yet another way in which conflict can be diffused throughout social "levels" (individual, small or large groups, community) is described by James S. Coleman.[18] Since conflict—its creation and its handling, its resolution or its escalation—is the very stuff of politics, studies of its relation to elite nature are absolutely necessary for the development of a meaningful broader comparative sociology.

Writings on China have generally avoided explicit and systematic discussion of conflict structure. One notable exception is Ezra Vogel's article, "The Structure of Conflict: China in 1967," in which the author isolates three issues that caused basic political cleavages: (1) the speed of collectivization; (2) the extent of mass mobilization in 1957–58; and (3) the degree of independence from the Soviet Union. In late 1965, when both domestic and international conditions were favorable, Mao decided to bring these cleavages to the surface "to regain control over the Party and government apparatus." [19]

Other writers have grappled with the same issue in fact if not in name. Franz Michael argues that a "battle for supremacy began in 1958" between a "rational communism moving forward or retreating within the confines of stages of development as hitherto understood by most Communist leaderships" and "Mao's radical, utopian communism, which preaches the attainment of the same Communist goals

[17] Seymour Martin Lipset, *Political Man* (New York: Doubleday, 1960), p. 88. Taylor and Rae give a systematic treatment of this problem in "An Analysis of Crosscutting between Political Cleavages."

[18] Keller, *Beyond the Ruling Class,* p. 246; Coleman, *Community Conflict* (Glencoe, Ill.: Free Press, 1957), pp. 22–23.

[19] In *The Cultural Revolution: 1967 in Review* ("Michigan Papers in Chinese Studies, No. 2" [Ann Arbor: University of Michigan Center for Chinese Studies, 1968]), pp. 97–98.

by means of a short cut replacing economic and political rationality with blind belief in doctrine and reliance on force and the power of human will." [20] Tang Tsou takes the conflict in effect back to 1949 as the "first and basic issue confronting a revolutionary regime" ("whether it should rapidly implement its revolutionary program or give priority to the consolidation of revolutionary gains and the newly established institutions"):

With the possible exception of the Hundred Flowers episode and the subsequent anti-rightist campaign, in which the roles played by Mao and the Party organization are still a matter of doubt, Mao has always been the promoter and initiator of new radical policies. With the possible exception of the controversial case of the Socialist Education Movement during 1964, Liu has always tried to consolidate the gains and tended to move more slowly. As the head of the Party organization, he was more a co-ordinator of activities than an initiator of new policies. In the process of policy-making as distinct from Party management, he generally played the role of approving, supporting, or rejecting ideas or programmes advanced by his subordinates. The programmes which he supported or approved were generally less radical than those later adopted by Mao. Liu was also the spokesman and executor of the more moderate policies of the regime, which in all probability he wholeheartedly favoured.[21]

John Lewis pushed the genesis of the Mao-Liu conflict back to an even earlier day. Interestingly, at least two scholars have found conflicts along different lines than a Mao-Liu split, one hypothesizing shifting coalitions, the other discovering significant differences within the ranks of the Liu camp itself.[22]

Only one analyst, to my knowledge, has drawn a distinction between levels of conflict by differentiating "certain domestic or foreign policy measures" from "commonly-agreed national objectives":

Presumed "hard-liners" [before the Cultural Revolution] have since been among those most severely criticized, while "soft-liners" have survived (some of them having actually been restored from previous disgrace). Nor were the divisions along institutional lines (as, for example, between Party and army); rather, they occurred *within* the major institutions. All of this suggests that the growing division among

[20] "The Struggle for Power," *Problems of Communism* (May–June, 1967), p. 12.

[21] "The Cultural Revolution and the Chinese Political System," *CQ*, No. 38 (April–June, 1969), pp. 66–67.

[22] Lewis, "Leader, Commissar, and Bureaucrat: The Chinese Political System in the Last Days of the Revolution," in Ho and Tsou (eds.), *China in Crisis*, pp. 449–81. The shifting coalitions are set forth by Parris Chang in "Disputes over Communes 1959–1962: A Case Study of Intra-Elite Conflict in Communist China (unpub. MS, 1968), pp. 2 ff.; Richard D. Baum studies the Liu camp in "Revolution and Reaction in Rural China: The 'Struggle between Two Roads' during the Socialist Education Movement (1962–1966) and the Great Proletarian Cultural Revolution (1966–1968)" (Ph.D. dissertation, University of California, Berkeley, 1970), pp. 126–37.

the leaders was not primarily the result of a split between proponents and opponents of certain domestic or foreign policy measures. It was a disagreement not so much over the particular methods, direction, and speed to be employed in order to attain commonly-agreed national objectives—such as "modernization" or "Great Power status"—as over the nature of those basic goals themselves and the general approach to them.[23]

Likewise, only one writer has suggested the usefulness of analyzing crosscutting cleavages: ". . . instead of analyzing Party and government bureaucrats as one group, a more rigorous analysis would examine the interests and power of the bureaucrats in the various functional systems into which the Party and government were divided; finance and trade, agriculture, forestry, and water conservancy, industry and communications, culture and education, law enforcement, and so on."[24] There is clearly room for more penetrating consideration of various concepts associated with the general variable group, structure of conflict.

Now, having looked at a small number of key problems associated with the conflict basis of political life, we are ready to take a third step, this one even more directly related to our overall concern with how to fulfill the essential condition laid down at the outset.

ELITE NATURE

The third variable group covers all possible descriptions of elites used in scientific propositions. Included are both observable characteristics of fixed-membership elite groups as well as other aspects of elites (fixed membership or not) that are taken by various writers as especially salient or meaningful. Some factors appearing in the existing literature are quite distinct and usable variables; others, as we shall see, suffer from the haziness that surrounds the concept of "the elite."

INDIVIDUALS, GROUPS, AND POSITIONS

To begin with, two major distinctions regarding composition are frequently disguised behind the single word, "elite": first, between individual persons and groups of people; and second, between people and impersonal ranks, statuses, or positions. One of Pareto's critics

[23] W. F. Dorrill, *Power, Policy, and Ideology in the Making of China's "Cultural Revolution,"* Memorandum RM-5731-PR (Santa Monica, Calif.: Rand Corporation, 1968), pp. 96–97. This hypothesis could be given greater sophistication by differentiating progressive stages of conflict.

[24] Michel Oksenberg, "Occupational Groups in Chinese Society and the Cultural Revolution," in *The Cultural Revolution*, p. 38.

addresses a portion of his commentary to the first distinction: "He does not resolve the question of how the two types of elite circulation —the ascent and descent of individuals, and the rise and fall of social groups—are connected with each other. He suggests, briefly, that if the governing elite is relatively open to superior individuals from the lower strata it has a better chance of enduring, and conversely, that the replacement of one elite by another may result from a failure in this circulation of individuals." [25] Similarly, it has been traditional for the American Jewish community to have at least one Supreme Court judge, although different individuals have been "circulated" through as the community's "representative."

Frederick Frey recently called attention to the second distinction: "We felt we had to come up with two basic structural notions, one of which I call structural isomorphism and the other I call personnel isomorphism. . . . This is what [Robert] Dahl means by dispersed inequalities of power. What he's really talking about is a system, in our terms, where there is high structural isomorphism but very low personnel isomorphism. The structure remains the same, but essentially the personnel switches as you move from issue area to issue area." Franz Schurmann recalls, along the same line, that in Russia even though the "old technical intelligentsia" of tsarist days was liquidated and replaced by "new young technocrats," the successor generation nonetheless "stepped into the positions of those liquidated." [26]

In China studies, even though appropriate data have been published, we have largely overlooked the first distinction. One laudable exception is William Whitson's study, "The Field Army in Chinese Communist Politics," in which the author shows that in spite of Cultural Revolution purges of individual military leaders, four "field

---

[25] T. B. Bottomore, *Elites and Society* (New York: Basic Books, 1964), pp. 46–47. The author quotes from Pareto himself: "Revolutions come about through accumulations in the higher strata of society—either because of a slowing down in class circulation, or from other causes—of decadent elements no longer possessing the residues suitable for keeping them in power, or shrinking from the use of force; while meantime in the lower strata of society elements of superior quality are coming to the fore, possessing residues suitable for exercising the functions of government and willing enough to use force" (Vilfredo Pareto, *The Mind and Society* [4 vols.; London: Jonathan Cape, 1935], 1431).

[26] Frey, in "Conference on Theory and Method in Comparable Elite Analysis," p. 67. Schurmann, *Ideology and Organization in Communist China* (Berkeley and Los Angeles: University of California Press, 1966), p. 282. Similar arguments can be found in Leonard Schapiro, *The Communist Party of the Soviet Union* (New York: Vintage Books, 1964), p. 462; and in Milovan Djilas, *The New Class: An Analysis of the Communist System* (New York: Praeger, 1957).

army systems" (all but Ho Lung's First) as groups retain their proportional representation at several important decision-making points. More commonly we take changes in individual fortunes as indicative either of shifts in the fortunes of collectivities which they represent or of general swings to the political right or left. With regard to the second distinction, the record is better. For example, in writing about the State Council, Donald Klein states that since 1949 the number of its ministries and other subordinate organs has doubled from twenty-four to forty-nine, while the number of ministerial or vice-ministerial posts (or their equivalents) has increased fivefold, from seventy-six to 366. But independently of this expansion in bureaucratic slots, Klein also finds that "by and large, the State Council has been marked by a rather high degree of continuity in terms of its personnel."[27]

In the future it would be helpful for us to keep these differences in mind. Is the reappearance of Ch'en Yün, for example, to be interpreted mainly as a personal triumph or mainly as a manifestation of renewed interest in his economic thought? To what extent is Chou En-lai's famed survival (or his performance of other political roles) a result of his personal political sagacity, to what extent a result of the need to keep the all-important State Council functioning during periods of political turmoil? When Red Guard members of revolutionary committees are "sent down" after a movement to "simplify administration," does this signify that their factional opponents have won a victory or rather that the importance of mass organizations in new local power structures has been reduced?

FORMAL AND INFORMAL CRITERIA

A separate but related matter is deciding what importance to attach to institutional affiliation when identifying elites. Morris Janowitz argues from a comparative study that "whereas formal criteria . . . permit the initial delimitation of an elite," there are additional "functional criteria" that should be applied as a second step:

These functional criteria identify those who wield influence without formal office or public recognition. They can be selected junior members of high influence in a hierarchy who have not yet achieved high office. Likewise, they can be specialized personnel who are indirectly influential and will have little chance of achieving high office; for example, the private secretaries of political leaders and the public-rela-

[27] Whitson, "The Field Army in Chinese Communist Politics," *CQ*, No. 37 (January–March, 1969), p. 14. Klein, "The State Council and the Cultural Revolution," in John Wilson Lewis (ed.), *Party Leadership and Revolutionary Power in China* (Cambridge: Cambridge University Press, 1970), pp. 352–53.

tions advisers of businessmen. Likewise, there are those who need to be excluded despite their formal rank or station because they have ceased to exercise influence.[28]

On the other hand, John Armstrong feels that in the Soviet system the factor of formal career is foremost in significance:

The relative importance of the members of the elite of the Ukrainian apparatus depends primarily on the positions they hold in the bureaucratic structures. Even the more subtle distinctions of influence arising from personal connections of the officials appear to stem indirectly from their careers. The member of the apparatus who exercises influence beyond that conferred by his nominal position is one who usually worked at an earlier stage of his career with, or for, a more powerful official who continues to act as his patron.[29]

This problem would become more resolvable were "object level of influence" to be specified.

In the China field few, if any, criteria of an informal nature are available; thus all elite identifications necessarily have been pinned to bureaucratically defined hierarchies. John Gittings departs slightly from form by approximately subdividing the People's Liberation Army leadership into three echelons "based on a study of the promotion, seniority, and activities of the officers in this command structure." Richard Diao goes even further by using criteria of multiple hat-wearing to break down 316 members of China's 1966 economic elite into five groups ranked by "political status." [30] Further experimentation with other categories of real influence should be rewarding.

ASCRIPTIVE BACKGROUND AND ROLE

No practice is more standard for elite analysis than cataloguing members' backgrounds, means of recruitment, and collective profile. One comparative study, for example, treats four "characteristics" (place of birth, education, age, parents' occupations) and three "attitudes" (unity, Marxism, nationalism and anticolonialism) as important for understanding the behavior of new elites in developing areas.[31] Zbigniew Brzezinski and Samuel Huntington express the widely held rationale for doing so: "The relatively humble social origin of the

---

[28] *The Military in the Political Development of New Nations* (Chicago: Phoenix Books, 1964), pp. 107–8.

[29] *The Soviet Bureaucratic Elite: A Case Study of the Ukrainian Apparatus* (New York: Praeger, 1959), p. 11.

[30] Gittings, *The Role of the Chinese Army* (London and New York: Oxford University Press, 1967), p. 282. Diao, "The Impact of the Cultural Revolution on China's Economic Elite," *CQ*, No. 42 (April–June, 1970), pp. 67–68.

[31] Fred R. von der Mehden, *Politics of the Developing Nations* (Englewood Cliffs, N.J.: Prentice-Hall, 1964), pp. 86 ff.

Soviet political elite and the middle class origin of the American have an impact on their respective political styles." [32] The magnitude of this impact, however, is controversial. Edward Dreyer wrote in June, 1969: "I feel that origins are not as important as group identification in determining behavior. A person's awareness of literati standing (as recognized by a formal title) is more important than the fact that he gained the station by *chin-shih* vs. nomination, or [came] from land-lord vs. peasant class origins. The same applies to other self-conscious groups (military, eunuchs)." [33] This, of course, is the major assumption of role theory, that once having taken a role, irrespective of how, the player's behavior is thereafter determined to a large extent by the various role-related pressures that impinge upon him. No scholar who relates either background or role identification to behavior should neglect to consider as an alternative explanation the possible effects of the other factor.

Understandably, role analysis has hardly figured prominently in research-from-afar on China; scholars have been inclined to work rather with available background and career pattern data (even though these too are rarely complete). It was early 1967 before the first instance appeared in the form of Ezra Vogel's essay on the accretion of bureaucratic roles to the position of cadre after 1949. Michel Oksenberg has subsequently taken an interest in the role concept. And most recently Richard Solomon has produced a full-fledged examination of "the role of the activist." [34] But there has yet to appear an explicit comparison of these twin factors for any single explanatory purpose.

PROFESSIONALISM, HOMOGENEITY, AND PUBLIC
"THEY CONSCIOUSNESS"

Modern society's growing division of labor in general has been accompanied by a growth of specialist political jobs and careers in particular. Significant variation, though, is observable not only between

---

[32] *Political Power: USA/USSR* (New York: Viking Press, 1963), p. 139.

[33] Private communication to the author, June, 1969.

[34] Vogel, "From Revolutionary to Semi-bureaucrat: The 'Regularization' of Cadres," *CQ*, No. 29 (January–March, 1967), pp. 36–60. For Oksenberg's studies on role concept, see "Getting Ahead and Along in Communist China: The Ladder of Success on the Eve of the Cultural Revolution," in Lewis (ed.), *Party Leadership*, pp. 306–8; "Local Leaders in Rural China, 1962–65: Individual Attributes, Bureaucratic Positions, and Political Recruitment," in A. Doak Barnett (ed.), *Chinese Communist Politics in Action* (Seattle: University of Washington Press, 1969), pp. 155–215; and "Policy Making under Mao Tse-tung, 1949–1968," *Comparative Politics*, III, No. 3 (April, 1971), 323–60. Solomon, "On Activism and Activists: Maoist Conceptions of Motivation and Political Role Linking State to Society," *CQ*, No. 39 (July–September, 1969), pp. 76–114.

electoral and bureaucratic hierarchies, but also between capitalist (liberal-democratic) and socialist (democratic-centralist) states. The apotheosis of this development is the appearance of the professional political classes in present-day Communist states. "The Soviet professional politician thus functions exclusively in a bureaucratic environment. . . . Since the Party apparatus is the most important bureaucracy in Soviet society, the power of the apparatchik depends upon his position in the Party bureaucratic structure. Organizational positions are to him what votes are to the American politician."[35] A 1957 curriculum for a four-year interoblast Party school in the U.S.S.R. reserved 41.5 per cent of its 3,200 total hours of instruction for strictly political subjects like dialectical materialism and Communist Party history, courses clearly designed to train "professional political leaders of society."[36] In the United States, institutions like the Lyndon Baines Johnson School of Public Affairs at the University of Texas cast only a faint shadow by comparison with their Soviet counterparts. Americans do forge political careers, but they ordinarily spend segments of their professional lives in private pursuits as well. And most importantly, Cincinnatus seems to view politics quite differently than does the Apparatchik.[37]

One writer further suggests looking closely at the distinction between an elite cadre "composed of specialists in the specific and technical ends of the organization" who owe their "top membership" to achievement of those skills, and an elite nucleus recruited from them and composed of a "very small group of prime leaders who are oriented toward the broadest social issues, including innovation, self-scrutiny, and interrelations with other elites. . . . The elite cadre and the smaller elite nucleus may display markedly different social profiles and career lines. Here we have the difference between the top cadre of technical personnel in manufacturing firms and the market-oriented managers. In the military establishment, here is the difference between the effective regimental and divisional commanders and the politically oriented strategists."[38]

For some purposes it would be helpful to know what portion of the elite is held responsible by the public-at-large for policy decisions and effects flowing from them, good or bad. The comparative problem has been articulated by Lipset:

[35] Brzezinski and Huntington, *Political Power,* p. 149.
[36] *Ibid.,* p. 143.
[37] *Ibid.,* pp. 150–73.
[38] Janowitz, *The Military,* p. 109.

The left in the European stable democracies grew gradually in a fight for more democracy, and gave expression to the discontents involved in early industrialization, while the right retained the support of traditionalist elements in the society, until eventually the system came into an easy balance between a modified left and right. In Asia, the left is in power during the period of population explosion and early industrialization, and must accept responsibility for all the consequent miseries.[39]

Lipset believes that in Asia, "as in the poorer areas of Europe, the Communists exist to capitalize on all these discontents in a completely irresponsible fashion . . ."; predicting Communist success in associating (in the popular mind) incumbent elites with existing social evils, he concludes that "the prognosis for the perpetuation of political democracy in Asia and Africa is bleak." [40] It remains a subject for empirical investigation to determine what tactics can be adopted by an elite to influence the public's perception of a single responsible "they" group in power.

Like the Soviets, the Chinese Communists made early efforts to provide training for a professional political elite through a system of Party schools. Even before the Cultural Revolution, however, leadership positions more often than not fell to old Party members with experience and seniority, members who had won their spurs in the field without undergoing much formal training. The Cultural Revolution period nevertheless has witnessed an uncompromising attack upon every small vestige of professionalism—academic, military, economic, and technical as well as Party.

In spite of all complications, China's political elite has nonetheless often been discussed as a unit which must collectively bear the burden of responsibility for their policies. Victor Funnel only slightly simplifies a widely held view of the Party's relation to the elite as a whole: "The further the distance from the mass base, and the greater the power and the policy-making capability, the higher the proportion of communists to non-communists holding office, until, at the very summit, the parallel hierarchies of State and Party finally merge in a common nucleus of leadership." [41] Townsend hypothesizes that before the Cultural Revolution the Party strove to preserve its collective

---

[39] "Some Social Requisites of Democracy: Economic Development and Political Legitimacy," *American Political Science Review,* LIII, No. 1 (March, 1959); selections reprinted in Roy C. Macridis and Bernard E. Brown (eds.), *Comparative Politics: Notes and Readings* (Homewood, Ill.: Dorsey Press, 1961), p. 474.

[40] *Ibid.,* pp. 474–75.

[41] "The Cadres: Methods of Mass Control in Communist China" (Ph.D. dissertation, University of London, 1968), p. 14.

image: ". . . the CCP's treatment of allegedly deviant top leaders (Politburo or senior Central Committee members) was cautious and restrained in an effort to minimize the impression of conflict at the top." And echoing the dilemma raised by Lipset above, Richard Pfeffer calls attention to Mao as "the great legislator, a *radical in power*. . . ." [42] Scattered evidence to the effect that many Chinese people had extreme difficulty comprehending the concept of "Party persons in authority taking the capitalist road" (one reason perhaps for publicly initiating in April, 1967, a relentless symbolic repudiation of Liu Shao-ch'i) suggests the prevalence of a unitary view of "the rulers" in China, a conclusion reinforced by responses obtained in the course of my own limited interviews with émigré cadres during 1968–69. As data become available, further exploration to determine how extensively both cadres and masses conceive of "the rulers" would be valuable.

DISPLACEMENT, REPLACEMENT, AND COUNTERELITES

To their supporters, one of the proudest achievements of capitalist liberal-democratic regimes is their ability to replace peacefully and regularly one set of leaders with a competing set. Conversely, the times of greatest instability and tension in socialist democratic-centralist regimes are thought to be the irregularly spaced "succession crises" during which competitors for maximum leader struggle viciously for power, winner take all.

When elite changes imply more thoroughgoing regime changes as well, then milder forms of changing the guard (called "elite displacement" by Donald Rosenthal) are those which allow members of the old elite to retain symbolic status, in an effort to minimize their active opposition to the new order. To Rosenthal, the originator of the concept, "this need not include displacement from positions of economic or ritual importance." [43] One prominent example of how the so-called crisis of elites can be solved in this way is Mexico: ". . . many of the Mexican aristocrats remained in that country during and after the Revolution of 1910 and in so doing not only won an important place in the expanding economy by entering new types of economic endeavor, but continued to play a constructive if indirect role in the

[42] Townsend, "Intra-Party Conflict in China," p. 295. Pfeffer, "The Pursuit of Purity: Mao's Cultural Revolution," *Problems of Communism,* XVIII, No. 6 (November–December, 1969), 21.

[43] "Deurbanization, Elite Displacement, and Political Change in India," *Comparative Politics,* II, No. 1 (January, 1970), 176.

political evolution of their homeland." [44] Another example is Japan.[45] The alternative, more severe form of changing the guard, of course, is revolution, a process in which power is seized unceremoniously from the old power-holders who are subsequently denounced, suppressed, driven into exile, or liquidated. Revolutions can be considered incomplete to the extent that elements of the old elite still retain some influence.

Identifying the elite is naturally more complicated for those societies where an "out" elite is in the process of displacing or challenging an "in" elite. Scholars typically skirt this difficulty by analyzing either one or the other—rarely are both treated as a unit. Charges of political or scholarly bias have been leveled at research which uniquely emphasizes either "in" or "out" elite groups. On the one hand, for example, Berkeley's Radical Student Union levels a doctrinaire attack at the University of California Comparative Political Elites Archive Program for overemphasizing "outs":

> As is indicated by the nature of the subject matter, these elite studies are not concerned with those who presently control the governments of the underdeveloped world and their policies [author's note: Chinese, Korean, and Vietnamese Communist elites have been studied], nor with their dependence on the western industrialized countries. No attention is paid to the process and mechanisms by means of which existing social-economic-political elite groups have retained control over their countries and the ways in which they have actually hindered development, permitting only those kinds of change which are beneficial to their own particular interests. These projects focus, rather, on the movements and individuals which threaten or could potentially threaten existing stability or foreign domination of those countries.[46]

On the other hand, Morris Janowitz spears the present trend in elite sociology for doing just the opposite: "Emergent elites and counter-

---

[44] Robert E. Scott, "Political Elites and Political Modernization: The Crisis of Transition," in Seymour M. Lipset and Aldo Solari (eds.), *Elites in Latin America* (New York: Oxford University Press, 1967), pp. 140–42.

[45] Some relevant works on the post-1868 Meiji modernizers are: Bernard S. Silberman and H. D. Harootunian (eds.), *Modern Japanese Leadership: Tradition and Change* (Tucson: University of Arizona Press, 1966); Robert E. Ward and Dankwart A. Rustow (eds.), *Political Modernization in Japan and Turkey* (Princeton, N.J.: Princeton University Press, 1964); Johannes Hirschmeier, *The Origins of Entrepreneurship in Meiji Japan* (Cambridge, Mass.: Harvard University Press, 1957). To complicate the Japanese case somewhat, historians have discovered several significant social changes that occurred in the early modern period under the Tokugawa Shogunate. See John W. Hall and Marius B. Jansen (eds.), *Studies in the Institutional History of Early Modern Japan* (Princeton, N.J.: Princeton University Press, 1968); and Robert N. Bellah, *Tokugawa Religion: The Values of Pre-Industrial Japan* (Boston: Beacon Press, 1970).

[46] *The Uses of U. C., Berkeley: Research* (Berkeley, Calif.: Center for Participant Education, 1969), pp. 37–38.

elites are obviously less discernible on the basis of formal characteristics. Therefore, the identification of elite groups on the basis of formal characteristics alone is likely to underrepresent emergent groups. There can be no doubt that social research to date on the stratification of elites has tended to emphasize formalized elites and therefore to concern itself with the status quo." [47] These two criticisms taken together underscore the point that not only existing elites, but emergent and counterelites as well are worthy of scientific attention; for many purposes, comparison of the two should be rewarding.[48]

In Schurmann's conception, China's "true elite" was already well along the road to decline by 1949:

> The traditional elite of China was attacked from two directions. The coming of modern organization deprived it of its leadership role in society. The erosion of the social system deprived it of its status. All it had left was naked power and naked wealth. The act of class destruction directed against the traditional elite at the time of the land reform in the late 1940's came when its position in a crumbling social system was already undermined.[49]

During the long period of time required by the Chinese Communist Party (CCP) to build up a new social system, elite recruitment would necessarily reflect contradictory needs to utilize old Kuomintang personnel and "old intelligentsia" while at the same time educating and training new cadres from among the Communist regime's lower-class constituency.[50] For eight years the new government recruited heavily from both Party and bureaucracy, and consequently "the rapid political recruitment and upward mobility following the seizure of power seem to have strongly boosted the prestige and legitimacy of the Communist leadership." [51] Afterward, though, upward mobility was slow by comparison, and even forms of downward mobility were increasingly common.[52]

---

[47] *The Military*, p. 108.

[48] A shortcoming of Allan Goodman's "South Vietnam: Neither War nor Peace," *Asian Survey*, X, No. 2 (February, 1970), 107-32, is that no Communist groups are included in a list of twenty-three political parties, national fronts, and non-Party political associations. The Vietcong, National Liberation Front (NLF), and Provisional Revolutionary Government are discussed only as threats, although Goodman makes clear that the non-Communist groups analyzed were much affected by their own comparisons between the NLF and the government of South Vietnam.

[49] *Ideology and Organization*, pp. 5-7.

[50] *Ibid.*, pp. 168 ff.

[51] Ying-mao Kau, "The Urban Bureaucratic Elite in Communist China: A Case Study of Wuhan, 1949-65," in Barnett (ed.), *Chinese Communist Politics in Action*, p. 262.

[52] *Ibid.* See also Michel Oksenberg, "Paths to Leadership in Communist China: A Comparison of Second Echelon Positions in 1955 and 1965," *Current Scene*, III, No. 24 (August 1, 1965).

As the situation has progressed, "two new elites appear to be developing"—educated professionals and red cadres.[53] In somewhat different analytical contexts, Vogel characterizes the 1957 bloomers and contenders as a "non-power elite" (and later as a non-Party elite). And Oksenberg distinguishes "potential leaders" in the late 1960's as "those who have access to the locus of power and periodically may influence policy; they also form a group from which the active leaders are drawn."[54] So far we have been able to identify, though incomprehensively, various counterelites in and out of the Party, but no systematic analysis of their political importance has yet appeared. What efforts at cooptation of counterelites have been made, and how is variation in these efforts explained? What political resources (such as prestige, technical expertise, or administrative experience) are counterelites able to withhold for purposes of bargaining with the elite? How much elite turnover in the past few decades is traceable to a long-term process of social disintegration in old China, and how much to the polarizing policies of the CCP itself?

Finally, having raised a number of crucial distinctions that might help clarify separate dimensions of the variable group, elite nature, we can proceed to the fourth and last step, a consideration of several important types of political outcome which it might reasonably be expected to affect.

POLITICAL OUTCOMES

I would summarize the argument so far in this way: since in general the concept of the elite implies an influential elite found at the top of a unitary political stratification, we could greatly improve our elite studies by first specifying the object level of influence (values, resource distribution, or decisions); second, by identifying which individuals, groups, or hierarchical positions are most influential in those terms; third, by characterizing the resultant elite by a variety of other descriptive factors; and finally, by explaining how it developed the way it did in terms of relevant input factors and changes in the community's structure of conflict. The remaining question is, where do elite studies lead us? What difference does it make whether a political community has an elite with this or that characteristic?

[53] Schurmann, *Ideology and Organization,* pp. 51–53.

[54] Vogel, *Canton under Communism: Programs and Politics in a Provincial Capital, 1949–1968* (Cambridge, Mass.: Harvard University Press, 1969), pp. 193–99. Oksenberg, "Local Leaders in Rural China," pp. 158–59.

This concern factors into two questions: (1) What are some important political outcomes that might stand as dependent variables? (2) How much variance in those outcomes can be predicted from knowledge of elite nature? The latter problem is obviously an empirical one; below I shall deal solely with the former.

CONFLICT HANDLING MIX

Competing interests in every society hope to prevail over their opposition at authoritative decision-making points. Only rarely are the conflict resolution institutions found at those points impartial, regularly favoring the side with the logically or ethically stronger case (even if either one could be neutrally determined). It is therefore of interest to both participants and scholarly observers alike to know not only whose interests are ostensibly served by the elite controlling such institutions, but also how conflicts involving various kinds of interests are customarily approached by the authorities in power.

Approaches could be operationalized, for example, in terms of a scalar five-step "mediation-suppression" variable like the following: [55] (1) Eliminate conflict by satisfying both parties. (2) Manage conflict by compromising, appealing to legal principles, appealing to external authorities or disinterested third parties, expanding the arena of bargaining, or employing other devices that both parties will accept as legitimate. (3) Postpone decisions on conflict through cooling-off periods, tabling, tokenism, study committees, pilot projects, or symbolic gratification. (4) Suppress conflict by authoritatively favoring one side (thus bringing to life an "opposition" side); banning opposition newspapers; restricting public gatherings by the opposition; restricting their telephone communications with wiretaps; characterizing their views as immoral, illegal, unpatriotic, irresponsible, or anarchic; infiltrating agents and provocateurs into their organizations; or engaging in police harassment on tax or traffic charges, including searches and arrests. (5) Eliminate conflict by suppressing one party (American Indians, German Jews, Greek Communists, Chinese landlords, Taiwan self-determinists, Saigon neutralists). Depending on the issue, all elites at some time engage in every one of these measures. Nonelites' responses to them obviously vary according to a variety of circumstances;

[55] See Daniel Katz, "Approaches to Managing Conflict," and Herbert A. Shepard, "Responses to Situations of Competition and Conflict," both in *Conflict Management in Organizations;* see also Dahrendorf, *Class and Class Conflict,* pp. 223 ff.

nonetheless, we are at least provided with a crude rank-order basis for comparing elites' approaches to handling conflict.

Our storehouse of scholarly literature on China is well stocked with passages about social conflict and its creation, exploitation, and handling; indeed, for the Communist period it would be difficult to treat any topic at length without encountering instances of noticeable contradiction, tension, or even open struggle. It is therefore all the more surprising to discover that we have no general study which attempts to pinpoint the decision-making points (institutional or otherwise) where different sorts of conflicts are dealt with, both to characterize resolution processes and to compare them to functional equivalents in other systems as a means of seeking explanation for Chinese approaches. How much observed variation is attributable to pre-Communist conflict resolution traditions? How much to CCP innovations, to particularities of the Chinese postrevolutionary phase, to universal bureaucratic pressures, or to poverty? Does "elite nature" have an independent effect?

Fortunately, while the absence of general work on these questions continues, legal scholars have seized the initiative and produced some innovative analyses in particular sectors, notably, contractual and criminal law.[56] In fact, the most imaginative article yet published comparing social processes in China with those elsewhere has emerged from an analysis of the processes by which "criminals" are identified and punished under Chinese and American systems of criminal law, processes which turn out to contrast less in reality than they do in theory. Armed conceptually with polar opposite "due process" and "crime control" models, Richard Pfeffer finds elements of each in both countries' criminal-law practice. While American defendants enjoy greater "due process" protection than their Chinese counterparts, this difference appears most sharply in latter stages of the process for that small minority of cases (5–10 per cent) actually brought to trial.[57] In the future, emulating the standard set by this interpretation, much valuable comparative analysis should be possible using conflict handling as a dependent variable.

[56] See Jerome Alan Cohen, *The Criminal Process in the People's Republic of China, 1949–1963: An Introduction* (Cambridge, Mass.: Harvard University Press, 1968); Stanley Lubman, "Mao and Mediation: Politics and Dispute Resolution in Communist China," *California Law Review,* LV, No. 5 (November, 1967), 1284–1359; and Stanley Lubman, "Form and Function in the Chinese Criminal Process," *Columbia Law Review,* LXIX (April, 1969), 535–75.

[57] Richard M. Pfeffer, "Crime and Punishment: China and the United States," *World Politics,* XXI, No. 1 (October, 1968), 165.

RELATIONS BETWEEN ELITE AND NONELITE

Aloofness of leaders from nonleaders is not uniformly held to be bad. Social distance can create a mystique of social rank, which in turn can induce a noncoercive deference for the august "statesmen" who rule. Or again, prior to impending tactical moves, official secrecy (especially in economic or foreign policy) can easily be defended. Yet there always is a danger that the conveniences of aloofness will prove too comfortable for the elite, causing them to lose all touch with the nonelite; and "for elites, isolation ultimately is a sentence of death." [58] Once isolated, even a charismatic leader may fall: according to Reinhard Bendix, while "charisma appears to occur frequently because the search for it continues . . . genuine charisma is a rare event, born as it is of a belief in the mysterious gift of one man, *which that man shares with those who follow him* (emphasis added).[59]

First of all, isolation can lead to the emergence of political interests articulated by the elite qua elite: ". . . the interests of the leaders are no longer fully identified with those of the rank and file, since they include the special interests of the leaders in maintaining their own leadership—an interest which is no doubt rationalized, but not always justly, as constituting the interest of the whole group." [60] Second, isolation can lead to a significant information gap, "a gap that nullifies many of the rights available to the public on paper."

Ignorance of the public often encourages leaders to resort to irrational methods of persuasion and communication. In an age of mass communications, the power of leaders to manipulate public opinion is extraordinary. "The spectacle of an efficient elite maintaining its authority and asserting its will over the mass by the rationally calculated use of irrational methods of persuasion is the most disturbing nightmare of mass democracy." The best safeguard against this danger is for the public to become literate, informed, and thus potentially critical of decisions and proposals made by leaders.[61]

On the question of how to contain elite isolation, Western scholarship has little to offer. The problem is apparently assumed in the West to be solved through the liberal-democratic, representational electoral process. While accurate in part, this assumption fails to consider the importance of nonresponsible bureaucratic power, concentra-

[58] Keller, *Beyond the Ruling Class*, p. 239.
[59] "Reflections on Charismatic Leadership," *Asian Survey*, VII, No. 6 (June, 1967), 352.
[60] E. H. Carr, *The New Society* (Boston: Beacon Press, 1951), p. 77.
[61] Keller, *Beyond the Ruling Class*, p. 264. The interior quotation is again from Carr, *The New Society*, p. 77.

tions of private influence, and even ways in which constituencies to which elected officials are responsible can be severely limited. Lucian Pye merely echoes the thoughts of Pareto when he advises governments negotiating the vulnerable "transition period" to maintain a flexible outlook and to coopt from among the mass group "those who have political aspirations" (a form of "political tutelage").[62]

This limited counsel is especially surprising since in the same context "the central cause of political instability in transitional societies" is identified by Pye as "the lack of an effective relation between the ruling elites and their peoples." [63] Contrarily, as shown by the experience of prewar Japan, stability in the short run may be only weakly related to elite-mass unity. The new bureaucrats (*shinkanryo*) of the 1930's and 1940's carried to an extreme the early Meiji ideal of a higher civil service (*kobun*) recruited by examination and trained largely at Tokyo University: "Their wartime appearance, the last stage of the history of the *kobun* official system, was an eruption of the worst features of elitism. The exaggerated elite consciousness of *kobun* bureaucrats who went hand in hand with the military elites contributed substantially to the collapse of Imperial Japan." [64] Stability became superstability in the Japanese case, and that in turn became expansive fascism, all apparently without "an effective relation between the ruling elites and their peoples." While this particular interpretation of Japan in the 1930's may be open to dispute, the two works cited do illustrate that much remains to be understood about the elite isolation outcome.

Though much has been written, little is understood about this problem in the case of China. Because all research has been focused on cadres or elites, we can at best talk about elite-mass relations from the

---

[62] *Aspects of Political Development* (Boston: Little, Brown, 1966), pp. 76–77.

[63] *Ibid.*, p. 78. "Stability" is widely taken as a desirable output in comparative studies of developing areas; it is rarely defined and almost never considered as a scalar quantity in relation to its natural converses, "change" and "good government." Cf. Robert A. Dahl, *Who Governs?* (New Haven, Conn.: Yale University Press, 1961), p. 311.

[64] Yoshinori Ide and Takeshi Ishida, "The Education and Recruitment of Governing Elites in Modern Japan," in Rupert Wilkinson (ed.), *Governing Elites: Studies in Training and Selection* (New York: Oxford University Press, 1969), p. 132. Sociologist Irving Horowitz draws a direct relation between *instability* and democracy in Latin America. "The military has increasingly surrendered direct political control, except for short interim periods. It has enough power to prevent governments unfavorable to itself from exercising authority, but not enough to rule for any length of time. This then is a basic reason for the instability of Latin American governments, which in turn may help to democratize these governments by preventing the hardening of any political complex and by minimizing the effects of already overdeveloped bureaucracies." See "The Military Elites," in Lipset and Solari (eds.), *Elites in Latin America*, pp. 149–50.

elite point of view alone. Is it possible to show that China's masses prefer Mao's policies to others? Do Chinese masses even know what Mao's policies are, as distinct from other central or local leaders' policies? At what level in the Chinese bureaucratic hierarchy do people become aware of what different positions are being advocated on policy questions, at any level of decision-making? Do the Chinese media engage in the "rationally calculated use of irrational methods of persuasion?" Is a "literate, informed and thus potentially critical" public an effective safeguard in the Chinese context?

For comparative purposes, do the Chinese elite's methods of gathering information and otherwise acquainting themselves with the effects of basic-level policy implementation compare favorably or unfavorably with different methods used elsewhere, particularly where the social and economic context imposes similar limitations? Measured against other systems, what degree of success have the Chinese elite achieved in identifying and responding to the interests of the public? Funnel suggests that "in the absence of a rival power centre, or any real political alternative, one source of pressure on the Party to formulate popularly acceptable policies may be removed, or at any rate become less urgent." [65] Is this a fatal flaw in the Chinese system, or have substitute means been adequate to the need, and if so, under what conditions? Pye writes that in China, "while the gap of alienation in most transitional societies has been between a Westernized and modern inspired elite and a still traditionalist mass, in China the gap of alienation has been between the dispossessed Westernized intellectuals and a political elite that has remained closer to the masses." [66] Was this ever true? In what sense might it still be true under the Communist regime in its different periods? Much data upon which answers to these questions could draw have already been published, but we have widely avoided ordering them in a meaningful fashion.

PYRAMIDING POLITICAL RESOURCES

"Political resources," like economic resources (land, labor, capital), are quantities exploitable by entrepreneurs to achieve influence (profits), often under pressure from competitors. Dahl defines them as "anything that can be used to sway the specific choices or the strategies of another individual"; Warren Ilchman and Norman Uphoff describe them as "things of economic, social, and political worth"

[65] "The Cadres," p. 12.
[66] *Spirit of Chinese Politics*, p. 38.

(akin to David Easton's "values"). Following Dahl's notion that almost everyone has some political resources, however unequally dispersed, Ilchman and Uphoff originated the concept of "sector" as "a group of persons who respond to political issues in a similar fashion"; sectors such as landlords, minority-group merchants, or high-ranking civil servants are then said to differ not only on the basis of their interests and degree of organization, but also according to "their resource position and its composition." Consequently, a regime constructs its supportive coalition through a process of political exchange, whereupon the various sectors can be arrayed from the highly influential "core combination" to the relatively ignored "unmobilized sectors." [67] In essence, the theoretical debate between proponents of elitist democracy and mass democracy hinges on the issue of how widely political resources should be distributed outside the "core combination." [68]

Sometimes the concept of political resource is crudely employed in fact if not in name. Irving Horowitz, for instance, argues that effective curbs can be applied to military takeover regimes in Latin America by civilian authorities with "weapons" (resources) of their own.[69] From his analysis, then, there would seem to be no enduring way for military elites to "pyramid" various civilian resources.

I regard the political resource concept as extremely valuable, if for no other reason than because it opens the door to more precise descriptions of how influence is dispersed than we are accustomed to make, a step prerequisite to analyzing bargaining relationships which most certainly occur in China as elsewhere. Little by little the concept fortunately has begun to appear in writing about the Chinese Communists. Richard Baum singles out "the instruments of coercion, the channels of social mobility, and the media of mass communications." Richard

[67] Dahl, *Who Governs?*, p. 226. Ilchman and Uphoff, *Political Economy of Change* (Berkeley: University of California Press, 1969), pp. 19, 39–40, 43. The intermediate categories are "ideological bias," "stability group," and "extra-stability group."

[68] See Peter Bachrach, *The Theory of Democratic Elitism: A Critique* (Boston: Little, Brown, 1967). "Widespread mass support of totalitarian movements in prewar Europe and the rise of powerful proletarian-based Communist parties in postwar France and Italy, of Peronism in Argentina and McCarthyism in the United States have badly shaken the confidence of liberals in the cause of democracy. The increased power of established elites in democratic countries consequently has not been entirely disapproved of from this quarter. In fact, reminiscent of the views of de Tocqueville, Burke, and de Maistre, elites are once again regarded not only as the energetic and creative forces of society, but, above all, as the source which sustains the system. The relationship of elites to masses is, in a vital way, reversed from classical theory: masses, not elites, become the potential threat to the system, and elites, not masses, become its defender" (pp. 8–9).

[69] "The Military Elites," in Lipset and Solari *Elites in Latin America*, pp. 157–58. Cf. Janowitz, *The Military*, pp. 83 ff.; and Max Millikan and Donald Blackmer (eds.), *The Emerging Nations* (Boston: Little, Brown, 1961), p. 36.

Walker selects a different set to compare the dawn of the Communist period with the outset of its third decade. And second on Oksenberg's list of necessary steps for getting ahead and along in Chinese official-dom is to "hoard resources; do not squander them"; for resources he includes "knowledge, influence, and personal obligations owed by others, as well as material goods." [70] As already suggested, though, much more can be done with political resources than simply offering a few examples; for China studies the opportunities all lie ahead of us.

INNOVATION AND DEVELOPMENT

Literature on problems of economic, social, and political development (however defined) often treats elite nature as a significant variable. But to learn just what elite characteristics affect causally just what elements of development, much work still needs to be done. The case of Japan is illustrative. On the one hand, the successful Japanese modernization begun in the second half of the nineteenth century is attributed in large measure to the composition and initiatives of the Meiji elite. "If these several studies collectively yield any large generalization it is simply this: the existence of a strong strategic elite in the initial stages of modernization is more important than a comprehensive design for change or a variety of politically articulate groups competing with each other." [71] Not only was the old samurai elite effectively retired by the Meiji genro (all of whom except Saionji Kimmochi were samurai themselves), but a new business elite was actively encouraged.[72] In addition, the education system was used to provide a new cadre of trained and highly motivated young people, as

[70] Baum, "Ideology Redivivus," *Problems of Communism* (May–June, 1967), p. 8. Walker, in A. Doak Barnett and Edwin O. Reischauer (eds.), *The United States and China: The Next Decade* (New York: Praeger, 1970), pp. 6–7. Oksenberg, "Getting Ahead and Along in Communist China," p. 338.

[71] Harootunian, "Introduction," in Silberman and Harootunian (eds.), *Modern Japanese Leadership,* p. 5. Sidney Brown reiterates the point in his contribution ("Okubo Toshimichi and the First Home Ministry Bureaucracy, 1873–78") to the same book: "The innovating bureaucrats of early Meiji guided Japan's modernization to a greater degree than their Occidental counterparts did in an earlier era. This political elite of informed, perceptive civil servants grasped power directly, and—particularly after 1873 —carried out plans for the modernization of the Japanese economy and polity. By contrast, the economic elites, among them the urban middle class, played relatively less prominent roles than did the European bourgeoisie or the American tycoon" (p. 195).

[72] Hirschmeier, *Origins of Entrepreneurship in Meiji Japan,* pp. 34–35. The author goes on to point out that "for the most part merchants remained unenthusiastic, and many of them participated in the scheme only under pressure. In Tokyo the government threatened noncooperating merchants with exile to Hokkaido." Because of previous policies, merchants were suspicious that investments in exchange and trading companies would be equivalent to a forced loan (*goyōkin*).

well as to enhance the status of occupations needed for modernization: ". . . the well-known preferential treatment and support existing between the *gakubatsu* (school clique) and the *zaibatsu* (used here in the rather broad sense of leading enterprises) really started in these years when the Keiō and shortly afterwards the Hitotsubashi University supplied the zaibatsu with talented and progressive managers." [73]

On the other hand, as William Lockwood contends, it is easy to exaggerate the effect upon Japanese development attributable to the Meiji oligarchy's vigorous initiative: ". . . the real drive and momentum lay in large measure outside the realm of national political ambition and State activity." [74] But as Lockwood himself points out, state and elite are not the same, and minimizing the impact of state activity does not necessarily detract from the importance of the composition of the elite:

> Given the temper of Japan's leaders, their control over wealth, and the strength of the Japanese social fabric, it was unnecessary to rely on State coercion extensively to mobilize resources for industrialization. Moreover, while different elements of the ruling coalition—for example, the military and the zaibatsu—often had divergent interests, they found it possible for a long time to harmonize their differences in a political regime with limited economic responsibilities; and no popular movement arose with sufficient power to wrest control and impose a different pattern.[75]

Some favorable influence upon development beyond the realm of state intervention was a product of the genro-dominated elite which managed the transition.

Development writers have also asserted that "in societies where values are antithetical to economic development," entrepreneurial roles must be introduced by social "deviants" in terms of the ongoing system values.[76] In Everett Hagen's formulation, the greatest innovational force can be expected to build up among those groups within the old elite that have suffered "withdrawal of status respect":

> . . . there gradually emerges a group of individuals, creative, alienated from traditional values, driven by a gnawing burning drive to prove themselves (to themselves, as well as to their fellows), seeking for an area in which to do so, preferably also one in which in some symbolic way they can vent their rage at the elites who have caused their troubles. . . . The fact that the disparaging group . . . was

[73] *Ibid.*, p. 259.

[74] *The Economic Development of Japan* (Princeton, N.J.: Princeton University Press, 1964), p. 574.

[75] *Ibid.*, p. 590.

[76] Lipset, in Lipset and Solari (eds.), *Elites in Latin America*, p. 23.

traditional is one of the reasons why the disparaged group rejected traditional values and turned to innovation.[77]

Data on the composition of the Meiji elite from 1868 to 1873, the earliest phase of the Restoration, reveals the prominence of lower samurai, imperial court nobles (*kuge*), and individuals from "outer" clans—all of whom were disadvantaged in status terms under Tokugawa rule.[78]

Since the publication of Marion Levy's two aging studies on Chinese entrepreneurship,[79] elite variables have generally been given subdued attention in the literature on China's economic development. Whether we compare the overall Chinese experience with that of other systems— Communist China with Republican China, the Mainland with Taiwan, or the development program of one CCP coalition with that of another —the most commonly discussed themes are self-reliance vs. foreign assistance, styles of state intervention, popular mobilization and incentives, or collectivization. To my knowledge only David McClelland has subsequently made an explicit empirical probe into a relevant elite-related factor—conscious use of primary education to instill new patterns of motivation. He devised a standard score to measure the relative emphasis that children's fiction from different countries devoted respectively to needs (n) for achievement, affiliation, and power. The following table presents McClelland's mean and standard scores for motivational themes in three sets of children's readers. Even without an explanation of how the scores were derived, variation is shown to be sharp ("a score of + 3.00 is about as wide a deviation from the mean as the standard score scale registers").[80]

	Republican China (1920–29)		China Taiwan (1950–59)		China Mainland (1950–59)	
	mean	score	mean	score	mean	score
n Achievement	0.86	−0.90	1.81	−0.25	2.24	+0.32
n Affiliation	0.38	−2.02	0.43	−1.91	1.05	−0.55
n Power	1.29	+1.53	1.00	+0.57	1.81	+3.27

[77] "How Economic Growth Begins: A Theory of Social Change," *The Journal of Social Issues,* XIX, No. 1 (January, 1963), 32–33.

[78] Bernard Silberman, "Elite Transformation in the Meiji Restoration: The Upper Civil Service, 1868–1873," in Silberman and Harootunian (eds.), *Modern Japanese Leadership,* p. 236.

[79] *The Rise of the Modern Chinese Business Class: Two Introductory Essays* (New York: International Secretariat, Institute of Pacific Relations, 1949); "Contrasting Factors in the Modernization of China and Japan," *Economic Development and Cultural Change,* II (October, 1953), 161–97.

[80] "Motivational Patterns in Southeast Asia with Special Reference to the Chinese

The current mainstream of related analysis, however, is to write variations on a general theme of incompatibility between (1) visionary equalitarian ideals and the radical politics they inspire, and (2) the twin phenomena of "development" and "bureaucratization," which are assumed to correlate invariably:

On the one hand, modernization is positively valued as a social goal, for modernization means economic development and economic development means national power. On the other hand, however, modernization entails bureaucracy, instrumentalism, and the consequent attenuation and ritual sterilization of ideological principles. Damned if they do and damned if they don't, the leaders of the CPSU and the CCP have thus been forced to steer a not altogether happy course between the Scylla of modernization-cum-revisionism and the Charybdis of atavism-cum-orthodoxy.[81]

Similarly, Ying-mao Kau avers that the Chinese leadership must "moderate its fanatic drive" toward giving prominence to politics if national development is to continue: "What appears to be particularly critical today in China's bureaucratic system is the regime's excessive emphasis on political priorities and hostility toward bureaucratic authority and professionalism. A more balanced system which pays equal attention to political leadership and to professional authority is probably what China needs most in its quest for modernization." [82]

However, a few imaginative students of the Chinese economy who have deserted their firm statistical ground to venture out into the vaguer realm of the Chinese political economy have found more than "many and profound" differences between capitalist and Maoist processes of economic development ("perhaps the most striking difference . . . is in regard to goals").[83] They also have found internal differences between "Maoists and the 'followers' of Liu Shao-ch'i" that involve "important political, social, and philosophical considerations" in addition to purely economic ones.[84] Finally, faint voices are even beginning to ask (perhaps prompted by our new awareness of the abominable waste and pollution which modernization has brought to

Case," *Journal of Social Issues*, XIX, No. 1 (January, 1963), 12–13. Cf. John W. Lewis, "Education and the Chinese Polity: Themes in Development," in James S. Coleman (ed.), *Education and Political Development* (Princeton, N.J.: Princeton University Press, 1963).

81 Baum, "Ideology Redivivus," p. 8.

82 "Urban Bureaucratic Elite," p. 264.

83 John G. Gurley, "Capitalist and Maoist Economic Development," *Bulletin of Concerned Asian Scholars*, II, No. 3 (April–June, 1970), 38.

84 Charles Hoffman, "The Maoist View of China's Development: Diagnosis and Prescription" (mimeographed; Chapter 1 of a forthcoming book tentatively entitled *The Chinese Worker*), p. 1.

America) whether the "modernization" process itself might have a wholly new meaning to the Chinese.

Will efficiency, specialization, and bureaucratic rationality eventually dissipate the appeal of revolutionary values? Is Mao one of the last great political romantics whose vision is ultimately doomed? It is tempting to . . . predict China's future on the basis of the experience of the early modernizers. But precedents are of dubious worth in this case. Not just in China (or in the developing countries), but throughout the world, the present is a time of great institutional flux. It seems likely that we shall see a proliferation of social experiments that will enlarge our vision of what modernity means. All we can do here is note some limiting factors which the Maoist experiment is likely to face.[85]

Above all this is a plea to go beyond considering China as a "transitional society" (as Pye urges) to ask "transition to what?"

Numerous factors have been proposed to explain observable configurations of policy views among China's elite on "development" issues: continuing strength of the "Yenan legacy," Chinese rejection of the "Soviet model" on nationalistic grounds, negative consequences of the Great Leap Forward, and long-standing antipathies among elite personages. But the considerably more rigorous exercises of specifying concrete criteria for economic and social "modernity" and of formulating alternative hypotheses as falsifiable statements have yet to be undertaken. Most interesting and most deserving of study in this regard are the experimental Chinese attempts to include the welfare of the countryside in their overall development program, instead of resigning themselves to the growth of modern, urban subcultures in coastal cities.

POLICY

Do variations in elite nature have any independent effect upon public policy decisions? In turn, we must ask whether answers to that question depend upon the level of specificity of the policy choice, such as: (1) laying down national priorities, for example, foreign war vs. investment at home, welfare vs. aid to business, housing vs. education; (2) implementing those priorities, as in research and trial programs, provision of legal recourse, assistance to localities, creation of new national administrations, launching major "moral suasion" campaigns; and (3) financing implementing programs.

Is it true that political elites of democratic-centralist governments

---

[85] Jon Saari, "China's Special Modernity," in Bruce Douglass and Ross Terrill (eds.), *China and Ourselves: Explorations and Revisions by a New Generation* (Boston: Beacon Press, 1969), p. 66.

in socialist countries, freed from accountability to big owners of land and corporate capital, are more humanistically inclined in policy than elites of liberal-democratic governments in capitalist societies?

Is it true that governing elites elected under Shumpeterian procedural formulas are more pluralistic and hence more peace-loving and less aggressive than dictatorships, even ones which can rally a mandate at the polls through an exercise in mass democracy?

Is it true that Communist elites, sprung from urban backgrounds and dedicated to the interests of heavy industrial growth and the welfare of the urban proletariat, are less able than their non-Communist counterparts to handle agriculture policy successfully?

In China studies it is more common to use visible policy stands to categorize the elite than it is to employ elite characteristics as predictors of policy preferences. Hypotheses such as the one that follows linking generational predominance with military policy views are exceptional.

Sharing professional values and goals with younger men of the fourth, sixth and seventh generations who served under them in a context of military expansion and combat with improving weaponry, this third generation will soon dominate field units throughout the PLA. From that status, their selection of officers from the fourth and fifth generations for promotion may be expected to reflect their fundamental disdain for People's War. With the advent of missiles for both strategic and tactical employment, their interest in military technology is likely to remain far more compelling than what must be considered a temporary and expedient obeisance to the thoughts of Mao.[86]

It would be valuable for us to explore which changes in "elite nature" usually have policy output consequences.

CONCLUSION

What I have attempted above is a listing of various distinctions and concepts applicable to Chinese elite studies which hold some potential for satisfying the condition laid down at the beginning of the paper: if the present movement away from classical elite sociology is ultimately to encourage discovery and refinement of generalizations about elites and their societies, then newly devised outcome concepts should make it easier for us to specify important effects wrought by variations in the nature of elites, a development which in turn should help us identify various dimensions of the "elite" concept itself. As Gerhard Lenski has noted, there are two exceptional ways of reformulating

---

[86] Whitson, "Concept of Military Generation," p. 947.

problems and concepts: transferring categorical concepts into variable concepts, and breaking down compound concepts into their constituent elements.[87] Both techniques have guided my effort here. My hope is that suggestions I have made will prove of equal assistance to future writers on Chinese elites.

[87] *Power and Privilege,* p. 20.

PART II

Elites on the National Level

DEREK J. WALLER

The Evolution of the Chinese
Communist Political Elite, 1931-56[*]

This paper is a study of the backgrounds of the Chinese Communist
political elite at two different points in time. The purpose of its first
part is to describe and analyze certain data concerning the elite operating during the Kiangsi Soviet period (1929–34). The second part of
the paper will compare and contrast these data with similar quantitative material relating to the Eighth Central Committee (CC) of the
Chinese Communist Party (CCP) in 1956. By drawing on material
presented, the second part of the paper will also be concerned with
the characteristics of and roles performed by the political elite in the
process of modernization and political development, and will examine
assumptions concerning the adaptations of the elite to the demands of
a postrevolutionary society.

For each time period, an institutional definition of "political elite"
is made. For the Kiangsi Soviet period, the elite is defined as being
the Central Executive Council (CEC) of the Chinese Soviet Republic,
and the postrevolutionary elite is defined as being the Eighth CC,
elected in 1956. An institutional, or "positional," definition is given
even though it cannot be assumed that membership on an organ is
necessarily congruent with a position of power. To assume this is to
believe that the legal prescriptions of organizational charts are accurate reflections of power relations, and to assume that power is

* I should like to thank the Vanderbilt University Research Council for the support
which made this study possible. My thanks also go to Robert Donaldson, Peggy Du-
Bose, Richard Pride, Jorgen Rasmussen, and Benjamin Walter, all of whom rendered
assistance in various ways. For all errors, I of course remain responsible.

equally distributed among all members of the organ.[1] However, since it is impossible to declare with accuracy that certain individuals constitute the "real" elite (power-holders), the elite is therefore defined in positional terms.[2]

In both cases, the CEC and the CC represent that "crucial upper-middle level" existing between the highest echelons and the masses. While the top elite were included, numerically it is the "upper-middle level" that predominates. Speaking of this level, Karl Deutsch says that they are the people "without whose cooperation or consent (or, of course, replacement) very little can be done in the decision system." The use of this kind of positional definition of the elite permits comparison over time, and also opens up the possibility of cross-national comparison with elites in other Communist systems.[3]

As has frequently been emphasized, background data on the social and career characteristics of the elite do not provide an infallible guide either to their attitudinal patterns or to their policy preferences. However, biographical analysis of such characteristics can reveal much information about the nature of the political system, particularly with reference to the role of elite recruitment as a response to systemic demands, and the degree to which the elite is representative of society as a whole.[4]

[1] For example, Article 37 of the 1956 CCP Constitution states that "the Central Committee elects at its plenary session the Political Bureau, [and] the Standing Committee of the Political Bureau. . . ." Most students of Chinese communism would agree that this situation is in fact reversed.

[2] For a consideration of this methodological problem, see Frederic J. Fleron, Jr., "Note on the Explication of the Concept 'Elite' in the Study of Soviet Politics," *Canadian Slavic Studies*, II, No. 1 (Spring, 1968), 111–15. Also, William A. Welsh, "Toward a Multiple-Strategy Approach to Research on Comparative Communist Political Elites: Empirical and Quantitative Problems," in Frederic J. Fleron, Jr. (ed.), *Communist Studies and the Social Sciences: Essays on Methodology and Empirical Theory* (Chicago: Rand McNally & Co., 1969), pp. 327–28.

[3] Karl W. Deutsch, *The Nerves of Government: Models of Political Communication and Control* (New York: Free Press, 1966), p. 155. A call for cross-national comparison was made in a review article by Dankwart A. Rustow in *World Politics*, XVIII, No. 4 (July, 1966), 690–717.

[4] For further considerations of the links between the political elite and the political system, see Carl Beck, "Career Characteristics of East European Leadership," in R. Barry Farrell (ed.), *Political Leadership in Eastern Europe and the Soviet Union* (Chicago: Aldine Publishing Co., 1970), pp. 157–94; Alexander Eckstein, "Economic Development and Political Change in Communist Systems," *World Politics*, XXII, No. 4 (July, 1970), 475–95; Lewis J. Edinger and Donald D. Searing, "Social Background in Elite Analysis: A Methodological Inquiry," *American Political Science Review*, LXI, No. 2 (June, 1967), 428–45; Frederic J. Fleron, Jr., "Cooptation as a Mechanism of Adaptation to Change: The Soviet Political Leadership System," *Polity*, II, No. 2 (Winter, 1969), 177–201, and "Representation of Career Types in Soviet Political Leadership," in Farrell (ed.), *Political Leadership in Eastern Europe and the Soviet Union*, pp. 115–16; Donald R. Matthews, *The Social Background of Political Decision-Makers* (New York: Random House, 1954);

This essay will examine, in a Chinese context, certain hypotheses concerning the functional relationship between the requirements of the political system and the social and career attributes of the elite. After 1949, China was in the grip of a "mobilization regime" committed to a rejection of the traditional order and its replacement by a program of forced industrialization and modernization. While in the Chinese case the mobilization regime was dominated by a revolutionary elite organized on democratic-centralist lines and imbued with a Marxist-Leninist philosophy, in other developing countries the revolutionary elite might well take the form of a nationalist non-Communist movement. Even so, the literature suggests that the "revolutionary intellectual" is a common element in the membership of both Communist and non-Communist mobilization regimes.[5]

The composition of this revolutionary intellectual elite has been described by John Kautsky as being made up of individuals who are "generally lawyers, journalists and teachers, students of the humanities and social sciences, philosophers, novelists and poets, they are men with a vision of the future and men who speak and write well." Furthermore, Kautsky concludes on the basis of observations from thirty societies that, unlike the mass of the population in these countries, the majority of the top revolutionary leaders were professional men, highly educated and with cosmopolitan perspectives.[6] In the following discussion of the Kiangsi Soviet elite, it will be apparent that the revolutionary intellectuals who created the Chinese revolution are clearly discernible in Kautsky's prototypes.[7]

William B. Quandt, *The Comparative Study of Political Elites* ("Comparative Politics Series," Vol. I, No. 4 [Beverly Hills, Calif.: Sage Publications, 1970]), pp. 179–84; Lester G. Seligman, "The Study of Political Leadership," *American Political Science Review*, XLIV, No. 4 (December, 1950), 904–15, and "Elite Recruitment and Political Development," *Journal of Politics*, XXVI, No. 3 (August, 1964), 612–26; and William A. Welsh, "Toward a Multiple-Strategy Approach," pp. 329–30.

[5] For further discussion of the "mobilization regime," see David E. Apter, *The Politics of Modernization* (Chicago: University of Chicago Press, 1965), esp. Chap. x; Chalmers Johnson, "Comparing Communist Nations," and Richard Lowenthal, "Development vs. Utopia in Communist Policy," in Chalmers Johnson (ed.), *Change in Communist Systems* (Stanford, Calif.: Stanford University Press, 1970), pp. 1–32 and p. 35, respectively. For the "revolutionary intellectual" concept see, for example, Samuel P. Huntington, *Political Order in Changing Societies* (New Haven, Conn.: Yale University Press, 1968), p. 290.

[6] John H. Kautsky, *Communism and the Politics of Development: Persistent Myths and Changing Behavior* (New York: John Wiley & Sons, 1968), p. 165; "Revolutionary and Managerial Elites in Modernizing Regimes," *Comparative Politics*, I, No. 4 (July, 1969), 446.

[7] These revolutionary modernizers can also be identified among the membership of the Seventh CC, elected in 1945. Speaking of this group, A. Doak Barnett has noted the middle-class origins, relatively high education, and extensive foreign travel of most of its

However, the modernization literature also hypothesizes that over time the modernization process and the concomitant tasks of organizing and administering a complex industrializing society may eventually lead to the replacement of the revolutionary intellectuals by a "managerial intelligentsia." [8] These managerial intellectuals will possess the technical training and expertise necessary to the operation of a society increasingly characterized by an advanced division of labor and the consequent emergence of new, functionally specific roles. The new managerial intelligentsia can be expected to search for more rational and efficient means of societal control and to place greater stress on material incentives with less reliance on coercion and ideology.[9] These new approaches may well bring them into conflict with the revolutionary veterans; Kautsky concludes that the revolutionary veterans will resist change and that if industrialization is to be successful, they might well have to be replaced by a new managerial elite.[10] The second part of this chapter will empirically test the degree of change in China by comparing the prerevolutionary with the postrevolutionary Chinese Communist elite.

THE KIANGSI SOVIET POLITICAL ELITE

Breaking out of the Kuomintang blockade of the Chingkangshan revolutionary base area in January, 1929, Mao Tse-tung and Chu Teh, with P'eng Teh-huai's Fifth Army guarding their rear, began campaigning in Kiangsi and spent the rest of that year consolidating their base in the southern Kiangsi and western Fukien area, centered on Juichin. By the end of 1930, nearly all of southern Kiangsi had fallen to the Red Army, and the base of the central soviet region had been established.

---

members. Few had followed a professional career prior to joining the revolutionary movement: the skills which they acquired in the long years of achieving victory in China were "those of military combat, political organization, and ideological mobilization, rather than technical or professional skills of other sorts." See Barnett, *China after Mao* (Princeton, N.J.: Princeton University Press, 1967), pp. 74–76.

8 Kautsky, *Communism and the Politics of Development,* p. 165.

9 For an excellent essay relating modernization to Chinese conditions, see Benjamin I. Schwartz, "Modernization and the Maoist Vision: Some Reflections on Chinese Communist Goals," in his *Communism and China: Ideology in Flux* (Cambridge, Mass.: Harvard University Press, 1968), pp. 162–85.

10 Kautsky, *Communism and the Politics of Development,* p. 165. See also his "Revolutionary and Managerial Elites," p. 441. This discussion of the relationship between modernization and elite composition has been drawn from Robert H. Donaldson and Derek J. Waller, *Stasis and Change in Revolutionary Elites: A Comparative Analysis of the 1956 Party Central Committees in China and the USSR* ("Comparative Politics Series," Vol. I, No. 11 [Beverly Hills, Calif.: Sage Publications, 1970]), pp. 621–27.

So began the period of the Kiangsi Soviet, one of the formative episodes in the history of the Chinese Communist movement. During this period many techniques (such as the mass line) and policies (such as land reform) were first tested, the experience of which was utilized to the full after 1949. Also during this time membership in the Communist Party grew from 122,000 in 1930 to an estimated 300,000 in 1934. In November, 1931, the Chinese Soviet Republic was established, a functioning "state" which operated primarily in the Kiangsi-Fukien area until the start of the Long March.

In this section of the paper we shall analyze the composition of the Communist elite operating during this crucial period through an investigation of the membership of the Central Executive Council of the Soviet government. The CEC was chosen to delineate the Kiangsi Soviet elite partly because an inspection of the characteristics of only the men forming the Political Bureau and Central Committee of the Chinese Communist Party would have provided too small a sample for an analysis of Communists active during this period, even omitting the difficulties of determining such membership. Furthermore, the histories and careers of many of these Party leaders have been documented as well as possible elsewhere. Widening the group to include all CEC members (not one of whom is known to have been a non-Communist) allows a more comprehensive analysis of the Communist movement of the time by providing some idea of the kind of people the leaders were and of the careers they followed. This analysis also furnishes clues as to the nature of the present-day Chinese Communist leadership, so many of whose members first rose to prominence in the Party during this period.[11]

[11] The major source of data used in this section of the paper was the *Shih-sou-shih kung-fei tzu-liao* (The Ch'en Ch'eng Collection of Communist Bandit Documents), microfilm, 21 reels (Stanford, Calif.: Hoover Institution on War, Revolution and Peace, Stanford University). On the microfilms, particular use has been made of issues of the Soviet government newspaper *Hung-se chung-hua* (Red China), Nos. 1–243, December 11, 1931–October 20, 1934 (incomplete); also, the Red Army organ, *Hung-hsing* (Red Star), Nos. 4–66, August 27, 1933–September 25, 1934 (incomplete).

Other sources include: General Ch'en Ch'eng (comp.), *Ch'ih-fei fan-tung wen-chien hui-pien* (A Collection of Red Bandit Reactionary Documents) (Taipei, 1935, reprinted in six vols., 1960); Chou-mo pao-she (comp.), *Hsin chung-kuo jen-wu chih* (Eminent Persons in the New China) (2 vols.; Hong Kong, 1950); *Fei-wei jen-shih tzu-liao hui-pien* (Collected Bandit Personnel Material) (Taipei, 1961); *Gendai chūgoku jinmei jiten* (A Biographical Dictionary of Contemporary Chinese) (Tokyo: Kasumigaseki-kai, 1962); Hua Ying-shen, *Chung-kuo kung-ch'an-tang lieh-shih chuan* (The Biographies of Chinese Communist Martyrs) (Hong Kong: Hsin-min-chu ch'u-pan-she, 1949); *Hung-ch'i p'iao-p'iao* (The Red Flag Waves), Nos. 1–13 (Peking: South China Press, 1957–60); Robert Rinden and Roxane Witke, *The Red Flag Waves: A Guide to the Hung-ch'i p'iao-p'iao Collection* ("China Research Monographs" [Berkeley, Calif.: Center for

The Central Executive Council, the supreme governmental organ of the Chinese Soviet Republic, comprised a total of 241 people elected either at the First National Soviet Congress in November, 1931, or at the Second Congress of January–February, 1934, or both.[12] The National Soviet Congress was the highest formal authority in the Soviet areas. The congress elected a Central Executive Council which was to have supreme executive power in the intervals between congresses. The CEC in turn elected a Council of People's Commissars as the highest administrative organ of the state. The statistics presented in this paper represent the information collected on the CEC membership of 241 individuals, expressed in percentage terms of the total number on whom data are available. At one time or another the CEC numbered among its membership virtually all the Chinese Communist leaders of the time, including Chang Kuo-t'ao, Chang Wen-t'ien (Lo Fu), Ch'en Shao-yü (Wang Ming), Ch'in Pang-hsien (Po Ku), Chou En-lai, Chu Teh, Ch'ü Ch'iu-pai, Fang Chih-min, Hsiang Ying, K'ang Sheng (Chao Yün), Liu Shao-ch'i, Jen Pi-shih, Mao Tse-tung, Shen Tse-min, and Tseng Shan.

In addition to acting as the government of the Chinese Soviet Republic, the Communist executive in the Soviet areas also aspired to being a potential government of all China, and a counterweight to Chiang Kai-shek in the national arena. However, at the foundation of the Chinese Soviet Republic at Juichin, Kiangsi, on November 7, 1931, little or no effort was made to bring delegates to the congress from outside the soviet areas; and although the government, when

Chinese Studies, University of California, 1968]); Tso-liang Hsiao, *Power Relations within the Chinese Communist Movement, 1930–1934,* Vol. I: *A Study of Documents* (Seattle: University of Washington Press, 1961), and Vol. II: *The Chinese Documents* (Seattle: University of Washington Press, 1967); Nym Wales, *Red Dust: Autobiographies of Chinese Communists* (Stanford, Calif.: Stanford University Press, 1952).

Material on the later careers of the elite has been obtained from *Who's Who in Communist China,* Vols. I and II (rev. ed.; Hong Kong: URI, 1969); Howard L. Boorman and Richard C. Howard (eds.), *Biographical Dictionary of Republican China,* Vols. I–IV (New York: Columbia University Press, 1967–71); Donald W. Klein and Anne B. Clark, *Biographic Dictionary of Chinese Communism, 1921–1965* (Cambridge, Mass.: Harvard University Press, 1971).

[12] A full listing of the 1931 CEC membership can be found in the *Chung-hua su-wei-ai kung-ho-kuo chung-yang chih-hsing wei-yüan-hui pu-kao, ti-i-hao* (Announcement No. 1 of the Central Executive Council of the Chinese Soviet Republic), dated December 1, 1931, on the Ch'en Ch'eng microfilm, reel 16; also printed in *Hung-se chung-hua,* No. 1 (December 11, 1931), p. 2. The 1934 CEC membership is listed in the *Chung-hua su-wei-ai kung-ho-kuo chung-yang chih-hsing wei-yüan-hui pu-kao, ti-i-hao,* dated February 5, 1934, on the Ch'en Ch'eng microfilm, reel 16; also printed in *Hung-se chung-hua,* No. 148 (February 12, 1934), p. 1. A cumulative list of all 1931 and 1934 CEC members can also be located in Klein and Clark, *Biographic Dictionary of Chinese Communism,* II, 1,075–77.

elected, claimed to be a national government, it was at best only representative of the various Communist-occupied areas of the country, since the CEC did include several persons from other soviet bases, such as Chang Kuo-t'ao from the Oyüwan border area (Hupeh-Honan-Anhwei), Ho Lung from Hsiangosi (Hunan-West Hupeh), Chang Ting-ch'eng and Fang Chih-min from Fukien, and P'eng Teh-huai from Hsiangkan (Hunan-Kiangsi), in addition to Mao Tse-tung and Hsiang Ying from the central soviet area in Kiangsi.

For the Second National Soviet Congress of January–February, 1934, far greater efforts were made to get delegates to come from other soviet areas, from the Nationalist-controlled regions of China, and even from foreign countries. Particular stress was placed on obtaining representatives from the industrial provinces and centers such as Hopeh, Manchuria, Shanghai, and Wuhan. These efforts met with some success, and delegates to the congress reportedly came from such places as Shanghai, Manchuria, and Amoy, as well as Hong Kong, Korea, Java, Taiwan, and Annam.[13] Even so, in terms of numerical strength, these delegates from the "White areas" were a tiny minority of seventeen as compared with 676 from the soviet areas.[14] Therefore, little concrete support was forthcoming from areas which the Communists did not directly control, although the inclusion of delegates from the "White areas" and from overseas did allow Communist propaganda to continue to claim that *"in the Chinese Soviet Republic all conditions and elements of a modern state, worthy of being called a civilised people's republic, already exist."* [15]

Demographic and Career Attributes of CEC Membership

It is unfortunate that, despite intensive investigation, in many cases nothing is known about some CEC personnel except their names and their election in 1931 or 1934. On the average, for any given characteristic, there is information on about 30 per cent of the total.[16] Many of the "unknowns" were probably military figures who were killed in

[13] *Hung-se chung-hua,* Special Edition on the Second Congress, No. 2 (January 24, 1934), p. 2.

[14] *Ibid.,* p. 3. The figure for the "White area" delegates includes those not only from the Nationalist-controlled areas, but also from foreign countries.

[15] Wang Ming and K'ang Sin [K'ang Sheng], *Revolutionary China Today* (London: Modern Books Ltd., n.d.), p. 20 (emphasis in original).

[16] The tendency is for the majority of characteristics to be identified for the same 30 per cent of CEC members, although there are individuals on whom isolated bits of information are available. All the tables on the CEC (1–6) therefore analyze approximately the same sample group.

action during the Kiangsi Soviet period, who did not survive the Long March, or who were only elected to alternate membership at the Second Congress and never fulfilled their earlier promise. Although 30 per cent is not a large sample, much of the information, particularly that from the Ch'en Ch'eng collection of documents, has not hitherto been brought to light, and it is believed that this biographical analysis, although it cannot furnish precise information, will provide new insights into this period in the history of the Chinese Communist movement. It is a period which remains in many respects as described by one leading scholar: "largely a myth, if not a blank, in our knowledge of the history of the CCP to date." [17]

We do not assume that the CEC as an institution wielded a great deal of power in Soviet China. It was too large a body for effective governance and, furthermore, its membership was scattered over too wide an area. Its functions were usually performed by the Council of People's Commissars or its Presidium. It is not as a measurement of power but of prestige that this organ assumes significance. CEC membership can be considered indicative of an individual holding a position of some standing in the soviet areas.

The CEC was an overwhelmingly male group, as might be expected of a revolutionary elite functioning under wartime conditions. Of the known females in the group, moreover, many were the wives of prominent Communists who were themselves elected to the CEC. These included Chang Ch'in-ch'iu (who had been married to Ch'en Ch'ang-hao and to Shen Tse-min), K'ang K'o-ch'ing (wife of Chu Teh), Li Chien-chen (married to Teng Chen-hsün), Liu Ch'ün-hsien (married

---

[17] Hsiao, *Power Relations*, I, 302. Some recent scholarship, however, has added to our knowledge of the period. See William F. Dorrill, "Transfer of Legitimacy in the Chinese Communist Party: Origins of the Maoist Myth," *CQ*, No. 36 (October–December, 1968), pp. 45–60; and the same author's "The Fukien Rebellion and the CCP: A Case of Maoist Revisionism," *CQ*, No. 37 (January–March, 1969), pp. 31–53. See also Ilpyong J. Kim, "Mass Mobilization Policies and Techniques Developed in the Period of the Chinese Soviet Republic," in A. Doak Barnett (ed.), *Chinese Communist Politics in Action* (Seattle: University of Washington Press, 1969), pp. 78–98; Tso-liang Hsiao, *The Land Revolution in China, 1930–1934: A Study of Documents* (Seattle: University of Washington Press, 1969); John E. Rue, *Mao Tse-tung in Opposition, 1927–1935* (Stanford, Calif.: Hoover Institution on War, Revolution and Peace, Stanford University Press, 1966); Henry G. Schwarz, "The Nature of Leadership: The Chinese Communists, 1930–1945," *World Politics*, XXII, No. 4 (July, 1970), 541–81.

See also the series of articles by Warren Kuo on Chinese Communist history in *Issues and Studies*, Vols. II–IV (1965–68), reprinted as Book 2 of Kuo's *Analytical History of Chinese Communist Party* (Taipei: Institute of International Relations, 1968); and Tien-wei Wu, "The Kiangsi Soviet Period: A Bibliographical Review," *Journal of Asian Studies*, XXIX, No. 2 (February, 1970), 395–412.

to Ch'in Pang-hsien), Teng Ying-ch'ao (married to Chou En-lai), and Ts'ai Ch'ang (wife of Li Fu-ch'un). It is not clear to what extent nepotism played a role in their selection.

As far as is known, the vast majority of the CEC were Han Chinese. The only known exceptions were Kuan Hsiang-ying, a Manchu, and Wei Pa-ch'ün, who was a member of the Chuang national minority. In the provinces of origin (for which information is available on eighty-five individuals, or 35.3 per cent of the elite), Hunan, Szechwan, and Hupeh were the most heavily represented—indeed, they account for over half the sample—followed by Kiangsu, Kwangtung, Kiangsi, and Chekiang. Taken together, these seven provinces of the south and central coast and central interior of China provided the birthplaces of 83.5 per cent of all CEC members whose birthplaces are known (see Table 1). The high percentage of the elite emanating from Hunan, Hupeh, and Kiangsi is no doubt explained by the strong Soviet organization in those areas. Truly, this was the heart of the Chinese Communist movement after the forced evacuation of the coastal urban centers.

The figures are particularly striking when the percentage of CEC members from a given province is contrasted with the percentage of the total population of China (in 1926) from the same province. Hunan is grossly overrepresented in terms of Communists coming from that province, as is Hupeh, and also Kiangsu and Szechwan (though to a lesser extent). The underrepresentation of the six northern provinces reflects the southern orientation of the CCP in its early years.[18] As Robert North notes: "An examination of Chinese upheavals since 1850 reveals South China as a revolutionary incubator, while the North has been more conservative." [19]

Of the eighty men whose date of birth is known (33.2 per cent of the total, although the sources conflict or are imprecise in the cases of some individuals), the great majority—81.3 per cent—were born between 1895 and 1909, making them twenty-two to thirty-six years old

---

[18] The figures for the 1945 Central Committee show a very similar distribution, with only a slight percentage decrease in personnel coming from the favored areas of Szechwan and Hupeh (there was actually a slight increase in the percentage from Hunan in 1945), and a slight increase from the northern provinces of Shantung, Shansi, and Shensi. See Robert C. North with Ithiel de Sola Pool, "Kuomintang and Chinese Communist Elites," in Harold D. Lasswell and Daniel Lerner (eds.), *World Revolutionary Elites: Studies in Coercive Ideological Movements* (Cambridge, Mass.: M.I.T. Press, 1965), p. 403.

[19] *Ibid.,* p. 402.

TABLE 1

GEOGRAPHICAL ORIGIN OF 1931–34 CEC MEMBERS

Birthplace	Percentage of Elite (N = 85)	Percentage of China's Total Population in 1926 *	Index of Proportional Representation †
South and Central Coast			
Kwangtung	8.2	7.6	1.08
Fukien	2.4	3.0	0.80
Chekiang	5.9	5.0	1.18
Kiangsu	9.4	7.1	1.32
			1.10
Central Interior			
Hunan	25.9	8.4	3.08
Szechwan	14.1	10.7	1.32
Hupeh	12.9	5.9	2.19
Anhwei	3.5	4.2	0.83
Kiangsi	7.1	5.7	1.25
Tsinghai	0.0	‡	§
			1.45
South Interior			
Kwangsi	2.4	2.5	0.96
Kweichow	0.0	2.3	§
Yunnan	1.2	2.3	0.52
			0.49
North			
Shantung	1.2	7.1	0.17
Hopeh	0.0	8.0	§
Honan	2.4	7.3	0.33
Shansi	1.2	2.5	0.48
Shensi	1.2	3.6	0.33
Kansu	0.0	1.5	§
			0.22
Tibet	0.0	1.3	§
Sinkiang	0.0	0.5	§
Mongolia	0.0	‡	§
Manchuria	1.2	9.9	0.12
Total	100.2 ‖		

* Post office estimate, from the *China Year Book,* 1931, p. 2, quoted in North with Pool, "Kuomintang and Chinese Communist Elites," p. 403.

† This column gives the degree of representation of the province (or sector) on the elite in terms of the percentage of the total population coming from the area. Overrepresentation is represented by a figure greater than one; underrepresentation by a figure less than one. Figures are given for each province and then averaged for the geographical section as a whole.

‡ Figures for Tsinghai and Mongolia not included in the post office estimate.

§ No figures can be obtained, as no members of the elite came from these provinces.

‖ This figure does not total 100 per cent because of the statistical error caused by rounding.

in 1931 (see Table 2). Only 15.1 per cent were over thirty-six years old. This is a remarkably young revolutionary elite, who joined the Party during the 1920's when nationalist fervor was running high.

The date of joining the CCP is known for seventy-six individuals, or 31.5 per cent of the total (see Table 3). The initial 1921–23 period

TABLE 2
AGE OF 1931–34 CEC MEMBERS

Date of Birth	Number	Percentage	Cumulative Percentage
1875–79	3	3.8	3.8
1880–84	2	2.5	6.3
1885–89	3	3.8	10.1
1890–94	4	5.0	15.1
1895–99	20	25.0	40.1
1900–04	21	26.3	66.4
1905–09	24	30.0	96.4
1910–14	3	3.8	100.2
Total	80	100.2 *	100.2 *

* These figures do not total 100 per cent because of the statistical error caused by rounding.

TABLE 3
DATES OF 1931–34 CEC MEMBERS' ENTRY INTO THE CCP

Date of Party Entry	Number	Percentage
1921	11	14.5
1922	7	9.2
1923	4	5.3
	22	29.0
1924	6	7.9
1925	15	19.7
1926	10	13.2
1927	16	21.1
	47	61.9
1928	4	5.3
1929	1	1.3
1930	0	0.0
1931	2	2.6
	7	9.2
Total	76	100.1 *

* This figure does not total 100 per cent because of the statistical error caused by rounding.

covers the interval between the founding of the CCP and the inauguration of its alliance with the Kuomintang (KMT). The 1924–27 time
span covers the period of the first KMT-CCP united front until its
collapse in 1927. Most (61.9 per cent) of the CEC members whose
date of membership is known joined the CCP during its alliance with
the KMT. It is probable that many of the "unknowns" were locally recruited from the revolutionary base areas in the early 1930's, as membership statistics indicate a considerable growth rate from 1928–33.

The high educational attainments of the Chinese soviet leadership
are illustrated by Table 4, which shows the educational stage attained
by the eighty-one men (33.6 per cent) on whom pertinent data exist.
Of these eighty-one, an extremely large number (sixty-one, or 75.3 per
cent), received some kind of advanced education. In a substantial number of cases, this was an education in one of the establishments in the
Soviet Union such as the University for the Toilers of the East or the
Sun Yat-sen University. Since these Soviet establishments were more in
the nature of indoctrination centers, and corresponded but little to
the Western concept of a university, they have therefore been classified
as "higher Party school."

TABLE 4

EDUCATIONAL LEVEL ATTAINED BY 1931–34 CEC PERSONNEL *

Education	Number	Percentage
None	7	8.6
Primary	4	4.9
Secondary (middle or normal school)	9	11.1
Advanced		
Military	5	6.2
Higher technical institute †	3	3.7
Higher Party school ‡	18	22.2
University (formal)	25	30.9
Higher Party school, plus other higher education	10	12.3
Total	81	99.9 §

* An individual is classified only according to the highest educational stage reached. Also, the fact of attendance at a higher Party
school does not necessarily imply a secondary education.

† For example, engineering school.

‡ This category also includes those who attended the Peasant
Movement Training Institute in Canton.

§ This figure does not total 100 per cent because of the statistical
error caused by rounding.

We must use the above data with care, however. No information is available on two-thirds of the CEC membership. Since education is a prestige characteristic in China, it is probable that a large proportion of this latter group received only a minimum of education or, at most, middle-school training. But since they had achieved some prominence in the soviet areas, it is unlikely that they were completely illiterate.

Table 5 covers the "foreign experience" of fifty-one men (21.2 per cent of the full group) and indicates that in most cases "foreign experience" meant a period of study in the Soviet Union. Then, in

TABLE 5

NUMBER OF 1931–34 CEC PERSONNEL STUDYING ABROAD
OR VISITING FOREIGN COUNTRIES *

Country	Study	Visits †
USSR	35	8
France	14	2
Japan	7	2
Other European country	6	5
USA	1	0
Total	63 ‡	17 ‡

* Of the total of 241 CEC members, fifty-one are known to have been abroad at least once by the time of the Second National Soviet Congress of 1934.

† "Visits" includes, for example, political visits or visits to other countries while studying abroad.

‡ An individual is counted more than once if he has visited more than one country, but not if he has visited the same country more than once (regardless of the purpose of the visit).

descending order, came study in France, Japan, some other European country, and the United States. In the case of visits abroad which did not involve study, the USSR was again the most frequented nation, followed by a European country, which was usually visited while the individual was based in France. It is clear that education abroad, combined with a stay in Russia, was a major factor in the revolutionary experience of a significant number of Communist leaders, as was the experience of the work-study program in France, under which many first came into contact with the CCP. It is probable that few of the "unknowns" had ever traveled abroad, thereby placing the cosmopolitans on the elite in a distinct minority and probably distinguishing the "top elite" in many cases from the "upper-middle level" types.

Into what revolutionary occupations did this youthful elite fall? Once in the CCP and operative in the soviet areas, not all those who had been teachers in "civilian life" remained in the field of education and training. The majority, in fact, became full-time Party workers, organizers, and administrators—pursuits offering a better chance for advancement (see Table 6). Journalists tended to put their skills to use in Party propaganda work. Without exception, those who were following military careers continued to pursue this calling in the ranks of the Red Army.

We have occupational data on 106 members (44 per cent). These data provide information about their main occupation while in the soviet areas. Of these, the largest single group (33.0 per cent) comprised military and police personnel, as might be expected in a situation where near-constant warfare marked the fate of the Chinese Soviet Republic. An additional 21.7 per cent were engaged in political work connected with the Red Army, either as members of the General Political Department or as political commissars. Over 50 per cent of the sample, therefore, were connected with the military arm of the Party. Of the remainder, 37.7 per cent were full-time Party workers within the CCP apparatus (including those engaged in organizing labor unions or peasant associations), and 7.5 per cent devoted their time to education and youth work.

TABLE 6
MAJOR OCCUPATIONS OF 1931–34 CEC PERSONNEL
IN SOVIET AREAS

Occupation	Number	Percentage
Party apparatus	40	37.7
Political work in army	23	21.7
Military or police	35	33.0
Education, youth work	8	7.5
Total	106	99.9 *

* This figure does not total 100 per cent because of the statistical error caused by rounding.

It is hazardous to advance freely generalizations concerning an elite when there are so many gaps in the data. Nevertheless, on the basis of this sample of CEC members, we can make the following summary. The data suggest that the Communist leaders of this period were predominantly male, Han Chinese, and youthful (with an average age of thirty-four in 1934). The majority, moreover, came from provinces in the central interior of China, particularly Hunan, Szechwan, and Hupeh. In terms of the percentage of the total population, these provinces, and particularly Hunan and Hupeh, were heavily over-represented. The provinces of the south and central coastal regions were also represented in greater degrees than mere population distribution warranted, indicative of the generally southern bias of the Communist movement of this period.

Educationally, this elite, or at least its most visible elements, were a remarkably well-trained group in comparison with the general Chinese populace, with much of their schooling having been obtained abroad, particularly at Russian universities. We would reiterate the fact, however, that if more information were available on the "unknowns," it would no doubt lower the average level of educational attainment considerably.

The majority of the sample tended to join the CCP when they were in their middle twenties, from 1924–27, prior to the split between the CCP and the KMT. Once in the revolutionary base areas, they tended to work in the Red Army, either as military specialists or frequently as political commissars attached to the Communist troops. Those not in the Red Army were primarily full-time Party functionaries.[20]

THE POSTREVOLUTIONARY POLITICAL ELITE

The importance of the Kiangsi Soviet period can hardly be overrated, as all students of the CCP know well. One study has shown that of the 97 men elected to full membership in the Eighth CC in 1956, no fewer than 82 (84.5 per cent) had participated in guerrilla warfare during all or part of the period.[21] Out of the 170 full and alternate members of the Eighth CC, 48 (28.2 per cent) were former CEC members, of whom 42 were full members (43.3 per cent of all full members), and there were only 2 out of the 17 men who were full members of the Political Bureau who had not been on the CEC.[22] Further-

[20] Not all CEC members were based in the central soviet district. Chang Kuo-t'ao and Shen Tse-min were in the Oyüwan (Hupeh-Honan-Anhwei) soviet area; Ch'ü Ch'iu-pai and Liu Shao-ch'i spent much of the period in Shanghai; Ch'en Shao-yü was in Moscow; Lo Teng-hsien in Manchuria; Wei Pa-ch'ün in Kwangsi; and Ho Lung, Hsia Hsi, Hsü Hsi-ken, Kuan Hsiang-ying, and Tuan Teh-ch'ang were active in the Hsiangosi (Hunan-West Hupeh) soviet area.

[21] Franklin W. Houn, "The Eighth Central Committee of the Chinese Communist Party: A Study of an Elite," *American Political Science Review*, LI, No. 2 (June, 1957), 400.

[22] P'eng Chen and Teng Hsiao-p'ing. However, this situation altered with the Ninth Party Congress of April, 1969, for at the present time (1972), of the twenty-one full

more, of the total Eighth CC membership, no less than 47.9 per cent came from the five provinces of Anhwei, Fukien, Hunan, Hupeh, and Kiangsi, their presence reflecting the intensive recruitment in the Chinese Soviet Republic prior to the Long March. Many of the Chinese Communist leaders, therefore, first became significant during the time of the Kiangsi Soviet, and an understanding of the nature of the elite during this period is essential to an understanding of later developments.

Not surprisingly, the elite characteristics of the pre-1949 period were very different from those of the period following the acquisition of state power. In the revolutionary period, military power had occupied the center of the stage, with a Party-army mobilizing the masses by means of land reform and appeals to nationalism. But from 1949 onward, the administration and modernization of a vast nation posed new problems for a Party that had now achieved a revolutionary victory.

By 1956 some of the early optimism had faded, as the Party began to realize the magnitude of the tasks imposed by modernization. The first five-year plan (1953–57), although successful in an overall sense, also revealed problems, especially in the agrarian sphere, and caused the Chinese to doubt the wisdom of mechanically emulating the Soviet economic model.[23] Further, Khrushchev's de-Stalinization speech at the Twentieth Congress of the Communist Party of the Soviet Union earlier that year had already caused reverberations in Peking. The Hundred Flowers bloom era had arrived—and was quickly to be replaced by an antirightist campaign. In this setting, in September, 1956, the CCP convened its Eighth National Party Congress and elected a new Central Committee.

Economic development and industrialization require increased divi-

---

Political Bureau members, only a minority of nine have had previous CEC positions. This statistic reflects the break-up of Party unity and a certain influx of new blood into the highest echelons of the CCP (Chu Teh, Chou En-lai, K'ang Sheng, Li Hsien-nien, Lin Piao, Liu Po-ch'eng, Mao Tse-tung, Tung Pi-wu, and Yeh Chien-ying). Still, however, of the five members of the Standing Committee of the Political Bureau (Ch'en Po-ta, Chou En-lai, K'ang Sheng, Lin Piao, and Mao Tse-tung), only one, Ch'en Po-ta, did not hold a previous position on the CEC during the Kiangsi period.

[23] By the end of 1956, the land of 90 per cent of all peasant households was collectivized. There had also been considerable progress on the industrial front, particularly with respect to heavy industry. During the 1952–57 period, the average annual rate of growth of industrial production was estimated to be between 14 and 19 per cent. China's economic problems at that time resulted partially from copying the Soviet model of concentration on heavy industry: as a result of this policy the industrial sector was relatively neglected, and the industries such as cotton, which were dependent on agriculture for their raw materials, suffered consequent setbacks following the years when harvests were poor.

sion of labor and normally produce a parallel differentiation and specialization within the bureaucracy, especially in command economies.[24] Accepting our previous dictum concerning the interaction between the political elite and the political system, one would expect that the systemic demands of modernization, as perceived by the elite, would be quickly reflected in the characteristics of that elite itself. Consequently, the Eighth CC, by comparison with its Kiangsi Soviet counterpart, should show significant differences in education, age, career patterns, and other attributes. Specifically, we might expect that younger men, more highly educated, frequently specializing in science and technology, and more appreciative of the problems of industrialization, would be brought into the elite at various levels. It might also be anticipated that in specific terms, the Party would seek to increase its legitimacy by giving additional representation to such skill groups, as well as to representatives from a wider range of geographical areas and ethnic groups.

In comparing selected variables between the Kiangsi Soviet elite and the Eighth CC, however, we find a surprising degree of continuity, even immobility, rather than change. Our data base is the total amount of information available with respect to each characteristic for all 241 CEC members (1931 and 1934) and for all 170 members (97 full and 73 alternate) elected to the Eighth CC of the CCP.[25]

With respect to geographical origin, the restriction of the CCP's recruitment base in the early years continued to foster a decided unevenness of recruitment, with the six central interior provinces of China, and particularly Hunan, still grossly overrepresented on the elite (see Table 7). While the south and central coast provinces suffered (in the aggregate) a slight decrease in their overrepresentation (and the southern interior became somewhat more underrepresented), most of the elite (50.3 per cent) still came from the interior, from areas distant from the Westernized urban coastal regions. In 1956, as in 1931–34, Mao's own home province of Hunan remained the out-

---

[24] For some details of this bureaucratic specialization, see A. Doak Barnett, *Cadres, Bureaucracy, and Political Power in Communist China* (New York: Columbia University Press, 1967), pp. 3–37; J. M. H. Lindbeck, "Transformations in the Chinese Communist Party," in Donald W. Treadgold (ed.), *Soviet and Chinese Communism: Similarities and Differences* (Seattle: University of Washington Press, 1967), pp. 84–89. See also Chalmers Johnson, "Comparing Communist Nations," pp. 15–26.

[25] Listings of the membership of the 1956 Central Committee can be found in Appendix 1 of *Who's Who in Communist China* (Hong Kong: URI, 1966); Klein and Clark, *Biographic Dictionary of Chinese Communism*, II, 1,081–89; and *Biographic Directory of Party and Government Officials of Communist China* (Washington, D.C.: U.S. Department of State, 1960), I, 2–3.

TABLE 7

GEOGRAPHICAL ORIGINS OF THE EIGHTH CENTRAL COMMITTEE
AS COMPARED TO THE KIANGSI SOVIET ELITE *

Birthplace	Percentage of Elite in 1956 (N = 169)	Percentage of Total Population in 1956	Index of Proportional Representation †	Degree of Change in Index ‡
South and Central Coast				
Kwangtung	5.9	5.9	1.00	—0.08
Fukien	4.7	2.2	2.14	1.34
Chekiang	1.8	3.9	0.46	—0.72
Kiangsu	5.9	8.1	0.73	—0.59
	18.3	20.1	1.08	—0.01
Central Interior				
Hunan	25.4	7.5	3.39	0.31
Szechwan	7.1	11.0	0.65	—0.67
Hupeh	7.7	4.9	1.57	—0.62
Anhwei	2.4	5.1	0.47	—0.36
Kiangsi	7.7	2.8	2.75	1.50
Tsinghai	0.0	0.0	§	§
	50.3	31.3	1.47	+0.03
South Interior				
Kwangsi	1.2	3.3	0.36	—0.60
Kweichow	0.0	2.5	§	§
Yunnan	0.6	3.0	0.20	—0.32
	1.8	8.8	0.19	—0.31
North				
Shantung	3.6	8.3	0.43	0.26
Hopeh	4.7	7.1	0.66	‖
Honan	3.0	7.5	0.40	0.07
Shansi	4.1	2.4	1.71	1.23
Shensi	7.7	2.7	2.85	2.52
Kansu	0.0	2.2	§	§
	23.1	30.2	1.01	+0.68
Tibet	0.6	0.2	3.00	‖
Sinkiang	0.6	0.8	0.75	‖
Inner Mongolia	1.2	1.0	1.20	‖
Manchuria	4.1	8.0	0.51	0.39
	6.5	10.0	1.37	
Total	100.0	100.4 #		

* It should be noted that 1956 provincial boundaries were not precisely identical to those of the 1930's.

† This column gives the degree of representation of the province (or sector) on the elite in terms of the percentage of the total population coming from the area. Overrepresentation is represented by a figure greater than one; underrepresentation by a figure of less than one. Figures for provincial populations in 1956 taken from Houn, "The Eighth Central Committee of the Chinese Communist Party," p. 396 (no figure is given for Tsinghai).

‡ The "Degree of Change" is the difference between the index of proportional representation in 1956 and that of the Kiangsi period given in Table 1.

§ No figures can be obtained, as no members of the elite came from these provinces.

‖ Kiangsi elite data not available.

This figure does not total 100 per cent because of the statistical error caused by rounding.

standing example of this phenomenon, as it continued to claim over one-quarter of all members of the political elite while possessing only 7.5 per cent of the population.

The only major change that took place was in the northern part of China.[26] The north now attained a membership on the elite roughly equal to its population, a substantial change from the underrepresentation of the Kiangsi period. This significant alteration, moreover, was due mainly to the larger number of individuals on the CC coming from Shansi and Shensi, since the northern provinces had been the Party's main base of operations following the Long March.[27] It should be noted, however, that the new northern representatives in the elite were Party veterans whose membership predated the Yenan era. Only four members of the Eighth CC are known to have joined the Party after 1934.[28] Thus, northern representation on the Eighth CC for the most part did not involve later recruits.

Table 8, comparing the ages of the two elites, shows remarkable stability in the age distribution of the CCP leadership. While it was true that the percentage of individuals born on or before 1899 was much lower for the Eighth CC (22.2 per cent) than for the Kiangsi elite (40.1 per cent), the largest single age group among the postrevolutionary elite consisted of those born during the 1905–9 period, and over one-half of the total elite were born prior to 1905. This had also been true with respect to the Kiangsi elite a quarter of a century earlier. Consequently, whereas the average age of the Kiangsi elite was thirty-four in 1934, the average age of the Eighth CC member had risen to fifty-three (fifty-five in the case of full members only). While the frequency distributions do vary, for instance, in the larger number of individuals born in 1910 or later (16.1 per cent of the Eighth CC, and only 3.8 per cent of the Kiangsi Soviet elite),[29] or in the decreased

[26] The autonomous regions of Tibet and Inner Mongolia were also overrepresented in 1956, although primarily because their populations were so small. In addition, eight members of the 1956 elite were non-Han, compared with two for the Kiangsi Soviet elite. With respect to sex distribution, 2.5 per cent of the Kiangsi Soviet elite were female; in 1956, 4.7 per cent of the CC and 10 per cent of all CCP members were female.

[27] A similar situation of dominance of central-south personnel also existed for Party provincial secretaries. Again, the tendency was for northerners to gain increasing representation over time. See Frederick C. Teiwes, *Provincial Party Personnel in Mainland China, 1956–1966* ("Occasional Papers of the East Asian Institute" [New York: Columbia University, 1967]), pp. 8–9.

[28] Of all known members of the Eighth CC coming from the six northern provinces, 54 per cent joined in the 1928–34 period, and most of the remainder (42 per cent) joined during the first united front. Furthermore, none of the four members of the CC who entered the Party after 1934 came from the north.

[29] Interestingly, 92.4 per cent of the 10.7 million members of the CCP in 1956 were born after 1910.

percentage born on or before 1904, the general picture shows a lack of change and a lack of upward mobility for younger men into the elite by comparison with the Kiangsi period. In 1934, more than half the elite were under the age of thirty-five, but in 1956 not a single person was under that age.

TABLE 8

COMPARISON OF THE AGES OF THE KIANGSI SOVIET ELITE
AND THE EIGHTH CENTRAL COMMITTEE

Date of Birth	Kiangsi Elite * (N = 80)		Eighth Central Committee (N = 162)	
	Percentage	Cumulative Percentage	Percentage	Cumulative Percentage
1875–79	3.8	3.8	1.2	1.2
1880–84	2.5	6.3	1.2	2.4
1885–89	3.8	10.1	1.9	4.3
1890–94	5.0	15.1	3.1	7.4
1895–99	25.0	40.1	14.8	22.2
1900–04	26.3	66.4	29.0	51.2
1905–09	30.0	96.4	32.7	83.9
1910–14	3.8	100.2 †	13.6	97.5
1915–19			2.5	100.0

* These figures are drawn from Table 2.
† This figure does not total 100 per cent because of the statistical error caused by rounding.

Our basic theme is underlined again in Table 9 which compares the dates of Party entry for the two elites. While the percentage of those joining the Party during the 1921–23 period had decreased, and of those joining the Party in 1928 or later had increased, those who had entered the CCP during the first United Front with the KMT (1924–27) and who continued to provide almost two-thirds of the members of the 1956 Central Committee remained the dominant group.[30]

A comparison of major occupations of the elite, the distribution of personnel over the three major institutions of the political system—Party, state, and army—showed little significant variation over time.

[30] By comparison, at one municipal level, the Party elite during the 1949–65 period drew only 27.8 per cent of its membership from cadres who entered the CCP from 1921 to 1935. See Ying-mao Kau, "The Urban Bureaucratic Elite in Communist China: A Case Study of Wuhan, 1949–65," in Barnett (ed.), *Chinese Communist Politics in Action,* p. 231. For the CCP as a whole, Liu Shao-ch'i reported to the Eighth Congress that more than 60 per cent of the membership had joined since 1949.

Two changes indicated by Table 10 were the rise of individuals identified with the state apparatus after 1949 (it being impossible to demarcate Party/state relations during the Kiangsi Soviet), and the

TABLE 9

COMPARISON BETWEEN THE DATES OF PARTY ENTRY OF THE
KIANGSI SOVIET ELITE AND THE EIGHTH CENTRAL COMMITTEE

Date of Party Entry	Percentage of Kiangsi Elite * (N = 76)		Percentage of Eighth Central Committee (N = 122)	
1921	14.5		5.7	
1922	9.2		4.9	
1923	5.3		4.1	
		29.0		14.7
1924	7.9		7.4	
1925	19.7		11.5	
1926	13.2		21.3	
1927	21.1		23.0	
		61.9		63.2
1928	5.3		5.7	
1929	1.3		4.1	
1930	0.0		2.5	
1931	2.6		0.0	
1932	0.0		3.3	
1933	0.0		2.5	
1934	0.0		0.8	
		9.2		18.9
1935	0.0		0.8	
1936	0.0		0.8	
1937	0.0		0.8	
1950	0.0		0.8 †	
				3.2
Total	100.1 ‡		100.0	

* These figures are drawn from Table 3.

† This is Saifudin, who was a member of the Communist Party of the Soviet Union from about 1940 before he joined the CCP in 1950.

‡ This figure does not total 100 per cent because of the statistical error caused by rounding.

demise of political commissars in the military as a major career pattern. The other variation of note is the decline in representation of the military on the postrevolutionary elite, reflecting some decline in the political relevance of military skills, and a rise in the importance of specialists in organization. Nevertheless, for both the Chinese Soviet Republic and the People's Republic of China, a rough balance was maintained between the major institutions.

TABLE 10

COMPARISON BETWEEN THE OCCUPATIONS AFTER PARTY ENTRY
OF THE KIANGSI SOVIET ELITE AND THE
EIGHTH CENTRAL COMMITTEE

Occupation	Percentage of Kiangsi Elite (N = 99) * (Occupation in Soviet Areas)	Percentage of Eighth Central Committee (N = 170) (Major Occupation 1949–56)
Party	37.7	29.4
Government	—	32.4
Military, police	33.0	22.9
Political work in Red Army	21.7	—
Other †	7.5	15.3
Total	99.9 ‡	100.0

* These figures are drawn from Table 6.

† In the case of the Kiangsi group, this category includes personnel active in education and youth work; for the Eighth CC, it includes those working in the mass organizations, as well as scientists, academics, and intellectuals.

‡ This figure does not total 100 per cent because of the statistical error caused by rounding.

The apparent rigidity of the political elite is reinforced by an examination of Tables 11 and 12 comparing the two elites in terms of their educational backgrounds and foreign travel.[31] In the case of education, the two distributions are remarkably similar. With respect to foreign travel, a higher percentage of the 1956 group than of the Kiangsi group has been abroad (as of 1956); but, significantly, a sizable majority of both groups are not known to have ever set foot outside of China.[32]

Thus, the data repeatedly illustrate the apparent "immobility" of the Chinese Communist political elite from 1931 to 1956. Even though

[31] A comparison of the limited data available on the social origins of the 1956 CC reveals little change from that of the Kiangsi Soviet period.

[32] For a more detailed breakdown of the foreign travels of the Eighth CC (which includes the period from 1956 up to 1961), see Donald W. Klein, "Peking's Leaders: A Study in Isolation," *CQ*, No. 7 (July–September, 1961), pp. 35–43.

there was a substantial turnover of personnel during the twenty-five years following 1931 (122 of the 170 members of the Eighth CC had *not* been on the Kiangsi Soviet CEC), the characteristics of the new men coopted onto the elite during this period are sufficiently similar to those of their predecessors of the Kiangsi era to signal little overall difference between the two elites (except for the aging process), when the frequency distributions are tabulated.

TABLE 11

COMPARISON BETWEEN THE EDUCATIONAL LEVELS ATTAINED BY
THE KIANGSI SOVIET ELITE AND THE
EIGHTH CENTRAL COMMITTEE

Educational Level	Percentage of Kiangsi Elite (N = 81) *	Percentage of Eighth Central Committee (N = 135)
None	8.6	2.2
Primary	4.9	5.2
Secondary (middle or normal school)	11.1	16.3
Military	6.2	11.9
Higher technical institute †	3.7	1.5
Higher Party school only	22.2	21.5
University (formal)	30.9	25.9
Higher Party school, plus other higher education	12.3	15.6
Total	99.9 ‡	100.1 ‡

* These figures are drawn from Table 4.
† For example, engineering school.
‡ This figure does not total 100 per cent because of the statistical error caused by rounding.

In spite of the dissimilarities between the political systems of the Kiangsi Soviet and the China of 1956, the elite remained remarkably immune to the changes predicted in the direction of bringing onto the CC younger, better-educated, and perhaps more cosmopolitan personnel, with careers in science and technology.[33] In this sense, no major effort appears to have been made to improve the capacities of the Party at its upper-middle level by increasing the representation of such skill groups among the political elite, or by enlarging the repre-

[33] However, a number of CC members had undoubtedly received some kind of "on-the-job training" in scientific procedures by virtue of being associated with the administration of technical enterprises during the 1949–56 period.

sentation of women, national minorities, or additional geographical areas (except for the northern provinces).

TABLE 12

COMPARISON BETWEEN THE FOREIGN EXPERIENCE OF THE
KIANGSI SOVIET ELITE AND THE
EIGHTH CENTRAL COMMITTEE

Foreign Experience	Percentage of Kiangsi Elite (N = 241)	Percentage of Eighth Central Committee (N = 170)
USSR, bloc only	11.6	25.9
Travel to non-Communist country	9.5	21.2
Not known to have been abroad	78.8	52.9
Total	99.9 *	100.0

* This figure does not total 100 per cent because of the statistical error caused by rounding.

CONCLUSIONS

This essay has been concerned with examining certain assumptions relating the composition of the political elite to the requirements of the political system. The political elite was positionally defined as either the Central Executive Council of the Chinese Soviet Republic, or the CCP Eighth Central Committee in postrevolutionary China.[34]

In 1956, postrevolutionary China was experiencing the phenomenon of "mobilization from above" type modernization. Our effort here has been to relate this type of modernization to elite composition and change. Wide agreement exists in the literature concerning a prototype first generation of "revolutionary intellectuals"—a prototype which aptly describes the early leaders of the CCP during the Kiangsi Soviet period.

However, is the proposition valid that in a postrevolutionary society the revolutionary veterans will be forced to relinquish power to a new generation of "managerial modernizers" if the industrialization and modernization processes are to be brought to a successful conclusion? The primary task of this essay has been to examine these propositions empirically, by means of quantitative comparisons be-

[34] Because of gaps in the data, conclusions drawn from this analysis must be heavily qualified, particularly those relating to the Kiangsi Soviet period.

tween the pre- and postrevolutionary elites, and to reveal the degree to which the Party leadership had been willing to accommodate those individuals with modernizing skills, as well as other sectors of society previously denied access to the elite.

Although it was anticipated that the systemic demands of modernization made by the postrevolutionary society, and as perceived by the elite, would be reflected in changed elite composition, a broad comparison between the attributes of the political elites of the Chinese Soviet Republic and the People's Republic of China (1956) reveals that there had been essentially a lack of response over time to external change, in spite of significant differences between two political, economic, and social systems. Instead, a comparison of the aggregate data compiled on the Central Executive Council and the Eighth Central Committee reveals primarily the similarities between the two groups.

Those individuals brought onto the Central Committee in 1956 as new members were younger than the incumbents both in chronological age and in years spent in the CCP. However, it must be noted that these "younger" members were usually middle-aged and had spent approximately three decades of their lives in the Party. Consequently, while the pattern of elite selection tended to maintain the homogeneity and therefore the stability of the aggregate characteristics of the elite, it also reflected increasing restrictions on the upward mobility opportunities of younger men to achieve a position at this level of the political elite. Although men of new talents were being brought into lower and middle echelons of the Communist Party, the upward movement of these cadres into the upper-middle strata and beyond was being blocked by the revolutionary veterans, who sought to resist a change in the composition and outlook of the top elite. One inference suggested by this is that the incumbent members of the Central Committee, and more particularly, perhaps, members of the Political Bureau, did not feel "threatened" by the "managerial modernizers" and therefore did not perceive any need to bring them onto the elite. Whether that group—or its dominant member(s)—held a positive antipathy to such modernizers is an intriguing question requiring different data.

Similarly, in the case of the post-1949 career variable, while the military continues to be a major road to membership on the Chinese political elite, the absence of any sizable body of elite members with a technical education or with scientific-technical career patterns in postrevolutionary China seems to reflect the top elite's lack of appreciation of the problems of administering a complex industrializing society.[35] Moreover, it is possible that the political leadership is consciously resisting any replacement of their own utopian goals and "Red" techniques by the methods of a new generation of "experts." In general, the political leadership up to this point was unwilling to put longevity aside when merit appeared lower on the ladder; they would not select more youthful individuals for the Central Committee if it meant passing over the men with whom they had shared so many experiences and group affiliations.

The implications of the Great Proletarian Cultural Revolution for these questions we must reserve for future study. At present, the indications are that Mao came to fear that a lessening of revolutionary zeal in concession to the managerial modernizers would lead the Chinese on the Soviet revisionist path of "restoring capitalism." Hence, he apparently resolved to resist the type of elitist change "characteristic" of earlier modernizing societies. Despite the Maoist effort, however, whether political power in China must eventually pass into the hands of the managers and Party bureaucrats is a question still very much at issue.

[35] Nor does there appear to be a greatly increased use of scientific and technical personnel at the lower levels of the elite. For the case of the Wuhan bureaucratic elite, see Kau, "Urban Bureaucratic Elite in Communist China," pp. 260–65.

ROBERT A. SCALAPINO

The Transition in Chinese Party Leadership: A Comparison of the Eighth and Ninth Central Committees*

Despite some exceptionally good studies on the subject, leadership in a Communist state remains an imprecise concept. "Who governs?" is still a partially answered question at best, and few general theories concerning the nature and evolution of leadership in a Communist state have been advanced. Building upon the pioneer work of others, we should like to probe certain aspects of the authority structure in contemporary China by drawing upon all available data concerning the members of the Eighth and Ninth Central Committees.[1]

The primacy of the Party continues to be a governing principle in

* I should like to acknowledge the financial assistance of the Institute of International Studies, University of California, Berkeley, in connection with the preparation of this paper and related research. Without the support of the institute, my work would not have been possible. I should also like to acknowledge the helpful criticism of members of the Banff Conference and, in addition, that of Robert Bedeski, Wu Chen-tsai, Ivars Lauersons, and George Yu. I am also indebted to David Baker, Monica Brown, Scott Glascock, Stuart Grief, Gerald McBeath, James Nickum, David Purdy, and Leslie St. John for aiding me in the collection of the data upon which this paper is based.

[1] I refer specifically to the important work of Howard L. Boorman, Donald W. Klein, John Wilson Lewis, Thomas W. Robinson, and William W. Whitson. Following are some of the Chinese sources used: Kuo Hua-lun (ed.), *Chung-kung jen-ming lu* (Biographical Dictionary of Chinese Communists) (Taipei: Institute of International Relations, 1967); *Fei chün k'an-pu jen-shih tsu-liao hiu-pien* (Biographical Data on Communist Military Personnel) (Taipei: Intelligence Agency, Ministry of National Defense, 1967); *Fei-tang chen k'an-pu jen-shih tsu-liao hiu-pien* (Biographical Data on Communist Political and Party Personnel) (Taipei: Intelligence Agency, Ministry of National Defense, 1966); Huang Chen-hsia (ed.), *Chung-kung chün-jen chih* (English title: *Mao's Generals*) (Hong Kong: Research Institute of Contemporary History, 1968);

China, even in the aftermath of the Great Proletarian Cultural Revolution (GPCR). The most accurate institutional measure of authority, therefore, remains that of status in the Chinese Communist Party (CCP), and membership on the national Central Committee (CC) constitutes the best available indication of high status.[2] In this study, it has been necessary to create a number of categories, each of which we shall seek to explain and justify. The first, and most simple, is the distinction which will be maintained between Politburo members and others, and within the Politburo, between members of the Standing Committee and the remaining members. The authority and decision-making differential among Standing Committee, full and alternate Politburo, and full CC members is sufficiently great to make such distinctions mandatory.

We are concerned here with two, partially overlapping elite samples, separated in time by an extraordinary thirteen years. The Eighth Central Committee, elected in September, 1956, consisted of ninety-seven full members, of whom twenty-three sat on the Politburo at the outset, as full or alternate members.[3] The Ninth Central Committee, elected in April, 1969, consisted of 170 full members, of whom twenty-five sat on the Politburo. Let us commence by comparing the Standing Committee members of these two central committees, the men at the summit of power and authority. Here we are dealing with six and five individuals respectively, with only two men—Mao Tse-tung and Chou En-lai—serving on both groups. The Eighth CC Standing Committee initially was composed of Mao Tse-tung, Liu Shao-ch'i, Chou En-lai, Chu Teh, Ch'en Yün, and Teng Hsiao-p'ing; the Ninth Standing

Huang Yu-ch'uen (ed.), *Mao Tse-tung: A Chronology of His Life, 1893–1968* (Hong Kong: URI, 1970).

Among the English sources are: *Who's Who in Communist China,* Vols. I and II (rev. ed.; Hong Kong: URI, 1969); Howard L. Boorman and Richard C. Howard (eds.), *Biographical Dictionary of Republican China,* Vols. I and II (New York: Columbia University Press, 1967–68); articles on developments in Mainland China in selected issues of *Current Scene* (Hong Kong); Joint Publications Research Service, *Translations on Communist China;* The American Consulate-General, *CB, Mainland Press Translations,* and *Biographical Data File;* and a variety of individual biographies and secondary studies. The primary Japanese source is *Gendai chūgoku jinmei jiten* (A Biographical Dictionary of Contemporary Chinese) (Tokyo: Kazan Kai, 1966).

[2] It is clear, of course, that some individuals sit on the Central Committee and yet have very limited power—as apart from status—as will be made explicit in our subsequent remarks. It is also important to note that a number of individuals with considerable status *and* power, especially at local and regional levels, do not (yet) sit on the Central Committee. Despite these caveats, however, we are prepared to defend the above statement.

[3] Our study deals only with the two central committees in their original formation, and does not include the interim changes that took place. Moreover, as will be noted, we include only the full members of the Central Committee, no alternate members.

Committee included Mao, Lin Piao, Chou, Ch'en Po-ta, and K'ang Sheng. The change in personnel can therefore be regarded as major, amounting to more than 50 per cent of the body, with what we might designate as the "ideological" and the "administrative" branches of government continuing, while the "Party" and "military" branches underwent change and upheaval. The alterations in the Standing Committee can thus be used to symbolize continuity and change in the total political structure of contemporary China.

At the outset, let us examine those features of both bodies which have been most commonly surveyed and are most easily quantified. Both Politburo standing committees have been all-male bodies. The average age of the membership in 1956 was 58.66; in 1969, it was 67.80, an increase of nine years in a time span of twelve and a half years.[4] At the summit, China is governed by old men, albeit men somewhat younger on an average than were Winston Churchill, Charles de Gaulle, and Konrad Adenauer toward the ends of their political careers. The age span of the Eighth CC Standing Committee went from 53 to 70, that of the Ninth Standing Committee from 62 to 75.

Reflective of their generation of revolutionaries, moreover, these men came predominantly from Central-South China.[5] The six men of the Eighth CC all came from this area, two each from the provinces of Hunan, Kiangsu, and Szechwan. In the case of the Ninth CC Standing Committee, one of the five was born in North China, and each was born in a different province—the only indication at this level that the geographic base of leadership in China is expanding. All members of both Standing Committees have been ethnic Chinese rather than members of any minority.

The question of their socioeconomic backgrounds, however, poses the first serious methodological and conceptual problems. A new approach to this issue is now warranted. As is well known, traditional

[4] In computing age, we have followed two rules. First, age has been computed on the basis of what is presumed to be the nearest age. Thus, a man born in 1913 has been considered nearer to 56 than to 55 on May 1, 1969. This may weight our data slightly toward the senior side. Second, when two or more sources which we consider equally reliable give discrepant ages for a person, we have taken the average of the various ages. We should indicate that we do not regard age discrepancies as a serious problem. In most cases, the discrepancy is merely of one or two years; there are a few, but very few, cases where it runs as high as seven to ten years.

[5] Our geographic designations are based on the following divisions. Central-South: Hupeh, Hunan, Kwangsi, Kweichow; Central-Southwest: Szechwan, Tibet; Central-Southeast: Kiangsu, Anhwei, Chekiang (Shanghai); North: Hopeh (Peking), Shantung, Shansi, Inner Mongolian Autonomous Region, Honan; Northeast: Heilungkiang, Kirin, Liaoning; Northwest: Shensi, Kansu, Tsinghai, Sinkiang-Uighur Autonomous Region; South: Fukien, Kwangtung, Kwangsi, Chuang Autonomous Region, Yunnan.

Marxist-Leninist concepts of class are very inadequate when applied to a society like China. So-called Maoist adaptations help, but serious problems remain. Two significant separable elements of the society, for example, have been insufficiently recognized and improperly designated by the Marxists. The student and the soldier, each so vital to the modern Chinese revolutionary process, must be given separate class status, equal to that of other categories.

The temporary nature of the student status does not alter the importance of identifying that status when it constitutes the one from which an individual's involvement in political action commences, especially when his subsequent career is wholly that of the professional revolutionary. Moreover, it is not helpful, particularly in the case of "late-developing societies," to subsume the student under the general rubric, "petty bourgeois." The latter term should be reserved for those categories more properly identified by that label: the small merchant, certain professional men, and some office personnel. Thus, we shall employ two terms to designate (and distinguish) the student-intellectual community. "Petty intellectual" shall refer to students of middle school level and above, together with schoolteachers at the primary and secondary levels, and individuals of similar level and occupation. "Intellectual" shall be used to designate journalists, writers, and professors at higher levels.

The separate designation, "military," shall be used for professional soldiers. Four labels shall be assigned to the rural community—"poor peasant," "middle peasant," "rich peasant," and "gentry-landlord"—with combinations when dictated by the data. The classifications of "bourgeois" and "proletariat" shall be reserved for their traditional uses, with "petty bourgeois" being used in the fashion indicated above. Finally, a separate category shall be employed for "official," with "petty official" used for minor officeholders.

It is not sufficient, however, even with this somewhat more complex status structure, to set forth merely the personal status of the individual concerned. The relation between the individual and his family, particularly that relation at the time of his entry into full-time revolutionary service, can be highly revealing. Thus, we will seek to provide a family/personal status equation in as many cases as possible. For example, Mao Tse-tung's class background can be depicted as follows: $\frac{\text{M./R. Peas.}}{\text{Petty Intel.}}$. This signifies that Mao came from a middle to rich peasant family and entered the Communist movement as a petty intellectual, against a background of having been a student, library worker, and primary-school teacher.

Lin Piao's background is not so dissimilar as might have been imagined: $\dfrac{\text{Petty Bourg. (DM)}}{\text{Petty Intel./Mil.}}$. Lin's father, contrary to certain Communist reports, appears not to have been a poor peasant; rather, at one point, he owned a small dye factory. This was lost, however, and he was subsequently reduced to various temporary jobs to provide some livelihood for his family.[6] In such circumstances, we can signal another phenomenon not uncommon among top Communists by the designation, DM—namely, downward mobility in terms of family fortunes. In addition, it might be noted that Lin's home, while quasi-rural, was also "suburban," being in the vicinity of Wuhan and hence susceptible to the "modernizing" influences of this major urban center —again, a factor of importance to be found in more than a few cases among top-echelon Communist leaders. We have designated Lin both petty intellectual and military at the time of his entrance into the movement because he had had a brief experience as participant in student activities and substitute teacher prior to embarking upon his military training and career.

What of the other Eighth CC Standing Committee members? Liu Shao-ch'i who ranked second, should be depicted as $\dfrac{\text{Gentry-Landlord? R. Peas.}}{\text{Petty Intel.}}$. Sources differ on whether Liu's family was actually gentry-landlord or merely rich peasant in status. There can be no doubt, however, that despite Liu's lengthy career in the labor movement, neither his family background nor his own status at the time of entry into the Communist movement warrants labeling him as proletariat. It is Chou En-lai, however, who most nearly approximates the traditional powerholder in China, as the following equation indicates: $\dfrac{\text{Intel./Gentry-Landlord/Petty Off. (DM).}^7}{\text{Petty Intel.?}}$ Chou's great-grandfather had been a county magistrate, and other members of his family had also

[6] I am much indebted to Thomas W. Robinson for his extensive research on Lin Piao, having had access both to his longer work, *A Politico-Military Biography of Lin Piao, Part I, 1907–1949* (Santa Monica, Calif.: The Rand Corporation, R-526-PR, 1971), and to the interpretative essay included in this volume.

[7] For a recent and extremely detailed account of Chou's life, see Li Tien-min, *Chou En-lai* (Taiwan: Institute of International Relations, 1970).

been involved in officeholding and intellectual pursuits; but in Chou's case, as in that of Lin, the fortunes of the immediate family had declined. Of the Eighth (and Ninth) CC Standing Committee members, moreover, Chou comes the closest to meeting the formal criteria for intellectual status. Chu Teh's background is as follows: $\frac{\text{Petty Bourg.}}{\text{Mil.}}$, and that of Teng Hsiao-p'ing is the same as that of Mao, with only Ch'en Yün fitting the classical Marxian model: $\frac{\text{Prol.}}{\text{Prol.}}$.

As can readily be seen, the members of the Eighth CC Standing Committee (1956) come predominantly from the middle and upper rural classes, with some petty bourgeois representation as well, but only a single member is of proletarian background. The members are also mainly of rural-suburban origin, as would be expected, with only two having urban antecedents. In terms of their own backgrounds, five of the six men can be classified as petty intellectuals, one of whom (Lin Piao) can also be classified as military. Thus, we can count two military men (with Chu Teh) and a single worker (Ch'en Yün).

The Ninth CC Standing Committee presents a remarkably similar picture: [8] three are $\frac{\text{M./R. Peas.}}{\text{Petty Intel.}}$ (Mao, Ch'en Po-ta, K'ang); one is $\frac{\text{Intel./Gentry-Landlord/Petty Off. (DM)}}{\text{Petty Intel./Intel.}}$ (Chou); and one is $\frac{\text{Petty Bourg. (DM)}}{\text{Petty Intel./Mil.}}$ (Lin). Four of these men came from rural or sub-urban backgrounds, only one (Chou) from an urban background. In the topmost level of Chinese Communist leadership we are dealing with men who come closer in their origins and background to the traditional type of Chinese leadership than they do to the type of leadership envisaged by Marx, although in most cases they fit the classic "unable to continue with studies" or "failed in examination" types so familiar in Chinese history.

This latter point is illustrated further when we examine the educational backgrounds of these men. Once again we are confronted with a problem of definitions. How does one determine a "poor" educational background versus a "good" one? At this point, a relatively crude measurement will have to suffice. We can deal with formal schooling

---

[8] In addition to other sources, note Hsiang Nai-Kuang, "An Analysis of the Personnel of the Ninth Central Committee of the Chinese Communist Party," published in English and Chinese by the Institute of International Relations, Republic of China, for the First Sino-American Conference on Mainland China, December 14–19, 1970.

only, taking some account of the reputation of the institution involved, especially in the case of universities. Five levels have been established: "poor"—three years of primary education or less; "modest"—middle- or normal-school education only; "fairly good"—normal-school education and some college or university work, or specialized training; "good"—substantial work or completion at a "second-rate" institution or institute; "excellent"—substantial work, or completion of higher education, at any institution of high repute.

Based on these standards, members of the Eighth CC Standing Committee had the following ratings: two modest (Mao, Ch'en Yün); three fairly good (Chu, Liu, Teng); and one good (Chou). Those of the Ninth CC Standing Committee were as follows: one modest (Mao); three fairly good (Lin, Ch'en Po-ta, K'ang); and one good (Chou). There are two ways of interpreting these particular data. On the negative side, it can be noted that the very top leaders of Communist China, whatever their native intelligence (which in most cases is undoubtedly considerable), have had a relatively meager formal education, less substantial than either the best of the traditional Chinese elite or of their long-time competitors, the "modernizing" elite who were educated to "Western-style" politics and economics.

It could be argued, of course, that neither traditional nor modern education as it reached these latter groups was suitable to the needs of Chinese society. And indeed, that was precisely what Mao did argue, his words being climaxed by the actions taken in the course of the GPCR. Whatever the rationally involved in Mao's contempt for most Peita intellectuals or Oxford graduates, clearly his own modest formal schooling, together with his lifelong "work-study" experience, formed the background against which the assault upon the intelligentsia was launched. Nor does Mao stand alone. While his formal education was less than most other top leaders, all of the Eighth and Ninth Standing Committee members (with the partial exception of Chou En-lai) have educational backgrounds that qualify them as petty intellectuals—or good soldiers. None, for example, did extensive work at Peking University or other eminent Chinese universities, nor did any of them complete the path of the well-educated Chinese intellectual, modern or otherwise.

To be sure, this was the era when many young Chinese sought a foreign education, and these men were not exceptions. Of the Eighth CC Standing Committee members, only Mao had no educational experience abroad. One studied in Germany (Chu), two in France (Chou and Teng), and three in the Soviet Union (Liu, Ch'en Yün, Teng). This record, however, may look better on paper than is justified by the facts. For example, reports concerning the University of the Toilers of the East are fairly dismal, and all three men studying in Moscow did their work there. For the most part, moreover, these men spent far too little time in Europe to receive a meaningful higher education. Only Chou En-lai, with work at an American missionary-supported institution in China, Waseda University in Japan, and several years in France, can be considered reasonably well educated in conventional terms; and even here some doubts can be permitted, especially regarding his French and Japanese education.

As noted above, the formal educational attainments of the Ninth CC Standing Committee members do not differ greatly. Four of the five men had foreign educational experience, three in the USSR (Lin, Ch'en Po-ta, K'ang), and one (Chou) in Japan and France. Once again, however, it is legitimate to question the quality of the institutions attended, both at home and abroad, and the length of time during which the institution was attended. In any case, none of these men (again, with the partial exception of Chou) was in the mainstream of the most prominent Chinese intellectuals of their times.

On the other hand, their education generally distinguishes them from the *average* Chinese of their generation and socioeconomic status. If they cannot compete with the "best-educated" elements, they are at least better educated than their contemporaries of similar background. As is the case in most "underdeveloped societies," in the Chinese People's Republic (CPR) education, whether formally acquired or derived from self-study, distinguishes the top political elite from the nonelite more than does any other single factor. Yet the point is still valid that for the most part these old revolutionaries are self-made men, generalists, and petty intellectuals, alternately jealous and contemptuous of those who received an excellent education as judged by the criteria of the day. This fact, together with the vastly greater need for low- and middle-level technicians, has had much to do with the educational policies which they—or at least, the "Maoists"—have championed in recent times.

If we turn from the personal backgrounds to the career patterns of these men, a new set of questions and challenges is posed. What constitutes an accurate and appropriate typology encompassing the individuals at the top of the Party in recent decades? What type of generational lines should be drawn? How do these correlate with Party seniority? And what weighting should be given to personal ties and, above all, to the relation of each individual to Mao?

Let us turn initially to the questions of generation and seniority. There are many ways in which to delineate generations in the Chinese Communist movement, and we have used a combination of several. The first factor is when the individual began to participate in the modern Chinese revolution. We have divided its sequences into seven parts: the T'ung Meng Hui and the 1911 Revolution; the May Fourth Movement, student and labor organizational efforts of the 1917–23 period, and the first CCP; the era of the Kuomintang (KMT)-CCP Alliance and its breakup (1924–27/28); the Kiangsi Soviet period; the Long March, and the Yenan era; the Civil War, 1945–49; and the Chinese People's Republic era. For our purposes, these eras establish a seven-generational sequence. The Eighth CC Standing Committee was composed of one first-generation (Chu) and five second-generation men, based on this division. The Ninth CC Standing Committee was composed of three second-generation and two third-generation men, with all first-generation men having disappeared from this level of Party leadership, making Mao, Chou, and K'ang Sheng the most senior revolutionaries.

Another method of measuring seniority is to relate each individual to the Communist Party itself, both by when he first joined and when he was elected to the Central Committee and to the Politburo, there being nine central committees up to 1970. Six separate periods have been established: 1921–24, 1925–27, 1928–34, 1935–45, 1945–49, and post-1949.[9] In the Eighth Standing Committee, 5 of the 6 members joined the CCP in the first period, 1 (Ch'en Yün) in the second period. One member (Mao) was a member of the Third (but not the Fourth) CC, 2 were members of the Fifth CC (Mao and Chou), 5 were members of the Sixth CC, and all 6 were members of the Seventh CC. One sat on the Fifth CC Politburo (Chou), 5 sat on the Sixth CC Politburo, and all 6 sat on the Seventh CC Politburo. In the Ninth Standing Committee, only 2 of the 5 members (Mao and Chou) had joined the CCP in the first period, 3 having joined in the second period; 1 had been a member of the Third CC, 2 of the Fifth CC, 3

[9] The reasons for choosing these particular dates are probably clear. The first dates include the first Party, and end prior to the KMT-CCP Alliance; the second period encompasses the Alliance period; the third covers the Kiangsi Soviet period; the fourth is the Yenan period; the fifth involves the Civil War era; and the sixth encompasses the period since the establishment of the Chinese People's Republic.

of the Sixth CC, and all 5 of the Seventh CC; 1 had been a member of the Fifth CC Politburo, 3 of the Sixth CC Politburo, and all 5 of the Seventh CC Politburo.

Seniority can be measured against still another criterion, namely, participation in certain events that served as milestones in the emergence of the Communist movement. Dividing the years between 1911 and 1969 into eight periods, we have selected a large number of events (304) against which to check each member of the Eighth and Ninth Central Committees.[10] For purposes of this study, we shall indicate only the total number of these events in which the individual participated down to 1942, and also his participation in four epochal events or phases of the Communist movement closely connected with both the Party and Mao Tse-tung: the so-called Autumn Harvest Uprising (AHU) in the early summer of 1927; the Nanchang Uprising (NU) in August, 1927; the Kiangsi Border Government (KG), 1931–34; and the Long March (LM), 1934–35.

Among the Eighth CC Standing Committee members, Mao participated in 18 events between the New People's Study Society of 1917 and the *cheng-feng* campaign of 1941–42; Liu Shao-ch'i and Chou En-lai both participated in 14; Chu Teh in 7; and both Ch'en Yün and Teng Hsiao-p'ing in 4. Only 1 (Mao) participated in the AHU, 2 in the NU, 5 in the KG, and all 6 in the LM. In the case of the Ninth Standing Committee, against Mao's participation in 18 events and Chou's participation 14, Lin Piao had taken part in 15, K'ang Sheng in 3, and Ch'en Po-ta in 2. Only Mao was involved in the AHU, Chou and Lin in the NU, 4 in the KG, and 3 in the LM.

Using these various tests, we can now draw several conclusions concerning "generationism" and seniority in the topmost leadership of the Chinese Communist Party today. The 1911 Revolution generation, never of vital importance to the Party except for some military leadership and great symbolic utility, has now passed from the scene. At the very top, the Party is controlled by a combination of second-generation revolutionaries who entered the political scene first in the years between 1917 and 1924, and third-generation men who came into political activity during the KMT-CCP Alliance era.

Second, three men—Mao Tse-tung, Lin Piao, and Chou En-lai—

---

[10] We shall not detail the lengthy list here, but merely indicate the divisions and the total number of events checked: (1) 1911–21, 7 events; (2) 1921–27, 18 events; (3) 1927–34, 6 events; (4) 1935–45, 20 events; (5) 1949–54, 35 events; (6) 1955–56, 33 events; (7) 1956–57, 47 events; (8) 1959–65, 84 events; (9) 1965–69, 54 events.

stood out as the foremost historic figures of the Party still in active control at the time of the Ninth Party Congress, with Mao having an edge, but one less pronounced than is often assumed. One other individual at the top—K'ang Sheng—also had great seniority in terms of Party membership, but he had not been involved to the same degree in the historic events that marked the Party's evolution, and his career pattern diverged considerably from that of other veterans. When all measurements are taken into consideration, Mao, Lin, and Chou were not merely the top three men in the Party hierarchy; they were also the men who had participated most actively in guiding and shaping the Party in war and peace over the previous forty years. In this there was a supreme continuity up to that point—despite the extraordinary changes in policy and in the personnel beneath them.

The major difference between the Eighth and Ninth Standing Committees as a whole lies less in factors of generation or seniority, and more in the degree to which the Ninth CC Standing Committee is Mao-centric. Previously, in men like Chu Teh, Liu Shao-ch'i, and Teng Hsiao-p'ing, Mao had either contemporaries or men with careers relatively separate from his, at least during certain periods. While there seems little reason to question their loyalty, these men were not intensely dependent upon Mao; hence, he might regard them as potentially competitive. In Lin Piao, Ch'en Po-ta, and even K'ang Sheng, Mao had men highly dependent upon him for a variety of reasons. This did not prevent them from falling out of favor, but such men are generally more amenable to orders—and more easily removed in cases where the supreme leader determines this to be desirable.

Let us turn therefore to the critical question of career patterns and begin by setting up a simple, broadly based typology which can be further refined as we proceed. It is essential, of course, to divide the Communist elite into its military and nonmilitary components, and the manner in which this is done is of great importance. If all individuals holding the rank of field officer are designated as military irrespective of their current roles, the true scene is distorted. Admittedly, this is a highly complex matter. Party-military linkage, both at personal and impersonal levels, continues to be intricate. Indeed, as is well known, the essence of Chinese politics today lies in that linkage.

Nevertheless, it is crucial to work toward functional categories if we are to explore role specialization and its impact upon the elite. With these considerations in mind, we will be operating with the three basic categories established by the Communists themselves, namely, Party-administration cadres, military cadres, and mass representatives (the latter category naturally being applicable only to the Ninth CC). We shall define Party-administration cadres as those individuals whose primary and essential roles lay in these fields at the time of their CC appointment. Under this category will come personnel working at various levels: municipal, provincial, regional, and headquarters; front organization representatives; and technicians and "special cadres," who are individuals deriving their authority and power from outside the institutional structure, either because they perform a unique function, generally "intellectual" in character, or because they possess a special relationship to Mao and/or a few other key leaders such as Lin Piao.

The subcategories under military cadres will include personnel at the military district, military region, and headquarters levels; branch of service; staff versus line officers; and roles essentially political commissar versus primarily command in character. Divisions within the category of mass representatives will include type of work; municipality or province represented; and level of political involvement.

One man, Mao Tse-tung, must be placed outside and above these categories at this point in time. His current role in Chinese politics can only be equated with that of the monarch in a period when it was fashionable to believe in the Divine Right theory, and when the ruler was bound by no social contract. At present, Mao can seemingly delve into the institutional structure or the decision-making process whenever and wherever he wishes, directly or indirectly, and without the necessity of having a permanent institutional base—although several have been accorded him.

We have been outlining the above categories with the understanding that they are applicable to the individual at the time of his appointment to the CC or its Politburo. But a more complicated matter deserves consideration, namely, the career pattern of the individual throughout his active involvement. For these purposes, eight points of reference have been selected, based upon the history of the Chinese Communist movement: (1) 1927–28, (2) 1933–34, (3) 1934–35, (4) 1940–44, (5) 1949–50, (6) 1956, (7) 1960–61, (8) 1968–69. For each individual, a career pattern has been constructed based upon these (eight) reference points. The answers to four questions have been sought for each period. In what region was the individual at that point in time? Was he rural- or urban-based? What type of role or roles was he playing in the Party? Was he playing this role (or these roles) at the local, district, municipal, provincial, regional, center, or headquarters level of the Party?

Based upon this information, we have constructed a career pattern chart and a career graph for each individual of the Eighth and Ninth Central Committees (data permitting). Let us illustrate each of these by citing those constructed for Mao Tse-tung.

Period	1	2	3	4	5	6	7	8
Region	SE/CS	CS	LM	NW	Pek.	Pek.	Pek.*	Pek.
Urban/rural	R	R	R	R	U	U	U	U
Role	M/F/P	P/A/M	P/M/A	P/M/A	P/M/A	P/M/A	P/M	P/M
Party level	L/D/R	C	C	C	C	C	C	C

* Evidently spent considerable periods of time out of Peking; used Shanghai as base in planning the GPCR.

An interpretation of the above career chart would be as follows. Mao's Party service began in the southeast and central-south, continued during the Long March, with the wartime years spent in the northwest, and thence to Peking with the Communist victory in 1949. Thus, he has seen service throughout China in the course of his career. Before 1949, his locus was primarily rural; after that, primarily urban. His opening roles were military, front, and Party, more or less in that order. From the Kiangsi Soviet period through 1956 (until 1958–59) he operated more or less equally at the top levels of Party, military, and administration. After that time, he remained a central figure in Party and military affairs (the latter by virtue of his presence on the Military Affairs Committee of the CC). Except for the initial period, his role was played at the center, irrespective of where that center happened to be at the time.

The graph is based upon the same eight periods, but it has a different purpose. Basically, the graph is an effort to trace the rise or fall of authority and power possessed by each individual within the Party in the course of his political career. The graph can only be used to compare an individual's status at one point versus another; it cannot be used to compare one individual with another. By means of the charts and graphs, however, we can advance certain hypotheses concerning the types of career patterns characteristic of various levels of the CCP hierarchy. The graph we have constructed for Mao follows:

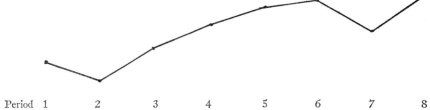

Period 1   2   3   4   5   6   7   8

Once again, some explanation is necessary. It will be noted that there are several points at which Mao's career graph takes a downward dip after 1928, namely, in the 1933–34 period when he was relieved from his post as political commissar of the First Front Army, being replaced by Chou En-lai, and again in the 1960–61 period, when the evidence suggests that he was out of touch for considerable periods of time with Party and administrative operations in Peking.

To facilitate the use of these graphs for comparative purposes, we have labeled six types covering most, if not all, of the cases. (1) The wave pattern: cases where there are one or more career dips, such as in the case of Mao, noted above. (2) The steady, regular progression pattern: cases where advancement is relatively regular, and without major obstacles or acceleration. (3) The steady, accelerating progression pattern: cases where advancement is unimpeded, and accelerating in the later stages. (4) The combined advance and plateau pattern: cases where there is little or no retrogression, but where advances are interspersed with periods when the individual remains at the same career level over a considerable period of time. (5) The mountaintop pattern: cases where there is a very rapid rise (and sometimes fall) in a very brief period of time. (6) The post-peak pattern: cases where the individual's career peak has been reached earlier, and subsequent stages are marked by a lower level of authority and/or power compared to some earlier point in the individual's Party career. This last type applies to several very different types of individuals: "burned-out" types like Li Li-san and most of the twenty-eight Bolsheviks who survived on the Eighth CC; ceremonial figures like Chu Teh and Tung Pi-wu; and the unique case of Chou En-lai who, if we apply our rules rigorously, was really at his all-time peak of authority relative to other Party figures for a brief time in the early 1930's—unless future developments in the post-Cultural Revolution era bring Chou to the very top. In view of more recent developments, this possibility seems increasingly to be becoming a reality.

Having set forth our methods and the principles governing them, let us now apply these, first to the Standing Committee members. With respect to the Eighth Standing Committee, Mao apart, four of the five remaining members were Party-administration cadres, one (Chu Teh) a military cadre. Of the four Party-administration cadres, all operated at the center, two were essentially Party administrators, two primarily state administrators, and one of the latter (Ch'en Yün) could be classified as the highest-ranking technician. The one military cadre (Chu Teh) also operating at the center was essentially a line officer, and the highest-ranking command officer of the People's Liberation Army.

When we examine the career charts of these individuals, some significant differences are to be noted. Once again, for the sake of convenience, certain labels will be assigned, although in this case clustering the samples is far more difficult than in the case of the career graphs. Our first labels apply to the geographic pattern of service. Here, three or four patterns appear to predominate. The orthodox senior pattern, namely, C-S, Cent or SE→LM→NW, or N→Pek, constitutes a movement from southern China via the Long March to northern China, and thence to Peking in 1949, with a corresponding movement from a predominantly rural to a predominantly urban base of operations. A second pattern we will label the regional to headquarters pattern, namely, service primarily in one or two areas, followed by movement to the center, again with mixed rural-urban service. A third pattern can be called the metropolitan or metropolitan-international pattern, involving service primarily in one or more major cities and/or abroad, heavily urban in character. Finally, there is a pattern of service wholly or almost wholly in one region, municipality or province, *not* extending to the center, or at least not primarily located in the center, which we shall call the localist pattern. In point of fact, few career patterns fit perfectly into one of these four types, but a substantial number approximate them closely enough so that they can be used for comparative and quantitative purposes.

Role changes are also very difficult to typologize. In general, however, we can describe four distinctive role patterns. The first can be called the generalist pattern, a pattern of consistent role-playing in all areas throughout the individual's career. The second we may designate as the generalist to specialist pattern, a pattern involving individuals who at an early point played roles interchangeably in Party, "state," military, and front affairs, but who came to be more differentiated in their roles, usually in periods 4, 5, and 6. Most of these individuals, it should be emphasized, did *not* become specialists in the commonly accepted sense of the term (these latter we shall call technicians); their field of operations, however, was narrowed in the course of their careers. The third type was that of a single- or dual-role pattern, involving individuals who consistently played roles in only one or two fields, a type involving most "technicians," "intellectuals," and similar cadres. A fourth type, most prominent among military men, is the specialist to generalist pattern, involving a broadening of role in the course of one's career, normally, the extension from military to military and Party/administration operations.

In the Eighth Standing Committee, 2 men fit perfectly into the orthodox senior service pattern (Mao and Chu), and 2 others approximate it closely (Chou and Teng). The final 2 (Liu and Ch'en Yün) come closer to the metropolitan-international pattern. With respect to roles, 1 generalist pattern (Mao), 3 generalist to specialist patterns (Liu, Chou, Teng), and 2 single- or dual-role patterns (Chu and Ch'en) are to be discerned. In their career graphs, 2 men fall into the wave pattern (Mao, Chu), 2 into the combined advance and plateau pattern (Liu, Teng), 1 into the steady, accelerating progression pattern (Ch'en), and 1 into the post-peak pattern (Chou).

In the case of the Ninth CC (once again, Mao apart), three of the men are Party-administration cadres (Chou, Ch'en Po-ta, K'ang) and one (Lin Piao) must be classified as a military cadre despite his major Party role, since his base of power and institutional position were essentially military. Again, all individuals were operating from the center at the time of their appointment (although intermittently in the course of the GPCR there may have been two "centers" in China). One significant difference from the Eighth CC Standing Committee, however, exists. Two of the four members (apart from Mao) had no visible institutional base (Ch'en Po-ta and K'ang), unless one is prepared to consider certain institutions hastily built in the course of the GPCR as adequate substitutes for the more traditional bases. (Perhaps incorrectly, we do not consider K'ang's security-intelligence role as providing an institutional base which can be wielded independently as a source of power, partly because K'ang's recent official position in that apparatus is unclear.)

The absence of an adequate institutional base puts an increased premium upon the individual's relation to "the Leader," as noted previously. It is not surprising that Ch'en Po-ta derived his position from his role as ideologue and long-time intimate (some insist, brain trust) of Mao, with K'ang Sheng also close to Mao and his wife, as well as a symbol of the security-intelligence operations so crucial in a period of trouble. When to this group is added Mao's "favorite general," the extraordinarily personal and potentially transitory character of the inner group is revealed.

If, with the partial exception of Chou En-lai, these men held in common a very special relation to Mao, in a number of other respects they were different, apart from the highly important difference in their institutional bases. While 3 of them fit or approximate the orthodox senior service pattern (Mao, Lin, Chou), 2 fit the metropolitan-international pattern (Ch'en and K'ang). With respect to roles, in addition to Mao's generalist pattern, 1 specialist to generalist (Lin), 1 generalist to specialist (Chou), and 2 single- or dual-role patterns (Ch'en and K'ang) are to be found. In their career graphs, 2 men follow the wave pattern (Mao and Lin), 1 the steady, accelerating progression pattern (Ch'en), 1 the combined advance and plateau pattern (K'ang), and 1 (Chou) the post-peak pattern (with the reservations noted).

In connection with career trends, one further type of data can be added to those presented above. Using the files compiled by the American consulate in Hong Kong, we can discern the number of recorded appearances of each individual, beginning in the early 1950's. These statistics must be interpreted with care and conservatism.[11] They do not reveal most meetings of a decision-making type, such as sessions of the Politburo, telephone conferences, and similar crucial sessions, but merely enable us to see how frequently an individual was reported by the media as a participant in various ceremonial, Party, state, or public functions. But this factor—which we shall label the individual's *visibility*—is very useful when combined with other data in indicating career trends and relationships. Table 13 records the visibility of the members of the Eighth CC Standing Committee.

As will be noted, all of the primary figures on the Chinese political scene attained greatly increased visibility beginning in 1955. Consistently, however, Chou En-lai, premier and head of active governmental operations, was the most visible leader during this period, with Liu Shao-ch'i, the key Party figure as well as head of the State Council, being in second position by a narrow margin. It is interesting, but somewhat misleading, to note that Mao was the least visible of the

11 Any attempt to use the consulate data to determine the power of a given individual at a given point in time is likely to end in failure, although these data can signal the disappearance, permanent or temporary, of an individual, whether because of illness or political difficulties. Obviously, it is important if a given individual does not appear at October first and May first ceremonies for several years.

six Standing Committee members in 1955, and ranked third in 1956, the year of the Eighth Party Congress.[12] The individual among the group who rose most rapidly in visibility during this period was Ch'en Yün. In considerable measure, this signified the increasing importance given to economic development and the chief technicians or administrators overseeing it. Clearly, however, the public role in these opening years of the Chinese People's Republic fell heavily to Chou, as premier, with limited distinction among the others.

TABLE 13

APPEARANCES OF EIGHTH CC STANDING COMMITTEE MEMBERS
JANUARY 1, 1952–DECEMBER 31, 1956 *

Name	1952	1953	1954	1955	1956	Total
Mao Tse-tung	19	24	18	51	111	223
Liu Shao-ch'i	13	18	33	69	124	257
Chou En-lai	44	46	34	204	267	595
Chu Teh	17	26	37	72	72	224
Ch-en Yün	11	15	27	53	110	216
Teng Hsiao-p'ing	9	24	32	60	78	203

* These figures do not include appearances outside China, or notices of exchanging messages, sending cables, or activities other than appearances.

How does the visibility of the Ninth CC Standing Committee compare with that of the Eighth CC? Note Table 14, which tabulates recorded appearances up to May 1, 1969, the period immediately after the Ninth Party Congress, and the new appointments.

As will be noted, for such central figures as Mao and Chou, visibility declined substantially in the course of the GPCR, no doubt because of successive crises and feverish activity behind the scenes. For such newcomers to the innermost circle as Ch'en Po-ta and K'ang Sheng, however, visibility in the mid- and later sixties was substantially greater than in the period prior to 1963. But of all key leaders, Lin Piao was consistently the least visible, with an extraordinary distance separating him from others in this respect. Far more than Mao, Lin Piao acquired the image of a man who worked behind the veiled curtain, whether for reasons of health, personality, or political style.

Assuming the basic accuracy of the data and evaluations presented here, certain conclusions relating to the careers of the major Chinese

[12] Since Mao is given massive visibility via all the media continuously whether he appears in public or not, the question of whether he makes frequent public appearances is less germane than in the case of all other individuals.

political actors can be advanced at this point. The first relates to Mao Tse-tung. When the various measurements are correlated, he clearly stands alone in combining the consistent role of generalist with a high degree of seniority and historical presence, an orthodox senior pattern of service involving mixed rural-urban experience, a substantial visibility, and a record of having suffered—and survived—setbacks. Given these assets, Mao does not need a concrete institutional base at this point, although he knows well that the men around him must be both loyal and dedicated to his principles, particularly the key military figures. To these ends, the Ninth CC Standing Committee was shaped, and now appears to be in the process of being reshaped.

TABLE 14

APPEARANCES OF NINTH CC STANDING COMMITTEE MEMBERS
JANUARY 1, 1952–MAY 1, 1969 *

Name	1952	1953	1954	1955	1956	1957	1958	1959	1960	1961
Mao Tse-tung	19	24	18	51	111	88	89	76	50	39
Lin Piao	3	0	3	1	2	2	13	39	24	7
Chou En-lai	44	46	34	204	267	375	242	237	235	252
Ch'en Po-ta	3	4	4	9	6	1	16	12	16	7
K'ang Sheng	0	0	0	6	19	17	35	41	15	16

Name	1962	1963	1964	1965	1966	1967	1968	May 1 1969	Total
Mao Tse-tung	35	75	93	55	24	34	28	8	917
Lin Piao	2	2	1	6	11	35	30	8	189
Chou En-lai	182	336	306	336	170	169	116	23	3,574
Ch'en Po-ta	5	14	17	17	26	42	47	9	255
K'ang Sheng	36	65	90	112	96	109	65	12	734

* The figures do not include appearances outside China, or notices of exchanging messages, sending cables, or activities other than appearances.

It is also worthy of emphasis that while the topmost leadership of the CCP continues to be numerically weighted in favor of Party-administration cadres against military cadres, the shift from Chu Teh to Lin Piao appeared to be a significant one, because Lin was at that point a Party activist whereas Chu Teh was always essentially a "pure" military man despite his high Party posts. In defining Lin's role pattern as that of specialist to generalist versus Chu's single- or dual-role pattern, we underline that fact.

The balance between orthodox senior service types and metropolitan-international types was also important because it shed light upon the rural-urban balance, and to some extent upon the broader element of political style. That balance remains tilted toward the mixed rural-urban type, but the key actors immediately before and after the Ninth Party Congress, Mao and Lin, had a decided rural flavor in their service patterns. All of the individuals at the top, however, had long operated at, or near, the center.

There remains one final measurement that can be applied, that of cosmopolitanism. By combining data on foreign training and foreign language capacities with information on foreign travel and interaction with foreign visitors to China, we have a basis for assessing the degree of cosmopolitanism that can be ascribed to each individual.[13]

On all counts, the least cosmopolitan figure of the Eighth CC Standing Committee was Mao Tse-tung: he has no foreign training or language capacity; one trip to the Soviet Union constitutes his total foreign travel up to this point; and meetings with foreign visitors to China have been relatively infrequent (except for 1956, the year of the Eighth Party Congress, when many delegations representing various Communist Parties and groups arrived in Peking). At the other end of the spectrum was Chou En-lai: he has had educational experience in two countries, with some capacity in four or five foreign languages; his travels total six visits to the USSR and eight visits to twelve other East Asian, East European, South Asian, and West European countries; and his sessions with foreigners, particularly in 1955 and 1956, were numerous.

Soviet influence upon the veteran Chinese Communists at this point is graphically illustrated by the fact that four of the six Standing Committee members spoke Russian with varying degrees of skill, three had received some training in the USSR, and, with the exception of Mao, each had made at least two trips to the Soviet Union. The Soviet orientation of Liu Shao-ch'i, Ch'en Yün, and Teng Hsiao-p'ing—the three Standing Committee members who did not reappear on the Ninth CC Standing Committee—is especially pronounced.

With the partial exception of Chou, however, none of the Eighth CC

---

[13] Clearly, foreign training and a capacity to use one or more foreign languages afford better indices to cosmopolitanism than foreign travel or interaction with foreign visitors to China. It can be argued that travel is not necessarily broadening, since most individuals carry their prejudices with them and reinforce them as they go along. On the other hand, even if the travel is limited as to time and area (often, only capital cities are involved), visual experiences are not easily forgotten, especially when involving radically different cultures. Similarly, a substantial number and range of foreign contacts may ultimately induce a more cosmopolitan style, even if the substance is little changed.

TABLE 15

EIGHTH CC STANDING COMMITTEE "COSMOPOLITANISM" INDICES

Name	Foreign Training	Foreign Language	Foreign Travels through September, 1956	
			No. of Trips	No. of Countries
Mao Tse-tung			1 USSR trip	
Liu Shao-ch'i	USSR	Russian	4 USSR trips 1 visit	1 East European country
Chou En-lai	Amer. missionary-connected school in China; France; Japan	Russian (speaks); Japanese (a little); French (some); English (a little); German (fragmented)	6 USSR visits 2 visits 3 visits 1 visit 2 visits	3 East European countries 4 East Asian countries 1 South Asian country 4 West European countries
Chu Teh	Republic of Germany	German (uncertain)	2 USSR visits 2 visits 1 visit 1 visit	5 East European countries 1 East Asian country 2 West European countries
Ch'en Yün	USSR	Russian (believed good)	4 USSR visits	
Teng Hsiao-p'ing	France; USSR	French (fair); Russian (fair/good)	1 USSR visit 1 trip	1 West European country

TABLE 16

FOREIGN VISITORS RECEIVED BY EIGHTH CC STANDING COMMITTEE
AS INDIVIDUALS OR AS A GROUP *

Name	Visitors' Homeland	1952	1953	1954	1955	1956	Totals
Mao Tse-tung	Communist Bloc †	2	0	2	3	10	17
	Asia ‡	4	3	3	9	18	37
	Africa §	0	0	0	0	0	0
	Latin America ‖	0	0	0	0	3	3
	Middle East #	0	0	0	0	3	3
	West **	1	0	0	2	5	8
		7	3	5	14	39	68
Liu Shao-ch'i	Communist Bloc	4	1	7	19	22	53
	Asia	2	5	6	36	51	100
	Africa	0	0	0	0	0	0
	Latin America	0	0	0	0	4	4
	Middle East	0	0	0	0	1	1
	West	0	0	1	7	13	21
		6	6	14	62	91	179
Chou En-lai	Communist Bloc	0	3	4	16	13	36
	Asia	4	6	4	34	54	102
	Africa	0	0	0	1	0	1
	Latin America	0	0	0	2	4	6
	Middle East	0	0	0	5	5	10
	West	1	0	1	17	12	31
		5	9	9	75	88	186
Chu Teh	Communist Bloc	5	4	8	17	14	48
	Asia	4	4	8	32	27	75
	Africa	0	0	0	0	0	0
	Latin America	0	0	0	1	0	1
	Middle East	0	0	0	0	0	0
	West	0	0	0	0	0	0
		9	8	16	50	41	124
Ch'en Yün	Communist Bloc	2	1	8	16	17	44
	Asia	0	2	2	22	40	66
	Africa	0	0	0	0	0	0
	Latin America	0	0	0	0	0	0
	Middle East	0	0	0	0	0	0
	West	0	0	0	2	4	6
		2	3	10	40	61	116

Name	Visitors' Homeland	1952	1953	1954	1955	1956	Totals
Teng Hsiao-p'ing	Communist Bloc	2	3	7	8	17	37
	Asia	1	3	7	22	19	52
	Africa	0	0	0	0	0	0
	Latin America	0	0	0	0	0	0
	Middle East	0	0	0	0	0	0
	West	2	0	0	8	7	17
		5	6	14	38	43	106

* Figures do not include contacts with embassy personnel or permanent foreign residents.

† Includes individuals from all Western Communist states, but not from Asian or other Communist states.

‡ Includes individuals from all South and East Asian states, both Communist and non-Communist.

§ Includes individuals from only Black African states.

‖ Includes individuals from all Caribbean and Latin American states.

Includes individuals from all states of North Africa as well as those of West Asia, up to and including Iran.

** Includes all individuals from Western non-Communist states, including Communist Party members.

Standing Committee members can be regarded as highly cosmopolitan, at least when measured in terms of training, skills, and experience. Mao and Ch'en Yün had only been to the Soviet Union. Liu at this point had had one brief visit to Hungary in addition to four Soviet trips. Only Chou En-lai had traveled much outside the Soviet bloc, and even his Asian trips were of recent vintage. In this era, the Chinese Communist elite were oriented toward the USSR, not toward the Afro-Asian world, and this important fact is strongly underlined by the data presented above. A transitional era had begun, however, as the statistics on foreign visitors indicate. With the Bandung Conference as a watershed, Peking increasingly turned its attention to the emerging world, and first of all to East and South Asia. The sharp rise in contacts on the part of all Standing Committee members with Asian visitors in 1955 and 1956 signals the new priorities.

Can the Ninth CC Standing Committee be considered more or less cosmopolitan? This question can be answered by examining the data set forth in the following two tables. Many of the same characteristics of the Eighth CC Standing Committee continued as of 1969. Mao might still be considered the least cosmopolitan of the Ninth CC Standing Committee members when all factors are weighed, but his "closest comrade-in-arms," Lin Piao, despite several years in the

TABLE 17

Ninth CC Standing Committee "Cosmopolitanism" Indices

Name	Foreign Training	Foreign Language	Foreign Travels through May, 1969	
			No. of Trips	No. of Countries
Mao Tse-tung	—		2 USSR visits	
Lin Piao	USSR	Russian (uncertain)	1 USSR visit	
Chou En-lai	Amer. missionary-connected school in China; France; Japan	Russian (speaks); Japanese (a little); French (some); English (a little); German (fragmented)	9 USSR visits 5 trips 8 trips 7 trips 2 visits 2 visits	6 East European countries 6 East Asian countries 5 South Asian countries 11 Middle East/African countries 4 West European countries
Ch'en Po-ta	USSR	Russian (believed good)	2 USSR visits	
K'ang Sheng	USSR	Russian (good); German (fair); English (fair to poor)	6 USSR visits 5 trips 1 trip	4 East European countries 1 West European country

Soviet Union in the late 1930's and early 1940's, has led an even more insular life than Mao in recent decades. Moreover, Mao's other confidant, Ch'en Po-ta, appears also to have led a highly cloistered life, except for a second visit to the Soviet Union, which was the source of his higher education, in late 1949 accompanying Mao.

In these men Mao appeared to have supplemented and recreated himself, with all of the advantages and hazards to them which that can represent. Even K'ang Sheng has scarcely traveled outside of the Communist world, and his contacts with foreign visitors since 1952 have been few. In the aftermath of the Ninth Party Congress, therefore, Chou En-lai, by virtue of both his role and personality, stood out even more clearly than in 1956 as the topmost leadership's hostage to the outer world. And at least in terms of those measures that we have used, the Ninth Standing Committee was considerably less cosmopolitan than its predecessor.

Nevertheless, the Soviet influence of earlier years lingers on. Visitations to Moscow may have ceased, and Soviet citizens may rarely have had an audience with Chou or the others at this point, but the signs of an earlier era are omnipresent in the pasts of the recent rulers. Despite the departure of Liu Shao-ch'i, Ch'en Yün, and Teng Hsiao-p'ing, three and possibly four of the 1969 five-man Standing Committee had Russian as their second language, three of them had some training in the Soviet Union, and in at least two cases that training was extensive. The patterns of travel and visitors, until the early 1960's, moreover, revealed the continuation of those ties.

As we noted earlier, however, even before the troubles with the Soviet Union emerged in the late 1950's, a conscious policy of cultivating the Third World was put into effect. For the first time, the CPR began to develop a foreign policy rather than seeking to live merely by a set of maxims. This fact was quickly reflected in the travel patterns of Chou En-lai and in the contacts made by most other Standing Committee members with foreigners coming to China. The decade commencing with 1955 was, in general, an Asian decade, with the emphasis variously placed upon India, Indonesia, Japan, North Korea, and North Vietnam. But the traumatic years between 1959 and 1963 also produced a concentrated wooing of Latin America, with Cuba both hero and symbol. Africa's day came in roughly the same period, with the Middle East sprinkled throughout the decade. A few Westerners, approximately two-thirds of them Communists, also dined and talked with China's supreme leaders at least until the events which began in

TABLE 18

FOREIGN VISITORS RECEIVED BY NINTH CC STANDING COMMITTEE AS INDIVIDUALS
OR AS A GROUP*

Name	Visitors' Homeland	1952	1953	1954	1955	1956	1957	1958	1959	1960	1961	1962	1963	1964	1965	1966	1967	1968	1969	Totals
Mao Tse-tung	Communist Bloc †	2	0	2	3	10	16	6	10	3	1	2	2	4	3	1	3	1	0	69
	Asia ‡	4	3	3	9	18	13	6	14	7	12	9	21	20	17	5	5	4	0	170
	Africa §	0	0	0	0	0	0	2	3	6	3	2	11	17	11	5	6	4	1	71
	Latin America ‖	0	0	0	0	3	0	1	11	17	5	10	11	8	2	1	0	0	0	69
	Middle East #	0	0	0	0	3	2	3	3	4	0	0	5	5	4	1	0	0	0	30
	West **	1	0	0	2	5	1	1	3	2	2	1	6	10	4	1	3	2	1	44
		7	3	5	14	39	32	19	44	39	23	24	56	64	41	14	17	11	1	453
Lin Piao	Communist Bloc	0	0	0	0	0	1	1	3	1	0	0	0	0	0	1	1	2	0	10
	Asia	0	0	0	0	0	0	0	4	1	2	0	0	0	0	0	5	2	0	14
	Africa	0	0	0	0	0	0	0	0	0	0	0	0	0	0	0	4	4	0	8
	Latin America	0	0	0	0	0	0	0	0	0	0	0	0	0	0	0	0	0	0	0
	Middle East	0	0	0	0	0	0	0	0	1	0	0	0	0	0	0	0	0	0	1
	West	0	0	0	0	0	0	0	0	0	0	0	0	0	0	0	0	0	0	0
		0	0	0	0	0	1	1	7	3	2	0	0	0	0	1	10	8	0	33
Chou En-lai	Communist Bloc	0	3	4	16	13	40	14	21	9	9	4	5	10	14	5	7	5	1	180
	Asia	4	6	4	34	54	71	20	35	28	42	31	48	54	40	29	20	12	2	534
	Africa	0	0	0	1	0	1	1	9	10	10	3	14	21	23	16	13	8	1	131
	Latin America	0	0	2	4	6	1	13	16	10	6	19	7	8	1	0	0	0	0	93
	Middle East	0	0	0	5	5	19	8	9	5	2	1	7	10	13	1	0	1	0	86
	West	1	0	1	17	12	17	8	5	5	3	2	10	9	5	1	3	3	1	103
		5	9	9	75	88	154	52	92	73	76	47	103	111	103	53	43	29	5	1,127

Ch'en Po-ta																		Total
Communist Bloc	1	1	1	0	1	3	3	0	0	1	1	1	2	2	2	1		23
Asia	0	1	1	0	0	0	2	0	3	1	1	3	3	0	0	0		15
Africa	0	0	0	0	0	0	0	0	0	0	0	0	0	0	2	0		2
Latin America	0	0	0	0	0	0	0	0	0	0	0	0	0	0	0	0		0
Middle East	0	0	0	0	0	0	0	0	0	0	0	0	0	0	0	0		0
West	0	0	0	0	0	0	0	0	0	0	0	0	0	0	3	0		3
	1	2	2	0	0	3	5	0	3	2	2	5	5	2	7	1		43

K'ang Sheng																		Total
Communist Bloc	0	0	0	0	0	1	1	0	1	0	1	4	4	2	6	2	1	18
Asia	0	0	2	3	0	0	2	1	0	3	7	15	16	6	5	0	1	61
Africa	0	0	0	0	0	0	0	0	0	0	0	1	0	3	1	2	0	7
Latin America	0	0	0	0	0	2	4	0	0	2	1	3	2	0	0	0	0	13
Middle East	0	0	0	0	0	0	0	0	1	0	0	1	1	0	0	0	0	2
West	0	0	0	0	0	1	0	0	0	1	3	4	9	5	7	3	0	35
	0	0	2	4	0	1	7	3	1	6	11	25	32	16	19	7	2	136

* Figures do not include contacts with embassy personnel or permanent foreign residents.
† Includes individuals from all Western Communist states but not from Asian or other Communist states.
‡ Includes individuals from all South and East Asian states, both Communist and non-Communist.
§ Includes individuals from only Black African states.
‖ Includes individuals from all Caribbean and Latin American states.
Includes individuals from all states of North Africa as well as those of West Asia, up to and including Iran.
** Includes all individuals from Western non-Communist states, including Communist Party members.

1966 drastically curtailed foreign contacts for all Politburo figures.

From the cumulative evidence set forth here, what final conclusions concerning trends in the inner circle of Chinese leadership are to be drawn? Perhaps it is possible to make up a balance sheet of continuity and change in comparing the Eighth and Ninth CC Standing Committees. On the side of continuity are the following factors:

1. Chinese leadership at the very top has been and still is composed of aging, ethnic Chinese, predominantly from Central-South China, the cradle of the modern Chinese revolution.

2. In strong proportion, these leaders have been petty intellectuals in background, as we have defined that term. They have come from the middle (or upper-middle) socioeconomic brackets of their society, although in at least several cases declining family fortunes were involved. They have been mainly rural/suburban in their geographic-cultural origins, and are generally men of the interior. Thus, on the one hand, they do not commonly come from the ranks of the poor peasant or the industrial working class. And, on the other hand, they are not primarily from the "old" rural gentry or the "new" urban bourgeoisie or intelligentsia. Their background, indeed, makes their political leadership both feasible and marked by some highly special qualities. It dictates that they will differ both from China's traditional leaders and from those envisaged in the classical Marxian model.

3. In the case of both the Eighth and Ninth CC Standing Committees, the educational median is within the modest-fairly good range measured by the standards we have applied. Better educated than their peers, the supreme Chinese leaders are far less well educated in formal terms than many modernizing elites. As is well known, however, the recent crisis in China revolves in part around precisely what is a good education for the new socialist man. Clearly, for Mao and most, if not all, of his "close" comrades, it is neither the Soviet nor the Western model, but one more closely approximating their own "work-study" background.

4. Party administration cadres predominate over military cadres, to the extent that this divison is legitimate, and men with a mixed rural-urban service record, always at or near the center, have dominated the top continuously, with those having a stronger urban or international record few, and no man reaching the summit yet who has made his career primarily as a regional power-holder. Indeed, role differentiation (inescapable in a modernizing society) has not yet had the type of impact upon the topmost organ of the Party that one might have anticipated. In broad terms, to be sure, the 1969 Standing Committee can be

defined as being composed of a supreme generalist, a military commander, a chief administrator, a Party theorist, and an intelligence-security operator. But no true specialist or technician has reached the topmost ranks, or at least survived there, suggesting that a long battle lies ahead as the Party—or important portions of it—resists the inroads of specialization. The key elite, at least as exemplified by Mao, seek to make organic politics a central objective, with the premium hence upon the type of generalists who can operate an organistic state. Of this, we shall have more to say later, after additional samples have been studied.

5. The Soviet flavor of the Stalinist era remains strong in the men closest to Mao, even though the individuals themselves have changed. Yet Mao and Lin Piao stood out as singularly indigenous, self-sufficient, quasi-rural, insular Chinese; and such qualities indeed have never been absent from post-1949 Communist leadership at the top.

These are the primary continuities to be discerned at present in China's most exclusive political club. What are the elements of change?

1. China is now governed by second- and third-generation revolutionaries—as we have defined her modern revolutionary eras—men who began their careers in the period of the May Fourth Movement and afterward. The 1911 Revolution generation, never vitally important to the Communist movement, is now fading from the scene, holding only ceremonial positions, as we shall see.

2. The Standing Committee has recently been a uniquely Mao-related group, a small band of men who in their careers and roles held a very special relationship to Mao, Chou En-lai being the only remaining partial exception. With the Ninth CC Standing Committee, the imprimatur of Mao was indelibly stamped upon the highest organ of the Party. In almost every sense, the other men of power were subordinate to and dependent upon Mao Tse-tung, although in most cases their ability could not be questioned. In these terms, the top of the Party came to reflect the Mao cult; and Mao himself, after having been edged toward retirement, represented the sun around whom all must revolve. The emperor system has been superimposed upon the Chinese Communist order. But by the same token, one's security at the top depended upon the emperor and the evolution of such an imperial system, an evolution inevitably involving court intrigue of a highly intricate nature.

3. While the class antecedents of the top leadership remained predominantly rural-suburban and petty intellectual, as we have

noted, the advent of political urbanism was signaled with the Ninth CC Standing Committee by several men whose antecedents were bourgeois and proletarian, to use traditional Marxist terms, and this phenomenon, as we shall see, was more pronounced in the lower ranks of the Ninth Central Committee. Gradually the class nature of Chinese politics is being changed. The first shift was that from the gentry-higher intellectuals to the middle/rich peasant-petty intellectuals (and peasant or petty bourgeois military). The more profound changes, changes involving a shift from rural to urban bases, lie ahead. Only the first signs of this latter change have appeared at the very top of the Party.

4. At a somewhat earlier point, another change could have been pointed out, namely, the movement from insularism to cosmopolitanism, from a Soviet-centered training and experience toward a combination of indigenous training and broader experience directed particularly toward the Third World. The economic-political travails of the last decade in China, however, produced an abrupt halt to this trend. For the moment at least, China's highest leaders as a group are less, not more, cosmopolitan than their immediate predecessors and, having been cut off from their Soviet (and West European) contacts of earlier decades, decidedly more insular. This appears to be a temporary phenomenon, as the most recent developments (1969–71) suggest, but later generations of potential Chinese leaders have also been affected by the events of the 1960's with uncertain long-range implications.

Any assessment of trends with respect to the Chinese political elite, however, cannot rest upon an analysis of the five or six men at the very top of the political scale, particularly since changes at this level have been occurring frequently. Let us now turn to the full and alternate members of the Eighth and Ninth Politburos (excluding the Standing Committee), applying the same measurements used above.

We are dealing here with 17 individuals of the Eighth Politburo and 20 individuals of the Ninth Politburo, whom we can describe as the second-highest echelon of the Chinese Communist political elite. In the Eighth Politburo, the full and alternate members were all male, with an average age of 58.57 at the time of their appointment, their ages running from 49 (2 members) to 75. Two of the members were in the 40–49 bracket, 11 were in the 50–59 group, 2 were in the 60–69 category, and 2 were 70 or over. As for place of origin, 12 of the 17 were born in Central China, 4 in the north, and 1 in the south. Eight provinces and 1 municipality were represented, with 5 from Hunan, 3 from Hupeh, 2 each from Szechwan and Shantung, and 1 each from Kiangsi, Suiyuan, Shansi, Fukien, and Shanghai. The Eighth Politburo full and regular members were thus males of late middle-age, predominantly from Central-South China, and in these respects they did not differ from the Eighth CC Standing Committee members.

In the Ninth CC Politburo, among the 20 members, there were 2 females. The average age at the time of appointment was 61.9 (with the ages of 2 members being unknown), and the age-spread went from 40 to 83. One member fell into the 40–49 bracket, 8 were in the 50–59 category, 4 in the 60–69 group, 3 in the 70–79 bracket, and 2 were 80 or over. Twelve of the members were born in Central China, 4 in North China, and 2 in South China, with the birthplaces of 2 unknown. Five were from Hupeh, 3½ from Kiangsi, 2½ from Szechwan, 2 from Honan, 1 each from Fukien, Shansi, Shantung, and Kwangtung, and ½ from Hunan and Chekiang.[14]

Again, the patterns of the Ninth Standing Committee are generally followed with some modifications. For the first time, two females sat at the Politburo level of the Party—but they were very special females, as is well known, being Mao's wife, Chiang Ch'ing, and Lin Piao's wife, Yeh Ch'ün. An innovation has thus been made via highly traditional means. Primarily as the result of one very young member, and a few members in their early fifties, the Ninth CC Politburo full and alternate members have a younger average age than the Standing Committee members. They too, however, average approximately 62 years of age, with eight members being over that age. Thus, the second-echelon Chinese Communist leadership has been aging in the course of the past decade, although at an appreciably slower rate than the first echelon. Its average age is now roughly comparable to that of Japanese leadership, slightly older than American leadership, and very considerably older than the average leaders of comparable rank in most of the Afro-Asian world.

This leadership, moreover, continues to come predominantly from Central-South China. The north, together with the "pure" south and southeast, continues to be underrepresented. From a different perspective, coastal China—whether north or south—had limited representation at the first and second echelons of leadership as of 1969. It was men from the interior that governed the nation. Yet the

[14] Where equally reliable sources report different birthplaces, we have given one-half credit to each. In the case of the Ninth Politburo, incidentally, this does not affect the regional distribution.

minorities of the interior were not represented at these levels of leadership. In the Eighth Politburo, one minority representative, Ulanfu, sat as an alternate member. The Ninth Politburo members were all ethnic Chinese.

Applying the class designations set forth earlier, we are able to identify with reasonable assurance the family antecedents of 13 Eighth Politburo members and the personal classifications of all 17. Of these 17, 9 can be classified as petty intellectuals, with 2 coming from the middle rich peasant or landlord background, 4 from a petty intellectual, intellectual, or petty bourgeois background, and 3 from unknown backgrounds. Four can be classified as military, with 2 coming from poor peasant backgrounds, 1 coming from a rich peasant background, and 1 with petty bourgeois antecedents. Of the remaining 4, the classifications assigned are as follows: $\frac{\text{Gentry/Bourg.}}{\text{Bourg.}}$; $\frac{\text{Poor Peas.}}{\text{Petty Bourg.}}$; $\frac{\text{Intel.}}{\text{Intel.}}$; and $\frac{\text{Poor Peas.}}{\text{Prol.}}$.

The first distinctive characteristic of these patterns is the dominance of the petty intellectuals, most but not all of whom came from rural or suburban backgrounds. Of at least equal importance are the signs of rising urbanization, as manifested by the antecedents of some of the petty intellectuals and by the fact that five members were classified intellectual, bourgeois, petty bourgeois, and proletariat. It is also significant, however, that all of the military men came from rural or suburban backgrounds, and two of the four came from poor peasant families.

In the Ninth Politburo, some important distinctions are to be seen. Here we have reasonably reliable data at present on only 15 of the 20 members, and even those data are incomplete in some crucial respects. With this basis, we can classify 10 members as of the military class, 5 as petty intellectuals. In striking contrast to the balance of the Eighth Politburo, the Ninth Politburo full and alternate membership as of 1969 had a strong military flavor. While we have data on the family backgrounds of only 11 of the 20 members, the general equations already established continue to be meaningful. Of the military, at least 5 came from poor or middle peasant backgrounds, 1 from a proletarian background. Of the petty intellectuals, 1 came from a landless gentry family, 2 from petty intellectual or petty bourgeois families, 1 from a bourgeois family, and the background of 1 was unknown.

Thus, the rising significance of men from the military class in post-GPCR CCP leadership was to be seen first in numerical terms at the second echelon of leadership. A corollary to this trend was the increasing importance of those from a poor and middle peasant background, since the correlation between such a background and the military class is high at this and lower echelons. On the other hand, an increasing number of the petty intellectuals who reached second-echelon leadership in the Ninth CC had urban, not rural, backgrounds —in contrast to the petty intellectuals of an earlier generation. Thus, the mix between the military and the petty intellectual has also become in considerable degree a mix between rural and urban antecedents.

At this point, then, we can assert that in contrast to the Eighth CC Politburo, the Ninth Politburo revealed the ascendancy of men with poor peasant-professional soldier backgrounds at the second level of leadership, with urbanization, however, reflected increasingly through the petty intellectuals of this echelon. Some compensation for the military rise could be found in the numerical superiority of the petty intellectuals at the first echelon, however, as subsequent events have indicated—although we cannot be certain of longer range trends in this respect. Prediction may be less hazardous after weaving other factors such as career patterns into the scene, as we shall shortly undertake to do.

First, however, let us examine the educational backgrounds of the two samples currently under study. Of the 17 Eighth CC Politburo members, 2 had a poor formal education, 4 are to be rated modest, 7 fairly good, 3 good, and 1 good to excellent. At least 10 of the 17 had some foreign study or training, 7 involving the USSR, 3 in France, 2 in Japan, and 1 in the United States (since in several cases an individual had an educational experience in more than 1 foreign country, these figures total more than 10). The type of study and time involved varied greatly, as in the case of Standing Committee members.

Like the Eighth Standing Committee, the second echelon of Eighth CC leadership had a median education that was fairly good at best, rarely involving higher institutions of first quality and frequently covering a very short span of time. Six of the members studied at Sun Yat-sen University or the Far Eastern People's University in Moscow, with most of them graduating; two attended Hosei and Chūō universities, respectively, in Japan; and one studied very briefly at the University of California, Berkeley, without registering. Only one member, however, studied at Peking National University, and he did not graduate. Nor are other prominent universities at home and abroad represented. There is a sprinkling of technical or vocational school representation: Hohai Engineering College in Nanking; the Shanghai "Labor University," and a polytechnic institute in Paris. Considerable advanced military training is also to be found. This includes both the more famous military academies of the pre-1930 era and those academies established by the Communists themselves—the Red Army Academy at Juichin and the "Anti-Japanese Political and Military University" (Kang-ta) at Yenan. From the evidence available, only one member attended the latter institution as a student, whereas three attended the pre-Communist military academies (Whampoa, Hunan, and Chengtu), with two of these men having additional military training in the Soviet Union.

Thus, Eighth CC Politburo members of the second echelon, like those of the first echelon, must be considered better educated than the average Chinese of their generation and status, but considerably less well educated in formal terms than classical Chinese standards (or most modern Western standards) would require. Theirs, moreover, was frequently the work-study type of education, involving short periods of schooling interspersed with work, revolutionary or otherwise, and education in vocational or political subjects, not infrequently conducted in an unorthodox manner and with makeshift facilities.

With respect to the 20 members of the Ninth Politburo below the Standing Committee, the data on education permit an analysis of 13, although we can hazard a guess about several others. Of the 13, 2 had a poor formal education, 2 must be classified poor to modest, 5 as modest, 2 as fairly good, 1 as good, and 1 as good to excellent. In addition, from family background, career pattern, and other data, we can guess that of the remaining 7, at least 3 had a poor to modest educational background, and 1 had a good background. According to the available data, only 4, and possibly 5, of the 20 are known to have had any foreign training. Of the 4, 3 studied in the USSR (1 of these studied also in Japan), and 1 had some training in Germany. Among those with some higher education, 4 had done work at a university—2 at home, 2 abroad—but in no case was a top institution of higher learning involved, unless one should classify Hosei University, Shanghai University, Sun Yat-sen University in Moscow, or the University of Göttingen in Saxony in that category.

At least five of these members and probably more did attend one of the Communist-established academies or "universities" at Juichin and

Yenan, with an additional three members attending pre-Communist military academies in China. Nonmilitary members in a few cases attended vocational-type schools such as the Shantung Experimental Drama Academy, and one member studied boxing in the Shalin Temple in his youth.

As can be readily seen, however, the Ninth Politburo members were actually less well educated on the average than the Eighth Politburo members, largely because a greater percentage came from peasant-soldier backgrounds, while several others were products of Mao-centrism with its unique requirements. The educational median of the Ninth Politburo at the time of its initial organization was no better than modest at the second echelon. When one realizes, moreover, that two of the better educated members, including Tung Pi-wu to whom we gave the highest rating, were now aged, ceremonial figures, the picture is an even more striking one.

Equally important is the fact that the second echelon of leadership, as of 1969, had had much less foreign training than was the case with respect to the Eighth Politburo, and more of its training, especially in the fields of "advanced military and political education," has been under Chinese Communist aegis. Thus, these were more *indigenous* leaders than the previous generation of Communist leaders.

Turning to questions of generation and seniority, and using our various scales, 3 of the 17 Eighth CC regular alternate Politburo members belonged to the first revolutionary generation, 7 to the second, and 7 to the third. In terms of Party seniority, 6 joined the Party in the first period, 10 in the second period, and 1 in the fourth. Six of the 17 had been members of the Sixth CC, 11 of the Seventh CC. Two of the 17 had been members of the Sixth CC Politburo, 8 of the Seventh CC Politburo, leaving 7 who were members of the Politburo for the first time in 1956.

Compared to the first echelon leadership, the second echelon could thus be described as having nearly the same seniority whether measured by revolutionary generation or length of Party membership. Only in time of advancement to the Central Committee did the first echelon have a slight edge. The three members of the 1911 generation in the Ninth CC Politburo, to be sure, were each men past their peak, even at this point. Thus, in 1956, the second echelon of Party leaders was composed mainly of individuals who belonged to the second and third revolutionary generations, who had joined the Party in the first or second periods, and who had become Politburo members either in

1945 or for the first time in 1956. We are describing men who became Party members in the early or mid-1920's, but who first achieved top Party roles toward the end of the Yenan era, or after the establishment of the Chinese People's Republic.

While relatively senior, these individuals played a less conspicuous historical role than did the leading figures of the Standing Committee— although not necessarily less than Chu Teh, Ch'en Yün, and Teng Hsiao-p'ing. Except for Tung Pi-wu, one of the Party elders, who had participated in ten of our selected events, and Chang Wen-t'ien, one of the few remaining twenty-eight Bolsheviks on the Eighth Central Committee, who had participated in nine, the range was between eight and zero, with the median being five to six. One member had participated in the AHU, six in the NU, ten in the KG, and ten in the LM. Clearly, these individuals must be considered very senior Party cadres, with more than one-half of them veterans of the Kiangsi Republic and Long March. And the relatively slight difference in seniority between first and second echelon members is prime testimony to the stability and prosperity of the Party in the years before 1956.

Turning to the 20 members of the Ninth Politburo below the Standing Committee level, we find 3 first-generation veterans, ranging in age from 77 to 83, who were now purely ceremonial figures, 1 second-generation man, 4 of the third generation, 1 and possibly 2 of the fourth generation, 2 of the fifth generation, and probably one of the seventh or last generation, with the generational status of 7 being unknown. In terms of Party membership, of the 14 who could be more or less positively identified, 3 belonged to the first era, 3 to the second, 6 to the third, and 1 each to the fourth and sixth periods. Of the full 20 members, 2 were first elected to the CC as members of the Sixth CC, 3 as members of the Seventh CC, 5 as members of the Eighth CC, and 10 as members of the Ninth CC. One member was a member of the Sixth CC Politburo, 1 of the Seventh, 3 of the Eighth, and 15 were first elected to the Politburo as members of the current Ninth Politburo.

Clearly, a major change had occurred in the character of the second echelon of contemporary CCP leadership, both in comparison with the same level of Eighth CC leadership and, in a lesser degree, in comparison to the Standing Committee of the Ninth CC. The Ninth Politburo second echelon reflected a much wider range of generations: the greatest representation was from the third to fifth revolutionary generations, namely, those who first became involved in the revolutionary movement from the period of the KMT-CCP alliance through the Yenan era, rather than from the group who had participated in the revolutionary movement during the May Fourth period and in the initial stages of the CCP. Except for the ceremonial figures, moreover, most of these individuals had joined the Party in the Kiangsi era or later and had come to occupy the highest Party positions only after World War II, half of them only after the Cultural Revolution.

As one would expect, the same patterns are to be discerned with respect to participation in historical events. Here, our data are undoubtedly incomplete, and full information would add to these figures somewhat. But based upon the available materials, except for Tung Pi-wu who, as noted, participated in ten of our selected events, the range was from seven to zero, with the median being one to two. One member participated in AHU, two and possibly three in NU, four and possibly five in KG, and ten and possibly twelve in the LM. While at least one-half of the members were Long March veterans, no more than one-fourth were associated directly with the Kiangsi Republic.

Thus, seniority more than age distinguished the first from the second echelon of Chinese Communist leadership at the close of the Cultural Revolution. That second echelon had a wide spread as of 1969 because it had been caused to encompass certain Party elders who were accorded prestige without power, having served the Party so faithfully for so long.[15] At the same time, it included the most successful post-1945 and post-1949 elements, individuals dramatically advanced by recent events, most notably, the GPCR. Its center, however, lay with individuals who first committed themselves in the Kiangsi Soviet era, who held middle-level positions at the end of the Yenan era, and who had become prominent only in the past, tumultuous decade.

We would expect such individuals to have different career patterns than their predecessors. Is that the case? Let us look initially at the situation with respect to the Eighth CC Politburo, using the measures we defined earlier. First, the 17 members can be divided into 11 Party-administration cadres and 6 military cadres. Among the former, we can subdivide the members into 4 whose careers up to 1956 had been essentially provincial or regional in character, as against 7 who had operated for some time at the center. The Party-administration cadres also included 4 men who could be labeled "technicians" at the time of their 1956 appointment, and 2 who were "special cadres."

15 There is some evidence subsequently that some elders, particularly among the military, were used very effectively by Mao and Chou in the political upheaval of 1971.

Among the military cadres, 4 were essentially command officers, 1 a political commissar. All currently served at headquarters. Thus, Eighth Politburo appointees, both Party-administration and military, were predominantly men of the center. It should not be overlooked, however, that 8 or 9 of the 17 had held extensive regional power apart from the center earlier, in the northeast, northwest, central-east, and Peking areas, regions where, for the most part, the Communists had held local power for a considerable period before their final national victory.

Among the career patterns represented, eight fit our orthodox senior model, and an additional three fit a combined orthodox senior-regional to headquarters pattern. Two follow the regional to headquarters pattern alone, and an additional one fits a combination of that pattern and the metropolitan-international patterns. One belongs to the latter category alone, and one fits the localist pattern.

Among the four role-change patterns outlined by us, 7 fit the single- or dual-role pattern, 5 the specialist to generalist pattern, 4 the generalist to specialist pattern, and 1 the generalist pattern. The career graphs of these men reveal 8 steady, accelerating progression patterns; 4 steady, regular progression patterns; 2 combined advance and plateau patterns; 2 post-peak patterns; and 1 wave pattern.

Let us provide a brief interpretation of these data. It has already been indicated that in 1956 military cadres played a more important role at the second echelon of Party power than at the first, as did men, both Party-administration and military, who had come from a regional base of power, rather than always having been part of the center. Nevertheless, the classic Communist career pattern—a career starting in Central-South China, involving the Long March, recommencing in the northwest or north, and moving to Peking at the time of, or shortly after the establishment of, the CPR—characterizes more than one-half of these men. Moreover, there is only one localist, and he, not by accident, also happens to be the house minority representative.

We do see, however, the beginnings of a typically third to fourth generation pattern, namely, the regional to headquarters pattern. This pattern is characteristic of men who spend their earlier careers largely or wholly in one location and then move to headquarters only when they are moving toward the top levels of power. In any case, as one would expect, the career patterns reveal a continuing balance in favor of rural as opposed to urban experience, a balance altered only when one puts greater emphasis upon service records since 1949.

With respect to role changes, a much greater diversity is found here than at the Standing Committee level. The dominant pattern is the single- or dual-role pattern, which together with the generalist to specialist pattern suggests a rising degree of role specialization. On the other hand, we must pay equal attention to the fact that in five cases the reverse pattern, namely, the specialist to generalist pattern, prevails, and in most of these cases the individual involved is a professional military man being converted into a more broadly gauged political-administrative-military man. In sum, two contrary trends were underway in 1956. Party cadres, and some military cadres as well, were being converted into specialists and technicians, their roles being narrowed and deepened. But in other cases, particularly in the case of military men with a wealth of combat and administrative experience, new roles were being added to old ones, with new generalists being created. These two trends carried within them, and more particularly, within their interrelation, the potentialities for major conflict within both the Party and the state.

At this point, however, few of the men at the second echelon of power had faced serious setbacks in their careers. Indeed, only one had had to overcome a serious setback, and the dominant pattern was that of either accelerating or regular advance. This was further testimony to the relative unity and harmony with the top elite that had prevailed during the years of phenomenal success from 1945 to 1956.

The picture with respect to the Ninth CC Politburo presented a radically different picture. Its 20 members below the Standing Committee could be divided into 10 military cadres and 10 Party-administration cadres. Among the former, 7 could be classified from their careers as essentially command officers, including 2 who were now aged, retired, presumably ceremonial figures; 3 could be classified as essentially political commissar and political administrator types. One navy and one air force man were included, 8 being army men. While 7 of the 10 military cadres were involved at the center at the time of their appointment in 1969, 3 were serving at regional or provincial levels, in Northeast, East, and Central China. Moreover, 1 had recently been transferred to the center from South China.

Of the 10 Party-administration cadres, 2 could be described as technicians and 4 as special cadres, the latter generally playing an "intellectual" or "cultural" role and having a special relation to Mao and/or Lin Piao. Only 2 of this group of 10 were playing their primary role in state administration at the time of their appointment, while 8 were operating primarily within the Party. Three were essentially provincial or municipal level cadres, the others were attached to the center.

In terms of their career patterns, 7 of the 20 members fitted the orthodox senior pattern, with an additional 5 representing a combination of that pattern and the regional to headquarters pattern. One fitted a combination of the latter with the localist pattern. An additional 5 members followed the localist pattern, 2 of them in combination with the metropolitan pattern. Nine of the 20 had pursued a single- or dual-role pattern, while 10 had followed a specialist to generalist pattern. In terms of career graphs, 7 had a mountaintop pattern, 1 of these combined with a wave pattern, another combined with a steady, accelerating pattern. An additional 5 had the latter pattern only, and 1 had that pattern linked with the combined advance and plateau pattern. Three fitted the post-peak pattern, and 2 had a steady, regular pattern.

Once again, let us turn to an interpretation of these data. The differences occurring at the second echelon of power in China in 1969 were more substantial than those that transpired at the first echelon at that time. First, the military cadres were advanced to a position of numerically equaling the Party-administration cadres, although of the three supposedly ceremonial figures, two were military and only one was Party-administration. More important, however, it is predominantly among the military cadres that one finds the specialist to generalist career pattern, with only the aged military men and the Party-administration cadres pursuing a single- or dual-role pattern. This means that key military men were acquiring Party and administrative roles while retaining their military posts, or at least some of these posts.

When the fact is added that none of the Ninth CC Politburo members had a generalist to specialist career pattern, it was logical to challenge the widely held thesis that the next era of Chinese Communist leadership would be one dominated by technicians. The trend established in 1969 was clear, namely, that the next generation of Chinese leadership would be dominated by former and active military men who had assumed the role of generalists by adding top Party and administrative roles to their military careers. Lin Piao was more than an individual—he was a type being encouraged and perpetuated into the third and fourth Chinese revolutionary generations.[16]

16 The evidence now suggests that Mao and/or Chou, alarmed by this fact, undertook to reassert Party (civilian) supremacy in 1971, aiming at Lin Piao and his followers, depending upon other military men to support them. At this writing, the details of this dramatic development are obscure, and the long-range results unclear.

Another aspect of this scene suggestive of the future was the presence of a number of "special cadres" and "technicians" many of whom were wholly or largely separated from an institutional power base, except for the institution of Mao Tse-tung. This would include Chiang Ch'ing and Chi Teng-k'uei, and probably Yao Wen-yuan and Chang Ch'un-ch'iao. Men like Tung Pi-wu, as Party elders, also had no institutional base. Yeh Ch'ün would have had to be included in this group as well, except for her ability—like Chiang Ch'ing—to use the power base of her husband.

When an individual reaches the upper levels of power within the Party without possessing a secure institutional base, the potential for a conflict of political styles, and for basic instability, increases. A fundamental, if largely obscured, competition exists at present between two concepts of leadership: one is highly personalized, noninstitutional, and leader-centered; the other, organizationally oriented, developmental, and post-Mao. It was always difficult to see how the former group could be maintained intact long, or at any rate, how it could survive Mao's death as a group, although certain individuals might successfully maneuver the transition. Whether Mao's imprimatur has sufficiently stamped itself upon his Party, however, to insure a continuing conflict of political styles after his death, irrespective of the personalities involved, may be the more significant question. Such a conflict would naturally interact with the perpetual adjustments that will be necessary between regional and centrist authority.

As can be seen from the data presented thus far, while men at the center were the dominant force within the Party as of 1969, the men who possessed, or who had recently possessed substantial regional power bases had assumed a new importance. For example, eight or nine of the twenty members of the Ninth CC Politburo as of 1969 could be placed in this category, involving four general regions—the northeast, center, east, and south—as well as two provinces, Honan and Anhwei, and one municipality, Shanghai. Four or five Party-administration cadres and four military cadres constituted the regional power-holders. This trend, should it continue, would be of the greatest potential significance.

Before turning from career patterns, however, let us examine the trends with respect to visibility for second echelon leaders. Once again, the data can be presented most economically in tabular form. It will be seen that the recorded appearances of all individuals were sparse for the opening years, down to 1955, perhaps partly as a matter of policy. Taking the period as a whole, however, we can label certain individuals as "the invisibles," and both their numbers and their identities are surprising. This group is led by Lin Piao, and includes Lo Jung-huan, Ch'en Yi, Lu Ting-i, Ch'en Po-ta, and K'ang Sheng; the media rarely reported their appearance. In the cases of Lin Piao and Lo Jung-huan, ill health was certainly one factor. Nevertheless, it is striking that all of these individuals except Lo, who died in 1963, were to become increasingly prominent in the years after 1956. Indeed, three of them were to serve on the Ninth CC Politburo Standing Committee.

TABLE 19

APPEARANCES OF EIGHTH CC POLITBURO MEMBERS, 1952–56 *

Name	1952	1953	1954	1955	1956	Total
Lin Piao	3	0	3	1	2	9
Lin Po-ch'ü	14	19	18	28	20	99
Tung Pi-wu	3	23	24	46	46	142
P'eng Chen	19	21	27	131	179	377
Lo Jung-huan	3	0	6	8	5	22
Ch'en Yi	2	3	2	11	13	31
Li Fu-ch'un	2	9	10	16	28	65
P'eng Teh-huai	0	2	7	49	76	134
Liu Po-ch'eng	14	19	18	28	20	99
Ho Lung	9	5	26	70	79	189
Li Hsien-nien	6	7	12	46	76	147
Ulanfu	12	9	23	38	72	144
Chang Wen-t'ien	2	9	6	56	99	172
Lu Ting-i	4	1	7	10	8	30
Ch'en Po-ta	3	4	4	9	6	26
K'ang Sheng	0	0	0	6	19	25
Po I-po	14	9	13	16	20	72

* The figures do not include appearances outside China, or notices of exchanging messages, sending cables, or activities other than appearances.

On the other hand, the most visible figures of the 1956 era generally fared badly during the upheavals of the 1960's. The leading figure, and in point of fact, the most visible man of the regime apart from Chou En-lai, was P'eng Chen, whose visibility increased remarkably in 1955 and 1956. A decade later, as is well known, P'eng was to be charged by the Maoists as the ringleader of a plot to seize power. Chang Wen-t'ien, an old rival of Mao and one of the twenty-eight Bolsheviks, also increased his visibility substantially at the close of this period, as did Ho Lung, Li Hsien-nien, and Ulanfu in lesser degree. Once again, with the exception of Li, these men did not survive the GPCR, suggesting that rapidly increasing visibility in this era was likely to place a man in jeopardy in the chaotic years that lay ahead.

Let us now look at the record of appearances made by the twenty Ninth CC Politburo members, which is given in Table 20. Considering the nature of the times in China, these are extraordinarily interesting figures. From them, several categories of individuals can be discerned. First, there are the individuals whose visibility seems not to have been affected by the political events of the period. In this category, we can place Chu Teh, Li Hsien-nien, Liu Po-ch'eng, and Tung Pi-wu. It is to be noted that three of these four men are Party elders. Liu's activities were never extensive in this period, and those of Chu and Tung have been greatly reduced in recent years, understandably, since both men were 83 in 1969. Li Hsien-nien's steady visibility, sharply rising from 1955, is both interesting and important because with the demise of Ch'en Yün, he became one of the leading economic spokesmen for the regime despite a lack of previous experience, and he apparently survived the GPCR when other "technicians" were going down.

The majority of the Ninth Politburo members, however, clearly acquired visibility in the course of the GPCR for the first time, or at least greatly increased their visibility. This group would include Chang Ch'un-ch'iao, Chiang Ch'ing, Hsieh Fu-chih, Huang Yung-sheng, Wu Fa-hsien, Yao Wen-yuan, and Yeh Ch'ün. For the most part these are our steady, accelerating progression or mountaintop types, whose rapid rise in prominence was intimately connected with the events that began to unfold in late 1965.

Some of the Ninth Politburo members continued to have relatively low visibility, such as Ch'en Hsi-lien, Ch'iu Hui-tso, Hsü Shih-yu, Li Tso-p'eng, Yeh Chien-ying, Chi Teng-k'uei, Li Te-sheng, and Wang Tung-hsing. As will be noted, these men fall into two categories: military cadres and men like Chi and Wang whose appointments appear to be connected with Mao's personal desires.

Will the developments after 1956 repeat themselves? Will the more visible figures of the Cultural Revolution era disappear in the course of the decade ahead, and the least visible figures acquire the resources for upward mobility? [17] That prospect seems slim indeed for a man like

---

[17] In some cases, the disappearance of the more visible figures appears now (December, 1971) already to have occurred.

TABLE 20

Appearances of Ninth CC Politburo Members, 1952–69 *

Name	1952	1953	1954	1955	1956	1957	1958	1959	1960	1961	1962	1963	1964	1965	1966	1967	1968	To May 1, 1969	Total
Chang Ch'un-ch'iao	0	1	3	0	0	1	5	3	4	7	6	5	11	10	28	64	47	7	202
Ch'en Hsi-lien	5	5	4	1	0	2	19	3	2	2	4	9	3	10	6	5	22	6	108
Chiang Ch'ing	1	0	1	0	0	0	0	0	0	1	1	4	8	3	21	64	39	5	148
Ch'iu Hui-tso	2	1	2	1	0	0	0	1	5	2	1	2	1	6	6	17	26	4	77
Chu Teh	17	26	37	72	72	157	113	124	124	81	54	110	131	109	75	5	4	0	1,311
Hsieh Fu-chih	1	1	2	3	6	14	7	6	1	2	2	7	4	59	54	95	67	8	339
Hsü Shih-yu	0	0	1	2	0	2	4	8	1	2	0	8	6	13	8	1	35	3	94
Huang Yung-sheng	6	3	4	2	3	5	3	1	1	1	2	12	17	15	7	15	100	9	206
Li Hsien-nien	6	7	12	46	76	74	68	73	112	88	69	119	175	199	134	81	68	18	1,425
Li Tso-p'eng	2	0	1	0	0	0	2	2	4	0	1	3	11	7	8	18	24	4	87
Liu Po-ch'eng	5	2	9	8	7	4	5	16	10	6	5	13	5	7	3	1	6	5	117
Tung Pi-wu	3	23	24	46	46	69	20	66	68	63	27	79	101	48	38	7	16	17	761
Wu Fa-hsien	1	1	5	2	1	7	13	8	8	8	8	15	22	9	6	33	57	7	211
Yao Wen-yuan	0	0	0	0	0	0	0	0	0	0	0	0	0	0	0	22	52	3	67
Yeh Chien-ying	0	0	0	3	1	2	2	2	2	1	1	1	0	2	0	7	15	6	45
Yeh Ch'ün	0	0	0	0	0	0	0	0	0	0	0	0	0	0	1	18	32	7	58
Chi Teng-k'uei	0	0	0	0	0	0	0	1	2	0	0	0	0	1	2	0	0	2	8
Li Hsüeh-feng	4	5	2	6	4	9	20	15	6	3	3	17	11	23	23	8	19	1	179
Li Te-sheng	0	0	0	0	0	0	0	0	0	0	0	0	2	0	2	0	11	0	13
Wang Tung-hsing	0	0	0	0	0	2	6	6	1	0	1	1	2	1	18	19	28	4	83

* The figures do not include appearances outside China, or notices of exchanging messages, sending cables, or activities other than appearances.

Chi Teng-k'uei, but not so slim perhaps for some of the military figures who now assume a low posture. In any case, one can note the same radical discrepancy with respect to visibility within the Ninth Politburo as was characteristic of the Eighth Politburo.

Finally, let us turn to those indices of cosmopolitanism which we earlier applied to the Standing Committee to determine how the second echelon figures of 1956 and 1969 compare with the first echelon of those periods, and with each other. From the information contained in the following tables, it is clear that at the second echelon of leadership, as at the first, members of the Eighth Politburo had had considerably wider experiences and opportunities for external contacts even *by* 1956 than had members of the Ninth Politburo as a group. Of the 17 Eighth Politburo members, 11 and possibly 12 had had some foreign training: 10 and possibly 11 in the USSR, 3 in Japan, 2 in France, and 1 in the United States. At least 9 and possibly as many as 12 had some capacity in the Russian language, 2 in French, 2 in Japanese, and 5 in English (although none appears to have had more than a rudimentary knowledge of English). Moreover, 16 of the 17 had made at least one trip to the Soviet Union, 7 had taken trips to East Asia, 8 to East Europe, 4 to West Europe, and 2 to the United States; in fact, only 1 Politburo member appears not to have been outside China as of 1956. Few of the Eighth Politburo members had had extensive contacts with foreign visitors in China, since the era of large-scale visitations lay ahead. P'eng Chen again was the primary exception, although Ho Lung, Li Hsien-nien, and Ulanfu also had a substantial number of contacts in 1955 and 1956 with Communist-bloc and Asian visitors.

Contrast this general picture with that prevailing among the 20 members of the Ninth CC Politburo below the Standing Committee as of May, 1969. Only 4 or 5 of the 20 appear to have had any foreign training, and with the possible exception of Li Hsien-nien, the one uncertain case, all the others were old men, already retired. Linguistic capacity also appeared to be quite restricted among this group, and again applicable only to the Party elders. Even with respect to travel, a sharp contrast was to be seen. Only one-half of the 20 members had visited the Soviet Union. Moreover, despite the extraordinary efforts after 1954 to cultivate the Afro-Asian-Latin American world, only 8 had been to East Asia, 1 to South Asia, and none to Latin America or Africa, so far as can be determined. Five had visited East Europe, 2 had been to West Europe (Chu Teh and Yeh Chien-ying, two elders),

TABLE 21

EIGHTH CC POLITBURO "COSMOPOLITANISM" INDICES

Name	Foreign Training	Foreign Language	Foreign Travel	
			No. of Trips	No. of Countries
Lin Piao	USSR	Russian (uncertain)	1 USSR trip	
Lin Po-ch'u	Japan; USSR	Japanese; Russian	1 USSR trip	
			2 trips	1 East Asian country
Tung Pi-wu	Japan; USSR	Japanese; Russian; English (a little)	1 USSR trip	
			1 trip	1 East European country
			3 trips	1 East Asian country
			1 trip	United States
P'eng Chen	——	——		
Lo Jung-huan	——	——	1 USSR trip	
Ch'en Yi	France	French; English (some)	1 USSR trip	
			1 trip	1 East European country
			1 trip	1 East Asian country
			1 trip	1 West European country
Li Fu-ch'un	France; USSR	French; Russian	2 USSR trips	
			1 trip	1 West European country
P'eng Teh-huai	——	——	1 USSR trip	
			1 trip	2 East European countries
			2 trips	1 East Asian country
Liu Po-ch'eng	USSR	Russian	1 USSR trip	
			1 trip	Hong Kong

Name		Languages	Travel	Destinations
Ho Lung	—		1 USSR trip 1 trip 2 trips 1 trip	1 East European country 4 East Asian countries 2 South Asian countries
Li Hsien-nien	USSR(?)	Russian(?)	1 USSR trip (uncertain) 1 trip	1 East European country
Ulanfu	USSR	Russian (probable)	1 USSR trip 2 trips 1 trip 1 trip 1 trip	2 East European countries 1 East Asian country 1 South Asian country 1 West European country
Chang Wen-t'ien	USSR; Japan; USA	Russian; English	2 USSR trips 1 trip 1 trip 1 trip 1 trip	2 East European countries 1 East Asian country 1 West European country United States
Lu Ting-i	USSR	Russian; English	1 USSR trip	
Ch'en Po-ta	USSR	Russian	2 USSR trips	
K'ang Sheng	USSR	Russian (good); German (fair); English (fair to poor)	1 USSR trip 1 trip 1 trip	1 East European country 1 West European country
Po I-po	—	—	1 USSR trip	

TABLE 22

FOREIGN VISITORS RECEIVED BY EIGHTH CC POLITBURO AS
INDIVIDUALS OR AS A GROUP

Name	Visitors' Homeland	1952	1953	1954	1955	1956	Total
Lin Piao	Communist Bloc	0	0	0	0	0	0
	Asia	0	0	0	0	0	0
	Africa	0	0	0	0	0	0
	Latin America	0	0	0	0	0	0
	Middle East	0	0	0	0	0	0
	West	0	0	0	0	0	0
		0	0	0	0	0	0
Lin Po-ch'u	Communist Bloc	4	3	5	1	0	13
	Asia	2	0	1	9	2	14
	Africa	0	0	0	0	0	0
	Latin America	0	0	0	0	0	0
	Middle East	0	0	0	0	0	0
	West	0	0	0	0	0	0
		6	3	6	10	2	27
Tung Pi-wu	Communist Bloc	0	4	6	3	4	17
	Asia	1	5	5	5	7	23
	Africa	0	0	0	0	0	0
	Latin America	0	0	0	0	2	2
	Middle East	0	0	0	0	1	1
	West	0	0	0	0	1	1
		1	9	11	8	15	44
P'eng Chen	Communist Bloc	1	7	3	23	11	45
	Asia	4	2	4	50	94	154
	Africa	0	0	0	1	0	1
	Latin America	0	0	0	7	5	12
	Middle East	0	0	0	5	2	7
	West	0	0	0	9	18	27
		5	9	7	95	130	246
Lo Jung-huan	Communist Bloc	1	0	0	0	0	1
	Asia	0	0	0	1	0	1
	Africa	0	0	0	0	0	0
	Latin America	0	0	0	0	0	0
	Middle East	0	0	0	0	0	0
	West	0	0	0	0	0	0
		1	0	0	1	0	2
Ch'en Yi	Communist Bloc	0	0	0	2	2	4
	Asia	1	1	2	1	1	6
	Africa	0	0	0	0	0	0

Name	Visitors' Homeland	1952	1953	1954	1955	1956	Total
	Latin America	0	0	0	0	0	0
	Middle East	0	0	0	0	0	0
	West	0	0	0	0	0	0
		1	1	2	3	3	10
Li Fu-ch'un	Communist Bloc	0	2	2	1	3	8
	Asia	0	1	1	3	2	7
	Africa	0	0	0	0	0	0
	Latin America	0	0	0	0	0	0
	Middle East	0	0	0	0	0	0
	West	0	0	0	0	0	0
		0	3	3	4	5	15
P'eng Teh-huai	Communist Bloc	0	0	1	2	3	6
	Asia	0	2	5	13	4	24
	Africa	0	0	0	0	0	0
	Latin America	0	0	0	0	0	0
	Middle East	0	0	0	0	0	0
	West	0	0	0	1	1	2
		0	2	6	16	8	32
Liu Po-ch'eng	Communist Bloc	0	1	1	1	0	3
	Asia	0	0	0	2	1	3
	Africa	0	0	0	0	0	0
	Latin America	0	0	0	0	0	0
	Middle East	0	0	0	0	0	0
	West	0	0	0	0	0	0
		0	1	1	3	1	6
Ho Lung	Communist Bloc	0	0	4	22	13	39
	Asia	0	2	8	22	47	79
	Africa	0	0	0	0	0	0
	Latin America	0	0	0	0	0	0
	Middle East	0	0	0	0	0	0
	West	0	0	0	0	0	0
		0	2	12	44	60	118
Li Hsien-nien	Communist Bloc	0	0	1	16	12	29
	Asia	0	0	0	17	29	46
	Africa	0	0	0	1	0	1
	Latin America	0	0	0	0	0	0
	Middle East	0	0	0	0	1	1
	West	0	0	0	0	3	3
		0	0	1	34	45	80
Ulanfu	Communist Bloc	0	0	2	6	5	13
	Asia	0	0	5	17	34	56

TABLE 22 (*Continued*)

Name	Visitors' Homeland	1952	1953	1954	1955	1956	Total
	Africa	0	0	0	1	0	1
	Latin America	0	0	0	7	0	7
	Middle East	0	0	0	4	1	5
	West	0	0	1	2	2	5
		0	0	8	37	42	87
Chang Wen-t'ien	Communist Bloc	0	2	2	1	3	8
	Asia	0	1	1	3	2	7
	Africa	0	0	0	0	0	0
	Latin America	0	0	0	0	0	0
	Middle East	0	0	0	0	0	0
	West	0	0	0	0	0	0
		0	3	3	4	5	15
Lu Ting-i	Communist Bloc	0	0	2	0	1	3
	Asia	2	0	0	2	0	4
	Africa	0	0	0	0	0	0
	Latin America	0	0	0	0	0	0
	Middle East	0	0	0	0	0	0
	West	0	0	1	0	0	1
		2	0	3	2	1	8
Ch'en Po-ta	Communist Bloc	1	1	1	9	0	12
	Asia	0	1	0	1	0	2
	Africa	0	0	0	0	0	0
	Latin America	0	0	0	0	0	0
	Middle East	0	0	0	0	0	0
	West	0	0	0	0	0	0
		1	2	1	10	0	14
K'ang Sheng	Communist Bloc	0	0	0	0	1	1
	Asia	0	0	0	2	3	5
	Africa	0	0	0	0	0	0
	Latin America	0	0	0	0	0	0
	West	0	0	0	0	0	0
		0	0	0	2	4	6
Po I-po	Communist Bloc	0	0	0	2	2	4
	Asia	1	1	2	1	1	6
	Africa	0	0	0	0	0	0
	Latin America	0	0	0	0	0	0
	West	0	0	0	0	0	0
		1	1	2	3	3	10

TABLE 23

NINTH CC POLITBURO "COSMOPOLITANISM" INDICES

Name	Foreign Training	Foreign Language	Foreign Travel	
			No. of Trips	No. of Countries
Chang Ch'un-ch'iao	——	——	1 USSR trip	
Ch'en Hsi-lien	——	——	1 USSR trip	
			1 trip	1 East Asian country
Chiang Ch'ing	——	——		
Ch'iu Hui-tso	——	——		
Chu Teh	Republic of Germany	German (uncertain)	2 USSR trips	5 East European countries
			3 trips	1 East Asian country
			1 trip	2 West European countries
			1 trip	
Hsieh Fu-chih	——		1 trip	2 East European countries
			2 trips	2 East Asian countries; 2 South Asian countries; 2 North African countries
Hsü Shih-yu	——	——		
Huang Yung-sheng	——	——		
Li Hsien-nien	USSR(?)	Russian(?)	1 or 2 USSR trips	3 East European countries
			5 trips	1 East Asian country
			1 visit	

TABLE 23 (Continued)

Name	Foreign Training	Foreign Language	Foreign Travel	
			No. of Trips	No. of Countries
Li Tso-p'eng	—			
Liu Po-ch'eng	USSR	Russian	1 USSR trip 1 trip	Hong Kong
Tung Pi-wu	Japan; USSR	Japanese; Russian; English (a little)	1 USSR trip 2 trips 3 trips 1 trip	3 East European countries 1 East Asian country United States
Wu Fa-hsien	—		1 USSR trip 1 trip	1 East Asian country
Yao Wen-yuan	—			
Yeh Chien-ying	USSR	Russian; German (some)	2 USSR trips 1 trip 3 trips 1 trip 1 trip	1 East European country 3 East Asian countries 1 South Asian country 1 West European country
Yeh Ch'ün	—			
Chi Teng-k'uei	—		1 USSR trip	
Li Hsüeh-feng	—		1 USSR trip 1 trip	2 East Asian countries
Li Te-sheng	—			
Wang Tung-hsing	—		1 USSR trip 1 trip	2 South Asian countries

TABLE 24

FOREIGN VISITORS RECEIVED BY NINTH CC POLITBURO AS INDIVIDUALS OR AS A GROUP

Name	Visitors' Homeland	1952	1953	1954	1955	1956	1957	1958	1959	1960	1961	1962	1963	1964	1965	1966	1967	1968	To May 1, 1969	Totals
Chang Ch'un-ch'iao	Communist Bloc	0	4	1	0	0	1	2	0	0	2	3	3	1	5	0	9	1	0	32
	Asia	0	0	1	0	0	0	0	0	1	0	3	0	1	0	5	3	0	0	14
	Africa	0	0	0	0	0	0	0	0	0	0	0	0	0	0	0	4	1	0	5
	Latin America	0	0	0	0	0	0	2	1	3	4	0	0	0	0	0	0	0	0	10
	Middle East	0	0	0	0	0	0	0	0	0	0	0	0	0	0	0	0	0	0	0
	West	0	0	1	0	0	0	0	0	0	0	0	0	0	0	0	1	0	0	2
		0	4	3	0	0	1	4	1	4	6	6	3	2	5	5	17	2	0	63
Ch'en Hsi-lien	Communist Bloc	2	3	1	0	0	1	8	1	0	0	0	0	0	0	0	0	0	0	16
	Asia	0	0	0	0	0	0	3	1	1	0	3	3	0	2	0	0	0	0	13
	Africa	0	0	0	0	0	0	0	0	0	0	0	0	0	0	0	0	0	0	0
	Latin America	0	0	0	0	0	0	0	0	0	0	0	0	0	0	0	0	0	0	0
	Middle East	0	0	0	0	0	0	2	0	0	0	0	0	0	0	0	0	0	0	2
	West	0	0	0	0	0	0	0	0	0	0	0	0	0	0	0	0	0	0	0
		2	3	1	0	0	1	13	2	1	0	3	3	0	2	0	0	0	0	31
Chiang Ch'ing	Communist Bloc	0	0	0	0	0	0	0	0	0	0	0	0	0	0	0	14	1	0	15
	Asia	0	0	0	0	0	0	0	0	0	3	1	0	4	0	0	5	1	0	14
	Africa	0	0	0	0	0	0	0	0	0	0	0	0	0	0	0	0	2	0	2
	Latin America	0	0	0	0	0	0	0	0	0	0	0	0	0	0	0	0	0	0	0
	Middle East	0	0	0	0	0	0	0	0	0	0	0	0	0	0	0	0	0	0	0
	West	0	0	0	0	0	0	0	0	0	0	0	0	0	1	0	0	2	0	3
		0	0	0	0	0	0	0	0	0	3	1	0	4	1	0	19	6	0	34
Ch'iu Hui-tso	Communist Bloc	0	0	0	0	0	0	0	0	1	0	0	0	0	0	0	5	0	0	6
	Asia	0	0	0	0	0	0	0	0	1	0	0	0	0	1	0	0	2	1	5
	Africa	0	0	0	0	0	0	0	0	0	0	0	0	0	0	0	0	0	0	0
	Latin America	0	0	0	0	0	0	0	0	0	0	0	0	0	0	0	0	0	0	0
	Middle East	0	0	0	0	0	0	0	0	0	0	0	0	0	0	0	0	0	0	0
	West	0	0	0	0	0	0	0	0	0	0	0	0	0	0	0	0	0	0	0
		0	0	0	0	0	0	0	0	2	0	0	0	0	1	0	5	2	1	11

TABLE 24 (Continued)

Name	Visitors' Homeland	1952	1953	1954	1955	1956	1957	1958	1959	1960	1961	1962	1963	1964	1965	1966	1967	1968	To May 1, 1969	Totals
Chu Teh	Communist Bloc	5	4	8	17	14	60	15	40	26	5	4	8	11	8	11	2	0	0	238
	Asia	4	4	8	32	27	31	16	15	37	35	19	53	39	43	20	0	0	0	383
	Africa	0	0	0	0	0	0	0	1	10	11	4	9	22	8	10	0	0	0	75
	Latin America	0	0	0	0	0	0	0	5	5	15	1	7	3	2	0	0	0	0	38
	Middle East	0	0	0	0	0	3	4	3	6	1	2	2	10	0	5	0	0	0	36
	West	0	0	0	4	5	2	2	4	2	0	3	3	4	1	0	0	0	0	30
		9	8	16	53	46	96	37	68	86	67	33	82	89	62	46	2	0	0	800
Hsieh Fu-chih	Communist Bloc	0	0	0	0	0	0	0	0	0	0	0	0	0	11	2	15	2	1	31
	Asia	0	0	0	0	1	7	1	2	0	1	0	0	0	10	15	9	2	1	49
	Africa	0	0	0	0	0	0	0	0	0	0	0	0	0	9	2	5	1	1	18
	Latin America	0	0	0	0	0	0	0	0	0	0	0	0	0	1	0	0	0	1	2
	Middle East	0	0	0	0	0	0	0	0	0	0	0	0	0	2	1	1	0	0	4
	West	0	0	0	0	0	0	0	0	0	0	0	0	0	0	0	0	1	0	1
		0	0	0	0	1	7	1	2	0	1	0	0	0	33	20	30	6	4	105
Hsü Shih-yu	Communist Bloc	0	0	0	1	0	2	0	0	0	0	0	0	1	0	0	0	0	0	4
	Asia	0	0	1	0	0	1	0	0	0	0	0	1	0	0	0	0	0	0	3
	Africa	0	0	0	0	0	0	0	0	0	0	0	0	0	2	0	0	0	0	2
	Latin America	0	0	0	0	0	0	0	0	0	0	0	0	0	0	0	0	0	0	0
	Middle East	0	0	0	0	0	0	0	0	0	0	0	2	0	0	0	0	0	0	2
	West	0	0	0	0	0	0	0	0	0	0	0	0	0	0	0	0	0	0	0
		0	0	1	1	0	3	0	0	0	0	0	3	1	2	0	0	0	0	11
Huang Yung-sheng	Communist Bloc	1	1	0	0	0	0	0	0	0	0	0	0	0	0	0	1	3	1	8
	Asia	1	0	0	3	1	1	1	1	1	2	0	1	5	2	0	0	4	1	24
	Africa	0	0	0	0	0	0	0	0	0	0	0	0	0	0	0	0	3	0	3
	Latin America	0	0	0	0	0	0	0	0	0	0	0	0	0	0	0	0	0	0	0

		1	2	3	4	5	6	7	8	9	10	11	12	13	14	15	16	17	Total
	Middle East	0	0	0	0	0	0	0	0	0	0	1	0	0	0	3	0	1	6
	West	0	1	0	0	0	0	0	0	0	0	0	0	0	0	0	0	0	1
		2	1	3	1	0	1	0	2	0	0	1	6	3	0	1	10	2	42
Li Hsien-nien	Communist Bloc	0	1	16	12	10	16	25	17	30	17	36	31	28	17	5	0	0	294
	Asia	0	0	17	29	15	17	43	32	24	47	41	62	50	14	3	0	0	407
	Africa	0	0	1	0	0	0	6	0	8	20	37	37	18	26	4	4	5	166
	Latin America	0	0	1	0	0	0	10	18	0	1	3	4	1	0	0	0	0	42
	Middle East	0	0	1	1	0	1	1	0	0	0	13	3	1	0	0	0	0	21
	West	0	0	3	3	0	0	0	0	5	5	9	3	5	14	0	0	0	40
		0	1	34	45	50	26	31	85	83	50	90	139	151	103	57	12	13	970
Li Tso-p'eng	Communist Bloc	2	1	0	0	1	0	2	0	0	1	0	0	1	0	0	0	2	10
	Asia	0	0	0	0	0	4	5	0	0	1	1	1	0	0	0	0	0	13
	Africa	0	0	0	0	0	0	0	0	0	0	0	0	0	0	0	0	0	0
	Latin America	0	0	0	0	0	0	0	0	0	0	0	0	0	0	0	0	0	0
	Middle East	0	0	0	0	0	0	0	0	0	0	0	0	0	0	0	0	0	0
	West	0	0	0	0	0	0	0	0	0	0	0	0	0	0	0	0	0	0
		2	1	0	0	1	4	8	0	0	2	1	1	1	0	0	0	2	23
Liu Po-ch'eng	Communist Bloc	0	2	1	2	1	0	3	0	0	0	0	0	0	0	0	0	0	9
	Asia	0	0	2	1	1	0	0	0	0	0	0	0	0	0	0	0	0	4
	Africa	0	0	0	0	0	0	0	0	0	0	0	0	0	0	0	0	0	0
	Latin America	0	0	0	0	0	0	0	0	0	0	0	0	0	0	0	0	0	0
	Middle East	0	0	0	0	0	0	0	0	0	0	0	0	0	0	0	0	0	0
	West	0	0	0	0	0	0	0	0	0	0	0	0	0	0	0	0	0	0
		0	2	3	3	2	0	3	0	0	0	0	1	0	0	0	1	0	13
Tung Pi-wu	Communist Bloc	0	6	3	4	13	5	15	5	5	6	7	6	5	4	5	0	1	90
	Asia	1	5	5	7	11	6	2	6	8	8	23	18	7	8	0	0	0	118
	Africa	0	0	0	0	1	3	0	5	3	12	6	2	2	6	3	0	3	41
	Latin America	0	0	0	0	1	2	2	6	2	4	2	4	1	0	0	0	0	26
	Middle East	0	0	0	2	1	1	1	0	3	3	3	3	1	5	0	0	0	20
	West	0	0	0	1	0	2	2	1	0	0	0	0	0	0	0	0	0	9
		1	11	8	15	31	22	23	23	21	41	46	16	17	4	13	2	8	304

TABLE 24 (Continued)

Name	Visitors' Homeland	1952	1953	1954	1955	1956	1957	1958	1959	1960	1961	1962	1963	1964	1965	1966	1967	1968	To May 1, 1969	Totals
Wu Fa-hsien	Communist Bloc	0	0	0	0	1	4	7	3	1	2	2	0	3	0	0	10	2	0	37
	Asia	0	0	0	1	0	2	2	1	1	2	2	5	8	2	0	2	0	1	29
	Africa	0	0	0	0	0	0	0	0	0	0	0	0	0	0	0	0	2	0	2
	Latin America	0	0	0	0	0	0	0	0	0	0	0	1	0	0	0	0	0	0	1
	Middle East	0	0	0	0	0	0	0	0	0	0	0	0	0	0	0	0	1	0	0
	West	0	0	0	0	0	0	0	0	0	0	0	0	0	0	0	0	1	1	1
		1	0	1	1	1	6	9	4	2	4	4	6	11	2	0	12	5	1	70
Yao Wen-yuan	Communist Bloc	0	0	0	0	0	0	0	0	0	0	0	0	0	0	0	11	2	0	13
	Asia	0	0	0	0	0	0	0	0	0	0	0	0	0	0	0	2	0	0	2
	Africa	0	0	0	0	0	0	0	0	0	0	0	0	0	0	0	0	1	0	1
	Latin America	0	0	0	0	0	0	0	0	0	0	0	0	0	0	0	0	0	0	0
	Middle East	0	0	0	0	0	0	0	0	0	0	0	0	0	0	0	0	0	0	0
	West	0	0	0	0	0	0	0	0	0	0	0	0	0	0	0	0	2	0	2
		0	0	0	0	0	0	0	0	0	0	0	0	0	0	0	13	5	0	18
Yeh Chien-ying	Communist Bloc	0	0	0	0	0	0	1	0	1	0	0	1	0	0	0	0	0	0	3
	Asia	0	0	0	0	1	0	1	0	0	0	0	0	0	0	0	0	0	0	2
	Africa	0	0	0	0	0	0	0	0	0	0	0	0	0	0	0	0	0	0	0
	Latin America	0	0	0	0	0	0	0	0	0	0	0	0	0	0	0	0	0	0	0
	Middle East	0	0	0	0	0	0	0	0	0	0	0	0	0	0	0	0	0	0	0
	West	0	0	0	0	0	0	0	0	0	0	0	0	0	0	0	0	0	0	0
		0	0	0	0	1	0	2	0	1	0	0	1	0	0	0	0	0	0	5
Yeh Ch'ün	Communist Bloc	0	0	0	0	0	0	0	0	0	0	0	0	0	0	0	0	1	0	1
	Asia	0	0	0	0	0	0	0	0	0	0	0	0	0	0	0	0	0	0	0
	Africa	0	0	0	0	0	0	0	0	0	0	0	0	0	0	0	0	0	0	0
	Latin America	0	0	0	0	0	0	0	0	0	0	0	0	0	0	0	0	0	0	0

	Category	Total
(continued)	Middle East	
	West	
	Subtotal	2
Chi Teng-k'uei	Communist Bloc	0
	Asia	0
	Africa	0
	Latin America	0
	Middle East	
	West	
	Subtotal	2
Li Hsüeh-feng	Communist Bloc	8
	Asia	11
	Africa	0
	Latin America	1
	Middle East	1
	West	0
	Subtotal	21
Li Te-sheng	Communist Bloc	0
	Asia	0
	Africa	0
	Latin America	0
	Middle East	0
	West	0
	Subtotal	0
Wang Tung-hsing	Communist Bloc	6
	Asia	5
	Africa	1
	Latin America	0
	Middle East	0
	West	1
	Subtotal	13

and the venerable Tung Pi-wu visited the United States in 1945 in connection with the founding of the United Nations.

Nor had this group had extensive contacts with foreign visitors to China since 1952. Most of them had seen very few visitors, at least in terms of recorded sessions. As Chu Teh and Li Hsien-nien had been the most active in this respect, with Tung Pi-wu involved to a lesser extent, the regime seems to have occupied the elderly with the ceremonial entertainment of foreigners. Insofar as the group as a whole was concerned, however, the data on "cosmopolitanism" correlates with that on education to indicate a less "worldly," more isolated elite at the second echelon of Chinese political leadership as of 1969 than at any time since the late nineteenth century.

Before looking at the third echelon of Party leadership, let us add a few additional conclusions to those already advanced concerning the second echelon. Once again, it may be useful to phrase our conclusions in terms of continuity and change, pointing out that at this level, change substantially outweighs continuity.

In respect to continuity between the Eighth and Ninth Politburo second echelons, in both cases the members were aging individuals, overwhelmingly male, and predominately from Central-South China, men of the interior, with the rural flavor still strong. But even here there are some exceptions to be noted. For the first time in its history, the Party had two women on the Politburo. Moreover, there was a wider provincial spread in the birthplaces of the Ninth Politburo members.

Far more important, however, was the shift in the class composition of Ninth Politburo membership: the peasant-soldier was numerically dominant, ahead of the petty intellectual, and the latter group was increasingly taking on a mixed rich peasant/gentry and urban intellectual/bourgeois flavor. Here one sees the two contradictory trends that have marked recent Chinese politics: the ascendancy of the military into the second (and third) echelons, and the increasing urbanization process, with its reflections in the petty intellectual as well as the intellectual, proletariat, and bourgeois classes.

The increase in peasant-soldier members was dramatically reflected in the weaker educational backgrounds within the second echelon and the more insular character of the new leaders. On the one hand the influence of the Soviet Union, while still to be seen in the backgrounds of the oldest members, had been decidedly reduced. Yet no other foreign experience had replaced that which older generations of radicals received in Russia, Japan, or the West. Now China had a truly indigenous leadership, with all of the strengths and weaknesses which that connotes.

It was also a leadership at the second level separated from the very top by not merely one, but several generations, measuring generations by political seniority and experience rather than age. Here again, the change between the Eighth and the Ninth Politburos is a major one. The leaders of the 1956 second echelon were men who had joined the Party in the early or mid-1920's, with one-half of them being involved in the Kiangsi Republic, and with most of them reaching positions of considerable importance during the Yenan era. They were second- and third-generation revolutionaries, with relatively similar career patterns, marked by mixed south-north, rural-urban service, always at or near the Party center. Their role pattern was generally that of the single or dual role, but with a considerable movement from generalist to specialist. In every respect, as a group, they characterized a movement highly unified and successful. Most of them had a career graph of the steady, regular or steady, accelerating type.

On the other hand, the men and women of the Ninth Politburo second echelon were, on the average, third- to fifth-generation revolutionaries who had joined the Party during the Kiangsi Soviet era and held top positions only after World War II, with no more than one-half reaching prominence prior to the onset of the Cultural Revolution. Their career patterns reflected these differences. Generally, they combined the orthodox senior pattern with one having regional beginnings and reaching headquarters at a later point. Many had sufficiently abrupt and steep rises to fall into the mountaintop pattern. Most important of all, their careers showed a considerable disposition toward the specialist to generalist route. These tendencies, together with the widely varying institutional bases (and political styles) underwriting the Ninth Politburo membership, spell out the latent instabilities at this crucial level of Chinese politics, and suggest the strongest probabilities with respect to future change.[18]

Let us now look at the third and final level of top political authority which we propose to survey, namely, the full members of the Eighth and Ninth CC (excluding all Politburo members). We are dealing here with samples of 74 and 145 respectively, since the Eighth CC had 97 full members, including 23 Politburo members, and the Ninth CC consisted of 170 members, including 25 Politburo members. Once again,

[18] And such changes have now (December, 1971) begun to make themselves manifest.

let us begin with the simple data pertaining to sex, age, and place of origin. The sex ratio changed only slightly, with 70 males and 4 females in the Eighth CC, 134 males and 11 females in the Ninth CC, with the percentage of females rising from 5½ per cent to slightly less than 8 per cent. In this, as in most other respects, however, figures concerning the Ninth CC are more meaningful if the membership is broken down into the three component elements noted earlier: Party-administration cadres, military cadres, and mass representatives. Eight of the 11 female members of the Ninth CC were mass representatives: 5 of them industrial workers, 3 of them peasants, 6 from northern China, two from Shanghai (C-E). The remaining three females were Party-administration cadres, each of whom was the wife of a prominent Party leader (namely, Li Fu-ch'un, Chou En-lai, and K'ang Sheng), and each of whom was herself a veteran Party worker. It is to be noted, however, that there were no truly independent women in key Party roles represented on the Central Committee. There were two such individuals on the Eighth CC, but one was purged and the whereabouts of the other is unknown. It could be argued, therefore, that women's liberation has retrogressed insofar as the CCP is concerned.

Turning to questions of age, we are handicapped by a paucity of data concerning the Ninth CC, particularly with respect to the mass representatives. This problem will confront us on most other questions as well, making a division of members into functional groups all the more essential. Regarding the Eighth CC, we have reasonably reliable data (with the usual discrepancies) for seventy-three of the seventy-four members, and their average age as of 1956 was 53.4 years, approximately five years younger on the average than the first and second echelon leaders of that period. If we divide the members of the Eighth CC below the Politburo level into two basic categories, Party-administration cadres and military cadres, the fifty-three Party cadres (with the age of one unknown) averaged 53.8 years of age, the twenty-one military cadres averaged 52.6—an insignificant difference.

For the Ninth CC, we have data on eighty of the 145 members, and the average age of these individuals is 61.1. On the basis of their current roles, we have also divided these cadres into basic categories: sixty-four military cadres, forty-six Party-administration cadres, and thirty-five mass representatives (below the Politburo level). Of the fifty-one military cadres for whom we have age data, the average age in 1969 was 61.2; for twenty-nine Party-administration cadres, it was 64.3. Data were available on only two of the thirty-five mass representatives, and they were 39 and 40 years of age.

While age statistics are incomplete for all categories, the implications of these facts are clear. Even if we assume that those military and Party-administration cadres upon whom we do not have data are somewhat younger than the others (almost certainly true), the principal figures in the third echelon of the Party as of 1969 were not young, probably averaging in their late fifties and possibly close to 60 years of age. It is likely that the military cadres were slightly younger than their Party-administration counterparts. We can also surmise that the mass representatives were considerably younger on an average, possibly being in the 40–49 age bracket. However, as we shall note, there is nothing to indicate at present that the top future leaders will come from this group.

The real power-holders of the Ninth CC third echelon—if we regard the mass representatives for the most part as symbolic—were considerably older than their Eighth CC counterparts, indicating a greater generational continuity than might have been anticipated. Let us now look at the geographic origins of both samples.

Looking first at the 74 Eighth CC members, 45 or 46 were born in Central-South China, 20 in North China, 7 or 8 in South China, and 1 in Japan. Of those from the central area, 22 or 23 were born in Hunan, 6 in Szechwan, 5 in Kiangsi, 5 in Hupeh, 4 in Anhwei, and the others in scattered provinces. Of those from the north, 6 were from Shansi, 4 from Shensi, and 4 or 5 from Hopeh, with the others from various provinces. When one divides the cadres into their nonmilitary and military components, one significant fact emerges. Only 1 of the 21 military cadres was born in the north, and only 3 or 4 in the south. Thus, almost all of the northern cadres were Party-administration cadres, while the military cadres came from the historic areas where the Communists held power in the pre-1934 era. In general, moreover, the third echelon —like the first and second echelons of this era—reflected the preponderance of veterans of all types from the central-south interior.

Turning to the Ninth CC, we have some birth data on 113 of the 145 members *if* we can assume that the present abodes of the mass representatives are also the provinces of their birth, which is strongly probable in an overwhelming number of cases. Taking the group as a whole, between 53 and 57 came from Central-South China, between 43 and 45 from North China, and between 11 and 14 from South

China. Once again, however, there was a considerable difference among the three categories of cadres. Between 23 and 27 of the 45 military cadres upon whom we have data came from Central-South China, 11 to 13 from North China, and 6 to 9 from South China. Of the 34 Party-administration cadres upon whom we have data, 21 came from Central-South China, 10 from North China, and 4 from South China. On the other hand, of the 34 mass representatives whose current abodes were known, 23 came from North China, 9 from Central-South China, and 1 from South China.

Thus, the center-south region continued to be dominant, even at the third echelon of power in 1969, with respect to both military and Party-administration cadres, with 4 provinces—Hunan, Hupeh, Szechwan, and Kiangsi—accounting for the great bulk of the center-south representation. Perhaps in partial compensation, the north had more mass representatives, mainly in the northeastern provinces of Manchuria and Hopeh-Peking.

As can be seen, if one merely compares the total figures for the Eighth and Ninth CC third echelons, it would appear that more balanced national representation had been achieved by 1969, with the north in particular making striking gains since 1956. When the situation is more closely examined, however, it becomes clear that the increased representation of northerners related largely to mass representatives. If they are excluded, there was considerably less change in the ratios since 1956. It is to be noted, however, that whereas only one of twenty-one military cadres in 1956 came from the north, by 1969, eleven to thirteen came from this area, representing approximately 25 per cent of the total military representation. These figures, together with the wider provincial representation in general, indicate that national representation was slowly being achieved. The "deep" south, however, and especially Kwangtung province, appears to have been consistently underrepresented at all top levels within the Party. While the data are too sparse to allow firm conclusions on another sociopolitical point of significance, it would also seem that few members of either the Eighth or Ninth CC were born in any of China's great cities. The overwhelming number appear to have come from rural areas or small- and medium-sized towns, influenced by, but not a part of, China's metropolitan centers.

If the geographic distribution of Party Central Committee members has expanded unevenly and to a considerable extent via the mass representatives, greater ethnic representation has developed within Party-military channels. In the Eighth CC, outside of Ulanfu at the Politburo level, there was only one other ethnic, a Moslem. In the Ninth CC, there were at least 7, possibly 8 ethnics, of whom 4 were Party-administration cadres (2 Moslems, 1 Uighur, and 1 Tibetan), 2 were military cadres (1 Chuang and 1 Mongol), and 1 or 2 were mass representatives (1 or 2 Mongols). Evidently, top Party leadership decided to take the ethnic question more seriously than in the past, in the light of internal and international developments. Thus, even if the ethnics were not represented on the first and second echelons as of 1969, they had greater representation at the third echelon of the Party than at any time in the past.

We turn now to the complex matter of class origins, using the typology set forth earlier. In the Eighth CC, we have some data on the backgrounds of 57 individuals at the time of their entry into the Communist movement. Of these, 23 can be defined as petty intellectuals, 20 as military men, 6 as proletariat, 6 as intellectuals, and 2 as petty bourgeois or bourgeois. As could be predicted, the majority of the soldiers came from poor and middle/rich peasant backgrounds, with the bulk of petty intellectuals also coming from such backgrounds or from the rural gentry (not infrequently, an impoverished gentry family). Once again, however, a number of petty intellectuals came from urban bourgeois, petty bourgeois, and intellectual households. The tabulation of all available data, showing 28 individuals from rural backgrounds, 14 from town or urban areas, gives evidence of considerable urbanization.

In those cases where the data are reasonably complete, the formulas which we set forth earlier continue to dominate this echelon of leadership: $\dfrac{\text{P. Peas.}}{\text{Mil.}}$ (or M./R. Peas.); $\dfrac{\text{M./R. Peas.}}{\text{Petty Intel.}}$ (Gent. or P. Peas.); $\dfrac{\text{Bourg. (Petty Bourg.)}}{\text{Intel. (Petty Intel.)}}$; $\dfrac{\text{P. Peas. (Prol.)}}{\text{Prol.}}$.

We have evidence of a somewhat different type to corroborate these data. An effort has been made to discern the route through which an individual joined the Communist movement. Four possible channels have been discovered: (1) via student-intellectual activities; (2) via defection or revolt (individual or group) from the National Army; (3) via peasant uprisings and rural recruitment; and (4) via the labor movement. These routes are not necessarily mutually exclusive, but generally it is possible to discover the primary or initial cause of conversion. The first channel, student-intellectual activism, is relatively broad, encompassing middle-school students, including peasant youth recently come to town, as well as university students and mature intellectuals.

For the Eighth CC third echelon, data have been obtained concerning 62 individuals. Of these, 34 entered the Communist movement via student-intellectual activism; 14 via military defection from KMT armies; 10 via peasant uprisings and rural recruitment; and 4 via the labor movement. This is additional, strong evidence supporting the thesis that the petty intellectual, often with a combined rural-county/ provincial capital background, played a major role in the third echelon of power at this point. Many of these student activists who came to communism, it should be emphasized, did so in middle or normal school, far from Canton or Peking.

The socioeconomic antecedents of Ninth CC third echelon members are considerably different, as one might expect. We have some data on 90 of the 145 individuals involved, including 34 of the 35 mass representatives. Taking the group as a whole, we can see a radical change from the Eighth CC: 36 could be classified as military, 25 as proletariat, 14 as peasant, 11 as petty intellectual, and 4 as intellectual. The numbers are more interesting and more meaningful, however, if we divide the Ninth CC into its three component elements. Of the 34 military cadres upon whom we have data, 31 were to be classified as professional soldiers. In most cases we do not have sufficient data on family backgrounds to make a judgment, but where such data are available, the poor peasant and middle/rich peasant backgrounds, in that order, usually prevail. Two individuals, classified as petty bourgeois and 1 proletariat, complete the military cadre group. Of the 22 Party-administration cadres upon whom data have been secured, 9 could be categorized as petty intellectuals, 5 as military, 4 as intellectuals, and 4 as proletariat. Again, the background patterns that predominate were those which were outlined earlier. Taking these two groups together, 24 could be identified as coming from rural backgrounds, 9 from town or urban areas.

When we come to the mass representatives, new circumstances are apparent. For the most part, these were postrevolution individuals, men and women who were not professional revolutionaries or full-time office-holders. Their primary occupation lay outside the Party, state, and military forces. Of the 34 whose occupations could be identified, 20 were workers (in factories, mills, construction) and 14 were peasants.

The above data clearly indicate the rise of the military and the decline of the petty intellectual in the Ninth CC (1969) as compared with the Eighth CC. Once again, there is supportive evidence. Data have been secured on 56 individuals (all of them military or Party-administration cadres) with respect to their conversion route. Of these, 27 came to communism via peasant uprisings and rural recruitment, 19 via student-intellectual activism, 8 via defection or revolt from KMT armies, and 2 via the labor movement. This is a striking reversal of the patterns prevailing among Eighth CC regular members.

As of 1969, the man of peasant-soldier background was the most prominent figure at the third echelon of power in China. In his values and in his political style, this individual undoubtedly reflected his rural antecedents in a variety of ways, despite the fact that in many cases he had now had substantial urban service on behalf of the Party, the state, or the army. The petty intellectual who was dominant both numerically and in the range of roles which he played in 1956 had lost ground, at least temporarily. Party "urbanization" now rested upon a mixture of forces, the largest of which in sheer numerical terms was the new proletariat—the factory, mill, and mine workers who had been awarded third echelon positions in the Party to provide evidence that this was, indeed, the Party of the working class and to symbolize the vital importance of worker-peasant productivity and loyalty. The petty intellectual, to be sure, has himself always been a hybrid, transitional figure: part rural, part urban; ambivalent, if not hostile, toward full urbanization, and, it might be added, toward the truly urbanized intellectual.

Despite his decline relative to the military, however, the petty intellectual is still a key element in the Party power structure, even at the second and third echelons. And we have sought to cast some doubt on the widely shared thesis that either he or the military man will be replaced in the near future by the true specialist or technician. It seems more likely that the petty intellectual will continue to be an important element within the Party-administration structure and the primary alternative or supplement to the military cadre.

Educational data pertaining to the third echelon tend to sustain the conclusions advanced thus far. Those statistics are meaningful only if used in conjunction with the basic categories of cadres we have established. In the Eighth CC, of the 45 Party-administration cadres upon whom we have data, 20 fell into the poor to modest education groups (a considerable number of these were ex-military men) and 25 were in the fairly good to excellent groups. On the other hand, of the 17 military cadres covered by some data, 13 must be placed in the poor to modest groups as against only 4 in the fairly good to excellent categories. The same trends prevail with respect to the Ninth CC, where our data are far less complete. We have material pertaining to the education of only 22 of the 64 military cadres; but of these 22, 15 were in the poor to modest categories, and only 7 in the fairly good to excellent groups. Of the 30 (out of 46) Party-administration cadres on whom we have some data, 12 were in the poor to modest groups, 18 in the fairly good to excellent categories. There remain the 35 mass representatives. Currently we have data on only 2 individuals from this group, and they are to be labeled poor. Naturally, one would presume that the overwhelming number of mass representatives would fall into the poor to modest categories, along with the bulk of the military cadres for whom no information is currently available. Generally, data are more readily accessible on the better-educated cadres.

We are thus justified in concluding that the Ninth CC third echelon, like the second, was less well educated in formal terms than its counterpart of 1956, even when the mass representatives are not included. And once again this change is directly correlated with the shift in weight from the petty intellectual to the military class, combined with the elimination of many of those educated overseas.

Because of its relevance, the data on cosmopolitanism can logically be presented at this point. Of the 74 Eighth CC members in the third echelon, at least 30 had had some foreign training: 24 or 25 had studied in the USSR, 9 in France, 5 in Japan, and 1 in Belgium (some individuals had studied in more than one country). Two of these individuals had also had preliminary work in American missionary-connected schools in China. Their linguistic capacities are less easily ascertained but from 14 to 23 had some ability to see Russian, 6 to 9 French, 7 English, and 4 Japanese. At least 50 of the 74 Eighth CC members had traveled abroad by the time of the Eighth Congress in September, 1956. A total of 40 had been to the Soviet Union at least once and in a number of cases, many times. In addition, 20 individuals had visited other countries or territories in East Asia, 20 in Western Europe, 17 in Eastern Europe, 3 in South Asia, 1 in Africa, and 1 in the United States. While the length of time spent in study and travel varied greatly, as noted earlier in connection with the first and second echelons, and for the most part involved short periods of time, the Eighth CC contained a number of individuals reasonably conversant with the external world. As might be expected, however, the influence of the Soviet Union was clearly preponderant, and those having educational experiences elsewhere without exception were the older members.

Of the 145 Ninth CC members, the available data would indicate that only 18 to 20 had studied abroad, 13 to 16 in the USSR, 5 in France, 2 in Japan, and 1 each in England, Germany, and Belgium. Between 6 and 10 had some capacity in Russian, 4 to 6 in French, 3 in English, 1 or 2 in German, and 1 in Indonesian. A total of 49 (all Party-administration or military cadres) had engaged in some travel up to May, 1969; but of these, at least 12 had only traveled to North Korea in connection with the Korean War. This accounts for the fact that the largest number, thirty-six, had been to some other part of East Asia, 19 to the Soviet Union, 19 to Eastern Europe, 11 to Western Europe, 5 to South Asia, 4 to Africa, and 1 to New Zealand. In comparison with the Eighth CC, the Ninth CC was remarkably less cosmopolitan in every respect, even though it was essentially after the Eighth Congress that China turned its attention strongly to the Afro-Asian-Latin American world. For the Party leaders of 1969, the task of getting to know that world, and the West, lay ahead.

What are the changes in generation and seniority between the third echelons of the Eighth and Ninth Central Committees? The picture of the Eighth CC is relatively clear; that of the Ninth CC is highly complicated. The Eighth CC third echelon was primarily composed of men of the third revolutionary generation, those who had become involved in the revolutionary movement during the era of the KMT-CCP alliance. A significant minority of second generation (May Fourth, Student-Labor movement, and First CCP) revolutionaries remained, and there were a few fourth generation elements making their first appearance at this level; but the center lay with the third generation, and there were no significant differences between the Party-administration and military cadres in this respect.

Further, the bulk of the Eighth CC members joined the CCP almost immediately upon becoming politically active, in the second period (1924–28), although some first and third period members are to be found. Once again, there were no differences here between the two types of cadres. In addition, slightly more than one-half of the Eighth CC regular members had been either full or alternate members of the Seventh CC or earlier central committees. Here, the Party-administration cadres showed somewhat greater seniority, with two having been in the Fifth CC and seven in the Sixth CC; whereas among military cadres, none had served on the Central Committee prior to the Seventh CC. A total of forty-four of the seventy-four Eighth CC regular members, however, had sat as full or alternate members of the Seventh CC.

This picture, then, complements the sketch of the Eighth CC second echelon drawn earlier. The typical third echelon power-holder of 1956 had joined the Party in the years between 1924 and 1928, had come to a high position in the Yenan era, and had been placed on the Central Committee in 1945. That individual also had taken part in some of the great historical events involving the Party. On the basis of our data, which in these respects are certainly incomplete, at least 53 of the 74 members had taken part in at least one of our selected events, and the average among these 53 was 3 to 4 events, with the most historic personages such as Teng Ying-ch'ao, Nieh Jung-chen, Ts'ai Ching, and Li Li-san taking part in 7 to 10 events. At least 12 individuals had participated in the AHU, 12 in the NU, 40 in the KG, and 36 to 39 in the LM. Again, the differences between the records of Party-administration and military cadres were negligible. This is the picture of a unified, successful movement, as we have indicated earlier.

The situation with respect to the Ninth CC third echelon was far more heterogeneous, and the data can be highly misleading unless constantly related to the basic cadre categories. Moreover, our statistics for this 145-man sample unfortunately are far from complete here, as in most categories. Of the 27 Party-administration cadres (out of 46) upon whom generational data exist, the second, third, and fourth generations were equally represented, with 7 to 8 individuals in each group. On an average, the military cadres were less senior. Of the 34 (out of 64) for whom we have data, only 3 were second generation, with 10 or 11 being third generation, 11 to 19 being fourth generation, and 1 or 2 being fifth generation. In sharp contrast were the 35 mass representative cadres. We have hard data on only 4 of these, with 1 in the fifth revolutionary generation and 3 in the seventh and final generation. Even without this clue, however, we could guess that the overwhelming number would fall into the fifth to seventh generations, and predominantly the latter.

As noted, the military cadre of the Ninth CC third echelon tended to be of a slightly younger revolutionary generation than the Party-administration cadre. Typically, he joined the Party in the third period (the Kiangsi Soviet era) rather than in the second (1924–28) as did the Party-administration cadre. With respect to association with historic events, however, the differences between the two groups were not great. At least fifty-four members of the Ninth CC, all of them from these two groups, participated in one or more of our selected events, the average number being two or three. Surprisingly, the Ninth CC third echelon contained at least six individuals who had participated in the AHU, eight in the NU, thirty-seven to forty in the KG, and forty-three to forty-seven in the LM.

The third echelon of power within the Chinese Communist Party of 1969 had a sizable number of far more senior individuals than has commonly been realized. Two matters of great importance must be kept in mind, however. First, our best data pertain to the more senior men among the military and Party-administration cadres, and full data would certainly reduce the seniority of each of these categories in terms of percentages. In all probability, the average military cadre of the Ninth CC was in the fourth revolutionary generation, with some fifth generation also present. In all likelihood, while the spread was greater, the average Party-administration cadre was also fourth generation, with fifth generation elements at least equaling those of the second generation. Even more importantly, we must not forget the introduction into this third echelon of thirty-five fifth to seventh generation types, largely devoid of historic association with the Party. In sum, with its Ninth Congress the Communist Party of China reached the maximum degree of heterogeneity possible with respect to revolutionary generations and seniority. This reflects the relatively short period of time which the modern Chinese revolutionary movement has encompassed as well as the rapid sequence of events which divided one generation of revolutionaries from another. Whatever merits the present heterogeneity of the Party may have, the situation is scarcely conducive to easy communications and understanding. Nothing would be more fascinating than to probe the generation gaps inside the CCP.

We come now once again to the important question of career and role patterns, seeking to apply to the third echelon the typologies used earlier in an effort to measure the first and second echelons. We have been able to construct career patterns for 72 of the 74 Eighth CC members below the Politburo level. Of these, 22 follow a "pure" orthodox senior pattern, and 17 follow a combined orthodox senior-regional to headquarters pattern, 7 a combined orthodox senior–metropolitan-international pattern, 6 a combined orthodox senior-localist pattern. Thus, 52 of the 72 members follow the orthodox senior pattern solely or in combination with some other pattern. Of the remaining 20, 8 follow a metropolitan or metropolitan-international pattern, 7 a regional to headquarters pattern, and 5 a localist pattern.

In their career graphs, of the full group of 74, 29 have a pattern of steady, accelerating progression, 16 one of steady, regular progression, 9 a post-peak pattern, 8 a wave pattern, 6 a combined advance and plateau pattern, and 4 a mountaintop pattern.

Finally, with respect to role patterns, 44 of the 74 can be classified as pursuing a single- or dual-role pattern, 14 as following a specialist to generalist pattern, with 7 midway between these two patterns, and 9 following the generalist to specialist pattern.

When these distributions are applied to the two major cadre categories, however, the results are far more revealing. First, the 52 Party-administration cadres for whom career patterns were constructed revealed a relatively wide range of patterns; the 20 military cadres, a restricted range. The former group included 33 who followed the orthodox senior pattern purely or in some combination, 8 who pursued the metropolitan or metropolitan-international pattern, 7 who followed the regional to headquarters pattern, and 4 who pursued the localist pattern. On the other hand, 19 of the 20 military cadres pursued the orthodox senior pattern, pure or in combination, and only 1 followed another pattern, the localist, solely.

The differences between the two groups of cadres in career graphs center upon two factors. The military cadres had only 2 wave patterns (and both of these happened to apply to elderly, "ceremonial" appointees), while the Party-administration cadres had 6 wave patterns. Moreover, the latter group had 7 post-peak patterns, with the military cadres having only 2.

The most substantial differences, however, were to be found with respect to role patterns. The Party-administration cadres had 40 single- or dual-role patterns, with only 3 specialist to generalist patterns and 2 individuals midway between these two patterns. They also had 9 generalist to specialist patterns. Among the 20 military cadres, 11 were pursuing specialist to generalist patterns, with 5 additional members fitting midway between that pattern and the single- or dual-role pattern; 4 were pursuing the latter pattern solely, and there were no generalist to specialist types.

How are we to interpret these data? First, the uniformly high incidence of orthodox senior career patterns illustrates the remarkable similarity of experience shared by the third echelon of Party power-holders in 1956. The overwhelming majority were closely knit by having gone through the same set of experiences and having operated in the same milieu. Starting in central or southern China, participating in the Long March or its equivalent, working in rural northern China or portions of the central region during the Sino-Japanese War, then gaining a massive victory in the years 1947–49, they had finally reached the capital. The only major variants were that some senior cadres were placed in regional or provincial headquarters after victory and in a few other cases military cadres had prolonged service in North Korea. In the main, however, the Eighth CC even at its third echelon was a center-oriented group.

Nevertheless, some Party-administration cadres illustrated the possibility of other career patterns, albeit ones outside the mainstream: the urbanized cadre whose primary service had been in metropolitan centers, or in a very few cases, abroad; or the purely regional or local cadre, supremely important in his region, but not as yet operating in the center. In contrast, the senior military cadres, as we have seen, showed remarkably uniform and orthodox career patterns, indicating among other things that regional or local military cadres had not yet reached the third echelon of Party power.

The very high incidence of steady or accelerating progression patterns among both Party and military cadres, however, is eloquent testimony to the extraordinary stability of this era, and also to the degree to which national triumph escalated the careers of all senior cadres who had survived the earlier, stormy periods. This was truly an age of victory and consolidation. Even some of those who had vied with Mao Tse-tung for leadership and lost, as, for example, some of the so-called twenty-eight Bolsheviks, were given third echelon positions in an effort to consolidate the Party (and also, possibly, to win Soviet approval).

It is in the remarkable variation of role patterns, however, that we may detect certain potentialities for the future. Three broad tendencies, not totally consistent internally, were underway. First, a number of Party-administration and military cadres were engaged in role change (and greater differentiation). These included cadres previously playing military roles who were now caused to set those roles aside and undertake purely administrative or Party work. Most of these individuals, it should be emphasized, were *not* becoming specialists or technicians. They remained general administrators but they operated without their previous military institutional base, and gradually they became incorporated either into the Party or the state apparatus. These individuals, together with those who had always been essentially Party-administration cadres, constituted the great proportion of the Eighth CC third echelon membership, and we have classified them as single- or dual-role types. A much smaller number we can classify as "specialists." Most of these individuals operated in the economic sector, although they were scattered throughout other areas as well. Many specialists were largely self-taught, but a few had acquired foreign training. The number admitted to the third echelon of the Party was small, but some played an extremely important role during this period.

However, a contrary trend was underway, namely, the creation of new generalists. As we have seen, this trend was almost exclusively confined to those military cadres who now took up Party and administrative functions without abandoning their military role (and institutional base). In this fashion, they could operate on a much broader, more diverse scale than previously. They were available for combined types of service, whether at the center or in crucial regions, with a mounting experience that encompassed the political, administrative, and military fields.

Naturally, the pure types outlined above were in fact often mixtures. Nevertheless, the processes themselves were underway, and of great significance. The first major crisis, that of 1957–62, affected all groups. The specialists, particularly if their newly developed specialty dealt with agriculture, industry, or the general economy, were exceedingly vulnerable and many were toppled, including some who sat on the Eighth CC. And since the struggles of this era centrally involved the army as well as the Party, both single- and dual-role and specialist to generalist types were struck down.

However, in the course of the next crisis, the GPCR, the single- and dual-role types were uniquely vulnerable, because the bulk of them were playing Party and administration roles, and among the ex-military, most had long been separated from their old institutional and personal ties. Thus, they were tagged with the Liu-Teng label, and if in desperation they sought to resurrect or construct a broader institutional-personal base by combining Party and military forces, they were exposed as counterrevolutionary plotters against Chairman Mao. In these circumstances, the purely military men as well as those who had never given up their military roles, but who had taken on more general activities, political and administrative in addition to military, were in a highly advantageous position *providing* they passed the loyalty tests.

Their institutional base, in comparison with that of the Party and state, remained basically intact.

The constituency of the Ninth CC third echelon is to be understood against this background. First, however, let us advance a few final observations about the third echelon of 1956. To an extraordinary extent, this was a center-based group, whether Party-administration or military in type, reflecting the firm desire of the Party to build a nation with its heart in Peking. In a number of cases, to be sure, the movement of the individual member to the center had been recent and also partial, in the sense that he retained many of his ties with the area from which he had recently come. In some cases, indeed, dual residences were maintained, with frequent trips between the capital and the regional base. Nevertheless, of the seventy-four Eighth CC members below the Politburo, we can positively identify only twelve Party-administration cadres whose primary post in 1956 was outside Peking (including one ambassador) and two military cadres. The Ninth CC, as we shall soon note, presented a major contrast.

Finally, to what extent is the third echelon in 1956 a Mao-centered group, a reflection of Mao's personal friends and favorites? Some seventeen of the fifty-two Party-administration cadres upon whom we have personal data had had sufficiently close relations with Mao to warrant their being considered intimate acquaintances. Such individuals included comrades from the 1917–19 era, the AHU, the Ching-kangshan days, and the Kiangsi Soviet era. They also included Mao's normal-school teacher, several of his students in the Canton Peasant Movement Institute, and two or three individuals reported to have been his private secretary at various points in time.

Obviously, an intimate relation to Mao could be, and often was, a vitally important asset to an individual's career. However, this point must be advanced with caution (and, as a result of the events of 1971, even more caution is warranted). Knowing Mao well and having been his close friend in the past did not necessarily save an individual when he got into trouble. It is one of the iron rules of any power structure, and one enforced with rigor in a Communist system, that an individual must pass repeated tests of loyalty, with each crisis posing a new test. Many "old friends" of Mao failed to pass the last test which extended over the years 1965–68. Moreover, intimacy does not necessarily generate trust or respect. For example, there is some evidence that though he had known Li Wei-han well since 1917, Mao never really liked or trusted him as a result of events in the 1920's and 1930's. The Eighth CC third echelon in truth represented a blend of "old Maoists," many of whom would not have achieved this level of power had it not been for their close association with Mao, *and* individuals selected for their particular talents and/or because of the roles which they were currently playing.

Of the 20 military cadres, Mao in his earlier career was closely related to, and reportedly especially fond of, 7. Yet some of these were violently attacked and purged after 1965. In more precise terms, we can identify various streams from which the military cadres came. At least 4 can be described as old Mao-Chu veterans, men with AHU and Chingkangshan ties. The mainstream, however, was comprised of men who had served in the 115th Division and/or subsequently in the Northeast Democratic Allied Army, later the Fourth Field Army. There were at least 8 in that group. Six individuals had long served under Liu Po-ch'eng, Ch'en Yi, or P'eng Teh-huai, two each in the respective units. Finally, there were several staff men who had specialized in military intelligence or other headquarters operations.

Thus, as early as 1956, whereas the Party-administration cadres might reflect the dominance of Mao (although the ranks were also filled with men who had long worked closely with Liu Shao-ch'i, Teng Hsiao-p'ing, and Chou En-lai), the military cadres already reflected the possibility of a Mao-Lin line. Each major military stream of recent times was represented, however, and above all, the group was strongly center-based, representing the desire of Party leaders to assert *national* authority vigorously.

There is no need here to detail the events between 1956 and 1969, a task well accomplished in many other sources. The upheaval involved at the third echelon is best indicated by noting that of the 54 Party-administration cadres, 32 were dismissed, purged, or caused to fade away, and 10 had died, leaving only 12 survivors in the Ninth CC. In percentage terms, the military cadres fared slightly better, but they too were hit hard. Of the 20, 8 were dismissed or at least not returned, 1 was demoted (to Ninth CC alternate membership), and 3 had died, leaving 8 survivors.

Before examining the new group, what could be said concerning these survivors? Of the twelve Party-administration cadres who survived, seven or eight must be regarded as old intimates of Mao, thereby providing strong evidence that this factor could be a crucial one, particularly since the group included individuals of greatly varying ability and vigor. Nevertheless, these particular individuals undoubtedly survived because once again, when put to the test, they demonstrated loyalty. In the other four cases we are confronted with special circumstances. In one instance, the individual was a Moslem who managed, albeit precariously, to separate himself from Ulanfu, and in some degree take his place. In two other cases, regional representatives of significance presumably proved their loyalty to Mao at the crucial time.

Interestingly, the eight who survived among the military cadres came from varied backgrounds. Two or three were brought back after retirement presumably to buttress the Mao-Lin forces and must be regarded as largely ceremonial appointments due to their age.[19] Of the eight, four had had service with the 115th Division and/or the Fourth Field Army of Lin Piao, but several of these had earlier been reported not to have been trusted by Mao. Again, the events of 1965–68 enabled a new test.

Turning once more to the Ninth CC third echelon, we find that the dominant career pattern remained the orthodox senior one if we exclude the mass representatives. However, that pattern had increasingly been "corrupted" by various combinations, as would be expected. Of the 93 career patterns we were able to construct (out of 110 military and Party-administration cadres), 27 had relatively pure orthodox senior patterns, with an additional 32 having such patterns predominating, but combined with another pattern. A total of 20 cadres followed our localist pattern, with an additional 6 having this pattern predominantly, but in combination. A new pattern had also emerged at this point, one we shall call the headquarters-regional alternation pattern, in which individuals were sent from Peking to the provinces with the prospect, of course, of returning at some point to the capital. Some 5 individuals had entered such a pattern. Finally, there were 3 metropolitan or metropolitan-international patterns, and 3 regional to headquarters patterns.

Once again, however, it was the relationship between these patterns and the cadre categories that provides the most interesting information. As in the case of the Eighth CC third echelon, the Ninth CC military cadres possessed much greater similarity in career patterns than

---

[19] Again, we should note recent evidence, still sparse, that these men were used in the struggles of 1971 on behalf of Mao and Chou.

did the Party-administration cadres. This time, however, two tendencies could be observed rather than one. While the majority of the military cadres had orthodox senior patterns with various combinations, localist patterns fit ten individuals, with an additional seven having mixed orthodox senior-localist patterns. No military cadre had primarily regional to headquarters or metropolitan-international patterns, but three did have the new headquarters-regional alternation pattern.

The Party-administration cadres once more had a much wider spread of career patterns: pure orthodox senior patterns accounted for only 11 of the 38 samples available, while there were 10 pure localist patterns, 3 pure regional to headquarters patterns, 3 pure metropolitan or metropolitan-internationalist patterns, and 2 pure headquarters-regional alternation patterns; the others were combinations.

Before analyzing the meaning of these new trends, let us apply our two remaining measures. It was possible to construct career graphs for 81 of the 110 cadres in our two basic categories. Of these 81, 25 had steady, accelerating progression patterns, 16 had steady, regular progression patterns, 14 had wave patterns, 11 had combined advance and plateau patterns, 8 had post-peak patterns, and 7 had mountaintop patterns. It will be noted that this is a much greater spread than existed in 1956.

The difference between the two groups of cadres, moreover, is highly significant. Of the 47 military cadres, 21 had steady, accelerating progression patterns, 8 had steady, regular progression patterns, and 4 had mountaintop patterns. This group had only 2 wave patterns, 4 post-peak patterns, and 7 combined advance and plateau patterns. The 32 Party-administration cadres, on the other hand, had 10 wave patterns and only 4 steady, accelerating, 8 steady, regular, and 2 mountaintop patterns. They also had 4 post-peak and 4 combined advance and plateau patterns.

The differences in role patterns were also major ones. Of the 89 cadres whose role patterns could be constructed, 42 had single- or dual-role patterns, 28 had specialist to generalist patterns, with an additional 10 adjudged midway between the two. Only 9 of the 89 had generalist to specialist patterns. Among the 54 military cadres, there was not a single instance of the latter pattern, whereas there were 24 specialist to generalist patterns, and all of the 10 determined to be midway were military cadres. In addition, 20 military cadres were of the single- or dual-role pattern type. The 35 Party-administration cadres, on the other hand, had only 4 specialist to generalist types, 22 single- or dual-role types, and 9 generalist to specialist types.

As can be seen, the passage of time and the events of recent years in China had produced radically different career and role patterns at the third echelon of Party power. Quite apart from the mass representatives whose precise power and role were dubious, local or provincial power-holders were now being admitted to the Party center. The old career patterns whereby an individual either started at the center or moved toward it as rapidly as possible were fading away. The new mode was the development of a career at the regional and local level which obtained recognition from the center when it had been sufficiently developed, or conversely, the movement from the center to the regional area upon long-term assignment. In either case, a localist institutional base was developed. Whether this was to be reflective of the strength or weakness of the national Party and state depends largely upon the balance achieved between autonomy and centralized authority. Whether membership in the third echelon of the Party can provide the necessary linkage now becomes a question of both urgency and importance.

How extensive is local or regional representation? As is well known, the Ninth CC was constructed in part from the base provided by the provincial and municipal revolutionary committees which had been built as "Three-Way Alliances" in the years 1967–68. Rather than analyze "localism" province by province, however, it is more meaningful to look at the current situation via our cadre categories. Once again, the emphasis must be upon the military and Party-administration cadres for obvious reasons. Of the 64 military cadres at the third echelon, 38 or more than one-half held posts outside the capital at the time of their appointment, with all military regions and most military districts represented. Of the 46 Party-administration cadres, 23 or precisely one-half held positions outside the capital at the time of their appointment, most of them at the provincial Party or governmental level.

It can be argued that as long as the top military command remains firm and united, this evidence of localism is of scant importance, since individuals can be transferred if any sense of danger develops and central commands will be obeyed, if the happenings of recent years are any criteria. Moreover, at most key military installations, the practice has been to have a newly assigned man in company with a veteran of many years, instead of having only long-term men at the top. Nevertheless, given the history of China—and even of the Communist Party —one cannot discount the risks of this experiment in "nationalizing" the Party, particularly since the Party itself remains weak and at this point lacking in clear institutional precedents. Indeed, the career graphs of the Ninth CC Party-administration cadres sharply reveal the trauma of the past decade for this group as a whole.

The problem for the Party-administration cadre at the close of the Cultural Revolution, however, was not merely a psychological one. As we have stressed, it was also a problem of role-playing. In a time when the top leadership had downgraded specialists, at least as candidates for top Party posts, and with the premium upon "new generalists," presumably in the image of Mao, such generalists were far more likely to come from the ranks of military cadres, given the events of recent years and the institutional base from which each group could operate.

There could be little doubt, moreover, that the military cadres in the third echelon of power as of 1969 had career patterns which in a sizable number of cases related them closely to Marshal Lin Piao. Here it should be emphasized that a close relationship to Lin need not have been fashioned only out of ties via the 115th Division during World War II, or the Fourth Field Army during the Civil War. It could have come both earlier or, more likely, later. Both the Korean War and recent service at headquarters provided excellent contact and screening opportunities. Of the sixty-four military cadres, at least twenty-six (and probably more) are Korean War veterans. After careful examination of each military man's record, we can set forth the "ideal" pattern for the rapidly accelerating career up to 1970: Party membership and military participation in the Kiangsi Soviet era; service in the 115th Division of the Eighth Route Army, in the Fourth Field Army, and in the Korean War; and subsequently an assignment in the Peking, Canton, or Foochow military regions, or more recently, in one of the real or potential "trouble spots" of Wuhan, Chengtu, or Shenyang. Such a pattern is "ideal" because it offered maximum opportunity for contact with Lin Piao and Huang Yung-sheng (who also appeared to be playing a major role in personnel decisions in 1969), provided the best chance for revealing one's abilities, and *also* could be regarded as a mark of trust in the individual by the highest military authorities.

Only a few of the Ninth CC military cadres had this "ideal" pattern in its entirety, but a clear majority partook of it in considerable part. Their advantage was that they could thus combine the protection of powerful mentors with a firm institutional base.[20] Unfortunately, for the Party-administration cadres there has been no "ideal" pattern in recent times, except that of complete loyalty to Mao and Lin—*as determined by them*.[21] Events seriously undermined the institutional base of such cadres, particularly those centrally serving the Party. Not merely their *esprit de corps* was affected, but also their collective security.

In the final analysis, the argument over whether the so-called Great Proletarian Cultural Revolution truly constituted a revolution is not very fruitful. It not only requires a prior agreement upon the meaning of the term "revolution," but more importantly, to pose the issue in these terms betrays an absolutistic, organistic bias making sophisticated analysis impossible. It is more meaningful to see the Cultural Revolution as a response to certain developments—"natural" and "accidental"—that accompanied the unfolding of the Communist era, with results that were partial, contradictory, and of questionable permanence. In some respects, it abetted and hastened trends already underway. In many more respects, it sought to stifle such trends, or reverse them. Like most political upheavals, it was productive of intended *and* unintended consequences, and the results flowing from it were by no means totally consistent. Most importantly, some of the dramatic immediate consequences may not be, and probably will not be, long-lasting. In all of these respects, the Cultural Revolution constituted a Maoist-directed effort at "reform" or "correction" taken in conjunction with an elitist power struggle. Thus, it deserves to be seen as a part of the evolution of communism, Chinese-style, illustrative of the causes of conflict, the nature of conflict, and the resolution of conflict accompanying the Chinese Communist system at this point in its development.

As our data indicate, the Cultural Revolution did have a powerful immediate effect upon political leadership. It is wise at the outset, however, to emphasize those elements of continuity with the past (the Chinese past, but more particularly, the Communist past) which still remain. Clearly, the emperor survives, stronger than ever. Mao re-

[20] If Lin and Huang have been removed, as seems probable, it will almost certainly affect the future careers of some of those who benefited from their era of power. At the very least, new loyalty tests will have to be passed.

[21] With Chou seemingly in ascendancy throughout 1971, past loyalty to him may be of great significance, and may be reflected in the greater upward mobility of Party-administration cadres, especially if elements of the military, such as the old marshals, provide their backing.

mains the sole authority figure for the Party and state, and indeed, he has less competition now, in his twilight years, than at any time in his long revolutionary career. So far as we can determine, he had no real competition in 1956 in personal terms; however, he did have competition in terms of impersonal institutional and career-role trends, and this he has sought (unsuccessfully, no doubt, when measured over a longer time span) to eliminate. Mao-centrism, as exhibited in the Standing Committee and elsewhere, can be viewed as a stopgap measure, an essential, "temporary" substitute while institutional experimentation continues. To facilitate this experimentation, certain old institutions including the Party were largely scrapped, but considerable difficulty attended the birth of new ones.

Meanwhile, as we have seen, China continues to be governed at the center by aging men, despite the premium which the initial stages of the Cultural Revolution placed upon youth. These men are the survivors of nearly one half-century of struggle and attrition—within as well as outside the Party ranks. One reason for the timing of the CPR's recent political crises, indeed, lies in the fact that because victory itself took nearly three decades, the revolutionary leadership aged rapidly in the aftermath of achieving power. The Chinese People's Republic did not commence with youthful leadership in the manner of most revolutionary movements, but with men already moving toward old age.

It can be argued that the quasi-rural, quasi-military, moderately educated, largely indigenous, "middle-class," self-made petty intellectual was the "ideal" type to preside over the initial stages of the renewed modernization drive which got underway in China after World War II, irrespective of the ideological banners to be flown. One formidable task was to unite in some fashion the great metropolitan and urban centers with the seemingly limitless peasant masses, or at least to prevent the gap from becoming rapidly larger. If there could be no perfect or final answer to this central problem, possibly such an elite would at least keep it always in the forefront of discussion and action.

Curiously, however, under Soviet inspiration, the initial thrust in the CPR was largely in an opposite direction, with the major premium upon heavy industry and hence urban development. Yet by 1956, as is well known, grave doubts concerning the direction and results of "modernization" Soviet-style were already being expressed, and from this point on, the interrelated issues of economic development and the basic cultural-educational system to be encouraged rose steadily as matters of the most serious contention and debate. Quickly, these issues—and the disastrous floundering that accompanied the first efforts to change course—abetted institutional rivalries, personal conflicts, and an elitist power struggle.

In the Ninth Central Committee, as it was initially constructed, were mirrored the immediate results. The precarious status of all political institutions at present is reflected in the extensive personalization that has taken place at the apex of power. To bolster authority, moreover, the soldier has been moved forward, occupying a much greater role within Party and administration, consequently moving from specialist to generalist. This in turn has perpetuated, even strengthened, the rural or quasi-rural cast to China's top elite, since the prototype is the peasant-soldier; such factors as the norms for elitist education and cosmopolitanism have been affected as well. The tendency of "modernization" to enhance the political role of the urban, industrial sector can perhaps be slowed, even temporarily reversed, by such an event as the GPCR, but it is very doubtful that this "iron law" of twentieth-century modernization can truly be overturned. Thus, it is more than likely that the historic role of the old peasant-soldiers is to provide the order and authority for as long as necessary while the effort to modernize goes forward, and that while their values and presence will ensure a continued attempt to walk on two legs—to push rural modernization more intensely than has been done in the Soviet Union, for example—the industrial, urban leg is still likely to be the stronger, especially given the degree of regional autonomy now prevailing.

Meanwhile, the worker and peasant are being introduced into the top Party structure formally, but with uncertain power, while the old intellectual—and to some extent, the new specialist—are held at bay. Specialists are strongly desired, especially in the technical and scientific fields, and hundreds of thousands are being trained. But there is also an intense desire to train new generalists who can command the political summits, and a deep distrust on the part of the petty intellectuals of the advanced specialist as well as the pure intellectual. (Ideally, to be sure, Communist training combines the qualities of Red and expert in each individual, but the issue of priority is omnipresent.)

At this point, however, nothing is fixed or final. The effort to encompass within the top Party echelons a wide range of generations, regional representatives, and even ethnic groups signifies a new, albeit precarious, stage in the nation-building process under Communist aegis. The studies of provincial and local developments in this volume and elsewhere indicate equally significant, and possibly challenging, efforts at the subnational levels. The introduction of "amateurs" (mass representatives) into the top Party structure—even if their roles be largely or wholly ceremonial—together with the wide mixture of roles and career patterns now represented by the "professionals" at the same level, represents a substantial contrast with the era of the Eighth Central Committee. A new era is underway, even before the old one has faded completely away.

If precise prediction concerning the future directions of the Chinese People's Republic cannot be drawn from our data, or other material currently available, perhaps a few hypotheses can be offered. First, Mao has literally made himself irreplaceable, since no one who follows him can play the same authority role; hence, a greater premium upon institutionalization must follow his departure, with all "special," non-institutionally based cadres at top echelons correspondingly affected.

Second, trends preclude the re-establishment of the same degree or type of homogeneity that characterized the top echelons of the Chinese Communist Party in the 1945–56 era; in the future, therefore, the Party will be forced to adjust to a greater element of diversity both within each geographic level and among levels—the great tests for nationalist *cum* ideological commitment lie immediately ahead.

Third, the prospects are strong that the military role within both Party and state will continue to be very substantial, possibly dominant, for the foreseeable future, with some combination of professional military and professional petty intellectual generalists running the system. Current role requirements, career patterns, institutional capacities, and value orientations all point in this direction.

Fourth, notwithstanding the advent of mass representatives, the distinction between professional decision-makers and amateur participants will be maintained rigorously, at least at the national level. And finally, the fear of specialists—and the type of intellectual which specialization breeds—is legitimate, for they constitute a challenge to the current system in certain of its vital aspects; and if the Cultural Revolution temporarily countered that challenge, it did not, and could not, remove it.

THOMAS W. ROBINSON

Lin Piao as an Elite Type*

Scholars of political elites adopt various approaches in eliciting and analyzing the characteristics of their subjects.[1] Most of the essays in the present volume utilize the aggregate analysis approach, gathering data on large numbers of Chinese Communist political elites on a geographic, institutional, or interest-group basis, and subjecting them to statistical or other kinds of numerical analysis. The advantages of this approach are obvious. Defensible judgments as to elite behavior in general can be obtained. Elite "types" are made manifest. Large-scale historical processes, as they affect and are produced by changing elite composition and behavior, become evident. And comparison among elite studies and across national boundaries is more easily made.[2]

There are some shortcomings in this approach, however.[3] Judgments statistically valid for a given political group often bear no certain re-

* Adapted from *Lin Piao as an Elite Type,* © 1971 by The Rand Corporation. Any views expressed in this paper are those of the author and should not be interpreted as reflecting the views of The Rand Corporation or the official opinion or policy of any of its governmental or private research sponsors.

[1] For example, psychological approaches (neo-Freudian, operational code); ruling class models (Marx, Pareto, Michels, Mosca, Veblen, Mills); straight political biographies; approaches linking elites to philosophies; aggregate (statistical) analysis; institutional-legal approaches; structural-functional approaches; leadership as a function of political system (developmental, totalitarian, democratic); and charismatic theories. See, in this connection, Dankwart A. Rustow, "The Study of Elites: Who's Who, When, and How," *World Politics,* XVIII, No. 4 (July, 1966), 690–717.

[2] See, for instance, Lewis J. Edinger and Donald D. Searing, "Social Background in Elite Analysis: A Methodological Inquiry," *American Political Science Review,* LXI, No. 2 (June, 1967), 428–45; and Donald D. Searing, "The Comparative Study of Elite Socialization," *Comparative Political Studies,* I, No. 4 (January, 1969), 471–500.

[3] For a thoughtful essay on how to join aggregate and individual elite studies, see William B. Quandt, *The Comparative Study of Political Elites* ("Comparative Politics Series," Vol. I, No. 4 [Beverly Hills, Calif.: Sage Publications, 1970]).

lationship to the behavior of individual members of that group. Sometimes the attributes of an important political decision-maker fall entirely outside the characteristics of the political group to which he would by statistical rights belong (charismatic leaders belong to this category). Even if a given political leader is found to be entirely representative of his group, it is not clear that he will act in a predictable manner in most given instances, if in any. Finally, aggregate data are background data; as such, they cannot take into account a decision-maker's immediate political surroundings, the dynamics of the decision-making small group, or the sometimes objectively defined "national" interests to which he is subject by virtue of his present office.

Aggregate elite analysis must, therefore, be supplemented, in the cases of leading decision-makers, by more detailed work on the political style, philosophy, biography, writings, and institutional position of individual elites. The political biography is the instrument employed here, and by now it is a well-honed device. There would seem to be a gap, however, between aggregate and biographic studies of political elites that only recently has been addressed, if not closed.[4] This chapter seeks to contribute to the process of relating these two levels of elite analysis by investigating the political character of Lin Piao, until September, 1971, minister of defense, vice-chairman of the Chinese Communist Party Central Committee, and announced successor to Mao Tse-tung. Lin makes a good choice for this endeavor. He combines a set of characteristics common to the Chinese Communist military officer and to the small group that has ruled the Party nearly constantly since 1928, with a set of personal idiosyncrasies that place him somewhat outside the "average" Chinese leader. Moreover, the data available in his case, while not voluminous, are rich enough to provide a basis for a detailed investigation. Finally, because of his historic importance to Chinese domestic and foreign policy, the simple task of reporting the basic facts themselves, together with the more difficult job of setting them in their proper context and drawing justifiable conclusions, provide ample justification for research.

In Lin's case, the following questions are pertinent. First, what are the elements in his biography that linked him to, and separated him from, his associates? This question includes consideration of the his-

[4] See, in this connection, the work of Fred I. Greenstein, *Personality and Politics* (New York: Markham, 1969); and some of the contributions in F. Greenstein and M. Lerner (eds.), *Source Book for the Study of Personality and Politics* (New York: Markham, 1971).

torical, institutional, personality, and interpersonal factors influential in determining his career pattern, as well as elements of accident and timing. Second, what were the main features of Lin's political style, and how did they compare with those of other well-known Chinese Communist leaders, such as Mao Tse-tung and Chou En-lai? Third, what philosophy of war, politics, administration, and education emerges from Lin's writings and speeches, as well as from his military campaigns and political ventures? Fourth, what about the character of his relations with peers, superiors, and subordinates over the years in both the Party and the People's Liberation Army? Was Lin an archetype or was he unique? Finally, what generalizations emerge concerning Chinese elite behavior from study of Lin as a particular case?

DETERMINATIVE FACTORS IN LIN PIAO'S CAREER

ELEMENTS IN COMMON

Comparing Lin's career with those of other leading Chinese Communist figures, and with the broad sweep of Chinese Communist history, it is obvious that, throughout, Lin is about as representative as one can find of the type of person who went into the Communist movement in China and emerged as a leader. Reading Lin's biography is akin to studying Chinese Communist history as a whole. The only exceptions are the years 1938–41 and 1951–55, when Lin was out of circulation for health reasons. Even a cursory listing of the high points of Lin's life demonstrates the congruence between the stages of his own career and those of the Chinese Communist Party (CCP) and the People's Liberation Army (PLA) themselves.

Lin shared, for instance, a common socioeconomic background with many Chinese Communist leaders. He was of nonpeasant, petty-bourgeois origin and came from the Wuhan environs of Hupeh province.[5] Like many others, he was subjected to the modernizing influences of the West from an early age and witnessed at least some of the major

---

[5] "Chairman Mao's Successor—Deputy Supreme Commander Lin Piao," Chinese Red Guard pamphlet (n.p., n.d.) (translation in *CB*, No. 894 [October 27, 1969]), p. 1; Howard L. Boorman and Richard C. Howard (eds.), *Biographical Dictionary of Republican China*, 4 vols. (New York: Columbia University Press, 1967–70), II, 374; and other sources listed in the author's *A Politico-Military Biography of Lin Piao, Part I, 1907–1949* (Santa Monica: The Rand Corporation, R-526-PR, 1971), p. 3. For full documentation of Lin's biography, see this reference and the sources contained therein, as well as its sequel, *Part II, 1950–1970,* forthcoming. Only essential documentation will be presented here.

nationalistic and anti-Western events in Wuhan and Shanghai.[6] His educational level and the kinds of training he received were again typical of his times and of the later leaders of the Party. He attended the local Chinese primary school in his native Huang-an, then later enrolled at a Western-oriented secondary school in Wuhan, transferred to an institution run by American Catholic missionaries, and finally received brief advanced training at the Nationalist Whampoa Military Academy in Canton.[7] This background and these influences caused Lin to turn radical at an early age, so that by his teens he, like Mao and others, was busy organizing socialist study groups in his locality, attending anti-Western rallies and meetings in Shanghai, joining first a socialist student party, attempting to enter the Kuomintang (KMT), and finally (in 1927) enlisting in the CCP.[8] These aspects of Lin's early history seem entirely typical of radicalized Chinese youths of the 1920's.

Lin's career pattern from the point of his entrance into the Party fold reads, with few exceptions, like the broader history of the Party and its army. While it is true that Lin often *made* that history, especially during the more recent stages of their common life histories, he was also carried along by Party policy and the exigencies of Chinese domestic turmoil and international involvement. While this is not the place to trace the details of Lin's career, it is useful to list the high spots of their common development in order to illustrate the congruence between Lin's own life and Party-army events. Lin was present at the original military uprising in Nanchang in 1927, and can thus claim, in some sense, to be one of the founders of the PLA.[9] He

[6] *CB*, No. 894, pp. 3–4, 5, 7; Boorman and Howard (eds.), *Biographical Dictionary*, p. 342; Huang Chen-hsia (ed.), *Chung-kung chün-jen chih* (English title: *Mao's Generals*) (Hong Kong: Research Institute of Contemporary History, 1968), p. 208; Edgar Snow, *Red Star over China* (New York: Random House, 1938), p. 95.

[7] Loren Fessler, "The Long March of Lin Piao," *The New York Times Magazine*, September 10, 1967, p. 127; Liu Yüen-sun, "Lin Piao chih hsien-tsai yü kuo-ch'iu" (The Current and Past of Lin Piao), *Fei-ch'ing yen-chiu* (Studies on Chinese Communism) (Taipei), I, No. 1 (January 31, 1967), 61 (translation by Robert Liang and Thomas Robinson, The Rand Corporation, p. 3671, September, 1967); *Whampoa Yearbook* (Canton: Whampoa Military Academy, 1926), p. 58.

[8] Ka-che Yip, "The Anti-Christian Movement in China, 1922–1927" (M.A. thesis, Columbia University, 1967), pp. 54–55; Donald W. Klein and Anne B. Clark, *Biographic Dictionary of Chinese Communism, 1921–1965* (Cambridge, Mass.: Harvard University Press, 1971), p. 559; Edgar Snow, *Random Notes on Red China* (Cambridge, Mass.: Harvard University Press, 1957), p. 26; Kuo Hua-lun (ed.), *Chung-kung jen-ming lu* (Biographical Dictionary of Chinese Communists) (Taipei: Institute of International Relations, 1967), p. 232.

[9] Huang (ed.), *Chung-kung chün-jen chih*, p. 208. For a detailed account of Lin's career, see Robinson, *Biography of Lin Piao, Parts I and II.*

was with Chu Teh and others as they retreated south from the defeat at Nanchang, and may have even been among those who attempted to aid the Canton Commune. He accompanied Chu Teh back to Ching-kangshan (some say he even helped persuade Chu not to give in to the Nationalists) and was therefore present at the historic linkup with the forces already there under Mao Tse-tung.[10]

Lin's activity during the Kiangsi Soviet period of Chinese Communist history reads like a history of the period itself. He participated in all five of the Communist defenses against Chiang Kai-shek's suppression campaigns and stood out militarily in all of them. At times, in fact, his forces were instrumental in saving Mao from ultimate defeat.[11] It is clear that the relationship of mutual dependence between the two—Mao relying on Lin's military exploits, Lin looking to Mao for intellectual guidance and political advance—had its origin during the early Kiangsi Soviet period. From available documents, it seems apparent that Lin also took part in all of the important political conferences of this period.[12]

Lin was a Long Marcher, almost a *sine qua non* for participation in top leadership after 1949. He led, and hence was responsible for the protection of, the central column of Party leaders, and was instrumental in effectuating the first breakthrough by defeating pursuing Nationalist columns, in seizing and then defending Tsunyi while the important conference (in which he participated) by that name was held in early 1935, and in fording the four major rivers that the Communist forces crossed.[13] It was Lin's own troops (under Yang Ch'eng-wu) who carried out the epic seizure of the Lu-ting iron cable bridge, thus opening the way to an escape westward and to linking up with Chang Kuo-t'ao at Maoerhkai. Lin led the march through the Grasslands and defeated Nationalist forces blocking the route to Paoan, Shensi.[14]

During the Yenan period, 1935–45, Lin's name often came to the

---

[10] Wang En, "Lin Piao," in *The Phenomenon of Communist China's Great Purge* (Hong Kong: Daily News Press, 1966), p. 39; Agnes Smedley, *The Great Road* (New York: Monthly Review Press, 1956), Chaps. xvii–xix; John Rue, *Mao Tse-tung in Opposition, 1927–1935* (Stanford, Calif.: Stanford University Press, 1966), Chap. iii.

[11] Robinson, *Biography of Lin Piao, Part I,* pp. 13–23.

[12] William F. Dorrill, "The Chinese Communist Movement, 1927–1935" (Ph.D. dissertation, Harvard University, 1969, draft, Chap. i, Research Note III, pp. 7ff., 44ff.; John Gittings, *The Role of the Chinese Army* (London and New York: Oxford University Press, 1967), pp. 102–5; *CB,* No. 894 (October 27, 1969), p. 11; Shanti Swarup, *A Study of the Chinese Communist Movement* (Oxford: Clarendon Press, 1966), p. 247; *Hung-se chung-hua* (Red China), No. 2 (December 18, 1931), p. 4.

[13] Robinson, *Biography of Lin Piao, Part I,* pp. 23–25.

[14] *Ibid.,* pp. 26–28.

fore. He was principal of Kang-ta, the famous Communist military academy at Yenan, and his was the first Chinese Communist force to inflict a defeat on a sizable unit of Japanese invaders, at P'inghsingkuan in the summer of 1937.[15] The first break between Lin's career and Party history then occurred, as Lin was wounded in battle. He was sent to the Soviet Union to recover and did not return until early in 1942.[16] In that year Lin participated in the Chungking negotiations with the Nationalists and the Americans.[17] During the later war years, he helped train large numbers of political and military cadres, who were to form the core of the force that at war's end went to the northeast and became the basis of Lin's Civil War operations. Finally, Lin participated in the *cheng-feng* rectification movement in 1942, having returned to Yenan from Moscow at the very outset of the campaign. In this instance, as in many others before and after, he gave important support to Mao and to the principle of Chinese adaptation of Marxist and Soviet precepts.[18]

The Civil War period (1945–49) can hardly be separated from Lin's name. After having contained the Nationalist offenses in 1945–46, Lin gradually wrested control of the northeast from the KMT and expanded his forces. He then moved to seize North China, using widely different strategies in the key battles at Tientsin and Peking, and subsequently racing south in pursuit of the defeated Nationalist armies in 1949 and 1950.[19] The result was Communist conquest of all of China and international prominence for Lin as an architect of the winning strategy. Lin thus arrived in South China at the head of the newly constituted Fourth Field Army, over a million strong, with a long list of political titles reflecting supreme regional power. While by then it was impossible to regard Lin as only one among many Chinese Communist military figures, his Civil War experience was not atypical

[15] For a good analysis of P'inghsingkuan, see Sidney Liu, "The Battle of P'inghsingkuan: A Significant Event in Lin Piao's Career," *The China Mainland Review,* II, No. 3 (December, 1956), 161–73.

[16] Haldore Hanson, *Humane Endeavor* (New York: Farrar, 1939), pp. 101–6; Konstantin Siminov, "The Fighting China," *Soviet Literature,* October, 1950, p. 19; *CFJP,* February 14, 1942.

[17] U.S. Department of State, *United States Foreign Relations, 1943: China; United States Foreign Relations, 1944: China; United States Foreign Relations, 1945: Far East* (Washington, D.C.: U.S. Government Printing Office, 1957, 1965, 1967, respectively); U.S. Department of State, *United States Relations with China, with Special References to the Period 1944–1949* (Washington, D.C.: U.S. Department of State, Division of Publications, 1949); and U.S. Senate Committee on Judiciary, *The Amerasia Papers* (Washington, D.C.: U.S. Government Printing Office, 1970), index entries on Lin.

[18] Robinson, *Biography of Lin Piao, Part I,* pp. 42–43, and the references cited therein.

[19] *Ibid.,* pp. 47–57.

of that of the Communist forces as a whole. Like its influence on other leaders, that experience would more and more come to be regarded as formative of Lin's attitudes and actions taken throughout the 1950's and 1960's.

Lin's career at the outset of the 1950's appeared to be entirely typical of a number (small by now, to be sure) of important Chinese Communist officials. An army leader, Lin now became a regional Party official, holding supreme authority in the central-south area of China, a pattern repeated in the case of similar personnel in other regions.[20] For Lin, however, this phase was cut short, possibly by the Korean War. Although there is no direct Chinese Communist evidence, considerable indirect source material indicates that Lin was directly involved in the Korean fighting and, at the least, shared in the planning of the Chinese intervention and in the strategy of the first phases of fighting against United Nations forces in late 1950 and early 1951.[21] Thus, what was an elementary experience to the Chinese leadership as a whole was also instrumental in forming parts of Lin's particular outlook, especially as it concerned foreign policy, modern warfare, and policy toward the United States.

With the initial phases of the Korean War, there is a second break in the parallels between Lin's career and the history of the Party. Apparently wounded in battle (or, possibly, removed because of disagreement over strategy), Lin was forced to retire from active political life for at least two and perhaps as long as four years.[22] He took a major part in political life again only in 1958 when he was appointed to the Standing Committee of the Politburo, and from 1959, when he assumed the post of minister of national defense. Despite this break in his career, Lin was active enough to keep himself in the top leadership group and to participate in most of the major events and decisions of the mid-1950's. For instance, Lin was apparently heavily involved in the Kao Kang–Jao Shu-shih affair in 1954; [23] he continued to be involved in central-south administrative matters until the "Great Regional" apparatus was abolished; he may have gone to the Soviet

[20] Robinson, *Biography of Lin Piao, Part II*, pp. 1–5.

[21] See *ibid.*, pp. 6–14, for comments and evidence, pro and con, on Lin's involvement in the Korean conflict.

[22] The possibility of a strategy disagreement causing Lin's temporary retirement is discussed in more detail below, in "Lin's Relations with Peers, Superiors, and Subordinates."

[23] Huang (ed.), *Chung-kung chün-jen chih*, p. 216; Huan Ming, "T'ou-mu Lin Piao ch'u-che sheng-chen" (The Twists and Turns and Ups and Downs of Headman Lin Piao), *Hsin-wen t'ien-ti* (News Scope) (Hong Kong), No. 586 (May 9, 1959), pp. 14–15.

Union; he attended the first National People's Congress in 1954, the 1955 Party Conference, and its Eighth Congress in 1956 (where he was re-elected to the Politburo and ranked ninth in number of votes cast), and the second session of the congress in 1958.[24] Thus, with health restored by 1958 and election to Standing Committee status, Lin managed to hold his own politically and to share enough in Party life to substantiate our claim of his representative status.

From late 1959, Lin again occupied a position in Chinese Communist history akin to that which he held during the Long March and the Civil War. Although, in contrast to these earlier eras, his public appearances seemed to indicate only sporadic involvement, his participation in critical decisions and behind-the-scenes administration of important campaigns within both Party and army demonstrated the central nature of his role.[25] It is not possible, for instance, to write the history of reforms in the PLA during the early 1960's, the "Learn from the PLA" campaign among the populace as a whole, or, for that matter, the Socialist Education Movement itself, without noting Lin's prominent role. In foreign policy, he emerged from relative obscurity in 1965 with his essay on revolutionary war.[26]

The Cultural Revolution was, of course, a period in which Lin departed from his previous role as one of the top leaders of the Party. At the Eleventh Plenum of the Central Committee in August, 1966, Lin replaced Liu Shao-ch'i as Mao's heir apparent. This status was later confirmed in official declarations and in the new Party Constitution passed at the Ninth Party Congress in April, 1969.[27] Nonetheless, from the point of view of common experience, the Cultural Revolution continued to be a period in which elements of continuity between Lin's own life and the histories of the Party and the army themselves could be seen. From a myriad of official documents and Red Guard posters it is clear that Lin shared in all major decisions regarding phasing of the Cultural Revolution.[28] Moreover, at Mao's behest, he directed the army's intervention in the domestic power struggle, beginning in January, 1967. Despite his absence from sight for lengthy periods, he evidently supervised many of the details of army involvement in poli-

---

[24] *TKP* (Hong Kong), August 19, 1954. NCNA, September 16, 27, 28, and 30, 1954; April 4, September 23, 1955; April 22 and 25, 1957; May 4 and 25, 1958. Gittings, *The Role of the Chinese Army*, p. 284, n. 10.

[25] Robinson, *Biography of Lin Piao, Part II*, pp. 27–36.

[26] *Ibid.*, pp. 36–42. Lin's People's War dictum was published first in *JMJP*, September 1, 1965.

[27] See *Peking Review*, XII, No. 18 (April 30, 1969), 36–39.

[28] Robinson, *Biography of Lin Piao, Part II,* pp. 42–55.

tics and the slow reconstruction of the Party at the central and regional levels after September of that year. He was present, perhaps directing troops, against the rebels at Wuhan in the summer of 1967 and took part in sessions purging many of his erstwhile comrades in the army and the Central Committee. Finally, he demonstrated his command over the details of Chinese policy (as well as his ability at least to read a lengthy speech) by delivering the major political report to the Ninth Party Congress in April, 1969.[29]

For much of its history, Chinese Communist politics has been group politics in the sense that, despite a growing domination by Mao Tsetung, decisions were usually made by a small group whose composition for over thirty years (until mid-1966) was amazingly stable. Lin Piao was part of that group for almost all of that period. It is not surprising, therefore, that his personal history parallels to a startling degree the history of the Party itself. While much of his time was spent in the field commanding troops or administering military and political bureaucracies, his political life was lived in the group of twenty or thirty top leaders and the institutions they dominated. Therefore, Lin was in many ways representative of the upper level of the Chinese Communist elite, as our outline of his activities demonstrates.

ELEMENTS UNIQUE TO LIN

Inspection in detail of a given leader's biography reveals, however, elements unique to his own personality and career pattern, others that are the manifestations of historically determinative elements, and still others the product of accident and coincidence. Among factors unique to Lin, his political radicalism, in contrast to that of many of his Communist peers, was at least partly explained by the influence of radical ideas in his immediate, and even in his extended, family. Some of Lin's brothers, cousins, and uncles were involved in the Communist movement almost from the beginning, and three of them rose to become important Party functionaries.[30] Lin's biography demonstrates that the

---

[29] For a detailed analysis of the Wuhan Incident, see the author's "The Wuhan Incident: Local Strife and Provincial Rebellion during the Cultural Revolution," *CQ*, No. 47 (July–September, 1971), pp. 413–38. See below, "Lin's Relations with Peers, Superiors, and Subordinates," for details on Lin's purge of Lo Jui-ch'ing, Hsiao Hua, and Yang Ch'eng-wu. For his report to the Ninth Party Congress, see *Peking Review*, XII, No. 18 (April 30, 1969), 18–35.

[30] These include Lin Yü-nan, Lin Yü-ying, Lin Ch'ing-fu, Lin Yü-chü, and Lin Hsiang-hung. Klein and Clark, *Biographic Dictionary,* has good biographies on Lin Yü-nan and Lin Yü-ying, and Boorman and Howard (eds.), *Biographical Dictionary,* Vol. II, discusses Lin Yü-nan.

direction of ideological influence was from relatives to Lin rather than the reverse. To some extent this was because Lin was younger than they, but it also may have resulted from personality differences. Lin was reticent and retiring; particularly in regard to family relationships, he was a receiver of influence, not the originator.

Another factor peculiar to Lin was his very early estrangement from his father and probable overdependence on his mother. Lin claimed not to have seen his father from age ten.[31] Whether or not this was the result of an early psychological break or whether Lin Ming-ch'ing merely abandoned his family is not known. In either case, Lin Piao was probably psychologically searching even as a boy for a substitute father figure. It is tempting to argue that he fixed himself upon Mao after failing to achieve such a relationship with Yeh T'ing (his first commander) and then Chu Teh (the Communists' first overall military leader). When combined with Lin's loss of economic, and concomitant social, status at an early age because of his father's inability to keep the family factory going, we have the basis for a psychological assessment that differs, at least in some details, from the familial factors that stood back of the psychological development of Mao, Chou En-lai, or Chu Teh (three Chinese Communist leaders about whom we know some relevant facts). In Lin's case, this can be supplemented by the obvious radicalizing influence of his cousin, Lin Yü-nan, who probably also served as a surrogate father figure. When he was unavailable to Lin after 1925, and when Yeh T'ing and Chu Teh did not fulfill Lin's needs, Lin turned to Mao.

A third unique element in Lin's case is his ability to stand out early in a given phase of operations. Thus, he quickly came to Yeh T'ing's attention during the Northern Expedition because of his exploits at Laiyuan, Hunan.[32] This led to his appointment as commander of the force guarding the chief of staff group at the Nanchang Uprising. Later, at Chingkangshan, Lin's military talents quickly brought him to the fore when on a number of occasions he defeated Nationalist forces that threatened to overcome Mao's small band. In this manner he came to Mao's attention at the outset of the Communist hegira. Again, in the Kiangsi Soviet period, Lin's political rise was (perhaps not surprisingly) related directly to his military importance. By the end of the period, Lin was the only major commander under Chu Teh not to

---

31 Snow, *Red Star over China*, p. 9.

32 *CB*, No. 894 (October 27, 1969), p. 8; Huang- (ed.), *Chung-kung chün-jen chih*, p. 208; Wang, "Lin Piao," p. 39.

have suffered at least one decisive defeat. In like manner, Lin was the only Chinese Communist military figure to best the Japanese in battle at the outset of the war. Indeed, so great was Lin's talent for winning, and winning first, that we have to wait until his 1947 debacle at Szup'ing before we learn of a military defeat.[33] Thus, despite Lin's well-known caution, he was able to pull off a successful military venture quickly and before other military leaders were able to do so.

Several other features separate Lin from the group. While he was not alone in having spent time in the Soviet Union, his stint was during the Second World War. The periodization of Lin's Soviet years is thus different from that of the "returned students," who, having gone to Russia in the late twenties and early thirties, were too much taken with what they saw and, overenthusiastic, came back wishing to impose Soviet institutions and methods on the CCP with little regard for local peculiarities. Lin could only have a healthy appreciation for the latter. Moreover, by the time he got to the Soviet Union, the divorce under Stalin between Soviet ideological pretensions and practical realities had proceeded far enough, and Soviet military defeats at the hands of the Germans were severe enough, to have convinced him of the undesirability of emulating that country too closely, either politically or militarily. Thus, when he returned to Yenan, Lin's report could only have been welcome to Mao, both in terms of the latter's emphasis during the *cheng-feng* movement and with regard to his enhanced confidence in Lin's judgments. Thus, Lin's fate was quite different from that of earlier Chinese Communist visitors to Russia.

It should also be noted that Lin's later illness in the 1950's conveniently kept him out of circulation during times of political difficulty and discord. His merely nominal position in the central-south military and administrative apparatus during the early 1950's was a possible asset during the Party debates on "independent kingdoms," for Lin (and Mao himself, who allegedly defended Lin from Liu Shao-ch'i's attack)[34] could well have argued that he was physically incapable of the kinds of activities for which Kao Kang and Jao Shu-shih were to be purged. Again, Lin was absent due to illness (he may even have been recuperating in the Soviet Union) during the critical period of the Hundred Flowers campaign in 1957, the antirightist reaction, the *hsia-fang* movement, and the debates leading to the Great Leap

[33] Robinson, *Biography of Lin Piao, Part I*, pp. 52–54, discusses the defeat, the reasons thereof, and Lin's own "lessons learned" self-criticism.

[34] Huan Ming, "T'ou-mu Lin Piao ch'u-che sheng-chen," pp. 14–15; and Huang (ed.), *Chung-kung chün-jen chih*, p. 216.

Forward.[35] Since much of the factionalism that followed the failure of the Great Leap stemmed from a given leader's role and declaratory position during this period, Lin's absence permitted him not to have to choose sides too early and to observe which side had the better political chance of survival. Some of his colleagues did not have this "opportunity," and many of them paid for it with the loss of their positions.

Finally, note should be made of Lin's unique pedagogical bent. From almost the very beginning of his career, Lin betrayed a pronounced inclination toward teaching and learning. He was once a substitute schoolteacher. More important, his insistence on acquiring a wide array of facts about a given situation before committing himself, his principalship at Kang-ta, and the constant themes of education, training, and self-preparation all indicated a strain not reproduced among many of his Party and military associates.[36] Lin's propensity to take the time to study the intimate details of a problem, plus his insistence on working out a plan and then practicing its execution may, in fact, have been one secret of his success. Without this quality, it is doubtful that he would have risen so steadily in the ranks or have rebounded so effectively when cast down.

HISTORICALLY DETERMINATIVE ELEMENTS

Mention should be made of the "tide of history" as one important variable in setting Lin's career. This historical milieu in which he, as well as other Chinese Communist leaders, found himself often aided, and sometimes held back, his progress. For instance, the proximity of his family's village to Wuhan, a national center for the spread of Westernization; the role of warlord taxes in closing down his father's factory; the existence in Wuhan of an American missionary school; and Lin's presence in Shanghai at the time of the May Thirtieth Movement all propelled him in the direction of extreme Chinese nationalism, anticlericalism, and anti-Westernism. The phenomenon of militarism and warlordism in the 1920's pushed Lin (who might otherwise have remained a schoolteacher) toward a military career, while it was the short-lived KMT-Communist alliance in the mid-1920's that made it possible for him to attend Whampoa and, from there, to participate in the Northern Expedition. It was the Japanese invasion of China in

[35] Huang (ed.), *Chung-kung chün-jen chih*, pp. 216–17; "Lin Piao: A Model for Application of Mao's Thought," *Tsu kuo* (China Monthly), No. 4 (July, 1964), p. 35.
[36] These themes are discussed in detail in Robinson, *Biography of Lin Piao, Part I*, pp. 63–70, and *Part II*, pp. 75–79.

1937 that drew Lin from his Kang-ta principalship and catapulted him to national fame at P'inghsingkuan, and the unavailability in Yenan of other equally experienced commanders in 1945 (among other factors) caused Mao to appoint Lin to head the forces leaving for Manchuria. Finally, the Korean War, over which Lin obviously had no influence, caused him to be sent out of the central-south region of China, thus (together with his war wounds) probably saving him from sharing the fate of Kao Kang and Jao Shu-shih. One must also include the accidents and coincidents of history. As two examples in Lin's case, he received a regimental command early because his superior was killed in a duel, while his first meeting of Mao was at the right time and at the right place—Chingkangshan in early 1928.

LIN PIAO IN THE CONTEXT OF AGGREGATE ELITE STUDIES

Three types of elements—common, unique, and historical—in Lin's background thus link him to and separate him from his peers. They provide one basis for making the transition from individual biography to the exposition of aggregate elite behavior. Another basis is to compare the details of Lin's career with the aggregate data on Chinese elites provided by other authors in this volume and by previous writers. In our own analysis, it has seemed that, despite his status until September, 1971, as Mao's designated successor, Lin Piao in many ways exemplified the kind of leader thrown up by the Communist movement in China and by the exigencies of twentieth-century Chinese history. By now turning to compare Lin with data on elites (as opposed to history) provided by others, the proposition of commonality—and hence Lin's representativeness—can be tested in a different, equally relevant manner.

Interestingly, only Derek Waller's data on the Central Executive Committee (CEC) during the mid-Kiangsi Soviet period show Lin to be somewhat atypical. The type and level of his education, for instance, were not entirely representative of his peers. In 1934, Lin, unlike most others on the CEC, had no foreign travel experience. And most of his peers, in contrast to Lin, did not come from a professional military background before joining the Party. In other cases, however, Lin was nearly typical or archetypical. He was from the central interior provinces, came from "petty bourgeois" background, had joined the Party before 1927, and in 1934 worked in the military. In fact, Lin well fits Waller's description of the "average" CEC member: male, Han Chinese, born in interior China, of nonpeasant background, relatively well-educated, having had no real career outside of the Communist movement, and following a military career after having joined the Party.[37]

Waller compares the Kiangsi elite with the membership of the Eighth Central Committee, elected in 1956. His theme is the widespread continuity not only of actual membership, but of the qualities and characteristics first noted with regard to the Kiangsi leadership. Inspecting Waller's list of identifying features, one is struck once again with Lin's representativeness. He was typical in regional origin, age (although still a bit young), date of entry into the Party, sex, nationality and, to some extent, in foreign travel. Only in regard to education, career channel, and post-1949 career pattern does Lin seem to be atypical, and even then the degree of his departure from Waller's norm is lessened by his holding Party, state, and army jobs and by his possible attendance at Soviet military schools during World War II.[38]

Heath Chamberlain's data for municipal elites in Canton during the early 1950's also provide a further test of Lin's typicality, for he was then in overall charge of the central-south region of which Canton was a part. Once again, Lin's sociological attributes mark him as near the median among the Communist rulers in Canton. He was a "liberator" and an "outside Red," was born in the region, grew up in one of the inland provinces of Central China, had foreign travel experience, took the "wilderness" route to power, was in the military as his pre-1949 task area, was a "generalist" leader, and in 1950 was an "elder" (that is, by then he was over forty years old). Only his urban-ruralite origin and more than average amount of education were departures from this norm.[39] As if to confirm this evaluation as of the early 1950's, Robert North's data once again place Lin squarely in the center of the distribution of elite characteristics. In his terms, Lin is typical in regard to his father's education, his own education, age, career pattern, date of Party entry, rural-urban origin, and provincial birthplace.[40]

Robert Scalapino's data on the Standing Committee of the Ninth Central Committee are difficult to use in attempting to discern Lin's degree of typicality, primarily because the number of committee mem-

[37] Waller, "The Evolution of the Chinese Communist Political Elite, 1931–56," this volume, pp. 41–55.

[38] Ibid., pp. 55–64.

[39] Chamberlain, "Transition and Consolidation in Urban China: A Study of Leaders and Organizations in Three Cities, 1949–53," this volume, pp. 255–71.

[40] Robert C. North, Kuomintang and Chinese Communist Elites (Stanford, Calif.: Stanford University Press for the Hoover Institution, 1952).

bers (five) is small and most of the men are members, to some extent, because they head major national institutions. Nonetheless, it is possible to state Lin's set of sociopolitical characteristics in Scalapino's terminology and to draw conclusions in several instances. For instance, Lin seems to exemplify the group in education ("fairly good"), foreign experience (USSR), generation of initial participation in the modern Chinese revolution (the third), generation of joining the Party (the third), date of first election to the Central Committee (the seventh, in 1945), date of first election to the Politburo (1955), and event participation to 1942. On the other hand, Lin does not seem to be typical in family/personal status, visibility, and "cosmopolitanism." On several of Scalapino's measures, no evaluation of typicality is possible; nonetheless, it is useful to set forth Lin's characteristics in these cases. His "career chart" and "career graph" can be constructed in this way:

Period	1	2	3	4	5	6	7	8
Location	SE/CS	CS	LM	NW	Canton/ Peking	Pek.	Pek.	Pek.
Urban/rural	R	R	R	R	U	U	U	U
Role	M/P	M/P	M/P	M/P/A	M/P/A	M/P/A	M/P/A	M/P/A
Party level	C	C	C	R/C	R/C	C	C	C

Period 1   2   3   4   5   6   7   8

In both these instances, it should be noted that, with certain specific exceptions, his career is very similar to that of Mao Tse-tung. His career chart shows differences only in period 5 (the early 1950's) when Lin was a combined regional administrator and central decision-maker, and in the relative priority of his military, political, and administrative roles. His career graph, like Mao's, is of the "wave" pattern, but with different periods of relative decline (in the late 1930's and again in the early 1950's). Each time he, like Mao, managed to recoup his losses and move still higher in the political hierarchy. In terms of "career pattern," Lin should be listed as "orthodox senior," while his "role pattern" is "specialist-generalist." [41]

Finally, William Whitson's data on military career patterns provide

[41] Scalapino, "The Transition in Chinese Party Leadership: A Comparison of the Eighth and Ninth Central Committees," this volume.

references for the thesis of Lin's typicality. In all four of his measures Lin again turns out to be representative. In military generation, Lin appears to be near the median for the first generation of military leaders (those who joined the Communist movement prior to May, 1928). He was born in Central China, had extensive war experience, adopted as values an emphasis upon guerrilla warfare and mass mobilization, and had reached the national level of power at least by 1966. His lack of foreign education prior to 1928, however, set him apart from his first military generation peers. In regard to field army origin, Lin is, of course, archetypical of the Fourth Field Army. In fact, in his case his degree of typicality is tautological, for one *defines* the Fourth Field Army lineage by reference to Lin's own career. The same can be said for his military region: Lin's career as a regional military administrator was spent in the northeast and in the central-south, which define, respectively, the Shenyang and Canton military regions. As to Lin's military elite level, he has been a member of the central elite (that is, Central Committee status) from at least the Seventh Party Congress in 1945, but probably much earlier. Like most other top military officers, he built his career in the field before 1949 and at the regional level in the 1950's. Finally, Lin's career channel is one indicator of why he occupied a position of authority to the very end of his career. The dominant path to power in the PLA has been the ground forces, not the other services—the militia, the public security apparatus, the General Political Department, or the General Rear Services Department. Lin spent his life in the ground forces.[42]

These comparisons, along with the previously supplied biographic data, help to explain how Lin attained his position of leadership. He seems to be representative so far as his participation in Chinese Communist history, his career pattern, and his sociological characteristics go. In fact, Lin seems too typical, almost as if he were an artificial composite creation. But if evidence is needed to support the proposition that a given leader emerges to supreme power *because* of his representativeness (in addition to traits that set him aside from, or above, his comrades), Lin Piao is an excellent case.

However, this can only be a partial explanation of why Lin was, to late 1971, Mao's heir apparent. Other factors must be used to explain why he managed first to get into the running for the Maoist succession and then to outdistance other competitors. While much of the answer

---

[42] Whitson, "Organizational Perspectives and Decision-making in the Chinese Communist High Command," this volume, pp. 383–405.

concerns recent Party history, especially that since the aftermath of the Great Leap Forward and the background to the Cultural Revolution, much of the rest had to do with Lin's own personal traits. These include his political style, his philosophy, and his relations with others, especially Mao. Understanding these aspects occupies the rest of this chapter. Our purpose, aside from assessing the importance of these three factors in Lin's own case, is to indicate the degree of emphasis that must be placed upon them in any comprehensive political elite study.

LIN PIAO'S POLITICAL STYLE

In contrast to Mao, we know comparatively little of Lin Piao's style of political leadership or even of his personality. Nonetheless, enough has been written about Lin, enough of his writings are available, and enough of his practical moves—both military and political—are known that it is possible to build up a picture of Lin complete enough for comparative purposes.[43]

Lin's political style can be inferred from his personality, from what we know of his work style, his relations with Mao, his ideological and national attitudes, and (most importantly) his writings and military campaigns. Personally, Lin was universally described as quiet, reserved, nontalkative, calm, unemotional, and modest. At the same time, he was said to be clever, calculating, deliberate, and astute. He drove himself very hard, sometimes losing much sleep in the process, was willing to learn both indirectly through books and directly through field experience and from his own and others' mistakes. He liked to bury himself in the details of his work and to pursue a matter, once begun, to its conclusion. At the same time, he was not a "public" figure in

---

[43] The following secondary sources have proven valuable: Liu, "Lin Piao chih hsientsai yü kuo-ch'iu," pp. 61–77; "China's Military Chief, Lin Piao," *The New York Times,* August 13, 1966; Fessler, "The Long March of Lin Piao," pp. 64ff.; Edgar Snow, "The Man Alongside Mao: Deputy Lin Piao's Thoughts and Career," *The New Republic,* December 3, 1966, pp. 15–18; Chu Wen-lin, "Lin Piao: Mao Tse-tung's Close Comrade-in-Arms," *Issues and Studies* (Taipei), III, No. 4 (January, 1967), 1–11, and III, No. 5 (February, 1967), 28–35; Li Tien-min, "The Rise of Lin Piao in the Chinese Communist Hierarchy," *Issues and Studies,* III, No. 1 (October, 1966), 8–19; Chingkang-shan Corps, Peking Industrial University, "Life of Lin Piao" (translation in *JPRS,* No. 41,801 [July 12, 1967] [*Translations on Communist China: Political and Sociological,* No. 406], pp. 1–24, and in *JPRS,* No. 42,503 [September 7, 1967] [*Communist China Digest,* No. 189], pp. 62–73); Ralph L. Powell, "The Increasing Power of Lin Piao and the Party Soldiers, 1959–1966," *CQ,* No. 34 (April–June, 1968), pp. 38–65; Colonel Robert B. Rigg, "Lin Piao: Portrait of a Militant," *Army,* XIX, No. 5 (May, 1969), 26–32; Robert B. Rigg, *Red China's Fighting Hordes* (Harrisburg, Pa.: The Military Service Publishing Co., 1951), pp. 201–7; and "Chairman Mao's Successor: Deputy Supreme Commander Lin Piao," pp. 1–24.

the sense of enjoying the public admiration of those around him. He preferred to work behind the scenes, for the most part, issuing instructions by telephone and handwritten order and calling officials to his residence instead of attending meetings.

While a believing Communist, Lin was not an independent political thinker, preferring to take his ideological orientation from Mao and concentrating upon an application of general theories to practical problems. Lin was accused of being a sycophant of Mao. In part this is true. But he was much more than a sycophant, and he even disagreed with Mao at least on one occasion, in 1936 after the Long March. Furthermore, his pre-1950 career reveals that he was very much his own man in the formulation and execution of military strategy and tactics. He probably did genuinely share with Mao a number of fundamental attitudes: aside from the standard Marxist-Leninist approach to basic questions, both exhibited a virulent anti-Americanism and anti-Sovietism, intense Chinese nationalism, a penchant for military solutions to political problems, and a propensity to overcome obstacles by main force—frontal attack using all the force at his disposal—if possible and by indirect action, waiting, or guerrillalike tactics if necessary. Lin was thought to be overly attracted to war and violence as solutions to problems. This penchant can certainly be inferred from his pre-1949 writings, his subsequent statement, and his career, almost all of which has been military. But one would expect little else, at least verbally, of a man with such a background.

Further insight into Lin's political style lies in analysis of his military writings in the pre-1949 period and in his actual military conduct.[44] Several principles of action emerge from such an analysis. First, Lin insisted on a long period of preparation and planning before any venture was attempted. He would rather play for time, paying for it by a series of small losses, than rush into an action before he was entirely ready. Training and indoctrination were critical elements in such preparation. Second, Lin did not usually strike at an opponent all along a given front; rather, he looked for the weakest point in the enemy's armor, disguised his moves by feints elsewhere, and then in a surprise attack put as much force and effort as possible into overwhelming the

---

[44] If we assume that Lin Piao used the same principles in politics that he found useful and necessary in military strategy and tactics, we then have an outline of some of the central elements of his political style. Although such an assumption has obvious shortcomings, it is nonetheless true that the formative period of Lin's political life was during the pre-1949 Civil War era. While it is true that he consciously subordinated himself to Mao, it was in the military sphere that he was most nearly independent.

enemy at this one spot. Surprise and concentration of effort were thus two central elements in his strategy.

Third, once his objective had been attained, Lin was quick to retreat, when necessary, to already prepared positions. Lin has been described as an artist at tactical disengagement, and he was wise enough to know that tactical success in a given area cannot necessarily be maintained there and that one tactical success was not necessarily followed by another. Thus, Lin's strategy can be described as aggressive, imaginative, and dramatic, but with much thought and preparation taken ahead of time and alternate courses of action thought out in case of failure. Lin was given to a generally characteristic pattern of action: long periods of deceptive inactivity were followed by lightning moves in specific directions using all the force at his disposal, which were then followed either by consolidation or quick retreat and, finally, by a further period of waiting and planning.

It is useful to compare the political styles of Chou En-lai and Lin Piao, who share a number of qualities. Both are outwardly calm and unemotional. Both were regarded as astute and clever men. Moreover, Chou's well-known political style provides, on balance, a healthy contrast to Lin's.[45] Both possessed great stores of energy and drive. Neither was an original political thinker, preferring to subordinate themselves rigidly to Mao. Each held the private goal of protecting the integrity and autonomy of their respective institutions and of their colleagues. Each was capable of moving quickly with the political current.

There are, nonetheless, some subtle differences in style and attitude. While each was adept at working behind the scenes and at political infighting, Chou is just as much at home working in the limelight; Lin was not. While both stressed the desirability of indirect means of attaining an objective, Lin, like Mao, attempted to surmount a goal directly when possible. Chou almost always takes a circuitous route. While both moved quickly with the political tide, Chou at times tries to swim against it if he thinks he can. Lin never did. Both men planned their avenues of retreat, but Lin was quick to move back, while Chou always fights a series of delaying actions. Finally, the brand of nationalism each evidenced was somewhat different: Lin's was almost wholly antiforeign to the point where he might have been termed a xenophobe;

[45] For Chou's political style, see the author's "Chou En-lai: A Statement of His Political 'Style,' with Comparisons with Mao Tse-tung and Lin Piao," *Asian Survey,* X, No. 12 (December, 1970), 1101–16.

Chou's nationalism is not necessarily antiforeign, stressing instead positive Chinese virtues.

In addition, there are areas where their styles differ dramatically. Chou is verbal; Lin was not. Chou revels in public appearances; Lin was at his worst under such circumstances. Chou prefers bureaucratic solutions to political problems; Lin may well have adopted such solutions (because politics is not, after all, war, and because he, too, had considerable bureaucratic experience), but he was not comfortable with them. He, like Mao, would rather have overcome problems by main force. There is a difference in the timing of their political involvement. Lin followed his military tendency to attack suddenly only after preparation, thereby seeming to be only sporadically involved. Hence, he disappeared from the scene for long periods and then suddenly exploded into view again. Chou, on the other hand, is more or less constantly involved. There is also an obvious difference in attitudes toward planning in politics. Lin planned to the extreme; Chou seems to adopt a posture of muddling through. Furthermore, Lin liked to simplify problems, whereas Chou tries to make them more complex. Finally, Lin and Chou differ fundamentally in their attitudes toward others. Lin appeared to treat others as enemies, at least initially. Chou does not seem to make this initial assumption. Thus, to Lin, politics was zero-sum; to Chou it is not.

But while these differences are fundamental, it does not follow that the political styles of these two men are diametrically opposed. They not only held in common a wide range of similar goals and policy means; they also complemented each other in important respects. Each needed, understood, trusted, and used the other. Hence, while their styles are different, they were still complementary, and it is that fact (aside from the Maoist framework) that kept them together until Lin's demise.

Lin Piao's Philosophy and Policies: Analysis of Writings, Speeches, and Interviews, 1932–70

Although Lin Piao spent most of his life in nonliterary pursuits and he was not overly verbal in public, available Chinese sources reveal that his written output was substantial.[46] At this writing, no less than

---

[46] Many of the Chinese publications in which Lin's writings appeared are in the Hoover Institution, Stanford University. In one or two cases, the Library of Congress has the original. Finally, some texts are available only in translation, usually in the U.S. Hong Kong Consulate-General series.

seventy-nine articles, speeches, and interviews are known to exist. Few have been available in English before, nor has the corpus ever been brought together; as a unit they provide valuable insight into Lin's philosophy and policies. For our purposes, a comparison between Lin's views on selected topics in the pre-1950 period of the Party's struggle for power and the twenty-year period of domestic rule after 1950 will assist in answering the question, what are the major continuities and changes in Chinese Communist elite outlook before and after coming to power? In Lin's case, we wish to know whether 1950 was as much an attitudinal watershed for him as it was an administrative turning point for the Party as a whole. Or did his philosophy, once formed, not change substantially over the decades? Or, finally, did his views evolve more or less continuously, being dependent either upon some inner psychological drives or, externally, on the exigencies of Party policy? Lin's views on three topics—ideology, politics, and education —provide a sufficient data base for addressing these questions.[47]

IDEOLOGY TO 1949

One basic question concerns the extent to which Lin reasoned in Marxist-Leninist categories. Although converted to socialism and then communism at an early age, Lin in his pre-1950 writings, with few exceptions, did not even refer to Marxism-Leninism, much less did he employ Marxist vocabulary in his writings.[48] This is not to say, of course, that before 1950 Lin was a Communist in name only. He no doubt believed in Marxism-Leninism to the extent that he was familiar with it. But it did not appear to have penetrated to the center of his being.[49]

[47] All of Lin's writings referred to in the following notes are found in the author's *Biography of Lin Piao.* Those dated 1949 and earlier are contained in *Part I* (The Rand Corporation, R-526-PR) ; those after 1949 are in *Part II* (manuscript). The date of each document is included in its first citation. A fuller analysis of all of Lin's writings and complete documentation for those cited below are contained in the author's forthcoming book, *Lin Piao:A Political Biography.*

[48] The two exceptions are Lin Piao, "Proclamation: Summary of the Exposure of the Counterrevolutionary Conspiracy of Huang Chung-yo/Hsiao Shi-chun and Others, Based on a Report by Representative of the Worker-Peasant Red Army Political Security Branch Bureau" (1933) ; and "On the Political and Military Situation in the Northeast" (1946).

[49] Lin's remarks on the limits of ideological understanding and on the need for unanimity in practical situations may give clues about the extent of his dependence on orthodox Marxism. In his "Report Made at a Meeting of High-Level Cadres from the Northeast Bureau of the Chinese Communist Party Central Committee" (July, 1948), he noted that "in taking action. . . we cannot afford to wait until there is complete ideological unanimity." Instead, in most practical situations, discipline, coercion, and unity through

What does come through clearly is that from the beginning Lin was a nearly xenophobic nationalist. Virtually all of the documents up to 1950 reflect this orientation. It is true that, during the Yenan period, the anti-Japanese nationalism felt by many Chinese was used by the CCP to gain adherents in guerrilla base areas and that, as a result, many of Lin's writings linked such sentiments with the details of how to fight the invader. But this theme also pervaded Lin's writing before and after that time. Before 1935 he denounced imperialism in general for denying China its national rights, and after 1945 it was Chiang Kai-shek who was "attacking the people." [50] But aside from this strident nationalism and his rather underdeveloped Marxism, Lin exhibited almost no concern for ideological categories. He seemed, rather, to have been a technician more concerned with *how* to instill right thinking and acting in people than with *what* they should be thinking.[51] This is not too surprising in a military man, even a Communist general. It is more difficult to explain of a man who spent much of his first four decades as an educator, and who was once the principal of Kang-ta, the central Communist military academy.

An important subsidiary topic is Lin's attitudes toward his mentor, Mao Tse-tung. From his biography, one would expect a fair number of favorable references to Mao. Lin's written pronouncements are indeed revealing, if largely negative, for his output to 1949 contains only a few references to Mao, the first not until 1944.[52] While this may not differ from the Party norm for the time, it is surprising that one commonly regarded as Mao's closest follower referred so little to the Party chairman. In his Civil War writings, though references increase, they are still few in number and mostly factual.[53] The July, 1949, speech, in fact, was the first instance of Lin's actually exhorting others to follow Mao's thought, and even that speech shows evidence of hav-

application of rules must substitute. This would make Lin more of a Leninist (a Marxist totalitarian) than a Marxist.

Lin's one solid Marxist concept, acquired early, seems to have been the centrality of the class basis of social organizations. See Lin, "Political and Military Situation in the Northeast," and "On the Struggle with Chiang Kai-shek" (ca. late 1946).

[50] Lin, "Proclamation"; "Political and Military Situation in the Northeast."

[51] "We should be pragmatists, not abstract theoreticians." Lin Piao, "Lin Piao's Talk at the Opening Ceremony of the First Artillery School in Yenan, August 1, 1945."

[52] Lin Piao, "How to Conduct Military Training This Year" (November 24, 1944).

[53] Lin, "Political and Military Situation in the Northeast"; "Strategic Evaluation before the Battle of Chinchow" (September, 1948); "Report Made at a Meeting of High-Level Cadres from the Northeast Bureau of the Chinese Communist Party Central Committee" (July, 1948); "General Lin Piao's Speech at a Meeting Welcoming Democratic Personages in Peiping on February 26, 1949"; "Interview with Lin Piao" (1949).

ing been rewritten for the contemporary reader.[54] Thus, in his writings at least, Lin was no more than formally correct in his attitude toward Mao.

IDEOLOGY SINCE 1950

After nearly a half-century as a member of the CCP, Lin Piao ought to have absorbed by the end of his career enough of the standard Marxist-Leninist categories of thought to have them permeate an increasing portion of his speeches and writings. While Lin was later than most of his peers in converting his inner thought processes, by 1970 it was possible to term him a committed Communist in the ideological as well as the operational sense. In particular, most of his works from the Cultural Revolution period forward were written strictly within the framework of the Chinese interpretation of Marxism.[55]

Of the concepts comprising the Marxian *Weltanschauung,* three—classes, contradictions, and class struggle—appeared to be of central importance to Lin. Each follows from the former. Classes arise on the basis of different economic conditions and explain all the variegated relationships among the elements of the noneconomic superstructure. Not to emphasize a class viewpoint in analyzing social relations was, to Lin, to fall into bourgeois "objectivism," which attempts to conceal the real class nature of society.[56] Classes give rise to contradictions; in fact, contradictions among socioeconomic classes are merely a reflection of natural contradictions in the universe itself: "From a grain of sand to the sun itself, whether macrocosm or microcosm, contradictions exist." [57] The human mind reflects this phenomenon and therefore is divided, like society, against itself.[58] The result is struggle, within the individual and within the class components of society. "Struggle is life—if you don't struggle against them [the opposite class], they will struggle against you; if you don't kill them, they will

[54] Lin Piao, "Comrade Lin Piao Reports on the Policy for Future Work of the Central China Bureau at the 'July 1' Commemoration" (1949). Since the first three documents cited in note 53 were published only recently, they could have been rewritten.

[55] Lin Piao, "Order of the Day" (1959); "Speech at Closing Session of National People's Militia Representative Conference" (April 27, 1960); "Lin Piao's Five-Point Directive for the Work of the People's Liberation Army in 1966"; "Lin Piao's Address at the Enlarged Meeting of the CCP Central Politburo" (May 18, 1966); "Speech at Peking's Mass Rally Celebrating the Great Proletarian Cultural Revolution" (August 18, 1966).

[56] Lin Piao, "Excerpts of a Speech at a Meeting of Army Level Cadres" (March 20, 1967).

[57] Lin, "Address at the Enlarged Meeting of the CCP Central Politburo."

[58] *Ibid.*

kill you." [59] Lin thus moved from struggle as a fact to struggle as a necessity and finally to struggle as a desirable goal.

Class struggle proceeds on three fronts: ideological, economic, and political. There are currents and countercurrents to class struggle: sometimes one class predominates, sometimes another. At any given time and in any given country, struggle will primarily be limited to two classes. But as there will also be remnants of the old, dying classes and sprouts of the new, emerging classes, class struggle is made much more complicated, even in the case of socialist societies.[60] The best way to deal with the difficulties thus produced is to utilize Mao's conception of internal versus external contradictions (those within "the people" and those between the people and their enemies). The main focus, however, is to view everything from the class struggle viewpoint and not from the "whole people" perspective or from the idea that the individual is an independent element. One's individual actions are nothing more than a manifestation of the attitudes of one's entire class.[61]

The residual influence of bourgeois ideology within a newer socialist society troubled Lin, for even within the proletariat many will often take on old attitudes, due to the continuing influence of old ideas and the old culture. The ensuing ideological struggle will continue in a protracted manner in each person's mind; the danger is that there will be a bit-by-bit retrogression to the bourgeois outlook. To prevent this otherwise apparently inevitable development, Lin recommended a violent, protracted ideological struggle. Only then would China be able to avoid a "slow change of color" or a violent revolutionary counter *coup d'état*.[62]

Lin catalogued various ideological sins: left and right opportunism; "mountaintopism"; individualism; factionalism; and small-groupism.[63] The most important, however, is revisionism (especially of the Soviet variety), for once a privileged stratum is allowed to exist within the Party, it will gradually lead to an unalterable situation. Lin knew well how revisionism operates: by promoting political privileges and allow-

[59] *Ibid.*

[60] Lin, "Excerpts of a Speech at a Meeting of Army Level Cadres."

[61] *Ibid.*

[62] Lin Piao, "March Ahead under the Red Flag of the General Line and Mao Tse-tung's Military Thinking" (1959), *Peking Review,* No. 41 (October 6, 1959), pp. 13–20; "Excerpts of a Speech at a Meeting of Army Level Cadres."

[63] Lin, "March Ahead"; "Talk to the Central Work Conference" (October 25, 1966); "On the Social Foundation of Revisionism" (1968); "Lin Piao's Speech at the Struggle Rally against Yang Cheng-wu" (1968).

ing factions to exist within the Party, Mao's thought is neglected, cadres are not permitted to participate in labor and mingle with the masses, the army-Party tradition of the hard, frugal life is undermined, class-based economic differentials are magnified, differences between workers and peasants grow, the cadre's will to fight degenerates, people become satisfied with the status quo, and class exploitation returns.[64] If a violent class struggle is not conducted at the beginning of this process, it will soon be too late and the proletariat will have lost through ideological means the power previously gained through military conquest.

Ideological campaigns must therefore be conducted constantly in the realm of art and literature, in the top leadership, and among the masses as a whole.[65] Ultimately, however, it is the people who determine the success, and the acceptability, of ideology. The leadership may err, but "the mainstream of the mass movement is always rational and suitable." [66] Ideology, to Lin, was therefore nothing more than the distilled essence of the creativity of the masses, and it is the duty of the leader to distill their views. Only then does he have the right to teach them.[67] However, when faced with a contradiction between the desires of the masses and Maoist policy, between populism and elitism, Lin always opted for the latter. He merely denied the contradiction by asserting that Mao's policy is entirely representative of the people's wishes.

Most of Lin Piao's public utterances after 1950 included at least some reference to the Party chairman. Not surprisingly, his favorable mention of Mao increased greatly with the onset of the Cultural Revolution in 1965. However, neither the frequency nor the quality of Lin's references to Mao differed much, if at all, from mention made of Mao in most Chinese Communist publications and speeches during the various periods of the post-1950 era. In the case of both Lin and the general run of Maoist praise, a rise occurred from an already high plateau in 1950 to a peak in the late 1950's, then a decline in the early 1960's, and a rise to new heights from 1965 on. This followed the general pattern of Mao's own political influence. In Lin's references to Mao, the decline was graphically portrayed in the available excerpts from the

[64] Lin, "On the Social Foundation of Revisionism."

[65] Lin Piao, "Directive on Literary and Art Work of the Armed Forces" (May 9, 1964); "Address at the Enlarged Meeting of the CCP Central Politburo."

[66] Lin, "Talk to the Central Work Conference."

[67] Lin Piao, Miscellaneous Military Directives (1961); "Talk to the Central Work Conference."

Kung-tso t'ung-hsün (Work Correspondence) in 1961, while the resurgence was evident in Lin's Cultural Revolution speeches as well as in his September, 1965, dictum on people's war.

Like most other Chinese leaders, then, Lin devoted part of his writing to extolling Mao personally, pointing out the efficacy of the "thought of Mao Tse-tung," emphasizing Mao's personal leadership and achievements, and advocating the study and application of the Maoist approach to politics.[68] To Lin, Mao was a "great proletarian genius," "the genius of the world revolution," a "pearl," and "the greatest contemporary Marxist-Leninist in the world." [69] Mao's thought should be used to answer practical questions, to help in military training, to develop basic technical skills, to learn to write, to eliminate the "four olds" and implant the "four news," to distinguish between friend and enemy, to promote the emergence of "public-minded people," to combat revisionism, to promote production, and to harmonize army-people relations.[70]

However, like the pre-1950 period, Lin only rarely quoted from Mao directly, repeated Mao's own analysis of a given matter, or applied Mao's methods directly.[71] To Lin, therefore, Mao's thought was more a general orientation, a diffuse guide to practical action, and a body of spiritual inspiration than a guidebook to be consulted for detailed advice on everyday affairs. It was good to memorize some of Mao's works, said Lin, but not very many, and it was better to use them as

[68] These themes are found in nearly all of Lin's writings in the 1950–70 period.

[69] Lin, "Address at the Enlarged Meeting of the CCP Central Politburo"; "Speech at the 11th Plenary Session of the 8th Central Committee of the Chinese Communist Party" (August, 1966); *ibid.;* "Talk to the Central Work Conference."

[70] Lin Piao, "Marshal Lin Piao on Political Work in Chinese People's Liberation Army" (1960), and "Lin's Important Instructions Concerning the PLA Work of 1961"; "We Must Understand Clearly the Important Changes Made in the Training of Our Army" (1961); "Important Instructions Concerning the PLA Work"; "Directive on Literary and Art Work," and "Five-Point Directive"; "Speech at Peking's Mass Rally" (August 18, 1966); "Speech at Peking Rally to Receive Revolutionary Teachers and Students from All Parts of China" (August 31, 1966); "Talk to the Central Work Conference"; "Speech at the Rally Celebrating the 18th Anniversary of the Founding of the People's Republic of China" (1967).

[71] Lin, "March Ahead"; "The Victory of the Chinese People's Revolutionary War Is the Victory of the Thought of Mao Tse-tung," *Peking Review,* No. 41 (October 11, 1960), pp. 6–15; "Directive on Literary and Art Work"; "Address at the Enlarged Meeting of the CCP Central Politburo"; "Report to the Ninth National Congress of the Communist Party of China (Delivered on April 1 and adopted on April 14, 1969)," *Peking Review,* No. 18 (April 30, 1969), pp. 16–35. "Victory of the Chinese People's Revolutionary War"; "Directive on Literary and Art Work"; "Speech at the Struggle Rally against Yang Cheng-wu"; "Report to the Ninth National Congress." "Six-Point Directive" (1960); "Address at the Enlarged Meeting of the CCP Central Politburo"; "Nine-Point Instructions Given by Vice Supreme Commander Lin during His Reception of All Comrades of the Party Committee of the Air Force" (1968).

background material for applied work.[72] Moreover, Lin admitted that Mao's thought was sometimes difficult for him to understand.[73] Nonetheless, he stated that it was his own, and every Chinese citizen's, duty to follow Mao: "We are the milling stones and must do everything according to the thought of Mao Tse-tung." [74]

However, Lin did have a definite, if still diffuse, interpretation of Mao's ideas. Mao's thought to him was a reflection of the class struggle in China, a development of Marxism-Leninism on the basis of Chinese practice. It was the science of revolution, "the most realistic form of Marxism-Leninism" and the summation of decades of revolutionary practice. It was, in fact, "Marxism-Leninism at its highest level," for Mao inherited and developed the teachings of Marx, Engels, Lenin, and Stalin, as well as critically absorbed the ideas of ancient China and "advanced ideas" from the non-Communist West. In international terms, therefore, Mao's thought was Marxism-Leninism in the era of collapse of imperialism, while in the domestic sense, it was the "locomotive for advance" running on the track of man's future material and spiritual path.[75]

On the surface, Lin thus appeared to be a blind follower of Mao. But that he considered Mao's ideas more a general guide to practical conduct than a detailed set of specific rules might mean that in a post-Maoist era he would have wished to interpret it in ways convenient for justifying the solution of problems worked out on the basis of other criteria. This has a lengthy tradition in Chinese politics, and it may prove to be used again. Lin, however, specifically warned that, as long as he was in control, there would be no de-Maoification or, as he put it, no Khrushchev-style secret speeches. He pledged "eternal allegiance to Mao" personally and the construction of a new (that is, post-Cultural Revolution) state machine "forever loyal to the thought of Mao Tse-

---

[72] "Talks by Vice Chairman Lin, Premier Chou, Chiang Ch'ing and Other Central Leaders at Reception Given to Comrades of the Political Work Unit, the Literary and Art Unit, and *Chün-pao* Unit of the Military Commission" (1968).

[73] In his "Speech at the 11th Plenary Session," Lin said: "There are many ideas [of Mao's] we do not understand. . . . Sometimes I cannot . . . follow the Chairman's thoughts. . . ."

[74] *Ibid.*

[75] Lin Piao, "Lin Piao's Letter to the Industrial and Communications Departments on Living Study and Application of Chairman Mao's Work" (March 11, 1966); "Instructions on Raising the Study of Chairman Mao's Works to a New Stage"; *ibid.;* "Speech at the Peking Rally Commemorating the 50th Anniversary of the October Revolution" (1967); "Talks by Vice Chairman Lin, Premier Chou, Chiang Ch'ing and Other Central Leaders"; "Speech at the 11th Plenary Session"; "Address at the Enlarged Meeting of the CCP Central Politburo"; "Important Directive: Speech Given at the Conference of High Military Cadres at Peking" (August 9, 1967).

tung." [76] Such statements have an ironic ring if we accept as true reports of Lin's anti-Maoist activities preceding his demise.

POLITICS

Amazingly, politics did not appear as a separate category of Lin's thought in the pre-1950 period. Why? It could be argued that Lin was too busy commanding troops in the field to write and think much about politics. But since he had time and interest enough to discourse on several other not strictly military topics, it must be concluded that either he was not particularly interested in strictly political topics before 1950 or he was deterred for some reason from writing about them in that period. The latter is unlikely, since Lin's writings in general do not betray a reluctance to discuss other relevant issues and since several of Lin's peers found no similar barrier to their own writing on political topics. It is possible, of course, that Lin deferred heavily to Mao and that he considered it a good division of labor for himself to take care of military matters, leaving politics to Mao.

The question may well be resolved, however, by noting that Lin's reluctance to discuss politics extended well into the post-1950 period. Only with the Cultural Revolution, in fact, did Lin appear to take an interest in the topic and then only because, as Mao's newly appointed successor, he had to say something about such matters. Nonetheless, Lin's latter-day discourses on politics were intrinsically interesting because they actually represent a rather well-constructed philosophy, because they bear a strong resemblance to the political *Weltanschauung* of another well-known political leader and political successor, Joseph Stalin, and because they may not be atypical of the political orientation of many of the political leaders who will rule China after Mao's demise.

Lin's theory of politics followed directly from his view of ideology. Since history is the history of classes and of class struggle, and since classes continue to exist in socialism, politics in socialist societies must also revolve around the class struggle.[77] Class struggle, like guerrilla war, will be protracted and continue even into the indefinite future.[78] This led Lin to emphasize the *beneficial* role of struggle. Contradictions between social classes can be resolved only by struggle, and progress comes about only through the dialectical relationship between contra-

[76] Lin, "Address at the Enlarged Meeting of the CCP Central Politburo"; "Important Directive."
[77] Lin, "Excerpts of a Speech at a Meeting of Army Level Cadres."
[78] Lin, "Talk to the Central Work Conference."

dictions and their resolution. The basic purpose of the CCP therefore must be to propagate struggle. To Lin, a philosophy that emphasizes the virtues of struggle guaranteed progress and dynamism: "Struggle is the only way that we will be able to correct anything." [79]

In all examples of class struggle, the fundamental problem is the seizure and maintenance of political power. It is relatively easy for the proletariat and their allies to seize power: the Yenan, country versus city, guerrilla-war path to power will, if followed correctly, guarantee success. [80] Lin did not concern himself unduly with the requisites for power seizure through military means, for not only had he already delivered himself at length on this subject in the pre-1950 period but, by the mid-1960's, the major problem was consolidation and maintenance of the Party's (or rather Mao's) pre-eminent role in China. He therefore devoted most of his later speculation on politics to the dangers of *losing* power, once having gained it, and how to prevent the opposition from regaining office.

This inevitably gave Lin's writing on the subject of power a negative cast. Quite obviously he was influenced by the power struggle that immediately preceded the Cultural Revolution. Thus, we find throughout his writings in 1966 and after such phrases as: "If we don't get rid of [revisionism], we shall see our Party and State perish and our heads will roll." "We cannot but attack [the revisionists], and if we do not overthrow them, they will overthrow us." "If we don't pay attention . . . and we act like fools, then they will win. If we are vigilant, they will not win. They want to cut off our heads, but they may not succeed. If they initiate a counterrevolutionary *coup d'état*, we are going to cut off their heads." [81] In fact, Lin defined political power negatively, as the power above all to suppress, to mete out death, prison terms, labor reform, expulsion from the Party, and dismissal from office. [82]

Lin was therefore very conscious of the necessity to prevent his opponents from ousting him and his allies from office. He had a fetish about coups. He talked about coups from below (people's revolutions, Communist revolutions by force of arms) and counterrevolutionary coups (court coups, internal collusion with the lowly, collusion with the

[79] "Speech on Ideological Struggle" (1966?). This philosophy is somewhat reminiscent of the views of Hitler and Stalin on the virtues of violence. We would not wish to push the parallel too far, however.

[80] Lin, "Speech at the Peking Rally" (1967); "Long Live the Victory of People's War!" *Peking Review,* No. 36 (September 3, 1965), pp. 9–30.

[81] Lin, "On the Social Foundation of Revisionism"; "Talk to the Central Work Conference"; "Address at the Enlarged Meeting of the CCP Central Politburo."

[82] "Address at the Enlarged Meeting of the CCP Central Politburo."

foreigner, invasion, coups following upon calamity). He gave statistics on the number of coups that had occurred since 1960 (to say nothing of earlier Chinese history) to support his contention that political power, once seized, could again be lost, and that the dictatorship of the proletariat could overnight be turned back into the dictatorship of the bourgeois.[83] "There is a likelihood of a counterrevolutionary *coup d'état*—killings, seizure of political power, capitalist restoration, and the doing away with all those associated with socialism," said Lin. "You must have smelled it—gunpower." [84]

Lin saw two requisites for a successful coup: control of the propaganda organs and control of the military.

When the civilian and the military are coordinated, and public opinion and rifles are in their [the revisionists'] hands, then a counterrevolutionary *coup d'état* can occur at any time. If a general election is needed, people can be called to cast ballots. If armed uprising is needed, the armed forces can be dispatched immediately. . . . Once the opportune time comes, a counterrevolutionary *coup d'état* will occur; once we have a natural calamity, or once a war breaks out, or Chairman Mao dies, this political crisis will come and this vast country of 700 million people will be in disorder and chaos.[85]

This last sentence, perhaps more than anything else that Lin has written, tells us what sort of personal political policy he would have favored in the post-Maoist period. Externally, he would have stressed avoidance of war; internally, he would no doubt have attempted to consolidate his power and purged any real or potential opposition until he felt he had ultimate control of both "rifles and inkwells." The important question is: Does one with Lin's seemingly excessive fear of plots and coups ever get to the point of feeling secure enough in his power to pursue socioeconomic policies for their own sake? [86] It may not be too far from the mark to conclude that Lin's political insecurity drove him, in the summer of 1971, to make a strong bid for enhanced personal power, a bid that Mao himself may have felt it necessary to deny.

In any case, the answer depends to some extent on Lin's views of the role of the Party in policy and administration. He regarded the Party as the center of all political, military, economic, social, and, especially, literary and ideological authority in the country.[87] His view of the

---

[83] *Ibid.*

[84] *Ibid.*

[85] *Ibid.*

[86] One is again tempted to draw a parallel with Stalin who, in his last days, purported to see "wolves" about him constantly closing in. See Wolfgang Leonhard, *The Kremlin since Stalin* (New York: Praeger, 1963), p. 49.

[87] Lin, "Talk to the Central Work Conference."

Party and its functions was therefore similar to those first put forward by Lenin in his *What Is to Be Done?* [88] In particular, there must be a high degree of Party membership within the army, for the PLA is a subordinate arm of the Party. There must be absolute obedience to the Party, and "nothing must be done behind the back of the Party." [89] When underhanded activities are discovered, they must be dealt with severely. As noted earlier, death, imprisonment, labor reform, expulsion from the Party, and dismissal from public office are the range of punishments Lin recommended.[90]

Of course, many of the mistakes made by individual Party members are due to misunderstanding and not to explicit anti-Party or anti-Maoist behavior. Most Party members are intrinsically good, and individual problems should be handled on an individual basis.[91] Nonetheless, the Party must have a constant turnover of personnel, the "stale" must be gotten rid of and the "fresh" taken in. And there can never be a situation in which class struggle within society as a whole is not reflected in the Party itself.[92] Thus, constant purge would seem to have been in store for the Party under Lin's leadership, a future that may not have endeared him to some colleagues. Moreover, to Lin the Party was an educational institution, teaching each member (and, through them, society as a whole) to be modest, prudent, free from arrogance and rashness, and to live in the style of "arduous struggle and plain living." [93] Lin was thus not only a Leninist and a Stalinist, but a Calvinist as well.

EDUCATION TO 1949: THE ROLE OF EXPERIENCE

Since the beginning, Lin had a well-formulated theory of education, in contrast to his views on ideology and politics, which developed slowly but continuously, and his policies, where there was no development at all until very recently, when it was explosive and relatively sophisticated. It is to be expected, of course, that Lin, an educator as well as a politico-military leader, would have thought and written about pedagogy. Of more interest to Chinese elite studies is that, while the whole of his views on this subject was expressed in nascent form very early, different parts emerged at different times and in accord with

[88] See Alfred Meyer, *Leninism* (New York: Praeger, 1962), Part I, "The Party."
[89] Lin, "March Ahead."
[90] Lin, "Address at the Enlarged Meeting of the CCP Central Politburo."
[91] Lin, "Talk to the Central Work Conference."
[92] Lin, "Report to the Ninth National Congress."
[93] *Ibid.*

differing practical demands. Thus, in the pre-1950 period Lin emphasized the role of experience, since that is what counted most in winning battles. In the period of Communist rule after 1950, on the other hand, he stressed the need for political education, since in a peacetime era of technological modernization many tended to forget the ideological and class bases of Communist political authority.

Lin's pre-1950 theory of education included opinions on where to obtain ideas, what to teach, and how. He noted three sources of ideas: commanders (personal authority), books (traditional authority), and combatants (individual experience). All are equally important and none should be emphasized at the expense of the others. Particularly concerned that past experience, while very important, not be regarded too highly, Lin advised that "formulaism" derived from books and "random education based on fragmentary personal experiences" be avoided, since future conditions were unlikely to be similar to those of the past. One must use formulas but must not apply them mechanically, and under no circumstances should one separate learning from application.[94]

Lin listed many educational methods: imparting knowledge through explanation and discussion; integrating theories learned from books with practice derived from experience; joint leadership and teaching by commanders and soldiers; incentives provided by competition, awards, honors, and models (hero figures); and on-the-job training.[95] He emphasized throughout the pragmatic approach, flexibility of methods, learning by participation, and realism. This is, of course, what one would expect of a leader always close to the scene of action and charged with the immediate safety of his men as well as with the success of his military operations. Lin was no different in this regard from other practical-minded members of the Chinese Communist political elite. But his insistence on two other qualities perhaps differentiated him from traditionally oriented Chinese educators. First, he wanted to replace the old Chinese method of rote learning from ancient written authorities with the "critical spirit"—asking questions and independent thinking—even if in the process doubts and disagreements arose.[96]

94 Lin, "How to Conduct Military Training."
95 *Ibid.*
96 Taken alone, such sentiments accord with liberal philosophies of education in the West. But in the Chinese Communist context, in which adherence to the new orthodoxy of Mao's thought came to be demanded, Lin's apparent invitation to free inquiry would have increasingly severe limits placed on it. Nevertheless, before 1949 at least, Lin Piao may have been as free from those limits as any Chinese Communist in recommending such a "critical spirit" to others.

Second, Lin stressed the practical content of the educational curriculum. Technique was what counted with Lin, and much of his pre-1950 writing on education concerned the details of tactics and techniques useful to the individual soldier and to the small unit. One pervasive nontechnical theme was the importance of "ideological work" (political indoctrination) in every aspect of training. From the very beginning of his immersion in military education, Lin stressed the correct ideological and political foundation of the soldier's practical training.[97] Though this is an old Maoist and Chinese Communist theme, the point is that even one who went to extremes over details took pains to emphasize the political basis of technical work.

EDUCATION AFTER 1949: STRESS ON POLITICS

Political (or ideological) education was, as might be expected, the central element in Lin's approach to politics in the more recent period. To Lin, political education had to take precedence over all other educational endeavors. "We must not slacken ideological [that is, political] work for a moment," for it is the "lifeblood" of all practical activity.[98] Within the army, for instance, political work is the "atom bomb of the spirit" that is much more important than the material atom bomb. "Once political work is well done, all other practical endeavors will be performed more efficiently." [99] It is the link between the two and although it need not take up as much time as practical study and work, it is in "supreme command" of the latter.[100] The best example of the correct relationship of political work to practical activity is to be found in the army itself, for the army is a "school of politics" and its history and work techniques—such as the three-eight style—can serve as examples for the population as a whole.[101]

Lin devoted most of his discourse on political education to methods, as perhaps befits a Maoist and a former schoolteacher and principal. He was, of course, well known for his insistence on placing the thought of Mao Tse-tung at the center of every educational endeavor. Proper application of Mao's thought was the primary method for instilling

[97] Lin, "Proclamation"; "How to Conduct Military Training"; "Political and Military Situation in the Northeast"; "Report Made at a Meeting of High-Level Cadres from the Northeast Bureau."

[98] Lin, "March Ahead."

[99] Lin, "Marshal Lin Piao on Political Work."

[100] Lin, "Important Instructions Concerning the PLA Work"; "We Must Understand Clearly." "Speech at the 11th Plenary Session"; "Talks by Vice Chairman Lin, Premier Chou, Chiang Ch'ing and Other Central Leaders."

[101] Lin, "March Ahead." "Marshal Lin Piao on Political Work"; "Important Instructions Concerning the PLA Work"; "On Writing Down Experiences" (1961).

discipline, evolving a good working style, and increasing industrial production. All complexities and situational differences were to be resolved by appeal to Mao's thought. "Everything is united by using the thought of Mao Tse-tung." [102] Many would have to devote a great deal of time to Mao study, Lin warned, for Mao's ideas sometimes are not easy to understand. It was often good, therefore, to memorize Mao quotations and even entire selections, for repetition gives rise to inner, psychological change.[103]

Yet it was not the actual rote memorization of the Maoist scriptures that Lin emphasized so much as their use as inspiration for correct practical activity. Book ideas, including those found in Mao's own writing, should be integrated with practice, and the emphasis should be on practice. If Mao's thought were used correctly, it would serve as the proper ideological base for answering practical questions.[104] But the important thing was to make Mao's thought a "living ideology," capable of energizing large numbers of people to solve practical problems. "Living ideology" meant emphasis on the questions of the moment, such as economic efficiency, on using Mao's thought to teach people how to cooperate and assist each other, and on propagating the "two remembrances and three investigations." [105] "Living ideology" was applied Maoism, with its stress on population mobilization, attacking and overcoming difficulties (and not avoiding them), gradual self-improvement through constant effort, elimination of one's own weaknesses, and a common concern for the other person's ideological level.[106]

In political education, as in fighting a battle, it was important to concentrate one's forces on one or a few essential objectives.[107] Like war, the principles of Marxist-Leninist-Maoist politics were few in number. One should therefore strive to master them thoroughly, despite their difficulty. Quoting Lao Tzu, Lin emphasized that it was best to

[102] Lin, 'Marshal Lin Piao on Political Work"; "Important Instructions Concerning the PLA Work"; "Instructions on Raising the Study of Chairman Mao's Works." The quotation is from the last-named source.

[103] Lin, "Instructions on Raising the Study of Chairman Mao's Works."

[104] Lin, "Marshal Lin Piao on Political Work"; "Important Instructions Concerning the PLA Work."

[105] "Six-Point Directive"; Miscellaneous Military Directives (1961); "Important Instructions Concerning the PLA Work." The two remembrances are of class bitterness and the nation's bitterness (against the foreign invader). The three investigations are of viewpoint, resoluteness in struggle, and work.

[106] Lin, "Victory of the Chinese People's Revolutionary War." Lin Piao, "Regulations for Improving the Methods of Supervisory Education in Army Units" (1961); Miscellaneous Military Directives (1961).

[107] Lin, "We Must Understand Clearly."

learn only a little, but to master that. If education were reduced to simple and easy ideas, and if formalistic, scholastic, and bourgeois methods were eschewed, even difficult concepts could be subdued.[108]

Through the concept of "supervisory education," Lin drew a clear line of connection between the necessity to purge the Party continually and the essentials of political education. Supervisory education was that branch of political education devoted to helping ideologically err-ing cadres return to the proper Maoist path. It was thus an educa-tional substitute for purge, and was Lin's term for the process known in the West as "coercive persuasion." [109] Lin castigated "rough" super-visory education, where cadres are unjustly accused of ideological shortcomings, where the sick are not cared for, and where punishment is disproportionate to the offense. He advocated criticism only when major errors had been committed, and then not in public accusation meetings.[110] It was better to rehabilitate a person "separately and in-dividually," by proceeding "slowly and patiently" in small peer groups, giving clear reasons for the accusations presented, and emphasizing the person's good deeds.[111] The resulting "new sense of working to-gether" would make everyone more successful as well as convince the erring cadre of his mistakes.[112] On the other hand, bad habits and excessive freedoms were not to be condoned. A combination of strict education and the compulsion of urgent need was what was desired. Together they would produce a sense of responsibility, the avoidance of extremes, and a set of good habits capable of being exercised in ad-verse situations.[113]

In sum, three different patterns emerge from an analysis of the links between the development of Lin's philosophy and the history of the Communist movement in China. His ideological outlook evidenced an ever-greater utilization of Marxist-Leninist categories over the years, with a major "breakthrough" coming in 1966, concomitant with the beginning of the Cultural Revolution. That is one pattern. A second is fashioned after the evolution of Lin's views on politics: the sudden

[108] Lin Piao, "On Educational Reform" (1967).
[109] See Edgar Schein *et al.*, *Coercive Persuasion* (New York: Norton, 1961).
[110] Lin, Miscellaneous Military Directives (1961).
[111] *Ibid.;* "Regulations for Improving the Methods of Supervisory Education"; "Com-rade Lin Piao's Four-Point Directive for the Work of Supervisory Education in the Army Units" (1961); Miscellaneous Military Directives (1961).
[112] Lin Piao, "Speech of Comrade Lin Piao at the Meeting on How to Carry on the Work of Supervisory Education for All the Army (Summary)" (1961).
[113] Lin, Miscellaneous Military Directives (1961); "Speech on How to Carry on the Work of Supervisory Education."

emergence of a well-thought-out philosophy after a long period of silence. Lin's ideas on education point out a third path for the evolution of his thought: the early emergence of an integrated attitude that was then applied to differing situations encountered over several decades. The existence of these three separate modes demonstrates that only in the third instance was 1950 a major dividing point for changes in Lin's philosophical outlook. Moreover, in no case (with the significant exception of the Cultural Revolution) were the other well-known partitions in Party history also dividing points in his own thought. Thus, what was administratively true of Party history was not necessarily true of the intellectual history of one of its important leaders.

A generalization might be risked at this point: analysis and explanation of the history—and the reasons for changes in policy—of the CCP as a whole must be sharply differentiated from the analysis and explanation of changes in outlook of some of its leaders. What is true of the whole, here as in other areas, is not necessarily true of its constituent parts; conversely, explanations for the behavior of those parts cannot necessarily be taken as explanations of that whole. While these may seem to be truisms, the implication for Chinese elite studies should be noted: conclusions drawn from aggregate elite studies should not be applied without qualification to individual members of that elite, even (or especially) when they are important members. Nor, of course, should the results of an investigation of the career, style, and outlook of one or a few elite members be generalized without constraint to the elite as a whole.

Elite studies need both the deductive generalizations produced from aggregate analysis and the inductive generalizations stemming from the study of individual leaders. Those places where contact between these two processes occur are the points that should be of increasing interest and concern to scholars. They should be on the outlook for results in one sphere that contradict or reinforce expected conclusions from the other. In Lin's case, the congruence between his own life and philosophy and that of the Party as a whole was usually quite close. Yet at times there was divergence. And it is often that divergence that makes political history a study more of unique events than statistical regularities and renders political forecasting a difficult art. The picture of the Chinese elite must be as accurate as possible; therefore it must be filled in "from above" and "from below" both by aggregate and by individual studies. Neither, in fact, is complete without the other.

LIN'S RELATIONS WITH PEERS, SUPERIORS, AND SUBORDINATES

One important question about any political leader is the kind of relations he maintains with other members of the elite. Is there a pattern discernible over a man's career that helps explain why he rose to prominence and why, in many instances, he either ceased to move up after a certain point or actually fell from power? In the case of many Chinese Communist leaders, we have very few data for this sort of analysis, which by nature depends as much on detailed and "inside" information as on known career patterns. The CCP before 1966 was, moreover, amazingly free (in relation, say, to the Soviet or East European parties) from large-scale purge, while the very fact of the lengthy Maoist leadership helped to hold down what would probably otherwise have been a higher rate of personal animosity, squabbles, and factionalism. With the Cultural Revolution, however, intraelite differences emerged with such a vengeance that we are now able to see clearly the smoke and flames from fires smoldering for over thirty years. While this aspect of Chinese elite behavior remains to be studied definitively, in Lin Piao's own case there is enough material, albeit fragmentary and inconclusive, to draw some general conclusions. It seems convenient to approach the subject by examining his relations with superiors, peers, and subordinates.

Mao Tse-tung, Chu Teh, and P'eng Teh-huai historically were Lin's three most important superiors. The story of Lin's life is, of course, the history of his fidelity to Mao as a person and, increasingly, to his ideas. In our second section, "Determinative Factors in Lin Piao's Career," we outlined the relations between the two, noting that a symbiotic dependence had emerged as early as the early 1930's and had grown with each succeeding decade. However, there was at least one departure, and perhaps two (three, if we are to believe recent charges against Lin), from this pattern, and these allow us to conclude that when Lin overtly disagreed with Mao, he was immediately disciplined, spent a period in relative disgrace, and then re-emerged all the stronger as Mao's supporter.

The first occasion was at the end of the Long March in 1935, when Lin made known his opposition to Mao's desire to resume military action so quickly, then indicated his reluctance to attend a Politburo meeting at Wayaopao, and finally opposed Mao's plan to break up his First Corps as cadres to be sent to other units.[114] The result was that

[114] For details, see Robinson, *Biography of Lin Piao, Part I*, pp. 30–32.

Mao removed Lin from field command and sent him to his administrative post at Kang-ta. It would be nearly two years before Lin would regain his field command, and then only at a lower level than he had originally held.

The second occasion, admittedly much more poorly documented, allegedly took place during the initial phases of the Korean War when Lin (and Kao Kang, according to assertions) found that current Chinese tactics were unsuited to countering American air-supported operations. He is said to have proposed to escalate the war by requesting Soviet tank and air cover and when this was not forthcoming, refused to carry out Mao's orders for a new offensive, commanding his troops instead to stand fast. Mao then removed Lin, replacing him with P'eng Teh-huai.[115] Whether or not these stories are true, their very infrequency demonstrates Lin's overall fidelity to Mao—a record of only two (if that) publicly known disagreements in forty-five years of association is difficult to match anywhere. With these exceptions, and pending definitive information on the events of late 1971, Lin was Mao's willing subordinate and, at least to this writer, it is doubtful even in the most recent instance that he departed from that status.

The same cannot be said of Lin's historical relationship to Chu Teh and P'eng Teh-huai. Lin was Chu's immediate military subordinate from 1927 until the mid-1950's and, superficially, the two seem to have gotten along well enough. Yet his relations with Chu were probably ambiguous from the beginning. Some reports indicate that Lin had to convince Chu not to give in to the Nationalists after the Nanchang defeat in 1927 and go instead to Chingkangshan. During the Nationalists' Fifth Encirclement Campaign in 1934, he had to walk a tightrope between Chu and Mao, when the former bent with the wind and accepted the Li Teh-Chou En-lai leadership while the latter was placed (for a time) under house arrest. Although Chu seemed to come around to the Maoist side at Tsunyi, at Maoerhkai he again disagreed with Mao, and Lin sided instead with Mao.

No more derogatory information is heard in connection with the Lin-Chu relationship until the Cultural Revolution. Then, for reasons as yet unclear, Lin allegedly loosed a fierce denunciation of Chu.[116] He

[115] Huang (ed.), *Chung-kung chün-jen chih*, pp. 215–16, and his unpublished manuscript, "Lin Piao," written in Hong Kong in conjunction with William Whitson. For an analysis of arguments for and against Lin's presence in Korea and responsibility for the Chinese military there, see Robinson, *Biography of Lin Piao, Part II*, pp. 5–13.

[116] Reported in a Peking Red Guard poster, February 8, 1967. Japanese translation in *Mainichi shimbun* (Tokyo), February 9, 1967; English translation in *Daily Summary of the Japanese Press*, U.S. Embassy, Tokyo, February 9, 1967, p. 1.

linked Chu with P'eng Teh-huai in attempting to overthrow Mao at the Lushan Plenum, said that Chu wished to replace Mao as Party chairman at the time of the Kao Kang incident, and attacked Chu personally for his "ambitions," his insincere self-criticism, and even for his alleged lack of military prowess. With regard to the last charge, Lin asserted (against all evidence) that Chu had not been a "general commander" for even a day since Nanchang—not at Chingkangshan, nor on the Long March, nor during the anti-Japanese resistance and the Civil War. Whether or not the charges are true, it is interesting that Lin evidently chose to strike at Chu when the latter was down, a (perhaps only temporary) victim of the Red Guard-initiated purge process.

Lin's relations with P'eng Teh-huai can be seen more clearly. There is not much doubt that Lin saw P'eng as his major personal competitor from almost the beginning of the Communist hegira. P'eng moved ahead of Lin in the military hierarchy as early as 1935, when he was appointed acting commander in chief at Maoerhkai, a change made permanent when he became deputy chief of staff to Chu Teh in the Eighth Route Army reorganization in 1937.[117] Lin remained a division commander. And although he managed to move up into a position of equal importance during the Civil War period (both headed field armies or their equivalents), P'eng took the lead again once Lin left the Korean War theater.[118] As the new minister of defense after 1954 and with Lin ill, P'eng seemed to have the inside track. However, miscalculating his strength, P'eng stumbled at Lushan in 1959, while Lin, having hung back during most of the 1950's, now moved up to replace him as minister.

Lin's reaction to P'eng's ouster and his attitude toward P'eng in the years immediately after Lushan contrasts with his attacks against P'eng during the Cultural Revolution. There is no evidence that Lin was directly involved in any of the disputes leading to the charges of P'eng's shortcomings in aspects of the Great Leap Forward, nor is there any indication that Lin took a major part in the debates at Lushan or, if he did, that he represented one side or the other, or spoke against P'eng. He probably felt that he was Mao's natural choice to succeed P'eng and had everything to gain from silence.

Lin's open concern about P'eng postdates the Lushan Plenum. He attacked P'eng directly at Military Affairs Committee meetings im-

[117] William W. Whitson, *The Chinese Communist High Command, 1927–71: A Political and Military History* (New York: Praeger, 1972); Klein and Clark, *Biographic Dictionary*, pp. 731, 732.
[118] Robinson, *Biography of Lin Piao, Part II*, pp. 11–13.

mediately following Lushan, indirectly through the pages of the *Kung-tso t'ung-hsün*, and in the few articles in publicly circulated journals that appeared under his name. But Lin never allowed his own name to be used openly in any of the written references and never attacked P'eng by name.[119] Instead, he concentrated on efforts to improve army efficiency and to restore Party control within the military. Thus, he seemed to be saying that he wished to be judged on his own merits, not by verbal attacks against P'eng, who could not reply openly.

Only in the summer of 1967 is Lin, for political reasons connected with the Cultural Revolution, first publicly on record as attacking P'eng by name. Even then, however, the brevity of his remarks and the lack of specific, detailed charges demonstrate that he did not wish to overplay his role in the anti-P'eng campaign. This is interesting for, aside from desiring to avoid the charge of senseless vindictiveness, Lin apparently wished to minimize his concern with personality matters once it was clear that P'eng was politically impotent. While quite sensitive to actual or potential attacks from his enemies, and even to possible competition from associates, Lin thus seemed more concerned with assuring administrative and military efficiency than with striking a rival when down.[120] Once a contender was eliminated from the running, he usually had nothing further to fear from Lin.

Do these generalizations hold for Lin's peers and subordinates, especially those purged during the Cultural Revolution? The very fact that three of Lin's erstwhile close associates—Lo Jui-ch'ing, Hsiao Hua, and Yang Ch'eng-wu—were purged at his own behest might lead to the conclusion that, once on top, Lin changed dramatically his attitude and methods for dealing with those who disagreed with him. After all, up to the Cultural Revolution, Lin had had a long history of

---

[119] For Lin's attacks at Military Affairs Committee meetings, see *CB*, No. 894 (October 27, 1969), p. 22; *Ke-ming tsao-fan pao* (Revolution Rebel News) (Peking), November 25, 1967. His published articles are "March Ahead under the Red Flag of the General Line and Mao Tse-tung's Military Thinking," "The Victory of the Chinese People's Revolutionary War Is the Victory of the Thought of Mao Tse-tung," and "Long Live the Victory of People's War!" cited in notes 62, 71, and 80.

For Lin's indirect attacks on P'eng, see the English translation of the *Kung-tso t'ung-hsün* in J. Chester Cheng (ed.), *The Politics of the Chinese Red Army* (Stanford, Calif.: Hoover Institution, 1966), pp. 4, 66, 281, 595–97, 617, 651, 727.

[120] Mention should be made of Lin's 1950 dismissal of Ch'en Kuang, a long-term associate and chief of staff to Yeh Chien-ying in the South China Military District. In this case, Lin seems to have taken a purely disciplinary action to prevent the usurpation of his position from below. As such, it bears comparison with Lin's actions in the case of Lo Jui-ch'ing. For details on the Ch'en Kuang affair, see Robinson, *Biography of Lin Piao, Part II*, pp. 3–4.

close relations with peers and subordinates—Nieh Jung-chen, Lo Jung-huan, and Li Tso-p'eng are good examples—and was known both for the loyalty of his following and his infrequent dismissal of subordinates.

With Chu too old to matter and P'eng safely aside, perhaps Lo, Hsiao, and Yang represented the real challenges to his newly found power, against which he reacted violently. Investigation of what Cultural Revolution material we have on the three reveals that at least in the case of Lo Jui-ch'ing there was an overt challenge to Lin's authority, which he had no choice but to oppose frontally. In the other two cases, while there were elements of competition for power, Lin's position was threatened only indirectly and he thus reacted less severely. Indeed, in the Hsiao Hua case he seems to have done his utmost to make the latter's demise as painless as possible. Even for Yang Ch'eng-wu, when he was accused of actually subverting the positions of important Cultural Revolution leaders, Lin moved more circumspectly than he might have. Since Yang (like Hsiao) had been a close associate of his for many years and since it was Lin's own actions that, to a large degree, had placed Yang in a precarious political position, Lin was reluctant to deal severely with him. Moreover, Lin himself was apparently under political pressure from the left at critical periods of the Cultural Revolution, and the removal of both Hsiao and Yang served to some extent as lightning rods to ground criticism of himself.

But in all three cases, Lin removed close associates for reasons stemming from competition for political power. This should demonstrate that Lin, like all major political actors, had to look first to his own political security and only then to the personal welfare of his colleagues. The two concerns are not contradictory, however, and at least in the cases of Hsiao and Yang, Lin attempted to make their removal as least uncomfortable as possible. A survey of the three instances will perhaps bear out these generalizations.

Lo Jui-ch'ing's case seems clear. Personal, ideological, administrative, strategic, and timing questions combined to make his removal imperative. To Lin, personal and administrative differences were the most important. Differences included Lo's relatively greater emphasis on training as opposed to the study of Mao, culminating in the now-famous argument over the "military tournaments" in 1964; the 1965 debate with Lin and others over the best means of defending China against possible American attack; disagreement over how and when to intervene in Vietnam, and over priorities concerning emerging domestic political problems (the emerging Cultural Revolution purge) versus foreign policy (the Vietnam conflict and possible military cooperation with the Soviet Union). These alone would probably have caused Lin to support Lo's removal. But Lo also allegedly attempted to supplant Lin personally, claiming to his face that Lin was too ill to hold office and should stand aside; he even went to the lengths of not consulting Lin on holding the military tournaments and of changing the content of Lin's directives behind his back.[121] If these accusations were true, Lin had no choice but to remove Lo. The timing of the purge, late 1965, was possibly pushed up because of the necessity to make the army as politically reliable as possible in light of Mao's believed necessity to purge large numbers of Party leaders.

Hsiao Hua's dismissal is more mysterious. One of Lin's closest associates from the early Kiangsi Soviet period (when he was a private in Lin's regiment), Hsiao in 1964 became director of the General Political Department of the army and hence was in charge of executing Lin's policy of emphasis on political training. He was apparently purged sometime in late 1967. The exact reasons are not clear. Mao stated that Hsiao "is a son of heaven without hope of being saved." Ch'en Po-ta said, "Hsiao Hua seems to be a gentleman, but he is not a good soldier. Especially, he possesses a strong sense of the elite. He tried to change the military . . . into a bourgeois force." Lin himself, in his only publicly known comment on Hsiao, stated that Hsiao had "made one mistake after another, and we tried again and again not to let him fall; now we are still trying to help him do well." [122]

Hsiao evidently was a victim of Cultural Revolution crossfire between the "May 16 Group" (of which he was sometimes alleged to be a member) thought to be supported by Chiang Ch'ing, and the Maoists headed by Chou En-lai and Lin. He may have made some administrative decisions that appeared, in retrospect, to have been ill-advised: he "withheld material" at the time of the Wuhan Incident; he supported Yü Li-chin (air force commissar), who in turn was supposed to have been associated with the erring Yang Ch'eng-wu; and he got tied up

---

[121] For details, see *ibid.*, pp. 44–46, and the references cited there.

[122] *JPRS*, No. 49,826 (*Translations on Communist China*, No. 90), "Selections from Chairman Mao," p. 20. Red Guard wall poster, January 20, 1967, reported in *Yomiuri* (Tokyo), January 21, 1961, and translated in *Daily Summary of the Japanese Press*, January 22, 1967, p. 2. Lin Piao, "Speech Given at the Conference of High Military Cadres in Peking," August 9, 1967, *Chu-ying tung-fang-hung* (Pearl Studio East-Is-Red) (Canton), September 13, 1967. Translation in *JPRS*, No. 43,449 (November 24, (1967) (*Communist China Digest*, No, 192), p. 63.

with the wrong Red Guard faction in Sinkiang.[123] It appears that Lin was quite reluctant to let Hsiao go, but probably felt he had no choice, given the pressure by Chiang Ch'ing from the left, Hsiao's connections with Yang, and undetermined ideological differences. But his case differs from that of Lo: unlike Lo, Hsiao did not try to oust Lin, and Lin did his utmost to arrange Hsiao's removal as quietly as possible. He was probably genuinely sorry to see Hsiao go.

Much more data are at hand concerning the purge of Lin's acting chief of staff and close associate, Yang Ch'eng-wu, since Yang's demise closely reflects (indeed, it formed the apex of) the central politics of the Cultural Revolution during 1968. By late 1967, political in-fighting between the Cultural Revolution Group and its detractors, within and outside the army, had reached the stage where previously close friends had to line up on opposing sides to enhance their own chances of political survival. While it is impossible in a short space to analyze these exceedingly complex events, which involved all important Cultural Revolution institutions and personalities, Lin's own role seems clear.

Yang's basic problems were organizational. On the one hand, he desired to consolidate his power within the military so as to remove the probationary nature of his appointment. For that reason, he tried to replace contemporary military region commanders with his friends in the former (1938–45) Shansi-Chahar-Hopeh Military Region. This could only incur the commanders' ire and cause discomfort to Lin in an era when no one's position was secure. On the other hand, Yang, like Hsiao, seemed to have been caught in the power struggle between Chiang Ch'ing and her supporters, who often wished to attack the army itself, on the one side, and, on the other, those who wished to pursue such less extreme policies as using the army to work out compromises between revolutionary factions and to promote the provincial revolutionary committees. Yang, in the center of the fighting, had to balance between the various sides and factions as well as make his own position secure. One way was to form his own group, move against too-leftist elements within the army, and cooperate with those who seemed willing to counter the moves of the Cultural Revolution Group. Therefore, he teamed up with Yü Li-chin and Fu Ch'ung-pi to move against Hsieh Fu-chih and, possibly, Wang Li and Ch'i Pen-yü.

By early 1968, Cultural Revolution politics were disorganized

---

[123] For further details on Lin's removal of Hsiao, see Robinson, *Biography of Lin Piao, Part II,* pp. 46–48, and the reference cited there.

enough that Yang (like Ch'en Tsai-tao in Wuhan) assumed that he had Lin's backing (because of their long association), while Lin had to withdraw his support in the face of pressure from the left. When Fu, at Yang's behest, failed (because of Chiang Ch'ing's opposition) to arrest Wang and Ch'i at the Cultural Revolution building in March, 1968, and when Yang allegedly bugged Mao's and Lin's own houses, Lin had little choice but to remove Yang. The fact that it was Lin himself who announced Yang's removal, together with his own and Chou En-lai's pandering of Chiang Ch'ing in their speeches, demonstrates the leadership's attempt to maintain a precarious unity despite obvious policy disagreements and personal animosity.

Yang's case, then, stands between those of Lo and Hsiao. Here was an admixture of personal ambition, administrative insecurity, and political differences. In the end, however, Lin probably felt he had to remove Yang more because of the latter's factional activities than for his political and administrative errors. As Chou En-lai put it, "Whoever is a bourgeois individual, an ambitious man, or a two-faced factional element, once found and exposed . . . will have nothing left . . . no matter who he is." [124]

CONCLUSION

What, in sum, have we learned from this exposition of Lin's experience as a member of the Chinese Communist elite? Four particular conclusions emerge. First, the congruence between Lin's own career, on the one hand, and Party history and the aggregate characteristics of the Chinese Communist elite, on the other, is quite close. This, aside from the particularly close relationship between Lin and Mao and the unavailability (for ideological reasons) of other leading members of the elite, goes a long way toward explaining Mao's choice of Lin as his successor. Second, Lin's political "style" differed markedly from that of such other top Chinese Communist political leaders as Chou En-lai and Mao himself.[125] Yet the character of those differences

[124] "Chou En-lai's Speech at the Struggle Rally against Yang Ch'eng-wu," *Chinese Communist Affairs: Facts and Features,* I, No. 21 (August 7, 1968), 23. Further details and references on Yang's removal are given in Robinson, *Biography of Lin Piao, Part II,* pp. 48–51.

[125] There is a need for two sets of comparative research. First, there should be comparative studies done of political styles. These can be interstate (for instance, between two Communist nations such as China and the Soviet Union, or a Communist and a non-Communist nation, as China and France); like styles may be compared (as, for instance, Chou-En-lai and J. Edgar Hoover); or similar levels of political authority may be examined. Second, there should be work on the views and styles of that set of leaders *just below* the very top. Here is where a great deal of political influence lies

was not such as to separate him from his peers; on the contrary, they complemented each other's administrative efforts and stylistic approaches to politics. The whole seemed to be harmonious, despite the apparent demise of Lin in 1971 while Mao and Chou remained on the scene. These differing styles were held together, until late 1971, as it were, by the "glue" of Mao's presence and by his charismatic leadership. But what until recently seemed to be an integrated complementarism may already have become one of the elements in a new competition for power.[126]

Third, the coincidence between the stages of evolution of Lin's philosophy and the turning points of Party history is not very close. While the content of Lin's views never differed much from the official Party outlook on important topics, the timing of the changes in Lin's philosophical and ideological orientation often led, lagged behind, or were seemingly unaffected by changes in Party status, policy, and historical direction. Thus, 1950 was not the philosophical-ideological watershed to Lin that it was, historically and administratively, to the Party. On the other hand, the initiation of the Cultural Revolution in 1965 was indeed a turning point for both. Fourth, Lin's relationships with other members of the Chinese elite varied considerably, both in time and with regard to their relative positions in the hierarchy. With Mao, with but two or three exceptions he was the model son. With Chou, he was the close colleague. Toward his military superiors, Chu Teh and P'eng Teh-huai, he was formally and properly subservient but, behind their backs, competitive and, when it paid him politically, derogatory and sometimes vindictive. With subordinates, he was always protective and fatherly as long as they accepted his leadership and did not attempt to compete with him politically or to maneuver behind his back. Once he perceived that a subordinate was moving against him, he quickly ousted the man. But even then he apparently did not entirely break with him personally or ideologically.

In addition to these specific conclusions, several generalities emerge. We have spoken above of the desirability of drawing lines of connec-

---

and here is where one often finds a definite administrative and decision-making style. For a perceptive and methodologically innovative study of this level of the Cuban Communist elite, see Edward Gonzales, Luigi Einaudi, Nathan Leites, Richard Maullin, and David Ronfeldt, "Divisions within the Cuban Leadership" (Santa Monica, Calif.: The Rand Corporation, R-754, forthcoming).

[126] For some further suggestions on comparative political styles, see pp. 293–95 of "Chou En-lai and the Cultural Revolution," Chap. iv of Thomas W. Robinson (ed.), *The Cultural Revolution in China* (Berkeley and Los Angeles: University of California Press, 1971).

tion between individual and aggregate studies of the Chinese Communist elite and of the dangers associated with assuming that generalizations found applicable in one area can without qualification be transferred to the other.

Second, elite studies need to be linked with the study of political succession. Consider the question: If Lin Piao was, as appears to be the case, a cross-sectional representative of the Chinese Communist elite, would not the probability of his succession to Mao Tse-tung's post seem to be quite high? A rather appealing argument could be made that, when a new revolutionary group comes to power and when that group is headed by a strong, sometimes charismatic leader, first-generation succession will go to one of a small number of individuals who are within the original revolutionary group, sociologically representative of that group, ideologically acceptable to various elements and factions within it and, possibly, to society at large, and whose power base and personal qualities fit the changing demands of administering and modernizing the society after the founder is gone.[127]

Lin seemed to fit this set of characteristics. Do others in the present ruling group? Both individual and aggregate studies are needed to answer this question. Moreover, the changing sociological character of society must be taken into account in determining the representativeness of certain individuals and the longevity of the first generation succession. In China, the original generation (or several generations) of revolutionary rulers is now passing from the scene, while that country is experiencing rapid modernization and, probably, increasing bureaucratization. These factors might greatly change the required characteristics of the successor generation of rulers. Once again, individual and aggregate elite studies are needed, but now of the emerging group of successor elites, and they must be researched in terms of the emergent and changing characteristics of Chinese society.

Finally, given the nature of the elite studies in this volume (which fill a large gap in our knowledge of the Chinese Communist leadership), the way is now much more open for comparative work. This can be done in terms of both aggregate and individual elite studies. It can also be done by comparisons between Communist, Western, and de-

---

127 Just to name a few instances: Soviet Union, Lenin-Stalin; India, Gandhi-Nehru; Egypt, Nasser-Sadat; Turkey, Ataturk-Inono; East Germany, Ulbricht-Stopf; Poland, Gottwald-Gomulka. This can even be extended to democracies in those instances where one party possesses (however temporarily) an overwhelming percentage of the vote. Thus, West Germany, Adenauer-Erhart; France, de Gaulle-Pompidou; England, Churchill-Eden.

veloping societies and politics. For instance, a number of generalizations have already emerged with regard to elite characteristics and trends in the Soviet Union and East Europe.[128] Rapid bureaucratization has meant the rise of rational-technical criteria for elite recruitment and the decline in the prescriptive role of ideology in decision-making. Once the Party stabilizes its rule, there is an increasing tendency to submerge intraelite conflict (which, to be sure, still continues) and a tendency to loosen gradually the interlocking bonds between state and Party machines. Members of the elite tend to be better educated, more homogeneous, less likely to be of proletarian origin, and more prone toward administrative (rather than ideological) posts. If we presume that China under Communist rule will eventually develop in a manner similar to that of the Soviet Union and East Europe, Lin Piao makes a good case study in several of these instances. Beginning as a "military specialist," by the end of his career Lin had to be regarded as a "political-military-administrative generalist." He surely regarded ideology as not so much prescriptive as justificatory. With regard to intraelite conflict, he was the last to publicize political disputes, although, given his declarations on politics, perhaps the first to fight. Perhaps this is what got him into trouble in 1971. He must be considered to have been a relatively well-educated administrator who liked, moreover, to surround himself with colleagues of the same views and background. Thus, even in the case of comparison between the profile of Lin Piao and of those who are possible future leaders of China, he stands out as one who well fits the demands of the times.

[128] See, in this regard, William A. Welsh's study, "Toward a Multiple-Strategy Approach to Research on Comparative Communist Political Elites: Empirical and Quantitative Problems," in Frederic J. Fleron, Jr. (ed.), *Communist Studies and the Social Sciences: Essays on Methodology and Empirical Theory* (Chicago: Rand McNally & Co., 1969), pp. 323–26.

PART III

Subnational Elites

VICTOR C. FALKENHEIM

Provincial Leadership in Fukien: 1949-66 *

This study addresses itself to the analysis of power and authority at the provincial level in the Chinese political system since 1949. The vehicle of the study is a detailed analysis of provincial administration in Fukien province between 1949 and 1966, with the objective of determining the degree of autonomy or latitude with which provincial leaders exercise their functions. It is, in short, an attempt to describe the nature of central-provincial relations and the determinants of that relationship using a single province as a case study.

We therefore focus on provincial *leadership* rather than on the traditional categories of elite analysis.[1] Most elite studies deal with the processes of elite recruitment, mobility, access, and training, relating them to the stability and performance of the political system. Two considerations have dictated the choice of an alternative focus for this paper. The first is the nature of the problem selected for study. Our goal is to describe the behavior of political leaders at the provincial level in an attempt to assess the nature of their power within the broader political system. Until more local and regional studies of this type are undertaken, studies of national elites will perforce be incomplete. Second, our understanding of provincial political processes is still so rudimentary that it is difficult to identify in a meaningful way who exercises what kinds of power at the provincial level. Until the

* I am indebted to Professors Michel Oksenberg, Robert A. Scalapino, and Richard Baum for their helpful comments on the initial manuscript.

[1] The term "leadership" used here refers to the top-ranking provincial cadres (*sheng i-chi kan-pu*) who manage provincial affairs as well as to the roles they perform in discharging their provincial management functions.

various perimeters and interrelations among subnational elites are established, most types of elite analysis are premature. Both of these problems are compounded by the ambiguities in the concept of power itself when that concept is applied to the analysis of provincial politics.

POWER AT THE PROVINCIAL LEVEL: PROBLEMS OF ANALYSIS

The contemporary literature on China is filled with references to the existence and exercise of provincial power. By most analysts provincial leaders are conceived of, either explicitly or implicitly, as separate and competitive power-holders, with significant interests to defend and the requisite resources to defend them. A number of writers have tended to describe the relationship between the provinces and the central government as in part a bargaining relationship. Central leaders are portrayed as trading policy concessions for provincial support in national political councils; provincial foot-dragging or oblique resistance to central demands are common themes in such discussions. In short, the intuitive conviction that the provinces are in some sense genuinely powerful has been widespread and compelling.

That this is the case should not be surprising. Provinces have traditionally been important political and administrative units in the Chinese bureaucratic state. As administrative units they have displayed a striking degree of administrative and territorial continuity; and such continuity suggests that they are more than artificial administrative contrivances. Many provinces in fact are natural topographic, economic, and linguistic units, which during periods of dynastic decline or interregnum have become virtually autonomous. All strong centralizing regimes in Peking have faced the problem of stemming the recurrent tendency to provincial separatism. The memories of twentieth-century warlordism are sufficiently sharp in our consciousness to lead many observers to doubt that even in the highly centralized Chinese state of today the problem of provincial loyalties has been fully solved.

In addition, it is an open question as to what degree power can be effectively centralized in a society at the particular stage of development marking China today. Marion Levy has argued that a high level of centralization can only be imposed on an integrated society with a modern communications and logistic network, two preconditions just beginning to emerge in contemporary China. Audrey Donnithorne, in her study of the Chinese economic system, has noted the presence of strong autarchic tendencies at the provincial level.[2] It therefore seems logical to assume that the conditions of early modernization, combined with the size of this massive state, dictate a large role for regional and provincial governments, the only agencies able to provide the flexibility needed in the successful implementation of central policy.

Evidence supporting a contention that regional administrators play a meaningful role in the policy process today can also be derived from Communist Chinese administrative theory. Chinese administrators at all levels are enjoined to adjust policy in accordance with complex realities. Flexibility and regional adaptation are maxims which guide administrators in the making of all decisions. Furthermore, the frequent criticism of policy "deviations," and the occasional purges of the administrators responsible, demonstrate that administrators often *do* overstep central guidelines in the process of making decisions.

However, these considerations, while persuasive evidence of the continuing importance of provincial-level administration, do not add up to a case for autonomous provincial "power." First, it is clearly necessary to distinguish between the formal statutory and discretionary powers delegated to provincial leaders, and their usurpation of additional informal powers in order to challenge or modify central policy. Most discussions of provincial power stress or, at a minimum suggest, the significance of the latter rather than the former; yet little evidence is adduced in support of the point.

Clearly, imperfections in central directives or inadequacies in the control system do cause administrators in China to make decisions that run counter to central preferences. Evidence that such "deviations" are occasionally deliberate and systematic, stemming from parochial interests and perspectives, can be found in the rare attacks on "localism" and "departmentalism" at both the local and provincial levels. During the antirightist campaign of 1959 and the Great Proletarian Cultural Revolution (1966–68), provincial leaders were charged with having consistently undermined central policies, in some cases by arguing for the exemption of their provinces from the effects of national policy on the ground of "special circumstances," and in other

[2] Marion J. Levy, Jr., *Modernization and the Structure of Society: A Setting for International Affairs*, 2 vols. (Princeton, N.J.: Princeton University Press, 1966), I, 17; Audrey Donnithorne, *China's Economic System* (London: Allen and Unwin, 1967), pp. 504–5.

cases by deliberate obstruction. Many provincial leaders were charged
with making "mountain strongholds" of their provinces, that is, making
them immune to central pressure. Though such charges are clearly
exaggerated, as the later vulnerability of these leaders demonstrates,
they do suggest some of the mechanisms by which provincial leaders
attempt to influence the policy process: the selective control of information; the selective reporting of data upward; the selective trans-
mission of central directives to subordinate units; and the cultivation
of "illicit" local and central alliances.

These categories of action correspond to those discovered in other
situations of bureaucratic policy-making. Modern administrative and
organization theory have demonstrated that even in the most centralized organizations, power is partially dispersed. Though in theory
power in such organizations is exercised from the top down, in fact
the middle echelons, by virtue of their strategic position astride the
channels of communications and their control of informational resources, do exercise influence in the policy-making process. The case
for provincial power, however, requires that it be shown to be autonomous. This case is difficult to make in the face of the clear ability of
the central government historically to exact compliance of provincial
leaders when desired and to remove them from office when deemed
necessary.

It is plausible to suppose that provincial leaders possess a distinct
set of perspectives and interests, but it is far from easy to see how
these are translated into action. What are the mechanics of provincial
influence? How can we distinguish between legitimate and illegitimate
influence, between formal and informal power? The distinction is both
critical and exceedingly difficult to draw. Some evidence on this point
is available in the rare instances prior to the Cultural Revolution when
provincial leaders were purged. But there are many provinces where
no such purges occurred between 1949 and 1966. Fukien was such a
province. What are we justified in inferring from such a record of
leadership stability? Are we entitled to take it as an index of central
confidence and satisfaction? To a degree, yes. However, purges are
an extreme and relatively infrequent manifestation of central dissatisfaction and as such are too gross an indicator to enable us to monitor
accurately central responses to provincial performance. They simply
show that the purge victims were guilty of exceeding tolerable limits
with respect to policy adaptation. Understanding the normal process
of provincial administrative leadership, however, involves understand-

ing what goes on within those limits and what precisely those limits are.

An additional research strategy might concentrate on studying the variations in timing or content of central programs in a number of provinces. Pilot studies along those lines show that variations in timing, both between provinces and within provinces, are quite common and that variations in the language of provincial directives are also frequent.[3] However, once it is demonstrated that such variations exist, the problem is to interpret their significance. In the absence of purges or criticism, it seems reasonable to infer that the variations occurring were not excessive.

In most political systems the most promising avenue of research is the study of conflict situations. Studies of intrabureaucratic conflict in the United States and the Soviet Union make it clear that allocational priorities are usually the stakes over which the most bitter battles are fought. In the case of provincial leaders in China, one would expect that they would be most acutely concerned over their share of budgetary resources, planned construction, and intraprovincial transfer balances. Some scholars have suggested, for example, that grain-deficit provinces, dependent on the central government for food, might be more responsive to central directives than net grain-exporting provinces. Similarly, one might argue that the economically advanced provinces would be more dependent on the supply capacities of the center and hence more amenable to central direction. While there are indications that such considerations are present in the relationship between the provinces and the central government, the data currently available do not permit us to go beyond speculation.

This leaves us with the problem of discovering some means of probing the complex relationship between the provincial and central governments. The first step in that direction, I would argue, lies in analyzing the different kinds of actual central-provincial interactions in terms of their concrete organizational and policy contexts, in the hope of specifying the different kinds of influence which provincial leaders are capable of marshaling. In general, my findings suggest that provincial leaders, like most upper-echelon bureaucrats, are caught in heavy cross pressures. These cross pressures are embodied in the demands of

[3] My own preliminary comparisons of Fukien with other provinces support this conclusion, as does an excellent study by Frederick Teiwes, "Provincial Politics in China: Themes and Variations," in John M. H. Lindbeck (ed.), *China: Management of a Revolutionary Society* (Seattle and London: University of Washington Press, 1971), pp. 116–89.

the central government for the execution of centrally assigned tasks on the one hand, and in the conflicting needs and problems of their provincial "constituency" on the other. Since the center is the prime source of both rewards and punishments for provincial-level leaders, compliance with central directives is the chief concern of provincial leaders. However, their ability to comply is dependent on a number of factors which reside in their constituency. The capacity of provincial leadership to operate effectively is closely correlated with the quality and number of the cadres it commands, the strength of Party organization at all levels, and the quality of its control system, all of which determine its ability to elicit a high performance level from subordinates. Similarly, the provincial resource base will serve as a source of both constraints and opportunities, conditioning the ability of leadership at this level to comply with central demands.

I therefore propose to begin with an examination of the "constituency," describing some salient elements of the Fukienese historical and social heritage which constituted one set of parameters for provincial leaders. The succeeding section will deal with the structure of provincial administration. In the third section I will discuss the policy-making process at the provincial level, specifying the kinds of roles played by provincial leaders. Finally, I propose to analyze some of the characteristics of the men who occupied the top provincial leadership roles between 1949 and 1966.

THE PROVINCIAL SETTING

In 1949 Fukien was the poorest of the coastal provinces. There were few roads, no railroads, and little industry. What wealth existed was concentrated in the coastal regions, and much of that had been destroyed during the war against Japan and in the last year of the Civil War. Internally, many remote counties could not be reached by motor traffic, and the only land links to neighboring Chekiang, Kiangsi, and Kwangtung lay across low-lying mountain passes.

The poverty of the province and its topography were inextricably linked. Fukien is a small province with a land area of a little over 123,-000 square kilometers. Of the major provinces, only Chekiang and Kiangsu are smaller. Further, only 5 per cent of Fukien's land area is arable plain, and that is concentrated along the coast and in the riverine valleys. The remainder of the province is mountainous and heavily forested. Thirteen million persons, predominantly of Han extraction, live in the region. Even though over 80 per cent of them are engaged in agricultural pursuits, the scarcity of land and the relatively large population has meant constant and chronic grain shortages.

While Fukien in the twentieth century has been a relatively impoverished region, it has enjoyed better days. One of the later-developing provinces, Fukien reached its high point during the Sung dynasty when it served briefly as the hinterland for the Sung capital at Hangchow. Its seaports were then the main ports of China, conducting a flourishing trade with Southeast Asia and the Indies. Intranationally, it was one of the chief suppliers of sugar, tea, and tropical fruits, its total agricultural production exceeding that of Kwangtung. The province's population during the Sung dynasty was relatively large, ranking fourth among the twenty-four provincial units. It was also an important cultural center, with its scholars renowned throughout the empire. During the Ming dynasty Fukien was ranked as a "large" province in the allotment of provincial degree quotas, and during the same era, its per capita production of *Chin-shih* degree-holders (the highest academic degree) was first in the nation.[4]

By the late sixteenth century, however, the province began to reach the ceiling of its growth and the beginning of its long decline. That decline was a product of several factors, most important of which was the rising population pressure on the land. Despite increases in productivity, the province was no longer able to support a growing population. All available land was already under cultivation by the end of the seventeenth century, and by the beginning of the next century it had become a chronic grain-deficit province. As early as the 1600's, Fukienese had begun to emigrate in large numbers to Taiwan, Southeast Asia, and the interior of China. Moreover, the economic decline was accelerated by a serious disruption in the province's external trade resulting from the rise of Turkish power which cut off European trade with Asia, and from the harassment of coastal trade by Japanese pirates. Gradually the major port of the province, Ch'uanchou, became silted in and lost its economic importance. The Ch'ing dynasty's embargo on trade off the Fukien coast during the seventeenth century and the later restriction of trade to the port of Canton dealt a blow to Fukien's trade from which it never recovered. Trade partially picked up again after the opening of Amoy and Foochow to foreign trade as a

[4] Ping-ti Ho, *The Ladder of Success in Imperial China: Aspects of Social Mobility, 1368–1911* (New York: Columbia University Press, 1962), p. 229.

result of the Anglo-Chinese War, but this contribution was offset by the impact of western imports on the traditional handicraft sector of the provincial economy.

Some limited industrialization went on under British and Russian auspices in the late nineteenth century, and the first modern ship-building industry was created by the Ch'ing court at Mamei in the Foochow region at the same time. However, the bulk of the new industrial investment was in light food processing plants, and these suffered heavily after 1894 from the Japanese competitors on Taiwan. The problem of chronic grain shortages and economic decline thus continued into the early twentieth century with little amelioration either by the efforts of the Ch'ing government or through foreign investment.

Little changed in the aftermath of the revolution of 1911. The Fukien civil governor, Hsü Shih-ying, an appointee of Yüan Shih-kai, wrote in the official governor's report of 1914 that the problems of the province were so overwhelming that the provincial government needed vast amounts of central aid to help deal with the problems of rampant disorder and corruption. He apologized for the "radical sound" of the report, saying, "I am sad and frightened and cannot remain indifferent." [5]

Yet little change was possible. Between 1911 and 1926, the province was the constant object of contention among the northern warlords, and between them and the revolutionary government of Sun Yat-sen. Because of its strategic location, both as a defensive barrier protecting eastern Kwangtung and as a path from eastern Kwangtung north into Chekiang, it was invaded three times between 1918 and 1926 by the forces of Sun Yat-sen. Even after its liberation from the control of northern warlords in 1926, the province was unable to shake the legacy of the warlord years. The rapid passage of the Eastern Route Army through the province in 1926 made it impossible to attain any real unification of the province.

Throughout the late 1920's and early 1930's, power remained divided among several groups. Formal control was vested with the navy which garrisoned Foochow and Amoy, controlled the provincial government, and served as the instrument of Nanking rule in the province. However, the government's effective control did not extend very far inland. Powerful militia forces occupied large sections of the province, and, allying themselves with the marine contingents which domi-

---

[5] *Fu-chien shih-ch'ing* (Fukien Affairs) (Tokyo: Ministry of Foreign Affairs, Commercial Bureau, 1917), p. 432.

nated several seacoast *hsien* (counties), they continued to threaten the stability of the Foochow government throughout the early 1930's. In the late 1920's, the Chinese Communist Party (CCP) also carved out a portion of western and northern Fukien which was incorporated into the central soviet. These territories were not recovered until the mid-1930's.[6]

As a result of the continuing political, military, and economic weaknesses of the Foochow government, and the preoccupation of Nanking with asserting control over the larger warlord groups in the north and in the southwest, central control was not effective in the province until 1934. Chiang Kai-shek's determination to expel the Communists from this region resulted in a series of military campaigns within Fukien that led to military unification of the province. The "Min incident" in 1933 was the real turning point, acting as the stimulus that led the national government to establish effective control in Fukien. In January, 1934, General Ch'en Yi, a Chekiang officer, was assigned to Fukien as provincial chairman. He held this post until 1941, and succeeded in a ruthless pacification campaign that genuinely united the region under provincial authority for the first time in twenty years. A series of effective administrative and financial reforms initiated what seemed to be a real development program, when the war with Japan began.[7]

Amoy was occupied in 1938, as was much of the coast in later years. Japanese control in the province, however, was largely limited to coastal sections, and the provincial government which retreated inland to Yungan continued to exercise fairly effective rule over the province to the end of the war. However, most of the bold programs developed during the late 1930's had to be shelved for the duration. During the war, Ch'en Yi was replaced as a result of conflict with the overseas Chinese leader, Ch'en Chia-keng. The new governor was a Hunanese general named Liu Chien-hsu. Liu's administration was unremarkable, and he left in 1948, being replaced briefly by a Fukienese, Li Liang-jung, and then, as the Civil War drew to a close, by Chu Shao-liang.

[6] For an excellent summary of Fukien's political history in the 1920's and 1930's, see *Fu-chien shih-ch'ing* (Taipei: Foreign Affairs Department, Taiwan Governor-General's Office, 1941), pp. 152–64.

[7] Some controversy surrounds the assessment of Ch'en Yi's governorship in Fukien. The findings of nineteen personal interviews with high-ranking former Fukien officials in Taiwan incline me to a charitable view of his performance. A good biographical treatment of Ch'en Yi is contained in Howard L. Boorman and Richard C. Howard (eds.), *Biographical Dictionary of Republican China*, 3 vols. (New York: Columbia University Press, 1967–70), I, 250–54. A summary of the achievements of his regime is to be found in *Fu-chien shih-nien* (Fukien Decennial) (Foochow: Fukien Provincial Bank, 1947).

Chu, a native of Kiangsu, though born and brought up in Foochow, took office in October, 1948. His comment upon his return, though perhaps unfair, might well serve as a conclusion to this section: "It is thirty-nine years since I left Foochow, but I found the city unchanged; if anything, it is even worse." [8] Two centuries of decline could scarcely be arrested by the efforts of the Nanking government after 1934. This fact was, in the most fundamental sense, the reality with which the new rulers of the province would have to deal.

PROVINCIAL ADMINISTRATIVE STRUCTURE

Provincial leadership operates through organization. To analyze leadership without some idea of the scope and nature of that organization is to approach the subject in a vacuum. The primary purpose of this section is to describe the scope of provincial bureaucracy in terms of size and personnel in order to establish those organizational boundaries that may facilitate analysis of provincial leadership. The following discussion is intended to suggest the complexity of provincial administration, not to mirror it. Neither the text nor the charts are exhaustive. Provincial administrative structure underwent a variety of changes as it evolved between 1949 and 1966, but I do not account for the varying organizational and jurisdictional realignments which occurred. Instead, I hope to portray some of the aspects of provincial administration as it stood midway in its development in the early 1960's.

The following charts are a composite portrait drawn from several sources. The most important material is derived from a detailed reading of *Fukien jih-pao* (Fukien Daily), supplemented by information from the press of other provinces. The materials were assembled and supplemented with the aid of refugee informants who worked during the early and mid-1960's in the middle levels of provincial government.

Provincial administration properly encompasses all provincial-level organs of the multiple hierarchies stretching from Peking to the localities. The three most important hierarchies are of course those of the Party, the state administration, and the military. I have omitted the last because information is relatively scarce and because the scope of this particular study is limited.

---

[8] Pai Feng-lou, "Fu-chien hsiang i ko wei-pa" (Fukien Is Like a Tail), *Hsin-wen t'ien-ti* (News around the World) (Shanghai), No. 66 (April 14, 1949).

The structure of provincial-level Party and governmental administrative organs is indicated by Figures 1 and 2. Let me reiterate that these charts are incomplete in several important ways. They omit the provincial-level organs of United Front Groups as well as of the mass organizations. Moreover, the charts barely hint at the complexity of the organs listed on them. Each department, bureau, commission, or staff office is itself a multitiered hierarchy consisting of many functional subdivisions.

When discussing provincial leadership, which organs are relevant to the analysis? Chinese administrative usage is helpful on this point. The Chinese distinguish between three kinds of "provincial organs": administrative organs (*hsing-cheng chi-kuan*), business organs (*shih-yeh*), and enterprises (*ch'i-yeh*).[9] The administrative category includes the vast majority of provincial departments, bureaus, commissions, and staff offices in both the Party and governmental hierarchies. These organs serve in administrative, supervisory, and coordinative capacities to monitor provincial performance of assigned tasks. The other two categories include operational organs involved directly in implementation.

Clearly, operational as well as administrative organs have an impact on policy. Certainly the problems and deficiencies of operational organs exert an influence over the speed and quality of policy implementation, and, in the process, affect subsequent policy decisions. Administrative organs are responsible for assigning tasks and overseeing their execution, and, since it is the administrative organs which bear the prime responsibility for any failure to reach assigned targets, and which in addition must articulate the needs and problems of subordinate units, a study of the leadership function may justifiably confine itself primarily to provincial administrative organs.

This distinction narrows the scope of the study significantly. While *Fukien jih-pao* in 1957 listed a total of 128 provincial-level organs, those with administrative responsibilities barely approached half that number.[10] According to my estimates, on the basis of scattered newspaper sources and refugee interviews, the total administrative staff at the provincial level in Fukien numbers no more than 10,000. This figure represents only a fraction of the total personnel employed in all organs under provincial jurisdiction. Shantung, for example, employed

[9] Refugee interview, Hong Kong, February 20, 1968, Interview Protocol, No. 38.
[10] *Fukien jih-pao*, November 5, 1957.

FIGURE 1

PROVINCIAL PARTY ORGANIZATION

Provincial Party Congress

Provincial Party Committee

Provincial Party Committee Standing Committee

Provincial Party Committee Secretariat
(First Secretary; Second Secretary; Secretaries; Alternate Secretaries)

Secretary General–Deputy Secretary General

Finance and Trade Political Department (*Ts'ai Mou Cheng Chih Pu*)	Industry and Transport Political Department (*Kung Chiao Cheng Chih Pu*)	Agriculture and Forestry Political Department (*Nung Lin Cheng Chih Pu*)	Political-Legal-Coastal Defense Department (*Cheng Fa Pien Fang Pu*)	United Front Department (*T'ung Chan Pu*)	Propaganda Department (*Hsuan Ch'uan Pu*)	Organization Department (*Tsu Chih Pu*)	General Office (*Pang Kung T'ing*)
					Provincial Party Committee Newspaper and Theoretical Journal	Fukien Intermediate Party School (*Fukien Chung Chi Tang Hsiao*)	Documents Office (*Tang An Shih*)
					Provincial Branch NCNA		Policy Research Office (*Cheng T'se Yan Chiu Shih*)

Social Affairs Department (*She Hui Pu*)

Control Committee (*Chien Ch'a Wei Yüan Hui*)

Education and Culture Department (*Wen Chiao Pu*)

Provincial Mass Work Department (*Ch'ün Chung Kung Tso Pu*)

State Organs Committee (*Kuo Chia Chi Kuan Wei Yüan Hui*)

Committee of Directly Attached Organs (*Chih Shu Chi Kuan Wei Yüan Hui*)

Provincial CYL Committee (*Kung Ch'ing T'uan Sheng Wei*)

Foochow City CCP Committee

Amoy City CCP Committee

Special District Party Committees (*Chung Kung Ti Wei Hui*)

FIGURE 2

PROVINCIAL GOVERNMENT ORGANIZATION

Provincial People's Congress

Provincial People's Council

Governor; Vice-Governors

Secretary-General; Deputy Secretary-General

Basic Construction Committee (*Chi Pen Chien She Wei Yüan Hui*)

Economic Construction Committee (*Ching Chi Chien She Wei Yüan Hui*)

Planning Committee (*Chi Hua Wei Yüan Hui*)

Personnel Department (*Jen Shih T'ing*)

General Office (*Pan Kung T'ing*)

Documents Office (*Tang An Shih*)

Statistical Bureau (*T'ung Chi Chü*)

Internal Affairs Office (*Nei Wu Pang Kung Shih*)

External Affairs Office (*Wai Shih Pang Kung Shih*)

Public Security Department (*Kung An T'ing*)

Establishment Committee (*Pien Chih Wei Yüan Hui or Chü*)

Religious Affairs Bureau (*Ts'ung Chiao Shih Wu Chü*)

Nationalities Affairs Commission (*Min Tsu Shih Wu Wei Yüan Hui*)

Civil Affairs Department (*Min Cheng T'ing*)

Overseas Chinese Affairs Commission (*Hua Ch'iao Shih Wu Wei Yüan Hui*)

Foreign Affairs Office (*Wai Shih Ch'u*)

Agriculture, Forestry, and Water Conservancy Office (*Nung Lin Shui Pan Kung Shih*)

- Meteorological Bureau (*Ch'i Hsiang Chü*)
- Aquatic Products Department (*Shui Ch'an T'ing*)
- Water Conservancy and Electric Power Department (*Shui Li Tien Li T'ing*)
- Agriculture and Reclamation Department (*Nung K'en T'ing*)
- Forestry Department (*Lin Yeh T'ing*)
  - Timber Industry Bureau (*Shen Lin Kung Yeh Chü*)
- Agriculture Department (*Nung Yeh T'ing*)

Finance and Trade Staff Office (*Tsai Mou Pan Kung Shih*)

- Marketing and Sales Provincial Cooperative (*Kung Hsiao Ho Tsuo She*)
- Price Commission (*Wu Chia Wei Yüan Hui*)
- Foreign Trade Bureau (*Tui Wai Mau I Chü*)
  - Port Customs (e.g., *Hsia Men Hai Kuan*)
- Food Grains Department (*Liang Shih T'ing*)
- Commerce Department (*Shang Yeh T'ing*)
- Provincial Branch of Agricultural Bank of China (*Chung Kuo Nung Yeh Yin Hang Fen Hang*)
- Provincial Branch of Bank of China
- Tax Bureau (*Shui Wu Chü*)

FIGURE 2 (Continued)

Finance Department (Tsai Cheng T'ing)

Lands and Buildings Bureau (Fang Ti Ch'an Kuan Li Chü)

Service Department (Fu Wu T'ing)

Provincial Construction Bank (Sheng Chien She Yin Hang)

Education and Culture Staff Office (Wen Chiao Pan Kung Shih)

Scientific and Technical Commission (K'o Hsüeh Chi Shu Wei Yüan Hui)

Broadcasting Enterprises Bureau (Kuang Po Shih Yeh Kuan Li Chü)

Cultural Relics Commission (Wen Wu Kuan Li Wei Yüan Hui)

Physical Training Commission (T'i Yü Yun Tung Wei Yüan Hui)

Department of Health (Wei Sheng T'ing)

Bureau of Culture (Wen Hua Chü)

Higher Education Bureau (Kao Teng Chiao Yü Chü)

Education Department (Chiao Yü T'ing)

Industry and Transport Office
(*Kung Chiao Pan Kung Shih*)

Department of Light Industry (*Ch'ing Kung Yeh T'ing*)

Department of Fuels (*Jan Liao T'ing*)

Chemical Industries Department (*Hua Hsueh Kung Yeh T'ing*)

Machine Industry Department (*Chi Ch'i Kung Yeh T'ing*)

Handicrafts Administrative Bureau (*Shou Kung Yeh Kuan Li Chü*)

Urban Construction Bureau (*Ch'eng Shih Chien She Chü*)

Geological Bureau (*Ti Chih Chü*)

Construction Engineering Bureau (*Chien Chu Kung Ch'eng Chü*)

Labor Bureau (*Lao Tung Chü*)

Posts and Telecommunications Bureau (*Yu Tien Kuan Li Chü*)

Civil Aviation Bureau (*Min Yung Hang K'ung Kuan Li Chü*)

Railways Bureau (*T'ieh Lu Kuan Li Chü*)

Electrical Industries Bureau (*Tien Kung Kuan Li Chü*)

Agricultural Machinery Department (*Nung Yeh Chi Ch'i T'ing*)

Metallurgical Industries Department (*Chih Chin Kung Yeh T'ing*)

Commodities Control Department (*Wu Tse Kuan Li T'ing*)

Navigation Department (*Hang Yun T'ing*)

Transport Department (*Chiao T'ung T'ing*)

Highways Bureau (*Kung Lu Kuan Li Chü*)

10,000 provincial cadres in 1957, though in the same year the Shantung industry and mining "system" alone was reported to be employing 400,000 persons.[11] Anhwei, during the 1957 *hsia-fang* campaign, reported that its administrative, business, and enterprise units were staffed by 400,000 persons of whom it was planned to "send down" 80,000.[12]

Thus, if we confine ourselves to those cadres working at the provincial level in administrative capacities, the number is far smaller. It is difficult, however, to be precise in determining the total number of provincial-level administrative cadres. Figures for Kiangsi and Hopei in the mid-1950's list less than 5,000 in the administrative apparatus (*hsing-chen pien-chih*).[13] These figures are significantly lower than the estimate of 10,000 noted above. The contradiction may reside in the fact that the larger figure includes state cadres listed not on the administrative apparatus but as part of subsidiary or attached units. It also may come from the fact that actual staffing at the provincial level often bore only a tenuous relationship to the actual establishment allotted. One pervasive practice of provincial-level organs was to add to existing staff by seconding to their own organs personnel from the enterprise levels. This was more widespread in units with subsidiary enterprises where the budgets were more flexible and where additional staff could be paid from enterprise profits. The Heilungkiang department of agriculture in 1957 had a total staff of 669, of which 217 were listed on the official establishment roster and 452 additional staff members were paid through enterprise appropriations, or profits.[14]

In short, I am eliminating from the empirical universe not only business and enterprise units, but also those provincial-level administrative organs which operate outside the province in liaison capacities, providing marketing, purchasing, and hosteling services. Some of the organizations which operate in the provincial capital are in fact resident service organizations of either central ministries, or liaison organs of *hsien* and special districts government, and are also omitted. Finally, I have omitted all "attached organs" (*fu-shu chi-kuan*), whether "dispatched" or "directly subordinate." While these middle- and basic-level organs of provincial government are operationally sig-

---

[11] *Ta chung pao* (The Masses) (Tsinan), January 22, 1958, translated in *SCMP*, No. 1723 (March 4, 1958), p. 26.

[12] *JMJP*, October 9, 1957.

[13] Michel Oksenberg, "Policy Formulation in Communist China: The Case of the 1957–8 Mass Irrigation Campaign" (Ph.D. dissertation, Columbia University, 1969), p. 53.

[14] *JMJP*, April 21, 1955.

nificant, they do not generate policy, however much their performance may influence it in the long run.

The organization structure described in the figures was the product of steady evolution through the 1950's and early 1960's. The dynamics of that evolution should be mentioned briefly here. The adoption of Russian administrative practices as well as the Russian economic model led to a rapid multiplication of state functions which automatically devolved upon the growing state-Party bureaucracy. Once created, that bureaucracy identified progress with its own growth and diversification, so that the administrative system was further bureaucratized. This bureaucratic growth was seen as dysfunctional to the regime's goals by the mid-1950's, and efforts were mounted to retrench in the state and Party administration, culminating in the movement to "simplify structures" (*ch'ing-chien chi-kou*) and retrench the establishment (*so-hsiao pien-chih*) in 1957 and 1958.

Data from Fukien, Shanghai, Kwangsi, and Hopei indicate practically a doubling of the number of organs attached to the provincial or municipal people's councils between 1952 and 1956, accompanied by an even greater increase in the number of personnel attached to those organs.[15] In the case of Fukien there was also a steady increase in the number of secretarial positions and vice-governorships as well as in the number of leading personnel. The maladies which attached to this expansion were described by Fukien Provincial CCP Committee Secretary Chiang I-chen as inflated organization, chronic overstaffing relative to work needs, overspecialization of functions, and the breakdown in coordination between organs. The problem was, he concluded, that "the province is taking charge of too many things." [16]

The answer to these problems was to abolish allegedly superfluous organizations, merging units wherever possible. Further measures involved compressing the number of levels within a given organization as far as possible and merging administrative and enterprise functions where possible. Provinces were urged to adopt a two-level system internally (*liang-chi-chih*), abolishing many of the smaller subdivisions within their own organizations. The effect of this reorganization in Fukien was a reduction in the number of provincial organs from 128 to 77.[17] The effect was equally drastic elsewhere. In Kwangsi, for ex-

---

[15] *Kwangsi jih-pao* (Kwangsi Daily), November 29, 1957; *Hsin-wen jih-pao* (News Daily) (Shanghai), December 28, 1956; Oksenberg, "Policy Formulation in Communist China," p. 52; *Fukien jih-pao*, November 5, 1957.

[16] *Fukien jih-pao*, November 6, 1957.

[17] *Ibid.*

ample, the number of offices under the provincial people's council was reduced from 48 to 27.[18] In accordance with the reduction of unit numbers and size, many provincial employees were eliminated by reassignment to local production or administrative roles.

The effect of the reforms was of brief duration, because after 1958, with the increase in provincial responsibilities caused by decentralization, the process of expansion began again, with differentiation and specialization the hallmarks of bureaucratic growth. It might also be noted, as a last caveat, that frequent changes in nomenclature occurred during these years, in many cases unaccompanied by any real organizational changes. I will not, except where necessary, discuss these changes.

POLICY-MAKING AND PROVINCIAL LEADERSHIP

Provincial leaders play a primarily prefectoral role within the broader administrative system. They are the agents of the central government in the localities and as such are responsible for overseeing the execution of central policies in the territory under their jurisdiction. Hence provincial leadership is for the most part exercised downward over subordinate units with the object of securing maximum compliance with central demands. To fulfill this responsibility requires that provincial leadership exercise the two related functions of supervision and coordination. In this section I propose to describe these leadership roles, focusing on those points in the implementation process at which provincial leaders may go beyond their simple supervisory and coordinative roles to modify central policy or assert the provincial "interest."

The pattern of provincial controls over subordinate units involves a complex process of interaction that is far from well known. Despite the risks of oversimplification, it seems to me that it is possible to identify and separate analytically four distinct processes in that pattern of control: (1) the process by which the provincial government communicates or assigns objectives or targets to its subordinate units; (2) the process by which the provincial level monitors the speed and effectiveness of implementation; (3) a process of feedback which represents efforts by the lower-level units to modify the assigned targets; and (4) the process of deviation control by which the province deals with the problems that have arisen during the implementation phase. Each phase within these processes creates different kinds

18 *Kwangsi jih-pao*, November 29, 1957.

of opportunities for provincial leaders, though the extent to which they are exercised varies according to organizational context as well.

The figures depicting provincial Party and state administrative structures in the previous section demonstrate the predominance of "branch type" organization based on function. The division of responsibilities according to concrete administrative specialization (*chut'i yeh-wu*) derives in part from Soviet administrative practices and in part from the imperatives of the command economy. These two pressures have created multiple hierarchies which are organizationally relatively self-contained and autonomous command and control systems with their own channels of upward and downward communication.[19] These hierarchies are responsible for the bulk of day to day routine implementation of central policy. One significant dimension of central-provincial relations goes on within these hierarchies between central ministers and the department heads at the provincial level. Intrabranch conflict is thus one aspect of the constant tug of war carried on between province and center.

What are the functions of provincial department or bureau heads? Their most important functions are defined by statute. Each vertical system of authority distinguishes between "leadership" (*ling-tao*) and "control" or "administration" (*kuan-li*). The center lays down the policy guidelines and goals but distributes the concrete administrative responsibilities to the lower levels. This principle is known as "unified leadership and level-by-level control" (*t'ung-i ling-tao fen-tseng kuan-li* or *chi-chung ling-tao fen-chi kuan-li*). Each department will follow a slightly different pattern in the allocation of responsibilities between the central, provincial, special district, county, and enterprise and subcounty levels.

In the early and mid-1950's, formal control over provincial departments' planned targets, staffing, and budgets was vested with the central level. The ability of provincial leaders to modify centrally fixed targets or resource allocations was limited. There were two stages at which provincial influence could make itself felt. One was during the planning stage, when the provinces were invited as part of the planning cycle to comment on and suggest modifications in the preliminary plan

[19] "Kuo-wu yüan kuan-yu sheng, tzu-chih ch'ü, chih-hsia shih jen-min wei-yüan hui kung-tso pao-kao chih-tu te kuei-ting" (State Council Regulations on the Work Report System of Provinces, Autonomous Regions, and Directly Administered Municipalities), in *Compendium of the Regulations and Statutes of the People's Republic of China* (Peking: Fa-lü ch'u-pan she, 1956), I, 542–43.

figures; the other opportunity arose during the policy implementation process.

Mao Tse-tung, in his talk on the "Ten Great Relationships," wrote that there were two kinds of central departments: those that exercised leadership down to the enterprise level, primarily industrial departments; and those which set down targets and working principles and depended on the localities for implementation.[20] The first kind of department makes its influence felt during the planning cycle, the second, during the process of implementation.

The process follows the steps outlined below. The typical department receives a directive specifying a task, laying down rationale as well as the overall goals, but leaving the concrete arrangements to the provincial officials. These officials generally establish some form of ad hoc working committee to rough out the schedule of implementation, estimating the personnel needed and the effect on the other responsibilities of the department. If the task is not top priority, the working committee will probably establish several experimental points to test their tentative program. They will also call on the lower levels to begin to set up similar experimental points of their own.

The experimental points (*shih-tien*) are intended to yield data on the impact and effectiveness of the policy in preselected regions with varying characteristics. If the program is economic in nature—for example, involving the application of a new agricultural implement or technique—experimental points are selected in mountain regions, hilly regions, and plains areas. If the program is political in nature—for example, involving an assault on "local superstitions"—the key points will be selected according to the strength of the local political organization and past performance in such campaigns, that is, advanced (*ch'ien-chin*) regions, median (*chung-chien*) regions, and backward (*lo-hou*) regions. Where the program or policy is successful, its experiences will be distilled into "models" for further application. Similarly, any difficulties encountered also yield their lessons and contribute to the final policy package. Once some preliminary experience is gained in the early stage of implementation, the scope of the campaign is extended to "key point" (*chung-tien*) areas, where continuing experimentation and refinement go on and where local cadres from other regions begin to train themselves to return to their own units to apply it. Finally the program becomes universal, with the lessons and experience acquired in the "experimental points" and the

[20] Jerome Ch'en (ed.), *Mao* (Englewood Cliffs, N.J.: Prentice-Hall, 1969), pp. 65–85.

"key points" being extended to the rest of the territory (*mien*).[21]

During this process there are considerable opportunities to influence the actual substance of policy. Some of the charges arising during the Cultural Revolution indicate that manipulating the experiences of experimental and key point areas to yield an outcome which would support one's own policy preferences is one technique available to provincial leaders or central leaders. I have found no evidence of such practices in Fukien, and refugee informants are skeptical about the frequency of them. They believe "models" are subjected to such close scrutiny that it is almost impossible to conceal any blatant manipulation of resources or personnel.

However, short of such manipulation, it is quite clear that directives acquire specificity and substance in the process of implementation and occasionally undergo modification. The provincial level is in constant touch with central authorities during this process. Its reports go up regularly, both at fixed intervals and on an unscheduled basis. Central investigating teams also send back reports. Provincial-level officials frequently seek guidance or aid (*ch'ing-shih*) from central officials by post or phone. The rationale of these "methods of work" lies precisely in the fact that they cut down on deviations (*p'ien-ch'a*). They are, however, slow and for that reason are not always observed.

The central level has several options for keeping especially close control over a given program. It can place responsibility for the program directly on the shoulders of the provincial Party first secretary. Or, alternatively, it can summon the responsible provincial department head to a conference at which the detailed work arrangements for a program are prescribed. In such cases, the study of official public directives is of no help to the researcher, for the specific central instructions will be presented either orally or in a restricted document. Of course, if the provincial departments have run "experimental points" prior to the conference, their views and experiences can have some influence on the outcome.

The course of a campaign may often extend over more than a year. In such cases, the accumulation of experience results in the ever tighter formulation of policy summarized in the experiences of various model units or regions. The longer the campaign runs, the less latitude is available to provincial leaders.[22]

---

[21] The term *"mien"* is a residual category including all territory which is neither part of an experimental point nor a concentration point.

[22] Refugee interview, Hong Kong, April 3, 1969, Protocol No. 56.

The crucial role of the provincial-level units is to ensure the implementation of central directives. During this implementation, provincial leaders may try to influence the character of the campaign in various subtle ways. If they fail to modify central targets or policy yet wish to evade the directives, their only recourse is to abdicate their supervisory functions and turn a blind eye to local-level "deviations." This form of evasion does not seem common.

To this point I have been examining one specific kind of central provincial interaction, that which occurs between two levels of the same hierarchy. It is useful to examine differences among hierarchies in this respect, for the patterns are almost certain to differ. For example, commercial departments with more budget flexibility probably have greater opportunities to circumvent central control than do departments without the same flexibility. Departments with critical political functions, such as the Public Security Department, maintain tighter control than does the Agriculture Department, for example. However, an even more important variable is the relationship between heads of provincial departments and their own regional superiors, that is, the Provincial People's Council and the provincial Party committee.

In any conflict between a provincial department head and his superiors at higher echelons, the natural ally of the department chief is his provincial Party committee. The members of the provincial committee are his superiors both in rank and political standing. An appeal for additional resources or for the funding of additional programs has a far better chance of succeeding if supported by the provincial first secretary. There is a natural identity of interest between the first secretary, who in a corporate sense represents the provincial interest, and the department head. It is to the former's interest to ensure that the province has the necessary resources for the multiple functions assigned to it; since he is judged on the overall performance of all sectors of the state administration. One important variable enabling provincial hierarchies to deal successfully with the center is the degree of support from the provincial committee.

The notion that the provincial Party committee represents the "provincial interest," however, requires further scrutiny, as does the relationship between the provincial committee and the Provincial People's Council and subordinate departments. The strength of "branch type" organizations in China created certain rigidities that were soon realized. The control that each departmental system exercised over the resources at its disposal made it difficult to plan regional programs that fully exploited available personnel, equipment, and transport facilities in a coordinated way. The difficulty of coordinating and concentrating resources often created situations of waste and underutilization. Aside from the political implication of such a situation, the economic consequences were also unhealthy, particularly in a system which stressed the "blitz" campaign to such a degree. The very essence of the "campaign" was the concentration of all available resources for a limited time to one or a few limited goals.

The answer was the principle of "dual control" (*shuang-fang ling-tao*) which imposed on provincial-level organs a dual subordination, both to the higher echelon within the department and to the provincial Party committee and Provincial People's Council. This principle posed some difficulties in operation, however. Given dual control, which was to prevail in any given instance of conflict? During the mid-1950's, vertical authority (*t'iao t'iao*) generally prevailed, so that a provincial department head could occasionally appeal an action of his regional authority through his own channels.

It was a foolhardy administrator, however, who would risk the displeasure of his provincial superiors.[23] The authority of the provincial Party committee was important because it was the responsibility of the collective leadership to set the overall priorities, allot available organizational and financial resources according to central priorities (*chung-hsin jen-wu*), and to set the agenda and timetable of provincial work as a whole. This coordinative function of provincial top-level leadership is probably one of its most important responsibilities, endowing it with real influence vis-à-vis its subordinate organs as well as with some leverage in provincial-central relations. However, the function is not vested so much with the provincial Party commitee as with "system" heads.

The term "system" (*hsi t'ung/chan hsien/ k'ou*) came into use in the early 1950's and became increasingly formalized over time. It refers to grouping of departments by similarity of function under a coordinating secretary and staff office. The more common "systems" are the finance and trade, industry and transport, education and culture, political and legal, internal affairs, and agriculture, forestry, and conservation systems. Systems leadership in the mid- and late 1950's became an important focal point in provincial-central relations. In the first place, the systems arrangement enabled provincial leaders to coordinate departmental functions more effectively. Second, it ran inter-

[23] Refugee interview, Hong Kong, November 10, 1968, Protocol No. 19.

ference between the provincial Party committee and the department heads by acting as a clearinghouse for departmental demands. It also provided guidance and support to the departments in their relationship to their own hierarchies. While system heads were staff men without some of the organizational resources of the working organs (*yeh-wu pu-men*), their key positions put them among the most powerful of the provincial leaders.[24] While intrabranch conflict was often mediated within each system, major issues were as a matter of course referred to the provincial Party committee as a whole, and the power of the provincial Party committee in relation to subordinate departments or systems, though relatively powerful, often fell short of the ideal.

Despite the coordinative power of systems and of the provincial Party committee, the rigidities of the highly centralized administrative system became more and more apparent by 1956. In February and March, 1956, the CCP Politburo held a series of hearings attended by thirty-four ministers to discuss administrative reform, among other things. Mao Tse-tung, summarizing part of the conclusions, criticized the system:

> Now there are dozens of hands interfering with local administration, making things difficult for the regions. Although neither the Center nor the State Council know anything about it, the Ministries issue orders to the offices of the provincial and municipal governments. All of these orders are said to have initiated from the Center, thus putting great pressure on the regions. Forms and reports are like floods. This situation must change.[25]

Mao's speech triggered a debate which continued through 1956 and well into 1957 in a variety of forms. Between May and August, 1956, the State Council held a series of national meetings on the problem of excessive centralization. The issue was raised by Chou En-lai at the National People's Congress in June, 1956, and by other central spokesmen at the Eighth CCP Congress in September, 1956. The problem was put most succinctly by Liu Shao-ch'i, who commented that during the past several years "some departments have taken on too many jobs, imposed too many tasks and too rigid restrictions on the local departments. . . . It is unthinkable that in such a big country as ours, the central government could take on itself all the various jobs of the state and do them well." Chou En-lai seconded his remarks in a some-

---

[24] Refugee interview, Hong Kong, September 16, 1968, Interview Protocol No. 10.
[25] Mao Tse-tung, "Ten Great Relationships," p. 75.

what more hesitant fashion, remarking that though provincial-central relations had on the whole been "appropriately" handled, there were some "shortcomings" which could be dealt with by an "orderly" process of decentralization.[26]

The solutions suggested involved a redemarcation of administrative responsibilities and jurisdictions between the central government and the localities, with an increase in the statutory responsibilities of both the provincial government departments and the provincial government as a whole. Liu suggested, for example, that in areas such as agriculture, small and medium industry, local transport, and primary and secondary school education, the central government should be free only to set forth overall policy and principles, with the process of implementation to be vested with the localities. At the same time the coordinative role of provincial government and Party leadership was to be strengthened by giving them the primary overall responsibility for plan fulfillment, and substantial power to shift resources within the region to accomplish that end. The universal implementation of the "dual leadership" principle was to be emphasized, with the understanding that, in general, regional authority was to supersede vertical authority where necessary.[27]

The detailed realignment of spheres of responsibility went on slowly through 1957 on a department by department basis, with administrative reforms in industry, commerce, and finance launched in the fall of 1957, prescribing the differential powers of each level. After the Third CCP Central Committee Plenum in 1957, the Communists began to transfer factories formerly under central management to provincial and local levels. At this stage, the process of decentralization was still somewhat haphazard. As the CCP Central Committee Work Report to the second session of the Eighth CCP Congress pointed out, though decentralization work had begun in 1956, "until quite recently [May, 1958] it was carried out slowly and not at all thoroughly."[28] Only after the Nanning and Chengtu work conferences of the Central Committee did the campaign gather steam with a mandate that the "au-

---

[26] Liu Shao-ch'i, *Political Report to 1st Session of the 8th CCP Congress* (Peking: Foreign Language Press, 1957), p. 77; Chou En-lai, *Report on the Proposal for the 2nd Five Year Plan for the Development of the National Economy* (Peking: Foreign Language Press, 1958), p. 275.

[27] Liu Shao-ch'i, *Report on the Work of the Central Committee of the CCP* (delivered at the second session of the Eighth Congress of the CCP) (Peking: Foreign Language Press, 1958), p. 54.

[28] *Ibid.*, p. 58.

thority to run other economic undertakings, as well as cultural, educational, political, and judicial affairs be handed over to local authorities." [29]

The actual legislation itself made it quite clear that the new provincial and local responsibilities were to be exercised under the very close scrutiny of the central government. Regulations passed at the eightieth meeting of the State Council in September, 1958, provided that the central government be responsible for the overall state plan, and that it retain control over such items as the production targets for the major agricultural and industrial products, the total national wage bill, and the total volume of railroad haulage.[30] The provinces, according to the conditions of the central plan, were to draft enterprise plans for both central and local units, and to take responsibility for the fulfillment of the prescribed state tasks. The central government retained control over the allocation of the principal resources and economic equipment, with some limitations, and was responsible for planning interprovincial transfers of goods "in consultation" with the provinces. The provinces, however, would have the right to reallocate goods and services within the region to ensure plan fulfillment, and in general were endowed with expanded financial resources to deal independently with their newly increased responsibilities. As they had increased control over personnel, labor supply, transport, planning, enterprise profits, and overall regional planning, the regulations provided that the "various enterprises and business units under the central government should apply to planning organs of the province when trying to assure the supply of resources . . . for production." [31]

What was the impact of these actions on central-provincial relations and on the configuration of power at the provincial level? Franz Schurmann argues that central ministries were the "heavy losers" and the regional governments, the gainers.[32] This conclusion is correct, though the reforms had some undesirable consequences as well. One

[29] *Ibid.*, p. 59.

[30] "The Ruling of the Central Committee of the Chinese Communist Party and the State Council on the Streamlining of Planning and Control Systems," adopted by the Eightieth Plenary Meeting of the State Council, December 24, 1958, *Compendium of the Regulations and Statutes of the People's Republic of China*, VIII, 98–99.

[31] "The Regulations of the Central Committee of the CCP and the State Council Concerning the Improvement of the System of Allocation of Resources," September 24, 1958, *ibid.*, pp. 100–1.

[32] *Ideology and Organization in Communist China* (Berkeley and Los Angeles: University of California Press, 1966), p. 210.

problem encountered in Fukien was the difficulty cadres faced in re-orienting themselves to the primacy of regional authority. They had long been accustomed to receiving their principal cues from higher echelons within their own ministries, and it was reported that through-out 1958, "some comrades" continued to act as though the vertical au-thority was superior (*k'uai-k'uai fu-tsung t'iao-t'iao*). Still another problem facing provincial leaders was the loss of control over resources and supplies from outside their regions. Though in theory the center still controlled interprovincial transfers of goods, in practice each region began to divert goods to its own local industries, with a di-sastrous impact on the heavy importers, who found that despite their new-found control over their own resources, their ability to fulfill cen-tral plans was diminished.[33]

The outcome was equally ambiguous for many provincial department heads. Though their administrative responsibilities had increased, they now had to depend on provincial authorities for many resources and services, and they were unable to whipsaw the regional government by appeal to higher echelons. For other departments the only real effect of the reform was to simplify the paper work involved in their relations with the central government, and hence speed up the decision-making process.

The major impact of the reform was on the provincial authorities, in strengthening their power vis-à-vis their own subordinate departments. Their coordinative powers were vastly increased to match their re-sponsibilities. Their latitude to develop innovative programs, lying out-side the scope of central plans, also increased substantially, though these of course were largely constrained by the local availability of re-sources.[34]

However, it is hard to argue that the provinces became more inde-pendent in the course of these reforms. Administrative decentralization had placed new powers in the hands of provincial leaders, but the con-tinuing pressures from a still centralized Party apparatus kept regional Party leaders in line. Provincial leadership came into its own in 1958 when it was given both large responsibilities and comparable powers, and the possibility of more than a narrow supervisory function became a reality. The political nature of provincial leadership also was thrust

[33] K'o Ch'ing-shih, "Ch'uan kuo i p'an ch'i" (The Entire Country Is Like a Chess-board), *Hung-ch'i* (Red Flag), IV (1959), 9–13.
[34] Refugee interview, Hong Kong, October 1, 1968, Protocol No. 14.

to the fore as provincial leaders became the focal point of the multiple pressures from below. In 1958, in many respects, the provincial Party secretary's desk was where the buck stopped.[35]

However, in two other ways, the provincial leaders were as weak in 1958 as they had been in 1955. They were unable or unwilling to depart from central guidelines, which were tightly drawn, and they were often unable to deal with the problems of their provinces. If central support was critical to local development efforts, then turning provincial leaders loose to create their own development strategies was to tie their hands in a much more subtle fashion than previously.

LEADERSHIP ROLES AND PERSONNEL

The preceding sections make it clear that the components of provincial leadership are far from simple. The provinces are responsible for translating central policy into action, and in doing so they must exercise at least three separate functions: supervision, coordination, and what might be called the representative function. These functions are shared by the provincial department heads, the provincial governor's office and staff offices, and the leading cadres of the Party committee. The first two responsibilities are largely in the hands of the staff committees below the level of provincial governor and the Party secretary. The representative function is vested almost wholly with the first secretary and his chief aides and consists essentially of distilling the various departmental demands, the economic and social pressures into a definition of the provincial interest, which it is the responsibility of this group to articulate and advocate. The channels through which such advocacy can take place are limited, and the pressures that provincial leaders can bring to bear are few; but it is a responsibility they must grapple with to perform their tasks well.

The ability of provincial leaders to carry out these multiple functions is shaped by four factors: organizational capabilities; leadership training and experience; political alliances; and leadership style. The first factor is the simplest. Clearly, provincial leadership can be no better than the quality and numbers of the cadres it commands, the strength of Party organization at all levels, and the strength of its control system, all of which determine its ability to elicit a high performance level from subordinates. Provincial leadership is also dependent on its ability to secure reliable information and to assess it accurately, a

35 "Industrial Development in China: A Return to Decentralization," *Current Scene,* VI, No. 22 (December 20, 1968), 3.

process in turn dependent not only on staff organization but also on staff training and experience. The ability to deal effectively with the leaders of specialized hierarchies requires not only some degree of specialized training but also highly developed administrative skills. The ability to "represent" the province requires that provincial leaders enjoy some degree of central confidence. While it may be stretching this relationship to call it "political alliances," this necessary confidence is built on long association and a long record of strong past performance which creates an almost personal and individualized structure of trust.

Finally, we should consider something that might be labeled leadership style, which would consist of one's orientation toward the functions performed. Leaders are individuals and surely vary according to the strength of their ambitions, their abilities, and their attitudes toward risk which must affect the way they play the game of politics in China. If this is the case, we should look to personal as well as organizational factors to explain leadership behavior.

In the remainder of this paper, I will try to sketch a portrait of the top-level leadership in Fukien in light of some of these considerations, discussing some of the experiential and personal characteristics of the provincial leaders during three separate periods: 1949–54 (the takeover generation); 1954–57 (the first five-year plan leaders); and 1958–66 (the Great Leap Forward and recovery). I also propose to discuss briefly intraleadership cleavages during these periods.

PROVINCIAL LEADERSHIP: 1949–54

The men who took up leadership positions in Fukien in 1949 were the leaders of a society in transition. It was their job to establish Communist political, economic, and military control in the province. What kind of men were they, and how well were they equipped for the delicate and arduous job they had assumed? One scholar has argued persuasively that east China, and Fukien as well, was "inherited" by the leading officers of the Third Field Army.[36] In this section I would like to examine the origins of the new provincial leadership in the light of this proposition.

Because this paper is concerned with an analysis of the exercise of provincial power, I omit from consideration two categories of provincial leaders—the Nationalist "holdovers" and the high-ranking and prestigious non-Communist sympathizers, often known as "democratic

---

[36] William W. Whitson, *The Chinese Communist High Command, 1927–71: A History of Communist Military Politics* (New York: Praeger, 1972).

personages." This category includes several high-ranking provincial officials, including provincial vice-governors such as Ch'en Shao-kuan and Ting Ch'ao-wu. Though the scarcity of well-trained cadres dictated the utilization of Kuomintang (KMT) "holdovers," and the imperatives of the United Front and the desire to create instant legitimacy dictated the prominent use of former high-ranking Nationalist officials, these men often served little more than ceremonial functions. This is particularly true with respect to well-known overseas Chinese leaders, like Ch'en Chia-keng, who were expected to ease the transition by maintaining the confidence of overseas Chinese communities and the flow of remittances as well.

If one exempts the above groups from consideration, the post-1949 Fukien leadership consisted of three groups: (1) the occupying military forces; (2) the cadres of the underground and guerrilla movement in Fukien; and (3) the southbound work teams which accompanied the Third Field Army into the province. These were the groups dominating the institutions from which power flowed—the provincial CCP committee, the provincial governor's office, and the local military control commissions. Table 25 indicates that over 60 per cent of the cadres in the Amoy municipal bureaucracy were either military cadres, guerrilla cadres, or southbound cadres. Though the data are derived only from Amoy, the proportions are likely to be similar at least in other urban coastal sectors like Foochow and Ch'uanchou. Furthermore, the top-ranking leadership at all levels was predominantly drawn from military and guerrilla cadres.

It is difficult to get figures for county-level government, but it is possible to document the fact that the ranking cadres in at least four counties were northerners, many of whom had come south with or in the train of the People's Liberation Army (PLA) forces.[37] Scattered evidence suggests that this is also true of special district offices. In the case, for example, of Min-hou Special District (in the Foochow region), the district CCP secretary, Ch'en Hsing-yuan, was a former central Fukien guerrilla leader; but the head of the district government (chuan-yuan), Wen Fu-shan, was a southbound cadre, as was the commander of the military subdistrict. A 1949 analysis by the Investigation Bureau of the Nationalist Ministry of Affairs has argued

---

[37] *Fu-chien sheng fei-wei ch'ing-k'uang tiao-ch'a ch'uan-pao* (A Special Report on the Bandit Situation in Fukien Province) (Taipei: Ministry of Internal Affairs, Investigation Bureau, 1949).

further that real power in Min-hou Special District was in the hands of Wen Fu-shan and that Ch'en, because of his lack of administrative experience and understanding of central policy, had been shunted almost exclusively into "support the front" work.[38] The implication is clear that even where local cadres held top Party positions, real power lay in the hands of the military cadres.

Actually, the top-level leadership was more complex in origin than the distinction between southbound and local cadres suggests. One

TABLE 25

DISTRIBUTION OF AMOY CITY GOVERNMENT CADRES
BY JOB AND ORIGIN (1950)

	Old Liberated Areas	Military Forces	Guerrilla Areas	South-bound Service Corps	KMT Holdovers	Total
Secretarial Office	20	11	4	1	11	47
Civil Affairs Bureau	7	—	6	1	2	16
Finance Bureau	20	1	11	2	59	93
Construction Bureau	4	—	11	2	5	22
Education Bureau	5	1	18	2	3	29
Industry-Commerce Bureau	2	—	9	11	—	22
Trade Bureau	6	2	5	10	5	28
Overseas Chinese Bureau	1	—	9	3	2	15
Health Bureau	1	21	4	20	20	66
Public Security Bureau	25	16	6	35	94	176
People's Court	2	4	5	1	16	28
Kai-yuan Ch'ü Office (*Kung suo*)	—	1	2	1	7	11
Ssu-ming Ch'ü Office	—	1	3	1	4	9
Hsia-kang Ch'ü Office	1	—	3	—	5	9
Hsiang-shan Ch'ü Office	4	—	5	—	2	11
Kulang-yü Ch'ü Office	2	—	2	—	5	9
Total	100	58	103	90	240	591

Source: Adapted from *Hsia-men shih-cheng* (Amoy City Government), June 1, 1950, III, 64.

[38] *Ibid.,* p. 2.

ought to distinguish at least four separate groups among the top-level leaders. One was composed largely of southerners, mainly Fukienese, who had joined the "revolution" in the late 1920's, served in the guerrilla or main force units in the central soviet region during the early 1930's, and remained in former soviet regions after the Long March in 1934. They proceeded to fight in what has become known as the "three-year guerrilla war" until the end of 1937, and regrouped into units of the New Fourth Army in 1938. Under this rubric, individuals in this group then fought in Central China for the rest of the war with Japan, with the New Fourth Army being reorganized into the East China Field Army, and later the Third Field Army during the Civil War. This group was stamped by the rigors of this long, isolated, and exceedingly difficult period of guerrilla activity during which they were often without any contact at all with the Party center. They differ in experience from what we might identify as a separate group of New Fourth Army leaders, who were recruited during the campaigns in Central China.

Chalmers Johnson's study of the growth of the New Fourth Army cites some revealing statistics compiled by the Japanese which indicate that of 210 officers listed for the third column of the New Fourth Army, only twenty-three were from Fukien, whereas two-thirds or 140 were from Kiangsu.[39] Thus at least one group of New Fourth Army personnel which took up leadership positions in Fukien was without roots in the early struggle in the central soviet region and without personal ties of any sort with the area.

A further group of leaders had the same career characteristics as the first group through 1937, but it was given the responsibility of carrying on the underground struggle in Fukien and in the border region after 1938. These men fought underground against great odds and without any real success for eleven years, almost totally cut off from central guidance. Their life of hit-and-run guerrilla raids kept them in constant motion and gave them little chance to acquire any administrative skills. During this period the local soviets were all but dismantled by vigorous KMT efforts, and virtually the only technique they were able to master was survival.[40]

The cadres in the fourth group were members of the southbound work teams which consisted largely of young activists or adminis-

[39] Chalmers Johnson, *Peasant Nationalism and Communist Revolution* (Stanford, Calif.: Stanford University Press, 1962), p. 155.
[40] See *Hung-ch'i p'iao-p'iao* (The Red Flag Waves), Vol. XI.

trators working in the regions under the New Fourth Army and the field armies, who came south with the main forces. Among this group were some high-ranking cadres who had spent years in the "early liberated" areas of North China and who were transferred south into Fukien in 1949 and 1950. Further distinctions without these groups would be valuable because the zones of guerrilla operations within Fukien were quite separate (south, southwest, east, central, and north Fukien), with different Party committees, such as the South Fukien Special Committee, leading separate guerrilla units. These zones formed the basis of regroupment into the different units of the New Fourth Army and later the field armies, and they formed separate bases of operations for those cadres who continued to fight underground after 1938. It seems likely that quite separate networks of personal loyalties were formed on these bases.

Because Fukien remained under "military control" until 1952 and because the military role was prominent in the province during the takeover years, it is appropriate to include the top posts in the Fukien Military District and the military control commission as well as the top cadre posts in the Fukien provincial government and provincial Party committee. Fukien was "liberated" in the summer and fall of 1949, with Foochow coming under PLA control on August 17 and Amoy in October. The leading Party and civil organs were staffed immediately after the provincial government was set up on August 26, 1949.[41] A provincial governor and two vice-governors were appointed, as well as the mayor and vice-mayor for Foochow city. On September 15, 1949, NCNA listed the occupants of the posts of secretary-general of the provincial government and fourteen major department heads. The provincial Party committee and the Amoy and Foochow city CCP committees were formed and staffed. The leading cadres of the Fukien Military District were announced somewhat later, as were some of the posts on the provincial military control commission. In 1951, after the First Provincial People's Representative Conference, the government was composed of one provincial governor, four provincial vice-governors, and thirty-eight members. Aside from the inclusion of a few new leading "democratic personages," its composition reflected few changes over the government appointed two years before.[42]

Of the fifty men I have identified in the top Party, government, and military posts, only nineteen are traceable in terms of their pre-1949

[41] NCNA, Peking, August 26, 1949.
[42] *TKP* (Hong Kong), January 9, 1952.

career lines, and of those nineteen only thirteen can be identified by provincial origin. It is largely profitless to attempt a portrait of this group in terms of education or social status, given the lack of data. They are, needless to say, almost all experienced in conventional and guerrilla warfare, which requires leadership and administrative skills that one presumes could be turned to account in a postrevolutionary society.

Of greater interest is the question of how the top leadership posts were distributed among the major groups mentioned before. I have listed them in the following table by career category and by position. The fact that one man may occupy multiple leadership positions accounts for the discrepancy in the totals.

TABLE 26

DISTRIBUTION OF TOP LEADERSHIP POSTS AMONG THE PRE-1949
CAREER CATEGORIES

Leadership Posts	I (Early New Fourth Army)	II (Late New Fourth Army)	III (Guerrilla Movement)	IV ("South-bound" Work Teams)
Provincial military district or provincial military control commission	3	4	1	—
Provincial governor or vice-governor	2	—	—	1
Provincial government department head or vice-head	—	1	4	1
Provincial secretary or deputy secretary	1	—	1	—
Provincial Party committee member or provincial Party department head or deputy	—	—	7	1

The figures, tentative as they are, indicate that the Fukien guerrillas were relatively well represented both in the Party hierarchy and at the departmental level of the provincial administration. They were far less well represented on the leading provincial military bodies, and they did not control any of the highest levels of any hierarchy. Native Fukienese were strikingly well represented, with eight of the nineteen born in Fukien or claiming it as their native area. The top three cadres in the province, Chang Ting-ch'eng, Yeh Fei, and Fang I, were all Fukienese.

Though these figures provide little evidence of discrimination against former guerrilla leaders in terms of job assignments, Nationalist sources have continued to describe the dynamics of Fukien politics in terms of a struggle between the two groups.[43] They distinguish between two groups which held power in Fukien in the early 1950's: the "newcomer" clique (*hsin-lai-p'ai*) and the "local" clique (*t'u-chu-p'ai*). The newcomers are represented by Yeh Fei and Chiang I-chen; the "locals," by Tseng Ching-ping, Huang Kuo-chang, and Liu Yung-sheng. According to these accounts, Tseng and Huang were aroused by the neglect of old revolutionary cadres and mounted an attack within the Party, calling for the creation of two provincial assemblies, one in Amoy and one in Foochow, with the latter to come under the leadership of the underground Party members and the former under the border region government. They allegedly dispatched a former guerrilla, Ch'en Chen-liang, once an aide of Mao Tse-tung's, to Peking to accuse Yeh Fei before Mao of having discriminated against the underground Party members during the rectification movement.

The Fukienese cadres I have questioned on this point provide no confirmation, though this is not necessarily conclusive. It is a fact that Tseng Ching-ping, a native of Hainan and leader of the Fukien-Kwangtung-Kiangsi column during the Civil War, was purged for localism in 1956 or 1957. The issue which led to his ouster dealt with the "localism" of the cadres in the old revolutionary base areas. Nationalist sources describe the situation as involving an attempt by former guerrilla cadres in leading positions in the Chin-chiang Special District to arrest and purge northern cadres accused of persecuting the former underground Party members. The accuracy of those reports is difficult to judge, but the following remarks by Yeh Fei at the second session of the First Fukien Provincial Congress lend credence to the report:

Our Party respects and is warmly concerned for those masses and cadres who firmly carried on the struggle in the old revolutionary base areas. During the period of victory in the final liberation, we relied on the great southbound army, utilizing the southbound cadres as our backbone elements . . . to win victory in the string of campaigns: land reform, suppression of counterrevolutionaries. . . . Since liberation, the Provincial Committee has unceasingly strengthened work at the old revolutionary base areas, and moreover has had striking success. . . . Moreover,

[43] *Fu-chien fei-ch'ing yen-chiu* (Research on Fukien Bandit Affairs) (Taipei: Fukien Provincial Government, 1959), II, 1–5.

in the wake of the progress of the revolution, the vast majority of cadres has been promoted [*te-tao le t'i-pa*], and at present more than a few local cadres hold important positions. . . . But some people who are carrying on anti-Party and localist activity deny these facts and slander the correct handling of the problem by the provincial committee and make use of the policy of localization of cadres . . . to damage Party unity, affecting the relations between the Party and the masses. *Last Fall, in the hsien and municipal organs of Chin-chiang Special Districts Ch'uanchou, Hsien-yu hsien, and Nan-an hsien, a high tide of antisouthbound cadre sentiment occurred* during the blooming and contending. . . . The localist elements' so-called concern for the Party, concern for local cadres, and concern for the old revolutionary base areas . . . have but one purpose, to use the people and cadres of the revolutionary base areas as their political capital, thinking of the central Fukien guerrilla areas as their own strongholds. . . . *Local cadres, particularly those who vigorously continued the revolutionary struggle in the north and central Fukien, must thoroughly purge themselves of the mistaken influence of Tseng Ching-ping, including the influence of having spent long years in the harsh conditions of guerrilla combat.* From now on we must continue to train and promote local cadres. Southbound cadres must learn the local dialect and become one with themselves until they are "localized" [*tso tao ti fang hua*] [emphasis added].[44]

Though this passage makes clear that deep-seated intraelite cleavages did exist, particularly at the local levels, with the exception of the purge of Tseng Ching-ping and Huang Kuo-chang, they do not seem to have penetrated to the upper levels. Liu Yung-sheng and Wei Chin-shui fought in central and southern Fukien through the 1930's and 1940's, yet both held positions on the provincial Party committee and in high-level government organs throughout the period 1949–66. Wei, in fact, became governor of the province in 1962. No widespread purges accompanied the attack on Tseng Ching-ping. The problem of localism in Fukien was far less serious than the comparable problem in Kwangtung, simply because the Pearl and East River columns in Kwangtung and the guerrilla movement led by Feng Pai-chü in Hainan were so much more vigorous in the 1940's than were those in Fukien. Guerrilla activity in Fukien after 1938 was never sufficiently widespread or powerful to plant roots.

From the outset of the takeover period a clear division of labor can be discerned among the top provincial leadership. Well before the emergence of the relatively structured systems of the mid-1950's, there clearly emerged a tendency to make individual leaders responsible for broad policy areas cutting across Party and state lines. These men, identifiable not only by their formal Party and state positions but by the frequency of their appearance at work conferences and their de-

44 *Fukien jih-pao*, February 15, 1958.

livery of the major work reports in their policy areas, were the working leaders of the province.[45] The top cadre in the field of military affairs was Yeh Fei, commander of the Tenth Army Group and native of Fu-an county in eastern Fukien. The ranking cadre in charge of finance policy was Fang I, also a native of Fukien with long administrative experience in the "liberated" areas of North China. The leading public security official was Liang Kuo-pin, a New Fourth Army veteran. The chief figure in agricultural policy was Chiang I-chen, a North China guerrilla leader associated during the 1930's and early 1940's with the Bethune Medical College.

Almost all of these men had acquired some experience in their area of specialization prior to 1949.[46] Fang I had held a variety of civil posts during the war against Japan and in 1946 was appointed director of the finance department of the Shantung-Anhwei Border Region government. Liang Kuo-pin had spent part of his career in the New Fourth Army in service on military tribunals. Shih Ying, the leading cadre in the field of commerce, had been director of the Customs Administration in the Northeast China People's Government prior to his assignment to Fukien in 1949. In large part, the top officials in the province were experienced administrators who brought both specialist and generalist talents to their new tasks. They served under the overall leadership of Chang Ting-ch'eng, deputy commander of the Third Field Army and ranking Party, administrative, and military leader in the province.

PROVINCIAL LEADERSHIP: 1954–57

A major redistribution of responsibilities and functions occurred in 1953 and 1954 in the wake of administrative centralization. First, the province came more directly under the supervision of the central government. Second, beginning in late 1952 the central government began to transfer leading cadres out of the provinces to staff the new central administrative apparatus. Between 1952 and the end of 1954, 34 per cent of the fifty top-ranking cadres previously identified in the

---

[45] For the first major series of work reports delivered at the first All Circles People's Representative Conference held in the province, see *Fukien jih-pao*, December 17–26, 1951.

[46] See the relevant biographies in Donald W. Klein and Anne B. Clark, *Biographic Dictionary of Chinese Communism, 1921–1965* (Cambridge, Mass.: Harvard University Press, 1971); *Who's Who in Communist China* (rev. ed.; Hong Kong: URI, 1969); Kuo Hua-lun (ed.), *Chung-kung jen-ming lu* (Biographical Dictionary of Chinese Communists) (Taipei: Institute of International Relations, 1967); Huang Chen-hsia (ed.), *Chung-kung chün-jen chih* (English title: *Mao's Generals*) (Hong Kong: Research Institute of Contemporary History, 1968).

key Party, state, and military posts had been transferred out of the province. Chang Ting-ch'eng, Fang I, Shih Ying, and Wei Kuo-ch'ing all were gone by late 1954.

As a result of these shifts a new leadership lineup emerged in the province. Yeh Fei succeeded Chang Ting-ch'eng in the top military, administrative, and Party posts. Yeh Sung moved into the foremost public security slot vacated by Liang Kuo-pin, and Yang Wen-wei inherited many of Fang I's responsibilities in the financial sphere. Most of the new department heads and system leaders who emerged during this period were men who simply moved up one rung in the hierarchies in which they had served as deputies during the preceding three years. In fact, 80 per cent of those top leaders who remained in Fukien after 1954 were promoted within the systems in which they had previously served. The number of intersystem transfers was remarkably small.[47]

As a result, the characteristics of this second generation of leaders are largely indistinguishable from those of its predecessors. As second-echelon revolutionary and military leaders, their pre-1949 career patterns largely parallel those of their superiors. Significantly, there is no evidence of a redistribution of the top Party, administrative, and military posts among those broad groups of cadres described earlier. A relative balance was preserved between cadres of New Fourth Army and guerrilla origins, despite the rapid fluctuations in career assignments. This balance continued to be preserved well into the 1960's as the personnel system stabilized and turnover rates declined.

PROVINCIAL LEADERSHIP: 1958–66

Despite the broad pattern of stability in the top leadership of the province in the late 1950's and early 1960's, some dramatic changes did take place at the very pinnacle of that leadership. In 1957 Yeh Fei stood at the top of his career: he was commander of the Fukien Military District, first secretary of the provincial Party committee, provincial governor, and had been elected in September, 1956, to the post of alternate member of the CCP Central Committee. In addition, success-ful completion of the Ying-t'an–Amoy railroad had changed the economic and strategic status of the province. For this last reason, among others, it was decided to establish a Foochow Military Region (FMR) consisting of two military districts, Kiangsi and Fukien. The commander of the FMR was also to serve concurrently as the commander

---

[47] See, for example, the career of Lin I-hsin, who transferred from work in Party affairs to political-legal work in the mid-1950's.

of the Fukien front forces. Yeh Fei was appointed to the post of commander as well as political commissar of the FMR.

The speed of Yeh's promotion is difficult to explain. Some analysts attribute his rise to the strength of a "Fukien clique" in Peking consisting of Chang Ting-ch'eng, Fang I, and Teng Tsu-hui, as well as other former Fukien guerrillas.[48] Others attribute his rapid ascent to the strength of his Third Field Army connections.[49] Whether such past career affiliations do pay off in these terms is impossible to verify, but they do make it difficult to explain Yeh's equally rapid descent. By the end of 1961 Yeh was replaced as governor by Chiang I-chen, as commander of the Fukien Front forces and the FMR by Han Hsien-ch'u, and in addition found himself sharing power in the provincial Party committee with a new second secretary, Fan Shih-jen.

There is no simple explanation for Yeh's relative loss of stature. Some sources have speculated on its connection with the failure of the Quemoy bombardment of 1958, which took place in the FMR, Yeh's bailiwick.[50] However, Yeh Fei did not bear operational responsibility for the bombardment. Han Hsien-ch'u, a veteran of the Korean War with experience in modern artillery warfare, had been assigned to the FMR in early 1958 to take charge of the operation. Since Han himself suffered no reprisals for the failure and since Yeh Fei did retain the post of political commissar in the FMR, the scapegoat theory does not seem valid.

It is even more difficult to explain Yeh's relinquishing of the position of provincial governor. It is entirely possible, given the dominance of the Party committee in decision-making after 1958 and the pressures of the dual responsibility, that the action was a voluntary one. Yeh did suffer heavily from a rheumatic condition contracted during the war with Japan, and he was hospitalized briefly in Peking in 1957. It is also possible he was pressured into the decision. Some writers speculate that the center was concerned as well over the potential dangers of a concentration of all local authority in the region in the hands of one man. Others point to Yeh's difficulties with the local cadres, which began to heat up again after his position weakened in 1958. Further, he was responsible, in the view of other analysts, for serious errors in the handling of the overseas Chinese dependents during the Great Leap

---

[48] Interview with Warren Kuo, vice-director of the Institute of International Affairs, Taipei, May 5, 1969.

[49] See Huang (ed.), *Chung-kung chün-jen chih*, p. 515.

[50] *Fu-chien fei-ch'ing yen-chiu*, p. 3.

Forward, and these factors taken together might have made him vulnerable.

Whatever the reasons, by 1961 Yeh held only the top Party position in the province. The second secretary assigned to Fukien in 1961, Fan Shih-jen, was a man with considerable administrative experience at both provincial and central levels. He also had been an old guerrilla colleague of Yeh's during the "three-year guerrilla war" in eastern Fukien. It is possible that Yeh requested his transfer to Fukien, and it need not be assumed that Fan was imposed on Yeh.[51]

Chiang I-chen, who had risen rapidly in prominence in the province after 1950, became governor in 1959. His term of office was cut short when in 1962 he was transferred to the central government as vice-minister of the Ministry of State Farms and Reclamation. There is some evidence that his shift out of the province was in part punitive, since he was condemned in 1961 within the province for his stand on communization and the Great Leap Forward. The evidence on this point, however, is obscure.[52]

Chiang's successor in 1962 was Wei Chin-shui, a native Fukienese from Lungyen in southwest Fukien. Wei had spent the three years between 1934 and 1937 in southeast Fukien leading guerrilla operations, and had remained in the province after the New Fourth Army contingents went north in 1938. He had been a member of the provincial Party committee from the start, specializing in rural work after the completion of land reform in 1952. He had risen steadily inside the Party, achieving the post of Party secretary by 1956. His elevation to the position of governor in 1962 provides a clear indication of the continuing political vitality of local guerrilla cadres.[53] The evidence thus suggests that while general personnel stability was obtained in the province during the late 1950's and early 1960's, the turnover, for reasons not entirely clear, was considerably more rapid in the top administrative post of the province.

The Cultural Revolution marked a sharp break in the continuity of provincial leadership. The accompanying purge struck cruelly at the established Party and state leaders. Virtually every political figure of significance in the province was swept from office under its impact.[54]

[51] *Who's Who in Communist China,* I, 203.

[52] Klein and Clark, *Biographic Dictionary,* pp. 174–75; Kuo (ed.), *Chung-kung jen-ming lu,* p. 101.

[53] Kuo (ed.), *Chung-kung jen-ming lu,* pp. 721–22.

[54] The most detailed though not always reliable list available of purged officials in Fukien can be found in *Shih pao* (Hong Kong), August 24, 1968.

The scope of the personnel removals was so sweeping as to make interpretation difficult. One would have expected the lines of cleavage emerging during the Cultural Revolution to reveal much about the dynamics of political conflict in pre-1966 Fukien. But in fact, they did not. No group was exempt from its impact, and old guerrilla leaders like Wei Chin-shui, relative newcomers such as Second Secretary Fan Shih-jen, New Fourth Army leaders like Yeh Fei—all fell during the Cultural Revolution. The only group to be significantly less affected by the purges was the professional military staff of the Fukien Military District (FMD) and the Foochow Military Region.

If little can be inferred from a list of the purged, it is not much more helpful to examine the composition of the survivors. Three of the eleven vice-chairmen of the provincial revolutionary committee established in August, 1968, were holdovers from the previous administration.[55] All three had been ranking provincial Party cadres since 1949, two of the three having been engaged in public security and procuratorial work and the third in Party organization work and youth affairs. The pre-1949 background of these men is obscure, though none of them seems to have had any connection with the New Fourth Army or the guerrilla movement preceding it. In terms of their post-1949 careers there is little to distinguish these men from their less fortunate peers on the provincial Party committee. The explanation of their survival undoubtedly owes more to their behavior during the course of the Cultural Revolution than their career affiliation before or after 1949.

The prime beneficiaries of the change in leadership were the professional military commanders of the FMR and the FMD. The new chairman of the provincial revolutionary committee was Han Hsien-ch'u, commander of the FMR for the previous ten years. The first vice-chairman was Pi Ting-ch'ün, deputy commander of the FMR. Also prominent on the new committee was Chu Yao-hua, an old New Fourth Army cadre, commander of the FMD, and commander of the 28th Division stationed in Fukien since 1949. Han Hsien-ch'u's emergence as the top provincial leader was not without its difficulties. Han had come under severe criticism in 1967 and 1968 for his rough handling of youthful rebel organizations. That he had substantial support at the center is indicated by Chou En-lai's remark to the representatives of

---

[55] The three men are Yeh Sung, Wu Hung-hsiang, and Lan Jung-yü. For a more detailed examination of the composition and origin of the revolutionary committee, see my "Factional Fukien," *Far Eastern Economic Review*, LXI, No. 35 (August 29, 1968), p. 379.

the mass organizations in which he said, "I don't oppose your attempts to beat Han Hsien-ch'u down, but when he is down you should help him up." [56] Central concern for Han's position is also reflected in a statement attributed to Mao Tse-tung in which he is reported to have said, "Tell Han that there are those who wish to knock him down, but that if he will go to the masses, I will protect him." [57] In a self-criticism delivered in Peking in May, 1968, Han, on behalf of the Standing Committee of the FMR Party Committee, declared his re-pentance and his willingness to reform.[58] Not long after, the new pro-vincial revolutionary committee was established under his leadership.

The leadership which emerged in the immediate aftermath of the Cultural Revolution was clearly a transitional one. Its composition owed as much to a desire to paper over the conflict of the preceding two years as it did to a desire to establish a genuinely new leadership in the province. This explains the unstable amalgam of old Party cadres, revolutionary cadres, leaders of rebel mass organizations, and military men which characterized the new leading provincial body. As a result of its transitional nature, however, it underwent considerable change in the ensuing two and a half years.

Within a year of the founding of the revolutionary committee, its rebel representatives were no longer prominent in its deliberations. And within a year and half the old cadres were playing a much dimin-ished role. By the middle of 1970 it was clear that a new slate of leaders was emerging in the province, staffed by men transferred into Fukien from other regions. These transfers, appointed to the provincial revolutionary committee and the FMR, came to form the nucleus of a rapidly changing leadership core. During 1970 T'an Ch'i-lung, a former Third Field Army cadre with roots in Shantung and the Tsinan Mili-tary Region, was transferred in as a leading cadre in the FMR. At the same time, Pi Ting-ch'ün was transferred to the Lanchow Military Region, possibly in connection with efforts to strengthen defenses in that vital region. Chou Chih-p'ing, a Fourth Field Army officer, former secretary of the Yunnan provincial Party committee, and since 1964 a vice-minister of metallurgical industry, also transferred to the FMR during 1970. At the same time, Wang Chien-an, a close former asso-

---

[56] For the text of Chou's remarks and a detailed chronology of Han's involvement in the Cultural Revolution, see *Chung-kung yen-chiu*, IV, No. 3 (March 10, 1970), 127–36.

[57] *Hsiao ping* (Little Soldier) (Canton), No. 23 (April 30, 1968).

[58] The text of Han's self-examination can be found in *Chan-wang* (Prospects) (Hong Kong), May 1, 1970.

ciate of T'an Ch'i-lung both in the Third Field Army and in the Tsinan Military Region, came to Fukien, possibly in the capacity of second political commissar of the FMR, replacing Liu Pei-shan. Ni Nan-shan, a former deputy commander of the Kiangsi Military District, also shifted to Fukien in 1970, as did Chuo Hsiung, a former Fourth Field Army officer, whose most recent assignment had been as vice-minister of geology between 1955 and 1963.[59]

Throughout 1970, and increasingly in 1971, these men came to play a dominant role in the province and, simultaneously, the holdovers from the former Party committee began to recede in prominence. These trends were confirmed by the composition of the new provincial Party committee elected in April, 1971.[60] Seven secretaries—a first and second secretary and five ordinary secretaries—were elected. None of the three holdovers was appointed to a secretariat position; only one revolutionary cadre obtained a secretarial slot. The remainder consisted of military men or new transfers. Four out of the seven secretaries— Chou Chih-p'ing, T'an Ch'i-lung, Chuo Hsiung, and Ni Nan-shan—had been in the province less than two years at the time of their appointment. Of the seven, five were from Central and North China. With the appointment of this committee the dominance of the old native Fukien guerrilla in the province was decisively broken. A new leadership had been created, one with far fewer ties to the province. Yet it was without question a skilled and experienced team which had been assembled, well able to serve the province. Their ability to do so, however, as in the case of their predecessors, was likely to be shaped not only by their political values and affiliations, but by the enduring constraints posed by the province itself.

CONCLUSION

The problem as originally stated was to investigate the degree of provincial latitude in policy determination. Can it be convincingly demonstrated that provinces do make substantial adjustments in central policy or, alternatively, that they contribute to the formulation of the policies they implement? If so, does the degree to which provinces exercise an independent role vary with socioeconomic, political, or strategic characteristics of the province or with the nature of its top-level leadership?

[59] The personnel movements described in this section derive from a reading of the daily radio broadcasts from Fukien between 1969 and 1971.
[60] NCNA, April 6, 1971.

I have argued that despite the unitary nature of the Chinese administrative system, regional leaders do, within narrow limits, adjust the timing and substance of central policy. To the extent that these adjustments arise from a mandated flexibility, it cannot be argued that provincial leaders possess power in any autonomous sense. The way provincial leaders respond to problems in the implementation of central policy suggests that the primary pressures and stimuli come from above rather than below. Provincial leaders operate within a framework which demands a successful reconciliation of the pressures and problems from below (problems which range from demands for lower targets, more staff, more financial support, and more resources to popular discontent and cadre passivity) with the even stronger pressures from above for plan fulfillment.

Though the provincial leader is clearly caught in heavy cross pressures, these pressures do not result in his independence. The primary avenue to rewards and upward mobility lies in satisfactory implementation of central plans. Provincial leaders are not entirely without resources to deal with the central government, but those resources consist mainly of the mutual confidence generated by long-standing political ties, common ideological bonds, and satisfactory performance over time. It may be that future evidence from other provinces will serve to modify the conclusion presented here, but this study suggests that the case against the "monolithic" model of Chinese politics in the 1950's and early 1960's still remains to be made.

HEATH B. CHAMBERLAIN

Transition and Consolidation in Urban China: A Study of Leaders and Organizations in Three Cities, 1949-53

In the early days of March, 1949, the Seventh Central Committee of the Chinese Communist Party (CCP) met together in the village of Hsipaipo, Hopeh province. For the fifty-odd full and alternate members present, it was a momentous occasion. Twenty years of armed struggle lay behind; total victory in civil war, ahead. "Very soon we shall be victorious throughout the country," said Mao Tse-tung in his report to the assemblage. "This victory will breach the eastern front of imperialism and will have great international significance." [1]

The meeting was more than a celebration of victory, however, for it marked a critical juncture in the movement of the Party to national power. With military victory in sight, Mao and the leadership now called upon members of the CCP and People's Liberation Army (PLA) to shift their attention to tasks of political and social reconstruction and to transform proven military prowess into capacity for effective governance. As Mao continued in his report, "country-wide victory is only the first step in a long march of ten thousand *li* . . . only a brief prologue to a long drama." [2]

For the new leaders of China, problems of political integration were

[1] Mao Tse-tung, "Report to the Second Plenary Session of the Seventh Central Committee of the Communist Party of China (March 5, 1949)," *Selected Works* (5 vols.; New York: International Publishers, 1954–61), V, 373.

[2] *Ibid.*, p. 374.

paramount. And nowhere were those problems more acute than in the urban areas, most especially the large cities of the coast and Yangtze valley. In prior years the essential ingredient of Chinese Communist success had been the effective integration of Party, Red army, and peasantry. Mao and the CCP had come to power through the villages and countryside. To transform that power into authority and thereby consolidate the fruits of military victory, the leaders now had to demonstrate their ability to mobilize and govern the cities. As John W. Lewis has observed, urban China constituted "the main arena for the legitimation of [Mao's] newly-won power." [3] Not until it harnessed the manpower and energy of the cities to its own purposes could the Party hope to achieve its stated goals: "to speedily restore and develop production, cope with foreign imperialism, steadily transform China from an agricultural country and build China into a great socialist state." [4]

How did the new leadership in Peking likely perceive problems of integration in urban China? Given these perceptions, what general strategies did the leaders employ? How did they pursue the goals of pacifying, mobilizing, and managing the cities, and linking the cities to the broader polity? How did strategies develop over time? And over time, how did they vary from place to place, from one city to the next?

Such questions are central to this essay. In brief, we are interested in the general purposes of the central leadership in the early years of the People's Republic, and the general strategies by which the Communist Party came to power in urban China. Our approach is to analyze urban elites—the characteristics of municipal leaders and their relationships to municipal tasks—by focusing upon the three Mainland China cities of Tientsin, Shanghai, and Canton, in the period immediately following liberation in 1949.

This essay is part of a larger study and is relatively limited in scope. Where the broader thesis examines developments over a four-year period spanning the *san-fan* (three anti) and *wu-fan* (five anti) campaigns of 1951–52, the present study concentrates on the period immediately subsequent to liberation. And where the former is partially devoted to a comparative analysis of events in Tientsin, Shanghai, and Canton, here we treat the leadership of these three cities as a single population. We shall have occasion to refer to developments

---

[3] "Political Aspects of Mobility in China's Urban Development," *American Political Science Review*, LX, No. 4 (December, 1966), 906.

[4] Mao, "Report to the Second Plenary Session," p. 373.

over time and variations over space. But the purpose of the present study is not to condense the larger into the space available here; rather, it is to develop a number of concepts and typologies and, most important, to demonstrate the potential value of elite analysis as one approach to the study of contemporary Chinese politics.

Several comments on the data are in order. The term "municipal leaders" refers to those individuals who held high-level positions in one or more of a number of organizational units in the three cities during the period under analysis.[5] The target sample exceeds one thousand individuals; the effective sample, or those who constitute the subject of analysis, is considerably smaller. Depending on the questions posed, it ranges from 450 to 800 leaders. In other words, there are gaps in the data. We have not been able to identify all office-holders; and of those we have identified, many remain "faceless names." [6]

These several hundred individuals by no means represent a "fair sample" of municipal leaders of the early years. An obvious bias arises from the fact that data are drawn from a particular kind of "municipality," that is, a heavily populated center located on the coast. Even within the cities under analysis, there is no way to guarantee that the effective sample is truly representative of all municipal office incumbents. In a sense, however, problems of "fair sampling" are not terribly relevant to our purposes. For it is the very fact of a given leader's "visibility" in the organization which concerns us. And why is this?

The student of elites makes a key assumption, namely, that there is some reason or purpose behind a given individual's presence therein. In his study of the Turkish legislature, for example, Frederick W. Frey makes this assumption quite explicit: "To learn what sorts of people are selected may provide some insight into the processes of selection—the behavior of the selectors." [7] Accordingly, we make the following assumption in the present study: more likely than not, an

[5] These units include not only the bureaucratic structure and municipal council, but also various party organizations, consultative committees, and the garrison command. For a more complete enumeration, see Tables 33 and 34.

[6] We have identified a total of 808 individuals holding office during the years 1949–53: 220 in Tientsin, 297 in Shanghai, and 291 in Canton. Discrepancies between target and effective samples are due, of course, to the nature of the sources available. Dealing as we are at the subnational level, such systematic sources as official appointment lists, directories, and "who's who"-type publications are few and far between. Positional and biographic information has come largely through a close reading of the local press: in Tientsin, *T'ien-chin jih-pao* (Tientsin Daily) and *Chin-pu jih-pao* (Progressive Daily); in Shanghai, *CFJP;* and in Canton, *NFJP, Wen-hui pao* (Cultural Exchange Daily), and *Kuang-chou jih-pao* (Canton Daily).

[7] *The Turkish Political Elite* (Cambridge, Mass.: M.I.T. Press, 1965), p. 23.

individual's presence in certain areas of municipal organization was the result of deliberate policy on the part of leaders at higher levels, specifically, the central Party leadership in Peking. In other words, to achieve certain purposes, the central leadership exercised its power over personnel selection and appointment in order to make "visible" certain types of leaders in certain areas of urban organization.[8] Moreover, as purposes changed, or as they varied with respect to different locales, so did relationships vary between leaders and organization. Thus, "visibility" of different types of leaders and "changing visibility" over time are critical phenomena. In effect, they constitute our major point of access for the analysis of purposes and strategies of central leadership.

The essay is divided into two major parts. In the first, we examine various types of municipal leaders to discover who they were and where they came from. Then, in the second part, we analyze the relationship between such leaders and their tasks in municipal organization. With these data we shall try to probe the broader political process.

The reader will note the reference to such entities as "leader types" and "organizational tasks." We develop two classification schemes in this study, one based upon certain factors of an individual's background, the other based upon the nature of office (or offices) he held in municipal organization. Each typology rests upon certain conceptions concerning the general nature of the "integrative process" and the essential business of political organization. Our study begins with the first of these conceptions.

INTEGRATION IN THE CHINESE COMMUNIST FRAMEWORK

We suggested above that problems of integration were paramount for the new leadership in the early years following liberation. What does that concept mean? More to the point, how were problems of integration likely perceived by the Chinese Communist leaders themselves?

As employed by many social scientists, the term "integration" is often equated with the notion of "unification."[9] But through the lenses of Chinese Communist ideology, and as they emerge in the writings of Mao Tse-tung, these two concepts have distinct meanings.

---

[8] By the term "central leadership" we refer to such bodies as the Party's Central Committee and Politburo.

[9] The terms are practically interchangeable, for example, in Amitai Etzioni's study, *Political Unification: A Comparative Study of Leaders and Forces* (New York: Holt, Rinehart and Winston, 1965).

In effect, unification (*t'ung-i*) is a necessary, but by no means sufficient, condition of integration (*hsiang-chieh-ho*). Of equal importance is the presence of "struggle" (*tou-cheng*). And it is the constant interplay of these two aspects—unity and struggle—which constitutes the genuinely integrative process. From the viewpoint of the leadership, in other words, integration is perceived in terms of "contradiction." It is a dialectical and unending process.

For example, Mao talks about the integration of leaders and led, the "linking of leaders with masses" (*ling-tao ho ch'ün-chung hsiang-chieh-ho*).[10] It is a linkage which ought to emerge through proper implementation of the "mass line"—the principle of "from the masses to the masses." [11] Such implementation demands equal attention to aspects of both unity and struggle. On the one hand, the leaders—cadres of Party and state—are to draw close to the masses, work among them, draw from them: there must be "unity." At the same time, leaders are enjoined never to lose their identity as "leaders"; as members of the "vanguard," they are charged with an obligation to "struggle" with the masses, to cajole, persuade—to "lead." Moreover, it is expected that those who lead will themselves become targets of struggle, open to criticism by the masses and the subjects of rectification efforts.

In Mao's eyes there is an inherent contradiction between leaders and led, a "nonantagonistic contradiction" amenable to peaceful resolution.[12] As in any contradiction, then, there are aspects of unity and struggle. The integration of leaders and led is, in effect, a "dialectical unity." The relationship is in constant flux and demands constant resolution.

By way of example, we have focused on Mao's concept of the correct relationship between leaders and led. But Mao has employed the term "integration" in a number of contexts: "integration of the general with the specific" (*i-pan ho ko-pieh hsiang-chieh-ho*); "integration of book knowledge and perceptual knowledge" (*shu-pen-shang te chih-shih ho*

---

[10] Mao Tse-tung, "Kuan-yü ling-tao fang-fa te jo-kan wen-t'i" (On Methods of Leadership), in *Mao Tse-tung hsüan-chi* (The Selected Works of Mao Tse-tung) (Peking: Jen-min ch'u-pan she, 1966), p. 899.

[11] For Mao's formulation of the "mass line" principle, see *ibid.*, p. 901. For a discussion of this concept see John W. Lewis, *Leadership in Communist China* (Ithaca, N.Y.: Cornell University Press, 1963), pp. 70–100.

[12] Mao Tse-tung, "Kuan-yü cheng-ch'üeh tui-li jen-min nei-pu mao-tun te wen-t'i" (On the Correct Handling of Contradictions among the People), in *Mao Tse-tung chu-tso hsüan-tu* (Selected Readings of Mao Tse-tung) (2 vols.; Peking: Jen-min ch'u-pan she, 1964), II, 444.

pien-yü kan-hsing te chih-shih hu-hsiang chieh-ho); "the integration of intellectuals and worker-peasant masses" (*chih-shih jen-tzu ho kung-nung min-chung hsiang-chieh-ho*); and so forth.[13] In each case, the correct relationship is a dialectical unity; integration is perceived as a constant dialectical process of interrelationship.

But interrelationship of what? In one sense, the question is meaningless. In terms of the ideology, this dialectical process of integration is inherent in all matter; it is conceptualized at many levels of abstraction. The list of "what is to be integrated" is endless. Theory and practice, Party and masses, Marxism-Leninism and the concrete practice of revolution in China, workers and peasants, education and productive labor—the overall process of integration encompasses the sum total of all such relationships. Rather than trying to define the specific components of the process, perhaps we should rephrase the question. Is it possible to identify certain constants? Regardless of specific components involved, can we discern some essential dimensions to the process?

A reading of Mao's thoughts and the general practice of revolution in contemporary China suggests that the integrative process is implicitly conceptualized in terms of two major dimensions, temporal and spatial. On the one hand, there is a process we might label "transition," which is a constant resolution of relationship between phenomena of the past, present, and future. At the same time, there is a concurrent process of "consolidation," which involves an unending search for correct relationship between the part and the whole. These aspects of transition and consolidation are constants. No matter how the problem may be defined in substantive terms, the process of integration is perceived as occurring along both dimensions; and in the eyes of the leadership, it ought to do so simultaneously.

Look again at the concept of the "mass line" as a statement of correct relationship, as integration between leaders and led. Dimensions of both time and space are implicit. On the one hand, leaders and masses, in leap-frog fashion, are enjoined constantly to recognize new problems, shape new concepts, come up with new techniques, and in so doing, constantly relate the new to the old. At times it is the leaders who are to leap the led; with goals in mind, they are to take

---

[13] "Kuan-yü ling-tao fang-fa," p. 899; "Cheng-tun tang te tso-feng" (Rectify the Party's Style in Work), in *Mao Tse-tung hsüan-chi,* p. 820; "Wu-szu yün-tung" (The May Fourth Movement), in *ibid.,* p. 546.

the lead in breaking down the restraints of existing culture and social structure. At other times, the masses are to be in the forefront, criticizing the "backward" ways of cadres, rectifying their "bourgeois" and "bureaucratic" attitudes. Cross-cutting this dimension of time is one of space. Problems of consolidation are especially evident in the relationship between leaders and led. For masses and cadres alike, what shall constitute the proper focus of identity? To what extent shall that focus be the immediate community and its particular problems? What shall be the proper relationship between the immediate community and the larger? How does the part fit into the whole? [14]

As dimensions of an overall integrative process, transition and consolidation share with that broader process an important characteristic: each is dialectical in nature. For example, transition involves aspects of both unity and struggle in calling for change and continuity. The new—be it a set of new values or a set of new techniques—ought not simply to obliterate and displace the old. Rather, the transition process involves a constant search for correct relationship between phenomena of the past, present, and future. For the new to take root and gain viability, it must be seen as emerging from the past-present.

Likewise, the correct resolution of problems of consolidation is not simply a matter of imposing the whole upon the part. The process again is one of unending search for proper balance. The whole is composed of its several parts, and each part must have its integrity. Be it family, small group, or territorial region, each community must have relevance to the members thereof. At the same time, however, the more immediate community, no matter how defined, must never become the ultimate focus of an individual's identity. The part must have its integrity; but the part must be subordinate to the whole. Mao himself has posed the problem in discussing the relationship between the center and region: "We must have both uniformity and individuality. For the development of regional enthusiasm, each region

[14] As a more immediate and concrete example of such phenomena, we can point to present-day efforts to rebuild the Communist Party in the wake of the Cultural Revolution. Mao seeks to create a newly integrated structure; and the phrase used to prescribe that structure is "revolutionary three-way alliance." Significantly, however, this phrase has been expressed in two ways: at times it is termed a "three-way alliance of PLA, revolutionary cadres, and revolutionary masses"; at other times, "a three-in-one combination of old, middle-aged, and young people." In other words, both spatial and temporal dimensions are involved. On the one hand, Mao clearly desires effective consolidation of leaders and led, center and region, Party, army, and masses. At the same time, he seeks to resolve the problems of transition—the integration of old and new, the passage of power from one generation to the next.

must have its individuality congenial to its local conditions, which is at the same time conducive to the interests of the totality and to the strengthening of the unity of the country." [15]

Because transition and consolidation are seen in dialectical terms, it follows that each process is continuing and unending. The search for proper relationship between old and new, between the whole and its several parts, is perceived as an on-going effort. The problems were not resolved in the early 1950's; nor have they been resolved by the recent Cultural Revolution.

One final observation is important. As dimensions of a single process, transition and consolidation are, by definition, closely interrelated. It is important to keep in mind, however, that they are not identical. From the viewpoint of the leadership, success in either process *ought* to result in successful resolution of the other: transition and consolidation ought to move in tandem. It is by no means inevitable that they will, however, and the two processes may well work at cross-purposes. The ways in which goals of transition are resolved, for example, may impede the desired resolution of consolidation goals.

To clarify our meaning, it would be helpful to focus on a more concrete setting and to pose these problems in the context of urban China of the early 1950's. In what guise did problems of transition and consolidation likely appear to the new leadership in those years? In general terms, what was it that had to be resolved in the overall process of integration? And given those perceptions, what general strategies did the central leadership adopt?

Transition, we say, involves a search for proper relationship between the new and old. For the Party leadership in 1949, problems of transition were tantamount to a search for proper linkage between values of a revolutionary ideology and an existing social ethos.[16] And in the specific context of urban China, that search involved a confrontation between purposes and goals of the Chinese Communist leadership on the one hand, and values not only of traditional China, but also of Western democracy and capitalism on the other. The reader may think it odd that we include all these latter elements in our delineation of "old order" values. Viewed through the lenses of Communist ideology, however, the values of "bourgeois democracy" merely occupy an in-

[15] Mao Tse-tung, "On the Ten Great Relationships," in Jerome Ch'en (ed.), *Mao* (Englewood Cliffs, N.J.: Prentice-Hall, 1969), p. 75.

[16] The terminology is drawn from Franz Schurmann, *Ideology and Organization in Communist China* (Berkeley and Los Angeles: University of California Press, 1966), pp. 1–8.

termediary stage between values of tradition and modernity, between the standpoints of "feudalism" and "socialism." To be sure, they represent values of a recent, rather than distant, past. But for that reason they likely pose the greater challenge to values of the "new order." And the forces of "bourgeois democracy" were concentrated, of course, in the coastal and Yangtze centers of commerce and industry, in such cities as Tientsin, Shanghai, Hankow, and Canton.

Problems of transition were compounded by those of consolidation. The essential question here was how the city as a "part" should fit into China, the "whole," that is, how the urban region should relate to the center.[17] As transitional problems did not emerge for the first time in 1949, neither did those of consolidation. "The problem of center versus region has bedeviled Chinese governments for centuries," writes Franz Schurmann. Within the traditional system, the relationship between central government and region was a precarious balance of power.[18] As a political force, regionalism became dominant with the decline of the Ch'ing dynasty, and regional-based power became a requisite for any genuine aspirant to the Mandate of Heaven. Such conditions made possible the rise to power of the Chinese Communists.

Ultimately, of course, the same conditions posed a severe challenge to Party control and authority. And as Chi Ch'ao-ting has pointed out, problems of regionalism were particularly acute with respect to the large urban centers of the coast: "The Treaty ports, serving as the base of economic and political operations of the powers, have grown into powerful economic and political centres of gravity, each port dominating a major section of China. The different ports, notably Shanghai, Hankow, Canton, and Tientsin, draw the economic and political life of the country in different directions and thus create a new situation of regional division and internecine struggle."[19]

Given the general guise of these problems, then, what general strat-

---

[17] Concepts of "center" and "region" are admittedly fuzzy. The center, for example, was likely defined in a number of ways, institutionally, geographically, ideologically: it was the Party and its central organs; it was Peking; it was often Mao himself, his thoughts and "world view." We cannot discount the possibility, of course, that the center was perceived differently by different people in different contexts. No doubt we oversimplify matters by talking about a "center" versus the "region" as a focus of identity.

[18] *Ideology and Organization*, p. 213; for a brief and informative discussion of center versus region, see Franz Michael, "Regionalism in Nineteenth-Century China," introduction to Stanley Spector, *Li Hung-chang and the Huai Army: A Study in Nineteenth-Century Chinese Regionalism* (Seattle: University of Washington Press, 1964), pp. xxi–xliii.

[19] Chi Ch'ao-ting, *Key Economic Areas in Chinese History* (London: George Allen and Unwin, 1936), p. 150.

egies did the leadership adopt? To resolve problems of transition, first of all, the principal order of business was to make "visible" the Party and its goals and purposes by positioning Party members in all areas of society, evincing the Party's willingness and capacity to control and govern, and mobilizing the urban masses through techniques of organization and propaganda. And an important corollary to these endeavors was the rapid development and expansion of local Party apparatuses. High visibility of the Party and its membership was essential to the aspect of change. But effective transition also involved due attention to the aspect of continuity. For purposes and values of the "new order" to take root, they had to have some linkage and relevance to values of the existing community. To this end, the leadership made every effort to coopt those individuals—businessmen, leading officials, intellectuals—with high status in the existing social structure. By their own "visibility" in the new order of things, such figures could lend their personal prestige to the leadership and thereby ease the transfer of mass loyalties to the "new." Thus, when Mao called for the entry of cadres to the cities, he placed great stress on forging a "united front" with all "patriotic" elements. It was the *combined* visibility of Party and non-Party which was essential to the overall process of transition.

What about problems of consolidation? What in general was involved in the search for proper balance between center and urban region? Again, the question was essentially one of visibility: how to make the center salient in the more immediate community; how to ensure widespread awareness of China as a total entity. The basic strategy employed was one familiar to students of Chinese history: the assignment to leadership positions in the community of those with few ties thereto.[20] Through the presence and visibility of such "outsiders" it was clearly hoped that loyalties within the community would be drawn toward the center itself. But as correct resolution of transition problems was not simply a matter of imposing a new set of values and perspectives on the old, neither was consolidation simply a matter of eradicating feelings of identity to the more immediate community. As Mao said, there must be "regional enthusiasm."[21] To generate such feelings, it was essential that the leadership recruit and employ indi-

---

[20] Under the imperial system, lower-level magistrates were never appointed to positions in their native provinces; and the so-called "law of avoidance" prohibited clan members from serving in the same administrative areas. See Ch'ü T'ung-tsu, *Local Government in China under the Ch'ing* (Cambridge, Mass.: Harvard University Press, 1962), Chap. ii.

[21] "On the Ten Great Relationships," p. 75.

viduals with roots in the specific locale. As Schurmann suggests, "Peking needed regional cadres with sufficiently deep roots in the local situation to permit them to operate effectively." [22]

Perhaps now the dilemma is clear. Successful resolution of *each* process demanded active recruitment of local cadres and the development of a strong local Party organization. Such endeavors were essential to the aspect of change in transition; they were also important for ensuring regional enthusiasm in the process of consolidation. As local Party leadership came into its own and gradually asserted its authority as spokesman for the "new order," however, it was entirely possible that the urban Party organization itself might become a terminus of local loyalties. The whole could well become subordinate to the part. Successful transition, characterized by an increased visibility of Party in all sectors of local society, could impede successful consolidation, and could operate to reduce rather than increase the visibility of the center.

Integration as a dialectical process of unity and struggle; integration as a process along the two major dimensions of time and space; transition as a search for a proper relationship between new and old; consolidation as search for balance between the part and the whole; transition and consolidation as processes related but not identical—such concepts are the backdrop of this study.

MUNICIPAL LEADERS OF THE EARLY YEARS: CHARACTERISTICS AND PROFILES

To analyze the backgrounds of municipal leaders and their relationships to organization, we have classified individuals in terms of several broadly defined categories based upon two major variables: (1) the degree of identification with the "new order," as evinced by one's membership or nonmembership in the Communist Party; and (2) the degree of identification with the immediate community, as evidenced by one's status of "outsider" or "local." The typology flows from our conception of the overall integrative process, namely, that through the eyes of leadership in Peking the most critical interchange of this early period was likely to occur between those with stronger and weaker commitments to the new order, having stronger and weaker ties to the specific locale.

Admittedly, the measures employed are not terribly precise; nor can they be. What we want to gauge, after all, are states of mind:

22 *Ideology and Organization,* p. 215.

commitments, identifications, perceptions. To what degree did a given leader perceive himself as a representative of the new order, or of the center? To what extent was he perceived as such by members of the immediate community, by fellow office-holders, by leaders at higher levels?

Needless to say, direct observation and measurement of such attitudes and perceptions are a virtual impossibility. We are obliged to rely upon circumstantial evidence, and such indicators are bound to be less than adequate. Is membership in the Party proof positive of one's "commitment to the new order"? Are Party members universally perceived as representatives of the new? Clearly the answers will vary with time and situation. What about the question of regional loyalty? How does one gauge the strength of a given leader's commitment to the immediate community? Such factors as place of birth and area of residence are no doubt important. But how important? [23]

We operate on certain assumptions. First of all, it is assumed that Party membership, *in most cases,* was evidence of commitment to the new order, *in the period under analysis.* We are dealing in the aggregate, and the relationship is qualified in terms of time. During the years following liberation, it is likely that Party members had, and were perceived as having, stronger feelings of identification with the new order than had non-Party members.[24] In like manner, it is assumed that factors of birthplace and residence were related to strength of regional identification. It is likely that individuals with little or no pre-1949 contact with the city in question had weaker commitments to the immediate community than did those who were natives of the city or those with long years of residence therein.[25]

Combining these several attributes, we emerge with a simple three-fold typology of municipal leaders: "outside Reds," "local Reds," and "local Whites" (there were no "outside Whites" to speak of). Of this basic scheme we make several modifications. Among outside Reds, first

[23] Michel Oksenberg confronts a similar problem in his article, "Local Leaders in Rural China, 1962–65: Individual Attributes, Bureaucratic Positions, and Political Recruitment," in A. Doak Barnett (ed.), *Chinese Communist Politics in Action* (Seattle and London: University of Washington Press, 1969), p. 177.

[24] The qualification of time is important. One need only look at developments of recent years. For Mao and those who share his perspectives, status of Party membership had all but lost its relationship to revolutionary standpoint by the mid-1960's. Indeed, during the Cultural Revolution, an individual was often called upon to evince his commitment to the "new order" *despite* his formal membership in the Party.

[25] An individual is considered "local" if born in the city in question, or if known to have lived in the city for ten years or more before 1949; all others are classified "outsiders."

of all, we draw a distinction in terms of time of entry. In the years following liberation, two separate waves of such leaders moved into the municipalities: a first wave of "liberators" who assumed office immediately after Communist takeover; and a "second wave" who began to move into municipal office during the *san-fan* and *wu-fan* campaigns of 1951–52.

Among local Reds, we distinguish between two categories based upon Party seniority. On the one hand were the "early organizers," those active in Party affairs in the years before liberation. On the other were the "local activists," or those individuals recruited to the Party after 1949. Finally, we differentiate two subcategories of local Whites: "early critics" and "late collaborators." The former leaders were those non-Party individuals who voiced their opposition to the Kuomintang (KMT) and Nationalist government in the years before 1949. And the late collaborators, in Nationalist Chinese parlance, were those White leaders who "joined the bandits after the fall of the mainland" (*ta-lu hsien-fei hou fu-fei*).

Table 27 shows the distribution of individual leaders among these various leader types, for each city and for all cities together. Of a total of 808 individuals identified as municipal office-holders, we have been able to classify 446 (55 per cent). These leader types constitute the primary focus of this study.

TABLE 27

MUNICIPAL LEADERS BY MUNICIPALITY AND LEADER TYPE

	Municipality of Leaders							
	Tientsin (N = 220)		Shanghai (N = 297)		Canton (N = 291)		All Cities (N = 808)	
Type	No.	% Total	No.	% Total	No.	% Total	No.	% Total
Liberator	21	10	23	8	17	6	61	8
Second wave	13	6	26	9	27	9	66	8
Total outside Red	34	15	49	16	44	15	127	16
Early organizer	7	3	23	8	24	8	54	7
Local activist	8	4	2	1	3	1	13	2
Total local Red	15	7	25	8	27	9	67	8
Early critic	2	1	38	13	14	5	54	7
Late collaborator	55	25	78	26	65	22	198	25
Total local White	57	26	116	39	79	27	252	31
Total classified	106	48	190	64	150	52	446	55

Where did these municipal leaders come from? What kinds of experiences did they have in the years prior to their assumption of municipal office? In the following pages we attempt to get behind the sterile labels and find out what we can about the members of these several categories. To this end our approach is twofold. First, leader types will be analyzed in terms of a number of different variables, such as age, place of origin, education, and revolutionary experiences, and the resulting characterizations will be compared. We shall seek to answer such questions as, Did members of a given category share certain characteristics, other than status of Party affiliation or prior exposure to the local community, which may have strengthened feelings of group identity? In a subsequent section, we shall then summarize the findings by sketching a number of leader type profiles and providing representative individuals for each category.

LEADER TYPES: CHARACTERISTICS AND ATTRIBUTES

Table 28 breaks down the leader types in terms of various background factors. These distributions will serve as a point of reference for the following survey.

TABLE 28

MUNICIPAL LEADERS BY LEADER TYPE AND BACKGROUND VARIABLES

Relevant Variables	Municipal Leaders by Leader Type					
	Outside Red (N = 127)		Local Red (N = 67)		Local White (N = 252)	
	Liberator (N = 61)	Second Wave (N = 66)	Early Organizer (N = 54)	Local Activist (N = 13)	Early Critic (N = 54)	Late Collaborator (N = 198)
Sex						
Total known	117 *		67		249	
Male	110 (94) †		54 (81)		241 (97)	
Female	7 (6)		13 (19)		8 (3)	
Age						
Total known	49	18	43	11	156	
Median age (as of 1950)	42	39	41	33	49	
Place of origin (relative to city of office-holding)						
Total known	80		52		165	
City itself	0 —		16 (31) †		33 (20)	
City's province	16 (20)		43 (83) §		83 (50) §	
City's region	35 (44) §		45 (87) §		123 (75) §	
Other	45 (56)		7 (13)		42 (25)	
Place of origin ‖						
Total known	46		39	7	152	
Urban-born	10 (22) †		21 (54)	6 (86)	80 (53)	
Rural-born	36 (78)		18 (46)	1 (14)	72 (47)	

TABLE 28 (*Continued*)

Municipal Leaders by Leader Type

Relevant Variables	Outside Red (N = 127)		Local Red (N = 67)		Local White (N = 252)	
	Liberator (N = 61)	Second Wave (N = 66)	Early Organizer (N = 54)	Local Activist (N = 13)	Early Critic (N = 54)	Late Collaborator (N = 198)
Degree of early urban exposure #						
Total known	46		46		152	
Urbanite	4 (9) †		17 (37)		47 (31)	
Urban-ruralite	17 (37)		23 (50)		91 (60)	
Ruralite	25 (54)		6 (13)		14 (9)	
Level of formal education						
Total known	42		22	3	153	
University +	16 (13) ‡		12 (22)	0 —	139 (55)	
Secondary +	32 (25) §		17 (31) §	0 —	153 (61) §	
Primary +	42 (33) §		22 (41) §	3 (23)	153 (61) §	
General foreign travel experience						
Known to travel	14 (11) ‡		10 (15)		90 (36)	
Known *not* to travel	23 (18)		27 (40)		4 (2)	
Travel unknown	90 (71)		30 (45)		158 (62)	
Specific foreign travel experience						
Total known travelers	14		10		90	
To USSR	10 (71) †		5 (50)		3 (3)	
To Japan	1 (7)		3 (30)		28 (31)	
To Europe	4 (29)		2 (20)		28 (31)	
To United States	1 (7)		1 (10)		45 (50)	
Earliest known participation in Communist Party						
By 1927	14 (23) ‡	1 (2)	10 (19)	N.A **	N.A. **	
By 1931	34 (56) §	10 (15) §	20 (37) §	N.A.	N.A.	
By 1935	49 (80) §	26 (39) §	27 (50) §	N.A.	N.A.	
By 1940	61 (100) §	42 (64) §	39 (72) §	N.A.	N.A.	
Revolutionary route of Party leaders #						
Total known	45	18	39	N.A.	N.A.	
Urban	0 —	0 —	20 (51) †	N.A.	N.A.	
Urban-wilderness	11 (24)	5 (28)	16 (41)	N.A.	N.A.	
Wilderness	34 (76)	13 (72)	3 (8)	N.A.	N.A.	
Revolutionary task area of Party leaders #						
Total known	59	24	54	N.A.	N.A.	
Red-military	24 (41) †	8 (33)	3 (6)	N.A.	N.A.	
Red-political	16 (27)	7 (29)	1 (2)	N.A.	N.A.	
Red-administrative	16 (27)	7 (29)	9 (17)	N.A.	N.A.	
White-organizational	0 —	2 (9)	34 (63)	N.A.	N.A.	
White-cultural	3 (5)	0 —	7 (12)	N.A.	N.A.	

* Where differences among subcategories are insignificant, we deal with them as single categories.

† Figures in parentheses equal percentage of total leaders for whom relevant data are known.

‡ Figures in parentheses equal percentage of total leaders in leader type category.

§ Frequencies are cumulative.

‖ We arbitrarily define as "urban" any population center of 50,000 or more.

See text below for explanation of categories.

** Not applicable to activists (who joined the CCP after 1949) or to non-Party local Whites.

Sex and age. In sex our leader types were overwhelmingly male. The distribution of their median ages, ranging from thirty-three to forty-nine years, suggests a division of leader types into three general age groups: elders (local Whites), middle-aged (liberators, second wave, and early organizers), and youths (local activists). We should point out, however, that the short separation between the median ages of liberator and early organizer on the one hand and of second wave on the other may be more critical than the first look suggests. One of our major concerns in this study is the possible impact of background variables upon an individual's revolutionary career and his tasks in municipal organization. The factor of age is important, for it governs the timing of an individual's exposure to certain historical events. It is entirely possible, in other words, that leaders of these several categories belonged to separate "revolutionary generations."

Place of origin. By definition, of course, this variable was a clear point of departure between outsider and local leaders. Among outside Reds (liberators and second wave), no individual was native to his city of office incumbency; a few were born in the province thereof; and a distinct majority came from altogether different regions of the country. Among both categories of locals, on the other hand, some 20 to 30 per cent were native to the city in question. At the same time, it can be seen that the vast majority of such leaders attained their status of local by virtue of prolonged residence rather than native birth.

From the table we find that local leaders were more likely than outsiders to have origins in urban areas, in population centers of 50,000 or more. Given the sizable proportion of natives among local Reds and Whites, however, the differences between various categories of leaders are not as pronounced as one might expect, with exception of the predominantly urban-born activist. If we were to remove these native-born individuals from the sample, moreover, we would find distinctions between leader types to be very slight indeed. A majority of members of each category (78 per cent of outside Reds, 63 per cent of local Reds, and 61 per cent of local Whites) came from the rural areas. On the whole, in other words, the individuals who emerged in municipal office after 1949 were not "urbanites" in the sense of having been born in large population centers. Be he Red or White, local or outsider, the municipal leader more likely than not had his origins in the country-side.

We should qualify that assertion, however. The term "rural setting" is ambiguous. To say that leaders tended to have rural origins is not to imply that they all came from isolated areas of the hinterland. In tracing the native origins of individuals in this study, we differentiated between those who were born in counties adjacent to major transportation and communication routes and those who came from relatively isolated counties. Among all categories of leaders, distinct majorities of rural-born individuals came from the less isolated—and one is tempted to say "more rapidly modernizing"—areas of the countryside. (The proportions among outside Reds, local Reds, and local Whites, were 61, 89, and 82 per cent, respectively.)

Regarding specific region of origin, it has been observed that an overwhelming majority of both local Reds (87 per cent) and local Whites (75 per cent) were native-born to the province or region of their city of office-holding (see Table 28). But what about the outside Reds? Some interesting patterns emerge from the data. First of all, in Table 28 we find that among such leaders of all municipalities taken together, some 44 per cent were native to the region of city of office incumbency. From Table 29 we see this same proportion held true among outside Reds of each municipality. Note, furthermore, that some 30 to 40 per cent of such individuals of each city were natives of the Central China region, specifically, the central interior provinces of Hunan, Hupeh, Kiangsi, and Honan.

TABLE 29

OUTSIDE REDS BY MUNICIPALITY AND REGION OF ORIGIN

| Region of Origin * | Municipality of Outside Reds | | | | | |
| | Tientsin | | Shanghai | | Canton | |
	N	% Known	N	% Known	N	% Known
North China	10	43	2	7	1	4
East China	3	13	13	43	1	4
South/Southwest China	1	4	5	17	12	46
Central China	8	35	10	33	11	42
Other	1	4	0	—	1	4
Total known	23	99 †	30	100	26	100

* North China includes Chahar, Hopeh, Pingyuan, Shansi, Shantung, and Suiyuan; East China includes Anhwei, Chekiang, Fukien, and Kiangsu; South/Southwest China includes Kwangsi, Kwangtung, Kweichow, Sikang, Szechwan, Yunnan, and Tibet; Central China includes Honan, Hupeh, Hunan, and Kiangsi; "Other" refers to Manchuria, provinces of the northwest, and overseas.

† Because we have rounded off individual percentages, the total does not equal 100 per cent.

The dominant presence of those native to the city's region is not at all surprising. Rural areas surrounding the cities of Tientsin, Shanghai, and Canton were important centers of Party and Red Army activity after the outbreak of war with Japan in 1937. Many of our liberator and second wave leaders were native to these regions and were swept up in Communist wartime activities. During the 1940's they served as Party and PLA cadres, and some gained prominence as administrators in various base-area governments. With the final defeat of the Nationalists in 1949, many of these individuals simply moved with the appropriate field army as the latter occupied the city.

The uniformly high proportion of central-interior natives demands a more speculative explanation. It should be noted, first of all, that the regional profile of our own leadership sample was strikingly similar to that of the national Party elite of the same period. As can be seen in Table 30, in terms of regional origin our own sample is a virtual mirror reflection of the CCP Central Committee membership elected in 1945. Of particular significance here is the fact that 30 to 40 per cent of each group were natives of Central China.

TABLE 30

COMPARISON OF OUTSIDE REDS AND CCP CENTRAL COMMITTEE
MEMBERSHIP (1945) IN TERMS OF REGIONAL ORIGIN

Region of Origin	Outside Reds		Central Committee *	
	N	% Known	N	% Known
North China	13	16	4	9
East China	17	22	9	20
Central China	29	37	19	43
South/Southwest China	18	23	9	20
Other	2	3	3	7
Total known	79	101 †	44	99 †

* Data are from Robert C. North with Ithiel de Sola Pool, "Kuomintang and Chinese Communist Elites," in Harold D. Lasswell and Daniel Lerner (eds.), *World Revolutionary Elites: Studies in Coercive Ideological Movements* (Cambridge, Mass.: M.I.T. Press, 1965), p. 403.

† Because we have rounded off individual percentages, the total does not equal 100 per cent.

As far as the national Party leadership is concerned, it is a well-known fact that natives of the central-interior have occupied, and continue to occupy, a prominent place in the Central Committee and Politburo. To some extent, of course, the phenomenon is simply due to historical circumstance. As high-level positions are by and large filled by those with greatest seniority, and as many of those with greatest seniority joined the Party during the early 1930's when Communist activities were concentrated in the central-interior region, we should expect a strong correlation between national prominence and Central China origin. Donald Klein makes this point in his analysis of Party leadership of the early 1960's. And Klein shows us, furthermore, that the regional profile of less senior and lower-echelon leaders reflects the shift of Party activities to the north after 1935.[26]

While strictly historical circumstance is important, it seems likely that common origin in the central interior served an important function for the new leadership, a function closely related to problems of integration. Mao himself is a native of the region, as are such past and present Party leaders as Li Hsien-nien, Lin Piao, Liu Shao-ch'i, and P'eng Teh-huai. It was on Chingkangshan and in the border region of Kiangsi-Fukien that Mao rose to prominence in the Party. It was during this period that his thoughts and perceptions began to fashion the structure and strategy of Party and Red Army. Those recruited from this area at this time, and who managed to survive the rigors of the Long March, ultimately became the core element of a greatly expanded Communist organization after 1937. This is all to suggest that common origin and shared experiences in Central China constituted an element of cohesion among Party leaders and likely strengthened their sense of common identity.

We now find this same core element visible among outside Red leaders of each of our three municipalities. And such evidence suggests that those with origins in the central interior region served as an "entering wedge" for the Peking leadership—an instrument by which the latter might forge the linkages between center and urban region. Through strategic assignment of such individuals, in other words, the central leadership might hope to strengthen the bonds between Party and state cadres at various levels within different regions. We shall return to these observations later.

Early urban exposure. To what extent did various leader types have contact with urban life at an early age? How did different categories compare in this respect? So far, we have examined the "urban-rural" dimension solely in terms of native origin. As George K. Schueller sug-

---

[26] Donald W. Klein, "The 'Next Generation' of Chinese Communist Leaders," *CQ*, No. 12 (October–December, 1962), p. 61.

gests in his study of the Soviet Politburo, however, it is important to ask also whether the individual moved to a metropolitan area at some early point in his life, for schooling, employment, and the like.[27] Our search here is for some indicator of "urban skills," the extent to which a given individual brought to office a familiarity with the urban setting and its particular problems. To this end, the relevant datum is not so much one's place of birth, but his place of residence during early and formative years.

With these considerations in mind, we have classified leaders in terms of three (admittedly arbitrary) categories: (1) "urbanites," who were born and raised in large population centers of 500,000 or more; (2) "urban-ruralites," either born or raised in lesser population centers of 50,000 to 500,000, or, if rural-born, known to have moved to some urban setting at an early age; and (3) "ruralites," who were rural-born, with no known movement to an urban center. The distribution of leader types among these several categories is shown in Table 28. Better than half of all liberator and second wave leaders qualified as ruralites, while an overwhelming majority of both local Reds and local Whites, if not native to major population centers, are known to have been urban residents by their late teens.[28]

Level of formal education. As various leader types differed with

[27] "The Politburo," Lasswell and Lerner (eds.), *World Revolutionary Elites,* pp. 110–11.

[28] Our findings seem to conflict with those of other students of urban China. In his study of Tangshan city, for example, John Lewis has observed that "the men who moved into positions of authority in Tangshan after the takeover had long ties with the city and had usually come from urban backgrounds" ("Political Aspects of Mobility in China's Urban Development," p. 905). Ying-mao Kau points to similar conditions in Wuhan where he finds "little sign of 'ruralism' in the top bureaucratic elite" of that city ("The Urban Bureaucratic Elite in Communist China: A Case Study of Wuhan, 1949–65," in Barnett [ed.], *Chinese Communist Politics in Action,* p. 228). We would suggest, however, that each of these studies is concerned with a particular leadership sample. Lewis is likely referring to those leaders we classify as both outside Reds and local Reds, that is, *all* Party members in higher-echelon office. And our own data support his findings: among both categories of Red leaders, two out of three were urbanites or urban-ruralites. Kau is dealing with a different sample, namely, the membership of the Municipal People's Government. As we shall see in a later section, this particular unit was an important component of the so-called generalist area of organization, which tended to be the most "balanced" in terms of leader type representation. To analyze the membership of this organ, in other words, is to analyze a cross section of all municipal leaders, regardless of type classification. If this were done with our own data, we would find, in agreement with Kau, that the incidence of ruralism was low. Among all identified leaders of this study, better than four out of five had experienced contact with city life before 1949. In other words, when we examine Party members as a group, or all leaders regardless of Party affiliation, a distinct majority were exposed to urban life at an early age. It is important to note, however, that among certain types of leaders—liberators and second wave—a substantial number had experienced no such contact.

respect to early urban exposure, so they differed in educational experiences. The two variables are closely related: movement to the city was often for the purposes of education, to permit attendance at one of the large metropolitan middle schools or universities. From the data of Table 28, we find that better than one-third of all leaders are known to have had at least the equivalent of a university education, and nearly one-half had completed secondary school. But there is a good deal of variation among separate leader type categories. On the average, local Whites enjoyed the longest period of formal education: a majority had achieved a university degree, and of these, a total of eighty-nine (35 per cent of all local Whites) are known to have had training at the graduate level. Among all leader types, those classified as activists apparently received the least amount of formal education: of our sample, none had attended secondary school, and only three (23 per cent of the activists) are known to have completed primary school. Outside Reds and early organizers occupied a middle ground between these two extremes.[29]

We should be careful in interpreting these findings. Most especially, we should avoid the simple equation of formal education *per se* to status of "expert." As students of contemporary Chinese politics are sorely aware, the essential traits of expertise are devilishly hard to define, for observer and participant alike. No doubt formal education is important; but equally important are such factors as on-the-job training and practical experience. From the viewpoint of leadership ideology, furthermore, expertise is rarely gauged by such an objective criterion as level of education. It defines the quality of a given individual—the way he perceives his fellow man and the manner in which he approaches his tasks in organization.

While an individual's education may provide us no accurate measure of his level of expertise, nevertheless it would be wrong to discount such experiences altogether. We mentioned above the close relationship in our sample between factors of education and exposure to urban life. In effect, these variables are very much of a common matrix. While his presence in the city may have sensitized the individual to specific problems of urban life, his attendance at an institution of higher learning likely exposed him to more generic questions of urbanization.

[29] In a sense, then, our own data are comparable to Kau's findings among the Wuhan elite: 52 per cent of his sample are known to have had formal education beyond the secondary school level ("Urban Bureaucratic Elite in Communist China," p. 233). What Kau's data do not reveal, however, is the significant variation between different types of leaders in this respect.

The thrust of such experiences, in other words, was not so much to "specialize" as to "generalize." The individual emerged not only as an expert in some given field of study, but also as a "cosmopolitan." These observations lead us directly to the next variable.

Foreign travel experiences. If those we classify as local Whites may be considered more cosmopolitan by virtue of early exposure to urban life and long years of formal education, this trait was likely reinforced by greater incidence and scope of travel abroad. As the data of Table 28 indicate, more than one-third of the leaders of this type are known to have traveled outside China; and all but a few of these travelers are known to have resided for some period of time in a country other than their own. Bearing in mind the scarcity of data in this regard, it appears that Party members of both outsider and local categories had considerably more limited travel experiences. Among outside and local Reds, only a handful of leaders are known to have traveled abroad; and, as a kind of reverse measure, we can see that proportionally more Party members (especially among locals) are known *not* to have traveled.

The data suggest that travel by Party members was limited not only in degree but also in kind. Especially among outsiders, the majority of known Party travelers had visited no country other than the Soviet Union. Thus, the leaders of this study share a common profile with Party leadership at the national level. As Donald Klein has shown in his analysis of the Eighth Central Committee, for example, pre-1949 foreign travel experiences of that group were mainly limited to countries of the Soviet bloc.[30] In contrast, the travel experiences of Whites were considerably more varied.

What impact did foreign travel have on an individual's career? To what extent did it shape his relationship to China's modern revolution? For many leaders, of course, travel abroad was simply a reinforcement of existing attitudes and commitments. Such was likely the case among those who visited the USSR. But could travel experience be a cause as well as an effect?

Prompted by this question, we focused on the local White. Was there any apparent relationship between specific foreign travel experience and the act of early or late identification with the Communist movement? There is an indication that such a relationship existed, and the critical nations appear to be Japan and the United States. As the dis-

[30] Donald W. Klein, "Peking's Leaders: A Study in Isolation," *CQ*, No. 7 (July–September, 1961), pp. 35–43.

tributions of Table 31 show, there was a better than even chance that the Japan traveler was later to be an early critic, in open opposition to the Nationalist government by the early 1940's. Among those who visited the United States, on the other hand, a substantial majority were to have no known association with anti-Kuomintang activity before 1949. Or, we might view the data from another perspective. Among early critics, former travelers to Japan outnumbered those to the United States by a margin of two to one; among late collaborators, it was the North American traveler who prevailed.

TABLE 31

TRAVEL EXPERIENCE OF LOCAL WHITES

	Travel Experience					
	To Japan/ Not U.S.		To U.S./ Not Japan		Total Known	
Type of Local White	N	% Known	N	% Known	N	% Known
Early critic	12	52	5	12	17	27
Late collaborator	11	48	36	88	47	73
Total known	23	100	41	100	64	100
	$X^2 = 10.11$		p = .001		C = .399 *	

* Very briefly, chi-square (X^2) is a measure of discrepancy between observed and expected frequencies. The greater the value of X^2, the more improbable that the distributions obtained occurred purely by chance. When we operate with bivariate tables of this kind, a large X^2 value signals a probable interdependence between the two variables involved. To express such a relationship, we have used a measure derived from X^2—the contingency coefficient. (For one description of such measures, see Sidney Siegel, *Nonparametric Statistics for the Behavioral Sciences* [New York: McGraw-Hill, 1956], pp. 104–11, 196–202.) Our employment of X^2 and C is not undertaken in the spirit of "proving" that one variable is interdependent with another. Furthermore, it is important that we take care in how we interpret a particular finding. Of itself, interdependence tells us nothing about "cause" or "effect." The primary purpose of these measures, we feel, is to suggest that one relationship is of greater theoretical interest than another, worthy of attention and additional analysis.

We cannot discount the possibility that travel experiences of themselves were largely irrelevant, that one's revolutionary proclivities predated and conditioned his travel choices. Thus, as we argued that travel to the Soviet Union was likely an effect rather than cause of identification with revolutionary ideology, so it could be argued that the more "radical" tended to sojourn in Japan. In this particular case, however, it seems more likely that the reverse was true, that there was something about the "Japanese experience" which had a "radicalizing" effect on the man.

It is certainly not our intent here to attempt an analysis of the complex relationships between Japan and the youth of China in the twentieth century. There is little question that Japan was an object of often intense feeling on the part of China's youth. Whether such feeling was predominantly one of identification or rejection—or both—is a problem more for the psychoanalyst than the political analyst.

One way or the other, however, it is unlikely that many felt untouched by their presence in Japan. Many of our local Whites were in their fifties and sixties by 1949, and many of those who visited Japan did so as students during a particularly turbulent period of China's history which saw the collapse of a dynasty and the rise of a short-lived republic. For Sun Yat-sen, Japan served as a staging area for revolutionary organization; and overseas Chinese students in Japan fleshed out the ranks of his T'ung Meng Hui. At the same time, many youth were attracted to the forces of radicalism and socialism which began to emerge in Japan during this period.[31] Finally, as Chow Tse-tsung has pointed out, these same students later provided much of the leadership of the 1919 May Fourth Movement.[32] But for the student in America, the environment, while not necessarily antiradical, was likely apolitical. The individual merely traveled to the United States to study, earn his degree, and gain experience in American business or industry; and he kept in touch with events at home through the pages of the American press.

Two interesting points of departure between local White visitors to Japan and the United States were their fields of study and later careers. The Japan traveler was more inclined to the social sciences and was more likely to follow a career in business or in such "communicating" specialties as law, teaching, or journalism. On the other hand, a majority of students in America concentrated their studies in the natural sciences or engineering, and they later pursued these specialties in government or industry.

Revolutionary experiences. Revolutionary experiences can be evaluated by the length of time leaders had been active in the Chinese Communist movement, in what general areas they were active before 1949,

[31] See Marius B. Jansen, *The Japanese and Sun Yat-sen* (Cambridge, Mass.: Harvard University Press, 1954), pp. 105–30.

[32] *The May Fourth Movement* (Cambridge, Mass.: Harvard University Press, 1960), pp. 31 ff.

and what general tasks they performed. For this evaluation, let us look first at the three Party member categories—liberators, second wave, and early organizers.[33]

Regarding length of service, we find in Table 28 that the liberators as a group were the most senior cadres in the municipalities. An overwhelming majority of such leaders are known to have been active in the Party by the Long March of 1934–35. We should treat these data with care, however. In the case of second wave leaders, for example, our knowledge of pre-1949 activity is rather meager; and it is possible that we have underestimated the number of such leaders who were active by the late 1930's and early 1940's.

In order to compare leader types in terms of general *area* of pre-1949 activity, we have classified individuals according to three broadly conceived categories of "revolutionary routes" which led to the assumption of municipal office after liberation. For certain leaders the route to office was solely or largely urban in nature. As we saw before, our sample includes a number of individuals who either were born and raised in the big city or, if rural-born, moved to the urban setting at an early age. Many such individuals simply remained in the cities until the time of liberation. They joined the Party during its "urban phase" of the late 1920's, and they subsequently served in the Party's urban underground apparatus. Joining this "urban route" in the late 1930's were a number of leaders who had previously served in the Kiangsi Soviet, perhaps having taken part in the Long March. During the Sino-Japanese War and Civil War, however, their revolutionary activities were concentrated in the cities: some of them engaged in United Front work, others worked in the underground among the proletariat.

A much different route was one which led through the "wilderness." Indeed, the wilderness route had many diversionary trails, and the scenery could be quite varied. Regardless of specific path, however, those who followed this route skirted the big cities until 1949. The route had its origins in the countryside and led successively through (1) early participation in a local peasants' association or guerrilla unit; (2) service with the Red Army in the early 1930's; (3) participation in the Long March or, barring this, continued activity in one of many "Red pockets" of resistance against the KMT military encirclement; (4) participation in the war against Japan as a cadre attached to the Eighth Route Army or New Fourth Army, or as a polit-

---

[33] The following discussion does not pertain to the local activist, who did not become active in Party affairs until after 1949.

ical worker in one of the many base areas which stretched from eastern Hopeh to the East River valley of Kwangtung; and (5) service with one of several field armies in the final confrontation between Communist and Nationalist forces after 1946.

Finally, as one might expect, there were a number of individuals who followed neither urban nor wilderness route alone, but some combination of the two. Typical of those who pursued the urban-wilderness route were leaders who served in the urban underground during the early 1930's, but who linked up with the wilderness route during and after the Sino-Japanese War.

In Table 28 we compare our three leader types in terms of these various revolutionary routes. Our purpose here is no more than descriptive. Given the kinds of people in each leader type, we should expect a strong relationship between wilderness route and outsider on the one hand, and between urban route and local on the other. It might be noted, however, that all categories included a fair number of individuals who enjoyed mixed experiences in the years before 1949.

Party leaders can be compared in terms of one final variable—general revolutionary task. Here our interest is not in how long or where the leader was active, but in what he was doing. The categories of Table 28 may be summarized briefly. Where the leader was a traveler of the wilderness route—where his pre-1949 activity was centered in the rural-based Party organization—he was assigned to the general category of Red area; otherwise he was classified as a White area worker. Red area leaders were further assigned to one of three categories: military, political, or administrative. Where primary functional ties were to the Red Army, the task area is military (we include herein not only members of the line-officer corps, but also such officials as political commissar and member of political department). Where the individual was primarily engaged in mass organizational activities and in the fields of propaganda and education, or if he held a leading post in some Party organization, he was assigned to the political task area. Finally, one's tasks are defined as administrative if the individual is known to have held a position in one of the Red area border governments. Among those active in White areas, on the other hand, tasks have been designated as either organizational (work with labor unions, "third parties," and so forth) or cultural (agitation and propaganda).

As can be seen in Table 28, leaders of the liberator and second wave categories were distributed fairly evenly among the three Red task areas, while the pre-1949 activities of the early organizer were very much concentrated in White area organizational work, as was to be expected. In a later section we shall look for possible relationships between these pre-1949 task areas and post-1949 assignment to municipal office.

Measured strictly in terms of identification with the Chinese Communist cause, the local White, of course, was the least "revolutionary" of all municipal leaders. At the same time, we ought not to allow this particular measure to obscure the fact that many such individuals experienced a rich history of revolutionary involvement. Among our sample there were several White leaders who played a role in the short-lived Fukien People's Government of 1933–34. Many were deeply involved in the events of late 1935.[34] And among the 128 about whom we have definite information, nearly one-fifth are known to have been in open opposition to the KMT by the early 1940's. These early critics were by and large travelers of the urban route, and their tasks were concentrated in the White areas.

Our purpose to this point has been twofold: (1) to compare and contrast leader types in terms of a number of variables, and (2) to search for any possible interrelationships among such variables which might enable us to understand better the life histories of our several leader types. While such an approach provides us with the tool for comparative analysis and helps us probe the possible significance of background variables, it has its disadvantage. In a word, we lose sight of the people themselves. Both by way of summary and as an attempt to rehumanize our categories, we shall now draw a number of leader type profiles.

LEADER TYPES: PROFILES AND REPRESENTATIVES

Liberator. In his early forties by the time of takeover, the liberator was likely born in the countryside and experienced little contact with urban life at an early age. Perhaps he received a formal education, but probably not beyond the secondary-school level. He joined the Party as a youth and was active in the Communist movement by the early 1930's. If he traveled abroad, it was to the Soviet Union for purposes

---

[34] Two individuals involved in the Fukien People's Government, for example, were Ch'en Ming-shu and Chang Wen. For an account of Ch'en's participation, see Howard L. Boorman and Richard C. Howard (eds.), *Biographical Dictionary of Republican China* (3 vols.; New York: Columbia University Press, 1967–70), I, 216. Sha Ch'ien-li, a local White leader of Shanghai after 1949, took an active part in the events of late 1935. His arrest at that time was something of a *cause célèbre*. See Lyman P. Van Slyke, *Enemies and Friends: The United Front in Chinese Communist History* (Stanford, Calif.: Stanford University Press, 1967), p. 73.

of political or military training. By definition, of course, the liberator had little, if any, pre-1949 contact with the city of his office incumbency.

Yet there was considerable variation among the ranks of liberator. Although all individuals were alien-born to the city in question, some were more "alien" than others. Many of these leaders experienced no prolonged exposure to the urban setting; but some are known to have lived in the big cities for purposes of education and/or employment. In other words, we seem to be dealing with two different kinds of liberators, one of these kinds sharing a number of traits with the local Reds and Whites. And the primary distinction between these subcategories is region of native origin.

TABLE 32

ANALYSIS OF OUTSIDE REDS BY REGION OF ORIGIN

	Region of Origin of Outside Reds			
	Central-Interior		Other	
Relevant Variables	N	% Known	N	% Known
Level of education				
More than secondary	5	36	15	88
Secondary or less	9	64	2	12
Revolutionary route				
Urban	0	—	0	—
Urban-wilderness	1	6	10	34
Wilderness	15	94	19	66
Revolutionary task area				
Red-military	13	59	11	30
Red-political	4	18	12	32
Red-administrative	5	23	11	30
White	0	—	3	8

In a prior section we made note of the pervasive presence of the central interior native and his possible role in the integrative process of those early years. Compared to other liberators, such leaders tended to have different experiences in the years before 1949. As can be seen in Table 32, the central interior native had relatively few years of education, was likely to travel the wilderness route, and was probably a pre-1949 specialist in military tasks. By contrast, among liberators from other regions of the mainland, many enjoyed formal education beyond the secondary school level, a number worked in the urban areas before liberation, and their revolutionary task area was as likely to be political or administrative as it was military.

A good representative of the central interior native is Li T'ien-huan, who served briefly as a political commissar with the Tientsin Garrison Command after January, 1949. Born in 1909, Li is a native of Huang-an *hsien,* Hupeh.[35] About fifty kilometers north of Hankow, this county, together with Huang-p'i to the south, became a center of intense Communist activity in the late 1920's. From this area came such prominent Party and Red Army figures as Lin Piao and Hsü Hai-tung; and the region itself was the seedbed for the Oyüwan (Hupeh-Honan-Anhwei) Soviet.[36]

Following completion of primary school in Huang-an, Li joined the local guerrilla forces and took an active part in the uprisings of the Autumn Harvest period in 1927–28. Active in the Oyüwan Soviet, and later in Szechwan, he emerged in June, 1933, as director of the political department of the Red Thirtieth Army. In 1937, after the end of the Long March, Li was sent to the Soviet Union for training in public security work. He returned to China in 1942 and for the duration of the war was active in the Shansi-Chahar-Hopeh Military Region. When military forces of this area were reorganized in 1948 as the North China Field Army, Li was appointed deputy political commissar of the Third Army Corps. He later moved with this unit to occupy Peking and Tientsin in the early days of 1949.

A much different type of revolutionary career was pursued by Li's fellow liberator, the first mayor of Tientsin, Huang Ching. Huang (original name Yü Ch'i-wei) was a nephew of Yü Ta-wei, former minister of national defense in Taiwan.[37] He was born in 1912 to a prosperous family in the coastal region of Shao-hsing, Chekiang. In terms of our study, Huang typified the urbanite. Shao-hsing itself was a thriving

---

[35] A detailed account of Li T'ien-huan's career may be found in Huang Chen-hsia (ed.), *Chung-kung chün-jen chih* (English title: *Mao's Generals*) (Hong Kong: Research Institute of Contemporary History, 1968). Various sources conflict on Li's birthplace. *Who's Who in Communist China* (rev. ed.; 2 vols.; Hong Kong: URI, 1969–70) (hereafter URI *Who's Who*) and Kuo Hua-lun (ed.), *Chung-kung jen-ming lu* (Biographical Dictionary of Chinese Communists) (Taipei: Institute of International Relations, 1967) both say Li is a native of Hunan. According to Tientsin *Chin-pu jih-pao,* January 18, 1950, however, Li was born in Huang-an, Hupeh. Our practice throughout this study is to accept the more local source as the more accurate.

[36] See, for example, Robert W. McColl, "The Oyüwan Soviet Area, 1927–1932," *Journal of Asian Studies,* XXVII, No. 1 (November, 1967), 41–60.

[37] Biographical data on Huang Ching are drawn primarily from URI *Who's Who,* Kuo (ed.), *Chung-kung jen-ming lu,* and *T'ien-chin jih-pao,* February 4, 1953.

population center of some 400,000 by the 1920's, and the center also of an "excellent rice spirit," the envy of travelers "from Friar Odoric to Abbe Huc." [38] By the early 1930's Huang was a student at Shantung University in Tsingtao and later graduated from Shanghai's University of Communications. While still a student, he joined the Party (1932), and for the next five years he worked among the theatrical circles of Shanghai and the students of Peking and Tientsin.[39] (One of his entourage during this period was the actress Lan P'ing—alias Chiang Ch'ing—who married Mao Tse-tung in 1939.)

Had Huang remained in Tientsin he would have emerged in 1949 as one of our early organizers. But Huang was a "straddler." With the outbreak of war against Japan in 1937, he joined the exodus of urban Party workers to the rural base areas and remained there until 1945. During the Civil War, Huang began to move back into the urban milieu. In 1945 he was named mayor of Kalgan; in 1946, mayor of Shihchiachuang. With the liberation of Tientsin in January, 1949, he was appointed mayor of that city and, concurrently, secretary of the municipal Party committee.

Second wave. Moving into the cities during the winter of 1951–52, leaders of the second wave were similar to the liberators in many respects. Most were rural-born and had little contact with urban life at an early age; few received training beyond the secondary school level; few traveled abroad. Like the liberator, the second wave leader was probably an active Party member by the mid-1930's and his revolutionary route, more likely than not, led through the wilderness.

At the same time, the typical second wave member was somewhat younger than his first wave counterpart. And as we suggested before, this age separation may have been important. The average liberator could recall the events of 1911 and had likely played an active role in the May Fourth Movement of 1919. For the second wave leader, however, initial contact with revolutionary events was probably delayed until the mid-1920's. In terms of "linkage" between various leader types, this lag in revolutionary exposure may have been critical. Despite profound differences in background, liberators and local Whites shared certain experiences: as teachers and students they

[38] Samuel Couling, *The Encyclopaedia Sinica* (London: Oxford University Press, 1917), p. 603. Population figures are from Boris P. Torgasheff, "Town Population in China," *The China Critic*, III, No. 4 (April, 1930), 300.

[39] For a brief account of Huang's activities during the December Ninth Movement of 1935, see John Israel, *Student Nationalism in China, 1927–1937* (Stanford, Calif.: Stanford University Press, 1966), pp. 147 ff.

once traveled together into the streets and "to the villages" during and after the events of 1919. Following takeover, the liberators likely made use of this common revolutionary heritage in their dealings with the local Whites. Between the latter and members of the second wave, however, that common heritage may well have been lacking. In this regard, then, the second wave of outsiders was likely perceived— both by the center and by members of the community—as a purer representation of the new order.[40]

Typical of the second wave leader was Ch'en P'i-hsien, a leading official of Shanghai.[41] Little is known of Ch'en's early life. Born in 1911, a native of Fukien, he received a primary education and by 1930 was active in local Party affairs. From the very beginning, Ch'en's revolutionary task area was Red-political. Active in Party youth work during the early 1930's, he emerged in 1935 as secretary of the Children's Bureau of the CCP Central Committee. During the Long March, Ch'en remained in the Kwangtung-Kwangsi border region to carry out guerrilla activities. Then with the outbreak of war against Japan, he was transferred to the East China region, and there he remained for the duration of the war and subsequent Civil War. By the late 1940's, he was identified as secretary of the South Kiangsu Party Committee and political commissar of the South Kiangsu Military Region.

In early March, 1952, Ch'en P'i-hsien first appeared in Shanghai politics as chairman of a local Party conference convened to denounce the then secretary-general of the municipal Party committee, Li Yü.[42] As fourth secretary of the Shanghai CCP Committee, Ch'en took a leading part in the on-going *wu-fan* campaign. Similar to T'ao Chu in the south, his intrusion into the Shanghai political arena was gradual but steady.[43] And as T'ao played an instrumental role in the purge of Fang Fang and others, so Ch'en took an active part in the attacks on

[40] In this regard, it would be interesting to analyze the format, content, and "tone" of successive celebrations commemorating the May Fourth Movement. How has the Party leadership depicted the contribution of White leaders to those events? Has the early linkage between Red and White leaders been stressed? Do we find changes in emphasis over time? We have not pursued these questions in the present study, but such data could give good insight into this phenomenon of "revolutionary generation."

[41] Background information on Ch'en P'i-hsien was drawn primarily from URI *Who's Who* and Kuo (ed.), *Chung-kung jen-ming lu*. For a brief account of Ch'en's activities during the mid-1930's, see Yang Shang-kuei, *The Red Kiangsi-Kwangtung Border Region* (Peking: Foreign Languages Press, 1961).

[42] *CFJP*, March 2, 1952.

[43] The entry of T'ao Chu into Kwangtung politics is described by Ezra Vogel in *Canton under Communism: Programs and Politics in a Provincial Capital, 1949–1968* (Cambridge, Mass.: Harvard University Press, 1969); especially Chap. iii.

Jao Shu-shih and P'an Han-nien in 1954. By the mid-1950's, Ch'en had attained a commanding position in Shanghai municipal organization, and he held that position until his downfall during the Cultural Revolution.

Early organizer. The early organizer's age was that of the liberator, and his revolutionary past as venerable as that of the second wave leader. In most respects, however, the life history of the early organizer looks like a negative print of the outsider. First of all, he was native-born, if not to the city itself, at least to the province thereof. If rural-born, he came from a county located close to major transportation routes. At an early age he made his way to one of the big cities of the coast. Like so many urban youth of his generation, he was caught up in the revolutionary events of the 1920's: the May Thirtieth Movement of 1925, the Northern Expedition, the Shanghai strikes, the Canton Commune. By the early 1930's he had become an active member of the CCP's urban organization, working among the proletariat, the "literary and art circles," or the youth. When Japanese forces advanced southward in 1937, the early organizer went one of two ways. Either he remained in the cities under Japanese control, or he temporarily joined the wilderness route, becoming active in one of the base areas in close proximity to his city of residence. With the defeat of Japan in 1945, he moved back to the urban setting and remained there until the entry of PLA forces in 1949.

The life of Yü Ling follows the above sketch closely. Forty-three years old at the time of liberation, Yü served for a number of years after 1949 as deputy director of the Shanghai Bureau of Culture.[44] He was born in I-hsing, Kiangsu, located at mid-point between the cities of Shanghai and Nanking. Yü first became involved with the Communist Youth League while a middle-school student in Soochow. Later, as a college student in Peking, he joined the Party and was active in organizational work among the Peking Left-Wing Writers' League. As Yü Ling was a playwright and theater critic, his primary task area was White-cultural. Except for a brief spell during the Sino-Japanese War, he served with the Party's organization in Shanghai from the early 1930's until the time of liberation.

Local activist. Youngest of all leader types, the activist was also the most local to the community. Perhaps native-born, in any event a resident of the city at an early age, he was a worker or shop employee

[44] Information on Yü Ling may be found in URI *Who's Who;* Kuo (ed.), *Chung-kung jen-ming lu;* and Ting Wang (ed.), *Niu-kuei she-shen chi* (A Collection of Ghosts and Monsters) (Hong Kong: San-chia-tien shu-wu, 1967).

in the years before liberation. He received little or no formal education and did not travel abroad. After 1949, he took an active part in the newly created labor, youth, and women's organizations. It was during the heat of the early mass campaigns that the local activist proved himself. "Flushed out" in the course of such movements, he was selected and recruited to the Party and municipal office.

Miss Li Chao-chen, a native of Tientsin, worked as a seamstress in a local bedding factory throughout the Sino-Japanese and Civil wars.[45] Only twenty-two years old at the time of liberation, she was placed in charge of a small group in her work section. She did well. And in recognition of her talents, Li was soon recruited to Party membership and selected a "special class model worker." She first appeared in municipal office as a standing committee member of the local trade union council in January, 1952. One year later she emerged as vice-chairman of the Tientsin Women's Federation and was elected a member of the municipal government council.

Early critic. Born before the turn of the century, the early critic was probably native to the region of his future city of residence, or at least knew the city at an early age. He most likely received a university education, and there was a good chance that he studied at the graduate level. The early critic who traveled abroad probably went to Japan, where he became active in some overseas revolutionary organization. On his return to China, he moved into such a career as teaching or business. In 1919 he was swept up in the wave of national emotion which marked the May Fourth Movement. If a teacher, he joined his students in protest against China's treatment at Versailles; if a businessman, he responded to calls for a boycott on Japanese goods. For him the events of 1926–27 were likely viewed as the first concrete steps toward national unity, and he was prepared to work with the new Nationalist leadership. But hope gave way to dismay as he felt the leadership either unwilling or incapable of dealing with civil strife and foreign aggression. By the early years of the Sino-Japanese War, he was in open opposition to the KMT and was working in behalf of the "third party" movement. From this position he moved ever closer to the Communist cause during the years of civil war.

Chang Ch'iung-po was an early critic in Shanghai.[46] He was born in the commercial center of Ningpo, Chekiang, in 1884. Following his

---

[45] Data are from *T'ien-chin jih-pao*, September 30, 1950.

[46] Information on Chang Ch'iung-po comes from *Fu-fei fen-tzu shih-lu* (A True Record of Bandit Collaborators) Taipei: Bureau of Security, Ministry of Defense, 1954).

graduation from a university in Shanghai, he went to Japan to continue his studies in economics at the graduate level. Upon his return to China, Chang became a lecturer in finance at the National University of Chekiang in Hangchow. In the aftermath of the May Fourth Movement, he moved from teaching into business and by the early 1930's was general manager of the Min Hua Bank in Shanghai. With the outbreak of war, Chang moved to Chungking where he became active in "third party" affairs.[47] He was one of the founders and leading supporters of the National Construction Association. Back in Shanghai after the war, however, Chang came under the pressure of Nationalist authorities and fled to Hong Kong in 1947. Two years later he returned to Shanghai where he played a leading role in local activities of the Democratic National Construction Association.

Late collaborator. In age, place of origin, early experiences, and education, the late collaborator was similar to the early critic. What distinguishes him is the lack of evidence of *open* opposition to the KMT before 1949. If the late collaborator traveled abroad, it was likely to America, where he received technical training at the graduate level. After his return to China, he usually moved into industry or government service and pursued this career until the time of the Communist takeover.

Representative of this type was Chao Tsu-k'ang. Born at the turn of the century in Sung-chiang *hsien* on the outskirts of Shanghai, he attended college and later specialized at the Tangshan School of Engineering.[48] He was then selected by the Ministry of Railroads for advanced training in the United States. Under the Nationalists, Chao held a variety of government posts dealing with public highways and roads, transportation, and communications. From 1945 until the Communist takeover, he served as director of the Public Works Bureau in Shanghai. With liberation, Chao was retained in office and put in charge of the process of change-over in his bureau. In this capacity he was appointed to the Shanghai Government Council in December, 1950.

On January 15, 1949, the city of Tientsin was liberated by Chinese Communist forces. Three months later, units of the PLA crossed the

---

[47] For a brief discussion of "third party" activities during the 1940's, see Van Slyke, *Enemies and Friends,* pp. 190 ff.

[48] Data on Chao are drawn from URI *Who's Who; Fu-fei fen-tzu shih-lu;* Kuo (ed.), *Chung-kung jen-ming lu;* and *Shang-hai-shih jen-chih* (Who's Who in Present-day Shanghai) (Shanghai: Chen-wang ch'u-pan she, 1947).

Yangtze and in rapid succession seized the cities of Nanking, Hang-chow, and Wuhan. Shanghai fell to forces under the command of Ch'en I on May 27; Canton was occupied on October 15. In the context of this study, the act of liberation marked the instant of contact between leader type and his office. It is to this phenomenon we now turn.

MUNICIPAL LEADERS AND ORGANIZATION OF THE EARLY YEARS

A typology of municipal leaders—leaders defined in terms of various background factors—is only half of the essential equation of this study. Our ultimate interest is in the individual as leader type *and* as occupant of municipal office. To analyze such relationships we have classified offices in terms of (1) general hierarchical ranking and (2) linkage to general task area. The resultant scheme is one wherein all offices of municipal organization are ranged along two major dimensions, vertical and horizontal.

To construct the vertical dimension, we assigned each municipal office to one of three general hierarchical levels. The distributions are shown in Table 33. The major difficulty here was in relating different organizational units to each other. And as is evident in the table, we ended by giving more weight to certain units. Thus, for example, the CCP committee was assigned a greater share of level one positions than was the political consultative committee; in the final scheme, in other words, the former unit occupies a higher "center of gravity" than the latter. Admittedly the process of assigning office to level involved a number of arbitrary decisions. What was truly arbitrary, however, was our decision to work with three levels, rather than, say, two or four. Having made that choice, it was a relatively straightforward task to rank-order positions from "highest" to "lowest."

To classify positions in terms of task area, we began with a question. What appear to have been the essential activities of municipal organization? What in general terms did the organization *do* in order to accomplish its substantive purposes? As we observed the organization in action—admittedly from afar and through the pages of the local press—four broad and interrelated areas of activity emerged: (1) a sphere of activity concerned with discussion and formulation of overall policy for the municipality; (2) an area related to the execution of such broad-gauge decisions through formulation of shorter-range policies and plans; (3) tasks related to problems of control and supervision over individual performance, so as to assure congruence between policy and its implementation; and (4) activities concerned with

TABLE 33

MUNICIPAL OFFICES IN TERMS OF MUNICIPAL LEVELS

Unit of Organization	Level One	Level Two	Level Three
Communist Party committee	Secretaries; secretary-general (+deputy); department head (+deputy); committee chairman (+vice-chairman)	Other leading posts	(None)
Garrison/public security force	Commander (+deputy); political commissar (+deputy); chief of staff (+deputy); department head (+deputy)	Other leading posts	(None)
Government council	Mayor (+deputy)	Member of council	(None)
Municipal bureaucracy	Secretary-general; bureau director; office director; commission chairman; chief justice of court; chief procurator	Deputy secretary-general; bureau deputy director; office deputy director; division director; commission vice-chairman; deputy chief justice	Division deputy director; commission member; court justice
Mass organization/democratic party	Chairman; secretary-general; chief editor of major paper	Vice-chairman; deputy secretary-general	Executive committee member; department head
Political consultative committee	Chairman; secretary-general	Vice-chairman; deputy secretary-general; standing committee member	Consultative committee member

mobilizing support among the population for whom such policies were relevant.

Given the limited scope of this essay, it is difficult to examine these various task areas in any depth. We shall simply give a brief description of each. The first sphere of activity, concerned with discussion and formulation of overall policy, we have labeled the "generalist" area. The separation of this sphere from all others is merely a restatement of the age-old dichotomy between "policy" and "operations." [49] No matter how expressed ("politics versus administration," "ends versus means"), the distinction between policy and operations is difficult to draw both in theory and practice. Yet we should like to retain the distinction in this study. Despite the problems involved, it is likely that in any organization there does exist a sphere of activity which has an intended relationship to discussion of overall policy. And performance of such generalist activities carries the expectation—on the part of all members—that resultant decisions will apply to the total organization and will serve as the organization's ends.

The other three spheres, then, are to be considered operational in nature. Activities in the areas we designate as "management," "control," and "mobilization" are together related to decisions and processes which are relatively narrow in scope and are geared to those policies which emerge from the generalist area.

Control activities impinge on the linkages between policy and operations, between higher leaders and lower, between leaders and led. To wield control in organization is to ensure that the sum-total of operations is congruent with general policy. And as Franz Schurmann suggests, control may be exercised in two ways: (1) through investigation and supervision of individual performance, to ensure that the individual "measures up to standards"; and (2) through the exercise of "restraint or direction upon the free action" of an individual in order to assure his compliance.[50] Implicit in the notion of control, then, is the threat of deprivation and/or the imposition of sanctions. Control, if you will, is the coercive side of organization.

Mobilization is its persuasive face. Again our concern is with linkages between policy and process, between leadership and compliance. Activities in this area, however, are directed toward generating feelings of loyalty and allegiance among members of the organization and the society at large. To mobilize is not to seek compliance through force

49 In this regard, see Schurmann, *Ideology and Organization,* pp. 223–25.
50 *Ibid.,* p. 310.

or threat of force; rather, it is to attempt to secure compliance by making the goals of the organization compatible with those of the individual.

What remains is the area of management. As used by Schurmann, the term "management" refers to "leadership concerned with operational ends and means. . . . Management is the functional side of executive position." [51] Where the areas of control and mobilization are concerned with problems of leadership and compliance, the area of management is more closely related to the substantive content of public policy. Given the goals which emerge from the generalist area, management decisions are essentially those of strategy and tactics: selection and allocation of resources; definition and assignment of tasks; selection of priorities, decisions on timing, and the like.

Each municipal office was assigned to one of these four task areas. How have we determined the linkages? How have we decided which office performs what task? Ideally we should have acted as participant-observers. Discounting the formal title of office, we should have watched what the individual did, probed his own perceptions of his tasks, and gauged the expectations of others. Needless to say, the proper course of action was impossible. In assigning office to task area, we were guided very much by the formal definition of office. At the same time, we tried to bring to bear our understanding and "feel" of municipal organization. In Table 34 we show the distribution of various municipal offices among the four task areas.

One final observation is important. As will become clear, there rarely occurred a simple one-to-one relationship between a given individual and a single task area. More often than not, leaders performed in more than one capacity, in more than one area.

What types of leaders were assigned to what areas of organization? What relationships do we discern between factors of an individual's background and his municipal level and task? What do such distributions suggest about the broader political process, about problems of transition and consolidation, interactions between the new order and old, and interrelationships between the center and urban region?

As mentioned previously, our focus is limited in this essay. We are concentrating on the immediate postliberation period, the months following Communist takeover of the cities, and treating municipal organization as a single entity, drawing data from all three cities. We assure the reader that the patterns we observe are roughly similar for

[51] *Ibid.*, p. 224.

each municipality; and where discrepancies do occur, we shall make note of them.

Looking at distributions of leader types among levels and task areas of organization, we first examine the degree to which an individual's type-classification itself may have governed his municipal assignment. Then, examining each leader type category in turn, we look for any

TABLE 34

MUNICIPAL OFFICES IN TERMS OF TASK AREAS

Task Area	General Unit	Specific Unit or Office
Generalist	CCP Committee	Secretary (+deputies)
	Government council	Mayor (+deputies); council members
Management	CCP Committee	Technical committees (e.g., Industrial Production Committee)
	Bureaucracy	Bureaus, offices, and divisions: real estate, works, labor, industry and commerce, civil affairs, finance, tax, public utilities, public health, supply, municipal construction, alien affairs Commissions: finance and economic, municipal construction
Control	CCP Committee	Secretary-general (+deputies) Departments and committees: social affairs, organization, discipline
	Garrison	All positions
	Bureaucracy	Secretary-general (+deputies) Bureaus and offices: public security, staff, personnel Commissions: people's control, political and legal affairs People's court/procuratorate
Mobilization	CCP Committee	Departments: propaganda, United Front work, youth/women's work
	Bureaucracy	Bureaus and offices: education, culture, news and publications Commission on Education and Culture
	Political consultative committee	All positions
	Mass organization/democratic party	All positions

possible relationships between municipal assignment and such background variables as degree of "localness," extent of prior urban exposure, level and type of education, quality of revolutionary experience, and so forth. These distributions will yield a rough profile of municipal organization which can give us insight into the general purposes and strategies of the central leadership in that early period. In conclusion, we shall talk briefly about variations over time and space.

LEADER TYPES, LEVELS, AND TASK AREAS

In Table 35, first of all, we show the distribution of leader types along the vertical plane. The data suggest the following general proposition: the more outsider and Red, the higher an individual's placement in the hierarchy; the more local and White, the lower; and where these particular characteristics are mixed, there is no discernible tendency one way or the other.

TABLE 35

LEADERS BY TYPE AND MUNICIPAL LEVEL

Municipal Level	Outside Red * (N = 57)		Local Red * (N = 47)		Local White (N = 163)	
	N	% Known	N	% Known	N	% Known
Level one	44	79	18	41	18	12
Level two	9	16	13	30	50	33
Level three	3	5	13	30	83	55
Total known	56	100	44	101 †	151	100

$$X^2 = 89.53 \ddagger \qquad p = .001 \qquad C = .513$$

* In the immediate postliberation period, the outside Red category includes only those we have designated as liberators; the local Red category, only those designated as early organizers. Leaders of the second wave and the local activists did not enter office until a later period.

† Because we have rounded off individual percentages, the total does not equal 100 per cent.

‡ For a note on X^2 see asterisked notation to Table 31.

In one sense, our findings are quite similar to those of Michel Oksenberg in his study of local leaders in rural China. The outsiders and Party members, he found, tend to congregate at the higher levels of organization, while the natives and non-Party members are found at the lower.[52] We should note an important distinction between Oksen-

[52] "Local Leaders in Rural China," pp. 177–80.

berg's data and our own, however. His conception of levels is based upon a hierarchical ranking of separate systems, such as counties, districts, and villages, while ours is based upon a rank-ordering of various offices within a single system.

What about distributions along the horizontal dimension? There are several ways we can approach the data. First, we can simply examine the proportion of each leader type assigned to each task area, as is shown in Table 36. This particular perspective enables us to say something about the degree of "balance" or "imbalance" in the distribution of a given leader type among various task areas. It is apparent, for example, that the outside Red category was the most balanced in terms of distribution: no more than half its membership was assigned to any single area, and sizable proportions of outside Reds were present in all four areas. In contrast, leaders of both local categories were highly concentrated, specifically, in the area of mobilization. Local Reds had proportionally more members than local Whites in the area of control; local Whites had proportionally more members than local Reds in the area of management.

TABLE 36

LEADERS BY TYPE AND TASK AREA

Task Area	Outside Red (N = 57)		Local Red (N = 47)		Local White (N = 163)	
	N	% Total *	N	% Total *	N	% Total *
Generalist	18	32	14	30	36	22
Management	10	18	7	15	47	29
Control	27	47	6	13	2	1
Mobilization	29	51	41	87	130	80

* Since many individuals were operating in more than one task area, total of separate numbers will exceed the total of each leader type.

We can approach these data from another angle, namely, in terms of over- or underrepresentation of each leader type in each task area. Given the total membership of each leader type identified in office, and given the total number of identified leader type members in each area, it is possible to calculate an "index of fair representation" which measures the degree to which each leader type had its fair share of positions in each area. We present such indices in Table 37. The reader will note one modification: we have added an area of "high management" tasks which encompasses all management positions at levels one and two. The reason for this modification is apparent. While outside Reds, for example, were somewhat underrepresented in the general area of management, they had a substantial degree of overrepresentation in management positions at the higher levels. In addition, we see that outside Reds were overrepresented in both generalist and control areas. With exception of the total management areas, local Reds had their fair share of positions in all municipal task areas. And of the three general leader types, local Whites had the highest incidence of underrepresentation. From the data of Table 37, the outside Reds emerge as the most "pervasive" leader type in municipal organization.

TABLE 37

LEADERS BY TYPE AND TASK AREA, MEASURED
BY INDEX OF FAIR REPRESENTATION *

Task Area	Outside Red	Local Red	Local White
Generalist	1.3	1.1	.9
Management	.7	.6	1.2
High management	1.5	1.1	.8
Control	3.7	1.0	.1
Mobilization	.7	1.2	1.1

* Closely related to chi-square (see note to Table 31), this "index of fair representation" attempts to gauge and express the degree of discrepancy between observed and expected levels of representation of various leader types in various municipal task areas. The index is calculated by the following formula: $I_{xy} = \dfrac{O_{xy}}{E_{xy}}$ where I_{xy} is the index of representation of a given leader type x in area y; and where O_{xy} is the observed level of representation, E_{xy} the expected level of representation of leader type x in area y. To calculate expected level of representation, we set E_{xy} equal to $\dfrac{N_x T_y}{T}$ where N_x is the total members of leader type x identified in municipal office as a whole, where T is the total members of *all* leader type categories in municipal office as a whole, and where T_y is the total members of all leader type categories identified in area y. Where the index for a given type category in a given task area equals 1.0, there is no discrepancy between observed and expected levels of representation: the leader type category in question has its "fair share" of positions. For example, an index score of 2.0 indicates overrepresentation by a factor of 2; a score of .5, underrepresentation by a factor of 2.

A third approach to the data is simply to construct a series of task area profiles in terms of identified leader type members in each area. Thus, from the patterns of Figure 3, we might make the following tentative observations: (1) the area of control was clearly dominated by the liberator, and we should therefore expect that particular area to be characterized by the qualities of outsider and Red; (2) the general area of management appears to have been the "Whitest" area of municipal organization; (3) the paucity of liberators in the mobilization area likely rendered that area the most local; and (4) the two areas of generalist and high management appear to have been the most balanced in terms of all those characteristics—Red, White, local, and outsider. We shall return to this profile later.

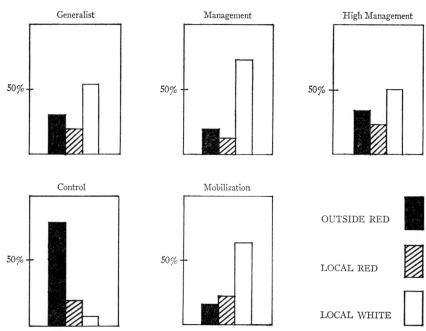

Figure 3. Task area "profiles" in terms of identified leader type members in each area

To what extent, then, did an individual's leader type classification *alone* govern his assignment to municipal office? Given knowledge that individual A was leader type X, would we thereby know his level and task assignment? Only to a limited degree. If he were a liberator, we would be safe in assuming that he held a high-level position. What about other leader types? As we saw, local Reds were distributed among all three ranks of organization; and while local Whites tended toward the lower ranks, a fair number held office at levels one and two. What factors, in addition to leader type classification, may have accounted for these differences in level assignment?

When we consider distributions along the horizontal dimension, the relationships between leader type classification and assignment become even more tenuous. Why did certain liberators move into the area of control, while others were located in the area of mobilization? Among local Reds, which leaders took up positions in the generalist area? Finally, within the ranks of the local Whites, were there differences between those who were managers and those who performed mobilization tasks? In the following pages we shall try to answer such questions by examining each leader type in turn.

OUTSIDE REDS: DISTRIBUTION AMONG LEVELS AND TASK AREAS

Among our sample of leaders, the category "liberator," of itself, was virtual assurance of assignment to high-level position, and little would be gained by examining differences within the category in this respect. The relationship of outside Reds to task areas is a different story, however. With possible exception of management tasks, the category was strongly represented in all areas of organization. What kinds of liberators moved into various areas?

Table 38, first of all, analyzes outside Reds in the area of control. As can be seen, leaders have been differentiated in terms of several background variables, the first of which demands a word of explanation. Although the liberator, by definition, was an outsider to his city of office incumbency, some members of the category were "more outsider" than others. No outside Red was native in birth; none had resided in the city for a long period before takeover; but some *had* experienced preliberation contact with the city in question. Huang Ching, whom we discussed previously, was one such individual; and Huang was clearly less an outsider to Tientsin than his fellow liberator, Li T'ien-huan. Apparently this factor of prior contact was to have a bearing on one's assignment to municipal office. The data suggest that lack of prior contact may have been an important qualification for assignment to the area of control. Moving into this area, in effect, were the "outsiders of the outsiders."

From what we know already about local politics in contemporary China, the finding is not surprising. Michel Oksenberg, for example, has found a high percentage of outsiders among "wielders of the instruments of coercion" at the local level. Ezra Vogel, in his analysis of land reform in Kwangtung, points out the important role played by outside northerners in the application of harsh, and often coercive, policies.[53] The argument here is quite straightforward: political or-

[53] Oksenberg, "Local Leaders in Rural China," pp. 187–88; Vogel, *Canton under Communism,* pp. 106 ff.

ganizations must perform the task of control, and the task can best be performed by those least likely to be compromised by former ties and associations with the particular population involved.

With fewer links to the city of their office incumbency, those liberators assigned to control tasks tended also to have less acquaintance with the urban milieu in general. As the data of Table 38 suggest, the ruralite (the individual with no early exposure to the urban setting) had a far better chance of assignment to that area than the nonruralite. Furthermore, liberators who traveled the wilderness route—those whose first sustained contact with the big city was to come only after 1949—were more likely to be controllers than those who worked in the cities at some point in their revolutionary careers. To summarize, of liberators active in the control area of municipal organization, overwhelming majorities were more outsider (88 per cent), ruralites (83 per cent), and travelers of the wilderness route (95 per cent).

TABLE 38

ANALYSIS OF OUTSIDE REDS IN CONTROL AREA

	Outside Reds in Control Area			
	Identified		Not Identified	
Relevant Background Categories	N	% Known	N	% Known
Status as outsider *				
"More" outsider	23	88	17	63
"Less" outsider	3	12	10	37
Total known	26	100	27	100
$X^2 = 3.38$ $.10 > p > .05$ $C = .284$				
Degree of early urban exposure †				
Ruralite	10	83	9	43
Other	2	17	12	57
Total known	12	100	21	100
$X^2 = 3.60$ $.10 > p > .05$ $C = .366$				
Revolutionary route †				
Wilderness route	19	95	12	57
Other	1	5	9	43
Total known	20	100	21	100
$X^2 = 6.04$ $.02 > p > .01$ $C = .404$				

* A leader is classified "more" outsider if he had no known contact with the city in question prior to 1949.

† These variables are discussed in the text.

This particular cluster of background attributes, it will be recalled, was characteristic of one of our outside Red subcategories—the central-interior native. Was it this individual, then, who moved into the control areas of municipal organization after 1949? If so, an interesting proposition comes to mind, namely, that the area of control was perceived by the national leadership as its prime "point of entry" into the locality, and that the assignment of central-interior natives to this particular area was to forge the major link between center and urban region.

The data give some, but not overwhelming, support to this proposition. What the distributions of Table 39 suggest is that the area of control served as a "center of gravity" for the central-interior native in municipal organization; while no means restricted to that area, he more likely than not was active therein. The same cannot be said for the other liberators. For them, in fact, there appears to have been another center of gravity, the area of mobilization. From this table there is no indication that the central-interior native dominated the

TABLE 39

REGION OF ORIGIN AND MUNICIPAL TASK AREA
OF OUTSIDE REDS

| | Region of Origin of Outside Reds | | | |
| | Central Interior * (N = 21) | | Other (N = 36) | |
Task Area	N	% Total †	N	% Total †
Generalist	6	29	12	33
Management	2	10	8	22
Control	13	62	14	39
Mobilization	8	38	21	58

* From Hunan, Kiangsi, Hupeh, or Honan.
† Since individuals may perform more than one task, the total of separate numbers exceeds the total of individuals from each of the two general areas.

area of control, at least in terms of numbers. But as effective control over a corporation's assets may be exercised by a tightly knit minority, so it was entirely possible that those from a distinct region of the country identified themselves as a group and perceived themselves as principal "guardians" of control tasks in municipal organization.

With ruralites and travelers of the wilderness route taking up position in the control area, a different kind of outside Red moved into the area of mobilization. While there is no indication from our data that the mobilizers were significantly "less outsider" than others, the distributions of Table 40 do suggest that they were more likely to have had prior contact with the urban milieu in general. Of those who were urban-born or who had moved to the city at an early age, all but a handful were active in the area of mobilization. Similarly, the liberator who had worked in the Party's urban apparatus at some point in his revolutionary career was very likely to move into this particular task area. Finally, when we differentiate liberators according to revolutionary task area, those with pre-1949 experiences in political tasks were far more likely to be mobilizers than were the military or administrative specialists.

The only other task area of significant liberator representation in this early period was that of generalist. And of the different back-

TABLE 40

ANALYSIS OF OUTSIDE REDS IN MOBILIZATION AREA

Relevant Background Categories	Outside Reds in Mobilization Area			
	Identified		Not Identified	
	N	% Known	N	% Known
Degree of early urban exposure *				
Ruralite	6	35	13	81
Other	11	65	3	19
Total known	17	100	16	100
	$X^2 = 5.37$ .05 > p > .02 C = .422			
Revolutionary route *				
Wilderness route	10	53	21	95
Other	9	47	1	5
Total known	19	100	22	100
	X^2 inappropriate			
Revolutionary task area *				
Red-political	14	56	1	4
Other	11	44	26	96
Total known	25	100	27	100
	$X^2 = 14.84$ p = .001 C = .500			

* These variables are discussed in the text.

ground variables we have examined in this study, only one, the level of formal education, appears to have been operative in the assignment of outside Reds to that area. Those with a higher level of education (university or more) were more likely than others to be active in generalist tasks. It is difficult to know what interpretation to attach to this finding, if indeed any should be attached at all. In a previous section, however, we suggested that formal educational experiences, in the final analysis, may have more of a "generalizing" than "specializing" effect on the individual. Regardless of his specific field of interest, the person in higher education is exposed to an entirely new realm of ideas and concepts which likely give him a more "cosmopolitan" outlook. To the extent that such is true, it is not surprising to find liberators with a higher education operating in the least specialized area of municipal organization, an area concerned with the discussion and formulation of broad-gauge policy for the total system. In other words, he who was generalist by virtue of former training and experience performed the generalist tasks of urban organization.

No other variable was operative in the assignment of liberators to the generalist area. Ruralites were as likely to be active therein as those with early urban exposure, those who followed the wilderness route as likely as those who worked in the cities before 1949, and so forth. The lack of any significant correlations in this regard suggests that the generalist area of municipal organization was the most balanced in terms of leader-type representation. We shall pick up the threads of this argument in a later section.

LOCAL REDS: DISTRIBUTION AMONG LEVELS AND TASK AREAS

We found in a previous section that one's classification as local Red was virtual assurance of assignment to the area of mobilization: of a total of forty-seven local Reds identified in office, forty-one were identified as "mobilizers." By itself, however, the category gave us little clue to the individual's placement in the hierarchy: a local Red was as likely to be at level three as he was at level one. Who among this category, then, were assigned to the higher levels? Moreover, which of our local Reds held a concurrent position in the area of generalist tasks, the only other area of substantial local Red representation?

The critical variable in each case appears to be length of revolutionary service. Local Reds with longer service (active by the Long

March period) were more likely than others to hold high-level positions and to be active in the generalist area. The relationships of Tables 41 and 42 may be expressed in negative terms: local Reds with briefer service were unlikely to hold positions at higher levels, and they were very unlikely to perform generalist tasks.

TABLE 41

MUNICIPAL LEVEL AND LENGTH OF PARTY SERVICE OF LOCAL REDS

| Length of Service * | Municipal Level of Local Reds | | | | | |
| | Level One | | Level Two | | Level Three | |
	N	% Known	N	% Known	N	% Known
Longer	14	78	6	46	4	33
Shorter	4	22	7	54	8	67
Total known	18	100	13	100	12	100
	$X^2 = 6.47$		.05 > p > .02		C = .358	

* Those with "longer" service are known to have been active Party members by the time of the Long March (1934–35).

TABLE 42

LENGTH OF PARTY SERVICE OF LOCAL REDS IN GENERALIST AREA

| Length of Service * | Local Reds in Generalist Area | | | |
| | Identified | | Not Identified | |
	N	% Known	N	% Known
Longer	12	86	13	41
Shorter	2	14	19	59
Total known	14	100	32	100
	$X^2 = 6.27$	.02 > p > .01	C = .385	

* See notation to Table 41.

Given our proposition concerning the relationship between liberators and the area of control, it would be fascinating to know what kind of local Red was assigned to that same area. Unfortunately, the numbers are too few, and no patterns emerge from the data. A similar condition holds for the local Reds identified in the area of management.

LOCAL WHITES: DISTRIBUTION AMONG LEVELS AND TASK AREAS

As a group the local Whites tended to cluster at the lower levels of municipal organization. Still, there were a number in this category who held positions at levels one and two. As might be expected, and as we found in the case of the local Red, the critical variable appears to be length of service, in this case, length of period of known opposition to the Nationalists. Relative to the late collaborator, the early critic had a high "center of gravity" in urban organization: nearly two-thirds of the latter type held positions at levels one and two, while all but a handful of late collaborators were located at levels two and three.

TABLE 43

LOCAL WHITES BY MUNICIPAL LEVEL AND TYPE

	Municipal Level					
	Level One		Level Two		Level Three	
Type	N	% Known	N	% Known	N	% Known
Early critic	11	61	14	30	14	18
Late collaborator	7	39	32	70	66	83
Total known	18	100	46	100	80	101 *
	$X^2 = 14.54$		$p = .001$		$C = .303$	

* Because we have rounded off individual percentages, the total does not equal 100 per cent.

Regarding distribution along the horizontal dimension, we have seen that the local White was very likely to be operating in the area of mobilization: four out of five leaders of this type were engaged in such organs as "democratic parties," "mass organizations," "political consultative committees," and the like. Another important area of local White activity was management. In the years following liberation, such non-Party personnel as former KMT officials and local businessmen were to play a critical role in the process of administrative change-over. In brief, the transfer of governmental responsibilities could not occur overnight. The Party leadership was the first to recognize this fact, and while anxious to train their own cadres and position them throughout the state apparatus, they were equally anxious to tap the knowledge and skills of the local White. To this end, they retained the services of many former officials and coopted a number of "democratic personages" into bureaucratic posts.[54]

The areas of management and mobilization were thus the two major loci of local White activity in organization. And from the data of Table 44 there is indication that different kinds of local Whites were moving into each. Those with a longer history of open opposition to

TABLE 44

ANALYSIS OF LOCAL WHITES IDENTIFIED IN MANAGEMENT
AND/OR MOBILIZATION AREAS

Background Variables	Local Whites in Office and Relevant Areas				
	Identified in Municipal Office	Identified in Management		Identified in Mobilization	
	N	N	% Total in Office *	N	% Total in Office *
Status of local White					
Early critic	42	1	2	41	98
Late collaborator	114	44	39	84	74
Field of formal education					
Social sciences, humanities	51	7	14	47	92
Natural sciences, engineering	49	23	47	29	59
Occupation					
Law, journalism, teaching	45	3	7	41	91
Business	57	17	30	54	95
Engineering, medicine	39	21	54	18	46

* A number of local Whites held positions in both management and mobilization areas; some held position in neither. As a consequence, the total number of any type identified in both management and mobilization areas may exceed or fall short of the total number of that type identified in municipal office.

the Nationalists—the early critics—were unlikely to perform management tasks but exceedingly likely to end up in the area of mobilization. The late collaborator, on the other hand, was far more likely than the early critic to be a manager and somewhat less likely to be a mobilizer. When local Whites are differentiated in terms of type of

[54] One statement of this policy may be found in "Nan-ching chieh-kuan kung-tso ching-yen" (Experiences in the Take-over of Nanking), in Lai Chih-yen (ed.), *Chieh-kuan ch'eng-shih te kung-tso ching-yen* (Experiences in the Take-over of Cities) (Canton: Jen-min ch'u-pan she, 1949), p. 34. See the discussion by H. Arthur Steiner in "Chinese Communist Urban Policy," *American Political Science Review,* XLIV, No. 1 (March, 1950), 49.

formal education and occupation, we again find different types of leaders moving into each area. Those with training and careers in the natural sciences and engineering had an even chance of assignment to either area. The leaders with formal education in the social sciences or humanities, who pursued careers in business, journalism, law or teaching, were far more likely to be present in the area of mobilization, and very unlikely to function as managers.

Might we conclude, then, that the more "Red" (less "White") were the mobilizers, while the more "expert" were the managers? It is a tempting formulation, but it obscures the fact that the local White mobilizer was an expert in his own right. Certainly the businessman was every bit as familiar with problems of urban planning as the engineer or doctor. And while the latter had familiarity with problems of housing and public health, the journalist or teacher was a specialist in communicating ideas. For the new urban leadership, one skill was as vital as the other. The division, in other words, was not so much between "Red" and "expert" as it was between different kinds of expertise.

With respect to local Whites in the generalist area, we again find no significant relationships between factors of background and fact of assignment. Early critics and late collaborators were present in similar proportions; level and type of education apparently had no effect; nor did occupation and type of expertise. Finally, the number of local Whites in the area of control was simply too small to analyze.

Summary and Conclusions

Given certain relationships between leader types, levels, and task areas of organization, can we now sketch a general profile of the municipal system of the immediate postliberation period? Which areas were dominated by what kinds of leaders? What do such phenomena suggest about linkages within the organization, and between the municipal system and those higher and lower? How were the processes of transition and consolidation manifested?

Regarding hierarchical placement, first of all, the most critical variables were length of identification with the Communist cause and degree of prior contact with the city of office incumbency. At the highest levels were the most Red and outsider; at the lowest, the most White and local. Party members with greater seniority (the liberators as a group, and those local Reds with longer revolutionary service) dominated positions at level one. As we saw, moreover, the quality

"Red" was not governed entirely by the fact of Party membership: among local Whites, a fair number of early critics were also located at the higher levels of organization. The relationship between level assignment and degree of prior contact with the city was especially pronounced: of all known outsiders in office (43), a total of 40 (93 per cent) held positions at level one; while among nonoutsiders (157), only 39 (25 per cent) were at this level.

Among the four task areas of organization, the area of control was the only one clearly dominated by a single leader type—the liberator, and in particular, the central interior native. Thus, individuals operating in this area shared the two dominant characteristics of those at the highest echelons of organization: they were Red and outsider. The "controller," however, had one additional attribute. Not only was he an outsider to his particular city, but he was very much a stranger to the urban setting in general. He typically came from the rural areas, had little exposure to the big city at an early age, and during his entire revolutionary career, his major center of activities was the rural hinterland. The controller, in brief, was a ruralite; his area of operation was the most "ruralized" area of urban organization.

A much different kind of individual moved into the area of mobilization. Compared to those operating in the area of control, first of all, the "mobilizer" was likely to be less Red, in terms of both CCP membership and length of revolutionary service. Non-Party members had a slight edge in this area; and among Party members, particularly among local Reds, "revolutionary juniors" were likely to end up in mobilization tasks. In this area also were the most local and urbanized leaders of the city. Local Reds and Whites were predominant; and among liberators, those who performed as mobilizers were likely to have had prior acquaintance with the urban milieu.

Leaders in the area of management had several attributes in common with those in the area of mobilization. First, they tended to be locals, especially in terms of prior residence. Second, they were urbanites who had knowledge of the problems of city planning and administration. Compared to the mobilizers, however, the managers were the "Whitest" leaders of the municipality. Not only were there many non-CCP personnel operating in this area, but an overwhelming majority of them were late collaborators.

Where each of the above areas was weighted toward one attribute or another (more Red, more local, and so forth), the generalist area was the most "balanced" of the municipal organization. As one examines the generalists, it is as though he had selected at random a sampling of all identified leaders in the city: in terms of nearly every attribute, the area was a microcosm of the entire leadership population. In only one respect was there a discrepancy: as a group, generalists were more senior, in both age and length of revolutionary service.

In other words, the generalist area was the only one not to serve as a "center of gravity" for particular leader types. The control area was a base of operations for the ruralite and outsider liberator; the mobilization area, for the local Red and early critic; the management area, for the late collaborator. The sphere of generalist tasks, on the other hand, served as a kind of bridge between all other regions of organization, as a common meeting ground for leaders of all types and of varying background experiences.

From these data we can begin to get a picture of the municipality as a system, and its place in the broader process. As Figure 4 suggests, the municipality may be conceptualized as one system in a series, held together and linked to higher and lower systems by the complex interplay of different kinds of leaders performing different kinds of tasks. Primary linkage between center and municipality was provided by the outside Red liberator, most especially, the native of the central interior. His "point of entry" into the municipality was the area of control; and in the capacity of municipal controller, he transmitted impulses from the center to all other areas of the system. In the generalist area, the liberator made contact with representatives of the other municipal leader types, the local Reds and Whites. Here leaders of all categories discussed and formulated policy for the system as a whole. Resultant policy was then carried into other areas of the system: back into the area of control, and on into the areas of mobilization and management. Finally, with the possible exception of those confined to the generalist area (very few indeed), leaders of all types in all areas forged the linkages between the municipal system and all lower systems—the districts, residential associations, and the like.

By way of conclusion, let us try to relate these findings to broader problems of transition and consolidation. As we do so, we shall give some attention to changes and variations over time and space. In pursuit of transition goals, the shift from old order to new, the Red leader was pervasive throughout the municipal system. Party members in general, outside Reds in particular, were dominant at the highest echelons; and along the horizontal dimension of organization, only in the area of management were such leaders underrepresented. Transition involved more than change and a high visibility of CCP members, however. The aspect of continuity was equally important. The old order was not to be obliterated, but (to paraphrase Joseph R. Levenson) "retired with honor." [55] In this regard, the local White played a critical role in the months after take-over. As technocrat or former KMT official, he was present in the area of management, where he could provide much-needed administrative and technical know-how.

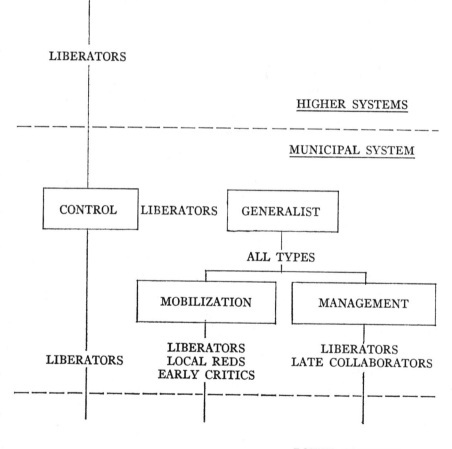

Figure 4. Linkages among Municipal Task Areas, and between the Municipality and Systems Higher and Lower

[55] "The Place of Confucius in Communist China," *CQ*, No. 12 (October–December, 1962), p. 16.

As businessman or intellectual, he was visible in the area of mobilization, where he could help bridge the gap between values of the "White past" and "Red future."

The transition process brought in its wake the development and expansion of urban Party organization; and the years following liberation witnessed a growing presence and visibility in municipal office of Red leaders in general, local Reds in particular. The change was most evident in the area of management, where Party members gradually displaced the local Whites. By early to mid-1953, White leaders, while still visible in municipal organization, were largely concentrated in the area of mobilization.

What about the process of consolidation? There is good indication from our data that the Peking leadership was deeply concerned about linkages between center and urban region. Outsiders, those with weakest ties to the immediate community, monopolized the highest and most visible positions of local organization. Here they could perform two critical functions. On the one hand, they could serve as "brokers" between the aspirations of central policy-makers and exigencies of the local situation. At the same time, their high visibility in the local community could help make visible the center itself. This strong relationship between outsider status and high-level municipal office persisted in the years after 1949, and the correlation held true in each of the three cities under analysis.

While the presence of outsiders in high-level office was a clear manifestation of the consolidation process, the distribution of outside Reds among task areas of organization reflected the manner in which goals of consolidation were pursued. Initially, the center's prime "point of entry" was through the area of control, through the exercise of violence and supervision over individual performance. In the months following take-over, in other words, "consolidation" was tantamount to "pacification." With time, however, linkages between center and urban region became more diverse. Members of the second wave, outsiders who assumed office in the winter of 1951–52, were far more likely than the earlier liberators to move into management and generalist areas of organization. This is to say, initial concentration in control tasks gave way to a growing emphasis on "utilitarian" modes of consolidation—effective performance in the deployment and allocation of urban resources.

Given the limitations of this essay, we have not examined similarities and differences between the three cities of Tientsin, Shanghai, and

Canton. Yet there is good indication that central strategies not only shifted over time, but also varied from place to place. In an early section of this paper, we argued that processes of transition and consolidation, while closely related, were not identical and could operate at cross-purposes. A key goal of transition, the development of a viable local Party structure, could ultimately reduce rather than enhance the visibility of the center, and thereby impede successful consolidation. Such appears to have been the case in Canton, the city most distant from the central leadership in Peking. For during the period of the *san-fan* and *wu-fan* campaigns, the Canton Party organization came under severe attack, and the outsider gained at the expense of the local Red. The closer to Peking—to some degree in Shanghai, to a greater extent in Tientsin—the more were goals of consolidation balanced by those of transition: a continuing high visibility of outsiders in municipal office was accompanied by substantial upward mobility of local Reds, and *all* Party members tended to gain at the expense of the local White.

This essay has developed certain concepts and typologies and through an analysis of relationships between urban leaders and organization has tried to shed light upon the general purposes and strategies of the Chinese Communist leadership in the early years. Our primary intent in this endeavor was to demonstrate the potential value of elite analysis for the study of contemporary China. Dankwart Rustow observed not long ago: "Neither elite studies nor any other method is likely to bring us closer to the deceptive ideal of behaviorism, of politics as a branch of mechanics. But individuals, families, and social groups *are* 'real and tangible.' They can offer a concrete island of refuge to a scholar who has seen old abstractions founder and who needs time and fresh materials to build a more seaworthy set of abstractions." [56] In this study we have tried to push away from the island of refuge and test some abstractions in the surrounding waters.

[56] "The Study of Elites: Who's Who, When, and How," *World Politics*, XVIII, No. 4 (July, 1966), 695.

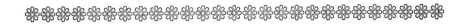

LYNN T. WHITE III

Leadership in Shanghai,1955-69 *

Politics is an elusive fish to catch in the net of social theory. In order to say anything of interest about specific short-term political conflicts, it is almost impossible to avoid discussing their relationship to social conditions. But it seems just as difficult to develop general theories that can show any firm, constant relationship between social structure and live politics.[1] If one kind of logic is used today to make us understand the contents of the newspaper, another different line of reasoning is all too likely to convince us tomorrow. For example, how can we make science out of the rises and falls of particular leaders?

* The author sincerely thanks the Foreign Area Fellowship Program, the Center for Chinese Studies at the University of California, Berkeley, the Universities Service Centre in Hong Kong, and the Center for Southeast Asian Studies of Kyoto University, all of which provided facilities that helped in the production of this essay. Donald Klein, Michel Oksenberg, Robert Scalapino, and William Whitson generously wrote comments to help revise the draft. The author is responsible for all errors of fact and attitude, and he is partially responsible for any misuses to which his information may in future be put.

[1] Biographical data for this paper come from many sources, which will not be specifically cited as authorities because assertions here are too often based on guesses between their differences. The most useful were: Kuo Hua-lun (ed.), *Chung-kung jen-ming lu* (Biographical Dictionary of Chinese Communists) (Taipei: Institute of International Relations, 1967); *Who's Who in Communist China*, Vols. I and II (rev. ed.; Hong Kong: URI, 1969); *Gendai chūgoku jinmei jiten* (A Biographical Dictionary of Contemporary Chinese) (Tokyo: Kasumigaseki-kai, 1962); Huang Chen-hsia (ed.), *Chung-kung chün-jen chih* (English title: *Mao's Generals*) (Hong Kong: Research Institute of Contemporary History, 1968); and the biographical files organized regionally in the St. John's Building, U.S. Consulate-General, Hong Kong.

[1] Two of the most famous modern efforts toward this end are presented in Barrington Moore, *The Social Origins of Dictatorship and Democracy: Lord and Peasant in the Making of the Modern World* (Boston: Beacon Press, 1966) and Talcott Parsons, *Politics and Social Structure* (New York: Free Press, 1969). A footnote will not suffice to criticize these masters' enormous and very different theories, which are necessarily open-ended, and are understandable in part because of analogies drawn from economics and other fields. Neither of these theories was designed to deal with leadership disputes at medium levels over short periods of time, of the kind with which this paper is concerned.

Most issues in social studies have proved amenable to one or the other of two techniques. The inductive, anthropological method would have us describe the characteristics we observe in human action and then construct them logically into a cultural whole that is less well defined. The deductive, sociometric method has us test the real extent of characteristics that have already been defined and organized ideally in our minds. This paper will use both of these methods. They complement each other and show different aspects of the question under study. But leadership disputes (and some other aspects of politics also) are too varied and too ephemeral to enable these techniques to work very effectively. Leadership conflicts do not follow simple patterns. If they did, elites in power might predict them better and prevent them. By the nature of their origin, they are unruly subjects for science. These conflicts nonetheless happen. Moreover, they cannot be ignored, even in broad theory. Social science must take them into account, because their particular outcomes—the leaders who rise to power—are such obviously important influences on society.

Nowhere could this be clearer than it is in contemporary China. The leaders of that country since 1949 have used their power without stint to achieve certain goals of modernism and morality. And for many purposes it is unrealistic (and sometimes unfair) to deal with the abstract characteristics of those leaders, with the passion of their differences, or with the sources of their power, unless reference is also made to their goals. This warning is somewhat too simple, because the aims of leadership—especially local leadership—are not always unified or national in practice. An action at any one level almost always mirrors interests at others, at least partially. The leaderships of Shanghai Municipality or of Huang-p'u district (*ch'ü*) may certainly be taken as units of study no less than China's national elite may be. The levels of government, and the imperfect unity of goals, will make an analysis of political leadership more complex, but they will also make it more realistic.

The word "leadership" has two meanings. In its behavioral sense, our title implies a set of events that occurred in Shanghai, 1955–69. It is a group of predicates, of descriptions. But it also implies a definable set of men, holding posts in Shanghai during those years, whose traits we can analyze sociometrically. Shanghai's "leadership" exercised "leadership." The ambiguity of this word will be apt and precise here, because it will continue to suggest a major problem: that leadership-action and leadership-men are things that cannot be defined separately from one another.[2] A really unified way to approach them together has not been invented. (Even the alternative noun, elite, also has a verb lurking behind it, the French *élire* or the Latin *eligere,* to choose. Leaders are selected as much as they lead.) It is possible to ask who governs a society, or to measure power and the sources of election to it; but even a satisfactory answer for these problems could only throw light on half of the larger topic of leadership, in the ordinary compound sense of that word. We must look at both the actions and the men, if we will really see either one.

The unified process of selection and governance is amenable to study by quantitative techniques, and it can also be examined inductively in historical cases. Sociometric aggregates will not offer much knowledge until some logic is shown to give them lively behavioral meaning. Logical patterns observed in specific cases cannot be considered important until they are seen to exist extensively. More data from Shanghai can be found for both of these methods at times of dispute among leaders than at times of apparent unity. The most relevant cases are derived quite naturally from our title: the socialization of the capitalists, the Hundred Flowers and Antirightist movements, the strains in Shanghai's elite after the Great Leap, and the Cultural Revolution.[3]

In the first part of this essay, Shanghai's leadership disputes will be described in whatever terms and categories seem most appropriate for each case. These conflicts can be analyzed according to the issues at stake, the functions of the participants, the administrative level at which they occurred, the number and fraction of the elite they involved, their duration in time, the changing size and tasks of the local government which they affected, the public or private character of

[2] It is not orthodox in current science to use words with specific ambiguities. This common tenet may help account for some of the research problems that are suggested in the first two paragraphs above. We are a bit like the astronomers, who had spent all their most brilliant passions thinking about the pure molecular dynamics of intergalactic gas clouds, and who then were presented with a rock from the moon and informed that they should say something interesting about it. In general, the Cartesian vision, to the effect that everything is perfectly organized, is not very useful to us in social science. Our typical basic data are human perceptions, which we know are often organized abominably. For example, the method of this paper will implicitly challenge the usual distinction between "power" and "legitimacy" in elite studies, on grounds that those two are not often well distinguished by actors, and that their separate effects cannot usually be distinguished in real behavior. Above, the distinction between two meanings of "leadership" is deliberately not made, because their fusion may be more useful in analysis of the actual leadership of Shanghai. But if any philosophy of science allows us to discuss the paper's topic, maybe it needs no more defense.

[3] The P'an Han-nien case is now not included in this paper. It involved only two leaders, and its causes arise from the early fifties.

motives which inspired them, the different techniques used to resolve them, and the differences in their outcomes. Leadership is always *of* something, and to be realistic we shall need to talk as much about the things (institutions, environments, groups) as about the leaders. That is why so many means must be used to characterize the specific situations in which leadership occurs.

We shall be dealing with groups of anonymous leaders as often as with personalities who are named in the local press. We should not begin with the assumption that initiatives for political behavior in Shanghai always rested with a few men only. Indeed, this is one of the main questions about leadership on which we hope to focus. We will try to deal with leadership as if it were a really political phenomenon, and as if it were behavior as much as institution.

After narrating the specific cases which the title implies, we shall make some rather primitive statistical analyses of Shanghai's definable elites, so as to measure the effects of the Great Leap and the Cultural Revolution upon them. Our objective here will not be to develop any grand theory. Rather, we shall attempt to sum up a few of the more obvious generalizations which emerge from these different cases of local elite conflict. These may suggest, on the basis of specific examples, the traits of leadership that might be useful in building more basic theory in the future.

JOINT OWNERSHIP AND SHANGHAI'S CAPITALISTS

Shanghai's elite before 1949 was thoroughly bourgeois. The new government's stated policy in the early 1950's was to "utilize, restrict, and reform" (*li-yung, hsien-chih, kai-tsao*) China's capitalists. They were to have self-respect, as elites do; and temporarily they were even to have a future. Speeches by Shanghai Communist leaders were sometimes less than candid about the speed at which this policy would be applied.[4] But despite severe political campaigns during the early 1950's, and despite many types of indirect control, Shanghai's capitalists long retained operational decision-making power at least within their own enterprises.[5]

The political aspects of this power were nevertheless almost extinct by December, 1953, when China was declared to have already begun its "transition to socialism." In late 1954 the first joint state-private

[4] Robert Loh, *Businessmen in China* (Hong Kong: "China Viewpoints," 1960, apparently a U.S. government front at Kowloon, P.O. Box 5217), pp. 1–12.

[5] Compare *ibid.*, pp. 45 ff. and Robert Loh, *Escape from Red China* (New York: Howard McCann, 1962), pp. 117–20.

enterprises were established. These pioneer joint firms were the ones in which either the government already held a share of the stocks (mostly confiscated from Kuomintang [KMT] refugees), or in which the capitalist leaders themselves were most willing to cooperate. These two categories included many of the largest companies in Shanghai, so that the movement for joint enterprises began with large firms and developed later to include small ones. Two capitalist leaders in particular, Jung I-jen and Kuo Lin-shuang, were persuaded to lend themselves to this movement. Jung, director of the Shanghai Shen-hsin Textile Company, was China's largest industrial capitalist. His enterprise had fallen into severe conflict with the Kuomintang (although not into love with the Communists) during the inflation of the late 1940's, when the price of cotton rose sharply and the total output of Shen-hsin's nine mills was officially commandeered at a fixed price.[6] Kuo Lin-shuang, manager of the Shanghai branch of the Wing On Company and China's largest commercial capitalist, also cooperated by placing his huge department store under joint ownership at an early date.

These two capitalist leaders had always been treated with consideration by the Communists, in part because of their overseas Chinese connections. Those relationships gave them some degree of independent power.[7] (Jung's cousin heads a huge textile company based in Hong Kong, and Kuo's brother is the head of the Wing On branch in that same city.) There is evidence that neither of them privately was highly enthusiastic about the prospect of joint ownership, but the patriotic appeal to cooperate with the government, together with more practical considerations, persuaded them to help lead other capitalists toward socialism.[8]

[6] Barry M. Richman, *Industrial Society in Communist China* (New York: Random House, 1969), pp. 904–6.

[7] Loh, in *Businessmen in China*, pp. 19 and 44, cites two separate minor instances in which Jung's independent power is evident. In one case he threatened to commit suicide unless some workers were restrained by the Party from tormenting one of his managers.

[8] In the spring of 1966, Jung's chief lieutenant, Wu Chung-i (who himself had owned 30 per cent of the Shen-hsin enterprise and during the sixties held many honorary positions in Shanghai), freely admitted to visiting management professor Barry Richman that severe economic pressure had been applied on the Shen-hsin directors in 1954 to accept joint ownership (Richman, *Industrial Society in Communist China*, p. 907). The evidence for Kuo is not quite so clear. On December 10, 1969, Hong Kong's *Hsing-tao jih-pao* (Singtao Daily) (hereafter *HTJP*) quoted a Red Guard paper to the effect that Kuo was attacked during the Cultural Revolution for having complained that the Party forced him to sign documents making his branch of Wing On a joint enterprise. *CFJP* of January 15, 1956, tells no such story; rather, it quotes Kuo's satisfaction with the socialist transformation, which he declared to be "democratic" and "consultative." The Communist *TKP* (Hong Kong) on June 13, 1959, said

Slowly the campaign was extended downward among smaller capitalists, and all Shanghai firms were induced to band together in large guilds (*hang-yeh*).[9] Some trades were organized with ease, particularly when the campaign for government supervision was concurrent with new market controls external to the firms themselves. For example, Shanghai's flour and rice-husking factories became joint-operated at almost the same time that the rationing of their output was instituted.[10] In trades that had smaller plants, producing less perishable products or with more disparate inputs, the guilds were formed more slowly. This was the case in such industries as electrical equipment, metals, paper-making, wood-processing, towels, blankets, brushes, and even chemicals. The Shanghai Bureau of Industry and Commerce uncovered some "illegal houses" (*wei-fa hu*) while investigating these particular industries in July, 1955. By late September, capitalist leaders in these trades had just begun to "learn and understand about patriotism and observing the law" in a course of study directed by the bureau.[11]

Most capitalists' resistance to this government pressure was not overt. The "transition to socialism" may have overthrown what little economic power had remained in the old elite, but the movement's style was really more banquet than revolution. Chairman Mao himself came to Shanghai for "secret" meetings with businessmen, to urge them to volunteer their cooperation. Guild members organized "good news reporting teams" (*pao-hsi tui*), which paraded to the city offices

---

Kuo had told visiting ex-Premier Fauré of France in 1957 that since joint operation had begun, Wing On's sources of supply had been made more abundant, that the amount of liquid capital at its disposal had increased substantially, and that staff and workers were more placid. Since these matters were largely in government hands, it is not difficult to find the implication that pressure was applied before joint status. No matter which of these reports is true, Kuo was not well used in both 1956 and 1966–67.

The notion underlying this paragraph, that Jung and Kuo were crucial in the drive for joint industries in Shanghai, is not the present author's own invention, nor did it originate with any capitalist source. It was suggested by a former Communist cadre, living in Hong Kong, in November, 1969. This was the government's own propaganda plan at that time: to persuade large and famous capitalists before small ones.

[9] Examples of Shanghai's *hang-yeh* during this period are the Textile Guild (*Fang-chih Hang-yeh*), Chemicals Guild (*Hua-hsüeh Hang-yeh*), Machinery Guild (*Chi-hsieh Hang-yeh*), Commercial Guild (*Shang-yeh*), and services guilds (*fu-wu-hsing hang-yeh*). Information comes from many sources, especially an interview in Hong Kong in October, 1969.

[10] *Hsin-wen jih-pao* (News Daily) (Shanghai), September 1 and 4, 1955 (hereafter *HWJP*).

[11] *Ibid.*, September 23, 1955. See Loh, *Escape from Red China*, pp. 211–13, for a description of the later (April, 1956) Shanghai Ideological Institute for Businessmen, at which Loh was a teacher. The earlier course, mentioned in the text, was apparently for the heads of smaller plants; but Loh's was for 1,000 businessmen in larger enterprises, who went through a four-week program of lectures, field trips, and movies with much less Party guidance than in the school for less important capitalists.

with red envelopes containing their petitions for joint status. These envelopes were accepted ceremoniously by high officials, who congratulated the capitalists on their love of country.

Socialization had often been forced, but the state came close to conveying apologies when some of the companies were transformed. At the very least, the government promised good management. For example, when the Chou-chia Ferry Company was socialized, local papers found it necessary to give explanations and reasons: so many workers and vegetables must cross the Whangpoo River at that point every day that the service should in any case be considered a public utility; fares would be cut by 40 per cent; the boats would run exactly on schedule, as in the past; "all" the ferries and piers would be repaired.[12]

On January 18, 1956, the last group of factories sent in its petitions for joint status, and on January 20, NCNA proudly reported that "a long line of shining motor cars," with capitalists inside and portraits of Chairman Mao outside, drove in celebration through the middle of Shanghai.[13] By January 21, the city as a whole was decreed to have made its happy landing in socialism. For managers, however, the operational meaning of this emerged only gradually during the course of 1956. Already by January 23, the industrial departments of Shanghai's government were dispatching teams to "lead work" in the factories.[14]

The procedure for socialization was as follows. The Shanghai Municipal Council would first give an enterprise permission to become joint. The firm would then compile an inventory of its assets "under the leadership of the state," and the guild's mixed appraisal teams would evaluate these (or, as few reports deny and many affirm, would often undervalue them). The share owing to each capitalist would then be "fixed" as a basis on which to compute his annual 5 per cent interest allowance. After these procedures had been completed, most small firms were amalgamated into larger units. Management and technical personnel were often shifted between plants. Finally, joint status was declared. In late 1956, Shanghai had two days of general vacation to celebrate the city-wide end of this process.[15]

12 *HWJP*, September 1, 1955.

13 NCNA, Shanghai, January 18 and 20, 1956; but other reports say a few capitalists never did agree to socialization and were punished.

14 *Chan-wang* (Prospects) (Shanghai), January 28 and 23, 1956.

15 Richman, *Industrial Society*, pp. 907–8. The socialization procedure is summarized in *HWJP*, September 3, 1955.

Socialization meant a major infusion of new leadership into management. When the managers of 223 medium-sized, district- (*ch'ü*) supervised general stores in Shanghai were surveyed in November, 1956, 48 per cent were still "private representatives," but 52 per cent were new managers either "appointed by the state" or "promoted from the workers." Of 801 section chiefs in these joint department stores, 39 per cent were former capitalists.[16] The papers ran lengthy articles when the municipal congress voted to appoint several "private representatives" to become managers of large Shanghai enterprises, some under municipal and others under national jurisdiction—a few of which were completely government-owned.[17]

Such developments did not tell the whole story, however. Crash training programs in business management had been set up by the Party in 1956. At the Shanghai Industrial and Commercial Circles Political School (*Shang-hai kung-shang-chieh cheng-chih hsüeh-hsiao*), in August, 1956, only 10 per cent of the students were from "bourgeois families." Only 18.6 per cent had university or junior college degrees; 17.9 per cent were below thirty years of age, but 99.4 per cent were less than sixty.[18] Clearly the state felt an urgent need for new cadres to staff its recently acquired interests in Shanghai, and it was training middle-aged workers to fill those posts.

The managerial power of the capitalists had been largely stripped away with socialization, but a few of them retained important overseas connections and were still wealthy. These individuals were treated with care. The government set up the Shanghai branch of the Overseas Chinese Investment Company in September, 1956—when the campaign to socialize industry was administratively still in full swing. After the transition to socialism, a series of bond issues was used to soak up capitalists' money so that it could be used for new investment.[19] A few of the ex-leaders of Shanghai were given honors and titles to suggest their former status. Occasionally they even displaced Communists in positions carrying some authority. Communist Deputy Mayor Liu Shu-chou had to explain to a group of Party activists in November, 1956, that certain "slight revisions and replacements" would be necessary in the candidate lists for the new Shanghai People's Consultative Conference. Liu told them that the Communist Party would have less

---

[16] These points are from several articles in *HWJP*, November 6, 1956.

[17] *Ibid.*, October 30, 1956.

[18] Figures constructed from *Shang-hai kung-shang* (Shanghai Industry), No. 15 (August 5, 1956), p. 6.

[19] *HWJP*, December 14, 1956; and Loh, *Escape from Red China*, pp. 191–92.

representation in the new conference than in the old one; but his reasons (that some of the old delegates had died or changed occupation, and that some had joined the Party) did not explain his subsequent emphasis that "intellectuals and non-Party members working in the commercial and industrial fields" had to be given more seats.[20] In the 1956 district elections in Shanghai, only 51 per cent among the 4,957 new urban district congress delegates were incumbents. In the Shanghai Municipal People's Congress elections that same year, 65.5 per cent of the members were incumbents, but only 29 per cent were workers.[21] Although the capitalists were finally dispossessed in 1956, many of them were given face-saving titles and roles.

The costs of the transition were not quite as low as these honors may suggest. Its real costs were economic. An elite had been dislodged from control of Shanghai's factories only because of government economic pressures that stemmed from profound ideological commitments. The old commercial-industrial elite, having lost official support over a period of years since 1949, could no longer operate their plants. In 1955, largely because of pressure against private enterprises, many factories operated at less than half capacity. In fact, that year saw the rare economic phenomenon of "disinvestment" in Shanghai: the industrial investment in the city was less than the depreciation of fixed capital.[22] The local Communist leaders may have allowed this as a temporary side effect of the means necessary to undermine their capitalist rivals, but they certainly could not approve of its continuance after they were in charge of the factories. In mid-1956, a local Shanghai magazine pointed out that the profits and revenue yielded by Shanghai had contributed "over one-fifth" of all capital invested in China's first five-year plan—whose funds were used largely to develop inland parts of the country. From 1950 to 1955, Shanghai had sent 210,000 workers, including 63,000 technicians, to other areas. But the city still retained over 30,000 engineers, and 320,000 residents qualified as technicians and experienced workers. The magazine frankly com-

---

[20] *HWJP*, November 6, 1956. None other than Robert Loh was on the Shanghai People's Consultative Conference that year, and predictably he assures us that it was (1) an honor and (2) quite meaningless in terms of power. See *Escape from Red China*, pp. 286–89.

[21] *HWJP*, October 30 and December 15, 1956.

[22] Kang Chao, "Policies and Performance in Industry," in Alexander Eckstein, Walter Galenson, and Ta-chung Liu (eds.), *Economic Trends in Communist China* (Chicago: Aldine, 1968), pp. 558–59.

plained that for some of Shanghai's industries, capital facilities were inadequate.[23]

The fall of the bourgeoisie thus allowed the rise of a patriotic Shanghai investment lobby. In an August, 1956, meeting of some Shanghai people's representatives, Municipal Party Secretary K'o Ch'ing-shih pointedly mentioned that "the industrial output of Shanghai makes up one-fifth of the nation's total industrial output; and aside from the small quantity sold locally, the bulk is used in meeting the nation's demands for export." This patriotic contribution was seen as good in itself. Pride in the city's production, for China's sake, made the local elite oppose any unreasonable discrimination against investment in Shanghai. About two years later, local administrators in many parts of China were assuming greater practical independence; and at that same time, K'o Ch'ing-shih became mayor of Shanghai.

It should be borne in mind that although the various elites in Shanghai all felt loyalty toward China, their practical independence in economic matters was not as restricted in this period as the rhetoric of planning and purges might suggest. The extent of local leaders' control over important economic decisions, even in the mid-1950's, was extraordinarily great in some instances. For example, in 1956 the national government ordered an overall reduction in the price of capital goods, presumably to decrease purchases from abroad and from non-state factories. But Shanghai's own local government set "temporary" prices above the decreed level, which helped the city's smaller, quickly developing capital industries, many of which were just then being made joint enterprises under municipal jurisdiction.[24]

Shanghai's independence in agricultural decisions was even more impressive. During the first five-year plan, Shanghai scored worse than any other province-level unit in fulfilling the *planned* increase of grain production—and it scored better than any other province-level unit in fulfilling the *planned* increase in cotton. By 1957, Shanghai's actual production of cotton was 114 per cent above the quota that had been planned and published five years earlier by the central government. Its production of grain was 35.6 per cent below the planned 1957 quota. Shanghai farmers were clearly producing the more profitable, industrial crop on their land, and were simply ignoring the plan. If the national authorities did not approve, local elites nevertheless had reasons for sanctioning such activities. Cotton could bring cash for the farmers, presumably raising their political support for the government, and local administrators would not have been eager to deny them this opportunity. In addition, the resulting textiles, milled in Shanghai and for the most part sold elsewhere, gave the city monetary credit; the municipal government would not have had much interest in enforcing orders to plant grain that would be consumed in the city, providing no such credit. Food grains could be bought from Yangtze Basin provinces.

A table showing how much Shanghai's production of grain and cotton fluctuated from year to year indicates that both had increases in 1953, 1955, and 1957, and both showed decreases in 1954 and 1956. The effect of weather seems obvious here. The chart also shows that for each of these five years the increase *or* decrease from the previous year is much less for grain than for cotton. There may be multiple reasons for this, but the evidence suggests that central planners could not enforce their specific dicta except through local leaders who could make some independent decisions even though they also needed central support on a wide range of issues. The main method, which the center apparently used in these years to encourage obedience, was to persuade Shanghai authorities that large unplanned quantities of state food would not be forthcoming from elsewhere if Shanghai needed grain in a bad year due to its own local policies. This was probably not an administrative warning, and in any case its effectiveness was not tested in

TABLE 45

GRAIN AND COTTON PRODUCTION IN SHANGHAI, 1953–57

	Percentage of Increase or Decrease over the Previous Year					1957 Increase or Decrease over 1952	Actual 1957 Increase or Decrease over Planned 1957
	1953	1954	1955	1956	1957		
Cotton	+69.5	−31.3	+115.5	−66.5	+94.5	+63.8	−114.0
Grain	+7.0	−12.7	+9.2	−18.4	+22.5	−19.4	−35.6

Source: These figures have been calculated from others in *Nung-ts'un kung-tso t'ung-hsün* (Rural Work Bulletin), No. 2 (1958), p. 21, for the grain statistics and *ibid.*, No. 4 (1958), p. 8, for the cotton figures. I must thank Mr. John Despres for telling me about the existence of these statistics on Shanghai agriculture.

those years. Even during the sharpest decrease of this period for each of these two commodities—in 1956, when local cotton production plummeted 66.5 per cent below the 1955 level—the output of grain was only allowed to drop by 18.4 per cent. There apparently was a partial bargaining relationship, rather than one based upon simple directives, between the leaders deciding agricultural policy in Shanghai and Peking. And this period, it should be noted, is early. After 1957, the long-term trend in Shanghai, as in other parts of China, was clearly toward more local autonomy, not less.

TECHNICIANS AND INTELLECTUALS CLAIM A LEADERSHIP ROLE

Local Communist leaders in Shanghai seemed to be in an enviable position in the mid-1950's: the power of their levels of government was not declining, and their main rivals, the capitalist managers, had been organizationally defeated. The very size of their success, however, now became their vulnerability. They were like Hobbes's monarch. Seemingly, no one could prevent them from having their way in any specific part of a huge thing. But they really wanted to *lead* Shanghai, not just to subdue it. In this respect, their position was not completely enviable, because their desire was not then matched by sufficient resources with which to accomplish it.

The challenge began even before the problem was clear, and it came first from intellectuals. This paper will not dwell on the purge of Hu Feng, even though his base was in Shanghai, because his case was more a part of national than of regional politics, and because the subject has already been well explored by other authors.[25] Many of the important men in Hu's organization had posts in Shanghai (for example, P'eng Po-shan was chief of the Municipal Party Propaganda Department and Liu Hsüeh-wei headed the New Literature and Art Publishing Company); but their animus was directed against "literary bureaucrats" elsewhere in China, not primarily against any other local faction.

The Hu Feng case did have local effects. In early 1955 an "elimination of counterrevolutionaries" campaign was aimed at certain intellectuals in Shanghai, and several of them committed suicide.[26] Many

---

[25] For example, see Merle Goldman's *Literary Dissent in Communist China* (Cambridge, Mass.: Harvard University Press, 1967), pp. 129–57, which invented the term "literary bureaucrats." See also Yang Yi-fan, *The Case of Hu Feng* (Hong Kong: URI, 1956).

[26] Loh, in *Escape from Red China*, pp. 165–70, uncharacteristically testifies that this campaign was not severe; but he characteristically cites one suicide which it caused.

had to compose autobiographies from the age of eight, and these documents were duly mulled in study meetings. But the events of 1955 are more prologue than plot, when they are seen alongside the intellectuals' later challenge to Communist leadership.

In 1956 all of Shanghai's latent elites—its intellectuals, its technicians, its businessmen, and even its ex-landlords in the rural areas—were offered political dispensation by the Party if they would live austerely and work loyally. In January some of Shanghai's non-Communist parties sponsored "way of life" reforms for their members to publicize this offer. "Unemployed" foreign-educated technicians and scientists in Shanghai were given jobs by the city's departments of heavy industry, which apparently decided that they were at least not unemployable.[27] Ex-landlords and ex-rich peasants in Shanghai's countryside were allowed to join cooperatives, or at least to work in them if their histories were "comparatively good." [28] Some intellectuals who had been "tested through a series of socialist reform movements" were even allowed to join the Communist Party.[29]

This policy toward eclipsed elites soon became overtly liberal. Government bureaucrats at the district level in Shanghai were instructed to set aside fixed times each week or month, during which elected district representatives (who were often non-Party, as we have seen) could come to "express opinions." [30] Liberalism and decentralism were both direct results of the fall of the old leaders in 1956. The socialization of industry had entailed immense amounts of new work for the officialdom. The resulting burden forced Shanghai's Communist Party to decentralize internal authority within itself (and in 1956, this began a trend that continued for several years). On-the-spot Party managers could not avoid assuming responsibility if they wished the huge, often unwieldy new economic structures to move. Central city offices were simply too distant from the streets and factories to be effective. Local administrators even worked on all-city problems in this period, assuming burdens that went far beyond the borders of their jurisdictions. A "slack in the fixed supply" of food was at one time frankly admitted to be general throughout Shanghai. An *ad hoc* committee of all the city's

[27] NCNA, Shanghai, January 17 and February 25, 1956.

[28] *CFJP*, Feburary 5, 1956.

[29] NCNA, Peking, March 17, 1956, and *Kuang-ming jih-pao* (Bright Daily) (Peking), March 18, 1956 (hereafter *KMJP*); but both articles concern Shanghai's intellectuals, not Peking's.

[30] *Hsin-min pao wan-k'an* (New People's Evening Gazette) (Shanghai), February 23, 1957 (hereafter *HMPWK*).

district chiefs (*ch'ü-chang*) was therefore created to serve as the operative decision-making group to see whether that "fixed" food supply could not be provided more regularly.[31]

The city-level Shanghai Public Enterprise Administration Bureau provided only limited guidance to its charges during this period. A vice-director's inspection tour was sufficient to produce a "satisfactory report" from the bureau.[32] Any real surveillance was apparently done at a lower level. Communist Youth League members were recruited to inspect factory record books and production methods. These reliable young sleuths did uncover several cases of business malpractice and inefficiency,[33] but this was clearly a makeshift for regularized control by the city's Party elite. Many new leaders had been sent down to run factories and schools during 1955 and 1956. Resources, however, were too scanty at higher levels to oversee these appointees on a regular basis—or even to supervise the less loyal men who often remained at subordinate levels.

It was important for the Party to secure cooperation from overthrown capitalist authorities. If the bourgeois people would not work hard at the tasks assigned to them, or if lower Party cadres attempted to take on all of the functions which capitalists could perform, then the administrative overload would only become worse. Liberalism was a handy device to inspire production in the intellectuals, technicians, and managers, and hence to reduce the dimensions of this problem.

In 1956 the Party attempted to set up an effective treaty of cooption with Shanghai's intellectuals. The Shanghai Party Committee called a conference from February 18 to March 9 of that year, and it announced a specific program of some ten points. Party organs would henceforth extend "constant aid and concern" toward technical and scientific projects. Experts and scholars would not be required to do administrative work, but in the future would receive administrative assistants and secretaries. Cornerstones would be laid within six months for a new library of philosophy and social science, two libraries devoted to medicine, a new historical museum, a museum of natural history, and several new publishing houses. The Party guaranteed that technological papers would be printed. Scientific workers would be supplied with club facilities, and they would receive better treatment in matters of health insurance, housing, and transportation. Senior pro-

[31] *Ibid.*, March 4, 1957.
[32] *Ibid.*, March 5, 1967.
[33] *CKCNP*, March 27, 1956.

fessors would be provided with research assistants, and any intellectual could appeal to Party organs if he felt that his position did not correspond with his talents.[34]

This was the Party's side of the bargain. For their part, the intellectuals were to work hard and strengthen their loyalty to the government. Evidence from the following year (March, 1957) indicates that the Shanghai Party tried sincerely to keep these promises; and in some ways, the policy worked. Under the slogan "marching toward science" (*hsiang k'o-hsüeh chin-chün*), Shanghai's specialized scientific societies had a total membership in excess of 10,000 by 1957. Seven hundred academic conferences were held in Shanghai during the year that began in March, 1956. A few intellectuals (for example, a lady holding a Ph.D. in physics from the University of Stuttgart) had simply lived at home since 1949, totally uninvolved in intellectual work. Such individuals were now brought out of seclusion and induced to take jobs. Nevertheless, during that year, only 566 intellectuals joined the Shanghai Communist Party, which then had a membership of about 150,000.[35] Despite the enthusiasm with which the Party press greeted this gain, it scarcely amounted to three-eighths of 1 per cent of the city's total membership. Up to this point, the Party's offer to the Shanghai intellectuals had been too limited in the political realm to mobilize them fully.

Party policy toward factory technicians also attained mixed results through early 1957. In March of that year, an Inspection Work Conference was held for 800 factory investigators, who were told that more suggestions and criticism should be forthcoming from non-Party personnel in factories. A few days later, Deputy Mayor Hsü Chien-kuo gave a speech urging Party cadres in factories to "accept advice" and to "depend on the people." He meant, largely, that they should listen to bourgeois experts.[36] But the city-level Party did not have sufficient staff to replace its lower cadres when they did not heed admonitions like this. There was only one leadership large enough to rival the new supervisors of Shanghai's factories, namely, the bourgeois leaders who had recently been ousted. As Hsü and his high-level comrades realized

---

[34] NCNA, Shanghai, March 12, 1956; see also *ibid.*, March 10, 1956. Some classroom and laboratory building projects at four specific Shanghai universities are mentioned in *HMPWK*, March 9, 1957.

[35] *HWJP*, March 7, 1957. The Shanghai Party's total size in mid-1956 is mentioned in Franz Schurmann's *Ideology and Organization in Communist China* (Berkeley and Los Angeles: University of California Press, 1966), pp. 137–38.

[36] *HMPWK*, March 12 and 20, 1957.

quite well, that was a wary leadership which would now not act without considerable circumspection. And it was definitely not a Communist leadership.

Under an impetus not originating in Shanghai, the municipal council on April 16 ordered that forums be held in all intellectual circles to stimulate free discussion.[37] Throughout May there was a constant barrage of exhortations that these forums be completely frank and unfettered. Conferences were held both for intellectuals and for other bourgeois elements, but many potential spokesmen remained silent. When the local paper *Hsin-wen jih-pao* sponsored a meeting for the sole purpose of asking businessmen why they would not express themselves, the responses were revealing: "We belong to a class that has to be transformed." "We fear someone will be writing it down." "Some people may pervert the truth." "We could air our views, but of course it would have no effect."[38] Shih Hui, a director and famous actor at Shanghai's T'ien-ma Movie Studio, could be coaxed into nothing more than a statement that "only lies are safe." This remark is worthy of Chuang Tzu, but it cannot have been very comforting or informative to the Party.[39] This new movement was not precisely like the campaigns that had solicited self-confessions. The Party was not quite prepared to force anyone to speak very dramatically against the Party.

Some leaders from each field nevertheless did express themselves in these forums. Local newspapers published much more criticism of the Shanghai Party elite during this period than can be detailed here, but a few examples should be given of the points raised by various types of bourgeois leaders. Artists complained about the Party's rigid puritanism and about censorship of their completed works. Hsü Chung-nien

---

37 *HWJP*, May 11, 1957. As the footnotes below will make clear, this author found the bourgeois-run local *HWJP* to be a goldmine of information for 1957.

The exact motive of Mao Tse-tung in calling for sharp Hundred Flowers criticism, and the exact attitudes of his central colleagues toward it, are still elusive after a dozen years of speculation. It is harder to talk about these things than about the organizational effects of the policy. There is no good evidence to show that Mao either did or did not consider his overture to the intellectuals a trap before May, if indeed he had any fixed ideas on that at all. According to one Cultural Revolution interpretation, P'eng Chen of Peking opposed the liberalization; so Mao had to come to Shanghai (already the land of K'o Ch'ing-shih) to experiment with the idea. It is probably true that units to which Mao had communications adopted the policy most readily—but such units would not necessarily be far from P'eng; they might include parts of Peking University, where 8,000 students on May 4 held a rally to accuse the Party of repressing freedom.

38 *Ibid.*, May 17, 1957.

39 *Ibid.*, November 28, 1957. Shih Hui's reticence may have been affected by the fact that his brother Shih Ching was, at least by November, serving a fifteen-year jail sentence for "counterrevolutionary activities."

of the Shanghai Foreign Languages Institute wrote a novel, *Niao, chou t'i!* (Bird, Cry When It's Dawn!) entirely during the Hundred Flowers period, in which he called Party members "monsters and freaks" (*niu-kuei she-shen*). The director of a department in the Shanghai No. 2 Military Hospital said he had "an office but no power" (*yu chih, wu ch'üan*), and other intellectuals complained frankly about their low salaries and perquisites. Schoolteachers criticized the Shanghai Education Bureau for placing no restraints on the new principals it had appointed over them in the mid-1950's. A scientist at the Academia Sinica's local Organic Chemistry Institute complained that the Party wasted scientific talent. He added that economy drives were sabotaging the institute's twelve-year research plan.[40]

Industrial scientists objected that they were too often sent out of their laboratories to do trivial work; that security regulations stifled the flow of professional contacts between factories, universities, and research institutes; that too many scientific libraries could not lend books; that laboratory equipment orders were filled too slowly; and that there was too much dogmatism about which countries' "foreign experiences" were advanced and which were not.[41] University scientists complained that many research reports were "immature" and based on very little work; that the Guozi Shudian (International Bookstore) was stingy and did not let scientists subscribe freely to foreign technical journals; and that Party cadres interfered too readily in the details of scientific research about which they knew nothing. A doctor working in a military hospital, who was himself a Party member, said that the *su-fan* rectification campaign had been "inhuman" (*pu jen-tao*) and that the Party was incapable of leading natural science.[42]

Jung I-sheng, the brother of Deputy Mayor Jung I-jen, said that factories which had been moved from Shanghai to inland provinces should be returned to the city now if they proved unworkable elsewhere.[43] Li K'ang-nien, nominal manager of the Hung-hsing and Ts'ui-chung textile companies and the China Watch Factory, all of which he had once owned, wrote a book entitled *Ting-hsi erh-shih nien* (Fixed Interest for Twenty Years). Li pointed out that the government's plan

[40] *Ibid.*, May 18, 1957. *Chan-wang*, No. 31 (August 7, 1957), p. 12. The expression *niu-kuei she-shen* was used prominently in Cultural Revolution documents to describe those same cadres Hsü had in mind. *HWJP*, May 19, 1957. *Ibid.*, May 15, 1957, two different articles.

[41] *HWJP*, May 19, 1957.

[42] *Ibid.*, May 4 and September 14, 1957.

[43] *Ibid.*, May 24, 1957.

to pay previous owners 5 per cent annually for seven years would compensate them for only 35 per cent of their socialized capital, and in good Shanghai tradition he demanded the other 65 per cent in addition.[44] Hu Shui-p'ing, ex-head of the Lien-huan-chou Bookstore and Publishing Company, had been retained after socialization to lead that same organization under its new name of "Lien-huan-chou Editorial Office of the Shanghai People's Press." By 1957 he was reportedly slated to hold high editorial posts in the New Arts Press and People's Arts Press. But in May he chose instead to speak his mind, asserting that the Party had used force against him in 1954 and that the new structure was no improvement.[45] Even Deputy Mayor Chin Chung-hua, a "bourgeois" and a professional editor, said that Party members had been employed in many Shanghai newspaper posts which they were not qualified to hold. Without using the word, Chin called for less censorship ("less contradiction between the news workers and the business departments"), especially when honest debate on an issue was taking place within the Party.[46]

These were all complaints from organs which had too much Party leadership, or from men who had specific alternatives to the Party's policies and who would have led Shanghai very differently. Their criticism was that the Party's men were too incapable, not that they were too few. But the worst attacks came from units which the Communists could not staff at all. As we have noted, the Party's leadership resources were much smaller than its ambitions in Shanghai during this era. The Chinese bureaucracy was rapidly changing, and it faced a huge range of pressing problems. In a large metropolis like Shanghai, some units could simply get lost in the shuffle when they were not involved in the immediate campaign. They could be forgotten almost completely by the small educated Communist elite of the city and district levels. As a result, they retained their staffs but had little money.

In March, 1957, certain leaders of such units were heard from, although in normal times it would have been dangerous for their careers

---

[44] *Chan-wang*, No. 31 (August 17, 1957), p. 12.

[45] *HWJP*, December 11, 1957.

[46] *HWJP*, May 16, 1957. Chin remained a deputy mayor until 1967 (in fact, he holds the record for tenure in that post in Shanghai); but in 1957 Chin ceased to be chief editor of *HWJP*, a position he had occupied since 1949. In 1958, curiously, he became "director" of both *Wen-hui pao* (Cultural Exchange Daily) (hereafter *WHP*) and *HWJP*. Chin has been a man for most seasons both before and after 1949, and he once had strong overseas Chinese connections. From 1938 to 1941 he was editor of Hong Kong's important *Hsing-tao jih-pao*, although both he and the paper would no doubt disclaim each other now.

to voice public demands for more funds and attention. The Morticians' Guild, for example, had not usually been the scene of Shanghai's liveliest politics. But at a forum chaired by Deputy Mayor Sheng P'ei-hua, the guild's director, Ch'en Ping-ch'üan, bitterly pointed out the implications of the fact that, "in our line of business, there is still no jointly operated company." The government had approved joint mortuaries in principle and had assumed charge of all related property; but it had not even begun to take inventories or assess valuations, much less pay interest. As Ch'en put it, "This is similar to confiscation."

The director of the Shanghai Car Wreckers' Guild was even more blunt. His entire membership had long since applied for joint status, and the petition had been accepted, "but up to now we have heard nothing more about it." [47] Until the bureaucracy got around to them, their businesses were in limbo. Resources were not available, and decisions could not be taken about investment and hiring.

At another forum, the vice-president of the Shanghai Middle-School Teachers' Training College read an indictment which was apparently too severe to be quoted directly, even in the newspapers of mid-May, 1957. He criticized bureaucratism in the Education Bureau and "also raised sharp criticisms against the municipal council." He suggested that the teachers' training college should get the "same treatment as universities" and that some rooms should be allotted in school buildings so that the college would have enough space to hold classes. Lower Party cadres had done nothing to resolve this problem. K'o Ch'ing-shih himself attended the meeting at which this tirade was read.[48]

At a forum called by the municipal council, the principal of the Experimental Primary School in I-miao district documented the rise and fall of leadership concern for his unit. "In the past, when the chairman of the local teachers' union was a Party member, the branch of the Party was more interested in union work and gave it more support. Now the chairman is not a Party member. . . ." The district Party committee had allegedly neglected schools in general ever since the *san-fan* (three anti) and *wu-fan* (five anti) movements, and it had not continued to assign work to lower units. The principal said that "as for the Experimental Primary School, the mission of the experiment is not clear." [49]

It must be understood that there was a deficiency of Party func-

[47] *HWJP*, May 18, 1957.
[48] *Ibid.*, May 15, 1957.
[49] *Ibid.*, May 15, 1957, a different article.

tionaries, not of cadres in general. Other studies have shown that Shanghai certainly had no shortage of bureaucrats after 1954.[50] In fact, periodic national campaigns to reduce their number affected Shanghai, even though the size of its officialdom per unit of population was lower than in any other large Chinese city.[51] But many of these functionaries sat in their offices reading newspapers and drinking tea.[52] They were not entrusted with work. There was a sharp shortage of competent Party cadres in Shanghai who had both the credit to receive important work and the ability to do it.

Sometimes the leadership crisis was treated in a humorous fashion, in the style of the Soviet magazine *Krokodil*. In mid-1957, Shanghai's own *Chan-wang* published an item entitled "Would You Believe It" about a certain Comrade P'an Min, a newly appointed member of the Yang-p'u district Blind Women's Aid Committee. She was in a quandary because she did not know what that work involved. She wrote for advice to *Chieh-fang jih-pao*, which in fine bureaucratic fashion did not answer her letter but passed it on to the city office of the Blind Women's Aid Committee. That headquarters similarly wrote to the head of its Yang-p'u district branch, asking this agent on the scene to help enlighten P'an Min. The trouble was, Yang-p'u's branch head was none other than P'an herself—a fact of which the headquarters staff had not been aware when writing the letter.[53] Yang-p'u was one of the largest of Shanghai's fifteen urban districts in 1957.

The Shanghai Party elite had organized a certain degree of liberalism in May, 1957, by means of forums, and the repression which followed proved to be no greater chore. Bureaucrats at middle levels naturally wanted an opportunity to bloom as colorfully as their critics and to rebut the complaints being made against them by potential rivals. It was unseemly to have actual Party members initiate this attack, and also unnecessary, since non-Party functionaries could easily be found to do it. On June 6, Deputy Mayor Ts'ao Ti-ch'iu presided over a forum of non-Party administrators. They did not attack the liberals directly. In fact, they themselves sounded like reformers, calling for a change in the current structure. They wanted more control over a host of specific activities in Shanghai. A vice-head of the Education Bureau said "the sections concerned" should supervise skating and dancing

---

[50] See Ying-mao Kau, "Governmental Bureaucracy and Cadres in Urban China under Communist Rule, 1949–1965" (Ph.D. dissertation, Cornell University, 1968), Chap. vii.

[51] See *ibid.*, charts on pp. 261 and 264.

[52] For a Shanghai example, see *ibid.*, pp. 227–28.

[53] *Chan-wang*, No. 26 (July 6, 1957), p. 18.

parties more strictly. A vice-head of the Shanghai Nationalities Affairs Committee bemoaned the fact that only one of the city's twenty-four minorities (the Muslims) had a special culture association to lead it. The head of the Engineering Bureau said ambiguously that "the thought of the leaders in various sections is not unified, and this leads to great difficulties." [54]

But Shanghai's workers were an even more effective balance to the critics. On June 5 Lai Jo-yü himself, chairman of the All-China Federation of Trade Unions, came from Peking to preside over a meeting of more than 11,000 advanced producers in Shanghai; [55] by June 9 the Party was being actively defended in workers' forums, and its critics were being attacked by name. The Shanghai General Trade Union was in charge of a June 9 meeting against a man who had criticized "unified distribution and purchase" in the Communist commercial system. A truck driver said that "everyone now has rice and meat to eat" and "I am able to enjoy labor insurance." A mail carrier said it was necessary clearly to distinguish the Communist Party from the reactionary elites of the past. [56]

The local newspapers still continued to quote speeches made at the forums, as if nothing had changed. Using these reports, it is possible to read how participants sometimes began to realize what was happening even during the course of a single meeting. At an East China Teachers' College forum of June 10, Professor Wu Ti-sheng said that an article in *Jen-min jih-pao* had given people the feeling that it was not enough for a man to retract what he had said, even if later he knew it to be wrong. Professor Wu suggested that in order to avoid this feeling, which he presumed to be a misinterpretation, counter-criticisms might be "slowed down a bit" (*huan-i-huan*). But Yao Shun-ch'ing (apparently a member of the college's Party committee) replied that forbidding people to speak was the only true type of retraction; and Chu Yüeh-wan said that the masses would never be satisfied unless the speeches of unreasonable critics were repudiated. Chu Cheng-k'un then countered that some speeches were different from others. But Wang Hsien-tan denied these fine distinctions, saying there was no sense in yielding to any speeches that "may shake the line of socialism." Mei Kung-yi asked for a clarification: Were the Party comrades actually saying that it was not suppression to suppress a bad

54 *HWJP*, June 7, 1957.
55 *Ibid.*, June 6, 1957.
56 *Ibid.*, June 10, 1957.

speech? And if they were saying that, weren't they failing to make the essential distinction between right and wrong? And wasn't that the main distinction on which the present Hundred Flowers movement was based? But then the meeting ended.[57] Mr. Mei apparently never received his clarification.

Not everyone in Shanghai had reason to be so surprised at the change in events. In a few instances the Party had found it necessary to stifle attacks even before the second week of June, although it surely did nothing to trumpet that fact. A member of the Political Consultative Conference of Hsü-hui district had produced evidence of "bureaucratism" in the Party leadership of the Chemical Materials Corporation. The secretary of the Hsü-hui Party committee counterattacked immediately, as early as mid-April, without waiting for any antirightist movement. The democrats quickly jumped on him for "suppressing criticism" and "taking revenge." One of them raised this issue in the all-city consultative conference and presented materials concerning the case to reporters of both *Wen-hui pao* and *Hsin-wen jih-pao* (ample evidence, incidentally, that the bourgeoisie still had some means to communicate grievances, even if alone they had no means to correct them). The Party supported its district secretary. It made an investigation and discovered that no undue revenge had been taken.[58]

The most important attacks of the antirightist campaign were against leaders who had not opened their mouths at all during the Hundred Flowers period. Professor Ch'en Tzu-chan was attacked as one of the "Four Tyrants of Futan University"; but the only specific charge against him was that he had *not* attended Futan's forums.[59] Because the full list of accusations and victims in Shanghai is extremely long, we will restrict examples here to that single university. Often the rightists of 1957 were attacked for their misdeeds before 1949, with little or no specific complaint against their activities since then. Wang Heng-shou, a Futan physicist, had once helped Chiang Kai-shek's defense department develop a bomb which could be used in cold climates— which of course was "aimed at the USSR." Yang Chao-lung, of the Futan Law School, had held three posts under the KMT, dealing consecutively with common crimes, war crimes, and "special" crimes. Many Communists had "met their fate" at the hands of his court. Incidentally, he had also wanted to reform Chinese Communist legal

[57] *Ibid.,* June 11, 1957.
[58] *Ibid.,* August 30, 1957.
[59] *Ibid.,* September 7, 1957.

procedures in May, 1957, but this was a secondary accusation. Wang Tsao-shih, another law professor and an "ardent admirer of Ch'en Kuo-fu," had praised the KMT as well as the Communists for resistance to Japan during the war. Professor Sun Ta-yü had known Hu Shih (and had also committed more recent crimes). Professor Ch'en Jen-ping had been a member of the KMT's Blue Coat Society and in 1948 had published an article entitled "The Naïveté of the Intellectuals" (*"Lun chih-shih-fen-tzu ti t'ien-chen"*).[60] In 1957 he had "passively advocated setting fires" (that is, stirring up political resentments) at a number of Shanghai movie studios.[61]

The rightists were usually attacked more because of their ideas than because of their organizational activities, but the exceptions are important and interesting. Li Hsiao-feng, a "convener" of the Peasants' and Workers' Democratic Party and an official of the Shanghai Cultural Press, allegedly tried to gather information about other units by placing his friends in them. Yen Wen-hsiung, a judge of the P'u-t'o district court, organized a "little consultative conference" and a study group in apparent hopes of dismissing his rivals from that bench. A Chiang-ning district tax secretary, who had been promoted since 1949, demanded to see personnel files from the *san-fan* and *wu-fan* campaigns.[62] Each of these cases suggests that the main issue in 1957 for many low-level leaders was their personal careers, even though more abstract principles were deeply involved in the speeches of some of the Party's critics.

When the challenge was organizational, or when the flowering critics pointed to systemic, organizational faults, the Party responded appropriately. Both of these conditions, for example, prevailed in the Shanghai court system. Consequently, in 1958 the personnel of the courts in Shanghai were reduced by half in a massive campaign.[63] Almost as spectacular was the purge taking place in the Shanghai *Wen-hui pao*.[64] Before 1957, this newspaper had been under editor Hsü Chu-ch'eng, a member of the Democratic League who conceived of it as a southern version of Peking's *Kuang-ming jih-pao*, an organ for

60 *Chan-wang*, II, No. 5 (May, 1948), 6 ff.

61 *Ibid.*, No. 31 (August 17, 1957), p. 12.

62 *HWJP*, September 21, 26, 29, 1957.

63 *CFJP*, November 9, 1958.

64 In February, 1970, the author interviewed a past editor of Hong Kong's *Wen-hui pao*, who is now residing in Taipei. This essay generally follows the account he gave. The two *Wen-hui pao*'s of Shanghai and Hong Kong originated from the same group of editors during the thirties and forties, and they have maintained (and apparently still maintain) personnel links, although in finances and editorial policy they are separate.

non-Party people. In 1957 Hsü was accused of rightism and was dismissed. Also ousted were the paper's assistant general editor, the manager of the Peking office, three junior editors, ten correspondents, and the administrative secretary.[65] Chairman Mao himself, writing under a pseudonym, published an article in *Jen-min jih-pao* criticizing *Wen-hui pao*.[66] For a time after this drastic purge, the newspaper had to be administered directly by personnel sent from the Party Central Committee in Peking. Then, for another period, it ceased publication entirely while the *Chiao-yü pao* (Education News) was printed on its presses.[67] *Wen-hui pao* was later reinstated, with non-Communist Deputy Mayor Chin Chung-hua as its nominal director.

In a few instances in Shanghai, organs of the Party itself simply refused to accept the antirightist campaign, on grounds that the flowering critics had been assured of safety and that promise had to be kept. Resistance of this sort was strongest in Hsü-hui district, the center of Shanghai's old Roman Catholic community, a district containing Chiaot'ung University, Shanghai Teachers' College, Shanghai Music Conservatory, the First Medical School, the Chinese Medical Institute, and also the East China Chemical Engineering College and the Textiles Institute (both of which are the best in their fields in China). Hsü-hui district has a high concentration of secondary schools also including the huge Shanghai Middle School.

The Hsü-hui Party Committee's Education and Culture Department, from Director Men Chang-hua and Deputy Director Ts'ao Mei-chiu down to lowly teachers, declined to participate in the antirightist movement. Director Men said that "there are no rightists on the District Committee or in its organs. The antirightist struggle is against conscience and is immoral." [68] Men had been a Party member since 1940. During the Hundred Flowers period itself, he had criticized the district Party committee (of which he was a member) in mild terms; he had taken the movement at its face value. When it was reversed, he defended both the committee and his own department unconditionally. The Party's higher levels had no choice but to replace this kind of leader. In this important Education and Culture Department, and in

[65] *HWJP*, March 13, 1958.

[66] *JMJP*, June 13, 1957. See also *ibid.*, July 1, 1957, and August 25, 1967, translated in *SCMP*, No. 4020 (September 13, 1957), pp. 15 ff.

[67] Interview with ex-cadre in Hong Kong, October, 1969. Interview in Taipei cited above.

[68] *HWJP*, October 24, 1957. Compare this to the Swedish Reformation, in which the whole hierarchy made a clean break—except that for reasons of size, in Sweden it was permanent and in Hsü-hui it was not.

ten government organs of Shanghai's central Huang-p'u district, widespread purges subsequently took place.[69]

Rectification within the local Party generally began at high levels, and when necessary it proceeded downward. But as early as May 24, Ma T'ien-shui and Wei Wen-po (never deputy mayors, but important Party functionaries) made speeches at a gathering of 13,000 low-level Shanghai Party cadres to assure them that they were not standing on the threshold of a major purge that would sweep them away. In December no less a figure than Chou En-lai addressed a Shanghai Party Congress on "The World Situation and the Purpose of Rectification." [70] That address was not published despite the distinction of the speaker, but it is clear that the Shanghai Party was not about to destroy completely the morale of its foot soldiers, who had been deeply embattled during the Hundred Flowers period.

The Shanghai Party Committee called upon a group of four hundred cadres from six of its departments, including the important Propaganda Department, to choose 80 per cent of their number to be sent down to the rural areas for at least a brief period. All departments, other than these six, were declared completely immune from this movement "because of their work." [71] At first the Shanghai First Commerce Bureau sent eight hundred cadres to become managers, factory heads, and secretaries at low levels permanently; but only 18 per cent of these were Party members, and 92 per cent were below the rank of deputy section chief (*fu k'o-chang*).[72] It was then decided to send no fewer than 140,000 Shanghai cadres to villages during the three months beginning in December, 1957—and as the sojourns became more temporary, the percentage of Party members in these groups went up sharply.

The regular Thursday meetings of all Shanghai district chiefs were canceled, because now "that day is for going deep into the basic levels." [73] By January, 1958, all of Shanghai's elites, Party and non-Party alike, were participating heavily in a temporary *hsia-fang* whose value was moral and political as much as economic. In a few of the smaller groups (for example, one from the Shanghai Foreign Languages Institute), half of the short-term rusticates were Party members and more than half had university degrees.[74] With few excep-

[69] *Ibid.*, November 27, 1957.
[70] *Ibid.*, May 24 and December 21, 1957.
[71] *Ibid.*, November 28, 1957.
[72] *Ibid.*, October 11, 1957.
[73] *Ibid.*, November 30, 1957.
[74] *Chan-wang*, January 19, 1958, p. 24.

tions, local elite disputes in Shanghai were now swallowed up in a huge mass movement, the Great Leap Forward.[75] They did not re-emerge openly again until the end of that movement—and because of it.

THE GREAT LEAP AND ITS AFTERMATH

The significance of the Great Leap in Shanghai is not identical with its meaning for China as a whole, and it affected Shanghai's elite differently from elites elsewhere. The main crisis of the Great Leap— its crippling of the distribution of food—is basically a rural problem, not an urban one. The failures in rural management, marketing, and industry did not originate in Shanghai, no matter how mightily they hit the city afterward when food and agricultural inputs were scarce. Of course, Shanghai itself has rural areas, in which the municipal Party leadership pressed energetically and early for large-scale units. When higher-level cooperatives were being formed, the city called a conference whose sole aim was to propagate the virtue of size.[76] At the beginning of communization itself, Shanghai's rural counties had the staggering average of 11,300 households per commune—much the highest of any province-level unit in China.[77] As G. W. Skinner has shown, even in areas with relatively modern local transport systems (and the canals around Shanghai are highly efficient, especially when the barges are motorized), the size of communes outran all rationale, with disastrous effects on the food market.[78]

But the Communist elite's policies for the urban areas as such were not disastrous, and that fact made a happy contrast with the widespread commercial failures elsewhere. The Great Leap looks different— and better—in terms of Shanghai's history than in terms of the history of China. No one could avoid seeing that Shanghai itself looked better during the Great Leap, at least before the shortages became acute. The metropolis was productive, for all of its cultural and political sins. Mayor K'o Ch'ing-shih was apparently trusted in Peking. The "coun-

[75] Goldman, in Chap. x of *Literary Dissent in Communist China,* cities one of the most interesting kinds of exception to this generality: the fact that some writers balked at having to produce set quotas of written output during the Leap. In Shanghai, Pa Chin, maybe with a bit of humor, promised to generate within a year one long novel, three medium novels, and several translations. Ho Ch'i-fang, based in Peking, had gone along with the literary authorities, and often participated, in criticizing writers for scores of ideological sins in the content of their works; but he perceived that a writer's choice of form was now being impinged, and his professionalism made him object publicly.

[76] NCNA, Shanghai, January 18, 1956.

[77] *1967 fei-ch'ing nien-pao* (1967 Yearbook of Chinese Communist Affairs) (Taipei: Fei-ch'ing yen-chiu ts'a-chih she, 1967), p. 1016.

[78] G. William Skinner, "Marketing and Social Structure in Rural China," Part III, *Journal of Asian Studies,* XXIV, No. 3 (May, 1965), 363–99.

try as a single chessboard" argument could be used to attract capital to Shanghai's concentrated market. And the center during this era was preoccupied with other matters.

The Great Leap also involved huge numbers of Communist cadres in the most gigantic "in-service leadership training" ever launched. It helped to reduce the Shanghai Communist elite's shortage of trusted manpower, and so gave local Party authorities more resources with which to care for the city. Between 1956 and 1959 the Party increased —by almost half—the number of its members per unit of population in Shanghai.[79] The Great Leap strengthened local Party leaders not only in terms of increased manpower, but also in terms of increased financial credit. From late 1957 through late 1959, an extremely complex series of management and tax regulations was issued, which this paper has no space to study in detail but which tended in their net effect to reverse the progressive centralization of taxes that had prevailed since 1950. One such decree, that of June 9, 1958, allowed regional governments to set up seven new kinds of taxes, the most important of which were an urban property tax, a stamp tax, and an interest-income tax. The revenue from all of these went directly into local government coffers.[80] Later, other local taxes were abolished, and

[79] Calculated from other figures in Kau, "Governmental Bureaucracy and Cadres," p. 267. See also pp. 261 and 264, which imply that the concentration of state cadres (i.e., mostly non-Party) in Wuhan's population as early as 1957 was triple the concentration in Shanghai in 1959. In fact, both Party members and state cadres remained scarcer in Shanghai than elsewhere even after the Great Leap, but the problem was not as great as it had been previously. Please notice that the figures given here and in the text are all corrected to discount the effects of Shanghai's huge population increase in 1958, which was caused by many factors including jurisdictional changes. They do not discount the other effects of the expansion of Shanghai's administrative borders in that year and so may slightly misestimate the increased concentration of cadres in the urban area proper. The statistics by which this estimate might be corrected are unavailable. For all too many matters, the statistical bases have proven fickle over time; so we are sometimes reduced to figures like "almost half" and "triple," because nothing more precise can be justified.

[80] Chinese Communist taxes come in many different kinds, and are collected by different levels, whose budgets receive different after-collection boosts from other levels; so the elusive political effects of the difference between 1957 and 1960 are no fit subject for dogmatism. The text's scanty information came from interviews in Hong Kong, November, 1969, and Taipei, February, 1970. In English, see also George N. Ecklund, *Financing the Chinese Government Budget: Mainland China, 1950–1959* (Chicago: Aldine, 1966). This useful book describes the 1958 simplification of the central tax system (pp. 67–71), but then speaks sparingly of the "other taxes" which "provided income only to local government units, supplementing revenue from taxes shared with the central government." See also the short paragraph on "miscellaneous local taxes," pp. 55–56. But as the "special surtax, applied to certain profitable industrial and garden crops" (up to 30 per cent of a basic tax) mentioned on page 54 implies, some locales' "only" may be quite a lot.

Shanghai has long sent a higher portion of its profits from local joint industries to the center than have most other province-level units in China. [81] The drain on Shanghai's surplus value was clearly less, however, during the Leap than before it; and this fact allowed the city's Communist Party elite to offer more jobs and education to ordinary citizens, and even to encourage better cooperation from the city's alternative leaders.

The Great Leap's emphasis on size was not restricted to funds and personnel alone. The city government now called for large factory units, just as it had earlier demanded large rural communes. The 1958–59 movement for technical innovations cannot be analyzed apart from the bureaucratic efforts to amalgamate small factories and to transfer small production functions to previously noneconomic units. These efforts further lessened the power of the factories' former leaders. Of course, many of the effects of this drive for unification, like those stemming from the effort to unify markets, were counterproductive from an economic standpoint—to the extent that they could not be avoided by extralegal actions. But a few important effects of the size-metaphysic were good for Shanghai. They provided the administrative basis for an expansion into heavy industry, just as the Great Leap's general localization of politics provided the financial basis for heavy industry. In broad terms, Shanghai was authorized to process iron and steel, as well as the customary textiles. The interagency politics of investment requires money, and now some money was available; 1958 gave new life to both parts of Shanghai's "political economy." They revived together in a new Communist setting, showing that politics was as primarily an economic topic in modern Shanghai as it had ever been in the old treaty port.

The Great Leap tended to change the structure of economic management in Shanghai, and so it determined which local leaders would obtain new resources and be trusted to solve new political problems. In Chinese enterprises, the various policies of finance, technique, procurement, and personnel may be administered separately or together by any combination of levels of government. The possible structures of management are numerous. There is evidence that Chinese regional government elites prefer to have new factories which are locally administered (rather than those which are more directly under the authority of ministries in Peking) because such factories provide more direct

[81] Audrey Donnithorne, *China's Economic System*, pp. 151–54.

and indirect income for local budgets.[82] No new joint enterprises were authorized after 1956, and old joint companies were prohibited from establishing any major new plants by themselves.[83] Most new Great Leap investment was thus in "state-owned" factories, whose administration was handled largely by local authorities. Shanghai spent as much money in its municipally run machine-building industry in 1958 as during the whole of the previous five years.[84]

The capitalists also benefited from these developments as long as there were still goods to buy. Deputy Mayor Chao Tsu-k'ang, who had been the KMT's caretaker mayor in Shanghai just before liberation, made a speech to celebrate the tenth anniversary of that event. It is a stockholders' report as smug as one could ask of any bourgeois company president. More than a million tons of steel were produced in the city last year. A railway has been laid southward to service our new investments at Min-hang in the suburbs. The staff is being given a technical education. Both Yat-sen and Han-min roads (named affectionately without surnames, in honor of questionable proletarians) are now four-lane. Best of all, the Wing On Company is doing five times as much business as a decade ago.[85] These were real accomplishments. What elite could ask for more?

Capitalist deputy mayors Chao and Chin went out to the fields of Shang-hai county (the rural *hsien* a short bus ride away from the city) in October to help the peasants reap their late rice.[86] This was a symbolic gesture worthy of China's old imperial leaders, but it also showed some economic interest. An expanded Shanghai municipality as early as 1958 had already shouldered a greater part of its agricultural needs than formerly, and this may well have been a corollary of its increased financial independence. In that year, the province-level unit was given jurisdiction over more counties on fertile Ch'ung-ming Island in the Yangtze, south along Hangchow Bay, and westward halfway to Soochow. By November, 1958, it was reported that Shanghai had greatly increased the percentage of its land planted in vegetables, and this was a continuation of earlier trends already noted above.[87]

---

[82] A Cantonese ex-cadre in Hong Kong, who had dealt with economic affairs and who was definitely not subject to any disaffection from centralism, told this to the author in November, 1969.

[83] *Ibid.*

[84] NCNA, Shanghai, January 10, 1959. The municipal machine-building industry led the worker education movement in Shanghai in 1958, and funds spent for this purpose were in addition to the capital investment mentioned above.

[85] *TKP* (Hong Kong), May 29, 1959.

[86] *HWJP*, November 1, 1959.

[87] *Ibid.*, November 28, 1958.

All of these preparations, however, were insufficient to prevent the disaster that followed. Beginning in late 1958, food imports coming to the city from the surrounding rural provinces began to diminish. In 1959 the problem was admitted publicly. The municipal Party committee, for which this was the first major setback of the Great Leap, called for quick increases in the production of meat, fish, and poultry so that Shanghai might become self-sufficient in "major non-staple foods." The committee vowed to "depend more on local production and less on supplies from other places," but someone was apparently still telling Shanghai's elite that the city would receive enough rice or wheat from elsewhere.[88] The enlarged Shanghai province-level unit claimed self-sufficiency in vegetables during 1959.[89] This claim undoubtedly reflects a failure of usual Yangtze Basin sources as well as the prowess of Shanghai in developing an intensive vegetable agriculture.

The crisis strengthened some kinds of leaders in Shanghai, particularly those in urban economic offices. The Municipal Economic Planning Committee made a survey of warehouses, and authoritatively cleared them out in order to provide light industry with materials in this time of shortage and to use the labor that had been inspired by propaganda and promises.[90] "Committees" and "trade departments" seem to have been engaged in entrepreneurial functions, while "industrial departments" were responsible for more ordinary administrative jobs. Local newspapers were overly enthusiastic regarding the productivity of these measures; but there was a buying spree for some products in the spring of 1959, apparently because the city's production could not be sold in its normal rural outlets. The February, 1959, Chinese New Year sales advertised everything from "Hawaiian" electric guitars to perfumed bedsheets.[91] The Great Leap seems to have been something less than a Cultural Revolution in Shanghai!

This temporary glut of some commodities was caused because surplus credit to buy consumer goods dried up in the countryside before the inventories of materials to make them dried up in Shanghai. But

---

[88] NCNA, Shanghai, June 30, 1959.

[89] *Ibid.*, August 20, 1963. The technical intensification on Shanghai's farms was nonetheless very real. By March, 1966, the whole of Shanghai was declared an "Outstanding Farming Unit" by the national government and was allowed to participate in an exhibition by such units held in Peking. Of course this was all very fine, but it is not quite how the city used to think of itself. See *ibid.*, March 30, 1966.

[90] *Ibid.*, June 9, 1959.

[91] *Ibid.*, February 3 and 7, 1959.

when the warehouses ran low, business cadres and light industrialists were hard hit by these input shortages. Their response to the implicit political crisis was less open and more constructive than that of the intellectuals, probably because more of the business cadres were now within Party ranks. The polity, for economic leaders, was no longer a vehicle for complaint; it was often something to hoodwink while obtaining the goods by extralegal means. In 1959 the city government held a campaign to foster the better filing of documents. An exhibit on this subject was held, and industrial representatives were among those invited to attend. Businesses were clearly expected thereafter to have papers which detailed all transactions on hand for inspection.[92] We may probably trust to the inventiveness of Shanghai business cadres that they found ways to circumnavigate restrictions of this sort.

By the early 1960's, however, the food and input shortages had sharp political effects in the city, about which the municipal leadership could do almost nothing. On March 1, 1960, *Jen-min jih-pao* published an editorial reminding businessmen that Party policy called for the "peaceful socialist transformation of the bourgeoisie," and implying that peace would also be the bourgeoisie's own wisest course. Deputy Mayor Ts'ao Ti-ch'iu escorted Madame Sun Yat-sen around Shanghai's new factories on inspection jaunts which were well publicized.[93] Jung Hung-jen, assistant manager of the largest Shen-hsin mill and the deputy mayor's brother, wrote an article in 1961 extolling the happy family life of the socialized capitalists: their concerts, their trips to Hangchow, their peace and security.[94]

By this time, discontent was obvious in the newspapers. Forums and meetings were held frequently to compare the bad old days before 1949 with the allegedly better new bad days. People were encouraged to recite in public the luxurious lists of consumer goods they had purchased during the early 1959 shopping spree, in order to show how successful the Great Leap had been. Light industrialists optimistically pledged to discover new sources of raw materials. Shanghai mechanics were brought to the countryside, usually for short visits, to see how much rural life had *improved*—and to help repair the trac-

[92] *WHP*, March 7, 1959.
[93] NCNA, Shanghai, March 18, 1960. No paper about Shanghai elites should fail to mention that one local resident, Soong Ching-ling, on paper now outranks everyone else in China except Tung Pi-wu (her fellow vice-chairman of the Republic, who since Liu Shao-ch'i's fall has been identified as acting chairman). But there it ends; it is information only for a footnote.
[94] *TKP* (Hong Kong), June 1, 1961.

tors which enthusiastic use had damaged.[95] As in 1957, the most open criticism came from Shanghai's intellectuals. The Party's United Front Work Department in 1961 took a firm attitude toward these dissident leaders. It called many of the third parties into conferences and used "a method of democracy, centralism, further democracy, further centralism" to induce acceptance of the proposition that all the Great Leap policies had been completely successful.[96]

In 1961 the political cadres in Shanghai's Academy of Social Science decided it was time to "implement a policy of letting one hundred flowers blossom together and one hundred schools of thought contend." [97] The response this time was not exactly overwhelming. The works of Mao were studied; but if any criticisms were raised, they were not published. The entire 1961–63 period in Shanghai was sprinkled with academic meetings whose themes had political import, in an esoteric way. For example, the Shanghai Economics Association met for more than a month to discuss how economic history should be periodized, how Western and Chinese business institutions interrelated before 1949, how the American economy was declining, how productivity has a dual character, and how monetary policy relates to planning.[98] These were all fine economic questions—and good political litmus paper, too, because loyal Marxist positions could certainly be worked out for each of them.

But something was missing. China's economic situation in early 1961, which might have stirred a more timely interest among the association's members was omitted from their scholarly agenda. Ts'ao Ts'ao was an approved topic at historians' meetings in this period. Biologists in Shanghai were supposed to discuss genetics. The editorial department of *Wen-hui pao* took responsibility for "promoting contention" on this topic, and the debates on it in Shanghai were important enough to receive coverage in *Jen-min jih-pao*.[99] The Party was definitely trying to test these intellectuals in a safe way, and they were definitely trying to object to the Great Leap in a safe way; but because of that concern for safety, candidness suffered. This was all real political debate, sponsored by the Party and argued by intellectuals

---

[95] These disparate details are all in *JMJP*, February 26, 1961.

[96] For example, a conference of twenty-seven Shanghai engineers is reported in *KMJP*, May 16, 1961, translated in *SCMP*, No. 2522 (June 22, 1961), p. 1.

[97] *KMJP*, March 10, 1961, translated in *SCMP*, No. 2479 (April 19, 1961), p. 17.

[98] *KMJP*, March 14, 1961, translated in *SCMP*, No. 2477 (April 17, 1961), p. 16.

[99] *JMJP*, April 23, 1961.

consciously as such—but hidden under so many layers of allusion that it was innocuous to policy.

In 1962 the author Pa Chin addressed the Second Shanghai Congress of Writers and Artists on "Courage and Responsibility in an Author." His speech is worth quoting both because it is in such sharp contrast to the surrealistic debates in Shanghai of that era and because its repercussions have still not faded entirely. In part, Pa Chin said:

I am a little afraid of those who, holding a hoop in one hand and a club in the other, go everywhere looking for men with mistakes. . . . If somebody lets them hear some new songs or see some new writings to which they are not accustomed, they will become furious with him and bring the club down right on his head. . . . At one time they hold literature in great contempt; at another they place literature in high esteem and hold writers responsible for all the actions of their readers—as if a novel can thoroughly transform the spiritual aspect of a man.[100]

Pa Chin was at least as hard on his fellow intellectuals as he was on the Party. Leadership would require more than they were giving. To be an elite the intellectuals would have to change, because now "they try to please everybody so that they will not expose themselves to fault-finding; they do not care whether their writings are useful or not; they only want to be left in peace." Concerning his own profession, Pa Chin said, "we have critics who specialize in ascertaining the direction of the wind and in acting on 'current market information.' Whether they write for or against an author, they always place themselves in a superior position. They seem to think that no review is possible without praise or condemnation." As we shall see, this was an implicit attack on specific Party writers in Shanghai. But Pa Chin's purpose was more to rally the intellectuals, both Party and non-Party, than to attack them. He called Mao's *Talks at the Yenan Forum* "a work of genius, a lighthouse for us at any time." He referred to the conference itself as a "conference of solidarity, of progress." He said that "solidarity is for the purpose of progress, and progress means the prosperity of creation." This speech, and the onset of a happier

[100] The full text of this speech was published in *Shang-hai wen-hsüeh* (Shanghai Literature) (hereafter *SHWH*), No. 5 (May 5, 1962), pp. 3 ff., under the title "Tso-chia ti yung-ch'i ho tse-jen hsin." A translation appears in *JPRS*, No. 15515 (September 28, 1962), pp. 15–20; this paper quotes it with adaptations because it is of a higher quality than some other translations in that useful series. But then, this kind of thing did not cross the Chinese desk at *JPRS* to be translated very often. Pa Chin is the main pen name of Li Yao-t'ang, one of China's greatest modern writers and a resident of Shanghai. Politically, Pa Chin has been an anarchist; the name is an acronym from *Ba*kunin and Kropot*kin*.

period in Shanghai's economy, tended to shift the emphasis of elite dispute from financial to cultural issues, portending the era that lay ahead.

LEADERSHIP IN CULTURAL REVOLUTION

A young Shanghai critic named Yao Wen-yüan led the attack against Pa Chin's ideas. Yao came from an educated family; his father was also a writer. As early as 1951 (presumably while he was still in his early twenties) Yao was a Shanghai Youth League cadre, and by 1952 he was on the staff of *Wen-i pao* (Literature and Art). Yao developed an amazingly sharp pen in rhetorical Chinese, and he may be one of the most powerful polemic writers of all time. By 1962 neither he nor Pa Chin was a newcomer to the business of personal criticism. In 1957, for example, they had together pinned the label "rightist" on the authors Ting Ling and Ch'en Ch'i-hsia.[101] Now it was Pa Chin's own turn to be the scapegoat. He had called for resistance to the hoop and the club, and he had to be answered.[102] The attack was not long in coming. Pa Chin was accused of "passiveness" and "lack of spirit," particularly in his early anarchist writings.

This dispute helped to crystallize factions among Shanghai's cultural leaders. At a July, 1962, conference of the Party group in the Shanghai Writer's Union, it was evident that Pa Chin's speech had won the support of many writers. For example, author Wang Jo-wang said that Pa Chin himself had been beaten by the club a good deal, and naturally the experience had had a deep influence.[103] Wang called for a reversal of the criticisms against Pa Chin. Even Wu Ch'iang, the secretary of Yao's Party group, failed to support Yao at this point.

Prominent cultural and political figures like Shih Hsi-min, Ch'en Ch'i-wu, Yang Yung-chih, Yeh Yi-ch'ün, Chou Yüan-ping, and K'ung Lo-sun also favored Pa Chin. At this time Shih was director of the Shanghai Party Committee's Propaganda Department, and Ch'en and

---

[101] Yao's articles against Ting Ling are "Sha-fei nü-shih-men ti tzu-yu wang kuo" (The Free Kingdom of the Ladies Sha-fei), *Shou-huo* (Harvest), No. 2 (March, 1958), and "Yi ko-ming-che ti tzu-t'ai so hsieh ti fan-ko-ming hsiao shuo" (The Counter-revolutionary Novel That's Written with a Revolutionary's Style), *Wen-i pao*, No. 3 (March, 1958).

[102] *JPRS*'s "hoop" is Pa Chin's *"k'uang-k'uang,"* which can also mean the end of a coffin.

[103] Interview, Hong Kong, December, 1969. Wang reportedly said "tui Pa Chin ta k'un-tsû pu-shao, ying-hsiang shen-yüan." Yang Hsi-kuang is added to the anti-Yao list (but most of the others are not mentioned) by *1969 chung-kung nien-pao* (1969 Yearbook of Chinese Communist Affairs) (Taipei: Chung-kung yen-chiu ts'a-chih she, 1969), V, 41.

Yang were among his deputy directors.[104] According to one rumor, Ch'en and Yang protested the publication of Yao's criticism of writer Chu Kuang-ch'ien, and Wu Ch'iang prevented the publication of a collection by Yao entitled *Hsiang-ch'i-lai kuo-ke* (Bringing to Mind the National Anthem).[105] It is significant that Mao Tse-tung launched the Socialist Education Movement in September, 1962, at the Tenth Plenum of the Central Committee. This movement did not affect cities until much later, but it may well have been related to the cultural debate that had already begun in Shanghai with Yao Wen-yüan and Pa Chin as the main antagonists.

This elite conflict already had a long history when it crystallized in 1962. Our narrative must therefore include some flashbacks. One early aspect of this debate concerned the maverick personality of Ch'en Ch'i-wu and his conflicts with Chang Ch'un-ch'iao and Yao Wen-yüan. Ch'en was director of the Propaganda Department of the Third Field Army in late 1949; but when the Party's own propaganda organs assumed greater significance than those of the army in Shanghai, Ch'en took secondary positions in them. In October, 1954, he was deputy head of the Propaganda Department of the East China Bureau.[106] Ch'en's political philosophy was liberal; he has referred to "incidents in [his] life in 1956–57" that prove this fact. He reportedly said, "I think that to live in our present day society . . . one must almost invariably be a rebel against social morals and law. I am willing to be a bold rebel. . . . If you accuse us of violation of moral principles and law, then you may pass judgment on us."[107] Ch'en (like Pa Chin) has expressed the greatest admiration for Mao's writings possibly because this same attitude is exhibited in some of them.

In 1958 Ch'en wrote a pamphlet called "On Cultural Revolution and Thought Revolution" (*Lun wen-hua ko-ming ho ssu-hsiang ko-ming*), but this auspicious title did not portend Ch'en's later career. He first ran afoul of Yao Wen-yüan because he supported a play by

---

104 U.S. State Department, *Directory of Chinese Communist Officials* (Washington, D.C.: U.S. Government Printing Office, 1963), p. 78. An interview source (Hong Kong, December, 1969) says that Chou Yüan-ping also had a post in the Propaganda Department; it may have been below the deputy director level and thus did not appear on the State Department list.

105 Interview, Hong Kong, December, 1969, with a Cantonese ex-cadre whose reliability was tested by many interviewers. He believed this rumor to be true.

106 Union Research Service, *Biographical Service* (Hong Kong) (hereafter URS *Biographical Service*), No. 1124 (November 25, 1966).

107 Quoted from a 1968 *WHP* article in *SCMP*, No. 4182 (May 21, 1968), pp. 14–15.

Hsüeh K'o entitled *Chan-tou ti ch'ing-ch'un* (Fighting Youth). Ch'en's personal taste for the play was apparently more important in starting this dispute that were his factional connections. The second occasion for quarrel between Ch'en and Yao was Ai Ming-chih's movie of the same drama. The third and most important difference came later, in 1962, when Lo Chu-feng published a play entitled *Ts'a chia* (Miscellaneous Writers) which Yao attacked immediately. Ch'en had private conversations with Yao, asking him to desist. When that tactic failed, a fellow liberal of Ch'en's named Liu Chin wrote a severe criticism of Yao, which was never published. This incident, and a comment against Yao from Lin Mo-han of the Central Propaganda Department the previous month,[108] was apparently the immediate inspiration for Pa Chin's public speech. Ch'en called the speech "moving" and said that he had "mass support from below" for a proposal to bring back from rural villages some of the "rightists" in Shanghai's propaganda system who had been sent there unjustly.

Chang Ch'un-ch'iao, head of the Literary and Art Work Committee under the Propaganda Department, sided with Yao rather than with Deputy Director Ch'en. The climax of the crisis came in the spring of 1963, when Mayor K'o Ch'ing-shih expelled Ch'en Ch'i-wu from the Party entirely. Mayor K'o also took advantage of a reorganization of propaganda units then occurring in many provinces to replace Shih Hsi-min with the more radical Chang Ch'un-ch'iao as director of the Propaganda Department.[109] While this act went unnoticed at the time, being regarded as a minor change within a small part of a merely local Party leadership, its implications are now obvious. This was the first power seizure of the Cultural Revolution.

It is difficult to know the precise factors behind K'o's crucial decision. Much of the evidence is circumstantial and personal; and it goes far beyond the boundaries of Shanghai. K'o Ch'ing-shih had a familial relation with Lin Piao, whose daughter, Lin Tou-tou, called K'o *"shu-shu"* (uncle) and was a pen pal of his son, K'o Liu-liu.[110]

---

[108] *1969 chung-kung nien-pao*, V, 41.

[109] *Ibid.* See also a summary of the same article in *HTJP,* December 29, 1968. Chang's accession to the propaganda directorship occurred in April. The author has found no exact month for Ch'en's dismissal.

[110] K'o always kept brush-written quotes from Mao under his deskglass. "Tou-tou" and "Liu-liu" are pet names. The big happy family also included air force chief Liu Ya-lou. An excellent commentary is Fr. LaDany's *China News Analysis,* Hong Kong, No. 570 (July 2, 1965), p. 7. Passionate (but revolutionary) letters between young K'o and Lin are quoted in *JMJP,* May 8 and May 12, 1965. See also URS, LI, No. 2 (April 5, 1966), 25, which quotes the Canton tabloid *Shout and Cry!* to the effect that K'o

K'o had worked with Ch'en Po-ta, and he had been in the same Party Small Group as Mao Tse-tung for a period in Yenan. There are also persistent unsubstantiated rumors that Yao Wen-yüan is married to a daughter of Mao Tse-tung.[111] Chang Ch'un-ch'iao had apparently sponsored some of Yao's literary projects in the fifties, and a close relationship had been built up between them. This "evidence" is mostly of the gossip variety; so lest science catch a sense of humor we had better label it "probabilistic." Nevertheless, emotional ties certainly did exist among some of the members of this group. It seems likely that K'o Ch'ing-shih consulted with his friends before firing Ch'en Ch'i-wu and replacing Shih Hsi-min.

Chang Ch'un-ch'iao was born into an intellectual family, probably attended a university, and by 1935 was doing left-wing cultural work.[112] When the war against Japan began, he joined the Red Army, and by 1942 he had specialized in political work in a border region. When the Communist Army took Shanghai in 1949, Chang became deputy head of Shanghai's new *Chieh-fang jih-pao*; and this newspaper, the Party's organ in East China, remained the center of his administrative work throughout the 1950's and early 1960's.[113] In this capacity he encouraged the careers of some young writers, including Yao Wen-yüan. In 1955 Chang joined Shanghai's Party Propaganda Department as head of its Literary and Art Work Committee, and in this capacity he was active in the antirightist movement, speaking out against movie directors and actors as well as writers.[114] But his rise in

---

Fa-ning and K'o Yu-shen, the mayor's offspring, accused Liu Shao-ch'i of "contempt and persecution" against their father. This bitterness is clearly expressed in terms of family revenge, not ideological orthodoxy—or even class familism.

[111] A subject for scholarship. The rumor first appeared in Russian newspapers. It was later picked up by some paragons of the Hong Kong free press, and was thus given suitably Oriental features. It is ardently believed on Taiwan. But problems arise. The discussants cannot agree among themselves which of the Misses Mao is Mrs. Yao. In the running are two daughters of Chiang Ch'ing, now named Li Na (sometimes Li Nuo, with a different character) and Li Min. A former editor of the Hong Kong *Wen-hui pao* told the present author in Taipei, January, 1970, that the lucky lady is one Mao Chih-yüan, a graduate of Peking University in 1966. (There may be some age difference between the Yao's.) The present author is concerned that this rumor, if true, would explain a few things—political not sociological—about Shanghai local leadership during the last ten years. He has no scoops. New China News Agency officials, popped the question at Hong Kong parties, only smile wryly; they usually do not deny it. They do not know, or it is a secret, or they are having the time of their lives.

[112] Huang (ed.), *Chung-kung chün-jen chih,* p. 394.

[113] *China Topics* (Hong Kong) (hereafter *CT*), No. 511 (January 8, 1969).

[114] Huang (ed.), *Chung-kung chün-jen chih,* p. 394, says it was in May, 1955; and I usually believe him. But URI's *Who's Who* and *CT* prefer October. Another source postponed it until 1956. Yet another biographical article could find no evidence of Chang's existence, in this or any other capacity, before 1964! It is really instructive to compare

April, 1963, was sudden despite the extent of his experience prior to that time.

The emergence of a new power center in Shanghai's cultural sphere in 1963, under the mayor's protection, had one amazing consequence: Yao Wen-yüan actually began to write some nice things about other authors. As early as May, Yao admonished youth to read proletarian books; he did not prohibit other books, but only objected that they would not give a good education.[115] In a sequel that October, Yao came out against love because it distracts people from revolution. He also suggested that youths might read the old romantic bourgeois novels as long as they do so critically, and he cited specific deficiencies in *Jane Eyre* and *The Sorrows of Young Werther* to show that he had done this himself.[116]

Later in the same month, Yao praised no fewer than thirteen separate books in a single review for *Shang-hai wen-hsüeh*.[117] (Several of them, including Chou Erh-fu's important novel *Shang-hai ti tsao-ch'en* [Morning in Shanghai], were attacked during the Cultural Revolution; Yao's earlier good opinion of some authors did not serve them later.) [118] Yao's own elitism is obvious in this brilliantly composed review. Parts of his article sound like the late theories of John Stuart Mill. Yao was quite aware of what is lost when writing becomes propaganda—yet he advocated that loss to achieve a revolutionary political effect. He admitted that if writers probe more deeply into the affairs of daily life than he would want, they may then make more truthful descriptions of what exists. They may describe complex, real "spiritual conditions." But they will also blur the distinction between classes, and thus will prevent or retard progressive action. Yao's Victorianism shows most clearly in his fear that the masses will not understand this problem. As yet, they are not clear about it morally. A popularization of art is therefore liable to lower its revolutionary value. Yao implicitly echoed one of the deadliest comments made by

---

even the three best accounts of Chang's early career: Huang, the *Who's Who*, and *1969 chung-kung nien-pao*, V, 36–39. Donald Klein's and Anne Clark's biographical dictionary, published after this essay was mostly finished, now provides us with something to trust in this field.

115 *CKCN*, No. 10–11 (May 18, 1963).

116 *Ibid.*, No. 19 (October 1, 1963).

117 "Wen-yi tso-p'in fan-ying she-hui-chu-yi ko-ming shih-ch'i ti yi-hsieh wen-t'i" (Some Questions about Literary and Art Works Reflecting Class Struggle in the Socialist Revolutionary Period), *SHWH*, No. 10 (October 5, 1963).

118 The author wrote to Guozi Shudian, the International Bookstore in Peking, asking to buy a copy of Chou's novel, which he needed. He mentioned Yao's favorable review in the letter. Back from Peking came a list of English editions of Chairman Mao's works.

his sometime foe, Ho Ch'i-fang: that the workers do not understand Lu Hsün.

The solution, therefore, is continuous, guided struggle to make them understand. The people who shared Yao's opinion in the early sixties needed an apt site in which to begin that task, and there are only two well-equipped sites in China. One is Peking. It is not true that Chiang Ch'ing's experiments in Chinese opera were entirely prohibited in Peking in 1963–64; her operas were performed there, even though members of the Peking Municipal Committee were strongly critical, calling them tasteless, "like boiled water." [119] It is easy to forget that in 1964 Lu Ting-yi gave the main speech at his own "Festival of Peking Opera on Contemporary Themes," and this was held in the capital.[120] Shanghai nevertheless offered relatively better logistical support for Chiang Ch'ing's campaign. Chang Ch'un-ch'iao was the Party's administrative overseer of Shanghai's many theaters, opera troupes, music and ballet schools, symphony orchestras, art academies —and reviewers.

As early as December 29, 1963, Mayor K'o gave a "very important" speech at the East China Drama Festival, suggesting that *hua-chü* (colloquial plays) were the drama forms most easily understood by the workers-peasant-soldier masses and hence should be revolutionized first. K'o warned his troupes that the bourgeoisie had no future.[121] The amount of dramatic activity in this period was phenomenal. In the month ending January 22, 1964, no fewer than twenty new plays were staged in East China, and one hundred reviews were written to praise them.[122] At the beginning of the year, Chiang Ch'ing herself directed a production at Shanghai's Peking Opera Academy.

The radical faction, however, certainly did not abandon Peking to their rivals at first. In mid-1964 Chang Ch'un-ch'iao personally led a Shanghai company to perform opera there. Chiang later asked a Peking ballet troupe to dance *The Red Detachment of Women;* but the deputy director of the Central Committee's Propaganda Department, Lin Mo-han, went to the same troupe and asked them to dance *Ta-chi and Her Father* instead. Chiang then visited Shanghai (this time apparently for medical as much as dramatic reasons), where K'o's independent political power made it somewhat easier for her to

[119] Chung Hua-min and Arthur C. Miller, *Madame Mao: A Profile of Chiang Ch'ing* (Hong Kong: URI, 1968), p. 104.
[120] URS, XL, No. 26 (August 13, 1965), 185.
[121] *JMJP*, December 29, 1963.
[122] NCNA, Shanghai, January 22, 1964.

work.[123] Her frustration was real, and in Shanghai she could depend on influential friends. In June, 1964, Mao Tse-tung announced that China's literary workers were "in the main" disloyal to the Party and should be reformed.[124]

The Great Leap had two meanings for Shanghai; it created both successes and resentments. The economic problems disappeared more quickly than the literary ones, and the distinction is essential for an understanding of what happened to different types of leaders in the city. Shanghai's economic elite was not affected in the slightest by the formation of a radical base in the Party Propaganda Department. During this period, Ts'ao Ti-ch'iu maintained his position as the unofficial "first deputy mayor," and he was concerned entirely with non-cultural problems. There is no evidence that K'o ever had an open dispute with Ts'ao, and the two of them worked mightily together to ensure the development of Shanghai's heavy industry.

The biennial local elections were held in 1963 and 1965, each returning about fifty thousand deputies to low-level people's congresses in Shanghai, and each with incumbency rates too embarrassingly high to admit in print.[125] Each New Year one deputy mayor or another would throw a lavish party for the foreign community.[126] And in mid-1964, Shanghai developed a taste for that classic trademark of elites, the garden party. Bourgeois-lining institutions like the Shanghai Red Cross called together their cadres, and especially their youth, to sip drinks in the warm summer nights. The city's street committees administered a new kind of campaign: "Enjoy the Cool Breeze Evening Parties" (*na-liang wan-hui*). These celebrations brought together many

[123] There may be some relation between all this mid-1964 activity and the early purge of High Party School President Yang Hsien-chen at that same time. The basis for the above paragraph is Chung and Miller, *Madame Mao,* pp. 110–12, and *1969 chung-kung nien-pao,* V, 37. There was some resistance to Chiang Ch'ing near Shanghai, but it was less strong than in the north and it was expressed later. In a public speech of mid-1965, Wei Wen-po, alternate secretary of the East China Bureau, bemoaned that the reformed operas were mostly not of a high artistic quality. He said that the actors had found no way of "breaking through the stylistic formalities of the Peking opera, and they were insufficiently willing to go among the workers entertaining them." Wei apparently said that the new plays were neither good nor popular. *WHP,* June 19, 1965.

[124] Philip Bridgham, "Mao's 'Cultural Revolution': Origins and Development," *CQ,* No. 29 (January–March, 1967), pp. 8–12.

[125] NCNA, Shanghai, on June 24, 1963, in reporting the local returns did say that "many of the deputies were re-elected for their good service in the last people's congresses." In the mid-fifties elections, as we have seen, the incumbency rates were reported.

[126] Mr. and Mrs. Ts'ao Ti-ch'iu took 1964 ("Shanghai Newsletter," *South China Morning Post* [Hong Kong] [hereafter *S.C.M. Post*], January 10, 1964). Mr. and Mrs. Sung Jih-ch'ang hosted for 1965 (NCNA, Shanghai, December 30, 1964). The entire foreign community was invited to both parties.

deputy district heads, street-office directors, Party branch secretaries, teachers, culture-station directors, street committeemen, and students. Local papers reported the singing and games, the telling of revolutionary stories, "the discussion of scientific principles," and "the activities of emulation and exchanging experience," although they do not say exactly what sorts of experience were exchanged on these evenings.[127]

The mid-1964 session of the Shanghai People's Congress raised no burning political issues. The talk was entirely about new investments, the importance of agriculture, "worker-activists" (which in this period meant producers), and technical innovations.[128] The most controversial task of the mid-level elite at this time was to send youth to the countryside, but even this policy in 1964 inspired almost as much pride as resistance because the terms of labor were often short. One "educated youth," a girl serving on the 1964 Yang-p'u District People's Council, had apparently gone to the countryside seven times before her election; so the stints could not have been too long.[129]

On April 3, 1964, the Party's Central Committee decided in Peking to transform its Department of Industry and Communications into a "Political" Department of Industry and Communications. In June, its Department of Finance and Trade became "political" in similar fashion. Finance cadres from all over China met in Peking that month and then returned to their provinces to set up political departments in their own commercial offices (*t'ing*) or bureaus (*chü*), but the old provincial organs were not abolished. Often members of the People's Liberation Army or of an elusive group known as the University Liberation Army (*Ta-hsüeh chieh-fang chün*) would join these new political departments. The whole idea was not entirely novel, since political departments (*cheng-chih pu*) had been used in the Party previously to strengthen discipline; but this was the first time the device had been applied over a whole functional system. Later the practice spread to other systems, and by the end of 1965, medium and small local-government units would often have political divisions (*cheng-chih ch'u*). Even handicraft co-ops and street factories might sometimes have political instructors (*cheng-chih chiao-tao yüan*) or political counselors (*cheng-chih chih-tao yüan*), although the move-

---

[127] *Hsin-min wan-pao* (New People's Evening Post) (Shanghai), July 17 and 18, 1964 (hereafter *HMWP*).

[128] *Ibid.*, September 20, 1964.

[129] *Ibid.*

ment reached such low administrative levels only slowly through the mid-1960's.[130]

These departments affected the leadership of Shanghai's bureaucracy in complex ways that at first may seem contradictory. First, political departments imported new personnel to lead the organs where they were established. Second, political departments sometimes tended to induce divisions between Party members who were outside the political departments and those who were inside.

Third, and most important, they upset the balance between horizontal Party and vertical government leadership. According to the theory which had operated previously, routine administrative control over any organ was in the hands of the government organ above it (*t'iao-t'iao ling-tao*). The job of organizing support for policies was in the hands of the Party committee within the organ (*k'uai-k'uai ling-tao*). When disagreements arose between a unit's Party committee and its government superior, they were to be resolved at least temporarily in favor of the committee, pending appeal to even higher levels; in slogan terms, "the vertical obeys the horizontal" (*t'iao-t'iao fu-ts'ung k'uai-k'uai*). But the new political departments now assumed from the Party committees this function of making interim decisions, and their leaders received more rapid approval of policies from higher levels, reducing the deviations from specific higher-level instructions for a time after mid-1964. Temporarily, more discipline was achieved within the bureaucracy.

Finally, while this new mandate restricted the independence of local units in the short run, paradoxically it increased the long-term prospects for such independence. Strong new departments authorized from above could control specific policies for a time—but after that, their very authority would give local interests a stronger position vis-à-vis the levels which had sent them. This had happened before the Great Leap; now in 1964, it occurred again.[131]

Elite tensions further developed in this period because the functions of specialists became progressively more difficult to exercise. Party representatives, on public-private committees running joint factories

---

[130] Interview, Hong Kong, November, 1969; and a personal communication from Donald Klein, September 10, 1970.

[131] Interviews with ex-cadres in Hong Kong, November, 1969, and Taipei, January, 1970. Political departments were specifically given the authority to order their organs' suspension of higher-level instructions (even instructions from ministries) "until" differences between the administrative levels in Party and government could be worked out. It was only necessary to send reports of such cases upward.

in Shanghai, gradually had to assume responsibility for the technical decisions they alone could authorize because politics was supposed to "take command." Despite China's historic habit of collective management, actual practice tended over time to resemble the Soviet single-director system, because distinctions between policy and operations became impossible to maintain.[132] The detailed leadership of commerce also tended to gravitate into the hands of certain Party officials. Even if they had wished to avoid power, the need to correct inefficiencies implicit in the fixed-price market forced them to assert control by political means. Lower, younger Party members, particularly those without much education who came from worker families, had much less of this power than did the higher comrades. Both the status and the future prospects of young Party members were ambiguous.

Some high leaders within the local Party were more successful than others in making liaison with these dissatisfied members. The tenth anniversary of Shanghai's basic-level Party organ *Chih-pu sheng-huo* (Branch Life) in June, 1964, provided an opportunity for the editors to call for more inner-Party democracy in local affairs. They promised that the magazine's "letter box" would really "discuss problems." The editorial board also put out a newspaper exclusively for posting on bulletin boards, entitled "Red Corner," to publish letters of low literary quality, written by Party members without education and not suitable for the magazine. The editorial office even stayed open twenty-four hours a day to receive and help Party cadres with problems.[133] If this basic-level newspaper was like others in China, it fell under the loose jurisdiction of the local Party Propaganda Department, which in Shanghai at that time was headed by Chang Ch'un-ch'iao.

The Socialist Education Movement had a negligible effect on leadership in Shanghai until it was combined with other urban class-struggle movements, at the instigation of a National Work Conference convened by the Politburo in January, 1965. After that, any really complete organ would have its own office, its political department, its Party committee, and its socialist education department—in addition to occasional visiting *ssu-ch'ing* ("four clean-up") work teams and sent-down administrative inspectors. This was all quite apart from its

---

[132] See Schurmann, *Ideology and Organization*, pp. 298 ff. Mr. Steve Andors suggested part of this concept to me, and his own research will throw light on these matters.

[133] *HMWP*, June 29, 1964; and *JMJP*, June 25, 1964. *Chih-pu sheng-huo* was then fortnightly and had a circulation of 690,000. The author knows of no copies outside China.

own subdivisions and superior agencies (always several of them, for different functions).

The work teams were the most effective, and politically the most unpopular, method by which high-level elites could control lower-level elites during this period. In Shanghai the teams were not mere formalities. When a thirty-man *ssu-ch'ing* work team of the municipal committee arrived to "clean up" the Shanghai Tobacco Company, it temporarily took over the functions of the deputy manager (who had been in charge), the ex-owner and manager, the Party committee secretary and his second secretary, as well as some lesser leaders. Detailed instructions for reform were issued by the high-ranking team members, and inspections were carried out.

Many employees were fearful that they might be classified "four unclean" (*ssu pu-ch'ing*), that is, unclean in their politics, history, economics, and thought. Party cadres were in practice immune from such labels in Shanghai; but they were wary, because the clean-up teams often investigated their family histories, and they knew that in some cases the files were bulging.[134] This temporary trauma, in the context of the permanent organizational cleavages listed above, sometimes produced formalism and often resulted in strains within the elite at many levels. Tensions of this sort greatly weaken leadership because they raise fundamental questions of identity in the minds of the elite members themselves. When higher authorities pressed hard after 1964, leaders at various levels in Shanghai no longer knew whether they were patriots or cogs. They found that the status of their own motivations had become ambiguous. Such subjective factors can have objective political effects.

Let us look at a further example, now at a higher administrative level. When input shortages eased after the early 1960's, the balanced war of wits between high and low economic leaders in Shanghai became no less intensive than in 1961, partly because somewhat similar relations existed between center and city. The municipal government still wanted to find local funds for new investment, having sent to Peking greater proportions of taxes and profits from various categories of enterprise than other Chinese provinces. Thus, a political understanding had to be reached between the central and municipal leaders on these problems of investment and tribute. Many of K'o Ch'ing-shih's speeches during the Great Leap suggested that he was instrumental in obtaining authority from the center to make large invest-

---

[134] Interview with ex-cadre, Hong Kong, December, 1969.

ments in Shanghai with retained capital, under certain conditions. After his death in April, 1965, evidence came to light of the formula which may have existed for some time before that: Shanghai was not to ask the national government for much new capital on the basis of its market-concentration and talent-pool advantages (which allow the city to bid for—and deliver on—more stringent "contracts" than other parts of China) without showing constant improvement in those advantages, and constant efforts to disperse them to other places. The innovation movements, the labor education movement, the technical *hsia-fang,* and some slogans of the period like "help the countryside" and "imitate Shanghai" are all related to this investment policy.

By the winter of 1965–66, however, after Mayor K'o died, the central-local understandings on investment and trade became more ambiguous. Ts'ao Ti-ch'iu became mayor; but no new first secretary of the East China Party Bureau was appointed to replace K'o, and Shanghai no longer had a vice-premier of the State Council. The expectation of sacrifices and the expressed desire for investment each became more extreme, and the need to re-establish a formula interrelating them became acute. Shanghai workers were caused to pledge explicitly that they would not ask the center for more capital and would not pressure city leaders to do so.[135] But there was also tremendous pride at this time in the city's technological level. Shanghai was "prepared for" the third five-year plan, which was moot at that time; and by implication the city deserved a substantial amount of the capital to be invested because of its good technology.[136] This issue undoubtedly relates to the general politics currently prevailing in Shanghai and in central-local elite relations then, but a better analysis must await additional data, since public mention of the new plan ceased totally in early 1966.

It is important to realize that the concerns of economic and cultural leaders in Shanghai remained separate until Yao Wen-yüan published his famous attack on Peking's Deputy Mayor Wu Han in *Wen-hui pao* on November 10, 1965. In February, 1966, Chiang Ch'ing chaired a "Conference on Literature and Art in the Armed Forces" in Shanghai.[137] These two events showed the acceleration of a movement that was now more frequently called "the cultural revolution." Early in 1966 at least part of the city's leadership was encouraging a more

---

[135] NCNA, Shanghai, December 27, 1965.
[136] *Ibid.,* December 31, 1965.
[137] *Ibid.,* May 28, 1967.

active campaign to control certain middle-level leaders by stimulating criticism of them from below. To accomplish this, the formation of political departments at very low levels was pressed forward. Branch secretaries were urged to exchange ideas with Party members prior to all meetings and to solicit opinions from them.[138] Shanghai's rural cadres, at and above the county level, were also pressured to "apply" Mao Tse-tung's thought, and to study his epistemological works on the relationship between knowledge and practice (this invariably meant they should labor with their hands).[139]

The earliest site of severe local criticism was in the industry where cultural and economic affairs most obviously converge, that is, the publishing industry. Li Chün-min, a member of the Party since about 1925, was the head of Shanghai's Chung-hua Bookstore in 1965. He apparently also had connections with the city-run No. 1 and No. 3 printing factories and was briefly a deputy director of Chang Ch'un-ch'iao's Propaganda Department. Li had worked in the "white areas" after 1927, writing for the Kuomintang and gathering intelligence for the Communists. During the war, he was personal secretary to Han Te-ch'in, head of the KMT organization in Kiangsu. Naturally, this background supplied vast amounts of material with which he could later be attacked.

In August, 1962, a children's magazine under Li's control published a short novel entitled *Tu Fu hui chia* (Tu Fu Returns Home) which applauded the poet's brave petitions to a T'ang emperor on behalf of the common people and described Tu's punishment, political exile. *Chieh-fang jih-pao* later said this was a case of "borrowing old things to satirize new" (*chieh-ku feng-chin*). No stranger to couplets himself, Li retorted that Yao Wen-yüan had "sold off his friends to seek personal glory" (*mai-yu ch'iu-jung*).

The attacks on Li began in June, 1966, and they came first from his own Chung-hua Bookstore. The rival Hsin-hua Bookstore quickly joined in and advertised in fine Shanghai-*cum*-rebel style that it would now stay open longer hours so that farmers and soldiers might more easily buy the books they would need to conduct the Cultural Revolution (and probably so that the store could fill its quotas more

---

138 *JMJP,* April 14, 1966, translated in *SCMP,* No. 3618 (January 17, 1966), p. 6.

139 Shanghai's *hsien* are extremely populous, and their cadres were later both the source and aim of much Cultural Revolutionary criticism. It is noteworthy that Wei Wen-po, who delivered a speech authorizing control of these cadres, was himself criticized later. See *SCMP,* No. 4388 (April 2, 1969), p. 9. On cadre study, see *JMJP,* March 7, 1966, translated in *SCMP,* No. 3600 (December 17, 1965), p. 1.

quickly, too). Typesetters and factory militia in two printing factories also joined the chorus against Li, and in time the local newspapers were publishing scores of condemnation letters from many kinds of units.[140]

The connections made by Chang Ch'un-ch'iao with press workers were of considerable importance in the "seizures of power" in *Wen-hui pao* and *Chieh-fang jih-pao* during the January Revolution later. The attacks upon Li Chün-min for his "abuse" of these workers were a prelude to those actions. The relationship Li had with his booksellers and typesetters was too tenuous to prevent them from forming groups against him, and Chang could use this organizational weakness to isolate and purge Li. This kind of situation recurred many times in Shanghai in the succeeding two years, and it illustrates one way in which elite change during the Cultural Revolution was related to group relations as well as issues.

The best-known cultural leader to be criticized early in Shanghai's Cultural Revolution was Ho Lü-t'ing, president of the Shanghai Music Conservatory and composer of "The East Is Red," a song written at Yenan and dedicated to Chairman Mao, which is all but officially China's national anthem. Ho had been professor of music at the Lu Hsün Arts Academy during the war, and he had received many government honors during the 1950's. Criticism of him began mildly with an open letter carried in both *Chieh-fang jih-pao* and *Wen-hui pao* on June 8, 1966, which said Ho had decried efforts to "force composers to become song-writing tools" and to "turn men into machines." In late June the attacks became more frequent and severe in local papers, and they came more often from workers and soldiers. Ho Lü-t'ing resisted. A year later it emerged that his wife and daughter had managed to obtain photostatic copies of the documents being used against him; and friends in his native Shao-yang, Hunan, had shadowed the team sent by his rivals to investigate his family history. These tactics did not work. Ho was eventually exposed, and he had to appear before a televised denunciation rally.[141]

The purge of these intellectuals, and several others, was accom-

---

[140] The text on Li is a synopsis of accounts in Ting Wang's superb *Niu-kuei she-shen chi* (A Collection of Ghosts and Monsters) (Hong Kong: San-chia-tien shu-wu, 1967), p. 106; *1967 fei-ch'ing nien-pao*, pp. 345 and 583; and *HMWP*, June 26 (two articles) and July 12, 1966.

[141] Ting Wang (ed.), *Niu-kuei she-shen chi*, p. 103; *KMJP*, June 9, 1966; *HMWP*, June 28, 1966; and *WHP*, April 24, 1968.

panied by an expansion of the Cultural Revolution at lower levels— apparently with the full support of local government leadership. Meanwhile, the number of workers allowed to join the Party in Shanghai expanded sharply in June.[142] The Party elite in the Shanghai No. 1 Electric Machines Company divided itself into groups in July, and each of these went to the production lines for one shift each day to lead the workers and "discuss technical problems." [143] There was some criticism of important bourgeois figures like Deputy Mayor Jung I-jen, even though the capitalists ceased to receive their fixed-interest payments in 1966.[144] The municipal Party committee, and especially Mayor Ts'ao Ti-ch'iu, gave many speeches about cultural revolution. On June 11, a rally for ten thousand was held on People's Square in the center of Shanghai. Mayor Ts'ao presided and read a "mobilization report" to encourage, as he put it, "all Party members, Youth League members, the masses of peasants and workers, revolutionary cadres and intellectuals to carry the Great Proletarian Cultural Revolution through to the end." [145]

In July, Ts'ao presided at a meeting to celebrate the forty-fifth birthday of the Chinese Communist Party, which had been founded in Shanghai in 1921. Yang Fu-chen (later prominent in a non-Party organization to be known as the revolutionary committee), a logistics expert from the Shanghai garrison, the head of a student organization at Futan University, and Mayor Ts'ao all gave congratulatory speeches.[146] On August 20, the mayor, with Shanghai Party Secretary Wei Wen-po and visiting writer Kuo Mo-jo, presided at another similar rally. Local papers said that "students and workers" also spoke there—but their names were not given.[147]

There is no need to recount here the detailed history of Shanghai's Cultural Revolution after August, 1966, since some writings on these events are already available in English.[148] We will try only to provide

[142] NCNA, Shanghai, June 30, 1966.

[143] *HMWP,* July 19, 1966.

[144] Interview, Hong Kong, January, 1970, with a prominent textile manufacturer who has bourgeois relatives in Shanghai.

[145] *HMWP,* June 11, 1966.

[146] *Ibid.,* July 1, 1966.

[147] *Ibid.,* August 20, 1966.

[148] For example, see Neale Hunter, *Shanghai Journal: An Eyewitness Account of the Cultural Revolution* (New York: Praeger, 1969); Evelyn Anderson, "Shanghai: The Masses Unleashed," *Problems of Communism,* XXVII, No. 1 (January–February, 1968), 12–21; and Gerald Tannebaum, "The 1967 Shanghai January Revolution Recounted," *Eastern Horizon,* VII, No. 3 (May–June, 1968), 7 ff. These are written respectively from socialist-humanist, capitalist-liberal, and Maoist viewpoints. All three are competent.

data about the changes in Shanghai elites that have not been emphasized in earlier studies.

The key figure of this period, Chang Ch'un-ch'iao, had abandoned most of his Shanghai work during late May to assume a deputy headship in the new Cultural Revolution Small Group in Peking; but he became more active in Shanghai affairs again in the autumn, as the municipal committee's power waned under the attack of local and imported radicals. On November 11, Chang reviewed Mao's seventh Peking Red Guard rally.[149] On that same day he was flown by military plane directly to An-t'ing East, a railway stop halfway between Shanghai and Soochow, just outside the municipal border. He had come to help resolve certain labor demands being pressed upon the municipal committee. These demands had arisen after the formation on November 9 of the Shanghai Workers' Revolutionary Rebel Headquarters, an anticommittee group. Acting on his own initiative,[150] Chang completely undercut the Party committee's negotiating position by signing the workers' petition in his capacity as a member of the Central Small Group. The municipal Party committee (to which Chang had been appointed by K'o Ch'ing-shih just before the latter's death) issued a statement declining to support Chang's action. Shanghai's official Party leadership had openly split.

Until November 25 Chang remained in Shanghai. He was attacked in numerous wall posters, and his office was ransacked.[151] On November 30, a group of radical students supporting Chang occupied crucial offices of *Chieh-fang jih-pao* to prevent publication of that important daily pending acceptance of some demands. They in turn were besieged, and their position became somewhat precarious. The siege was lifted only gradually after December 6, when a large independent workers' group called the Scarlet Guards was created.[152]

Shanghai's earlier elites seem almost to disappear during the Cultural Revolution's most turbulent months, December, 1966, and January, 1967. The city of course had leaders at this time—*many* leaders.

[149] NCNA, November 11, 1966.

[150] I follow Hunter's fine evidence for this in *Shanghai Journal,* pp. 137–43. On Ch'en Po-ta's role in it, see Gordon Bennett, "The Old Teacher," *Far Eastern Economic Review* (Hong Kong) (hereafter *FEER*), LXIX, No. 10 (March 7, 1968), 410–11.

[151] Interview, Hong Kong, March, 1969, with an ex-Red Guard who had been in Shanghai in November, 1966. He had seen the posters but only heard about the events at Chang's office.

[152] Hunter, in *Shanghai Journal,* accepts his sources' interpretation that the Scarlet Guards were a tool of the Party committee. This acceptance is strange, because his Chapters ix–xii provide more fine details to prove their independence than any other single source this author has seen; and some of his sentences do suggest this.

Relations between the changing heads of various student, worker, and bureaucratic groups were in constant flux. Even factions having a close ideological affinity were often unable to unite under a single organizational leadership. It was thus impossible to develop any unified power center in the city, and the Shanghai Party Committee was completely demoralized. On December 10 a huge rally was held in Hongkew Stadium to denounce Yang Hsi-kuang. On December 13 Deputy Mayor Shih Ying committed suicide.[153] By December 20 it was commonly known in Shanghai that Peking Party Secretary Teng T'o had done the same.[154]

On December 27, a group of antiradical Scarlet Guards laid siege to the East China Party Bureau building, with Mayor Ts'ao inside, because they feared he would go over to "the left-wingers" and join forces with Chang.[155] On the last few days of the year, while the radicals were holding huge demonstrations inside the city, a group of Scarlet Guards started out by road for Peking to petition that Chang Ch'un-ch'iao make a self-criticism. They were attacked at K'un-shan (near An-t'ing) by a larger force of radicals. Apparently none of the combatant groups in this major battle was under the firm control of any of the top leaders mentioned in this paper. On January 3, Mayor Ts'ao was indicted before a rally in Culture Square. Chang returned to Shanghai by air on January 6, and the next day another rally was held to criticize members of the Shanghai Party secretariat. On January 10 deputy mayors Sung Chi-wen and Chang Ch'eng-tsung were arrested and paraded through the streets.

Chang's civilian base of power in the city was not large, but military commanders in the local garrison clearly stood behind him. In addition, Chiang Ch'ing was in Shanghai at least briefly during early January, and her husband may have accompanied her.[156] Even if

---

[153] "Shanghai Newsletter," *S.C.M. Post,* December 28, 1966. Shih's suicide is a widely accepted rumor, not a proven fact. The official report, not stating a cause of death, came on December 20, a week after the event. Shih was an economist, aged 58, "well known to international trade delegates." The *Post*'s correspondent, a White Russian resident in Shanghai, was imprisoned shortly after filing this story—and probably in part because of it. The ex-director of the Shanghai Party's Education Department, Ch'ang Hsi-p'ing, also committed suicide much later in May, 1968, according to a notice of the Shanghai Revolutionary Committee reprinted in Canton *Hung-ssu t'ung-hsin* (Red Headquarters Communiqué), No. 4–5 (July 12, 1968). All Red Guard papers used for this essay are in the files of URI, Hong Kong.

[154] Sophia Knight, *Window on Shanghai: Letters from China 1965–67* (London: André Deutsch, 1967), pp. 236 ff.

[155] Hunter, *Shanghai Journal,* p. 192.

[156] Chiang flew from Shanghai to Canton on January 10, 1967. She is reported to have said she left Peking for Shanghai in Mao's company, so that they could check on

Chang had this kind of help, however, his problems remained difficult. A worker-leader in the "rebel" organization, Keng Chin-chang, had led a large faction of radical workers away from Chang's loose control in December; and the most active of the power-seizing student groups (especially those from Futan University) had always been under their own independent captains, not under Chang. The Scarlet Guards (which, like Keng's groups, seem to have largely been reincarnations of early factory militias) maintained some of their organization and leadership at low levels even after their general movement began to decline.[157] Demobilized soldiers also formed independent groups.

Chang's most important power base was undoubtedly military, but the garrison under Commander Liao Cheng-kuo was much quicker to use its presence than its guns. It did not participate violently in any of the occasional public brawls during this period. On January 24, local air force units rode ninety trucks through the city in a public demonstration to "join the revolutionary masses" and "show their strength to the reactionaries." [158] But this did not deter Futan radicals from establishing a "Committee to Examine the Chang Ch'un-ch'iao Question" the very next day. On February 1, moreover, they stated that Chang should be "bombarded" and "struck down," and as we shall see later, some of Chang's pre-1949 activities might indeed provide a basis for struggle against him. But a Peking poster in early February suggested a clear warning to Chang's detractors. It said, "The necessary steps must be taken if this meeting to attack Chang Ch'un-ch'iao is held. . . . One must certainly take steps to arrest people." [159]

Possibly to stifle these investigations and confirm his leadership, Chang set up the Shanghai People's Commune on February 5. At the time it was hailed as a "creative application of the thought of Mao Tse-tung." It appears in fact to have been a bit too creative. The concessions to workers' demands at An-t'ing suggest that Chang had authority from Peking to initiate very important policy suggestions, and

disturbances in Nanking and Shanghai. *HTJP,* January 12, 1967. Mao's whereabouts was not officially released until May; his last publicized appearance had been on November 26, 1967, when he received the Cambodian defense minister, Lieutenant General Lon Nol.

157 Hunter, *Shanghai Journal,* Chap. xi. The idea about militias is based on a release from NCNA, Shanghai, January 9, 1967.

158 *Shang-hai wan-pao* (Shanghai Evening News) (formerly *HMWP;* henceforth *SHWP*), January 25, 1967.

159 *CT,* No. 511 (January 8, 1969), p. 8.

at least the timing of the commune may have been his decision after telephone conferences with the capital. Point nine of the Central Committee's Sixteen Points of August 18, 1966, had called for the establishment of election and recall procedures as in the Paris Commune; and a wall poster indicated that Shanghai alone had received the Central Committee's approval to set up this form of local government.[160]

But clearly Chairman Mao had second thoughts. In mid-February he invited both Chang and Yao (head and deputy head of the commune) to come to Peking and review the situation. One poster in that city put Mao's name under these questions to Chang, the substance of which may not be entirely apocryphal: "The people's commune has been set up. Since its foundation, have you considered a whole series of questions? If the country sets up communes, then the Chinese People's Republic will have to change its name to the Chinese People's Commune. . . . The Chairman suggests that Shanghai should change a little. . . ."[161]

Chang may also have been required to explain events in his history before 1949, or to explain why it had been necessary in Shanghai to purge so many more members of the Party committee than had been purged elsewhere. On February 24, Chang gave a televised speech in Shanghai to clarify certain critical issues: the "provisional committee to organize the Shanghai Commune" would now become the revolutionary committee; Shanghai could not use the name "commune" because it had not yet set up a proper three-way alliance; technical experts had to be protected; "students alone could not possibly take power"; and most importantly, the Army must participate "before anything revolutionary can be achieved."

On February 25, the revolutionary committee declared that the army would assume control of Shanghai's harbor, airport, post office, radio station, secondary railroads, newspapers, and some factories. Another resolution two days later forbade "raids on airfields, radio stations, prisons, detention centers and offices containing secret docu-

[160] *CCP Documents of the Great Proletarian Cultural Revolution, 1966–1967* (Hong Kong: URI, 1968), Chinese text, p. 38. The wall poster is quoted in *CT*, No. 511 (January 8, 1969), p. 4.

[161] See *CT*, No. 511 (January 8, 1969), which presents both available versions of these events. The quoted one has Chang and Yao going to Peking on February 20. The other, which gives February 12, suggests that Chang may have had to do considerable explaining of his participation in the Shanghai Party Committee debates since 1965. Alexandra Close, in "Mao Plays His Last Trump," *FEER*, March 16, 1967, says mid-February posters in Shanghai asked why Chang and Yao had left and why *JMJP* had not mentioned the Shanghai People's Commune.

ments and files." [162] The committee also vowed to suppress people who dared to oppose "Chairman Mao and Vice-Chairman Lin"—and the second danger clearly worried them more than the first. Shanghai's elite now included some military officers who had not previously been so active in it.

Open season was declared not on all Party members, but on all Party bosses. Deputies, even at very high levels, might be spared if they criticized their chiefs. For example, the former deputy head of Ch'ang-ning district, whose high position had given him a constituency of several hundred thousand people, was accepted into the ranks of rebel legitimacy after making a recondite confession and censuring his former boss. [163] Pardonable cadres were invited to cry "I was duped" and to be excused from most of their crimes on grounds of the wily hoodwinking abilities of their former superiors. [164]

Experience, which had previously been considered a good quality in leaders, now became a dubious quality. Mao was cited to have said that the down-trodden are in many situations the wisest, and the intellectuals are often the most stupid. A worker in the Shanghai Flux Factory undertook to prove, on the basis of past critiques of novels, that People's Liberation Army soldiers could write better literary criticism than the literary critics. [165] A group of fifty amateurs, mostly workers, formed an organization during the January Revolution to take charge of Shanghai's entire economy, so that the planners could be dismissed. [166] The Shanghai Ink Factory reduced its bureaucratic staff by one-half and cut its levels of organization from three (factory-workshop-brigade) to two (factory-brigade). It also authorized less bookkeeping (which would almost inevitably lead to illegal black-market transactions) and insisted that administrative personnel work manually for two days each week. [167]

This trend against certain leaders was accompanied by higher-level actions to mute it. And both persisted over many months. On February 18, 1967, a *Wen-hui pao* editorial dealt with the necessity of welcoming government cadres who came forward to rebel after they realized their mistakes. An editorial in *Chieh-fang jih-pao* of April 2 stressed the need to attack Liu Shao-ch'i—and to leave lesser Party

[162] Close, "Mao Plays His Last Trump." NCNA, Shanghai, February 27, 1957.
[163] *JMJP*, March 6, 1967.
[164] For example, see *WHP*, April 12, 1967.
[165] *Wen-i pao* (Peking), No. 2 (February 16, 1965), pp. 24–26.
[166] NCNA, Shanghai, February 10, 1967.
[167] *Ibid.*, November 21, 1967.

men in relative peace. But New China News Agency, representing more radical central views, wrote its stories differently. On April 1, it reported forums in Shanghai of new, proletarian leaders, whose role as the "core and mainstay" of the January Revolution should now be recognized by giving them more power. The next day it reported forums of "revolutionary leading cadres" (that is, former power-holders who had been coopted, but who were often not quite as "revolutionary" as their less expert colleagues might like). These leaders had "decided" to overcome the "erroneous tendency of neglecting the roles played by the responsible persons of mass organizations." By late spring, the attacks on low-level leaders in many organs had subsided. In some schools and factories there was still spectacular disorganization; but even in these, the revolutionary committee by spring was at least trying to make the group leaders sit down together and form alliances even when their followers did not like the idea.

In many units, this attempt did not produce results. It was openly admitted that although Shanghai's chemical factories (largely created during the Great Leap) had established "revolutionary alliances" among their leaders, most were still split into "two or more organizations holding differing views and engaging in internal feuds." [168]

Analytical rather than chronological treatment of Shanghai leaders' behavior in 1967–68 will make their tensions easier to understand. Government policies and Party authorities did not have the capacity to shape social behavior after 1966 to the same extent as previously; therefore, conflicting policies and ideas could coexist for a long time. For this reason, an analysis of the Cultural Revolution in Shanghai cannot follow a neat time sequence after February, 1967. There were few clean divisions of trends in time; few things simply began or ended. Rather, there were only rising and waning tendencies. For at least sixteen months, "rebels" disagreed among themselves on how far the purge of leaders should be allowed to go, and this disagreement was evident in Shanghai's leading newspapers. Two editorials from widely separated dates will suffice to illustrate it, although a myriad could be cited. As each appeared at a time when the policy it recommended was *not* in fact generally being followed, they serve to emphasize the simultaneous existence of the opposite policy. (In fact, campaigns within the Cultural Revolution were frequently efforts by the revolutionary committee to reverse behavior that was current in lower-level rectification meetings at the same times.)

[168] *Ibid.*, June 8, 1967.

On March 17, 1967, for example, *Chieh-fang jih-pao* pointed out that the people in every unit best understood their own cadres and would be scrupulously fair in judging them without requiring much active outside help. Some local chiefs would of course have to be overthrown, but only the duly constituted revolutionary three-way alliance of the accused leader's own unit was competent to decide that matter. To interfere in this process was to contravene Chairman Mao's injunction about relying on the masses. Practical application of this advice would have greatly restricted the sources and forums of accusations; and it would have saved a good many low-level leaders from criticism.

Wen-hui pao in its editorial of June 9, 1968, however, took exactly the opposite tack.[169] It used the ambiguous word "masses" more abstractly and defined it in terms of theoretical "proletarian" interests rather than in terms of the numerical majority of any unit. This editorial scoffed at the fear of "making mistakes" in criticizing innocent leaders. It charged that this fear itself was a more serious mistake, indicative of apathy in defending the "masses." Outsiders were not told to abstain from accusation meetings. On the contrary, the virtue of "vigilance" was praised. *Wen-hui pao* may have been defending student (largely bourgeois-background) participants in nonstudent politics. The paper even admitted that its own critics "pretend" to be the masses—possibly because they are the majority—and it reported the "public opinion" that *Wen-hui pao* was carrying out a "new bourgeois" line.

These editorials revealed that no leader in Shanghai could be certain of the precise meaning or direction of the Cultural Revolution, at least through mid-1968. The movement's language was inexact, and many different groups sought to lead it by their own gyroscopes so that the total effect was always hard to predict. Shanghai had more real capitalists and more real proletarians than any other place in China, and they were participating in their own ways to overthrow the parts of a leadership that had put pressure on them. Various abuses from before 1966 now generated political energy in diverse groups, changing relations from those of coordination and compromise to those of conflict. Naturally, these groups openly disagreed on what leadership should emerge in the new postrevolutionary state. Some authorities demanded new posts for the real proletariat, on grounds that Shanghai's workers had been exploited and now deserved better. Other local leaders

169 Translated in *SCMP*, No. 4211 (July 5, 1968), p. 10.

pleaded for a more immediate criterion of worth, based upon the possibility of redemption from the stigma of a bad family background through faith in Marxism and a present decision to do good.

The issue was not theoretical but very practical. Who should assume posts made vacant by the Cultural Revolution? There was no possibility of an abstract choice between the rival criteria just set forth. The tension engendered by the struggle to control the revolution enforced a certain discipline within each group. To a surprising extent, the contending groups maintained the different criteria, and also remained separate from each other as long as possible. For example, rebels in the water conservancy and communications departments of the Shanghai Party Committee wanted to "seize power" as soon as the commune replaced that committee; so they quickly took possession of the big seals (*ta yin*) of those offices. The empress dowager, an inveterate seal-snatcher, would have understood that perfectly. In practice, however, the Party bureaucrats' work was not usually hampered by a lack of chops.[170]

Often power seizure was no joke. Throughout February and March, Shanghai Radio reported many attacks on cadres at the grass-roots level. Low-level leaders in both Party and government were liable for criticism if they held the rank of branch secretary, street-office director, or any higher post, even though the actual purge of cadres was less at the district or lower levels than at the city level.[171] Indeed, a number of the old district leaders continued to hold office, and only their titles were changed. The Huang-p'u District Revolutionary Committee was formed only three weeks after the Shanghai Revolutionary Committee; [172] and Wang Tzu-hua, its chairman, had held the post of district chief before the January Revolution. The next such group to be established (the Preparatory Committee for Ch'ang-ning district's revolutionary committee) had as its new chairman Hu Hua-ch'ing, who had previously been deputy district chief. Chang Chen-yen, the new "responsible person" (*tse-jen che*) of Shanghai's Ch'uan-sha County (*hsien*) Revolutionary Committee, had previously been deputy

170 *Chi-tien chan-pao* (Machine and Electricity Battle Report), published by the Ti-i chi-hsieh kung-yeh pu, Shang-hai shih ko-ming tsao-fan lien-ho wei-yüan-hui (Shanghai Joint Committee of Revolutionary Rebels of the First Machine-Building Ministry), February 2, 1967. In URI library. An ex-cadre from Canton, whose seals had been taken, reported to the author that in Canton also, the work of the bureaucracy generally continued even without chops.
171 *China News Summary* (Hong Kong) (hereafter *CNS*), No. 161 (March 15, 1967), p. 3.
172 *SHWP,* March 20, 1967.

county chief. In Sung-chiang county, the former chief and three of his Party secretaries all joined the new revolutionary committee. The heads of revolutionary committees in the Shanghai No. 1 Steel Company and the Shanghai Instruments and Telecommunications Industry Bureau had both been deputy heads of those units before. Wang K'un, "responsible person" of the Shanghai Foodstuffs Corporation, had even been chief Party secretary in that large municipal company.[173]

Terminology for the new leadership varied among committees. Chang Ch'un-ch'iao was at least initially called the "responsible person" of Shanghai's Revolutionary Committee; and he, Yao Wen-yüan, Hsü Ching-hsien, and a few others were also its "leading members" (*chih-tao chi-ch'eng yüan*). But Huang-p'u district had a "director" (*chu-jen*) at the head of its committee; Yang-p'u district and Sung-chiang county preferred "responsible people." [174] Sometimes preparatory revolutionary committees, or even full-fledged ones, would be announced without any leaders being named at all, as in Hsü-hui district on March 6, 1967 (although by November it was announced that Hsü Ch'uan-ssu was in charge).[175] Revolutionary committees were announced in Nan-shih, Lu-wan, P'u-t'o, Cha-pei, and Ching-an districts —and in most of Shanghai's counties—without any publicity being given their leaders.

Many leaders in Shanghai tried to retreat from participation in this new and uncertain political activity, particularly after they came under sustained attack. For example, the rebels of Yang-p'u district left no stone unturned exploring the background of Chang Ch'ing-piao, who had been secretary of the district Party committee. They investigated the history of his family going back as far as a decade before his birth. They read through the full minutes of the 539 district Party committee meetings over which Chang had presided during his eleven-year tenure, and they used this material to criticize him in a long series of struggle sessions. Understandably, Chang sought to retire, but he was persuaded to stay on. Ch'en Ta-tung, director of the Shanghai No. 3

---

[173] All in *JMJP*, April 3, 1967.

[174] The fad for titles was most elaborately developed in the Cultural Revolution Small Group itself, which initially had five categories of participants: a head, a first deputy, advisers, ordinary deputy heads, and ordinary members. It is interesting to note that by late 1968, purges had reduced the group's entire membership to that same number. (Some of the titles had been abolished.)

[175] See *Chūka jinmin kyōwakoku soshikibetsu jimmei hyō* (Organization and Personnel of the People's Republic of China) (Tokyo: Naikaku Kanbō, 1967), p. 93. Hsü's appointment is mentioned in *1969 chung-kung nien-pao*, IX, 92.

Steel Mill, also wanted to step out of politics after the attacks on him. He reportedly said, "If I become top man again, I will once more become the main target in the next campaign." Only after this reluctance was struggled out of him did he resume his previous duties, through which he then became a member of the mill's revolutionary committee. The ex-Party secretary in a municipal department expressed his desire not to become "top man" there again but to retire as a "general cadre or an 'old good' cadre." The principal-*cum*-Party secretary of Shanghai's T'ien-shan Middle School was similarly struggled before he would resume work. Even the deputy head of the Political Department in the Shanghai Party's Communications Bureau privately advocated "struggle-criticism-departure" (*tou-p'i-tsou*) rather than "struggle-criticism-transformation" (*tou-p'i-kai*)—until he was enlightened on this point by some additional struggle-criticism.[176]

Central authorities were clearly alarmed at the extent to which middle level leaders had been dismissed in Shanghai. As early as January 15, 1967, Premier Chou is reliably reported to have said at a meeting in Peking, "We should not promote the style of workers taking over management as they have done in Shanghai." He insisted that managers must not be allowed to "conceal themselves," and that workers should only supervise them, not assume their functions.[177] The *Wen-hui pao* editorial of March 7 told "proletarian revolutionaries" to accept any old cadre into their ranks—even cadres who had been called bourgeois—as long as they "show their colors" and declare for Mao. Again on August 19 the newspaper informed them to "push the cadres to the front—only in struggle can we identify and test cadres." It said that the old cadres were "politically mature" and "capable of holding power and running business operations." Such former leaders should therefore be accepted into "three-way alliances" if they were revolutionary.

Chang Ch'un-ch'iao's policy of encouraging alliances stirred the ire of some radical group leaders because it gradually lessened their own power, and they were quick to censure him. Almost as if nothing had changed since January, they continued throughout 1967 and even early 1968 to post handbills in which they accused Chang of spreading the doctrine of the extinction of classes, of supporting capitalists and rightist elements, of buying off some workers who put economics in com-

[176] All in *JMJP*, November 12, 1967.
[177] *CNS*, No. 154, January 19, 1967, p. A8; based on the January 16 dispatch of an *Asahi shimbun* reporter who was there.

mand, of attacking revolutionaries, and of advocating an "independent kingdom" in Shanghai (that is, independent of policies expressed by some members of the Central Cultural Revolution Small Group).[178]

Moreover, *Wen-hui pao* and Chang's fellow propagandist, Hsü Ching-hsien, were special objects of calumny at the hands of a Shanghai organization known as the "Wild Whirlwind of the Artillery Command" (*P'ao-ssu k'uang-piao*).[179] Strong anarchist, antileadership ideals stood behind much of this opposition. To some extent, as has been widely recognized, the mainstream of the Cultural Revolution sponsored such notions; but for the most part it opposed them.[180] In Shanghai, some factions advocated that social property and political power be redistributed on a continuous basis.[181] On August 3, 1967, elements opposing Chang Ch'un-ch'iao insisted that "Shanghai must have a second period of chaos which will thoroughly reform the Revolutionary Committee." [182]

According to *Chieh-fang jih-pao*, political disputes were "acute" during the two or three months before Chairman Mao's August trip to Shanghai and other trouble spots.[183] Even after that time, however, radical group leaders were certainly not defeated. In March, 1968, Shanghai newspaper editorials had to explain, apparently to radicals who believed they deserved Party membership, that not all of them could be admitted. It also indicated that not all of the Party members whom the young leaders wanted to replace were going to be expelled.[184]

Chang's campaign to crush independent local leaders was mounted slowly and carefully. As with the 1957 antirightist campaign, its civilian power base lay with the workers, now organized in a restructured system of militias. During the first few days of December, 1967,

---

178 This list is from *HTJP*, May 20, 1968; but there had also been earlier, less continuous abuse of Chang.

179 *Hung-se tsao-fan-che* (The Red Revolutionary), published by the Third Commanding Force of Shanghai Technical University and the Third Commanding Force also of Shanghai Municipality's Chia-ting *hsien*, May 13, 1967. In URI library.

180 A set of ten regulations set forth by the Shantung Revolutionary Committee were praised by NCNA, Peking, June 23, 1967 (in *SCMP*, No. 3963 [June 20, 1969], p. 11) as national models. These rules forbade many sorts of indulgences to the new elite (the committee members): no public praise; no welcomes or send-offs when they travel; no photographs of them in newspapers; no gifts; their names should not appear in the press except when absolutely necessary; they should answer all letters personally; every two months or so a self-criticism and rectification session should be held, to which members of various organizations are invited. These strictures were not by any means followed in Shanghai, but they were in the air.

181 *WHP*, July 23, 1967, rebuts this "reactionary idea."

182 *Ibid.*, July 30, 1967. See also *1969 chung-kung nien-pao*, IV, 22.

183 Anderson, "Shanghai," pp. 12–21.

184 *WHP*, March 22, 1968, translated in *SCMP*, No. 4170 (May 3, 1968), p. 13.

Chang and his labor-organizer, Wang Hung-wen, called a conference of worker representatives at which Wang spoke in strong, communal, nativistic terms about the need to establish a government led by real proletarians. His words evoked the image of class or caste pollution: nonproletarian persons (largely bourgeois students) had attempted to lead factories; but the real workers would be poisoned by their evil influence, so they had to be expelled.[185] In March, Wang announced that "recently, on the basis of education in the thought of Chairman Mao, we have violently assaulted anarchism." He said he had a little list of three thousand "enemy agents, traitors, and turncoats," who would shortly be investigated in Shanghai, although only "seven or eight" of them had actually been arrested at that time. He further stated that "these figures are far from complete."[186]

Chang's own speeches emphasized the more positive aspect of his leadership policy. Some of the old elite members, he indicated, would be retained. The Shanghai Revolutionary Committee was probably more "revolutionary" (in the sense of having new faces) than any other at the provincial level in China; but it did include three members from the old Shanghai Party Committee, namely, ex-Secretaries Chang Ch'un-ch'iao and Ma T'ien-shui and ex-Alternate Secretary Wang Shao-yung.[187] There is scant evidence that either Ma or Wang could be considered radical. Nevertheless, they were regularly present in high positions on the rank-list at Hung-ch'iao Airport and at revolutionary committee banquets to meet visiting dignitaries. Their constantly reported presence throughout 1967–68 may have reassured lower-level Party leaders that the flag was still there, that the Party as an institution had not been completely abandoned.

Wang Shao-yung was the model resurrected leader in Shanghai. To some extent it was only a repeat performance for him, since in 1955 he had been purged from his posts in the Shantung provincial Party for membership in a "sectarian clique." This clique was reportedly headed by Hsiang Ming (the only East China leader other than Jao Shu-shih important enough to have his name mentioned in the Central Committee communiqué announcing the famous Kao Kang purge). For nine years after that, Wang Shao-yung's name did not appear in

---

[185] NCNA, Shanghai, December 6, 1967.

[186] *Wen-ko t'ung-hsün* (Cultural Revolution Bulletin), Canton (hereafter *WKTH*), No. 13 (March, 1968). In URI library. Also found in *SCMP*, No. 4166 (April 29, 1968), p. 12.

[187] On these men and others who were purged, see *Chung-kung tung-t'ai fen-hsi* (Analysis of Chinese Communist Activities) (Taipei), No. 48 (November 30, 1967), pp. 4–5; and *Chūka jinmin kyōwakoku soshikibetsu jimmei hyō*, p. 93.

the press. In June, 1964, he re-emerged as a deputy director of the Propaganda Department of the Party's East China Bureau. By May of the following year, he was already an alternate secretary of the Shanghai Party Committee; and by October, 1966, he was deputy head of Ts'ao Ti-ch'iu's local cultural revolution group in Shanghai, an organization that was toppled soon thereafter.

Yet this cat appeared truly to have nine lives. He managed to change his line very quickly, so that in February, 1968, Chang made a speech extolling the method by which Wang had been redeemed and then retained in an elite position. Rebel groups first held small meetings with him. Then he was sent to "units which had committed mistakes" to criticize other leaders and to conduct self-criticism. Following this, a huge rally "of 20,000 people" was televised throughout the city. Viewers could phone in their criticisms of Wang "from where they were," in the manner of an American late-night show. Wang would duly explain himself on television: McLuhan had reached Shanghai. In Wang's case, the entire ordeal lasted for more than two months, at the end of which time he presided over a rally of 10,000 persons and was given a seat on the municipal revolutionary committee. Chang averred that "there is no triple-alliance behind doors or in small rooms." [188]

In February of 1968 it was publicly announced that Chang Ch'un-ch'iao had spent a good deal of the second half of 1967 investigating the histories of 2,086 individuals, most of whom were to be purged.[189] In June the *Shang-hai kung-jen tsao-fan pao* (Shanghai Workers' Rebel News) announced that a special new set of public security regulations had been approved in Shanghai to facilitate these purges and to extend the investigations of revolutionary committee members at all levels back to the Civil War period.[190] Post-1946 participants in KMT units at or above the district and county levels were to be "dealt

[188] *Hsin-hsing hung-se* (Newly Emerging Redness), published by the Hsin-hsing Kung-jen (Newly Emerging Workers), Canton, February 27, 1969. In URI library. URS *Biographical Service,* No. 1226 (September 15, 1967), is very useful on Wang. An even bigger cat with nine lives was P'an Fu-sheng, who was purged in 1958 from Honan due to his opposition to some Great Leap policies. P'an reappeared in November, 1962, as acting chairman of the Supply and Marketing Cooperatives Federation, and by July of 1963 he was the regular chairman. P'an later moved to the northeast and headed China's first province-level revolutionary committee in Heilungkiang. Thanks are due to Donald Klein, who helped gather this information.

[189] *WKTH,* No. 13 (March, 1968), but not the article cited in note 186.

[190] Quoted in *HTJP,* December 19, 1968. These springtime regulations followed the outlines of national rules laid down in Peking earlier.

with," as were ex-company commanders and individuals who had held higher ranks in the Nationalist Army, speculators, KMT police and *pao-chia* security system officials, young hoodlums, those who had been dismissed in the *ssu-ch'ing* movement, some dependents of escaped counterrevolutionaries, "five-bad-class" persons who had become leaders in rebel organizations, and (lest anyone feel left out) "those who cannot be reformed." Hsü Ching-hsien borrowed an old phrase to call this an "open-door" purge, and he claimed that it was the first Party rectification movement in China that had ever been truly public.[191]

Chang Ch'un-ch'iao's rivals were not idle as the storm gathered over their heads. In fact, as we have suggested, resistance sputtered irregularly from the time that Chang first came to power. For reasons which are not clear, a hostile group of one thousand people gathered at a meeting of the Shanghai Revolutionary Committee on December 19, 1967.[192] After this incident, more evidence began to emerge about the investigations which had been made of Chang Ch'un-ch'iao's own history before 1949. His enemies' need to advance this evidence against him was now very obvious because of his own preparations. The indictment against Chang contained two major counts: (1) that Chang's book concerning a visit he made to the Soviet Union in 1954 was a revisionist piece because it praised that country after the death of Stalin, and (2) that Chang had been captured in Shansi before 1949 by KMT troops and had briefly been an informant renegade.[193]

The ex-first secretary of the Shensi Party Committee, Huo Shih-lien, had made this accusation in a letter to Chairman Mao, presumably on the basis of what he knew about affairs in the adjacent province. Ma T'ien-shui spoke at the first enlarged session of the Shanghai Revolutionary Committee to deny that Chang had ever been arrested, or had ever been in Shansi before liberation. The second part of Ma's assertion is extremely dubious, because Chang was doing political work after 1942 in the Chin-Ch'a-Chi guerrilla region and once had responsi-

---

[191] *WKTH*, No. 16 (July, 1968), translated in *SCMP*, No. 4237 (August 13, 1968), p. 1. Hsü's claim is invalid if he meant that this was the first time the Party had ever sponsored non-Party criticism of its members.

[192] The meeting was said in later Communist sources to have been supported by Lu Wen-ts'ai, who was purged from the committee the next spring; but the present author does not have enough material to interpret this event. Possibly it was a protest by students against the workers' meeting earlier the same month. An anti-Communist but straightforward account is in *HTJP*, December 10, 1968.

[193] Chang's book is *Fang-su chien-wen ts'a-chi* (Record of Sights and Sounds on My Visit to the Soviet Union) (Shanghai: Hua-tung jen-min ch'u-pan she, 1954).

bilities in the Pei-yüeh area of Shansi province.[194] The statement that Chang was never arrested may also be inaccurate. Chang went to Peking in mid-April, possibly to exonerate himself from these charges or to undergo indoctrination. In any case, he suffered no loss of power. History was of no utility to Chang's rivals, although he certainly was able to use it often and effectively against them.

Purges of the Shanghai Revolutionary Committee came in at least two waves, which are simultaneous with some of the events noted above. In December, 1967, revolutionary committee members Hu Chih-hung, Chu Ken-fu, and Min K'ao-ssu were "dragged out." [195] All three had been "bad leaders" (*huai t'ou-t'ou*) in a mysterious group named the *Kung hsiang tung* (Communists Facing the East). Hu had been deputy head of the revolutionary committee's Political Propaganda Group (*cheng-hsüan tsu*), of which both Min and Chu were members. These first purgees seem to have run afoul of Chang on both organizational and policy grounds, to judge from their reported functions inside and outside of the revolutionary committee.

The more important purge, which followed in mid-1968, was possibly a continuation of the first one. Chu Hsi-ch'i, head of the Political Propaganda Group, mobilized an organization known as the Red Military Arts Rebel League (*Hung wu-yi tsao-fan t'uan*) to criticize Chang on the basis of his pre-1949 history. They held a demonstration in Shanghai on April 12, 1968, at which Chu called Chang a "left opportunist" and reportedly accused him of doing immense damage to Shanghai's administrative organs. After Chu's attack failed, he was in turn accused of having had close relations with the purged central radicals Wang Li and Kuan Feng and of having caused political chaos in Shanghai. At about this same time, Lu Wen-ts'ai, Party secretary of Huang-p'u district and second secretary in the Shanghai Social Sciences Academy, was also purged from the revolutionary committee. It is difficult to establish a firm relationship between these two purges be-

194 Huang (ed.), *Chung-kung chün-jen chih*, p. 394; *1969 chung-kung nien-pao*, V, 38–39. Donald Klein pointed out to me that the *Chin-Ch'a-Chi jih-pao* (Shansi-Chahar-Hopei Daily) of March 1, 1946, states that Chang was Teng T'o's deputy in the NCNA office of that border region. The Taipei people apparently could not locate any of their own records on Chang's arrest, although they certainly would be qualified to decide the issue. A different Red Guard source, for essentially the same tale, is cited in *CT*, No. 511 (January 8, 1969), p. 8.

195 *Tung-fang-hung tien-hsün* (The East Is Red Telegram) (Canton), No. 3 (July, 1968), translated in *SCMP*, No. 4234 (August 8, 1968), p. 15. Another source, *1969 chung-kung nien-pao*, III, 71, includes a "Li Fu-ken" with this group. The present author feels certain that Shanghai has no such man. This is a misprint or a spurious interview report (it uses the characters in other purgees' names) for Chu Ken-fu.

cause Lu was only called a "renegade." On an unknown date and for unknown reasons, Feng Kuo-chu, a "responsible person" of the air force based in Shanghai, was also expelled from the revolutionary committee.[196]

Another wave of purges came slightly later in mid-1968, when committee member Li Yen-wu was dubbed "the biggest capitalist roader in Shanghai's finance and trade system" and a follower of the "dead party" of Ts'ao Ti-ch'iu. Li had supervised Party branches in the city's economic and commercial departments in 1964 and was an old cadre. Revolutionary committeeman Chu Kang was also called similar names in the same period. This purge was apparently based on economic policy differences and did not stem from an organizational conflict— and the change of cause shows that Chang's own organization in mid-1968 was beginning to give Shanghai a cohesive elite once again.

The Cultural Revolution had caused major changes in Shanghai's leadership personnel, particularly at high levels. This "revolution" had also tried to change the style of leadership action, but the same repression that consolidated the new elite must also have brought back memories of the deposed work teams of the "Liuist" era. The circulation of Shanghai's elites alternated with their stasis, and the pressure and fear of the cycle made any incumbents work very hard on all of the problems that confronted them.

A QUANTITATIVE LOOK AT SHANGHAI'S ELITE
BEFORE AND AFTER 1967

A brief statistical analysis of the characteristics of Shanghai's elite before and after the Cultural Revolution should help us to define the

---

[196] *1969 chung-kung nien-pao*, III, 71, and *Chiu-i-liu t'ung hsün* (September 16 Bulletin) (Canton), August, 1968, translated in *SCMP*, No. 4240 (August 16, 1968), p. 10. The present author does not know what to make of a Taipei interpretation of factional divisions on the Shanghai Revolutionary Committee. Chung-yang she (Central News Agency), October 9, 1968, and *HTJP*, October 11, 1968. As always in Taipei, the real issue has been between Chiang Ch'ing and Lin Piao. Lin's faction supposedly consisted of the committee's soldiers—only. Chiang's was headed by Feng Kuo-chu (but he is an airman, and they do not mention that); and it included Ch'en Lin-hu, Hsü Ching-hsien, Li Yen-wu, and Lu Wen-ts'ai, three of whom were indeed purged. This would be an unusual group of bedfellows. The model's complete omission of Chang, Yao, Wang Hung-wen, Wang Shao-yung, Ma T'ien-shui (and at the national level, Mao Tse-tung) leaves something to be desired, unless one sees these last figures as the astute balancers of two opposing factions, the *tertii gaudentes*. The Taipei account does not do so. Nor is that theory dynamic in any other sense; it only states factional coalitions. After all this has been discounted, a problem still remains: the Taipei people have many sources of information. They may even be right. Lin Piao as of late 1971 was certainly not in the same faction as Chiang Ch'ing.

effects of that event on the city's politics.[197] The study which follows is preliminary, simple, and designed to discover things about Shanghai's leaders, not to prove any more general ideas. This limited goal dictates that the methods should elicit many different kinds of information and that the samples should be chosen for their importance and variety. With this limitation and understanding, we will be able to use samples which are mathematically small.

It should actually be no easier to select an elite sample in behavioral science than it is to separate leadership from social problems in historical narrative. It is simplest to equate "elite" with a particular political office and to say that the incumbents were all leaders. The trouble with generating "leadership" from any single institution, however, is that some political factions and functional systems may be underrepresented or overrepresented. The converse trouble of *not* equating leadership with a single institution is that "leaders" who are defined more broadly also run a greater risk of being incommensurable mathematically. If all the members of our sample have held the same post, then we know they have at least one thing in common; in at least one definite sense, there are no oranges mixed with the apples. But if our criterion is more free (and maybe more realistic), then the leaders' characteristics may be added together less justifiably. The basis of the numbers we find in conclusion is then less sure, and we can less easily derive political meaning from the statistical aggregates.

This is no mere technical problem. Indeed, it goes to the heart of the main dilemma in elite studies, a dilemma that concerns nothing less than the relation between politics and society. How can leadership be treated like other social functions? When we find the distribution of Chinese leaders' various characteristics, what can it tell us about live Chinese politics? How can we know the relation between the elite a society chooses and the leadership that governs policy? If we categorize all of an elite's sociological traits, by what logic can we deduce its will for the future, or indeed any of its intentions at all? These questions will be answered only when we can construct a sample of leaders in some way that is the obverse of a method to predict leadership-action from an elite's social traits.

If we could find a sure sociological procedure to make a list of leaders, then the statistics we derived from that list could be given

---

[197] The sources used for this study, in addition to those cited in footnote 1, are occasional data in *WHP, CFJP, HMWP,* and *HWJP.* A very few of the data on revolutionary committeemen come from *SHWP* and the places in Red Guard newspapers already cited.

social meaning by the same logic. In politics, we will not be really successful at making either "anthropological" or "sociometric" conclusions until we find a way to make them both together. In this specific case, the seemingly technical problem of constructing a leadership sample is inextricable from the qualitative lines of reasoning that can make behavorial sense out of a statistic.

We will not be able to solve this multifaceted problem in a single essay about Shanghai, but the specific case can at least suggest some ways to neutralize the larger dilemma. In practice, we can choose samples that are justifiable by the same reasoning that shows them to be less than perfect, and we can simply decide to treat behavioral conclusions from them with some caution.

The first group that we will use consists of Shanghai's twenty-one mayors and deputy mayors (to be called only "deputy mayors" for short) between 1950 and the Cultural Revolution. Two of the deputy mayors appointed in May, 1949, namely Tseng Shan and Wei Ch'üeh, assumed important national positions as soon as the People's Republic was founded in October. Because their local functions effectively ceased at that time, they are not included in our survey. Except for them, the deputy mayors constitute a plausible, if incomplete, high elite for Shanghai. Historically observed leadership is one means to generate a leadership sample; and any narrative of modern Shanghai politics must certainly deal somehow with P'an Han-nien, Jung I-jen, Liu Shu-chou, Hsü Chien-kuo, Sheng P'ei-hua, K'o Ch'ing-shih, Chin Chung-hua, Chao Tsu-k'ang, Ts'ao Ti-ch'iu, Shih Ying, Sung Jih-ch'ang, and Li Kan-ch'eng, to name some of the leading figures in this group.

These men had administrative as well as ceremonial responsibilities. Their status allowed them to voice opinions as often as anyone could (we have seen that even the non-Communists among them sometimes took somewhat independent lines, emboldened by the belief that the Party could not remove them from office without discrediting itself). And their names appeared frequently in the newspapers. The function of leadership is to represent as well as to act, and the capitalist deputy mayors in this very capitalist city were definitely visible in politics. Even when they did not make decisions or advise on decisions, the attitudes which they shared no doubt influenced the process of leadership in Shanghai. Our historical description has also mentioned other civilian leaders (for example, some Party secretaries who were not concurrently deputy mayors), and if the information sources were better, we would probably also have mentioned more military officers. But the deputy mayorship is a loosely structured, high-level institution, drawn from several parties and functional systems in Shanghai. For this particular group, the problem of defining leadership by a single institution may not be too severe.

Since a great deal of information is available about each of the deputy mayors as defined above, their whole population can be explored. It will be possible to state findings in simple definite percentages without a check against the randomness of sampling, since no sampling has taken place. Cautions against bias need be raised mainly in the process of inducing conclusions which go beyond the specific group to apply to more general situations.[198]

The deputy mayors were classified in ten different ways. For some of them in certain of the categories, more than one result could be supported; but a best result was always found to be available. These tests are not logically exclusive of each other. For each man, we considered (1) whether his political career prior to becoming a deputy mayor lay predominantly in the government, the Party, or army organs; (2) his tenure in office and date of appointment; (3) whether he was a Party member or not; (4) whether he might be considered a native of the Shanghai area, either because he was born in the Wu-dialect region or because he spent most of his life in Shanghai; (5) his professional skill, if any; (6) whether most of his administrative work had been outside of Shanghai at any time; (7) whether his name (or his memory) appears in newspapers after the Cultural Revolution without unfavorable mention; (8) whether he is known to have traveled abroad; (9) whether he is known to have had any military background; and (10) which of the main functional systems represented his main area of jurisdiction during the period he was deputy mayor. (The simplest list of these functional systems is five-part: politics-law, culture-education, finance-trade, industry-communications, and agriculture-forestry-hydraulics. It was possible to combine the last two categories for this study, because in Shanghai the deputy mayors concerned with rural problems all turned out to have responsibility in industry-communications also.) [199] The worst of several omissions from this list

---

[198] All percentage figures in this study have been rounded to the nearest whole number and often do not total exactly 100 per cent.

[199] The names for these systems, respectively, are *cheng-fa, wen-chiao, ts'ai-mao, kung-chiao,* and *nung-lin-shui.* The military one, introduced later, is *chün-shih.* Sometimes additional systems are introduced for united-front work and appointments, but it was not found necessary to account these here. Kau, "Governmental Bureaucracy and Cadres

is a test for educational attainment; but we must be content at present to use the material available in documentary sources, and these did not contain enough information on that topic to provide data for each of the members even of this small group.

When the deputy mayors are divided by functional system, they distribute themselves as follows: politics-law, 33 per cent; culture-education, 19 per cent; finance-trade, 14 per cent; industry-communications, 33 per cent. The party affiliations of the deputy mayors were Communist, 76 per cent, non-Communist, 24 per cent. By multiplying these two matrices, it is possible to find the percentages of Communist and non-Communist deputy mayors that would be in each system if the posts were distributed proportionally among them. The actual distribution of Communists was: politics-law, 29 per cent; culture-education, 10 per cent; finance-trade, 19 per cent; industry-communications, 19 per cent. Non-Communist representation was: politics-law, 5 per cent; culture-education, 5 per cent; finance-trade, none; industry-communications, 14 per cent.

The real distribution was therefore extremely close to the expected proportional one, differing by more than five points (about one deputy mayor) only in industry-communications, where non-Communist participation was higher than expected and Communist participation was lower; but even here, the difference from a proportional distribution was not great. The only other deviation was in the finance-trade field, where Communist participation was slightly higher than expected. The Shanghai Party tended to concentrate its high-level economic leadership talents somewhat in the financial and commercial sectors. Apart from this, work in Shanghai's functional systems was distributed evenly among the deputy mayors, without much obvious regard to whether they were Communists or not, once they had been chosen as deputy mayors.

When a similar test was applied to compare native deputy mayors with those not born in the Shanghai area, there was only one functional system in which the real distribution differed from the proportional distribution by more than five percentage points of the total: non-native deputy mayors tended to work in the finance-trade field more than expected. All of the functional systems had both Shanghainese and non-Shanghainese deputy mayors in them at one time or another during this period.

---

in Urban China," p. 163, gives a list of the functions of Shanghai's eleven deputy mayors in 1957, reprinted from a Canton newspaper of that time.

These leaders can be grouped much more naturally by their backgrounds than by the nature of their work. All of the non-Communist deputy mayors were natives of the Shanghai area. Moreover, none of the non-Communist deputy mayors had ever held a major administrative post outside Shanghai. Six leaders had important military experience before 1949: all of these were Communists; all were also nonnatives; all had previously held administrative posts outside Shanghai and had traveled abroad; and all but one were appointed before 1956.

The great majority of Shanghai's deputy mayors had at least some experience abroad; only three of them are not known to have traveled to foreign countries. These three were all Communists; but that fact does not contravene the expected percentages according to party affiliation, which were fulfilled almost perfectly.

Tenure in office as a deputy mayor was much higher among non-Communists (10.2 years) than among Communists (5.75 years). Tenure also varied among the functional systems: culture-education, 9.3 years; finance-trade, 6.8; politics-law, 6.7; industry-communications, 5.8. Deputy mayors in Shanghai's culture-education system definitely retained their positions longer than those in other systems, but the cases are too few to allow any generalization beyond that. It was also an advantage in terms of tenure to be a native. The average tenure of the twelve local-born deputy mayors was 7.5 years, whereas that of the nine outsiders was 5.9 years. The import of this difference is accentuated by the fact that a disproportionate number of the Shanghai-native deputy mayors were appointed in the few years before the Cultural Revolution, when their tenures were brought to an unnaturally quick end.

The appointments of deputy mayors were not continuous; for example, four new ones were announced in January, 1957, and four more in July, 1962. These were the largest two contingents to be appointed, and each included Communist and non-Communist members. No real deputy mayors were appointed in the years between 1957 and 1962, although K'o Ch'ing-shih became mayor in November, 1958. Only one event, the Great Leap, is of sufficient import to divide the accession dates into two groups. Their percentage distribution, on the base of the whole, was as follows: Communists appointed before the Leap accounted for 52 per cent, and non-Communists, 19 per cent; after the Leap, Communist appointees accounted for another 19 per cent, while non-Communists were another 10 per cent. More Party than non-Party deputy mayors were appointed in each period, and the distribution of seats between them was maintained very roughly at 2:1 during the time span with which this paper deals. But a very different result emerges between the two large periods if the deputy mayors are compared with regard to their place of origin. Of all the appointees, Shanghai natives before the Leap accounted for 33 per cent, and nonnatives made 38 per cent; but the post-Leap nonnative appointees accounted for only 5 per cent, while those from Shanghai represented 24 per cent. Appointments after the Leap comprise only 29 per cent of the total, but the portion of new appointees who were natives definitely increased at that point. This could be interpreted as an aspect of the trend toward local independence which we have already observed. It could also be interpreted as evidence that the Party had gradually overcome the relative lack of trusted leadership manpower which it suffered in East China during the early years after liberation, and even these very high levels of the elite were affected.[200]

None of Shanghai's pre-1967 deputy mayors survived with banners flying into the Cultural Revolution. The only partial exceptions to this rule were both ex-mayors: K'o Ch'ing-shih and Foreign Minister and Marshal Ch'en I. The former's memory is often honored in newspapers now, for the good historical reasons which have already been presented; the latter's qualifications for survival rest on considerably more than his experience in Shanghai. All of the other names on our list are now either unmentioned in the press or vilified there, and none of the deputy mayors now has any visible position in Shanghai.

Statistical analysis of Shanghai's revolutionary committee is harder than for the pre-1967 leadership. That committee is in some ways not comparable to the deputy mayors, but a juxtaposition of the two groups may help test their comparability as well as their similarity. We must make at least some attempt to answer the important question: How did the Cultural Revolution change local leadership? The present author has collected about fifty names of members of the Shanghai Revolutionary Committee. The list is incomplete; many of the worker members on it seem rather inactive; some important soldiers in Shanghai are not included; and at least eight members have been purged.

For twenty-two of the members—who form a more credible new

---

[200] Frederick C. Teiwes, in his pioneering *Provincial Party Personnel in Mainland China, 1956–1966* ("Occasional Papers of the East Asian Institute" [New York: Columbia University, 1967]), pp. 8–9, found that East China (not including Shantung) was underrepresented among Party provincial secretaries, 1956–66, relative to its population.

elite than the whole committee would anyhow—information is available regarding the main locus of their previous careers: Party, 45 per cent; army, 41 per cent; government, 14 per cent. The corresponding distribution among the deputy mayors was Party, 38 per cent; army, 5 per cent; government, 57 per cent. It will come as no surprise that the army has "increased its representation" enormously, but this fact points up the partial incomparability of the two sets as much as anything else. The drastic decline of government personnel is equally important, and it shows that the revolutionary committee cannot be considered a government organization in the same sense as the old deputy mayoralty was—although we will see below that their comparability increases if a larger sample of the revolutionary committee is used.

Most important, the proportion increased of men who had worked their way up in the very institution supposedly under attack during the Cultural Revolution, namely, the Party. This Party-career group, indeed, contains many of the most visible leaders on the committee, including Chang Ch'un-ch'iao, Yao Wen-yüan, Hsü Ching-hsien, Wang Shao-yung, and Ma T'ien-shui. Present leaders whose major posts lay in government, such as Ch'en Lin-hu, are fewer and less prominent. All of the members of the Shanghai Revolutionary Committee are believed to be Communist Party members, while 24 per cent of the deputy mayors were not. Most revolutionary committeemen seem to have less specialized functions than the deputy mayors had. These two facts still do not vitiate the differences between the two distributions given above, which indicate an increase in military men and an impressive decline in the number of high leaders whose career lay within the government bureaucracy. This is statistical confirmation, if any be needed, that the revolutionary committee was constituted of leaders whose experience prepared them to supervise the functions of the Party as well as of the government.

This same sample of committeemen can also be examined with respect to the functions in which the members used to work, with the military now added to the list of systems. The result is: army, 41 per cent; education-culture, 27 per cent; industry-communications, 18 per cent; politics-law, 9 per cent; finance-trade, 5 per cent. If the sample is representative, and if military officers are excluded from the tabulation, politics-law has a much smaller proportion of the committeemen than it did of the deputy mayors. As befits the aftermath of a "cultural" revolution, writers, publishers, educators, and propagandists now constitute almost half of the new obvious civilian elite in Shanghai (as compared with less than one-fifth of the previous deputy mayors).

The Shanghai Revolutionary Committee may consist entirely of people considered Shanghai natives. It has several members with cosmopolitan experience. Of the twenty-two committeemen mentioned above, almost two-thirds are already known to have met foreigners in Shanghai; one of them (naval commander Kao Chih-jung) is legally an overseas Chinese himself, and another (Li Kuo-chün) has lived in Hong Kong for extended periods. But these facts are hardly earth-shaking; they do not reflect the fact that Shanghai was once a very foreignized place, and they represent a sharp decline in cosmopolitanism as compared with the previous regime of deputy mayors. They indicate only that the Cultural Revolution has not banned leaders who have some non-Chinese cultural experience.

There is insufficient evidence on the ages of Shanghai's revolutionary committeemen to make numerical generalizations. On the basis of photographs, Chang Ch'un-ch'iao is reputed to be "about 60," Yao Wen-yüan, about 40, and Wang Hung-wen, about 35. Clearly some of the important new committeemen are young. The general impression may be false, however, that China's post-Cultural Revolution leaders have come to power at an earlier age than did their predecessors. Since the Shanghai evidence is scanty on this point, we may turn to a national sample. The average age of thirty pre-Cultural Revolution province-level government heads (provincial governors or special municipality mayors, each of whose personal ages was measured at the time of his accession) was 52.8 years. The average of the personal ages of eighteen heads of province-level revolutionary committees (also measured separately at the times their committees were formed) turned out to be 57.9 years—that is, about five years older. Note that we are dealing here with average personal ages, measured not in any single year but at the various times when these leaders came to provincial power. Men apparently rose to these headships at younger ages during a time of bureaucratic stability than at a time of cultural revolution. Two disclaimers should be filed immediately: first, the sample of revolutionary committee heads may well be biased in favor of old men on whom some information is available; second, the ages of committee heads do not necessarily reflect the ages of committee members. The average difference is nevertheless surprisingly large, and it suggests some qualification to the idea that the post-Cultural Revolution elite is extremely youthful.

Available data allow us to use much larger samples to study the contemporary statuses of members of the Shanghai Revolutionary Committee than to study their pre-1967 backgrounds. For example, a sample of forty-three Shanghai revolutionary committeemen can be divided easily into the parts of the "three-way alliance." The result is: military, 19 per cent; mass organization leaders, 44 per cent; leading cadres, 37 per cent. These three may be analyzed separately.

The sample suggests that military members of the committee are one-half land soldiers and one-half sailors or airmen. Even more obviously, the small representation of military people in this sample (less than one-fifth) does not express the apparent importance of military men in policy decisions—we may compare it with the much higher proportion in our smaller sample of the same committee. And some important Shanghai military leaders were absent from the committee altogether.

The mass organization leaders are basically of two types, labor-organizers and student-organizers; but since the news reports do not always make that distinction, the matrix of percentages within this part of our sample has a compartment for the unknown: labor-leaders, 37 per cent; student-leaders, 26 per cent; unknown, 37 per cent.

The revolutionary leading cadres, on the other hand, can be sub-divided clearly into two groups, those who work at administrative tasks in either Party or government and those who deal with cultural matters such as propaganda and art. The result is 63 per cent in administrative work, 37 per cent in cultural work.

This sample of Shanghai Revolutionary Committee leaders gives a much greater weight to administrative cadres than did the relatively small sample of important committee leaders that we examined earlier. The whole committee includes a number of administrators; but they did not usually hold high positions in the previous regime, and their backgrounds have not been publicized so much as have the backgrounds of more important committee leaders who previously specialized in cultural work.

The revolutionary committee is not the only possible locus of the "political elite" in current Shanghai. An alternative indicator might be the delegation sent by Shanghai to the Ninth Party Congress in

Peking during April, 1969.[201] Predictably enough, all six *full* delegates from Shanghai elected to the Central Committee were also members of the Shanghai Revolutionary Committee. (The head of the Chekiang Revolutionary Committee, Nan P'ing, was concurrently a political cadre in the Shanghai garrison; but of course he was not part of Shanghai's delegation.) Only one of the alternate delegates, Ma T'ien-shui, was a member of the revolutionary committee. The other alternates included four army men, a worker, and a Red Guard. In other words, almost half (46 per cent) of the total delegation sent to Peking was not on the Shanghai Revolutionary Committee.

Equally startling is the fact that two very high-ranking military men in Shanghai were not either delegates to the Ninth Congress or members of the revolutionary committee at its founding. These were Li Shih-yen, second political commissar of the Shanghai garrison (Chang Ch'un-ch'iao is first political commissar), who was much later reported to be on the committee; and Tuan Te-chang, political commissar of the East China Fleet, who participated actively in the Cultural Revolution in 1967 but is not named on the committee.[202] These men, who are most certainly in Shanghai's new elite, seem to have sent subordinate military officers—and mutually exclusive sets of them at that—to the Ninth Congress and the revolutionary committee. For this reason and others, the quantitative analysis which we can now make of Shanghai's post-Cultural Revolution elite is only preliminary and tentative.

SUMMARY: A DEFINITION FOR LEADERSHIP

Statistical and historical approaches have both confirmed the effect of the Great Leap in making Shanghai an increasingly prominent and separate center of political leadership within China, although this change resulted less from the breaking of ties with other centers than from the establishment of new kinds of ties. Both approaches confirm that the Shanghai Party needed some "bourgeois" representatives to hold at least ostensible leadership positions in a wide variety of government fields, and they have both indicated the replacement of

[201] Aside from a lady textile worker named Yang Fu-chen, there was no overlap between the thirteen-person Shanghai delegation to the Ninth Party Congress in 1969 and the 140-person group which went to the Third National People's Congress five years earlier. (Three prominent national figures officially in the Shanghai delegation at the 1964 congress are excluded from this: Ch'en Po-ta, Ch'en I, and Ch'en Yün.)

[202] URS *Biographical Service*, No. 1274 (March 1, 1968).

those representatives in recent years by professional soldiers and political writers.

A study of elite disputes can shed light on the variables of local leadership in China, because these conflicts show the political elite in action clearly, and because the disputes have differed in many dimensions. First, they have come in waves, and their issues and styles have been no more consistent than the changing ambitions that motivated them. Second, they have varied among the separate functional areas within which the elite operates. We have seen conflicts which engulfed all of Shanghai's functional areas at once, but we have also seen conflicts which concentrated almost exclusively in literary criticism or finance—while the city's other elites continued their business with total unconcern. Third, the disputes have affected different levels of leadership. The socialization of industry and the Hundred Flowers episodes involved fairly large numbers of people at middle levels. Only a few high leaders participated in the complaints of 1961–62, but many resisted the government less openly. The Cultural Revolution began among fairly high leaders but then spread both upward and downward to include all levels. Fourth, the combination of personal and social reasons for these disputes has varied greatly. Li K'ang-nien and some other Hundred Flowers critics reflected individual or factional interests. But many of the Party's critics in 1957, and Pa Chin in 1962, joined elite disputes for reasons which were more public than personal; and their criticisms did cause organizational changes. Chang Ch'un-ch'iao's rise to effective control cannot possibly be explained without invoking broad sociological concepts. It was a carefully planned and slowly executed masterpiece of social engineering. Chang knit factions into alliances and alliances into administrations. He aligned these forces with soldiers and with workers who were buttressed by a new communal ideology, so that finally these groups in concert provided the foundation upon which Chang and his friends constructed a new leadership for Shanghai. If we wish to develop theory in political science to explain elite changes, we will have to talk both about leaders and about society. This need has been evident no matter whether logical or statistical methods have been used, and in each case it has presented severe practical difficulties.

This problem arises in part because of the inherently complex relation between politics and society, but perhaps it also arises because of current preconceptions about science. Elite analysis often begins with distinctions that do not apply very closely to behavior. It sometimes suggests the importance of many different abstract categories which fail, even after investigation, to help define in essential terms what leadership is. The four broad variables of elite disputes in the list above may provide a common thread to tie together the occasions on which apparent leadership has been exercised in Shanghai, because they all refer to the relationship between social-political problems and leaders' own situations. Real actors attach more importance to the effects of action than to any of its other traits, or to their own traits. The main characteristic of leadership is elusive and difficult to measure, but it can be induced from the Shanghai data we have examined. It can be induced from Chin Chung-hua's or Chao Tsu-k'ang's continuing ability to maintain their good social values in many contexts; from Jung I-jen's or Men Chang-hua's clarifications that they could be pushed only so far before they would defend their subordinates against arbitrary demands from above; from Pa Chin's statement that a prosperous solidarity is dependent on differences; from Yao Wen-yüan's honest admission that something real will be lost while the revolution is being gained; or from K'o Ch'ing-shih's arrangement of an economic understanding between Shanghai and the Chinese central government so that investment and production could boom. The main deductive characteristic of an elite, after all, must also be the quality of its leadership in action. This is not any set power or legitimacy or even a combination of the two, but it is an appropriateness of leaders' behavior to the problems that people face.

PART IV

Elites in the Functional Sphere

WILLIAM W. WHITSON

Organizational Perspectives and Decision-making in the Chinese Communist High Command

For the sake of brevity and simplicity (if not for lack of hard data), the great majority of existing strategic analyses of the Far East begin with the fiction of "China" as a purposive actor, its collective behavior treated as if it were an individual possessing clear objectives, clear alternatives, and a set of rational criteria with which to choose among alternatives. Indeed, such a model of state behavior has been the traditional assumption for most international political analysis.[1] While it has served some purposes in the past—and will continue to do so in the future—this model clearly offers limited returns to research in Chinese decision-making; in fact, it constitutes an obstacle to such investigations because it tends to deny either the existence or the significance of controversy in the intranational decision-making process.

Students of international political behavior have been increasingly interested in two alternative models of decision-making. The first is based on the assumption that decisions and viewpoints within any government are structured by groups of organizations, members of which develop special interests and career investments in the survival and power of those organizations. Competition among these groups must inevitably invade the arena of national policy and may be

[1] For some general comments on this model, see Graham Allison, "Conceptual Models and the Cuban Crisis," *American Political Science Review*, LXIII, No. 3 (September, 1969), 689–718.

expected to inject special interests into what might otherwise be "rational" choices. As Graham Allison has perceptively put it:

> The happenings of international politics are, in three critical senses, outputs of organizational processes. First, the actual occurrences are organizational outputs. . . . Government leaders' decisions trigger organizational routines. . . . Second, existing organizational routines for employing present physical capabilities constitute the effective options open to government leaders confronted with any problem. . . . The fact that fixed programs (equipment, men, and routines which exist at the particular time) exhaust the range of buttons that leaders can push is not always perceived by these leaders. . . . Third, organizational outputs structure the situation within the narrow constraints of which leaders must contribute their "decision" concerning an issue. . . . As Theodore Sorensen has remarked, "Presidents rarely, if ever, make decisions—particularly in foreign affairs—in the sense of writing their conclusions on a clean slate. . . . The basic decisions, which confine their choices, have all too often been previously made." [2]

The second model is what Allison calls the "bureaucratic politics model." [3] According to this model,

> The decisions and actions of governments are essentially intra-national political outcomes: "outcomes" in the sense that what happens is not chosen as a solution to a problem but rather results from compromise, coalition, competition, and confusion among government officials who see different faces of an issue; "political" in the sense that the activity from which the outcomes emerge is best characterized as bargaining. . . . The actor is neither a unitary nation [Model I], nor a conglomerate of organizations [Model II], but rather a number of individual players [Model III]. Groups of these players constitute the agent for particular government decisions and actions. Players are men in jobs. . . . Answers to questions: "What is the issue?" and "What must be done?" are colored by the position from which the questions are considered. For the factors which encourage organizational parochialism also influence the players who occupy positions on top of (or within) these organizations. . . . Thus propensities of perception stemming from position permit reliable prediction about a player's stances in many cases. . . . Government behavior can thus be understood . . . as outcomes of bargaining games. In contrast with Model I, the bureaucratic politics model sees no unitary actor but rather many actors as players, who focus not on a single strategic issue but on many diverse intra-national problems as well, in terms of no consistent set of strategic objectives but rather according to various conceptions of national, organizational and personal goals, making government decisions not by rational choice but by the pulling and hauling that is politics. [4]

[2] *Ibid.*, p. 699.
[3] *Ibid.*, p. 690.
[4] *Ibid.*, pp. 707–9.

MAJOR FORMAL AND INFORMAL GROUPINGS
IN THE PEOPLE'S LIBERATION ARMY

Just as most of the literature about many national policies of Communist China portrays China as a unitary state, so literature about internal politics in China usually portrays the People's Liberation Army (PLA) as a unitary institutional actor. Terms such as "the army," "the PLA," and "the military" abound in both academic and government analyses. These terms do nothing to clarify the question of the high command's perceptions of their strategic problems. For, as in the larger sphere of national political analysis, "collective rationality" cannot be ascribed to a large group of men whose separate functions and career opportunities in any given case may be expected to generate compromise, coalition, competition, and confusion, to echo Allison's statement quoted above. For purposes of Model II speculation, we must, therefore, examine the less abstract groupings of senior leaders in the PLA.

At least six major career channels existed in the PLA before the Cultural Revolution: (1) local forces (militia and public security); (2) ground forces; (3) General Political Department; (4) General Rear Services Department; (5) navy; and (6) air force. These channels tended to be mutually exclusive; that is, between the ending of the Korean War in 1953 and the 1966 Cultural Revolution, officers generally did not move back and forth among these six career channels. By 1966, therefore, we could expect officers in each channel to have developed a distinctive set of organizational interests, values, attitudes, and goals. According to the fundamental premises of Model II, each of these organizations would tend to encourage its members to behave in such a way as to enhance their own collective interests.

Five factors, however, which cut across career lines, tend to confuse each career group's definition of collective priority interests. The first, military generations, has divided the PLA leadership into eleven major groups of individuals who have shared distinctive political and military crises. The second, field armies, consists of five groupings based on the affiliation of individual officers with the field armies which conquered China during the 1945–50 Civil War. The third, military regions, has divided the PLA leadership into eleven geographic groupings, which remained remarkably stable between the ending of the Korean War and 1966. The fourth, the central elite, has constituted a special geographic and functional group, the majority located in Peking with a minority scattered around the country for brief periods. (In principle, any member of the central elite who spends more than two years in a regional locale must be expected to undergo a shift in perspectives that tends to conform to those of his military region.) The fifth factor, personal relationships, has distributed the PLA leadership into an infinite number of obscure loyalty groupings that generally lie beyond our analytical and data collection capability. Yet their importance for Model III analyses demands that we appreciate this factor as a major cause for error when we attempt to explain behavior within the high command.

We shall first consider each of the informal factors because they help provide an historical context within which current, formal organizational values and interests may be discussed more realistically. It has been principally these informal obstacles to collective, formal institutional perspectives which have generated individual differences in values, viewpoints, and goals among about 1,000 senior officers of the PLA, where each of these men acts as a player in a bargaining process in which his informal and formal organizational affiliations could be expected to influence his choice of the issues on which he might bargain, his perspectives toward such issues, and his ultimate bargaining behavior.

After discussing informal affiliations, this paper will identify probable, if not actual, differences in organizational viewpoints toward the following questions of continuing importance to the high command: (1) the priority of security values and goals; (2) the priority of perceived threats to those values and goals; (3) the "best" organization of available systems and resources for coping with perceived threats; and (4) the preferred strategy and tactics for deploying available resources.

INFORMAL FACTORS

MILITARY GENERATIONS

If a military generation is defined as a group of officers who (regardless of age) *entered* the PLA at the same time and shared a given period of military professional and political experiences, the history of the Chinese Communist Party and the Red Army may be divided into eleven periods of major crises.[5] From the perspective of

---

[5] Employing the three principal criteria of political crisis, military ethic (role of the military in society, authority of a commander, promotion criteria for younger officers), and military style (organization of military power, strategy, and tactics), it is possible

this study, the most important generations are the first four: first, before May, 1928; second, from June, 1928, to November, 1931; third, December, 1931–July, 1937; and fourth, August, 1937–December, 1940. The first four military generations are the most important because these men occupy about 98 per cent of the 1,000 key military positions by which we may define the high command.

Among the six career channels enumerated above, how are these generations distributed? Within the ground forces, the majority of the military regional command and staff positions of significance are occupied by second- and third-generation officers with first-generation people found principally in Peking and fourth-generation people found principally at army (corps) and military district levels or below. The approximate distribution in the ground forces (and probably in local forces, the General Political Department, and the General Rear Services Department) of the first ten generations in 1969 is shown in Table 46.

---

to divide the PLA officer corps into eleven military generations, each characterized by one or more differences in their perceptions of the foregoing six factors of ethic and style. Since the first four generations are the focus of this chapter, the rationale for that particular periodization is provided as follows.

The first period or generation includes all officers who entered the embryonic Red Army before June, 1928. That date divides the first from the second generation by marking the reorganization of the combined forces of Mao Tse-tung and Chu Teh at Chingkangshan and also brought major changes in tactical style, from Mao's "guerrillaism" to Chu Teh's more conventional tactics. Nevertheless, a mixture of the two styles and of political and professional criteria for promoting younger officers characterized the period from June, 1928, to November, 1931 (the second military generation), when the Red Army faced a succession of offensives, including the first three Encirclement Campaigns in Kiangsi. The third generation begins with the founding of the Central Kiangsi Soviet in November, 1931, when the organization of the Red Army as well as all other aspects of ethic and style changed radically in favor of more conventional procedures. These procedures prevailed until the next major crisis for China as well as Chinese communism: the Sino-Japanese War.

We set the beginning of the fourth generation in August, 1937, because that date marked the reconcentration of all major Communist military forces following the Long March. It also marked the influx of many new recruits from North China universities to Yenan, students imbued with patriotic anti-Japanese, rather than pro-Communist, motives. The tactics and strategy of the Eighth Route Army and the politico-military relationships among border regions and the center at Yenan, all in the context of the Second United Front and a war against a foreign invader, distinguished the earliest professional experiences of this fourth military generation from the first three. A fifth generation began to enter the Eighth Route Army in January, 1941, the year in which the Japanese "three all" campaign, the Communist *cheng-feng* rectification movement, and the consequent dispersion of the Communist regular forces into small pseudo-guerrilla units encouraged a mass influx of peasants into the army, whose style was suddenly altered radically in order to survive against the Japanese onslaught.

For a more detailed discussion of military generations in the PLA, see William W. Whitson, "The Concept of Military Generation: The Chinese Communist Case," in *Asian Survey*, VIII, No. 11 (November 1968), 921–47.

TABLE 46

ESTIMATED PERCENTAGE OF COMMAND-COMMISSAR POSITIONS OCCUPIED BY TEN MILITARY GENERATIONS *

Geographic Origin		Central & South China			North China			All Regions			
Average Age 1967		62	57	54	50	46		Unknown			
Level	Date	1	2	3	4	5	6	7	8	9	10
National level †	Aug., 1966	60	34	6							
(100 positions)	Dec., 1967	50	44	6							
Military region ‡	Aug., 1966	27	42	31							
(104 positions)	Dec., 1967	20	39	41							
Military district §	Aug., 1966	10	49	35	5		1				
(138 positions)	Dec., 1967	6	39	49	5		1				
Corps level ‖	Aug., 1966	3	39	52	6						
(102 positions)	Dec., 1967		38	53	9						
Division level #	1966		5	50	45						
Regimental level	1966			5	60	30	5				
Battalion level	1966					25	65	10			
Company level	1966						5	50	30	15	
Platoon level	1966								10	55	35

Source: William W. Whitson, "The Concept of Military Generation: The Chinese Communist Case," *Asian Survey,* VIII, No. 11 (November, 1968), 945.

* Estimates of age, geographic origin, and national, military regional, military district, and corps-level distribution are derived from 500 biographies surveyed by the author in 1967.

† National-level positions include the Military Affairs Committee, the Ministry of National Defense, general staff, General Political Department, air force, navy, armor, artillery, chemical, engineers, General Rear Services Department, public security forces, railway engineers, and signal headquarters.

‡ Military regional positions include commander, commissar, three deputy commanders, and three deputy commissars.

§ Military district positions include commander, commissar, two deputy commanders, and two deputy commissars.

‖ Corps positions include commander, deputy commander, and commissar.

Estimates of distribution at division-level and below are based on promotion regulations and an extrapolation from incomplete biographic data.

Although data on the other five career channels have not been assembled, a spot check of senior officer biographies in the General Rear Services, General Political Department, and so-called local forces suggests that these career channels have not offered younger men a relatively better rate of advancement than the ground forces. Only the air force and the navy seem to have provided such a preferred rate of advancement up to military regional level. At the national level (central elite), senior air force officers (all former army military officers) appear to be drawn principally from the second and third military generations, based on a preliminary survey of available biographies. Thus, Table 46, if drawn for the air force, would probably show more fourth, fifth, and sixth military generation figures at army (corps) levels and above, a point worth further investigation since it would reinforce other factors that have tended to distinguish air force from ground force viewpoints.

Since the bulk of the high command falls within the first four military generations, it is important to underline those aspects of experience which might be expected to distinguish one generation from the other. We should recognize that the time spread between the entry of the oldest member of the first generation into the Communist Party in 1923 and the entry of the youngest member of the fourth generation in late 1940 would be eighteen years. Quite apart from variations in generational experiences of the post-1940 period, it is argued than an officer's *earliest* experience profoundly directs, shapes, and dominates lifelong viewpoints toward such crucial questions as the role of the military in society, the authority of a field commander, the proper criteria for selecting future generals, the proper organization of military power, the most effective strategic and tactical techniques for applying military power, and all four contemporary questions raised at the beginning of this paper.[6]

Based on their collective experience, it seems likely that there is a broad generational viewpoint toward each of those questions. That viewpoint would be based principally on early military and political experience and education, later modified by other broad factors of developing personal ties, affiliation with a particular field army leadership, prolonged assignment to a particular military region, and, perhaps most

---

[6] For theoretical and factual evidence in support of this assumption, see Davis B. Bobrow, "Chinese Communist Response to Alternative U.S. Active and Passive Defense Postures" (paper delivered at conference in Oak Ridge, Tenn., December, 1965), pp. 31-32.

important, long-term membership after 1953 in one of the six major career channels.

At the risk of oversimplifying differences, a summary judgment would propose that each successive generation, as a group, tended to veer progressively further away from the philosophy, style, and viewpoint of unconventional warfare, the so-called Maoist People's War. The first two generations were drawn predominantly from the poor central Yangtze Valley peasantry, and the second generation in particular had had minimal formal education, having spent their personal and professional formative years in a context of guerrilla warfare in which almost every political or military act aimed at the political mobilization of the masses. Already strongly tied to local customs and organized into local units (one county in Hupeh, for example, has produced approximately 150 second- and third-generation generals), these men may have abjured warlordism; but they probably acquired many of the politically myopic features of the warlord outlook: a strong sense of local loyalty, reinforced by a traditional peasant (and Chinese) suspicion of "strangers," perhaps best stated by James E. Sheridan: ". . . a bandit became a warlord at the point where he acquired acknowledged control over a specific area and assumed the tasks of governing it." [7]

This sense of political role, rather than the performance of a primarily professional military function, should have been reinforced by the early experiences of the first two military generations. Furthermore, since their objective was clearly revolutionary, their style necessarily demanded assumption of control over all available resources, including ideology, in their desperate struggle against adverse odds. To label these men opportunists would be to miss the point that, in a struggle for survival, opportunism is the very essence of the struggle and "opportunist" is a compliment to the victor. In their early campaigns before November, 1931, when the Central Kiangsi Soviet was formally established, the defensive strategy and the offensive guerrilla tactics of People's War were imposed by circumstances. These men at the outset thus tended to be local and regional (rather than national) in political perspective, political rather than military-

---

[7] *Chinese Warlord: The Career of Feng Yü-hsiang* (Stanford, Calif.: Stanford University Press, 1966), p. 19. For excellent discussions of the warlord outlook, see Hsi-sheng Chi, *The Chinese Warlord System: 1916 to 1928* (Washington, D.C.: Center for Research in Social Systems, 1969), Chap. iii; see also Sheridan, *Chinese Warlord*, esp. Chap. i, pp. 16 ff.

professional in their sense of role, and oriented to the relatively independent strategic defense of a particular locale through offensive, small-unit, irregular tactics.

Conversely, the third and fourth generations entered the Red Army in a context of increasing division of labor between the military and the Party. The Party had grown to such an extent by late 1931 that it was possible to replace many military-political administrators in Kiangsi villages with Party cadres, who were largely removed from military affairs. After November, 1931, a variety of developments tended to instill new concepts that should have distinguished the military values of the third and especially the fourth generations from the first and especially the second: the establishment of professional military schools; an emphasis on conventional tactics and a more conventional defense of the entire "country" (that is, the Kiangsi Soviet before 1934 and much of North China after July, 1937); and a greater emphasis on the professionalization of the officer corps under Russian auspices. The two later generations should have been less confident of the power of the untutored masses as a military force, of their own skill as political manipulators (at which they have had considerably less experience than the first two generations), and of guerrilla warfare or, broadly, People's War for national defense. Furthermore, because of their entry into the Red Army during a period of great national crisis (after the Japanese invasion of Manchuria in September, 1931), the third and fourth generations (the latter including a large number of students from North China) tended to be motivated by significantly different arguments for joining an army. Confronted by a foreign enemy and drawn from a wider, better-educated cross section of Chinese youth, these men might be expected to perceive their loyalties on a more national rather than a regional or local scale.

As suggested earlier, these broad comments about four major generations in the PLA high command could hardly establish more than a general foundation for differences in viewpoint toward contemporary problems of China's national security. After their first few years in service, later influences could be expected to alter generational stereotypes. Of these influences, the field army institutional evolution should have been of crucial importance.

THE FIELD ARMIES

In 1954, with the reorganization of the PLA after the Korean War, all large organizations formerly labeled "field armies" were deactivated.[8] Thereafter, the three-division "army" (*chün*) became the principal ground force operational command, directly under the control of a military region headquarters. At the same time, air force and navy units were being organized under the local operational control of air defense districts and three major fleet headquarters. Between military regions, air defense districts, and fleet headquarters on the one hand, and the general staff in Peking on the other, there were no intervening levels of military bureaucracy.

Nevertheless, the senior officers who had led the earliest guerrilla units of the Red Army from their 1927 origins through the operations of the 1930's against the Nationalists and, after 1937, against the Japanese, then against the Nationalists, and finally against United Nations forces (from 1950 through 1953), had had careers marked by one unique and highly significant characteristic. Less than 15 per cent of the high command had served in more than one stream of institutional evolution (see Figure 5 for the five field army institutional streams). That is, the five field armies which defeated the Nationalists between 1945 and 1949 had evolved through essentially independent processes of development over the previous twenty years. Among 85 per cent of 700 key military leaders analyzed, an officer who had first joined a unit, for example, from the Oyüwan Soviet (Central China) in 1928 had become a senior commander or commissar in the Second Field Army in 1949. An officer who had joined Ho Lung in central Hunan in 1928 had become a senior commander in the First Field Army by 1949.

Translated into American experience, the Chinese senior leadership would be comparable to an American leadership if the six American continental armies were being led by officers who had served together (and nowhere else) for forty years. Even if the continental armies were suddenly deactivated, we may imagine the strong informal bonds of shared victories and defeats which would remain active among former comrades, especially if deactivation did not actually remove leaders from the geographic locale which their old army had occupied.

MILITARY REGIONS

The year 1954 brought a new geographic dimension to loyalties which had been founded informally on traditional generations and

8 For a more detailed discussion of field armies, see William W. Whitson, "The Field Army in Chinese Communist Military Politics," *CQ*, No. 37 (January–March, 1969), pp. 1–30.

FIGURE 5

INSTITUTIONAL STREAMS OF THE FIVE FIELD ARMIES

1927–30 (RED ARMY PERIOD)	1931–36	1937–45 (8TH ROUTE ARMY PERIOD)	1946–54 (LIBERATION ARMY PERIOD)	1955–68 MILITARY REGIONS
HSIANG-O-HSI SOVIET				
Red Fourth Corps (West Hunan) Red Sixth Corps (West Hupeh) — Red 2nd Army →	SECOND FRONT ARMY Red 2nd Army, Red 6th Army →	120TH DIVISION Shansi-Suiyuan Military District, Shensi-Kansu-Ninghsia Military District, 358 Brigade, 359 Brigade →	1st FIELD ARMY (North-West China Military Region)	Sinkiang, Lanchow, Szechwan
OYÜWAN SOVIET				
Red New Fourth Corps — Red 4th Army → Red Fifteenth Corps	FOURTH FRONT ARMY 4th Corps, 9th Corps, 30th Corps, 31st Corps, 33rd Corps, 25th Corps, 28th Corps	129TH DIVISION Shansi-Hopeh-Honan Military District, 385 Brigade, 386 Brigade →	2nd FIELD ARMY (Central China Military Region)	Wuhan, Tibet, Kunming
	(Stay behind group in Kiangsi) Red 7th Corps (Fang Chih-min)	New 4th Corps North Kiangsu Military District, North Huai River Military District, Central Kiangsu Military District, Southern Kiangsu Military District, Hupeh-Honan-Anhwei Military District, Central Anhwei Military District, Kiangsu-Chekiang Military District →	3rd FIELD ARMY (East China Military Region)	Nanking, Foochow
CENTRAL (KIANGSI) SOVIET				
Red Third Corps, Red Fourth Corps, Red Fifth Corps, Red Seventh Corps, Red Twentieth Corps	FIRST FRONT ARMY Red 1st Army, Red 3rd Army, Red 5th Army	115TH DIVISION Hopeh-Jehol-Liaoning Military District, Shantung Military District, 343 Brigade →	4th FIELD ARMY (Manchuria Military Region)	Shenyang, Canton
		344 Brigade, Independent Regiment, Shansi-Chahar-Hopeh Military District, Hopeh-Shantung-Honan Military District →	NORTH CHINA FIELD ARMY ("5th") (North China Military Region)	Shantung, Inner-Mongolia, Peking

Source: William W. Whitson, "The Field Army in Chinese Communist Military Politics," CQ, No. 37 (January–March, 1969), p. 27.

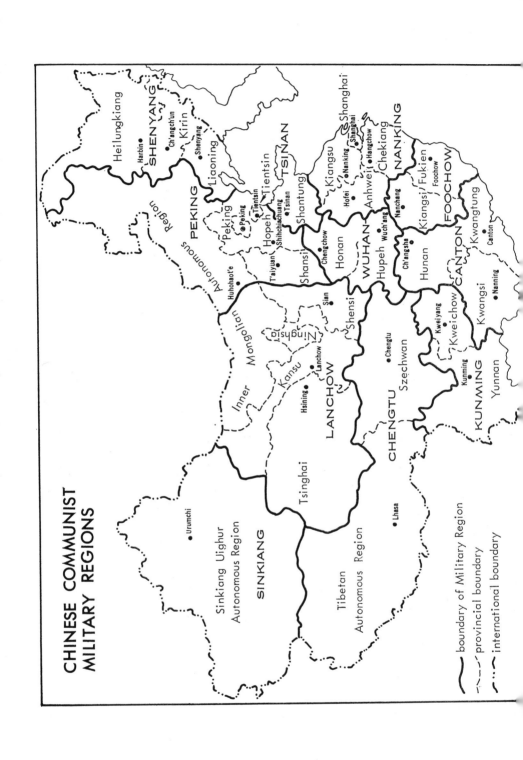

CHINESE COMMUNIST
MILITARY REGIONS

Heilungkiang

SHENYANG
Ch'angch'un •
Harbin • Kirin
Shenyang •
Liaoning

Shanghai
Shanghai •

Kiangsu
Nanking •

NANKING

Chekiang
Hangchow •

FOOCHOW
Foochow •

Region

PEKING
Peking
Peking • Tientsin
Tientsin

TSINAN
Tsinan •
Shantung

Anhwei
Hofei •

Wuch'ang

WUHAN
Hupeh

Kiangsi / Fukien

Autonomous

Huhohaot'e •
Shihchiachuang •
Hopeh

Taiyuan •
Shansi

Chengchow •
Honan

Ch'angsha •
Hunan

Nanchang •

CANTON
Kwangtung
Canton •

Inner Mongolian

Sian •
Shensi

Kweiyang •
Kweichow

Kwangsi
Nanning •

Ningsia

Chengtu •

Kansu
Lanchow •

LANCHOW

Szechwan

CHENGTU

Kunming •
KUNMING
Yunnan

Hsining •

Urumchi •

Tsinghai

Sinkiang Uighur
Autonomous Region

SINKIANG

Lhasa •

Tibetan

Autonomous Region

boundary of Military Region
provincial boundary
international boundary

institutions (the field armies). Based on their own origins and operational areas, the following relationship (Table 47) existed between field army senior leaders and the new military regions from 1954 to 1968. In general, these relationships changed very little over those fifteen years. The table shows the relative stability of field army representation in thirteen military regions even between August, 1966, and December, 1967, a year which brought the greatest number of personnel shifts in the entire post-1953 history of the PLA.

By October, 1968, when all the revolutionary committees had been formed to replace the former Party committees in each province in China, the distribution of power among field army representatives on revolutionary committees was as shown in Table 48. On the lower section of the table it may be noted that, with the exception of the First Field Army base where Ho Lung's former subordinates had suffered an unusual loss of status, other geographic power bases retained between 40 and 60 per cent of the representatives of any given field army elite. In other words, the informal loyalty groups which had emerged from field armies have apparently retained significance in the on-going intranational competition for status and influence.

THE CENTRAL ELITE

Just as the field armies acquired geographic power bases after 1949, so many field army senior leaders assumed posts of national importance in Peking. In one sense, such men at once represented military regional and old field army interest groups; in another sense, the senior figures in Peking were channels of communication and coercion from the center to their regional colleagues. However, the post-1945 process of central-regional negotiation, competition, and compromise over such matters as political and material resource allocations gradually brought an influx of regional figures into central positions. This process is reflected in Table 49, which shows the make-up of three successive Central Committees over a twenty-four-year period from 1945 to 1969.

Several interesting points emerge from this table. First, the high command as a whole has moved from a status of 50 per cent representation on the Seventh Central Committee through a loss of power on the Eighth Central Committee (only 37 per cent) to an increase of power on the Ninth Central Committee (65 per cent). Second, men whose careers had been built at the center, as contrasted with men whose careers had been built principally in "the provinces" (local

TABLE 47

DISTRIBUTION OF MILITARY ELITE MEMBERS AT EACH MILITARY REGIONAL LEVEL (1966–67)
(Percentages of all elite members known at that level)

Level	1st F.A. '66	'67	2nd F.A. '66	'67	3rd F.A. '66	'67	4th F.A. '66	'67	5th F.A. '66	'67	Mao* '66	'67	Unknown '66	'67	Double† '66	'67	Southern‡ 1,2,3 '66	'67	Northern‡ 4,5,M '66	'67	Total Percentage '66	'67
National	13	6	18	17	9	9	32	36	6	8	2	—	1	2	19	22	40	32	40	43	100	100
Mukden Mil. Rgn.	12	7	7	14	7	4	33	27	—	7	2	3	10	21	31	17	26	24	35	38	100	100
Canton Mil. Rgn.	3	—	3	—	3	10	62	57	—	—	—	—	8	7	18	23	8	10	62	57	100	100
Chengtu Mil. Rgn.	30	—	14	—	21	25	14	25	7	—	—	—	14	25	—	25	64	25	21	25	100	100
Kunming Mil. Rgn.	4	5	75	67	—	—	—	5	—	—	—	—	17	18	—	—	79	72	—	5	100	100
Tibet Mil. Rgn.	—	—	38	25	8	10	38	38	—	—	—	—	12	25	12	12	37	25	37	38	100	100
Wuhan Mil. Rgn.	15	10	46	30	31	44	4	5	—	—	—	4	23	40	4	5	69	50	4	15	100	100
Nanking Mil. Rgn.	—	—	17	16	43	42	12	4	—	4	—	—	6	12	34	16	49	69	11	8	100	100
Foochow Mil. Rgn.	8	—	4	—	22	24	16	25	—	—	—	—	8	25	21	8	54	42	17	25	100	100
Tsinan Mil. Rgn.	—	—	11	12	13	18	22	12	17	23	—	—	11	17	17	12	33	35	39	35	100	100
Peking Mil. Rgn.	6	4	9	7	—	25	6	7	37	38	—	—	13	11	13	11	28	30	44	45	100	100
In. Mong. Mil. Rgn.	—	—	—	—	—	—	14	25	14	—	—	—	72	50	—	—	—	25	29	25	100	100
Lanchow Mil. Rgn.	48	49	3	11	—	—	13	11	3	—	—	—	26	25	7	7	51	60	16	11	100	100
Sinkiang Mil. Rgn.	64	64	—	—	—	—	12	12	—	—	24	24	—	—	—	—	64	64	36	36	100	100

Source: William W. Whitson, "The Field Army in Chinese Communist Military Politics," *CQ*, No. 37 (January–March, 1969), p. 28.

* These leaders were judged to be personally loyal to Mao Tse-tung.

† The "Double" column shows figures for men whose careers have straddled two field army systems over such long time periods that it is impossible to assign them to a single field army system.

‡ A "southern" faction might consist of leaders whose 1966–67 power bases lay in the military regions of South China (Chengtu, Kunming, Wuhan, Foochow, and Nanking) plus the Tibet and Sinkiang Military Regions. The "northern" faction would consist of leaders of military regions in North China plus the Canton Military Region and a few men personally loyal to Mao Tse-tung.

TABLE 48

PARTY-MILITARY POWER DISTRIBUTION (1966–68) AMONG FIELD ARMY LOYALTY SYSTEMS

	1st F.A.		2nd F.A.		3rd F.A.		4th F.A.		5th F.A.		Unknown		Total	
	N	%	N	%	N	%	N	%	N	%	N	%	N	%
August, 1966 (pre-Cultural Revolution)	50	15	67	21	45	14	89	27	23	9	44	14	318	100
December, 1967	27	12	46	18	39	16	64	26	21	10	46	18	243	100
October, 1968 (military on revolutionary committees)	7	8	16	19	14	17	22	26	12	15	13	15	84	100
October, 1968 (military *and* Party members of committees)	10	7	26	19	25	18	25	18	16	11	38	27	140	100
October, 1968 (chairmen of revolutionary committees)	3	10	6	21	5	17	9	31	2	7	4	4	29	100

Field Army Elite among Field Army Power Bases *

	1st F.A.		2nd F.A.		3rd F.A.		4th F.A.		5th F.A.		Unknown		Total	
1st F.A. power base †	9	32	4	14	1	4	4	14	—	—	10	36	28	100
2nd F.A. power base ‡	—	—	15	60	1	4	4	16	—	—	5	20	25	100
3rd F.A. power base §	1	2	3	8	19	50	4	11	4	11	7	18	38	100
4th F.A. power base ‖	—	—	2	7	2	7	13	42	3	10	11	33	31	100
5th F.A. power base #	—	—	2	11	2	11	—	—	9	50	5	28	18	100

Source: William W. Whitson, "The Field Army in Chinese Communist Military Politics," *CQ*, No. 37 (January–March, 1969), p. 29.

* This section of the chart portrays the distribution of each field army elite among all field army power bases in October, 1968. For example, 32 per cent of the 28 key civil and military members of revolutionary committees of provinces in the former First Field Army power base came from the First Field Army.

† Includes the Sinkiang, Lanchow, and Chengtu Military Regions and the revolutionary committees of Sinkiang, Kansu, Ninghsia, Shensi, Chinghai, and Szechwan.

‡ Includes the Kunming, Tibet and Wuhan Military Regions and the revolutionary committees of Yunnan, Kweichow, Tibet, Hupeh, and Honan.

§ Includes the Nanking, Foochow, and Tsinan Military Regions and the revolutionary committees of Chekiang, Anhwei, Kiangsu, Shanghai, Fukien, Kiangsi, and Shantung.

‖ Including the Mukden and Canton Military Regions and the revolutionary committees of Liaoning, Kirin, Heilungkiang, Hunan, Kwangsi, and Kwangtung.

Including the Peking Military Region and the revolutionary committees of Hopeh, Peking, Tientsin, Shansi, and Inner Mongolia.

TABLE 49

Commanders, Commissars, and Field Army Representation on Three Central Committees, 1945–69 *

Committees and Members	Central		1st F. A.		2nd F. A.		3rd F. A.		4th F. A.		NC F. A.		Known Total†		Unknown		Grand Total	
	N	%	N	%	N	%	N	%	N	%	N	%	N	%	N	%	N	%
Seventh Central Committee (1945)																		
Full members	23	52	3	7	5	11	6	14	3	7	4	9	44	(100)			44	100
Commanders	2		1		3		3		2		1		12	(28)			12	
Commissars	1		1		1		2		1				6	(13)			6	
Both commanders and political commissars	1				1		1				1		4	(9)				
Total military													22	(50)				
Civil party ‡	19		1		0		0		0		2		22	(50)			22	
Alternate members	5	15	6	18	6	18	7	21	5	15	4	13	33				33	100
Eighth Central Committee § (1956)																		
Full members	34	37	8	9	16	18	11	12	8	9	14	15	91	(100)			91	100
Commanders	3		3		4		4		2		1		17	(18)			17	
Commissars			2		3								5	(6)			5	
Both commanders and political commissars	3				3				4		2		12	(13)			12	
Total military													34	(37)				
Civil party	28		3		6		7		2		11		57	(63)			57	
Alternate members	15	17	14	16	20	22	13	15	15	17	12	13	89				89	100

Ninth Central Committee (1969)

	(21)	(5)	(22)	(14)	(27)	(11)	(100)		
Full members ‖	27 (21) 16	7 (5) 4	29 (22) 17	18 (14) 11	36 (27) 21	14 (11) 8	131 (100)	39 23	170 100
Commanders	5	4	12	11	20	5	57 (44)		57
Commissars	3		2	1	11	2	19 (15)		19
Both commanders and political commissars	1		5		1	1	8 (6)		8
Total military	9	4	19	12	32	8	84 (65)		84
Civil party	18	3	10	6	4	6	47 (35)	39	86
Alternate members	4	9	8	16	17	9	63	46 42	109 100

Source: William W. Whitson, The Chinese Communist High Command, 1927–71: A History of Communist Military-Politics (New York: Praeger, 1972).

* These figures are based on an evaluation of the career of each member of the Seventh, Eighth, and Ninth Central Committees.

† The majority of the "unknown" figures were peasants and workers whose status as Central Committee members suddenly brought them from political obscurity to the center during the Cultural Revolution.

‡ As of April, 1945, "civil party" cadres were men who had spent most of their careers in nonmilitary political and administrative work in villages and cities.

§ By 1956, many men who had been "commissars" in 1945 had now been "civil party" cadres for as much as a decade because they had doffed uniforms, abandoned military units, and received responsibility for civil party policy and administration between the end of the Sino-Japanese War and the end of the Civil War in 1950. Teng Hsiao-p'ing would fall in this category, for example. Such a change of status meant, among other things, that they would not necessarily sympathize with the interests of contemporary commissars or commanders.

‖ Percentage figures in parentheses are a percentage of the 131 full members of the Ninth Central Committee whose biographies permit an evaluation of career specialty and field army affiliation.

soviets, border regions, or military regions), have suffered a persistent decline in relative representation from 52 per cent on the Seventh Central Committee to a maximum of 21 per cent on the Ninth Central Committee (only 27 full members out of a total of 170). Third, the accretion of power by the Second and Fourth Field Army representatives has brought them from a base of 11 per cent and 7 per cent, respectively, in 1945 to 22 per cent and 27 per cent in 1969. In effect, these two field army groups, backed up by their very powerful and wealthy military regional power bases, could dominate the Politburo and the Central Committee after 1969.

If these figures have any validity, they should suggest to aspiring career officers and Party cadres that it pays to establish one's credentials at the regional level first before entering the vicious struggle for power and privilege in Peking. A reputation and a political foundation in a military region plus, of course, useful contacts within a particular career channel (see below) would appear to be an object lesson from the past twenty-four years of intranational conflict.

But given this process of gradual vertical movement along career channels and across geographic lines toward Peking, what effect may such a process have on the perspectives of any given officer, already obligated to other sets and subsets of loyalties? Unquestionably, our hypotheses about Chinese high command perspectives must account for this process. Indeed, it is precisely because the outlook of the central elite *is* believed to be different from regional viewpoints that we must qualify our hypotheses when we speak of "the Chinese." Undoubtedly, military (and probably Party) leaders at the center are under the greatest pressure to perceive their problems in terms of the national interest. Yet, they are also dependent on the continuing close support of their regional comrades to sustain their political leverage in Peking. It would not be easy, for example, for them to detach forces from their own military region for some allegedly national purpose if such a detachment would clearly erode their popularity within their region, thereby weakening their status in the eyes of their old regional comrades and, in the long run, imperiling their own political flexibility in Peking. As Allison has suggested, in Model III these central figures *must* engage in a bargaining process in which institutional and geographic affiliations and related military resources have real significance as intranational political resources. As we have already suggested above, such a perspective might be especially characteristic of first- and second-generation leaders, now dominant in Peking and likely to remain so for the next decade.

The problem for the analyst, therefore, is to assess the extent to which local obligations among central figures may impinge on their dialogue over national issues and produce outcomes which are "rational" principally in terms of the cross-purposes of local interests and goals, mutually balanced to maintain or reflect a prevailing intranational power relationship. We would suggest that the experience of the second generation and their relatively local, traditionally peasant perspectives, as contrasted with broader, more nationally oriented perspectives which we have ascribed to third- and especially fourth-generation leaders, would underscore a continuing concern for local loyalties among those second-generation leaders, whose arrivals in Peking during Cultural Revolution personnel shifts were the most recent. Indeed, various scholars have seen the Cultural Revolution as a sociopolitical trauma in which the near destruction of the Party apparatus and the purge of many central leaders brought a dramatic shift of power over routine decisions and resource allocations toward regional authority at the expense of a confused central elite.[9]

While this trend may have been reversed after mid-1968, perhaps partly in the name of "war preparedness," the continuing absence of a national Party machine suggests that the military region and its burdened but largely undamaged hierarchy through military district, armies, People's Armed Departments, and Public Security Bureaus have become and are likely to remain a locus of major political as well as military decisions. We must, therefore, assume that the perspectives of the central elite, now (according to Table 49) increasingly dominated by figures transferred from regional posts, strongly reflect their military regional origins and obligations.

[9] For judgments underscoring a revival of regionalism in China after the Cultural Revolution, see Leonard Schapiro and John W. Lewis, "The Roles of the Monolithic Party under a Totalitarian Leader," *CQ*, No. 40 (October–December, 1969), p. 62; and, for an excellent survey of factors which tended to erode the totalitarian unity of the central elite, see Michel Oksenberg, "The Institutionalization of the Chinese Communist Revolution: The Ladder of Success on the Eve of the Cultural Revolution," *CQ*, No. 36 (October–December, 1968), pp. 61–92. For contrasting judgments (to the effect that the Cultural Revolution's politically centrifugal trends were only temporary), see Victor C. Falkenheim, "The Cultural Revolution in Kwangsi, Yunnan and Fukien," *Asian Survey*, IX, No. 8 (August, 1969), 580–97; and Gordon Bennett, "China's Continuing Revolution: Will It Be Permanent?" *Asian Survey*, X, No. 1 (January, 1970), 2–17.

PERSONAL AND FAMILY ASSOCIATIONS

Despite Communist assertions to the contrary and a certain success in weaning children away from Confucian notions of filial piety, among the four older generations that are the subject of this analysis, personal and family connections have remained of major significance in their approach to the jungle of political and professional career competition. Indeed, during the Cultural Revolution, Red Guard accusations against Ho Lung and others for their preferential treatment of relatives managed to side-step comment on the far more obvious role of Mao Tse-tung's wife, Lin Piao's wife, and the assorted cousins and in-laws of various senior figures on the Central Cultural Revolution Group which attempted (largely unsuccessfully) to stage-manage the Cultural Revolution. Unfortunately, this critical dimension of Chinese intranational political competition has remained largely unresearched, if not disdained, among political analysts. This factor must weigh significantly on the decisions of senior figures about promotions, preferred assignments, preservation of local interests, and so forth. But the dearth of reliable data demands that we also ignore this factor in this study and accept whatever margin of error that results.

FORMAL CAREER INSTITUTIONS

LOCAL FORCES

A brief analysis of each so-called career channel in the Chinese armed forces should complete our analysis of major groups and organizations engaged in China's high-command intranational competition. Beginning at the lowest level, taking the most locally oriented forces within the military and paramilitary hierarchy of China, the militia has hardly been a career channel in the customary sense of the word.[10] However, it has acquired a set of functions under the leadership of aged or aging Party and military leaders who have been released from service in the regular forces. By 1957, the militia and reserves

---

[10] For a standard, though dated, reference on the militia, see Ting Li, *Militia of Communist China* (Hong Kong: URI, 1955). For updated analyses, see John Gittings, *The Role of the Chinese Army* (London and New York: Oxford University Press, 1967), Chap. x, and Samuel B. Griffith, *The Chinese People's Liberation Army* (New York: McGraw-Hill, 1967), Chap. xvi. For a remarkably perceptive comparison of the role of local military forces, see the excellent master's thesis by Michael M. Lent, "Local Military Control in Communist China, 1949–52 and 1967–68" (University of California, Berkeley, 1968).

were merged into a single organization under the local control of the Party, aided by the PLA. For the vast majority of China's rural youth, the militia is the closest that they will ever get to a military organization.

In actual practice, the militia has fielded few effective units, has received minimal training, has been and remains responsive principally to military district and People's Armed Department (commune-level) control, and has performed only local guard and patrol duties which would not detract from their principal duties in agricultural production. Although the precise distribution of military generation and field army representatives within the militia is yet unresearched, it seems likely that overage officers and noncommissioned officers from local regular and public security ground force units have moved into the preferred senior posts of the militia "paper" units (regiment, battalion, and company). Thus, the collective loyalties and perspectives of these men are likely to echo those of units and senior leaders who have traditionally (since 1953) occupied relatively fixed garrison posts throughout China. Further, it seems likely that the majority of the senior figures in the militia organization are first- and second-generation PLA leaders.

These assumptions are approximately accurate, and given a natural career interest in fostering the growth and power of their own organization, these men should have consistently favored People's War as a philosophy and should have argued for more resources with which to equip and train the militia. Despite China's claim to a strategy of People's War, the militia has received minimal attention since the late 1950's. Only since 1968 has it again received increased, though still marginal, attention, primarily in the name of war preparedness, local security, and population control and discipline.

Better trained and equipped than the militia, public security forces have been almost equally concerned with local security problems ranging from criminal investigations to local guard duty on railroads, at warehouses, and at Party headquarters. Originally drawn from regular PLA units toward the end of the Civil War, public security forces were temporarily separated from PLA control between 1955 and 1962. Thereafter, they were gradually reassimilated by the PLA, the process being largely completed by late 1966. On the one hand, border defense forces probably have been under the direct control of military region headquarters since 1953. However, military internal security and municipal garrison forces have probably fallen under the control of military district headquarters (and now revolutionary and new provincial Party committees).

On the basis of a cursory survey of key biographies, it appears that key leaders of public security forces have spent their lives as ground force commanders (or commissars) and today reflect approximately the same generational and field army distribution found in regular ground force units (see Table 46). However, there appears to have been minimal transfer back and forth from public security to regular forces. Thus, public security channels seem to have provided a career stream for officers, a stream tied very closely to the fate of local Party and military leaders.

In consequence, we would expect that, like militia leaders, the top priority security values and goals of public security force commanders would be in consonance with local interests. Such local perspectives would be expected to identify internal (nonlocal) threats (from other Chinese) as the most significant. Indeed, these tendencies were criticized frequently during the Cultural Revolution, when "local forces" were under persistent Red Guard attack for simply performing their job of protecting local Party leaders.[11] Relatively immobile and rarely shifting from one district, not to mention one province, to another, these forces suffered a temporary eclipse during the Cultural Revolution but appear to be returning to many functions and posts of traditional responsibility.

From the viewpoint of organization and preferred strategic deployment of available military resources to cope with perceived threats, local forces and their leaders, armed with only light infantry weapons, minimal artillery, and very few vehicles, have probably retained a view of warfare only slightly more sophisticated than their country cousins, the militia. Consequently, we would expect them to be most concerned with local political and internal security problems, the impact of any national decisions (domestic or foreign) on such problems, and their ability either to mobilize or control the peasantry in the event of major crisis. At best, they would probably perceive their

11 The literature of the Cultural Revolution, especially during 1967, is replete with criticism of the entire public security apparatus in addition to the "local forces." For especially useful analyses of local force responses to central elite directives during the Cultural Revolution, including "fake power seizures," see Chalmers Johnson, "China: The Cultural Revolution in Structural Perspective," *Asian Survey*, VIII, No. 1 (January, 1968), 1–15; Charles Neuhauser, "The Impact of the Cultural Revolution on the Chinese Communist Party Machine," *ibid.*, VIII, No. 6 (June, 1968), 465–88; and Jürgen Domes, "The Cultural Revolution and the Army," *ibid.*, VIII, No. 5 (May, 1968), 349–63.

responsibility to be provincial (or at most military regional rather than national) and their "strategic" combat function to be either guerrilla command or light infantry conventional local defense.

From the viewpoint of political leverage, public security leaders had a voice at the national (Peking) level until 1962, when the gradual PLA assimilation of public security forces stripped those forces of top-level representation since, for most purposes, they fell under the control of military regions. A few forces remained under the minister of public security. However, Hsieh Fu-chih, the minister, eloquently expressed the situation when in 1967 he asserted that he really did not know his subordinates in the public security system sprawling across China nor could he evaluate their reliability.[12] In truth, their loyalties and career interests probably diminished substantially as they moved toward the State Council and Peking.

GROUND FORCES

The high command appears to be dominated by career ground force officers of the first three military generations.[13] Not only is the ground force hierarchy the dominant one among all career channels; all other career channels are also currently controlled by former ground force officers. This situation is least evident in the air force (see below) and the navy.

As noted earlier in the discussion of field armies and military regions, until the Cultural Revolution, army units rarely moved between provinces within a given military region and almost never between military regions. Possessing several basic military schools in which to train their officers, military region staffs probably could assume that they and their subordinates would spend the majority of their careers within the same military region. Only specialized training in artillery, communications, armor, airborne engineering, and political operations would normally require an officer's *temporary* absence from the

[12] See *SCMP*, No. 4023 (September 19, 1967), pp. 21–22, for excerpts from Hsieh Fu-chih's speech of July 22, 1967, when he "noticed" that the Public Security Bureau, the Procuratorate, and the Courts of Justice (all ostensibly subordinate to Hsieh as minister of public security) had been deeply poisoned by Lo Jui-ch'ing and others.

[13] For general descriptions of the role of the ground forces up to 1966, see Gittings, *The Role of the Chinese Army,* and Griffith, *The Chinese People's Liberation Army.* For post-1966 roles, all previous references pertaining to the Cultural Revolution underline the expansion of power in the hands of ground force commanders at all levels. For a more recent analysis, Charles Neuhauser's "The Impact of the Cultural Revolution on the Chinese Communist Party Machine" is of special value, together with the excellent tabulation of key leader backgrounds in Richard Baum's "China: The Year of the Mangoes," *Asian Survey,* IX, No. 1 (January, 1969), 1–17.

military region, since he would attend a special school under national control. Certainly, among the four military generations with which we are most concerned, widespread shifts among military regions were unusual before the Cultural Revolution, and actually they were held to a minimum during the Cultural Revolution. A survey, for example, of officers assigned to revolutionary committees by September, 1968, revealed that a maximum of fifteen out of about 140 chairmen and vice-chairmen (including about eighty military officers—see Table 48) were newcomers to the military region. The remainder had served either at the same military region or at subordinate provincial levels before and during the Cultural Revolution.

Several implications follow from the Chinese Communist high command's "ground force syndrome" and from the relative immobility (after 1954) of ground force units and senior commanders. The ground force high command's priority of security values and goals has probably reflected the ambiguity of national versus local defense responsibilities, depending upon the military region. Military regional commanders and staffs most threatened by external military forces (the six military regions stretching from Shenyang to Canton along China's east coast) have probably been most conscious of a dynamic priority relationship between internal and external security responsibilities. Further inland, seven other military regional commanders and staffs have probably been more intent on preserving internal stability, since external threats to them have been relatively minimal since 1950.

In all cases, however, it seems likely that the security values of these commanders and their staffs have ascribed primary importance to their own political survival within their military region, regardless of the temporary source of greater threat, internal political or external military. In brief, it would appear that a proprietary concern for their own status, their own resources, and their own political survival, especially among the now dominant first and second military generational leaders, would have linked their perspectives very closely with those of local force leaders.

As to their preferred organization of available resources, we have already noted the translation of field armies into a military regional organization during the 1950–54 period. It appears that the military regional headquarters gradually acquired powers over recruiting, logistics, personnel and unit assignments, operational planning, maneuvers, and, generally, military resource control that reflected a probable focus on the military region as a potentially self-contained theater of operations.

This is not to say that military regions have enjoyed equal power in their ability to negotiate with the central elite. In fact, a review of the Ninth Central Committee leadership would suggest that those military regions which traditionally controlled the greatest wealth and the most powerful ground forces emerged from the Cultural Revolution with the greatest political stature. Thus, in 1969 the commanders of the "top three" most powerful military regions (Shenyang, commanded by Ch'en Hsi-lien; Nanking, commanded by Hsü Shih-yu; and Canton, commanded by Huang Yung-sheng, now chief of general staff) were "elected" to membership on the Ninth Politburo. Although all military regional commanders were on the Ninth Central Committee, those three commanders would appear to have special powers, backed up by their dominant share of ground force units.

As to the dominant ground force leadership's preference for strategy and tactics, the following points seem worth noting.

1. The high command has failed to accent the long-range projection of military power, either through naval or strategic air forces. Instead, they have designed force levels best equipped to defend China against external ground threats on her borders and against internal threats. We spell out this point in greater detail under our discussion of the other career streams.

2. The modernization and professional development of the other services have probably been delayed by a general high command concern for a ground-oriented defense posture. Even ground force professionalization has proceeded fitfully, the majority of the regular ground units having experienced minimal combined arms maneuvers (with naval and air forces).

3. Indeed, the accent in the PLA during the past decade seems to have shifted away from massed artillery and infantry-armor-artillery coordination to a ground defense strategy oriented on separate military regions and a tactical scenario of infantry conventional combat supported by limited artillery and armored forces in selected areas. Apparently, in 1959 a decision was made to trade this delay in the modernization of PLA mobility, and fire support has been traded for greater resource allocations to the advanced weapons program, a bluff that the Russians called in the spring of 1969.

GENERAL POLITICAL DEPARTMENT

First organized in the late 1920's as a kind of institutional conscience to insure that commanders would not take advantage of their power to abuse either their authority or their peasant subordinates, the GPD ("the commissars") has evolved through forty years of political and military campaigning as an important career channel for military men with intramilitary political duties ranging from indoctrination of recruits to surveillance of senior officers whose behavior suggests unreliability.[14] Normally acting as secretary of the unit Party committee, a political officer (or commissar at army level and above) had become a specialized careerist by 1950. In spite of the conventional belief that PLA officers were equally adept at either political or military tactics, a survey of about 800 high command biographies shows that only about 10 to 15 per cent had been worthy of high marks in both specialized fields. Indeed, by 1950 the majority of the first four generations had served either in a professional military command or staff role or in the military political sphere, with little concern for troop management.

As a consequence of their concern for civil-military relations, and especially the role of the peasant in providing combat service support to combat units, many commissars tended to acquire expertise at primitive logistical operations and moved, after 1949, into the new General Rear Services Department (see below). Aside from this relatively more technical field, however, their concern with nontechnical subjects tended to bring them into conflict with commanders over priorities at various periods in the history of the PLA. During the Korean War their utility was challenged successively by United Nations forces, their own commanders, and finally their own troops. After the war, their status gradually declined to a point where, in 1960, 6,000 companies in the PLA did not have Party branches, and commissars were denied jeeps to use on field maneuvers.[15]

From 1960 through the Cultural Revolution, the traditional competition between the commanders and commissars for power and control over resources waxed and waned. Although the entire senior staff of

14 For an excellent account of the role of the commissar in the Korean War, see Alexander George, *The Chinese Communist Army in Action* (New York: Columbia University Press, 1967). For an account of more recent commissar roles and conflicts with commanders, see Ellis Joffe, *Party and Army: Professionalism and Political Control in the Chinese Officer Corps* (Cambridge, Mass.: Harvard University Press, 1965).

15 For this figure, see J. Chester Cheng (ed.), *The Politics of the Chinese Red Army* (Stanford, Calif.: Hoover Institution, 1966), Document No. 23.

the GPD was finally purged in August, 1967, probably much to the satisfaction of senior career commanders, their institutional function remained too important to be turned over to nonprofessionals. Furthermore, not all commissars have necessarily been primarily loyal to the GPD career channel. Biographic evidence suggests that, like the ground forces, commissar mobility between military regions and field army loyalty groups has been minimal. Thus, patterns of obligation have probably not been too different from those prevailing in the local and regular ground forces already discussed.

It was probably partly a consequence of those parochial loyalties that commissars suffered a notable decline in status during the Cultural Revolution. In addition to their temporary loss of their formal voice in Peking, they lost representation on the new (Ninth) Central Committee, as compared with prior representation on the Seventh and Eighth Committees (see Table 49). If we assume that men equally adept at command and commissar roles should be rated a commissar, they held 22 per cent of full memberships on the Seventh Central Committee (28 per cent held by commanders) and 19 per cent of Eighth Central Committee full memberships (18 per cent held by commanders). In 1969, however, while still holding 21 per cent of the available full memberships, they had lost heavily to commanders, who now held 44 per cent of such memberships.

Although limited evidence exists to show that, at any given level of the military bureaucracy, commissars have traditionally been slightly older than commanders at the same level, it is likely that the generational distribution of commissars throughout all services would approximate the distribution shown on Table 46. In general, commissars of the first four military generations have been better educated than commanders insofar as formal civil education is concerned. They have also had more experience with the Maoist concept of People's War, since they were normally charged with the training of militia, self-defense forces, and peasant mobilization, while commanders tended to focus their energies on the organization and training of regular forces.

Later generations of commissars, especially after 1946, shifted their functions away from mass mobilization and logistics because the entire PLA experienced a process of professionalization. Younger recruits into the GPD could thus expect to attend specialized political staff schools where they could study such technical subjects as intramilitary broadcasting, leaflet design and writing, mass warfare, stratagems, psychological warfare, and counterintelligence. All increasingly technical and complex, these subjects also tended to encourage a sense of professional status and expertise in younger commissars, who could prove their utility to contemporary commanders without threatening commander roles and specialization.[16] Thus, one former political officer told the author that his contemporaries (sixth generation) had little interest in leaving the professional military context, where their duties were clear, their status was coequal with commanders under most circumstances, and they did not have to worry about the risks of "politics" present in the civil community. Truly, the routine of military life had clipped the wings of potential revolutionary followers of Mao.

Despite the risk of being purged for excessive local loyalties, the fate of the GPD at the national level during the Cultural Revolution probably has encouraged commissars at the military regional level and below to remain sensitive to their status in the eyes of regional leaders. Indeed, just as the apex of a commander's career might be considered a post as deputy commander of a military region, so the commissar might be equally pleased with such a post as a cap to his career. In short, despite a tendency toward a broader, "national" commissar perspective due to the vaunted separate channel which the GPD has provided for the "Party within the army," the Cultural Revolution probably reinforced a practical concern for career equities and interests based on local and military regional ground rules of behavior and promotion. This judgment is speculative, however, since only limited evidence from interviewing can be adduced to support this thesis.

Nevertheless, by virtue of their collective knowledge of Maoist military principles, their long experience in applying those principles on the Chinese stage, their historic concern for the "correct" use of local military power to achieve local political objectives, the generally higher survival rate of local (military regional) commissars as contrasted with national-level commissars, and the post-Cultural Revolution shift of further nonmilitary administrative powers to military regional and provincial military district authorities during the 1970's, the General Political Department senior leaders are likely to share many of the viewpoints set forth below.

---

[16] Many of these views about younger commissars in the General Political Department derive from interviews held with refugees, who were former political officers, in Hong Kong in 1968.

Possessing only limited representation in Peking, where a new GPD has been painfully emerging from the ashes of the Cultural Revolution, they are likely to emphasize the security of their own military region and subregional status, especially with respect to the new Party organs that have been undergoing cautious revitalization since late 1968. Given the strong focus upon their own power status with respect to both local commanders and civil Party figures, they are also likely to perceive radical Red Guard and other dispossessed groups as primary threats to their own status and to the stability of their local political sphere. Indeed, their professional experience with internal political mobilization has probably reinforced their focus on internal threats while encouraging commanders to shift *their* emphasis to real or imagined external threats, particularly in northeast China.

In the ongoing search for salience among a multiplicity of threats, commanders and commissars will probably continue to contend over the question of "correct" resource organization. However, the commanders will probably be glad to assign to commissars the responsibility of mobilizing the military potential of the peasant masses and the millions of disgraced Red Guards who have been sent into the countryside. To the extent that the General Political Department can mobilize the paramilitary strength of those people, the regular ground force commanders may be persuaded to return troops to professional routines. That such a process has already become a nationwide movement is suggested in the 1969 creation of youth companies which appear to be releasing regular soldiers from the menial tasks of farming on PLA-managed farms.

In consonance with the foregoing, the older (first four generations) leaders of the General Political Department will probably continue their historic preference for a strategy of local People's War, a strategy which affords them maximum opportunity to extend their own political power at the expense of both commanders and civil Party competitors for local status and privilege. Thus, for different reasons, they are likely to share with many local and ground force professional commanders a preference for a defense decentralized among relatively independent military regions. Such a preference must be expected to clash with the tendency of coastal military regional commanders to look further outward rather than inward, as China's weapons technology promises a capability to project her military power beyond the Asian arena.

GENERAL REAR SERVICES DEPARTMENT

There is some doubt about the career dimension of the GRSD channel, since schools seem to be quite limited in this field. However, given the existence of a Rear Service College in Peking and the increasing complexity of the logistical system and the defense mobiliza· tion base, over which the GRSD has acquired increasing responsibility, it seems likely that both the senior and the younger members of this corps of logisticians have gained a sense of professional self-awareness and an expertise that must have laid the foundation for routine selection and promotion procedures.[17]

We are not clear on the relationship between military production (advanced weapons, conventional weapons, and military research and development) and the General Rear Service Department elite. While the GRSD probably has responsibility for the procurement of military hardware and for its distribution, their control over the production of such hardware is probably minimal. Thus, the GRSD is primarily concerned with distribution, not production, logistics.

Despite the evidence of their performance during the Cultural Revolution, there is great doubt that the available logistical system and its personnel could sustain a major campaign beyond China's borders or could even transfer resources in significant numbers from current locations to other areas inside of China. Despite the national performance of China's railroads during the Cultural Revolution, when more than a million Red Guards were shifted around the country to and from Peking, it appears likely that the high command has allocated key GRSD senior officers and matériel to local regions most likely to consume large quantities of ammunition and other resources in a war of defense.

The point of this surmise for our purposes is that many, perhaps most, GRSD senior officers probably share key military regional command perspectives about the priority of allocation of intranational and intramilitary regional resources. Yet, we must recognize that the planners of military production logistics perceive the national security problem in broader terms than local distribution of military consumables. Their concern with advanced weapons production as well

[17] It is very difficult to obtain reliable data on the role, strength, and status of the GRSD. Interviewing in Hong Kong has provided much of the information contained in this section. For an exceptionally useful treatment of military production economics, see Chu-yuan Ch'eng, "Growth and Structural Change in the Chinese Machine-Building Industry," CQ, No. 41 (January–March, 1970), pp. 26–57.

as the less complex conventional weapons production cycle must reflect a national or central elite vision of priorities.

Thus, within the GRSD, as in the navy and air force, there is unquestionably a younger generation of technocrats who must seek the most efficient nationally (not locally) rationalized production of heavy military equipment. In so doing, they would probably oppose the apparent defense strategy of independent military regional theaters of operations and any tendency toward the creation of eleven separate tank, artillery, aircraft, and missile production centers. Since small arms and small arms ammunition seem to have been produced in excess to date, evidence should soon emerge pointing up a definite conflict between advocates of conventional heavy weapons production and those favoring more complex weapons systems. The victors in such a conflict would receive increased power over budgetary resources and strategic decisions. The conflict should divide less educated second-generation leaders from the more competent technocrats of the third and fourth military generations, men whose air force and naval colleagues probably share similar views. Furthermore, to the extent that defense industrial facilities are located in separate military regions (Szechwan, Lanchow, Sinkiang, and others), the hinterland political parochialism of regional commanders and their staffs in those regions must be attenuated by the sense of national weapons priorities that probably influences their "captive" military industrialists.

We must therefore conclude that the GRSD, especially first- and second-generation senior leaders, probably retains a strong and pervasive element of localism in its collective outlook, in its selection of younger men for promotion, and in its preference for conventional weapons modernization. But the preferences of the more technically advanced services (air force and navy) have already begun to erode such a perspective in favor of viewpoints more generally associated with the central elite.

THE NAVY

Of the six career channels discussed in this paper, the navy is the smallest. By an accident of post-Civil War troop distribution (1949–50), most of the first appointees to the fleet headquarters along China's east coast came from the Fourth Field Army (in Canton, providing the South Sea Fleet's initial senior officers, and in Shenyang, providing North Sea Fleet leaders) and from the Third Field Army (in

Nanking, Foochow, and Tsinan military regions, providing officers for the East Sea Fleet). Second- and third-generation army officers from the better educated Third and Fourth Field Armies soon assumed the responsibility of creating a new navy with the help of Russian advisers. In spite of some Cultural Revolution changes within the navy in Peking, the fleets remain dominated by the same generations that control the rest of the high command. However, younger men are obviously bringing new skills to the navy along with a new respect for "weapons over men," the antithesis of the Maoist military ethic.

As these young men advance, we may expect them to argue that the fleet, as an organization, must be conscious of a national orientation, consonant with a national mission of coast defense. Although the fleets have not received heavy budget allocations for a deep-sea navy, it must be anticipated that larger allocations will be forthcoming during the next decade or so. And they will be in response to a national and international perspective that the navy high command may be expected to sustain in opposition to more parochial local force, ground force, commissar, and rear service force viewpoints and interests.

That time is yet to come, however, even though the navy's political commissar won a seat on the Ninth Politburo. The navy's fate has been a hostage to a ground force viewpoint, which has presumably been responsible for a shortage of deep-draft vessels and an emphasis on many small, high-speed patrol boats and torpedo boats, designed for short-range coastal defense. Even China's submarines have remained within her coastal waters, and her few destroyers have never ventured into the game of flag-showing and international visits normally associated with a global power. At best, the navy seems to perceive its mission in Asian regional defensive rather than offensive terms.

On the intranational stage, its officers evidently rallied behind Peking in order to help stabilize some of the more chaotic situations that developed during the Cultural Revolution. In so doing, the navy probably expressed a sense of technical superiority over not only the ground forces but also over the peasant masses, from whom the navy has generally been remote. This Cultural Revolution behavior notwithstanding, the navy's future would not appear to be tied to its role on the intranational stage, but rather to its ability to demonstrate a need for its services (and improved equipment) along China's coasts against Asian regional enemies and across the Pacific and Indian oceans against China's global enemies. Thus, in contrast with the leaders of the ground forces, still preoccupied with limited projections of power internally to solve problems of internal stability, the navy's leaders may be expected to seek increasing support for naval modernization and nuclear weapons development in order to achieve strategic projections of power to cope with problems of external threats.

THE AIR FORCE

Boasting more than three thousand aircraft in their inventory by 1969, including over two thousand jet fighters, the air force leadership, like that of the navy, was shifted from the ground forces in 1949–50 to build a new air force with the help of Russian advisers. Although a few pilots had been trained during World War II, the majority of the top leaders of the air force are nonrated. Nevertheless, the experience gained against United Nations forces in Korea provided a new generation of rated leaders who gradually assumed command of operational units. Between 1953 and 1969, these younger leaders moved quickly into key positions in air armies and divisions. As a result, fourth-, fifth-, and sixth-generation air force members of military region and air defense district staffs tend to be among the youngest members of those staffs and, therefore, the entire high command. As suggested earlier, this fact would tend to create certain frictions between the air force and other career channels, even if other factors did not help reinforce such frictions.[18]

The gradual spread of air bases around the east coast of China and then westward across her borders with Vietnam, Thailand, and Burma has reflected a primary concern with the mission of air defense against a conventional external threat. "Conventional" is stressed because the Chinese air force seems to have minimal defensive capability against nuclear-tipped missiles. Despite the obsolescing of many of their aircraft, the air force and its antiaircraft artillery and radars could probably give a creditable performance against manned fighter and bomber attacks. Thus, like the navy, the air force perspective seems to have been focused outward rather than inward.

The record would suggest that the air force has been more responsive to central elite directives than has the army, General Rear Services Department, General Political Department, or local troops. On the other hand, the probable subordination of air defense district commanders to military regional headquarters and the long-term gar-

---

[18] For the most recent, unclassified treatment of the Chinese air force, see Richard M. Bueschel, *Chinese Communist Airpower* (New York: Praeger, 1968).

risoning of air bases by the same air force units suggest that before 1968 unit commanders and air force deputy military regional commanders (air defense district commanders) probably established closer bonds with local ground force and Party leaders than the navy did. Because of the importance of his air power for the coordinated defense of his military region, the military regional commander probably has enjoyed relatively direct, routine, and uninterrupted control over most available air force units within the region. Such relatively independent military regional control of jet fighters would be more likely than regional control of the more limited bomber and transport units. These units, and their bases, probably have been more directly responsive to the central elite.

Just as the majority of the air force leaders have been concerned with air defense, so their perspectives have probably not focused on problems of strategic (global) air power. Instead, strategic *Asian* threats have probably been the focus of the leaders and operational units. That focus should have taken priority over any problems of internal security and would thus join senior air force and navy commanders together in their search for solutions to a common problem, the external threat to China's borders and border military regions.

Looming on the horizon as a competitor for funds and resources devoted to modernization, the advanced weapons program has reached a stage in China where career equities within the high command have already been affected. Still a relatively small elite of military scientists and engineers plus a few unit commanders concerned with organization and training of missile units, since 1959 these men have played an increasingly significant role in the interelite process of negotiation and compromise over resources and rewards. The April 26, 1970, public announcement of China's successful satellite launch tended to confirm a time schedule predicted earlier by Robert McNamara and Melvin Laird, who anticipated Chinese possession of around twenty-five ICBM's by 1975.[19]

CONCLUSIONS

As we suggested at the outset, any attempt to predict Chinese behavior in terms of the rationality of "China" as a unitary, purposive actor must be challenged by the fact of controversy among contending domestic personalities and institutions. For the policy-maker, however, it is not helpful to outline the basic viewpoints and interests that prob-

[19] For these figures, see the *Washington Post*, April 26, 1970, p. 1.

ably motivate separate interest groups within the Chinese military establishment. For, despite the existence of controversy, decisions *are* made in China, and their rationale, especially in the military sphere, usually seems to be discernible to foreign military observers, frequently on the spurious basis of professional insights.

It has not been the purpose of this chapter to deny the utility of such insights for describing or predicting Chinese military behavior. Indeed, an American air force planner must draw heavily on his own professional experience in seeking to understand his Chinese counterpart. Truly, in some measure, "an air force is an air force is an air force." But it is precisely the "Chineseness" of the People's Liberation Air Force that may be expected to confound the American planner when he might least expect aberrant behavior. And that Chinese quality in the behavior can be understood only to the extent that we appreciate the informal factors discussed above, that is, those factors which have constituted the unique experience of Chinese military leaders.

Among those factors (generations, field army affiliations, military regions, the central elite, and personal relationships), the phenomenon of the military region would appear to offer the greatest promise as a tool for prediction; the military region appears to have evolved into a *political* unit with remarkable staying power in the face of political instability. While regional and provincial political entities have enjoyed temporary ascendancy in the past, only the military region has enjoyed an unbroken record of institutional viability since 1954. As a focus for the practical expression of career equities in each of the six career fields, of personal loyalties stemming from field army experience, of a more traditional Chinese administrative-political style of "localism," and even of personal and family relationships, the military region provides the analyst with a unique qualitative aspect of the Chinese military-political scene. In oversimplified terms, prediction is likely to be more accurate if it is based on the comparative analysis of eleven military regions, each treated as a unitary, purposive actor, rather than on the analysis of China as one vast collectivity. This is only to say that Chinese military leaders, especially those generations at the top during the 1970's, are most likely to reach operational compromises among their many contradictory loyalties and interests through the focal institutional mechanism of the military region. It remains for research to discover greater refinements in the distinctive characteristics of each military regional elite.

JUNE DREYER

Traditional Minorities Elites and the CPR Elite Engaged in Minority Nationalities Work

Communist China officially recognizes fifty-four minority nationalities with a total population of approximately thirty-eight million. Although they constitute less than 6 per cent of the population of China as a whole, these minorities occupy 60 per cent of the Chinese land area, much of it in strategic border regions. Thus Peking has directed greater attention toward them than their mere numbers would warrant.

In their policies and programs relating to minorities, Chinese Communist leaders have had a range of objectives. Basically they have sought acquiescence to the Party's rule—"law and order"—in minority areas; but their ultimate goal has been a popular voluntary acceptance of Party leadership and enthusiastic support for its particular vision of a Communist society. Implicit in this vision is some degree of minority assimilation, varying in accordance with the toughness of the Party line at a given time.

Consonant with these aims, the leadership has created organizations within both Party and government to deal with what it refers to as "the nationalities problem." On the highest level, these include the Party Central Committee's United Front Work Department (UFWD), the Nationalities Affairs Commission (NAC) of the State Council, and the Nationalities Committee of the National People's Congress. On lower levels, a system of "autonomous areas" has been established through which minorities theoretically exercise self-government. These autonomous areas range in importance from the five provincial-level autonomous regions for the more numerous nationalities (Mongols, Uighurs, Chuang, Hui, and Tibetans) down through the autonomous *chou* (districts) and the autonomous *hsien* (counties). A short-lived experiment with autonomous *hsiang* (townships) begun in late 1955 was ended when units of such small size proved impractical in the agricultural collectivization of 1957.[1]

The most important of the national-level organs dealing with minorities affairs has been the UFWD. It was this department which interpreted and applied the Party line in establishing policy for minority areas. Its directives were sent to the Nationalities Affairs Commission, which had the responsibility of implementing them, in addition to its duties of handling more routine business concerned with minorities affairs. Despite its subordination to the UFWD, the commission, functioning on a daily basis in much the same manner as a regular ministry, wielded considerable powers.

The Nationalities Committee of the National People's Congress met approximately once a year to register approval of previously decided Party policy; its operations were limited to discussion functions only. While its members did not possess any special powers by virtue of their participation on the committee, their selection is nevertheless a good index of the Party's assessment of the various individuals' prestige in their own respective areas. Thus, though the committee itself is little more than a rubber stamp, its members constitute an important element in the Party's minority work.

The institutional differences between autonomous areas and regular subnational units are not major ones. Apart from a few minor concessions on control of finances and provisions requiring the election of a certain percentage of members of minority nationalities to public offices, the autonomous areas function much as do their counterpart organizations on the provincial, district, and county levels in the Han areas of China.

At this point we shall define the elite engaged in minorities work as the personnel of the national Party and government units set forth above, plus those individuals working at various levels within the autonomous area system, both in the Party and in the government. It is, of course, axiomatic that Party members at any given level will wield more power in the Communist hierarchy than do their non-party

---

[1] See Hsien I-yuan, "Delineation of Administrative Regions of the Chinese People's Republic" (Peking, February, 1958), in *JPRS*, No. 650-D.

counterparts, although the former do not necessarily outrank the latter in prestige among the members of a given community. Particularly in the early days of the Chinese People's Republic (CPR), Party members often were able to work in the minority areas only on the sufferance of local leaders, and were very much aware of the limitations of their guest status.

Our basic purpose in this study is to examine the relationship between the elite engaged in minorities work, as outlined above, and the traditional, pre-1949 minorities elite, in order to explore the following questions:

1. To what extent have the Chinese Communists relied upon the traditional elite for Party and governmental leadership, and with what results?

2. What methods has the Party employed to recruit non-Han talent, and how successful have such methods been?

3. What are the backgrounds of Han and non-Han elites engaged in minorities work?

4. How has the blend of Han and non-Han elites worked out in practice?

5. To what extent have the Communist-trained minority elites tended to identify with (a) the Party and (b) their own nationalities?

6. To what extent have pro-Communist minority elites been accepted or rejected by their own nationality groups?

7. How has the composition of the elite groups engaged in minorities work under the Chinese Communist Party (CCP), Han and non-Han, changed over time?

8. As measured by their participation in the Chinese Communist elite structure, are there significant differences among the minority nationalities in terms of successful adaptation to Communist rule?

Statistical comparisons will be used where possible, but as adequate biographical data are available on only a small portion of the group examined, the significance of such comparisons must necessarily be limited.

THE PARTY ELITE

The elite group which became engaged in minorities work after 1949 emerged from a variety of backgrounds. Looking first at the Party elite, those holding Party posts in the post-1949 era can be divided into six basic categories. First to join the Party in point of time was a group of young intellectuals who became interested in socialism during the period of the May Fourth Movement. Though members of minority nationalities, these young men were highly unrepresentative of their communities. Since knowledge of communism at this time was virtually confined to an urban intellectual elite, it is hardly surprising that the earliest converts from minority nationalities were also from this group. As children of families with the financial means and the inclination to send their children to Peking or Moscow for an education, these individuals tended to have weak ties to their own nationalities and to be of wealthy or even noble background. Often they were sons of that hereditary minorities elite which had cooperated with both imperial and republican governments.

Despite their lack of a proletarian background, however, this group was to prove extremely important in future CCP work. The background of the most prominent minority member of the CCP prior to the Cultural Revolution, Ulanfu, exemplifies the pattern described above. Scion of a leading Mongol family which had been ennobled by the Ch'ing for its service to that dynasty, Ulanfu was so assimilated that he did not speak Mongolian. He first became interested in left-wing activities while a student at the Mongolian and Tibetan school in Peking in the early 1920's. Ironically, the school had been founded in the latter days of the Ch'ing dynasty to ensure an adequate supply of imperial officials trained in the special problems of minority areas. It had been preserved by the warlord government to serve its own purposes. After a period of study in the Soviet Union and many years of work building a Communist Party in Inner Mongolia, Ulanfu rose to become an alternate member of the Politburo—the only member of a minority nationality to achieve so high a position. At this point, he was a leading national spokesman on minority affairs, chairman of the NAC, and in addition held a monopoly of key positions in the Inner Mongolian Autonomous Region.[2]

Two of Ulanfu's fellow students at the Mongolian and Tibetan school, Chi Ya-t'ai and K'uei Pi, also Mongols and of backgrounds

[2] Biographical data on Ulanfu and other members of the elite group under study may be found in Howard L. Boorman and Richard C. Howard (eds.), *Biographical Dictionary of Republican China*, Vols. I-III (New York: Columbia University Press, 1967–70); *Who's Who in Communist China*, Vols. I and II (rev. ed.; Hong Kong: URI, 1969); and Japan Foreign Office, *Chūgoku jinmei jiten* (Biographical Dictionary of Contemporary China) (Tokyo: Gaikō Jihōsha, 1962). I am also deeply indebted to Mr. Donald Klein, research associate, East Asian Institute, Columbia University, for making available his files for purposes of this study.

similar to his, joined the Party at the same time. Both held a variety of important positions in Inner Mongolia, K'uei Pi also becoming an alternate member of the Central Committee and ambassador to the Mongolian People's Republic.

Chou Pao-chung, of Pai nationality, was converted to communism while attending Chu Teh's alma mater, the Yunnan Military Academy, from which he was graduated in 1923. Unlike the Mongol group mentioned above, he did not return to his native area to proselytize fellow Pai, but distinguished himself as a military leader. Assigned to minorities work only after liberation, he held several positions in the central government minorities hierarchy and was in addition an alternate member of the Party Central Committee.

Chu Teh-hai, the son of a well-to-do Korean family apparently native to Kirin province, is reported to have first joined the Communist Party in Korea in 1929, and to have become a member of the Chinese Communist Youth League a year later. After serving as secretary of a local league branch, he was sent to study in the Soviet Union. During the Yenan period he held posts in nationalities work and was an officer of the Eighth Route Army. After liberation, Chu became first Party secretary of the Yen-pien Korean Autonomous District, a vice-governor of Kirin province, and an alternate member of the Central Committee.

Such individuals as these represent the minority "pioneers," and in certain respects their backgrounds parallel those of the initial Han recruits to the Communist cause: upper, or upper middle, class, generally urban-oriented, and well educated.

After 1927, as is well known, all elements within the Communist movement were involved in a great political crisis. Forced from their urban bases after Chiang Kai-shek began his anti-Red campaign, those Communists fortunate enough to escape with their lives either went underground or retreated to the rural hinterlands. Although the Party claims to have done some work with neighboring Miao at this time, no major successes have been reported and no prominent figure in later minorities work emerged from the Kiangsi Soviet period.

The Long March represents a second basic stage in the Communist recruitment of minorities talent. In undertaking the march to escape Chiang Kai-shek's progressively tightening encirclement of their rural base area of Chingkangshan, the Communists had to avoid areas controlled by Nationalist forces. Thus the marchers were often forced into regions of extremely rugged terrain inhabited by minority nationalities. Typically, these peoples did not live in their inhospitable surroundings by choice, but because they had been forced there by the pressure of Han Chinese military power and by progressive waves of Han emigration. Cherishing a deep hatred for those who had deprived them of their lands, they were not likely to distinguish between the political views of one Han group and another.

Thus, as a matter of sheer survival, the Communists had to convince these peoples that they were Han of a different sort—not the land-greedy exploiters of past acquaintance, but the harbingers of a new life of "freedom and equality for all." Although postliberation historians have exaggerated the successes of this propagandizing almost beyond recognition of the actual events—clashes rather than conversions being the rule—the mere fact that a part of the Communist group was able to survive to reach Yenan speaks well for the Long Marchers' efforts. It is also a fact that the Party was joined on the march by at least twenty members of various nationalities—chiefly Hui, Yi, and Eastern Tibetans.[3]

The most eminent member of this group was a Tibetan, Sang-chi-yueh-hsi (also known as T'ien Pao), who joined the march as a teenager. Sang-chi-yueh-hsi, as opposed to the rest of the group, had received some prior education, and he so favorably impressed veteran Party members that in 1956 he became the youngest person ever elected to the Party Central Committee. Over the years he was also appointed to an impressive array of positions in minorities work and in his native area. Another Tibetan, Cha-hsi-wang-hsu, has had a similar, though slightly less impressive, career.

This second group was quite different from the urbanized intellectual minority group which had joined the Party in the 1920's. The newcomers, typically the "have-nots" of their respective communities, were generally totally illiterate and had an extremely low level of political awareness. In most cases, they understood no Chinese, nor could the

---

[3] For a near contemporary account of the relations between the Long Marchers and minorities, see Nym Wales, *Red Dust: Autobiographies of Chinese Communists* (Stanford, Calif.: Stanford University Press, 1952), pp. 70, 217. Also, Edgar Snow, *Red Star over China* (New York: Grove Press, 1961), pp. 202–3, 214; and Robert Ekvall, "Nomads of Tibet," *Current Scene* (Hong Kong), I, No. 2 (September 23, 1961), 3. Though Eastern Tibetans, generally called Khambas, are of the same ethnic stock as inhabitants of Tibet proper and share a common religion with them, their dress, dialect, and life style set them apart somewhat from the inhabitants of Tibet proper. There has been a good deal of tension between Khambas and the Lhasa government over the course of history, though it has usually been overshadowed by the tensions between Tibetans as a whole and the Chinese government.

Han Long Marchers understand their languages. It became the task
of the Party at Yenan to reshape this group, making them into good
Communists. More importantly, perhaps, this task presented the Party
with the opportunity to experiment with the methods and institutions
which were to become the pattern for minorities work after liberation. At first the new minorities group attended the Higher Party
School headed by Li Wei-han, being placed in a special class because
of the deficiencies in their academic backgrounds. A few years later,
in 1941, the Yenan Nationalities Institute was founded in order to
undertake more intensive and specialized work with the minorities.[4]

It was during the Yenan period also that Han first began to be
assigned specifically to minorities work. Liu Ch'un, later to become a
vice-director of the Party UFWD, a vice-chairman of the NAC, and
president of the Central Minorities Institute in Peking, began his
career in minorities work in 1941 as director of the Research Department of the Yenan Nationalities Institute. Li Wei-han was made
director of the UFWD in 1944, commencing his long association with
minorities affairs at this time. Wang Feng, later a vice-chairman of
the Nationalities Committee and a deputy director of the UFWD,
also began his association with minorities work at Yenan, as director
of the UFWD of the Party's Northwest Bureau.

Various members of the earliest minorities group to join the CCP
also gathered at Yenan, either fleeing there to escape capture by
secret police, as was the case with Ulanfu and K'uei Pi, or returning
there after study in the Soviet Union, as did Chu Teh-hai.

Recruitment of minorities talent was also carried on in the Shen-
Kan-Ning border region, and those nationalities who became involved
with the Party during the Yenan period may be considered to constitute a third group in the Communist elite engaged in minorities
work. Since the chief minorities in the Shen-Kan-Ning area were Hui
(Chinese Muslims) and Mongols, inevitably individuals from these
communities constituted the majority of the Party's new nationalities
converts. As might be expected in a situation in which the Red government controlled an entire geographical area and wished to gain

---

[4] Nym Wales interviewed both Li Wei-han (referred to as Lo Man) and many of the
minorities students at the Higher Party School, including an unidentified Tibetan who is
almost certainly Sang-chi-yueh-hsi. Her recollections are contained in *My Yenan Note-
books* (Madison, Conn.; mimeographed, 1961), pp. 104–10. A short history of the
Yenan Nationalities Institute may be found in Tsung Ch'un, "Cradle of Minority Nationalities Cadres," *Min-tsu t'uan-chieh* (Nationalities Solidarity) (hereafter *MTTC*),
No. 7 (1961), pp. 15–19.

support from all available quarters, the Hui and Mongol converts spanned a wide range of socioeconomic backgrounds. Everyone from the lowliest peasants to high-ranking religious personages and land-owners was welcomed, with the simple provision that they showed sympathy with the Party's cause.

The most eminent member of the post-1949 Party minorities elite to emerge from the Yenan period is the Hui, Yang Ching-jen, originally a high imam (Muslim prayer leader) in Kansu province. After joining the Party, he became chief of staff of a Hui cavalry brigade and held various posts in minorities work administration in the Shen-Kan-Ning border region government.[5] After 1949 he became a vice-chairman of the NAC and first secretary of the Ninghsia Hui Party Committee.

Another Hui of good family, Ma Yü-huai, joined the Party after graduation from middle school in the mid-1930's and pursued an early career in Party-backed Hui organizations in the Shansi-Chahar-Hopei (Chin-Ch'a-Chi) border region government. After consolidation of Party control on the mainland, he, like Yang Ching-jen, became a vice-chairman of the NAC, serving in addition as deputy secretary of the Ninghsia Hui Party Committee. Wang To, a Mongol, also began his Party career at this time, serving as secretary-general of the Yenan Nationalities Institute; after 1949 he held various Party and govern-ment posts in the Inner Mongolian Autonomous Region.

Having set up the Nationalities Institute, the United Front Work Department, and Nationalities Affairs Commission, the Party pro-ceeded to work out a system which was to become the pattern for its minorities work after 1949. The prospect of autonomy within a unitary Chinese state was offered to attract minority converts and appears to have been moderately attractive to them, though a precise definition of autonomy was never publicly advanced. Groups of minority workers might be sent from Yenan to propagandize in their native areas when the situation seemed to warrant it. A case in point is the dispatch of a Mongol group headed by Ulanfu to Inner Mongolia in 1945. In 1947, over two years before the establishment of the CPR itself, the found-ing of the Inner Mongolian Autonomous Region (IMAR) was pro-claimed.[6]

By the time of the liberation, the Communists had trained a fair-

[5] At this time the Party allowed Hui to serve in separate army units in deference to the religious beliefs and customs which are especially sensitive issues to Hui. After 1949 these units were gradually absorbed into regular PLA units.

[6] There are indications, however, that the IMAR led a precarious existence until late 1949.

sized elite of Han and perhaps half a dozen other nationalities—the large majority of them Mongols and, to a somewhat lesser extent, Hui—in minorities work. Well-trained and politically reliable despite its generally upper-class background, this group was nonetheless far too small for the tasks it was to be called upon to perform. Many more politically reliable persons who either had some knowledge of minorities areas or would be otherwise acceptable to members of minority nationalities were needed.

The Party solved this problem in various ways. In some cases, Communists who were technically members of minorities, though well assimilated and with no previous experience in minorities work as such, were pressed into service. Chou Pao-chung, the Pai mentioned earlier, had had a long and successful career as a People's Liberation Army (PLA) commander, chiefly in Manchuria. After 1949 he was transferred back to his native southwest and given various positions in nationalities affairs work. Wei Kuo-ch'ing, of an assimilated Chuang family from Kwangsi, had also earned his reputation as a military commander, under P'eng Teh-huai. He later became head of the Kwangsi Chuang Autonomous Region. Though we know nothing of the preliberation background of the Hui, Liu Ko-p'ing, except that he joined the Party in 1931 and spent many years in Kuomintang (KMT) prisons, it is highly likely that he also falls into this category. He served as chairman of the NAC, president of the Central Minorities Institute, and first secretary of the Ninghsia Hui Party Committee. Thus, assimilated members of minority nationalities who had gained a reputation as reliable Communists and capable leaders in other fields and were assigned to minorities work after liberation primarily because of their ethnic backgrounds form the fourth source of recruitment of the top-level elite in this field.

A fifth source of recruitment was the non-Yenan guerrilla bases. Members of minority nationalities who participated in such bases and Han who had learned the ways of minority peoples through experience in guerrilla bases in minority areas had received excellent practical training in minorities work. The best-known member of this category is Feng Pai-chü. Long a leader of Communist guerrillas on his native Hainan Island, Feng chanced to hear in 1944 that the Li nationality indigenous to Hainan had rebelled against mistreatment by KMT officials. After the rebellion failed, Feng made contact with the leader of the dissident Li, Wang Kuo-hsing. The two decided to join forces against their common enemy and by the end of the civil war Feng's guerrillas were being actively helped by several thousand Li.[7] Feng's position on Hainan was later formalized in the title of first secretary of the Hainan CCP District Committee; he also held various other posts in Kwangtung. Wang Kuo-hsing became chairman of the People's Government of the Hainan Li-Miao Autonomous District and a member of the Hainan Military and Administrative Committee. Other, less well-known personnel were drawn from bases in Kwangsi and elsewhere.

PLA members assigned to minorities areas constitute the sixth and final source of the Party elite engaged in nationalities work. Shortages in Party personnel knowledgeable in the conditions of given areas were sometimes remedied by assigning PLA officers to the regions. The Party was not, of course, content to let these men rest on the laurels of their political reliability, but ordered them to familiarize themselves with local conditions immediately and thoroughly.

The best-known members of this group were the PLA commanders assigned to Tibet, Chang Kuo-hua and Fan Ming. Fan Ming's career indicates the Party's effort to appoint generals with at least some experience in the problems of the areas to which they were sent. In 1949 he had been named deputy chairman of the Kansu Provincial Nationalities Affairs Commission, Kansu having a substantial Tibetan population. Thus his assignment to command PLA forces entering Tibet in 1952 appears to have been a carefully reasoned choice.

The elite formed from these six sources—urbanized minorities intellectuals who began interpreting communism to fellow members of their nationalities in the 1920's, minorities who joined the Party during the Long March, members of the minorities work apparatus at Yenan, members of similar organizations in other base areas, assimilated minorities who had made their mark in fields other than minorities work, and PLA commanders in minorities areas—was to dominate nationalities work for the next seventeen years.

THE GOVERNMENT ELITE

Still noticeably absent from the composition of this emerging Party elite were representatives of Sinkiang's many nationalities, of those groups who lived in remote southwest areas, and of Tibetans from

---

[7] Feng's own account of this may be found in his "Five Red Clouds on Five-Finger Mountain," *MTTC*, No. 2 (1957), pp. 20–22. After Feng's removal from Hainan following charges that he had treated it as his "independent kingdom," a slightly different version appeared in which his role is minimized. See Liao Chih-hsiung, "Red Flag Waving on Five-Finger Mountain," *MTTC*, No. 6 (1961), pp. 39–42.

Tibet proper. For one thing, these were the ethnic groups living farthest from the Party's historic bases of operations. And with the Party about to assume power, there was a greater need than ever for administrators who thoroughly understood these areas and their unique problems. Army commanders unfamiliar with the territories under their jurisdiction needed advice, and the consequences of a mistake could be serious. Inadvertent violations of minority customs could discredit the Communists' image with the very people they had come to liberate. Thus a policy of Red cooperation with "expert" elements was clearly needed.

This was easily developed via the concept of the "people's democratic dictatorship" and subsumed under the rules governing the United Front. At the very outset of Communist rule, it was announced that all traditional leaders of the minorities who had "maintained close connections with the masses" and who were sincerely desirous of reforming themselves would be allowed to stay in office.[8] In practice, not only most traditional minority leaders but also many KMT administrators of minority areas were allowed to stay on. Obviously the political loyalties of such people were highly suspect and they did not, with very few exceptions, become Party members. Rather, they retained or assumed posts in the government minorities work hierarchy consonant with the Party's assessment of their prestige with the masses and potential value to the Party.

These people, in addition to a small group of scholars, chiefly anthropologists and sociologists who had some knowledge of minority peoples, formed the initial basis of the government elite engaged in minorities work. Though the United Front policy was applied throughout China and in all minority areas, it was particularly important, and its administrators especially powerful, in areas where the Party had little strength prior to 1949: Sinkiang, Tibet, and the southwest.

Sinkiang had been ruled from 1933 to 1944 by the pro-Soviet government of warlord Sheng Shih-ts'ai. Its Communist movement was clearly oriented toward the USSR and not toward China during this time. In 1942, Sheng, convinced that the Soviet Union would lose World War II, abruptly broke his alliance with the USSR and began to mend fences with the KMT. After a brief, disastrous encounter with KMT government, a group of Turkic Muslims commanding widespread

[8] See, for example, *Hsin-hua yueh-pao* (New China Monthly) (hereafter *HHYP*), I, No. 4 (1950), 876-77.

popular support staged a successful rebellion. A *de facto* independent East Turkestan Republic was set up, reportedly with Soviet backing, though its leaders continued to negotiate with the KMT on the precise terms whereby the republic might be incorporated into "Free China." Major stumbling blocks proved to be the KMT's intransigence regarding autonomous status for the area, and its attempt to force an unpopular governor on the province.

Eventually a compromise governor, a Tatar named Burhan, was accepted by both sides and an uneasy alliance between the East Turkestan Republic leaders and the KMT was reached. By this time, however, the Communist Party was virtually assured of victory in the Civil War, and the CCP's offer of autonomy was attractive to Sinkiang.[9]

When the East Turkestan leaders decided to attend the Chinese People's Political Consultative Conference (CPPCC) being held in Peking to discuss the form of the future Chinese People's Republic, Burhan and T'ao Chih-yueh, the Nationalist garrison commander in Sinkiang, decided to surrender to the CCP, whose armies were expected to take over Sinkiang soon in any case. In return, Burhan remained governor of liberated Sinkiang and T'ao, only slightly demoted, was made deputy commander of the Sinkiang Military District.

The Party was relieved of the task of finding positions for the potentially troublesome East Turkestan Republic leaders because all but one died in a mysterious plane crash en route to the Peking conference. The sole survivor, Saifudin, a Uighur, is a rather special case. He was educated in Moscow, first became a member of the Soviet Communist Party, and subsequently had an interesting career fomenting anti-Han rebellions in Sinkiang during the 1940's, almost certainly acting on Moscow's orders. Although it can be argued that these uprisings were aimed at the overthrow of the KMT government, not of Chinese rule as such, it is significant that the Turkic mobs involved attacked Han Chinese regardless of political persuasion. In addition, as later events have indicated, the USSR's interest in Sinkiang was not erased by the presence of a Communist government there. This was true even during the period of overt Sino-Soviet friendship. For example, a treaty signed in Moscow in 1950 calling for

[9] The most complete account of these events may be found in Allen Whiting and Sheng Shih-ts'ai, *Sinkiang: Pawn or Pivot?* (East Lansing: University of Michigan Press, 1958).

joint Chinese and Soviet exploitation of Sinkiang is thought to have been particularly irritating to Mao.[10]

Saifudin had gone to Moscow to help negotiate this treaty, and it was while he was still in the USSR that Peking announced he had become a member of the CCP. Despite this late switch, he eventually succeeded Burhan as governor of Sinkiang, serving concurrently as deputy secretary of the Sinkiang Party Committee. The PLA commander in the area, who by 1952 was Wang En-mao, became first Party secretary.

In Tibet, the Party's situation was even more difficult than in Sinkiang. Untouched by Communist influence from any quarter, devoutly religious, and suspicious of Party offers of autonomy, the Tibetans had been *de facto* independent for forty years and wished to remain so. However, the military strength of the Lhasa government was insufficient to uphold that desire. After its small army, commanded by a leading noble named Ngapo Ngawang Jigme, was literally wiped out at the Battle of Chamdo in November, 1950, the Tibetans had no choice but to negotiate.[11] Their decision was influenced by the fact that, despite PLA military supremacy, the Chinese position had several weak points. At this time, there was not a single Party member in Tibet. Moreover, the Tibetan population was overwhelmingly hostile, PLA supply lines were seriously overextended, and the Korean War had begun. In addition, there was considerable uncertainty about the international status of Tibet, which the Chinese feared might prove an excuse for "imperialist intervention."

Thus the Tibetans were able to exercise some leverage in the negotiations, and the resultant so-called Seventeen-Point Agreement on the Peaceful Liberation of Tibet provided that the existing political structure should remain intact.[12] The position of the Dalai Lama, who possessed both the highest secular and religious powers in Tibet, was to remain unchanged. All officials of the Lhasa government would be allowed to remain in office, provided they did not engage in sabotage or resistance. The Chinese promised not to force reforms on Tibet, saying they would be carried out by the Local Government of Tibet, and only when desired by the local people. Official press releases always referred to the Lhasa government as the "Local Government of

10 Allen Whiting, "Sinkiang and Sino-Soviet Relations," *CQ*, No. 3 (July–September, 1960), p. 34.
11 The events of these days are detailed in Robert Ford, *Wind between the Worlds* (New York: D. McKay Co., 1957).
12 The English text of this agreement was released by NCNA, Peking, May 27, 1951.

Tibet," thus distinguishing it from the "People's Governments" established in the rest of China.

The discrepancy in conditions between Tibet and the rest of China was further underscored by Tibet's total lack of an indigenous Communist Party. In order to create at least the rudimentary basis for a dual Party-government structure, a Party Work Committee was organized to build a native Communist Party. For several years this committee had no Tibetan members at all. With the exception of its original head, Chang Ching-wu, moreover, its top officials have continuously been predominantly military officers.

Meanwhile, relations between the Han invaders and the Local Government of Tibet were kept from being completely hostile by the presence of a small group of collaborators led by Ngapo Ngawang Jigme, whose defeat at Chamdo had opened the way for Chinese Communist penetration of Tibet. The Party, naturally, could not be sure whether their conversion had been sincere or whether it had been simulated in order to make the best of a bad situation.[13] However, the group proved valuable as a liaison between the PLA and the Local Government of Tibet.

In Yunnan, the Party was able to take advantage of a split between the local warlord and Chiang Kai-shek. The province had been ruled for many years by Lung Yun, a sinicized Yi whose half brother, Lu Han, served as his chief lieutenant. Lung, who appears to have been sincerely anti-Japanese, allied himself with Chiang during World War II, while maintaining the integrity of his army as a separate force. Yunnan also had a separate currency and several other appurtenances of an independent regime. At the war's end, Chiang, desirous of bringing Yunnan under his direct control, ordered Lung's troops, commanded by Lu Han, into Indochina to receive the Japanese surrender there. This left Lung Yun in a weakened military position, easy prey for Chiang's troops. KMT troops entered the provincial capital, arrested Lung, and packed him off to Nanking where he was held under surveillance. In accordance with a prearranged agreement with Chiang, Lu Han returned to Yunnan as governor.

Though Chiang obviously expected Lu to remain loyal to the man to whom he owed his governorship, Lu's allegiance in fact waned with every Communist success, and it became clear that he was gradually severing his ties with Chiang in order to be better able to negotiate

---

[13] For their part, anti-Communist Tibetan refugees have indicated that they are equally unsure of the enigmatic Ngapo's motives.

with Mao Tse-tung. To make matters even worse for Chiang Kai-shek, Lung Yun managed to escape from Nanking and, from the sanctuary of Hong Kong, began to issue pro-Communist, anti-KMT statements.[14] As a result of these, and because he still wielded a good deal of power in Yunnan, Lung was invited to the Chinese People's Political Consultative Conference. He was subsequently made a member of the Central People's Government Council, a vice-chairman of the National Defense Council, and a vice-chairman of the National Defense Council, and a vice-chairman of the Southwest Military and Administrative Committee (SWMAC). Lu Han was also made a vice-chairman of the SWMAC and head of the military and administrative committee for Yunnan as well.

In other areas, similar developments took place. Those who resisted the inevitable, such as Kazakh leader Osman Bator and Mongol Prince Teh Wang, or who were thoroughly unacceptable to the people because of corruption and/or past cruelties, were removed by force. In general, however, a strenuous effort was made to persuade the traditional elite to cooperate. Of such politically doubtful material was the government apparatus engaged in minorities work formed.

MINORITIES WORK AFTER 1949

Up to this point, our discussion has centered on the upper echelons of the Party and government elite engaged in minorities work. There is, of course, very little information available for the lower levels, but since Party members were few and rewarded with higher positions, one must conclude that the pattern of collaboration with the local traditional elite was even more marked on lower levels of administration.

Politically reliable members of minority nationalities were often seriously overworked. For example, Sang-chi-yueh-hsi, the young graduate of the Yenan Nationalities Institute mentioned previously, was simultaneously chairman of what are now known as Kan-tzu Tibetan Autonomous District and A-pa Tibetan Autonomous District. He was a member of both the Sikang Provincial People's Government and the Szechwan Provincial People's Government, the SWMAC, and the Standing Committee of the CPPCC's National Committee.

Obviously the Party's task was to expand this minorities elite which was both Red and expert. In many areas resentment against Han was a serious problem, and in order to ensure that a minority people did

---

[14] See A. Doak Barnett, *China on the Eve of Communist Takeover* (New York: Praeger, 1963), pp. 282–95.

not simply reject communism out of hand as a creation of the hated Han, it was necessary for them to receive it through cadres of their own nationality. Thus Mao Tse-tung stated in 1949 that the solution to the nationalities problem lay in training a large number of minorities cadres.[15]

The place to begin nurturing such an elite was clearly at the lowest level. Because native Party organizations were generally nonexistent at the grass roots level, the organization best suited to carry out the task was the PLA. Tactics differed somewhat according to area, but in general the procedure was for the PLA to send in a work team to pay a call on the local leader. As the persons responsible for the fate of their communities vis-à-vis the outside world, headmen typically had had experience in dealing with outsiders as spokesmen for their respective groups. Often they could speak some Chinese when other members of their group could not. Even if it had been possible for PLA men to communicate directly with "the masses," however, it would have been useless in many cases, for the common people considered political matters far beyond their comprehension. Thus, the dictates of ideology aside, the most efficient way to reach the masses was generally through the local headman.

If a headman was not disposed to cooperate, the work team would not force itself upon him, but would move on until it found a person more amenable to the group's presence. The team would then ask what the problems of the area were and suggest solutions. For example, if drought were mentioned, they might describe and offer to help build a small irrigation project. If it were malaria, drugs would be supplied and a plan outlined for killing mosquitoes and draining swamps. The work team would also try to find out local customs from the headman so as to avoid offending local sensitivities. Such gaucheries as sitting to the right of a campfire when custom dictated the left or preparing food in a manner considered unclean could prove major setbacks to the Party's good relations campaign.

The work team's slogan was "work together [with the minorities], eat together, live together." Daytime was devoted to working together with the people at such homely tasks as hauling water and cutting firewood. In the evening, work teams would occasionally entertain the others, generally with simple morality plays which linked what had been found out about the area's past history with the idea of class exploitation. For example, if the nationality's land had been stolen by

[15] Quoted in *MTTC,* No. 8–9 (1961), p. 10.

Han, the play's villain might be an avaricious Han official who, it would be made clear, had been simultaneously oppressing the Han masses of the area. When one headman was impressed with what the work the team was doing, it was hoped he would tell one of another area, who might then be persuaded to accept a team also. This was called the "point and area" system—building a point of trust and then expanding into the surrounding area.[16]

While dispensing free seed, tools, labor, and entertainment, team members learned the local language and propagandized Party doctrine and Party nationalities policy. Minority individuals who appeared especially receptive to Communist propaganda and who gave evidence of leadership qualities might be singled out for special treatment, some being sent to a PLA-run cadre school in the area. Having proved themselves there, these activists might be sent on to one of the regional minorities institutes or to the Central Minorities Institute in Peking. Often people on the lowest rung of society were especially propagandized on the grounds that being the most exploited members of their groups, they would be particularly receptive to the Party's point of view. For example, there was a disproportionately large number of blacksmiths elected to Tibetan people's councils, blacksmiths representing a kind of pariah caste in Tibetan society.

For the community as a whole, propagandizing laid the groundwork for a series of mass meetings culminating in democratic reforms. Where possible, agreement on such reforms was reached by peaceful discussion at a meeting of the entire community conducted by the leader of the work team. People's councils would be elected, theoretically with representatives from "all strata of society." Meetings of the councils would be scheduled at regular intervals to discuss the government's policies and to make suggestions as to adapting them to the minority areas. Meanwhile, the slower and more demanding task of creating a Party organization could proceed.

The people's councils as originally set up were, of course, never conceived of as more than first steps toward the type of peasant-run organizations the Party hoped to achieve eventually. Though the head of the PLA work team would generally occupy a position nominally secondary to a member of the minority nationality of the area, he was nearly always a Han Chinese and the real power in the council. The

16 See, for example, "Chairman Mao Has Sent a Very Valuable Person to the Lisu," *MTTC,* No. 8–9 (1961), p. 10; also, Alan Winnington, *Slaves of the Cool Mountains* (London: Lawrence and Wishart, 1959), pp. 141–43.

holder of the nominal first position was apt to be the traditional local headman, or another traditional leader of some standing in the community. Typically, to maximize the prestige of the people's council, as many traditional community leaders as could be persuaded to participate would be included in its membership. The activists, on whom the Party placed its hopes for the future, were naturally also included.

The Party branch, when it was set up, would generally have the PLA work team head as first secretary, and those activists who had proved themselves would be among the members. Here, the latter could gain the experience necessary before they could take charge of the area themselves.

Naturally, the scheme outlined above represented the ideal. In actuality, work team members faced many problems and frustrations. For one thing, conditions in minority areas were often incredibly primitive, even when measured by the standards of rural China. Malaria and other diseases were a constant problem to the newly arrived cadres. Since many minority peoples lived in the mountains, the bitter cold often caused much suffering. In the case of Tibet, the altitude as well as the weather made for severe hardships. As mentioned, frequently the minorities did not live in such areas of their own free choice, but because they had been forced there by Han who had usurped their land, sometimes centuries earlier. Thus they were extremely suspicious of the newcomers. One work team member found a local saying, "As a rock does not make a pillow, a Han does not make a friend." [17] Another, with orders to teach the Hani minority to read, was told by them that "reading is a Han custom only. If we read, our stomachs will ache, our crops won't grow, and our women will become barren." Having been refused permission to teach by all the local headmen, he tried a people-to-people approach, but found that the natives would simply say, "I don't understand" in their own language and walk away. [18]

In nomadic areas, whole villages decamped overnight, leaving startled cadres with no one to propagandize. [19] One cadre, sent to an area inhabited by the Lisu nationality, took his first step in gaining the trust of the people by learning to chew the local tobacco, a mixture of grass, lime, tobacco, and sand which was to him utterly repulsive. He later

[17] *MTTC*, No. 7 (1962), p. 41.
[18] Li Chiang-chen, "Local Girls Teach Han," *MTTC*, No. 12 (1963), pp. 37–38.
[19] Ma Ta-chün, "Democratic Reforms and the Socialist Transformation in the Nationalities Areas of China," *Chiao-hsüeh yü yen-chiu* (Teaching and Research), No. 6 (1958), pp. 62–75.

found out that what had sealed their acceptance of him was the fact that he would sleep under the same quilt with them although they were dirty and had lice.[20] Given the sort of working conditions described above, it is hardly surprising that very few cadres were eager to work in minority areas. Indeed, the shortage of trained personnel became a persistent complaint of Party spokesmen on the minorities problem.

Also, particularly in areas inhabited by traditionally warlike minorities, the cadres who were sent there tended, irrespective of Party edicts, to exclude them from participation in Party and governmental affairs as much as possible. An angry editorial in *Kansu jih-pao* (Kansu Daily) of October 1, 1949, noted that in Ho-cheng county, an area in which Hui were concentrated, there was not one single Hui cadre, and in fact the People's Government had refused to allow Hui to enter the county capital. In neighboring Lin-hsia county, the government had arbitrarily decided that Han were to form two-thirds of the militia, although Hui were more numerous and better soldiers. It was further revealed that in some unnamed areas, Hui were being arbitrarily shot at and killed. This was not, the editorial warned, the way to win the trust of the masses or to gain Hui converts to communism.[21]

Under such circumstances, progress was slow and there was perhaps more compromise with the traditional elite than had originally been intended. It was explicitly admitted that minority areas had "special characteristics" and that Party policy would have to be reinterpreted to accord with them.[22] Han cadres were warned not to apply mechanically the policies developed for Han areas. In practice, this meant that the Party person in a given area had a good deal of leeway in interpreting Party directives. The "special characteristics" theory also favored the position of the traditional elite: in return for recognition of their very real authority, the traditional elite served as guarantors of the population and smoothed relations between populace and Party. As applied in this period, the policy of compromise was indeed the most efficient way to establish good relations with the masses and seems to have been accepted as such by all of the "top Party persons in power."

Although Party policy differed in accordance with the assessment of the characteristics of a given area, reforms in this early period were generally quite moderate and headmen were often allowed to keep

20 "Chairman Mao Has Sent a Very Valuable Person to the Lisu," p. 38.

21 Quoted in *HHYP,* I, No. 4 (1950), 376.

22 See, for example, "CCP Kweichow Committee Rectifies Deviations in Implementing Nationalities Policy," *JMJP,* October 11, 1953.

their best land. Democratic reforms in Inner Mongolia were carried out under the slogan "herdsmen and herdowners both profit," and indications are that the traditional elite retained its prestige as well as its livestock.[23] A British leftist traveling in southwestern Szechwan in 1957 met a slave-owning member of the Yi nobility who was his area's delegate to the National People's Congress.[24] Democratic reforms had taken place there only a few months before. In Tibet, as has been stated, the traditional elite structure remained virtually untouched, and in Sinkiang it was announced that public functionaries of the old regime had been kept on en masse and reformed by means of such mass movements as those to eradicate special agents, oppose corruption, and increase production through labor.[25]

Of course the Party could not hope to carry out its economic and social policies if it compromised extensively with too many of the traditional elite, and saw cooperation with it as an alliance of convenience to be endured no longer than necessary. Thus, although the position of the majority of the traditional elite remained theoretically unchanged during this early period, the Party was already taking steps to undercut the bases of their power. In general, its policy was to avoid frontal attack on the ruling class while diminishing the sources of its preeminence—principally, landholding, moneylending, and religious functions. The "peaceful negotiations" under which democratic reforms were carried out resulted in reduction of the elite's real property, and state-issued low-interest or interest-free loans undercut their ability to hold the peasantry in bond through debt. Antireligious propaganda during this period was low-keyed and concentrated on demonstrating the superiority of modern scientific techniques to imploring the gods to cure disease and protect crops and livestock.

Obviously the traditional elite was well aware of what the Party was doing, but protest generally accomplished nothing except removal from office on charges of refusal to reform. Rebellions were quickly suppressed by vastly superior PLA forces, and the rebel leaders sent to jail or to labor camps. The majority of the traditional elite seem to have chosen the path of nominal cooperation with the Party while doing everything possible to retain its preliberation prestige. This program was not dissimilar to the application of the United Front in Han areas of China, but the Party's official admission that minority

[23] Ulanfu, "Success in Nationalities Work and Questions of Policy," report to third session of first NPC, June 20, 1956, in *CB*, No. 402 (July 10, 1956), pp. 17–22.
[24] Winnington, *Slaves of the Cool Mountains*, p. 85.
[25] As reported by Wang Chen, "Last Year in Sinkiang," *JMJP*, October 1, 1950.

areas had "special characteristics" which would have to be taken into consideration strengthened the minority elite's case.

While it is highly unlikely that many members of the traditional elite were glad that the Communists had come to their areas, relations between individual members of the traditional elite and Party members cannot automatically be assumed to be hostile. Party and traditional elite shared responsibility and concern for their area's stability and prosperity. Given the Party's rather moderate initial policy, moreover, a community of interests was likely to produce not only alliances of convenience but genuine friendships as well.

Meanwhile, however, the "Red and expert" successors of the traditional elite were continuously being trained. In 1957 the Party proudly announced that it now had the core of a minority nationality Party leadership: 400,000 CCP members, 400,000 cadres at or above the township level, and 600,000 members of the Communist Youth League. On July 1, 1956, seven Tibetans had been admitted to the Party—the very first CCP members from Tibet proper.[26]

Not surprisingly, Mongols, who had had the best-developed Communist movement prior to liberation, also had a higher percentage of CCP members than any other minority. Three per cent of the Mongols in Inner Mongolia were Party members, as opposed to a Party membership of 2.3 per cent of the population of Inner Mongolia as a whole.[27] By contrast, the Chuang—if anything, a more advanced nationality than the Mongols—had a Party membership percentage of only 1.2 per cent.[28] The number of Tibetan Party members relative to the population of Tibet was negligible.

The number of Mongols in leadership positions in the Party was greatly disproportionate to their total numbers in the IMAR. As of 1960, for example, four out of five IMAR Party secretaries and deputies were Mongols, while the Han population of Inner Mongolia was estimated to have outnumbered the Mongol population by a ratio of approximately seven to one. In the Ninghsia Hui Autonomous Region, where the population was about 35 per cent Hui, three out of six secretaries and deputy secretaries were Hui.

In the Kwangsi Chuang Autonomous Region, with a Chuang population of about 32 per cent, two out of six secretaries and deputies were

26 *MTTC*, No. 2 (1957), p. 8; NCNA, July 2, 1956.
27 "Great Victory for Nationalities Policy in Inner Mongolia," *JMJP*, May 1, 1962.
28 *Kwangsi jih-pao* (Kwangsi Daily), July 1, 1959.

Chuang. In the Sinkiang Uighur Autonomous Region, where the Han population was probably no more than 10 per cent of the total and the Uighur population about 75 per cent, there was only one Uighur deputy secretary out of a total of six secretaries and deputies; the others were all Han. In Tibet, where the population is virtually all Tibetan, there were no Tibetan secretaries or deputies.[29]

The Mongols' privileged position in Inner Mongolia is further indicated by statistics on numbers of cadres. Of the minority nationality population of the IMAR, 1.7 per cent were cadres, whereas Han cadres were only 0.93 per cent of the total Han population of China. With the exception of Kirin, where 1.3 per cent of the minority population (chiefly Mongols and Koreans) were cadres, minority nationality cadres were always underrepresented in relation to the total minority population of the area.[30]

Toward the latter half of the 1950's, when the first group of minority Party members trained after liberation began to assume positions in Party and government, a third group was added to the elite engaged in minorities work. The uneasy nature of this balance among the traditional elite, most of whom were of minority nationalities and in the government administrative hierarchy, and the Party elite engaged in minorities work, most of whom were Han, plus the fledgling minority Communists being trained by the CCP, is detailed in the revelations of the Hundred Flowers period. Members of the traditional elite who had been coopted into the local government structure complained that their Han comrades failed to consult them on issues or simply ignored their advice.[31] Others complained that being given so-called self-government had been as useful to them as a "deaf ear"; they were simply messenger boys for the Han. They demanded a rectification of the situation of "many rights in theory, few in practice." [32] Some went further, demanding complete separation from the CPR. Hui insisted they could not accept the Party committee as leaders: their real leaders were the traditional religious elite.[33]

A widespread attitude was that members of minority nationalities who had been receptive to Party propaganda had betrayed their people.

[29] *Biographic Directory of Party and Government Officials in Communist China* (Washington, D.C.: U.S. Department of State, 1960), pp. 8–11.

[30] Yeh Hsiang-chih, "Some Questions in the Work of Fostering Minority Nationality Cadres," *JMJP*, February 6, 1957.

[31] *SCMP*, No. 1362, p. 19.

[32] *NFJP*, May 5, 1957.

[33] *MTTC*, No. 6 (1958), p. 1.

Saifudin frankly admitted that Kazakhs and Uighurs who cooperated with the Party were taunted as "jackals serving the Han."[34] In Tibet, those who helped the Han in such minimal ways as agreeing to work on PLA highway construction projects in return for wages considered high by Tibetan standards risked mutilation or death at the hands of their fellow Tibetans.[35]

Problems between conservative minority factions on the one hand and Han and those who were willing to cooperate with them on the other were not the only tensions revealed by the Hundred Flowers campaign. Minorities who had proved receptive to the socialist message also found themselves at odds with their Han comrades. The Han, they complained, were arrogant and overbearing. They were unwilling to learn minorities languages, loath to observe local rules of etiquette when it did not suit their convenience, and in general exuded an air of what the Party called "Great Han chauvinism." Borrowing yet another phrase from Communist terminology, the minorities accused their Han comrades of not allowing them to be "masters in their own house."[36] Particularly during the period of the Great Leap Forward, some minorities cadres criticized Han cadres for forcing premature reforms on the people, such as assigning Muslim Hui to eat in communal dining halls where pork dishes were served. A solution advocated in several different areas was that all Party committee members and all cadres must be of minority nationality.

Considering the provocations with which it had been confronted, the Party's response was surprisingly mild. Although it engaged in a torrent of criticism of local nationalism, the Party made a real effort to avoid destroying the fragile structure it had put together with such difficulty in minority areas. Teng Hsiao-p'ing, in his report on the rectification campaign, warned that criticism of nationalist tendencies must not be made too hastily and that support should be given to the majority of Party functionaries and non-Party activists from minority nationalities.[37] If Teng's suggestion was indeed followed, it was not extended to the traditional elite who had been absorbed into the CPR structure; they became the main targets of the *cheng-feng* movement in minority areas.

However, any suspicions that this meant the end of cooperation with the traditional elite were quickly dispelled. Wang Feng, then vice-

[34] *JMJP*, December 26, 1957.
[35] NCNA, March 28, 1959.
[36] *JMJP*, December 26, 1957.
[37] NCNA, October 19, 1957.

chairman of the Nationalities Committee and a deputy director of the UFWD, emphasized that the Party would "continue the United Front and unite with all those who [could] be united with." While admitting that "quite a number of persons in the upper strata of nationalities object[ed] to socialism," their problems were still to be regarded as "within the ranks of the people." Whether the traditional elite who had served as officials of the CPR were to receive re-education or to perform labor was to be decided "on a voluntary basis and according to their physical condition and other conditions." [38]

Areas in which the socialist transformation had not yet been completed were exempted from the antirightist campaign. In Tibet, the chief news in 1957–58 concerned the withdrawal of a number of Han cadres and the promulgation of the Party's policy of "no democratic reforms" in Tibet for at least six years. No mass criticism and no purges were carried out.[39] This came, moreover, as the demands of other minorities for the withdrawal of Han cadres were being criticized as bourgeois nationalism.

The position of the traditional elite actually became more precarious during the Great Leap Forward than it had been during the antirightist campaign. In the drive to increase production, simplify administration, and eliminate bureaucracy, the congeries of compromises which had been worked out in minorities areas seemed to represent only so many more obstacles to success. The idea that minority areas had special characteristics to which the Party should adapt came under severe attack. Cadres only recently criticized as local nationalists during the antirightist campaign feared to disagree and assured higher Party organs that indeed their areas could catch up with the Han in three to five years or even less. Traditional dress was to be discarded, customs reformed, and the Chinese language learned in the same short period required to completely revamp and communize the local economy.

While the Great Leap did not directly attack either the United Front or the position of the traditional elite, it assaulted everything for which they stood. Of course, the traditional elite well understood the nature of the threat, but before much could be done against them, the Great Leap's weaknesses had become glaringly apparent. Its failure strengthened the hand of the moderate faction in the Peking leadership and also the position of the traditional elite in minority areas. The earliest

[38] Wang Feng, "Report to the 5th Enlarged Meeting of the Nationalities Committee of the 1st NPC," February 9, 1958, in *CB*, No. 495 (March 14, 1958), p. 16.

[39] See the collection of reports from *Hsi-tsang jih-pao* (Tibet Daily) for this period carried in *CB*, No. 490.

indication that the position of the traditional elite was being reassessed in view of the Great Leap's deficiencies may be found in the lament of a *Kuang-ming jih-pao* (Bright Daily) editorial of 1958 that "at present there are still very few Communist hard-core elements who are capable of political leadership among the minority nationalities." [40] Several members of the traditional elite who had been purged were rehabilitated in the wake of the Great Leap, the two most prominent being Lung Yun and a Hui leader, Ma Sung-t'ing.[41]

In March, 1962, the lead article in *Min-tsu t'uan-chieh*, the most prominent of the journals devoted to nationalities work, was entitled "Continue Good United Front Work with Nationality Religious and Upper Classes." Its author, Lü Chien-jen, a member of the NAC, maintained that past experience had proved that a policy of compromise and peaceful negotiations with the upper classes could achieve the best results—diminution of resistance to socialism, reduction of losses in production, avoidance of nationality and religious strife—while producing the greatest benefits for the workers. This would hold as true in the period of socialist construction as it had in that of democratic reforms. The Party's best course, he argued, was to "persuade the masses" to work with the upper classes: it was most important to choose "relatively compromising methods" and not to carry out class struggle. This policy would "continue to smooth the socialist road." [42] Since one of the crucial reasons Lü had advanced for cooperating with the nationalities' upper classes was the great amount of influence they had over the masses, it seems likely that he was actually trying to convince a faction of the Party and not the minority masses of the wisdom of this antistruggle, procompromise policy.

From the first realization of the Great Leap's deficiencies through the mid-1960's, the clear implication of policy decisions is that although the traditional elite participating in government had disappointed the Party by proving more of a hindrance to reform than a center around which reform could take place, they would continue to be tolerated out of necessity. This could be seen as a bowing to the inevitable, as the moderate group probably saw it, or as a selling out of the Party's interests, as the more leftist faction definitely did see it. The emergent Party line held, however, that though re-education of the traditional elite was certainly still needed, "People of Nationalities

---

[40] Cheng Hung, "Nationalities Institutes Are Political Schools for Fostering Autonomy," *Kuang-ming jih-pao*, December 17, 1958.

[41] *SCMP*, No. 2644, p. 4; *ibid.*, No. 2775, p. 16.

[42] *MTTC*, No. 3 (1962), pp. 2–5.

Upper Strata See a Bright Future," as the title of a *Jen-min jih-pao* article phrased it.[43]

Even the Tibetan revolt in 1959 did not end the policy of cooperation with this upper strata. Those surviving nobles who openly opposed the Party either escaped to India or were imprisoned, and their estates were confiscated. However, those who did not join the rebellion retained their previous positions on such organizations as the Preparatory Committee for the Tibetan Autonomous Region and received financial compensation for lands taken from them during the subsequent land reform. Government organs created after the revolt were also staffed by nobles.[44]

The continued existence of the United Front did not, of course, mean that the position of any one individual therein was secure. For example, although the Tibetan governmental structure remained continuously in the hands of nobles, the Dalai Lama was replaced after the revolt by the Panchen Lama. And while the Panchen Lama was widely regarded as a Chinese puppet, he was removed from office in 1964 on grounds that he "represented a clique of reactionary serf-owners" who were plotting against "the people, the motherland and socialism." [45] The Panchen Lama was succeeded by Ngapo Ngawang Jigme, who had been the Party's most enthusiastic collaborator since 1951. In Sinkiang, Burhan, though remaining in public life as chairman of various Islamic associations, was removed from the region's governorship, his position of real power, in 1955.

There is no doubt, however, that there was substantial continuity among the traditional elite engaged in minorities work. An examination of the Nationalities Committee of the National People's Congress, for instance, shows that forty-three out of eighty-four members elected in 1965 had also been members in 1955,[46] a holdover of better than 50 per cent. When one notes that many members of the original body were local patriarchs of advanced years, the continuity becomes even more striking. However, this continuity indicates that the men involved had proved successful collaborators rather than that the Party had decided their talents as individuals were indispensable.

---

[43] *JMJP,* June 14, 1959.

[44] Ngapo Ngawang Jigme, "Great Victory of Democratic Reforms in Tibet," *JMJP,* April 10, 1960. Nevertheless, an effort was made to introduce some ex-serfs into positions on the lower levels of people's governments.

[45] Chou En-lai, "Report on the Work of the Government," speech to first session of the Third National People's Congress, NCNA, December 30, 1964.

[46] Compare the 1955 *Jen-min shou-ts'e* (People's Handbook) with the 1965 edition.

While there was substantial continuity in the traditional elite engaged in minorities work, there was virtually no change at all in the Party elite engaged in minorities work. Li Wei-han, head of the Party Central Committee's UFWD since 1944, remained head until 1965. He had been assisted since 1949 by Hsu Ping (also known as Hsing Hsi-p'ing). In 1952 the NAC had a chairman and five vice-chairmen who were Party members. Thirteen years later, five of the six still held these or other high positions in minorities work; the sixth, Liu Ko-p'ing, had been demoted only a few years before.

Of the first Party secretaries of the five autonomous regions in 1966, Ulanfu had held his post in Inner Mongolia since 1947 and Wang En-mao had held his in Sinkiang since 1952. Wei Kuo-ch'ing had been governor of Kwangsi since the founding of an autonomous region there in 1958; three years later he assumed the post of first Party secretary as well, the original incumbent being transferred to a similar position in Honan. Chang Kuo-hua, who became first Party secretary in the Tibet Autonomous Region when it was founded in 1965, had been in Tibet since 1951. Yang Ching-jen, who had held important positions in minorities work since the Yenan period, had become first secretary of the Ninghsia Party Committee in 1960, replacing Liu Ko-p'ing, the purged member of the NAC who had been accused of being a rightist.[47]

A by-product of this extreme stability in the elites engaged in minorities work is the relegation to low-level positions of those minorities activists trained by the Party since liberation.[48] Of twenty-three vignettes published by the Chinese Communist press about such persons, none held a Party office higher then the *hsien* level or a government post higher then the *chou* level. Five had been named delegates to provincial or autonomous region people's congresses, but these were positions of little consequence.

In addition, it is evident that members of minority nationalities, whatever their backgrounds, had little prospect of success outside the Party-government minorities structure, or indeed outside their own minority area. One Szechwan Yi, Wang Ch'i-mei, was chosen to serve on the Party work committee in neighboring Tibet, and Chi Ya-t'ai, a Mongol, was named ambassador to the Mongolian People's Republic;

[47] NCNA, November 22, 1960.

[48] As shown by A. Doak Barnett, *Cadres, Bureaucracy, and Political Power in Communist China* (New York: Columbia University Press, 1967), this lack of mobility was by no means confined to minority nationalities.

however, these are exceptions to the general pattern that minorities serve either among their own nationality or as spokesmen for it in some Party or government body. Cadres who received training at one of the central or regional minorities academies were returned to their native areas as a matter of policy.[49] One does not find Uighurs assigned to Han or Pai areas, or Mongols serving in South China.

This pattern recurs in all professions. Tibetan soldiers cited for bravery have invariably performed their meritorious deeds in Tibet; those minorities trained as historians and authors write exclusively on the history and literature of their own nationality. One must conclude that the minorities' chances for advancement were highly circumscribed by geography and that their integration into the CPR had taken place in only a limited sense.

THE CULTURAL REVOLUTION AND ITS AFTERMATH

The policy of the United Front which had proved so durable showed its first crack in 1965. In what retrospectively seems a portent of the accusations of the Cultural Revolution, Li Wei-han was removed as director of the UFWD on charges of capitulationism in United Front work.[50] He was replaced by Hsu Ping, his long-time deputy director, and for a short period everything appeared to be functioning normally.

It should be noted that it was not the United Front itself which had been attacked, but the allegedly capitulationist activities of one member, albeit the director. However, with the coming of the Cultural Revolution a year later, the entire United Front came under attack as a screen behind which Liu Shao-ch'i and his agents had pursued their allegedly capitulationist schemes.[51] Moreover, those singled out for most vehement attack were not those minority nationality "remnants of the old society" whose positions in the new society had been tolerated under the United Front concept, but those Party members who had been associated with United Front work. Party membership actually seems to have rendered its holders more vulnerable to attack than membership in the traditional elite cooperating with the Party would have made them.

The explanation for this may lie in the reasoning that, while those remnants of the old society were simply doing what historical necessity

---

[49] *SCMP,* No. 3381, p. 9.

[50] Peking, *Chui ch'iung k'ou* (Pursue the Desperate Foe), No. 4, May 20, 1967, in *SCMP,* No. 3970, p. 1.

[51] *Ibid.*

expected of them—that is, trying to salvage their old positions insofar as was possible—the Communist "new men" had actually sold out the interests of the revolution: the traitor within is more to be feared than the enemy without. In rectifying this situation, the CPR's structure for dealing with minority nationalities as a group separate from the Han population was destroyed, and most of the elite staffing it were purged.

Not surprisingly, those Party members most closely associated with United Front work bore the brunt of the attack. Hsü Ping was charged with following in Li Wei-han's path and "surrendering to the bourgeoisie and upper strata of national minority and religious groups . . . and forming cliques for private ends." [52] Liu Ch'un, a deputy director of the UFWD and concurrently vice-chairman of the NAC and president of the Central Minorities Institute, was accused of "completely controlling the business of the Nationalities Affairs Commission" while collaborating in Liu Shao-ch'i's plots.[53] Wang Feng, another long-term member of the UFWD who was also an important figure on the NAC and first secretary of the Kansu Party Committee, was removed from all his positions on grounds he had abetted the schemes of China's Khrushchev.[54] Party General Secretary Teng Hsiao-p'ing was accused by Red Guards of complicity in the Tibetan revolt: in 1952 he had, they said, "under the guise of the United Front" arranged passage to India for a prime minister of the Tibetan local government after the latter had outspokenly disagreed with Party policy in his country. The ex-prime minister later played an important part in planning the Tibetan revolt of 1959.[55]

The attacks extended beyond central government organs to those whose chief bases of power were at the provincial and autonomous *chou* level. Ulanfu was purged following accusations he had plotted to split Inner Mongolia from China, forced people to study Mongolian to the neglect of Chinese studies, and connived to replace the thoughts of Mao with the thoughts of Ulanfu.[56] With the single exception of Wang Tsai-t'ien, all the well-known Mongols previously

---

[52] *Ibid.*

[53] *Ibid.*, p. 2.

[54] Canton, *Chih-k'an nan-yüeh* (Surveying South Kwangtung), No. 3, October 27, 1967, in *SCMP*, No. 4057, pp. 6–7; see also Radio Kansu, January 25, 1968, in Foreign Broadcast Information Service, *Daily Report* (Communist China) (hereafter FBIS), January 26, 1968.

[55] *Chih-k'an nan-yüeh*, in *SCMP*, No. 4086, pp. 6–10.

[56] *Kung-jen chan-pao* (Workers' Combat News), No. 16–17, June 29, 1968, in *JPRS*, No. 42,933; Radio Huhehot, January 12, 1968, in FBIS, January 17, 1968.

involved in Party and government work were purged with Ulanfu, including K'uei Pi, Chi Ya-t'ai, and Wang To.[57]

Yen Hung-yen, first Party secretary of Yunnan, is said to have committed suicide when confronted with a list of his crimes, including advocating special privileges for minorities and allowing their cooperatives to be disbanded in the reorganization which followed the Great Leap. He was also alleged to have colluded with the traditional elite in allowing them to "ride roughshod" over the peasants seventeen years after liberation. Yang Ching-jen, first Party secretary of the Ninghsia Hui Autonomous Region, and other prominent Hui Party members including Ma Yü-huai were also purged.[58]

Those who were attacked but survived include Wei Kuo-ch'ing, first Party secretary of the Kwangsi Chuang Autonomous Region, who was later confirmed as chairman of the KCAR Revolutionary Committee, and Saifudin, deputy secretary of the Sinkiang Uighur Autonomous Region, who became a member of the SUAR Revolutionary Committee. Chang Kuo-hua, first Party secretary in Tibet, was abruptly transferred to Szechwan where he became chairman of the revolutionary committee there.[59] Ngapo Ngawang Jigme, virtually the symbol of Party cooperation with the Tibetan upper classes, was severely attacked by the Red Guards. The Cultural Revolution Group intervened directly on his behalf, saying he had gained merit by exposing the treachery of the Dalai and Panchen lamas and was henceforth to be protected. He became a vice-chairman of the Tibet Revolutionary Committee.[60] Sang-chi-yueh-hsi, possibly the only powerful member of the Party elite engaged in minorities work who was not attacked, became a vice-chairman of the Szechwan Revolutionary Committee in 1968. Less than a year later, it was announced he had become a vice-chairman of the Tibetan Revolutionary Committee.

In some cases survival was only temporary. Wang En-mao, former first Party secretary in Sinkiang, managed to survive repeated attacks

---

[57] Wang Tsai-t'ien (Mongol name: La-mu-chi-se-leng), a pre-1949 convert to communism, had been a secretary of the secretariat of the IMAR Party Committee from 1960 to 1967. At the formation of the IMAR Revolutionary Committee in 1967, he was listed as a "responsible person" of that region.

[58] Radio Kunming, November 30, 1967, in FBIS, December 5, 1967. Radio Yin-ch'uan, April 10, 1968, in FBIS, April 12, 1968.

[59] Though Chang was transferred after severe Red Guard criticism in Tibet, his position in Szechwan suggests promotion rather than demotion.

[60] *I-yueh feng-pao* (January Storm) (Canton), No. 23–24 (March, 1968), in *SCMP*, No. 4150, p. 10.

to become a vice-chairman of the Sinkiang Revolutionary Committee—
itself a demotion—and has apparently been demoted still further since
then. Liu Ko'p'ing, the vice-chairman of the NAC and first Party
secretary in Ninghsia who had been purged as a rightist in the early
1960's, managed to become a champion of a Red Guard faction and
was subsequently confirmed chairman of the Shansi Revolutionary
Committee. He has since been removed from office, however, presumably because he was too leftist for the PLA group in the province.[61]

As can be seen, the survivors of both the traditional minorities elite
and the Party elite engaged in minorities work represent no single,
clear-cut ideological pattern. It is significant that two of the most
prominent survivors, Saifudin and Wei Kuo-ch'ing, had no connection
with the United Front Work Department of the Party. The political
situation within a given province at a given moment appears to have
been an additional factor of importance. Wei Kuo-ch'ing, for example,
was allowed to repent his errors only after Red Guard factionalism
in Kwangsi had disrupted railway transport to the extent of causing
serious shortages of supplies throughout the southwest and delays in
China's shipments of war matériel to Vietnam.[62] Saifudin, the only
prominent Uighur Communist in the Sinkiang Uighur Autonomous
Region, had in addition been particularly vigorous in his denunciations
of both Uighur nationalism and of the Soviet Union. His continued
activities as a representative of his people during this nadir in Sino-
Soviet relations must have seemed especially desirable. Sang-chi-yueh-
hsi, a man of proven talents and the only prominent Communist to
have arisen in eastern Tibet, and Ngapo Ngawang Jigme, one of the
few successful collaborators the Party has been able to produce in
Tibet proper (where there have been *no* prominent native Communists), had similar symbolic value.

The toll taken by the Cultural Revolution, however, was heavy in
this field as in many others. Only a handful of Party members who
had been prominent in minorities work and a similarly small number
of the traditional minorities elite have been identified as still in favor
since 1969. These few hold offices at the various levels of revolutionary
committees which were established in minorities areas as in Han areas.
The United Front Work Department, the Nationalities Affairs Com-

[61] *Tung-fang-hung t'ien-hsün* (The East Is Red Telegram) (Canton), No. 3 (July,
1968), in *SCMP*, No. 4243, pp. 15–16; Tillman Durdin, "Local Army Role Widened in
China," *New York Times*, June 14, 1970, p. 8.

[62] Liu-chou, *Kung tsung* (Workers' General [Headquarters Bulletin]), July 12, 1968,
in *SCMP*, No. 5226, pp. 1–3.

mission, and the Nationalities Committee of the National People's Congress apparently became completely defunct. Suggestions for a new Party constitution supposedly put forth by the Shanghai masses in early 1968 contained the accusation that the United Front and other nationalities work organs had created nationality schisms and stood in the way of the unity of nationalities. It was suggested that the new Party constitution should stress Mao's dictum that "national struggle is in the final analysis a question of class struggle." [63] This in effect was a call for minorities to be treated just as were other citizens of China, with class background and not ethnic origin the determining factor. The validity of the "special characteristics" theory was again disputed, as it had been in the Great Leap period.

An examination of these and other charges made during the Cultural Revolution shows them to have at least partial validity. The contention that previous policy had created nationality schisms was clearly overdrawn. Such schisms as exist under the CCP are simply continuations of historic internationality tensions exacerbated by the Party's more rigorous and comprehensive methods of dealing with minorities. It is, however, undeniable that the United Front and other nationalities work organs had contributed to the perpetuation of the nationalities as separate entities. In this sense they did, as the framers of the Shanghai draft constitution contended, stand in the way of nationalities' unity. From the radicals' point of view, while some arrangements of this sort might have been necessary when the Party was consolidating its control over minority areas, the need for them had passed by the time of the Great Leap. Those who insisted they must remain were simply trying to protect their own vested interests.

There were other accusations. The Red Guards charged that those in power in the United Front had surrendered to the minority upper strata and formed cliques for private ends. While the plots that United Front members were said to have perpetrated in collusion with this upper strata were hardly unlikely to have been as well planned or as far-reaching as the Red Guards portrayed them, it is true that in establishing an apparatus for minorities work, the Party had in effect created an organization with a vested interest in the perpetuation of minority separateness in order to perpetuate its own power. The necessity for a certain amount of cooperation with or "capitulation to" the minority upper strata was built into the concept of the United

---

[63] *Wen-ko feng-yun* (Cultural Revolution Wind and Cloud) (Canton), No. 2 (February, 1968), in *SCMP*, No. 4151, p. 3.

Front. It is not unlikely that this cooperation became the basis for a certain amount of what could be construed as factionalism or clique-ism.

In the eyes of the radicals, errors of judgment became tantamount to premeditated crimes. Thus Teng Hsiao-p'ing's desire to avoid provoking bloodshed in Tibet by allowing its dissident prime minister to leave the country unmolested was seen as complicity in the revolt which occurred seven years later. As for Ulanfu, charges that he was a secret nationalist who plotted to detach Inner Mongolia from China and join it with the Mongolian People's Republic under the protection of the Soviet Union were patently absurd. A member of the CCP since his youth and so unnationalistic that he had never bothered to master Mongolian, Ulanfu had not taken advantage of his numerous chances to join with the Soviet Union and Mongolian People's Republic when CCP power in his area was so weak that he could have done so with impunity. His protection of the Mongolian language and culture are more likely to have been an attempt to attract conservative citizens of the Mongolian People's Republic away from their increasingly Russified government and back toward China.[64] This was magnified into a plot to promote "national splittism."

Suggestions of the Shanghai masses notwithstanding, more recent developments indicate that the high ideals of the Cultural Revolution on minorities policy have, as on so many other issues, fallen short of fulfillment. Perhaps in deference to radical insistence that nationality problems be regarded as no more than class problems, the constitution agreed upon at the Ninth Party Congress made no mention at all of the United Front, or even of the existence of minority nationalities. As might be expected, Russian propaganda alleges that this indicates a Maoist plot to exterminate the minorities.[65]

However, neither actual minorities nor the concept thereof has been erased. Minority names appear on lists of provincial revolutionary committees in rough proportion to the population strength of the minority in a given region. (Though Uighurs and Tibetans are under-represented, this scarcely constitutes a change from past practice.) Because of the obscurity of their backgrounds, it is difficult to tell

[64] Stuart Schram, in *Mao Tse-tung* (New York: Simon and Schuster, 1966) p. 236, lists several instances of Mao's desire to win back Outer Mongolia.

[65] The English text of the constitution can be found in *Peking Review*, No. 19, April 30, 1969, pp. 32–35. For the Russian comment see, for example, T. Rakhimov, "The Great Power Policy of Mao Tse-tung on the Nationalities Question," *Kommunist*, No. 7 (1967); Radio Peace and Progress (Moscow), September 18, 1968.

whether the new minorities elite is present as window-dressing or by virtue of its members' excellent records as Maoists. If the latter situation prevails, they might be expected to wield some power. The case of Tsering Lam seems to indicate that at least one minority new-comer has distinct prospects. A Tibetan who was virtually unknown prior to the Cultural Revolution, Tsering became a vice-chairman of the Tibetan Revolutionary Committee and has written several articles on the progress of the socialist revolution in Tibet.[66] In contrast, Rev-olutionary Committee Chairman Tseng Yung-ya, a PLA man, and Ngapo Ngawang Jigme, perennial spokesman for socialist Tibet, have been notably silent.

Although the new Party constitution does not mention the existence of minority nationalities, members of minorities continue to be iden-tified as such in official press releases, and the system of autonomous areas continues to function. There are other signs that elements of the old system may be re-emerging. The fact that Tan Tung, a member of the NAC previously thought to have been purged, was listed as among those "leading comrades and representatives of the revolu-tionary masses in various departments under the State Council" who attended the 1970 May Day rally in Peking [67] indicates that the com-mission may be re-forming. Recently, too, references to the United Front have begun to reappear: an April 20, 1970, broadcast by Radio Tsinan indicated that, at least in Shantung, its functions have been taken over by a department under the jurisdiction of the provincial revolutionary committee.

While it can safely be assumed that the desire of the more radical group in the Cultural Revolution to ignore all nationality differences has not been achieved, it seems equally certain that the Cultural Rev-olution has resulted in minorities' losing power and cohesiveness *as minority groups*. Han military leaders serve as revolutionary committee chairmen in four out of five autonomous regions and, due to the deterioration of China's relations with many foreign countries, partic-ularly the USSR, there has been an increased PLA presence in the border areas where most minority peoples live. In addition, and possibly more important in the long run, there has been a sharp rise in the numbers of Han permanently transferred to border areas.

To the extent that this situation is conducive to further integration

[66] *JMJP*, November 18, 1968; *ibid.*, January 16, 1969.
[67] "Great Leader Chairman Mao and His Close Comrade-in-Arms Vice-Chairman Lin Join Peking Workers and Masses in May Day Evening Festivities," NCNA, May 1, 1970.

of minorities into Han-Chinese society, the Cultural Revolution goals regarding minorities policies may have been partly achieved, in the fashion of Lenin's "two steps forward, one step backward." But whether at some point the new minorities elite now taking form will be subject to the same criticisms of perpetuating separatism as the old remains to be seen. Minority problems in most societies have proven enormously resistant to easy or rapid "solutions," irrespective of the broad goals enunciated or the concrete policies applied. It is not yet clear that the People's Republic of China constitutes an exception.

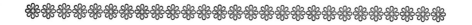

SIDNEY LEONARD GREENBLATT

Organizational Elites and Social Change at Peking University

Of all the types of data which biographical sources on Communist Chinese personnel yield, none comes in greater quantities than raw position data. And, lacking direct access to the personal files of decision-makers in Communist China, no form of aggregate data is more essential to an understanding of the exercise, allocation, and consequences of power than the long lists of appointments, transfers, and dismissals that constitute the bulk of biographical material. Yet few works utilizing position data derive maximum utility from the one true quantitative characteristic they possess, namely, the sheer number of positions. This is so despite the fact that sociologists concerned with social stratification and role analysis have developed a significant body of theory that owes much to the enumeration of social positions. Georg Simmel, writing in the first decade of this century, went so far as to suggest that enumeration could define an individual.[1] That is, if all the social positions each person in a large population occupied were enumerated, only some would be found to share sets of exactly the same size, containing the same specific positions (or, more accurately, statuses). If the amount of time and energy expended on each status were calculated, then the number of shared sets would diminish appreciably, for no two individuals would be likely to handle their statuses in exactly the same way.

What Simmel was describing, in contemporary terms, were the di-

[1] Reinhard Bendix (trans.), "The Web of Group-Affiliations, in Georg Simmel, *Conflict and the Web of Group-Affiliations* (New York: Free Press of Glencoe, 1964), especially pp. 124 and 140. Also Kurt H. Wolff (ed.), *The Sociology of Georg Simmel* (New York: Free Press, 1964), p. 107.

451

mensions and properties of "status sets."[2] His point was not to deny the importance of personality or of the unique in human behavior, but to pursue the logic of social structure as far as reasoning would take it. Nor is it our point to diminish the importance of analyses of policy statements, the contents of publications, interviews, and other methods applied to the study of Chinese Communist elites. Structural information on the composition of status sets and the distribution of statuses within them tells us little about what power is and the multitudinous ways in which it can be and is exercised. If power is, as some would argue, zero-sum,[3] then data concerning statuses and their distributions can tell us a great deal about how groups are structured around the exercise of power, who is likely to have access to the resources power-holders command, and how the structure of access changes over time.

If such information is considered crucial for the study of elites in any context, it is that much more critical, given the sheer weight of positional data compared to any other form of information, in the Chinese Communist context. Even more, it assumes a special significance for studies of those Chinese Communist subsystem elites located in organizations that are not specifically subunits within the state and Party apparatus. For these elite groups, data of any kind are relatively rare, so that we cannot afford *not* to take full advantage of aggregate structural information when and where it appears. More important, where such subsystem elites are concerned, one must start with the assumption that power is at least partially derivative, that is, that subsystem elites exercise power through resources allocated by superordinates in command positions within the state and Party apparatus. Measuring status sets is important because it permits us to determine where the interface between command elites and subsystem subordinate elites is located.

Maximizing the utility of aggregate positional data is but one major problem in the study of Chinese Communist elites. Another equally important issue relates to problems in the definition and measurement of change. Most frequently, analysts approach elite change in Communist China by comparing a predefined elite group at time 1 to the

---

2 Robert K. Merton, *Social Theory and Social Structure* (New York: Free Press of Glencoe, 1949), pp. 252–72.

3 For an example, with refinements, see Ralf Dahrendorf, *Class and Class Conflict in Industrial Society* (Stanford, Calif.: Stanford University Press, 1959), pp. 169–70.

same group at time 2.[4] Such studies are valuable contributions to our knowledge of elite behavior, but they mask the continuous dynamism of social behavior in general and the remarkable dynamism of change in China in particular. Research designs which start with the assumption that change is continuous are of little value to modern Chinese studies because of the rigor they demand and the weaknesses inherent in data derived at a distance and secondhand. Yet there is adequate evidence of the dynamic and continuous nature of social change in China in at least one form: the recurrence of political campaigns.

Few works written about Communist China fail to mention the recurrence of campaigns as a predominant facet of social life in that society. But despite the attention given to campaigns, only a few works describe them in detail, and these few draw a tiny sample from a huge universe. Furthermore, they are more often treated as discrete historical events than as part of a continuous process intimately linked to social change.[5] If what I suggest is indeed true, then the analysis of campaign behavior has an important role to play in the study of elite structure and particularly elite change. While limitations on data prevent me from adopting models of continuous change, I shall aim at breaking the hold of dichotomous treatments of aggregate data on Chinese Communist elite analysis to suggest how temporal space may be broken up into less discrete segments.

[4] Robert C. North, *Kuomintang and Chinese Communist Elites* (Stanford, Calif.: The Hoover Institution, 1952), is a leading example of this genre.

[5] Of the works that deal directly with campaigns as a continuous process or from a comparative perspective, three are especially notable: G. William Skinner, "Compliance and Leadership in Rural Communist China," a paper prepared for delivery at the annual meeting of the American Political Science Association, Washington, D.C., December 8–11, 1965; Merle Goldman, *Literary Dissent in Communist China* (Cambridge, Mass.: Harvard University Press, 1967); and Thomas Bernstein, "Leadership and Mass Mobilization in the Soviet and Chinese Collectivization Campaigns of 1929–30 and 1955–56: A Comparison," *CQ*, No. 26 (April–June, 1966), pp. 1–48. This generalization does not deny the great value of the many studies which treat campaigns as discrete historical events. Those particularly relevant to the study of Peking University are: Roderick MacFarquhar, *The Hundred Flowers Campaign and the Chinese Intellectuals* (New York: Praeger, 1960); D. W. Fokkema, "Chinese Criticism of Humanism: Campaign against the Intellectuals," *CQ*, No. 26 (April–June, 1966), pp. 68–82; Rene Goldman, "Peking University Today," *CQ*, No. 7 (July–September, 1961), pp. 101–12; Merle Goldman, "The Unique 'Blooming and Contending' of 1961–62," *CQ*, No. 37 (January–March, 1969), pp. 54–84.

The number and variety of campaigns is enormous and each could presumably be classified along some or all of the following dimensions: (1) local versus nationwide campaigns, (2) short-term versus long-term campaigns with variations in (3) goals, (4) target populations, (5) timing, (6) scope, (7) intensity, (8) degree of organization, and (9) the degree to which participants' life activities are encompassed by demands for participation in campaign activities.

Scope of the Study

I am then dealing with two central problems: elite structure and elite change for a specific organizational subsystem, that is, Peking University and its faculty elites from 1949 to 1965. My purpose is to present a research design and preliminary findings in what must necessarily be a tentative form subject to a great deal of refinement and revision. In the pages that follow, I shall examine the sources from which relevant biographical data have been drawn, the nature of the population our samples claim to represent, the characteristics of our samples, and some findings derived for a selected subsample of the faculty elite. Although I shall attempt to test one hypothesis, this is not intended as an exercise in hypothesis testing, for that would require a degree of rigor in our data that we do not yet lay claim to.

Since I am approaching these materials from an empirical point of view, then one might ask why I chose a university for a research site and why Peking University in particular. Although factory and commune organizations would be equally serviceable research sites, my choice of a university meets some special requirements. There is, obviously, no regulation requiring that researchers choose sites in which they have had some personal experience. Relatively few students of industrial organizations have ever served as factory workers or managers, though one has drawn special attention by bringing to the sociology of industrial organizations the unique and edifying experience of technological expertise.[6] On the assumption that all institutions of higher learning share some processes in common, and that the familiarity that only a perpetual graduate student could have would be a useful aid in interpreting both documents and interviews, the choice seems justified.

Among the universe of universities, Peking University (hereafter referred to as Peita) was a logical choice. As the most prominent of China's universities, with a long and reasonably well-documented history, news from Peita appears with regularity in the national and local press, academic and political periodicals, and policy documents.[7] Pre-

[6] See W. H. Scott *et al.*, *Technical Change and Industrial Relations* (Liverpool, England: Liverpool University, 1956).

[7] Peita produced two editions—one in natural sciences, the other in humanities and social sciences—of an all-university journal, *Pei-ching ta-hsüeh hsüeh-pao* (Peking University Journal). With the onset of the Great Proletarian Cultural Revolution, both editions were withdrawn from publication and replaced by the organ of the Peita May Fourth Commune, *Hsin peita* (New Peking University). I have also been told that there was a periodical edited by students in the middle 1950's with the title, *Peita chou-*

liminary surveys of the literature, in and out of translation, promised documentary access. Higher-ranking members of Peita's faculty and staff occupy prominent places in the standard biographical reference works from Hong Kong, Japan, Taiwan, and the United States, and a significant sample of their published works can be found in library collections here and abroad, in both book and article form.[8]

Opportunities for interviews seemed particularly promising. A number of Western scholars, students, and journalists have been in and out of Peita for periods ranging from weeks to years. A few, particularly from the Soviet Union, served as resident faculty experts and played critical roles in Peita's early reorganization into a comprehensive university.[9] Preliberation graduates of Peita are well represented in the United States, Taiwan, and Hong Kong. They form readily accessible alumni associations wherever their number warrants. Postliberation graduates continue to make their way into Hong Kong, the United States, and Canada. Language was no small matter in the choice of Peita (as against other types of organization), for Peita students and staff are guaranteed speakers of the Mandarin dialect. Since this is my own second language, I was able to establish contact and carry out interviews without the aid (or interference) of interpreters. From this point of view the choice of Peita was expedient.

Since the purpose of the study is to develop a design for the study of social change in Communist China, its temporal scope confines it to the period after 1949. But temporal boundary lines are fluid. Students and faculty were actively involved in the Communist movement before liberation. The hunger strikes of 1948 formed the commitments of many whose activities in later years were subject to criticism or approbation. For older members of the faculty, formative experiences refer to the years of the Long March and before. Their experiences were also subject to scrutiny in postliberation campaigns. Thus, biographical data must account for developments that precede the period most central to our analysis.

In organizational terms, Peita did not take form as a comprehensive

---

pao (Peking University Weekly), but I have never been able to secure copies of this journal.

[8] A discussion of the limitations of these sources will appear in subsequent pages of this paper.

[9] In a brief trip to the Institute of the Peoples of Asia in Moscow during the summer of 1969, I met several "experts" who had served at Peita in the 1950's. Interviews were impossible then, but access was promised for another time. The names and affiliations of several Soviet experts at Peita are separately constituted in a file of foreign visitors to that institution.

university until the reorganization of 1952. For an understanding of the significance of this reorganization, the study must include the years immediately preceding. While biographical data begin with the earliest references found in the sources, 1949 marks the starting point for an analysis of organizational data. Biographic data were likewise collected from Red Guard publications through 1967, even though the study of Peking University draws to a close in 1965. Peita changed form once again in 1965 to become the New Peita Commune. The whiplash of the Great Proletarian Cultural Revolution (GPCR) brought down numerous well-known Peita figures and carried unknown figures to places of public prominence. A flood of Red Guard literature shed light on earlier events and personalities at Peita. While sources provided by the GPCR are of crucial value in this study, the events of this movement are still shrouded and obscured.[10] At the time research was underway, the complexity of cultural revolution at Peita was a severe handicap to this project. Thus, although Red Guard sources inform this study at all points, the events of the GPCR are themselves not included, and the study draws an arbitrary terminal date at 1965. The research design is, however, amended to include organizational and biographical data after 1965 so that the analysis may be extended as further and more reliable information emerges.

THE PEITA CASE: SOURCES AND SAMPLES

Under the auspices of grants from Fulbright-Hays and the Joint Committee on Contemporary China, I journeyed to Taiwan and Hong Kong to undertake a survey of resources on organizational change at Peita. During a six-month period in Taiwan (from November, 1967, to May, 1968), the resources of the Institute of International Relations, the library of the Ministry of Justice in the Department of Public Security, the Military Intelligence Library of the Ministry of Defense, and the Library of the Sixth Section of the K.M.T. Central Committee were placed at my disposal. While in Hong Kong (from June, 1968, to June, 1969), the voluminous files of the Union Research Institute, the biographical files of the U.S. Consulate-General, and the library holdings of Universities Service Centre provided the greater part of my documentation. In Taiwan and Hong Kong a total of

---

10 Victor Nee's fascinating account of the Cultural Revolution at Peita does little to remedy this situation. The sources he utilized parallel, but do not duplicate, my own. There are many contradictions, and partisanship obscures some important problems. See Nee, *The Cultural Revolution at Peking University,* special issue of the *Monthly Review,* XXI, No. 3 (July–August, 1969).

twenty-four interviews were conducted with former Peita students and staff. Although they overlap, the data derived from these sources can be classified into two broad categories, biographical and organizational. Organizational data are subdivided into two more categories: (1) organizational structure and behavior and (2) campaign structure and behavior. Since the study of elites is our principal concern here, I will restrict my discussion to the biographical data.

SOURCES OF BIOGRAPHICAL DATA

All sources were scoured for references to any individual who held Party, administrative, teaching, or research posts at Peita at any time between the years 1949 and 1965. Some students are also included, but their entries form a tiny proportion of the total and are primarily for future use. As of this date, a total of 568 individuals, excluding students, occupy the biographical file, and over twenty-five hundred entries have been recorded for this group.

The quality of the biographical entries reflects biases inherent in both major and minor sources. If only because of size limitations, few of the major sources of biographical data offer representative samples of the intelligentsia, much less of any particular organization's academic elite. The biographical files of the U.S. Consulate-General in Hong Kong provided data for about one-half of the Peita sample. Few, however, were under fifty years of age, and the majority of these were either in the social sciences or the humanities (the latter providing the lesser number). The reason for this is probably not that academic elites are constituted by social scientists and specialists in the humanities over the age of fifty, but that, for the period being analyzed, age and specialization are closely associated with the political prominence of academicians. Even though the young and the natural scientists, particularly those in specialized theoretical branches of the sciences, are underrepresented, a few notable exceptions do find their way into the files.[11]

Entries vary in composition. Social background information for academicians is seldom available except for academicians of advanced age and considerable political prominence. The consulate's files yield little information on personal associations, campaign behavior, sanctions applied as a consequence of campaign behavior, or the content of

---

[11] Those few include the noted mathematician, Hua Lo-keng; rocketry expert, Ch'ien Hsüeh-shen; and nuclear physicists, Ch'ien San-ch'iang, Wang Kan-ch'ang, and Ch'ien Wei-ch'ang.

published articles (although dates and titles of publications are often listed). Despite all of these limitations, the Hong Kong consulate files do produce a nearly exhaustive list of Party, state, mass organizational, academic, and international positions. There is an exception here, too, for Party and administrative positions below the level of university chancellor, vice-chancellor, dean, assistant dean, and first and second secretaries of the school Party committee are seldom listed. An occasional departmental chairmanship does get into the files, as do teaching positions. The latter, however, are seldom recorded if they are below the level of full professorships or lectureships. Again, age and political prominence are partially accountable for these deficiencies.

Not available at the time this paper was first written were biographical files maintained at Columbia University by Donald Klein, now partially reproduced in his *Biographic Dictionary of Chinese Communism, 1921–1965*.[12] While only six new and previously unknown figures were added as entries to the Peking University sample, the Klein files were of immeasureable value to this study, providing the most exhaustive cross check of both major and minor sources available anywhere. The inaccuracies of the Hong Kong consulate files, and particularly in the biographical sketches published by the URS, have been corrected, and all entries have been updated. Most important, the Klein files systematically record and conveniently label the innumerable changes in the titles of organizational units and the dates and durations of appointments that cause such endless confusion for all students engaged in aggregate biographical analysis. These files contained the most exhaustive compilation of academician's biographies of any of the sources used, and their unique feature—background information drawn from some of the biographical files of the American Embassy in Chungking in 1944—filled a good many blank spaces in the Peita file. To take advantage of these features, each entry in the Peita sample was compared to those in the Klein file for updating and correction before being recorded on IBM cards.

An additional 25 per cent of the sample was drawn from other English-language, Chinese, and Japanese sources. Howard Boorman's *Biographical Dictionary of Republican China* yielded very useful information for a few of the older Peita faculty.[13] Social background

---

[12] Donald W. Klein and Anne B. Clark, *Biographic Dictionary of Chinese Communism, 1921–1965* (Cambridge, Mass: Harvard University Press, 1971).

[13] Howard L. Boorman and Richard C. Howard (eds.), *Biographical Dictionary of Republican China*, Vols. I–III (New York: Columbia University Press, 1967–69).

information such as date and place of birth, primary, secondary, and undergraduate educational background were offered, as were excellent summaries of article and book publications, political experiences undergone and positions occupied during the Republican period, travel and representation abroad, personal associations and, in a few cases, details of postliberation campaign experiences. But dates of birth conflict sharply with those reported in other sources. The editors often declined to date educational background, educational positions held, and some preliberation political experiences recorded. Postliberation positions are sampled rather than exhausted.

One of the sources with which Boorman's dates are most in conflict is the URI's *Who's Who in Communist China,* another major source for Peita biographies.[14] The institute's entries, like those of the Chinese and Japanese sources in general, give greater space to academicians than do the Hong Kong consulate's files. Positions are exhausted in this case, and greater attention is given to dating each item.[15] The *Who's Who* lacks the attention to preliberation detail that Boorman's dictionary gives and it lists rather than analyzes publications. Some commentary is occasionally appended to items concerning campaign behavior, but they are not detailed.

For academicians at least, entries in Taiwan's *Chung-kung jen-ming lu* (Biographical Dictionary of Chinese Communists) are carbon copies of those in URI's *Who's Who.*[16] One exception concerns commentaries explaining campaign behavior or those appended to items describing the content of publications. The commentaries are evaluative and very biased.

Among the major sources used was the Japanese *Gendai chūgoku jinmei jiten* (A Biographical Dictionary of Contemporary Chinese). I found no better a coverage of academicians here than in the Taiwan and URI biographies, though a few more natural scientists were included. Though I was not able to determine who erred most, there are indications that errors are common in the Japanese listings of academic personnel.[17]

All the major sources were highly selective at least by age and political prominence. Conflicts in reported dates can be found among

---

[14] *Who's Who in Communist China,* Vols. I and II (Hong Kong: URI, 1966).

[15] The Hong Kong consulate frequently appends URS bulletins to their file entries.

[16] Kuo Hua-lun (ed.), *Chung-kung jen-ming lu* (Taipei: Institute of International Relations, 1967).

[17] *Gendai chūgoku jinmei jiten* (Tokyo: Kazan Kai, 1966). For one criticism of this source, see Ting Wang (ed.), *Niu-kuei she-shen chi* (A Collection of Ghosts and Monsters) (Hong Kong: San-chia-tien shu-wu, 1967), pp. 202–6.

all the sources cited. Social background and detailed campaign behavior data are relatively scarce. Only the Boorman dictionary gives information on personal associations, but for too few cases. This is a serious deficiency, for knowledge of personal associations is critical to any measurement of cohesion among members of the academic elite and between elites and nonelites. The most serious deficiency in all these sources is the total absence of information for academic organizational administrators—the men and women who staff the bureaus, offices, sections, and departments that make up school administrative structures.

In an effort to compensate for the deficiencies in the major sources, "minor" sources were also used. These included URS *Biographical Service* bulletins to supplement the *Who's Who* of 1966 and the biographical appendix to Cheng Chu-yuan's study of scientific and engineering manpower.[18] The latter source warrants a comment. For all the trouble it took to list twelve hundred scientists and engineers, the biographical index yields only the most meager results and must be supplemented by other sources. No sequential dates are provided; only positions held as of 1964 are listed. Dates of birth are in sharp conflict with other sources (ten years' difference in two cases). Dates of graduation refer only to graduate education and give only the date upon which the highest degree achieved was awarded. Of the positions possible, only positions in academic associations and in the Academy of Sciences, representation at national congresses or consultative conferences, and teaching positions are given. Some of this information can be supplemented by references in the text, since names are included in the index to the book. Despite its weaknesses, it is the only large-scale study of scientific personnel available.

Additional information on one particularly weak link in the sciences, the nuclear physicists, comes from British sources. Information on campaign behavior was supplemented by data from Ting Wang's study of victims of the GPCR.[19] Although this material postdates the period in which we are most interested, Ting Wang's review of historians' writings and their advocacies reflects earlier experiences of his subjects that are directly relevant to this study. Position data were checked and supplemented with the listings of every annual *Jen-min*

18 Cheng Chu-yuan, *Scientific and Engineering Manpower in Communist China, 1949–1963* (Washington, D.C.: U.S. Government Printing Office, 1965).

19 "Chinese Nuclear Scientists, Appendix A," *China Topics,* June 19, 1968; also, William L. Ryan and Sam Summerlin, *The China Cloud* (Boston: Little, Brown and Co., 1967). Ting (ed.), *Niu-kuei she-shen chi,* pp. 1–202.

shou-ts'e (People's Handbook). A search for both additional biographical data on scientists and for publication positions was undertaken by surveying three major academic bulletins for articles written by Peita professors, students, and staff, and all editorial positions occupied by Peita faculty and staff.[20] In order to increase the number of lower-ranking faculty and administrators included in the file, every item of organizational or campaign data that referred to Peita students, faculty, and staff was recorded as a biographical entry.[21]

A unique source from Taiwan which was central to this task was an article by Wang Chün in *Fei-ch'ing yen-chiu* (Research on Communist Bandit Affairs) detailing Peita's structure.[22] In the article, the author claimed to give a complete listing of the faculty as of 1965, including all administrative and teaching positions from the school level, through departments, teaching and research offices, programs, and specializations to small groups. It is unfortunate that a good many entries included faculty members long since deceased. Serious errors occurred in the subunit listings: some faculty members listed were definitely not at Peita, and an irrelevant ideological theme pervaded Wang's study. Despite these failings, Wang's article is still the most exhaustive single academic organizational listing available. Some errors can be checked against more reliable primary sources, others must await additional information.

Finally, interviews were an important source of information entered into the biographical file. Student informants and interviewees were asked to name their teachers and to indicate their knowledge of faculty campaign behavior, the sanctions applied to faculty personnel, associations, life styles, attitudes, living and working conditions, and the authority of teaching personnel. Student interviewees proved about as knowledgeable in these areas as their American counterparts. Unless special circumstances allowed (teaching assistantships, graduate

[20] *K'o-hsüeh t'ung-pao* (Bulletin of the Natural Sciences); *Pei-ching ta-hsüeh hsüeh-pao,* natural sciences and social sciences editions.

[21] The principal sources were: *CKCN; CKCNP; JMJP; Kuang-ming jih-pao* (Bright Daily) (hereafter *KMJP*); *Pei-ching jih-pao* (Peking Daily); *Pei-ching wan-pao* (Peking Evening News); *Pei-ching ta-hsüeh hsüeh-pao; Hsin peita; Chingkangshan* (The Chingkang Mountains), the organ of the cultural revolution group at Tsinghua University; *Hsin chien-she* (New Construction); and *Jen-min chiao-yü* (People's Education). Six individual biographies were constructed wholly from this type of information yielding fairly complete career listings from student days to occupancy of full professorial status. In other cases, these entries either duplicated or supplemented biographical data from major sources.

[22] Wang Chün, "Fei-kung k'ung-chih hsia ti pei-ching ta-hsüeh" (Peking University under Communist Bandit Control), *Fei-ch'ing yen-chiu,* July, 1967, pp. 63–67.

work, family connections, inside information), most students were only vaguely familiar with faculty life. Aside from special contributions from informants who commented on the entire Peita name list, the most valuable information interviewees were able to supply was the extent to which punitive sanctions were employed against the most prominent of Peita's faculty in the course of successive campaigns, and much of this information was secondhand.

These minor sources and interviews provided the final 25 per cent of the Peita sample. As in the case of major sources, older, more politically prominent, higher-ranking faculty in the fields of social sciences and humanities are overrepresented. The supplementary data provided by minor sources did, however, yield a better balance than would have been obtained had only major sources been utilized, and some totally void areas were given substance, if only for a few cases.

COMPILATION OF BIOGRAPHICAL DATA

All biographical information was recorded from primary and secondary sources onto file cards and then transferred to IBM data cards. The latter are subdivided into several categories, each introduced by an alphabetical code. Each category represents a different type of information organized into a format peculiar to that type. Hence, for every individual biography, entries are divided into the following categories: social background, associational positions, Academy of Sciences positions, state positions, Communist Party positions, Third Party positions, Youth League positions, mass organizational positions, international positions, publication positions, university Party positions, university administration positions, university teaching positions, campaign behavior, status adjustments, publications content, and coalition behavior. A brief description of the format for each category follows below.

Social background cards begin with a four-digit identification code assigned to each individual in the file. A combination of numerical and alphabetical codes designates birthplace, home town, and the locus of education from primary to graduate training. Location codes identify region of the globe, country, and type of location (a code combining primary function of the locality and population size) for locations abroad. For locations in China, province and type of locality are indicated. Dates of birth are read literally, as are dates for education at each educational level, dates of graduation, and dates marking the receipt of degrees and diplomas. For education at all levels, alphabetical and numerical codes indicate the type of school attended (such as public, private, Christian, other religious, nonsectarian, graduate, undergraduate, military, polytechnical, or liberal arts), whether the individual graduated or merely attended, the field of study (by discipline, subdiscipline, and specialty), and the title of the degree awarded. Ethnic, marital, and religious statuses are designated by alphabetical codes, and an alphabetical code indicates whether the individual was living or dead in the last year for which information was accepted—1967. Dates of death are likewise indicated. Age at the time of death or for those still living in 1967 is classified into ten-year intervals beginning at the age of fifteen and ending at seventy-five and above.

Position cards follow essentially the same format, though there are variations in the information entered and the codes utilized. Associational positions refer to all academic associations in which the individual has ever occupied a position (for example, the Peking Society of Historians or the China Physics Association). Every entry of the associational type is recorded until all such entries are exhausted. Dates indicating when occupancy of the position began and terminated are read literally. Where only one date is given, a judgment must be made as to whether it represents the initial or terminal date. Alphabetical codes then designate the title of the association, the name of the position, and the subunit of the association for which the position applies. Position codes allow for varying degrees of membership, directorship, chairmanship, secretaryship, or presidency. Subunit codes permit a wide range of variations including committees, conferences, presidiums, congresses, councils, groups, and secretariats. A levels code indicates the territorial level of the position (from village to central), and the region and province code provides an indication of its specific location. Any change in any one of these items requires a new entry. Thus, if a person was a delegate to a conference of the China Physics Association in Peking from 1954 to 1955 and simultaneously a member of its standing committee, two separate entries will be recorded using the same dates and titles but reporting two different position titles.

The format alters slightly for other types of positions. Academy of Sciences position cards carry the same information, but allow for research positions. Publication position cards use codes identifying the title of the publication, editorial board membership or directorship (in two degrees), and an identification of the contents and target of the publication. International position cards indicate degrees of membership and whether the organizational unit with which the position is associated is an international conference, an international mission, an international organization, or a friendship association. Codes also indicate whether the organizational position is primarily political or academic. Finally, the non-China region code indicates the countries to which international positions refer.

University Party, administrative, and teaching position cards are more detailed. A code naming each school supplements dates, unit, and subunit information. Party position entries rely on the same code as all other Party positions, but administrative and teaching position entries use separate codes specific to universities. This is also true for the designation of subunits. The same code indicating types of schools and fields of study in the social background cards is applied to each entry on the university Party, administration, and teaching position cards. As is true for all types of data, cards are repeated until all information in each category is exhausted.

The format for the remaining cards differs in each instance. Cards containing entries on campaign behavior begin with the date on which the action cited took place. Where that date is not given, which is frequently the case, the date on which the reference was published serves in its stead. An alphabetical campaign code identifies the campaign to which the reference applies. What follows is an index of behavior coded into scores which designate what direction the action was deemed to have taken and its intensity. Three degrees of response are allowed both for direction and intensity. Thus, an action may be labeled positive, negative, or neither positive nor negative in direction; high, low, or medium in intensity. Each combination of direction and intensity yields a score. If a label has been attached to the individual as a result of his actions, an alphabetical code indicates the direction of label in three degrees: positive, moderate, and low, along with a code designating the specific label applied (such as rightist, left-opportunist, or right-opportunist).

Finally, if sanctions are said to have been employed because of the action an individual is alleged to have taken, a code designates the nature of the sanction. This code also allows three degrees of direction: positive, negative, and mixed. Finally, a gross indication of the nature of the sanctions applied follows in coded form, showing whether any number of political positions increased, decreased, or were totally eliminated because of the sanction, whether any number of academic positions were affected in the same way, whether rank was so affected, and whether salary was so affected. Any permutation of any of these possibilities is read out of a code book containing all possible permutations.

Status adjustment cards describe class and family origins whether estimated from biographical data or known and confirmed. An alphabetical code designates the particular class or family status that applies. If an individual's status is known to have changed at any time, the change is dated in the same way that dates are applied to positions. The nature of the change is indicated in code, and the reason for the change is given if known (punishment for ideological errors, administrative adjustment, reward for ideological commitment, or some other reason).

Publications content cards record every known published article and book. The date of the publication (month and year) is given, and the title of the periodical, the target population, and content of the publication (political for academicians, academic for academicians) appear in code. A code also indicates the type of article (ideological, organizational, technical, policy, general description) and whether or not an ideological preface accompanies the publication.

Coalition behavior cards complete the biographical "deck." Every mention of association between the subject and any other individual, in documentary or interview sources, is a datum for coalition entries. As in the publications content cards, if the date of the alleged association is mentioned, it is recorded; if not, the date of the publication in which an association is alleged serves the same purpose. Codes indicate whether the association is within Peita or outside, Peita elite or nonelite, and the nature of the relationship (personal friendship, teacher-student, joint research, political clique). Finally, an identification number is assigned to the person with whom a relationship is alleged, and that number is entered on the card.

CHARACTERISTICS OF THE SAMPLE

At the date of this writing, the 568 cases constituting the Peita file are recorded onto IBM cards. Organizational data, including aggregate statistics on the changing size and composition of Peita's staff and student body, are simultaneously being prepared for the computer. Until the data are fully recorded and enumerated, we can only provide estimates of the relationship between the sample and the larger population it represents. How scientific a sample these cases really are must await an analysis of the computer's output. We can, however, make some tentative statements about the sample's relationship to its universe.

Sources reporting the size of Peita faculty and staff vary both in the scope of their enumerations and the manner in which statistics are reported. The same sources report staff and faculty in separate calculations for one year and then embrace both in the same figure the following year. One source of constant frustration is the absence of any definition of "staff," though statistical breakdowns make it reasonably clear that teaching ranks are not included in that category. Another frequent source of confusion, common to all statistics of the period, is the expression of increases in the size of the faculty and/or staff as percentages of some prior, unreported total. A spot check of those academic terms for which authoritative numbers are available suggests that such percentages are "guesstimates" published in anticipation of official statistical reports. They are notoriously unreliable. Finally, reports of the size of faculties are frequently rounded out to the nearest thousand. But where authoritative reports are available, secondary and primary sources are in reasonable agreement, and a sufficient number of authoritative reports cover the years with which we are concerned to permit broad comparisons between sample and universe.[23]

23 Authoritative statistics on faculty size and composition are available for 1949, 1952, 1953, 1955, 1956, 1958, 1959, 1961, 1962, 1964, and 1965. The reported figures have been rounded to the nearest hundred for those over one thousand. Sources include the following: Wang, "Fei-kung k'ung-chih hsia ti pei-ching ta-hsüeh," p. 72; Lu P'ing, "Peking University Now Trains for Communism," *Communist China Digest*, No. 19 (1959), pp. 70–71; Tsun Chieh-t'ang, "Wo-men k'o-ai ti hsüeh-hsiao pei-ching ta-hsüeh" (Peking University, the School We Love), in Ma Yin-ch'u *et al.*, *Chung-kuo chi-ko kao-teng hsüeh-hsiao chieh-shao* (An Introduction to Several Institutions of Higher Education in China) (Hong Kong: San-lien Bookstore, 1957); "Pei-ching ta-hsüeh tsung-ho hsing ta-hsüeh" (Peking University: A Comprehensive University), *TKP* (Hong Kong), February 25, 1955; "Chin-jih pei-ching ta-hsüeh" (Peking University Today), *TKP*, May 18, 1964; "Pei-ching ta-hsüeh ch'ing-nien chiao-shih pien kan pien hsüeh hsün-su ch'eng-chang" (Young Teachers at Peking University Mature Rapidly through Both Work and Study), *CKCNP* (Peking), January 25, 1961; "Pei-ching kao-teng hsüeh-hsiao hsün-li" (A Tour of Peking Higher Schools), *Chung-kuo hsin-wen t'ung-hsün ch'ao* (China News Bulletin), August 12, 1959.

The most comprehensive single volume I have yet found is a Taiwan source listing all higher schools in all categories as of 1958. For each school listed, departments and courses are given. A brief history is appended to the description of its organizational structure, and in some instances student and faculty data are appended. Peita is included in the volume. Administrative Department of the Ministry of Justice, *Fei-ch'ing tiao-ch'a chüan-pao: fei-wei ko-chi chiao-yü chi-pen ch'ing-k'uang tiao-ch'a* (A Special Investigatory Report on Communist China: An Investigation of the Basic Situation at Various Levels in Communist Chinese Education) (Taiwan: Ministry of Justice, 1958). An allegedly updated version of this same source was published in May, 1963, by the same authors but bearing a new title: *Fei-ch'ing yen-chiu chüan-pao: kung-fei ti kao-teng chiao-yü*

COMPOSITION

When Chinese Communist troops entered Peking in 1949, the first of a series of measures to reorganize the university for service to the new society began. Peita was moved from its former site (now the address of the Peking Industrial Academy) to a new campus on the grounds where Yenching University once stood. At the time, Peita was headed by six faculties (*hsüeh-yüan*): humanities, theoretical sciences, law, engineering, agriculture, and medicine. Under the faculties, 213 faculty members in 25 departments (*hsi*) and 21 teaching and research groups (*chiao-yen tzu*) offered a total of 370 courses to a student body varying between 1,824 and 2,349 members, 7 per cent of whom were female and 23 of whom were foreign students. Twenty laboratories (*shih-yen shih*) served the science departments of the university, and the Peita library serving all departments calculated it holdings at one million volumes.[24]

By contrast, the Peita of 1965, the last year for which comparable statistics are available, was headed by two faculties (humanities and social sciences, and theoretical sciences.) [25] Under these two faculties some 2,300 faculty members in 20 departments, 107 teaching and research officers (*chiao-yen shih*), 22 programs (*chüan-yeh*), five specializations (*chüan-men hua*), and two teaching and research groups offered over 400 courses to some 9,300 students, 50 per cent of whom were said to be of worker-peasant origin and 25 per cent of whom were female. Some 400 foreign students attended Peita that year. One hundred twenty-nine experimental laboratories serviced the science departments, and the Peita library, with both departmental branches and central collections, calculated its holdings at 2,400,000 volumes. University buildings covered an area of some 315,000 square meters, including 40 factories and 30 agricultural fields. Besides the university proper, Peita's administration assumed responsibility for at least one Marxist-Leninist night school, a worker-peasant accelerated middle school, a regularly affiliated middle school, and a correspondence school.

These figures give some idea of the magnitude of the change in

(A Special Report of Research on the Communists: Communist Bandit Higher Education) ; however, apart from updated commentaries in the introduction, the text is borrowed almost verbatim from the 1958 version.

[24] Apart from the sources mentioned above, see Feng Yu-lan, "Wo-men ti meng pien-ch'eng le hsien-shih" (Our Dreams Have Become a Reality), *Wen-hui pao* (Cultural Exchange Daily) (Hong Kong), May 18, 1955, p. 5.

[25] The statistics are in Wang, "Fei-kung k'ung-chih hsia ti pei-ching ta-hsueh," p. 73.

Peita's size and structure after 1949. Faculty ranks had increased by nearly ten times the 1949 figure. If the statistics are in any way reliable, faculty growth at Peita occurred in four separate phases. In the first phase, between 1949 and the reorganization of the university in 1952, the number of teachers quadrupled. Though a small proportion might have included young graduates returning to China from Europe and the United States, most of the increase reflected the absorption of senior scholars from departments of surrounding colleges melded into Peita's structure. These were academicians whose teaching careers spanned the interwar period between the Sino-Japanese and Civil wars. By reason of political prominence, age, and rank, the increase in their number is well represented in our sample.

Faculty ranks maintained a steady rate of growth in the second phase, from 1952 to 1956, reflecting both natural increases from absorption of new graduates of Chinese institutions of higher learning (shown in aggregate statistics, but not in the sample presented here) and the addition of returned students from the United States. By the end of the period in 1956, one hundred additional people entered Peita's faculty. The most publicized among the new entrants were those drawn from the pool of nearly five hundred professional scientists, engineers, and qualified graduate students who returned to China in the aftermath of the Korean War and the McCarthy period. The most neglected group, from the point of view of the sample, were those who graduated from Chinese institutions of higher learning in 1949, 1950, and 1951. There are a number of reasons why this might be so. They were politically transitional, bereft of the possible protection that rank and notoriety might have provided against sanctions applied in early campaigns. Their opportunities for mobility might well have been displaced by the returned students, especially those in the sciences. It is also possible that their involvement in revolutionary activities just after the take-over led to their absorption into nonacademic careers. For whatever reason, relatively few are found in the sample, and those few seldom achieved full professorial rank. The returned students, however, are represented. They received considerable attention in the press and rose through faculty ranks in rapid succession. They are not, however, equally well represented. Returning natural scientists and engineers of known rank won greater attention than social scientists and specialists in the humanities or first year graduate students and graduates of American liberal arts colleges.

In the third phase of faculty growth, Peita's teachers nearly doubled in number. Unlike the first phase, which is attributable to the reorganization of higher education, and the second, which reflects external events, the third phase was almost entirely the result of a succession of overlapping campaigns which swept Peita between the end of the second phase in 1956 and the end of the third in 1960. One of the purposes of this series of campaigns, among others, was to bring young graduates and staff assistants into faculty ranks at the utmost possible speed. Thus, the period from 1956 to 1960 witnessed the most significant increase since the reorganization of 1952. Faculty ranks swelled over the 1,000 mark to nearly double the 1956 count.

Relaxation of entry requirements, advanced graduation, revised placement schedules, and open recruitment into the ranks of the elite yielded vast changes in the composition of the faculty. Of the 1,554 teachers in 1959, the peak year of expansion, only 200 or 13 per cent occupied the ranks of professors (*chiao-shou*) or associate professors (*fu chiao-shou*). The remaining 87 per cent were either lecturers (*chiang-shih*) or assistants (*chu-chiao*). The 1961 figures confirm this expansion of lower faculty ranks: 85 per cent (close enough to our 87 per cent) of the faculty were said to be "young" teachers, more than 50 per cent of whom assumed their posts after the educational revolution of 1958. Of this group, 70 per cent were in the natural sciences. Since the title of "lecturer" was most often reserved for faculty members drawn from the Academy of Sciences, central ministries and departments, or from other universities, we can assume that the bulk of the expansion focused even more narrowly on the ranks of the assistants. The press paid special attention to the training of young postgraduates, so this group is represented in the files. But the emphasis is on young scientists serving under ranking faculty of public note. Younger men and women serving under lesser figures do not appear in the published accounts of the period. A smaller number of young social scientists and humanists earned similar attention before the Antirightist Campaign, and young rebels of the Hundred Flowers period as well as critics of the Antirightist era enter the files as signatories of *ta-tze pao* (big-character newspapers) and critical articles.

None of this information yields complete entries. Dates of graduation, current faculty status, field of study, association with senior faculty, and department of affiliation are the maximum such references provide. Their inclusion is all the more important because young graduates of this period were deeply influenced by Sovietization of the sciences, the leadership of students returned from Europe and the United States, and, in the social sciences and humanities, the continued influence of faculty born and bred in China. For the young and old alike, it was a period of crisis and ambivalence. The failure of the sample to fully represent young faculty is an important weakness, though interviews and limited documentary sources permit some generalizations about them.

Little change occurred in the growth of faculty ranks during the first four years of the fourth and final phase from 1960 to 1965. Some four hundred additional persons entered teaching positions between 1964 and 1965. By 1965, members of the faculty bearing professorial or associate professorial rank numbered 318, but our figures are unclear as to the sources of this expansion. It may reflect promotions among new entrants of the third phase, the appointment and promotion of students and faculty returned from the Soviet Union, the promotion to faculty rank of graduates who had been passed by in the second and third phases, or possibly all three.[26]

The final period is the most incomplete from the point of view of the sample's representativeness. The impact of the Antirightist Campaign is revealed in that sector of the sample most accessible to public view. Young scientists returning from study in the Soviet Union and Eastern Europe are known only as aggregate numbers. Young social scientists and specialists in the humanities of this period are occasionally mentioned, but little social background information can be derived for this sector of the sample. With the decline of Soviet influence and the growing age gap between the returned students of the

---

26 "Pu-che chao-sheng jen-wu shih mei-yu tso ch'u cheng-ch'üeh ku-chi kao-teng hsüeh-siao p'u-pien fa-sheng fang-shih pu-kou hsien-hsiang" (Those Who Were Responsible for Carrying Out Enrollment Tasks Did Not Make Accurate Estimates—Shortage of Housing Space Is Widespread), *KMJP*, October 27, 1956, URI files 11705; Chang Ching-shan and Hsü Ts'ai, "Chin-chien pan-hsiao, k'o-fu k'un-nan, pei-ching ta-hsueh, ssu-ch'uan i-hsüeh yuan ts'ai-ch'u chi-chi shih-shih pan-ti tao ti k'uai-pan, pan-pu-tao ti t'an ch'ing-ch'u" (Manage the Schools with Diligence, Overcome Difficulties: Peking University and Szechwan Medical School Adopt Positive Approaches to Handle Quickly What They Can and Clarify What They Cannot), *CKCNP*, November 24, 1956, URI files 36520; "Ch'ao-chu kuo-wai ti t'ung-hsüeh men, p'eng-yu men, hsi-wang ni-men tsao-jih cheng-ch'u hui-kuo" (Fellow Overseas Chinese Students Abroad: Friends, We Hope You Will Strive to Return to Your Homeland Soon), *KMJP*, April 2, 1957, URI files 42118; "Chi-nien pei-ching ta-hsüeh liu-shih chou-nien" (Commemorating Peking University's Sixtieth Anniversary), *China News Agency Dispatch*, April 24, 1958, URI files 42116; "Ch'ung-fang chung-kuo: Wen Teh chiao-shou hai tsai pei-ta" (Return Interview in China: Professor Winter Is Still at Peita), *Wen-hui pao*, April 27, 1958, URI files 42116; "Ch'ien-chin! kuang-jung ti chiao-shih tui-wu" (Forward, Ranks of the Glorious Teachers), *KMJP*, September 30, 1959, URI files 42110311. Additional sources from the same files provide departmental figures.

mid-fifties and their students of the sixties, knowledge of the young elite becomes strategic. By comparison it is a generation increasingly subject to native Chinese influences. The Nieh Yuan-tzu's of the GPCR owe their socialization to the events of the Antirightist Campaign and the Great Leap recovery period. Generalizations based upon this sector of the sample must be most tentative. Interviews and the revelations of GPCR publications are prime sources of information on the academic generations of the 1960's.

The representativeness of the Peita biographical file varies from period to period. After 1959, entries in the file are decreasingly representative of the universe of Peita faculty. Minor sources help to compensate for the deficiencies in the file, but for limited categories of information only.

However much faculty ranks in general expanded between 1949 and 1965, that expansion was sporadic. It brought disparate groups into Peita's academic elite, and added disproportionately to lower faculty ranks. The four phases of growth opened the doors into Peita's elite for four different generations of academicians who were diverse in background, experience, socialization, and outlook. Phase one placed faculty members of prewar and wartime standing, as well as early returned students, into the new Peita elite. Many were in their forties and fifties, and were personal witnesses to or active participants in the Civil War. Both those who were directly involved in wartime activities and those who were not were subject to the first Chinese Communist attempt to socialize the academic elite to the new society's norms in the course of the campaigns designed to revolutionize the intelligentsia in the early fifties.

Phase two belonged to the returned scientists: the products of Cal Tech and M.I.T., whose personal commitments to the goals of the new system were high, but experience with it, minimal, and socialization under it, negligible. Most were in their twenties and thirties. Phase three introduced a new generation, almost wholly the products of education under the new regime. They were young, eager to assume roles of responsibility in Peita's growing elite, and subject to pressure from three sources: Sovietization of the early and mid-fifties, academic superiors trained in Western Europe and the United States, and anti-Western revolutionization in the course of intensive campaigns against bourgeois idealism in the late fifties. Phase four is more difficult to assess. Many who entered in this phase were trained in the Soviet Union and absent from China during the big push of the late fifties.

Cohesion between generational groups in elite ranks was probably low, though we are not entitled to draw a final conclusion until we know what measures were taken to bridge the generational gap.

Finally, while mobility across the status gap between the faculty elite and the student body of lower participants was high during the four phases, and particularly high during phase three, interrank mobility and probably cohesion within faculty elite ranks was extremely low. We have already pointed out the disproportionate expansion of lower faculty ranks. In 1954, of a total of 744 faculty members, 130 (18 per cent) were full professors, 80 (11 per cent) were associate professors, and an estimated 534 (72 per cent) were teaching assistants and staff. Ten years later, and well after the big push of the third phase, there was no change at all in the number of professors or associate professors. Their percentages of the total faculty of that year (1,900), however, were a mere 7 per cent and 4 per cent, respectively. Five hundred (26 per cent) of the faculty occupied the rank of lecturer, and an estimated 1,190 (63 per cent) were assistants or staff.[27] If I am correct in suggesting that a fair proportion of lecturers did not include young graduates, then faculty status was clearly malapportioned.

But it was not only faculty status that was poorly allocated. It was the full and associate professor, particularly the former, who concurrently served as university administrator, Party committeeman at the university, municipal, and central levels, committeeman of the State Planning Commission and Commission for Science and Technology, member of the board of the Academy of Sciences and of the editorial boards for important publications, and national and international delegate to conferences and congresses. The power of academic spokesmanship—the power to plead the cause of one's own academic interests and to draw upon the resources of the state for their pursuit—was their privilege. One might respond that higher status means greater visibility, and greater visibility means greater vulnerability. The Feng Yu-lan's, Fang Chih's, and Ma Yin-ch'u's appear far more often as the villains in the public press than lowly assistants. But, as one interviewee put it, "full professors like Feng Yu-lan might be vulnerable, but young faculty members were expendable. When Feng Yu-lan came before the entire school to hear the accusations against him,

---

27 "Shou-tu kao-teng hsueh-hsiao chin san-ko yüeh lai ti-shang le san-pai ming chiang-shih ho chiao-shou" (Capital Higher Schools Promote Three Hundred Lecturers and Professors in the Past Three Months), *KMJP*, February 26, 1956, p. 3; Wang, "Fei-kung k'ung-chih hsia ti pei-ching ta-hsüeh," p. 65.

everyone stood up out of respect and read from prepared statements. He did not have to dig ditches, carry heavy loads in midwinter, or even suffer violent face-to-face criticisms despite the violence of written attacks upon him. Young teachers like myself were not so fortunate." [28]

Though this was but one case among many, and although the author of the statement was a victim of the Antirightist Campaign, his point merits consideration. Judging from the fate of a good many rightists, the protective function of faculty eminence supplemented the power of academic spokesmanship, and the prestige of professorial rank.

THE SUBSAMPLE

These generalizations about the nature of academic spokesmanship and those who exercised its powers must remain merely impressions until they can be confirmed by more systematic methods. It was with this intent in mind that a subsample of Peking University faculty was drawn for a much more rigorous analysis. It is not, unfortunately, a scientific subsample, and indeed it could not be given the conditions imposed upon the data. The criterion for selection was simple. The most complete entries in the Peita faculty file were selected for preliminary analysis and in order to test computer programs. One hundred four individuals of the 586 in the initial file constitute the faculty subsample.

Choosing the best entries imposed an immediate bias, for as would be expected, the best were by definition the most prominent, and the most prominent were likely to be found among male faculty members above the age of 45 in the theoretical and social sciences and the humanities. The sample is then weighted against younger men and women in the applied sciences and professions. It tells us a great deal more about men who began their tenures at Peita before 1958 than after, and is weighted against those who returned from the Soviet Union to accept lower-level teaching positions in the natural sciences and those whose training was all or mostly indigenous in whatever field. Despite these failings, however, we do obtain a good sampling of men whose status sets are above the minimum size (that is, contain more than one position) and for whom some background data are available.

[28] Interview No. 17 (September 4, 1968). Interviewee was an assistant in the Department of Chinese Language and Literature from 1956 to 1958.

Specifically, the sample stresses the upper middle and older age brackets. Of the 104 cases in the sample, the ages of 63 (60.6 per cent) are known. None fell into the 15–25 or 26–35 age group, and only 3 (2.9 per cent) fell within the 36–45 age group. Eighteen (17.3 per cent), 24 (23.1 per cent), and 15 (14.4 per cent) fell into the 46–55, 56–65, and 66–75 age groups, respectively, and only 3 (2.9 per cent) were 76 years of age or older.

Twenty-nine (28.9 per cent) of the total were known to have been born in China, and only one abroad. Those who traced their origins to East and Central-South China dominate the sample. Only three-quarters of the twenty-nine China-born came from these two areas: thirteen from East and nine from Central-South China, about evenly distributed between the provinces of Shantung, Kiangsu, Anhwei, Chekiang, Fukien, Honan, Hunan, Kiangsi, Kwangtung, and Hupeh. The largest single contributor was Chekiang province, with five Peita faculty members out of the total. The number was too small to warrant inclusion of specific localities.

The sample is also sexually lopsided, with males constituting 76.9 per cent (or 80 cases). Female academicians number a mere ten (9.6 per cent), which is close to the 7 per cent said to have been present in faculty ranks in 1949, but far from the 25 per cent reported in 1965. Fourteen (13.5 per cent) are of unknown gender, which simply means that informants identified them by the characters in their names, if at all. Only two members of non-Han minority groups found their way into the sample.

Information on primary and secondary education is too sparse to warrant its inclusion in the sample. But for higher education a sufficient amount of data exists to permit some generalization and cross comparison. One word of warning applies to the data presented here: since most faculty members in this sample obtained their higher education in several different schools, often in China and abroad, and received multiple degrees, the total number here refers to higher educational statuses rather than to individuals. This factor inflates 104 individuals into 146 statuses, but it does not seriously misstate the relationships described.

If all these statuses are grouped by date of entry into and graduation from higher institutions of learning, they describe event cohorts—in this case, entry and graduation cohorts.[29] Dates of entry are more elusive than dates of graduation. Only 45 of the 146 cases (30.8 per cent) bear dates of entry, but 109 (74.7 per cent) bear dates of graduation. Expressed in terms of decades, the Peita entry cohorts span the first to the fourth decades of this century, and graduation cohorts, the first to the fifth. Ten (22.2 per cent) of the subsample entered higher institutions in the first decade of this century, 19 (42.2 per cent) in the twenties, 12 (26.7 per cent) in the thirties, and only 4 (8.9 per cent) in the forties. Nine (8.3 per cent) graduated within the first decade, 30 (29.5 per cent) in the twenties, 40 (36.7 per cent) in the thirties, 20 (16.4 per cent) in the forties, 9 (8.3 per cent) in the fifties, and only 1 (.9 per cent) in the sixties. The entry cohorts and graduation cohorts of the 1920's and 1930's constitute the overwhelming majority of the subsample. We are thus talking, almost exclusively, about phase one faculty (see discussion above under "Composition"). The returned students of the Korean War and McCarthy periods (phase two) and those whose experiences were shaped by the early campaigns (phase three) are poorly represented. The returned students from the Soviet Union (phases three and four) and the indigenously trained (phase four) are virtually nonexistent in the subsample.

Phase one graduation cohorts were overwhelmingly products of the American educational system. Of the 146 cases, 95 (65.4 per cent) obtained their education primarily outside of China, 29 (19.9 per cent) primarily in China; and of those who obtained their education abroad, 71 (74.4 per cent) went to American schools. Twenty-one (22.1 per cent) either attended or graduated from schools in England, France, and Germany, and only 2 built their academic qualifications on Soviet experience. Phase one graduate cohorts were as likely to have obtained college and graduate degrees abroad as they were to have obtained college degrees in China and graduate degrees abroad. Thus, a significant number of those who spent any part of their college years abroad were abroad for a decade or more. Those who returned in the thirties and forties accepted teaching positions almost immediately and

---

[29] For a brief discussion of cohort analysis, see Norman Ryder, "The Cohort as a Concept in the Study of Social Change," *American Sociological Review*, XXX, No. 6 (December, 1965), 843–62. A cohort is an aggregate of individuals who experience the same event within the same time interval. A "birth cohort"—all those born in the same time interval and aging together—is a unit in demographic studies. One can also speak of an "event cohort" as, for example, the "Great Depression cohort."

moved rapidly into full professorships. A few were already assuming administrative positions in the forties. A smaller number stayed abroad for postgraduate work, and a few others, whose higher education was primarily obtained in China, built careers in politics and publishing.

Phase one graduation cohorts were predominantly products of modern rather than classical schools, public as opposed to private institutions, and nondenominational rather than Christian schools. For 115 (78.8 per cent) of the 146 cases, the type of school attended is known: 77 (67.0 per cent) attended or graduated from graduate schools; 27 (23.5 per cent) were products of liberal arts colleges; 6 (5.2 per cent) earned their qualifications in polytechnical schools or institutes, 2 (1.7 per cent) in cadre-training institutions, and 1 each (0.9 per cent) in commercial institutes, comprehensive universities, or professional schools.

The 29 who stayed at home attended a variety of institutions. The Peking College of Education, Chiaotung University, and Nan-k'ai University each contributed 2 (6.8 per cent) to the phase one graduation cohorts. Peking Union Medical College (PUMC), Ningpo Normal College, Peiyang University, Sun Yat-sen University in the Soviet Union, and Southwest Central University (Chungking) each provided 1 additional entrant to those cohorts. But the largest proportion traced their pedigrees to Tsinghua University and Peking National University: 9 (31.0 per cent) from the former and 5 (17.2 per cent) from the latter.

In terms of the fields in which phase one graduation cohorts earned their statuses, the theoretical sciences occupy a dominant place. Sixty (41.1 per cent) of the 146 cases were specialists in the theoretical sciences and most of them (28, or 46.7 per cent of the 60) were physicists, with 6 nuclear physicists among their number. Biology, chemistry, and mathematics follow in rank order. The social sciences are the next most prominent disciplines. Twenty-eight (19.2 per cent) straddled the fields of economics, philosophy, history, political science, psychology, anthropology, and archaeology and geography, in that order of magnitude. Ten (6.9 per cent) specialized in the humanities, in languages and literature and in poetry. Nine (6.2 per cent) were professionals in education, law, library science, and cadre-training. The smallest contingent was made up of 6 (4.1 per cent) applied scientists in the fields of geology and metallurgy. Here, too, the biases of the subsample are at least partially evident: while some of the phase two scientists are among the theoretical scientists listed here, few of the engineers who returned in the fifties and none of the applied scientists of Soviet training appear in the subsample. It does, however, parallel the phase one group in the larger sample from which it is drawn.

As Table 50 indicates, a shift away from the social sciences and toward the theoretical sciences is apparent through all the graduation cohorts in the subsample, and the ratio of theoretical to social scientists reversed in the thirties until the theoretical scientists dominated the graduation cohort of the forties. Since the numbers are small, these figures must be treated with caution, but a strictly *Gestalt* comparison between the larger sample and the subsample would suggest that the trend for the subsample was paralleled in the larger group. Whether the shift resulted from changed rules of admissions in American institutions that served most often as their alma maters in this period, or from the coming of age of polytechnical training centers and theoretical science curricula in China, from increased opportunities for scholarships or changing commitments and aspirations are possibilities that remain open to speculation.

TABLE 50

HIGHER EDUCATION FIELDS OF STUDY OF PEKING UNIVERSITY
FACULTY ELITE SUBSAMPLE

Field of Study	Decade in Which Higher Education Was Completed (percentages in parentheses)				
	1910–20	1921–30	1931–40	1941–50	1951–60
Natural sciences	2 (28.6)	11 (39.3)	17 (46.0)	13 (65.0)	9 (100.0)
Social sciences	3 (42.9)	13 (46.4)	9 (24.3)	3 (15.0)	0
Applied sciences	0	0	4 (10.8)	1 (5.0)	0
Humanities	1 (14.3)	2 (7.1)	4 (10.8)	2 (10.0)	0
Professions	1	2	3	1	0
Total	7 (100.1)	28 (99.9)	37 (100.0)	20 (100.0)	9 (100.0)

Finally, as Table 51 makes clear, for those for whom both age and field of specialization were known, theoretical scientists included more of the younger age group than the social sciences did. Twenty-nine (63.0 per cent) of the theoretical scientists were 46–65 years of age as opposed to 12 (46.2 per cent) of the social scientists.

In terms of highest academic degrees earned, doctoral degree holders dominate the subsample. Sixty-three (43.2 per cent) held a Ph.D. or Doctor of Science degree. Nineteen (13.0 per cent) earned a

B.A. or B.S. degree, and 12 (8.2 per cent) obtained an M.A. or M.S. Three earned teacher's college degrees, and 1 held a special degree. Ph.D. degree holders formed the overwhelming majority among both theoretical and social scientists.

TABLE 51

HIGHER EDUCATION FIELDS OF STUDY OF PEKING UNIVERSITY
FACULTY ELITE SUBSAMPLE BY AGE
(percentages in parentheses)

Age	Natural Sciences	Applied Sciences	Social Sciences	Humanities	Professions	Total
36–45	4 (8.7)	0	0	0	0	4 (4.3)
46–55	14 (30.4)	3 (60.0)	4 (15.4)	0	1 (11.1)	22 (24.2)
56–65	15 (32.6)	0	8 (30.8)	4 (80.0)	2 (22.2)	29 (31.9)
66–75	10 (21.7)	1 (20.0)	12 (46.2)	1 (20.0)	4 (44.4)	28 (30.8)
76	3 (6.5)	1 (20.0)	2 (7.8)	0	2 (22.2)	8 (8.7)
Total	46 (99.9)	5 (100.0)	26 (100.1)	5 (100.0)	9 (99.9)	91 (99.9)

We are dealing then with two phase one Peking University faculty graduation cohorts centered in the 1920's and 1930's, most of whom were males above forty-five years of age at the time this study was begun, originating from East and Central-South China, educated in the United States, and holding doctoral degrees primarily in the theoretical natural sciences and secondarily in the social sciences. Data on family origin are not included here because of the small number of cases for which such information is available and the fact that family origin or class status must be estimated from general biographical data, a most unreliable method. Our background data center on two variables: age and educational status.

ORGANIZATIONAL STATUSES

The largest single type of information contained in the subsample, and indeed in the larger sample from which it was drawn, is positional. The 104 Peking University faculty members with whom we began held a total of 3,408 positions between the years 1949 and 1965. More accurately, they held 3,408 "statuses." A "status," as it is used here, refers to several data: (1) the date when the position in question was first noted, if it was; (2) the date until which the position was held, if known; (3) the title of the parent organization in which the position was located; (4) the title of the position itself; (5) the title of the subunit to which the position applied; (6) the level, either territorial or organizational, at which the unit was located; and (7) the province in which the unit was located. A typical status might thus read: 1952–53, China Democratic League, first secretary, standing committee, special municipality, Hopeh province. A change in any one of the seven items mentioned above yields a new status. There are twelve categories of organizations in which statuses might be found, and the definition of status varies according to the type of organization, though most follow the pattern given here. The variations are described above under "Compilation of Biographical Data." Records of campaign behavior, status adjustments, publication content, and coalition behavior are not included, as the codes and the methods for scoring them are in the midst of revision.

A status set describes all the statuses a person occupies at any given time. For the phase one Peita elite, the total number of statuses occupied from 1949 to 1965 represent the group's status set. As the individual position totals in Table 52 indicate, well over half (54.6 per cent) the group's status set consisted of essentially academic statuses represented by those in organizations of known academic relevance, in this case, academic associations, the Academy of Sciences, university administrative units, and teaching units. More than a quarter (28.9 per cent) were located in expressly political statuses counting only third party, state, Chinese Communist Party (CCP), and university Party positions. The remainder—mass organizations, international units, and publications—could be either expressly political or essentially academic. Mass organizations included unions of writers and educational workers as well as celebrations of the birthdays of important historical personages. International organizations embraced both friendship associations and attendance at various scientific conferences, and publications included scientific journals, the popular press, and journals pronouncing policy and propaganda. In sum, phase one Peita elites were primarily academicians with strong secondary political qualifications.

The yearly total column in Table 52 shows the cumulative growth of the group's status set from year to year. Few changes mark the years between 1949 and 1951, immediately prior to the reorganization of the university system. Status sets grew in increments of about twenty-seven new positions per year between 1951 and 1954 as phase one faculty were gradually absorbed into the reorganized universities and preparations were begun for new expansions in curriculum and

TABLE 52

ANNUAL TOTALS OF FACULTY ELITE SUBSAMPLE IN POSITIONS AT PEKING UNIVERSITY, 1949–65
(Percentage of annual total in parentheses)

Year	Academic Associations	Third Parties	Academy of Sciences	State	Mass Organizations	CCP	International	Publications	University Party	University Administration	University Teaching	Totals
1949	10 (10.2)	1 (1.0)	1 (1.0)	34 (34.7)	22 (22.4)	8 (8.2)	8 (8.2)	1 (1.0)	0 (0.0)	5 (5.1)	8 (8.2)	98 (100)
1950	1 (1.0)	1 (1.0)	0 (0.0)	41 (42.3)	16 (16.4)	10 (10.3)	5 (5.2)	0 (0.0)	0 (0.0)	12 (12.4)	11 (11.3)	97 (99.9)
1951	4 (4.2)	1 (1.1)	0 (0.0)	38 (40.0)	14 (14.7)	11 (11.6)	7 (7.4)	0 (0.0)	0 (0.0)	9 (9.5)	11 (11.6)	95 (100)
1952	6 (4.9)	3 (2.5)	2 (1.6)	42 (34.4)	16 (13.1)	12 (9.8)	15 (12.3)	2 (1.6)	0 (0.0)	10 (8.2)	14 (11.5)	122 (100)
1953	6 (4.9)	2 (1.6)	2 (1.6)	47 (30.9)	32 (21.1)	12 (7.9)	15 (9.9)	5 (3.3)	1 (0.7)	12 (7.9)	18 (11.8)	152 (100)
1954	3 (1.7)	3 (1.7)	4 (2.2)	58 (32.4)	23 (12.8)	13 (7.3)	17 (9.5)	5 (2.8)	0 (0.0)	17 (9.5)	36 (20.1)	179 (100)
1955	5 (2.8)	3 (1.7)	35 (19.9)	21 (12.0)	19 (10.8)	14 (8.0)	16 (9.1)	3 (1.7)	0 (0.0)	16 (9.1)	44 (25.0)	176 (100)
1956	8 (3.3)	10 (4.2)	34 (14.1)	30 (12.5)	28 (11.6)	18 (7.5)	24 (10.0)	1 (0.4)	2 (0.8)	26 (10.8)	60 (24.9)	241 (100)
1957	8 (3.0)	6 (2.3)	33 (12.5)	32 (12.1)	14 (5.2)	20 (7.6)	18 (6.7)	26 (9.8)	1 (0.4)	27 (10.1)	80 (30.1)	265 (99.9)
1958	14 (4.5)	13 (4.1)	35 (11.2)	47 (15.2)	28 (9.1)	24 (7.7)	15 (4.8)	16 (5.2)	4 (1.2)	31 (10.0)	83 (26.8)	310 (99.8)
1959	7 (2.8)	6 (2.4)	32 (12.0)	40 (16.1)	11 (4.5)	27 (10.9)	10 (4.0)	3 (1.2)	2 (0.8)	31 (12.6)	78 (31.6)	247 (98.9)
1960	14 (6.1)	5 (2.2)	34 (14.9)	11 (4.8)	12 (5.3)	29 (12.8)	17 (7.5)	2 (0.9)	1 (0.4)	28 (12.3)	75 (32.9)	228 (100)
1961	14 (6.3)	6 (2.7)	37 (16.6)	7 (3.1)	11 (4.9)	29 (13.0)	11 (4.9)	6 (2.7)	1 (0.5)	27 (12.1)	74 (33.2)	223 (100)
1962	16 (6.9)	5 (2.1)	37 (15.9)	9 (3.8)	5 (2.1)	29 (12.3)	14 (6.0)	2 (0.9)	2 (0.9)	36 (15.3)	80 (34.0)	235 (100)
1963	10 (4.7)	5 (2.4)	32 (15.0)	6 (2.8)	3 (1.4)	31 (14.6)	12 (5.6)	2 (0.9)	2 (0.9)	34 (16.0)	76 (35.7)	213 (100)
1964	21 (6.1)	7 (2.0)	81 (23.5)	60 (17.3)	4 (1.2)	29 (8.4)	11 (3.2)	2 (0.6)	3 (0.9)	40 (11.6)	87 (25.2)	345 (100)
1965	3 (1.7)	4 (2.2)	17 (9.3)	10 (5.5)	8 (4.4)	30 (16.5)	7 (9.3)	2 (1.1)	4 (2.2)	33 (18.1)	64 (35.2)	182 (100)
Total	150 (4.4)	81 (2.4)	416 (12.2)	533 (15.6)	266 (7.8)	346 (10.2)	222 (6.5)	78 (2.3)	23 (0.7)	394 (11.6)	899 (26.4)	3408 (100)

research. While virtually no change is registered in the total for 1955, entries in the cells for that year indicate that the preparations of the 1951–54 period reached fruition. The number of state positions declined by more than half their 1954 number, while the Academy of Sciences grew eightfold, and steady though relatively small increments boosted teaching and academic associations statuses. These changes reflect less the creation of new statuses than the shift of academicians from research under state auspices to the newly organized Academy of Sciences by appointments made in 1955. The small numbers in the Academy of Sciences cells between 1949 and 1955 count those few phase one people who officered preparatory committees in anticipation of the academy's formal organization.

By 1956, and the inauguration of the twelve-year plan for scientific development, growth in state positions resumes, reflecting the appointment of academicians to state units for scientific and technological planning, new appointments in academically related ministries and state offices, and the absorption of theoretical scientists into Party ranks. Since "status" in teaching units is defined not only by date, school, and the title of the position itself, but also by the department in which it is located, additions to teaching statuses reflect changes in curricular and departmental organization. Thus the increments registered in 1956 also measure expansions in the science curriculum and in the university administrative units created to govern its development. Increases in 1956 statuses further reflect the absorption of those few phase one faculty among the returned students of the Korean War and McCarthy periods.

Few changes are registered in the period 1956–58. Statuses in academic associations continue to expand, as do those in state positions, CCP, university administrative, and teaching. The one area where expansion is especially marked is among publications statuses in 1957 and 1958; but these cell numbers must again be viewed with caution. To spur both the Great Leap Forward and the Antirightist Campaign, Peking University's academic journals published special issues for which the editorial boards were deliberately enlarged. This enlargement was not evident before 1957 or again after 1958.

By 1959 the consequences of the Antirightist Campaign for phase one faculty are felt in the composition of their status sets. Academic associational statuses drop from a peak established in 1958, but recover by 1960 and, with one exception, reach a new high shortly before the GPCR gets underway. Third party statuses fall sharply to pre-1958 levels and remain virtually unchanged through 1965. No significant changes in Academy of Sciences statuses take place until 1964. The high figure for academy statuses in that year (81) and the inflated total of statuses for 1964 (345) are partly spurious. Many of the references for the generation of the post-Leap recovery period were drawn from Cheng Chu-yuan's *Scientific and Engineering Manpower in Communist China, 1949–1963.* Academy of Sciences statuses were given as of 1964, though many of the individuals in his biographic index had undoubtedly held such positions since 1955. If no data were found to confirm an earlier appointment, the position was counted only for that year. The most significant change in 1959 is the decline in state statuses continuous until the reappointments of 1964. Phase one faculty no longer played major roles in domestic affairs of state after the Antirightist Campaign except for their brief recovery in 1964. Mass organizational statuses show a similar decline, though less pronounced.

What is startling on first appearance, however, is the increase in CCP statuses during the same period. While phase one faculty were no longer welcome among state circles, Party membership was; or, more accurately, their performance in the course of the Antirightist Campaign enjoined Party membership upon them. International statuses never recovered the peaks established in the pre-1958 period. The larger figure in 1960 reflects phase one faculty participation in the international physics symposium of that year. Publications statuses return to pre-1957 levels, and university Party statuses (though not the personnel in them) remained unchanged. Finally, university administrative and teaching positions show a brief decline between 1959 and 1962 as departments were either consolidated or temporarily disbanded and courses were cut back to meet demands for austerity in the early years of the post-Leap recovery. The figures for 1962, 1963, and 1964 represent their revival, reorganization, and expansion just prior to the GPCR. The decline of the 1965 figures is only partly attributable to the revolution; good information on faculty statuses was difficult to come by in that year, and confusion still surrounds much of the data on the phase one group.

With suitable caution applied to the Academy of Sciences statuses in 1964, publication statuses in 1957 and 1958, and the 1965 statuses, some idea of the distribution within status sets can be gleaned from year by year percentages. Specifically, academic statuses combined with those in mass organizations, international units, and publications constituted the largest segment of the 1949 status set, with expressly political statuses playing a strong supporting role. In the status sets of 1950 and 1951, the weights are reversed. Expressly political statuses dominated the sets in those years, with specifically academic statuses and statuses in mass organizations, international units, and publications in support. The distributions of 1952, 1953, and 1954 more nearly resemble that of 1949, though teaching and university administrative statuses as well as international statuses increase their relative weights. After 1955 and the new appointments to the Academy of Sciences, specifically academic statuses outweigh nonacademic and semiacademic statuses combined. That pattern continues through 1959, though by 1958 a decline in the importance of mass organizational and international statuses is apparent. From 1960 to 1965, academic statuses formed the overwhelming majority of the status sets. The role of state positions is eclipsed by the growing importance of Party statuses, reversed only briefly in 1964.

Nothing in this description of changing weights within status sets or in the table itself tells us who allocated what proportions of time, energy, and emotional commitment to the statuses he held. It does, however, suggest that phase one faculty were becoming less and less visible to the nonacademic community as their most "public" statuses declined after the onslaught of the Antirightist Campaign. In the light of what has been written about the relationship between scholars and the Party, this is not a very startling revelation. But it is important to note that while public non- or semiacademic statuses declined, statuses visible to the academic remained surprisingly stable and indeed grew despite the Antirightist Campaign. This is not to say that the content of courses taught, the authority of administrators in their departments or of teachers in their classrooms, the content and style of research at the Academy of Sciences and in the universities, or the policies pursued within academic associations remained unchanged. But even in these respects, the evidence suggests that by 1962 the theoretical sciences revived theory to its pre-1957 honors; the social sciences and humanities were enjoined to be more politically and ideologically relevant, but these disciplines did not succumb to political command; and the applied sciences reached out to new areas. Classroom authority appears to have been not merely restored but enhanced, and university administrators won the right to make academically related decisions without the benefit of interference from Party branch secretaries.

CAMPAIGN BEHAVIOR

What effect, if any, did the Antirightist Campaign, or for that matter any political movement, have on the phase one group? In the period between 1949 and 1965 no less than sixty-three campaigns have been recorded and dated for the nation as a whole. Forty-two of those campaigns struck Peita with varying degrees of intensity and for varying durations. To simplify matters, the full panoply of campaigns was collapsed into six campaign periods. The first period, 1949–51, includes, among others, the 1949 Land Reform Campaign, the Party rectification campaign of 1950, thought reform, the "resist America, aid Korea" campaign, the beginning of the Democratic Reform Movement and *san-fan* (three anti) campaign as well as the campaigns "to increase production and voluntary contributions" and "to suppress counterrevolutionaries." The second period, 1952–55, embraces the second and third stages of the *san-fan* campaign, the new *san-fan* campaign, the *wu-fan* (five anti) campaign, the Patriotic Health Movement, the *su-fan* campaign and the campaigns "to increase production and economize," "to criticize the thought of Hu Shih," "to criticize bourgeois idealism," "to petition against the use of atomic weapons," and "to eliminate illiteracy."

The third period, 1956–57, is witness to the Hundred Flowers, the national rectification campaign, national *su-fan*, the 1957 *hsia-fang*, the Socialist Education Movement, the first, second, and third stages of the Antirightist Campaign, and the campaign "to study the Soviet Union." The fourth period, from 1958 to 1960, begins with the fourth stage of the Antirightist Campaign, the *hsüang-fan* (double anti) campaign, the Educational Reform Movement, the "campaign for academic criticism and academic reasearch," the "campaign against emphasizing the old and slighting the new," the Great Leap Forward, the commune movement, the Scientific Great Leap, the 1958 *hsia-fang*, the first stages of the Three Combined Movements, the "campaign against rightist tendencies," the 1960 Great Leap, and ends with the "campaign to increase production and economize." The fifth period, 1961–64, includes the Party rectification movement of 1961, the new Hundred Flowers, the Socialist Education Movement of 1962, the "campaign to learn from Lei Feng and the People's Liberation Army," the 1963 *hsia-fang*, and the Four Cleanups Campaign. Finally, for purposes of comparison a sixth period, 1965 and beyond, was appended to include both the "campaign to study the works of Chairman Mao" and the GPCR.

This form of periodization distinguishes, though imperfectly, between those times when campaigns were of relatively high intensity, scope, duration, and rate of succession from those when all four were relatively low. From the point of view of the Peita faculty, the period from 1949 to 1951 was mild compared to the rapid succession of campaigns that struck between 1952 and 1955. The distinction blurs for the following two periods. Faculty involvement in the Hundred Flowers campaign was certainly intense in the 1956–57 period, and the Antirightist Campaign began in mid-1957. But severe criticism and sanctioning mounted in 1958 and did not subside until the end of 1959. Thus 1956–57 marked a period of mild campaign activity compared to the periods immediately before and after. Though campaigns continued through the post-Leap recovery, Peita's faculty were only sporadically involved, and until 1965 most of the activities in which they engaged were of low or moderate intensity—a pattern the GPCR was to reverse.

The activities and behaviors in which Peita faculty engaged in the course of these campaigns are classified along two axes representing direction and intensity. A behavior designated as positive in direction followed the Party line as described and approved in authoritative sources. If negative, its line of direction was disapproved by those same sources. The second axis, intensity, is measured in three degrees: high, low, and moderate. Intensity is described as low if the behavior involved was limited to presence at meetings, speeches, or rallies on behalf of (positive) or in opposition to (negative) approved policies, standpoints, or groups. Behavior was designated as moderate if it involved: (1) formal speeches supporting (positive) or opposing (negative) approved policies, standpoints, or groups, but mentioning no specific names; (2) the writing of big-character posters or articles supporting (positive) or opposing (negative) approved policies, standpoints, or groups, but mentioning no specific names; or (3) the signing of petitions supporting (positive) or opposing (negative) approved policies, standpoints, or groups, but mentioning no specific names. Behavior was recorded as high intensity and positive in direction if (1) one engaged in a personal attack orally or in writing; (2) one was involved in "struggle" (*tou-cheng*) against another person or group, or (3) one was a member or leader of a campaign organization designed to implement approved policies or standpoints or to support approved groups. Finally, behavior was labeled high intensity and negative in direction if (1) one was criticized personally in writing or orally; (2) one was subjected to "struggle"; or (3) one was a member or leader of an alleged opposition group.

Since a single individual might be reported to have behaved in exactly opposite ways in any one campaign, and because a number of different campaigns are collapsed into single campaign periods, a judgment had to be made as to which report should be counted. Two separate evaluations were carried out. In the case of multiple reports for any one campaign, the report closest to the terminal date of the campaign was selected as the significant entry. Then, of all the entries during a single campaign period, those with reference to minor campaigns were pulled out. Since the number of reports were few to begin with, the last step in the evaluation yielded one report for every individual in the subsample. Obviously, these devices would not suffice for a larger sample. Thus methods for scoring are being tested in order to provide a more accurate measure of campaign performances.

Of the 104 individuals in the phase one subsample, 60 were reported to have engaged in positive actions and 44 in negative actions for the entire period from 1949 to 1965. Twenty-seven of the 60 positive were of high intensity, 30 moderate, and 3 low. Thirty-six of the 44 negative cases were of high intensity; 8 were moderate, and none were low. In short, a majority of the phase one group had a pretty good official record, though a sizable minority were deemed not only bad, but very bad. If we examine the statistics across the six periods, well over half of the subsample recorded positive high or moderate performances with gradually increasing proportions of highly intense negative behaviors in those periods between 1949 and 1958. Of the 46 cases recorded for the 1958–60 period, 8 were positive and high, 13 were negative and high; 8 were negative and moderate, and 17 were positive and moderate. Thus, the general pattern in pre-1958 campaign performances continued during the peak years of campaign activity, but the proportion of negative, high-intensity cases registered a fourfold increase. That only 8 cases were reported for 1961–64 reflects the lull in campaign activities during this period. But in the sixth, 1965 and beyond, the pattern reversed. Of the 25 recorded in that period, 17 were negative and high-intensity performances; 4 were positive and high, 2 positive and moderate, and 2 positive and low. Finally, for the entire period from 1949 to 1965 only 6 of the 104 individuals were known to have been purged from their positions or to have lost rank, salary, title, or some combination of the three.

The data examined above must be viewed with the utmost caution not only because of the methods employed, but also because of the rather large number of unreported cases. We have reason to believe, however, that even if additional instances were added to the file, the general distribution of campaign performances would not alter appreciably. A considerable proportion of the phase one group performed in approved ways, through the Antirightist Campaign, and despite the expansion in the ranks of the ideologically backward in the aftermath of that most intense period of campaigning, decreasing political reliability did not lead to any significant alteration in the academic statuses of the group as a whole. It did, as we have seen, lead to a significant change in the distribution of nonacademic statuses after 1959.

STATUS AND POWER

It was suggested earlier that men of high teaching rank were those most likely to exercise the power of academic spokesmanship—the power to plead the cause of one's own academic interests and to draw upon the resources of the state for their pursuit. If we permit this statement to serve as our principal hypothesis, we must accept, at least tentatively, an underlying assumption that status is related to power. To be more specific, we must assume that high rank in those nonacademic or semiacademic organizations which are known to have been the prime distributors of resources to subsystem elites provides access to power. We have chosen to label that access "academic spokesmanship" in order to indicate not only that the command politicians to whom academic spokesmen related chose those upon whom resources would be bestowed, but that academicians exercised resources of their own by influencing such decisions. We are looking then for those among the subsystem elite who were likely to have confronted command politicians with demands for resources and suggestions pertaining to their distribution. Assuming that this definition of academic spokesmanship makes sense, how can it be measured? Furthermore, with the knowledge we already have that distributions within status sets altered over time, how do we measure those changes in the ranks of academic spokesmen that are likely to have accompanied changing distributions of statuses?

Our answer to these questions was to perform two statistical operations on data already presented: a multiple correlational analysis and a step-wise multiple regression. For both steps, each item of background information (where numbers were sufficient to permit) and each item of information concerning organizational statuses was dichotomized to form a 30 x 30 matrix. Each operation was performed six times in order to yield separate measurements for each of the six time periods into which campaign performances were collapsed.

Age and higher education composed the two groups of background variables tested in these operations. Age was read literally for each of the six campaign periods, and the average age was calculated for each period. Region of higher education formed the second variable, dichotomized into education in China and abroad. A variable indicating the subregion in which subsample members received their higher education followed, dichotomized into "United States" and "Europe" (the latter including the Soviet Union). Field of higher educational study formed the next variable dichotomized to differentiate between the theoretical natural sciences and the nonnatural sciences (including the social sciences, humanities, professions, and applied sciences). The last of the background variables indicated whether the highest degree obtained was a Ph.D. or some other higher educational degree.

Organizational statuses formed the second group of variables. Since there were no statuses recorded for the Chinese Communist Youth League, this set was left out. For all the others, excepting third party statuses, the type of organization and the rank of the status held within that organization were separately considered. For example, state statuses were measured by two variables, one recording whether the organization was academically related (such as the Planning Commission for Science and Technology or the Ministry of Education) or nonacademically related, and the other recording the rank of the status held as either high or low. CCP positions were similarly classified, but the terms differed. The variable measuring the type of CCP unit differentiated between statuses in central CCP organs (central CCP units at the national level or CCP units on the provincial, regional, or special municipality levels); and statuses in noncentral CCP units (all those units at levels below those designated as central). A second variable measured those statuses as either high or low. Variables measuring international statuses distinguished between permanent units (friendship associations, regularly scheduled congresses, and international agencies) and ad hoc units (international missions and irregularly scheduled conferences), high and low statuses, those statuses that were held with reference to European countries and those that were held with reference to non-European countries, those statuses held with reference to Communist countries and those with reference to non-Communist countries. Publications positions were labeled high or low, political or academic. Variables measuring university Party, administrative, and teaching statuses distinguished between those held primarily at Peking University and those held primarily at other universities, the rank of the status being high or low; and in the case of teaching positions, the department in which the position was located was either in the theoretical natural sciences or the nonnatural sciences. Third Party statuses were simply recorded as high or low.

Determining whether a status was high or low was left to a good deal of subjective judgment. For any period of the six, the status judged highest in terms of rank, level, and subunit designation was chosen as the item to be measured. State, mass organizational third party, and CCP statuses were the most problematic in this regard. For other positions these decisions were more clear-cut. Editors and deputy editors were labeled high; editorial board members low. University administrators at the level of the departmental chairman and above were labeled high; below the level of the departmental chairman, low. Full professors and assistant professors were classified as high; lecturers and assistants as low. Directors of institutes, bureau chiefs and their deputies, and standing committee members in Academy of Sciences units were regarded as high; members of academic departments in the academy were regarded as low. In due time, these judgments will be supplanted by a panel of expert judges for those statuses most open to bias, and weighted scores will replace the designations now in use.

The thirtieth and final variable measured temporal prominence before and after 1958, but it proved an unworkable measure and was dropped. Finally, the step-wise multiple regression was performed on only one dependent variable in this case to determine which of the twenty-nine independent variables best predicted high CCP status. Ultimately, all of the high nonacademic statuses will be similarly treated, and the findings will permit cross comparisons between elite subgroups.

FINDINGS

Who were those in the phase one group who held high-ranking teaching statuses throughout the six campaign periods? If the correlations for each period are placed in rank order, and if those correlations which refer to cases too small in number to be meaningful are eliminated (both procedures have been applied to the reports given below), the groups among the phase one faculty who were found to have held high-ranking teaching statuses are shown in Table 53.

TABLE 53

IDENTIFICATION OF PHASE ONE FACULTY MEMBERS
WITH HIGH-RANKING STATUS

Time Period	Description	Correlation	Degree of Significance
1 (1949–51)	Those who held university administrative positions at universities other than Peita	−.413	.01+
	Those who obtained their higher education primarily in Europe	.345	.01+
	Those who held low-ranking university administrative positions	−.345	.01+
2 (1952–55)	No significant correlations		
3 (1956–57)	Those who held high-ranking third party positions	.345	.01+
	Those who held high-ranking Academy of Sciences positions	.284	.01+
	Those who held positions in academically related mass organizations	.236	.05
	Those who held high-ranking university Party positions	.224	.05
4 (1958–60)	Those who held university administrative positions primarily at Peking University	.224	.05
5 (1961–64)	Those who held high-ranking positions in the Academy of Sciences	.405	.01+
	Those who held university administrative positions primarily at Peking University	.344	.01+
	Those who held high-ranking university administrative positions	.284	.01+
	Those who were officers (not members) of academic associations	−.251	.05
	Those who held positions in academic associations serving the social sciences	.227	.05
	Those who held positions in nonnatural science fields in the Academy of Sciences	.225	.05
6 (1965 plus)	Those who held low-ranking university administrative positions	−.196	.05

Our hypothesis is partially upheld if we define high-ranking university Party positions and high-ranking university administrative positions as two locations for an interface between command elites and subsystem elites. In the two moderate periods of campaign activity, time periods 3 and 5, those who occupied high-ranking statuses in university Party units, and in university administrative units at period 5 alone, occupied significant places among high-status faculty. But for time periods 1 and 6, the correlations show low-ranking administrators among faculty of high status. High status in third parties, the Academy of Sciences, and academic associations, also in time periods 3 and 5, indicates the possibility that some academic spokesman of high faculty rank had opportunities outside the university proper to influence command elites; but until we can relate those positions to known centers of power, this finding must be held aside.

While high university Party status correlates with high faculty rank, the numbers are small and any conclusions we draw must be tentative. We do have a far larger sampling of high-ranking university administrators. High-status faculty included ranking administrators in period 5, but definitely not in time periods 1 and 6. Who, then, held high-ranking statuses in the university administrations through the six campaign periods? To save time and space we shall not replicate the correlation tables, but the procedures are the same.

High university administrative status correlates with teaching rank only in time period 5. Ranking university administrators were more likely to derive support from positions held outside the university proper, and they were, from time period 1 through time period 5, more likely to have been Peking University administrators than administrators in other universities (this is not a foregone conclusion, since a large proportion of the Peita administrators spent some part of their careers in administrative posts elsewhere). In time period 1 (1949–51), correlations significant beyond the .01 level indicate that high-ranking university administrators included those who held high statuses in state organizations that were academically related, those with positions in social science academic associations, and those who held high statuses in mass organizations that were academically related. Thus, prior to the reorganization of 1952, phase one faculty elite in Peita's administration probably faced command elites both through their positions in the university proper and through their positions as academicians in the apparatus of the state. Their positions in mass organizations may have served as supports, but again we are not entitled to draw such a conclusion without further evidence.

For the campaign periods following the reorganization of 1952, state positions are no longer significant. Nor do we find any correlations linking high university administrative status to the CCP. Peita administrators in these periods faced command elites through their positions in the university and possibly through high-ranking offices in organizations outside the university and independent of both the state and Party apparatuses. While this factor remains stable, the distribution of statuses alters. In time periods 2 and 3, high rank in academic publications provides our strongest correlations, and representation from the natural science branches of the Academy of Sciences increases in importance. By period 4, those who hold high statuses in the social science branches of the Academy of Sciences provide our strongest correlations, and in period 5, high-ranking international statuses come second only to occupancy of Peita administrative positions. No significant correlations derive from the data for time period 6.

To cumulate our findings thus far, a subgroup among the phase one faculty constitutes a possible elite within an elite. Those holding high-ranking university, Party, and administrative statuses are included among ranking faculty in the two periods of moderate campaign activity, suggesting the possibility that high faculty rank supported their influence through the university to command elites. We cannot confirm that this is so with the data at hand, nor can we ask, given the small numbers in our files, how important faculty rank was by determining who were most likely to hold high university Party positions. We do have a sufficient number of cases to raise this same question for highly placed university administrators. Here we find another elite within an elite: Peita administrators of high status exercising their influence indirectly on command elites through their positions at Peita and directly through their positions in state organizations up to the reorganization of 1952. The composition of statuses important to this elite subgroup changes over time, and influence (if it is legitimate to imply its presence) is dependent, after the reorganization of 1952, upon one channel provided by their university positions and another set of channels through high statuses in organizations that are not subunits of the Party, the state, or the university. Thus academic spokesmen in a third elite subgroup of postreorganization administrators emerge through our findings for this segment of the subsample.

It should now be clear that elite statuses for the Peita faculty need not depend upon rank in the university proper. In order to determine whether we also have elite subgroups outside the university we posed the same questions to the distribution of statuses in state and CCP units, the two units assumed to be the most important centers for the distribution of power to academic subsystem elites.

Who were the phase one faculty who held high-ranking state positions throughout the six campaign periods? Our findings in this instance resemble those for ranking Peita administrators. In time period 1, their positions in academic associations identify them as social scientists not of high rank. The same applies to time periods 2 and 3, although representation from the natural science branches of the Academy of Sciences increases in importance. The strongest correlations in time period 3 show that those of high state rank were not high in other organizations outside the university during this time and that the high statuses they held were in those units of the state apparatus dealing with academic affairs. In time period 4, high status in academic associations yields the only measure of significance. Background characteristics relate importantly to high state rank in the fifth time period. Those who held such positions were above the average age (57.13 years) and more likely to hold B.A.'s or M.A.'s than Ph.D's. No significant correlations derive from the data for time period 6.

Combined with the findings on university administrators, our results here suggest that academic spokesmen to command elites in the state apparatus form an elite subgroup different from the three we have already identified. With the exception of the 1949–51 period when university administrators also held high state positions, those high in state rank derived little support from either university statuses or statuses in organizations outside the university, state, and the Party. A departure is registered in the 1958–60 period reflecting the state's effort to enlist ranking natural scientists in the planning of the Great Leap Forward. In sum, after the reorganization of 1952, high-ranking status in state organizations was important in its own right. In this respect members of the state elite subgroup differ from those whose access to power depended upon the university or a combination of positions including the university. They also differ from the subsample as a whole in so far as they were more likely to be social scientists, older than average in age, and holders of degrees other than the Ph.D.

We turn, finally, to those among the phase one group occupying high-ranking CCP positions. The same measures show that academic spokesmen to the CCP were likely to have been social scientists, in their early or mid-forties (younger than the average age of 48.03 years), with M.A. or B.A. degrees, holding important statuses in mass organizations in the two campaign periods between 1949 and 1955. In 1956–57, the role of the academic disciplines is reversed. Those who held positions in academic associations serving the theoretical natural sciences with low third party statuses and positions of indeterminate rank in academically related mass organizations constitute the ranks of academic spokesmen to the CCP. A second reversal takes place in the 1958–60 period as members of academic associations serving the social science disciplines provide the most powerful correlations. No significant findings derive from the data for the fifth period. But, in the sixth, the correlations reverse once more as those in the theoretical natural sciences resume the most important place among academic spokesmen to the CCP, and the Academy of Sciences emerges as the most important location for their statuses.

Like high-ranking state positions, high status in the CCP was a channel for academic spokesmanship in its own right. Those with high CCP statuses derived some support from high rank in academic associations and third parties in the two periods from 1949 to 1955, but not afterward. But, unlike any of the other statuses we have measured, CCP statuses are far more sensitive to the fluctuations induced in the course of political campaigns. The rotation of social and natural scientists reflects the CCP's choice of academic spokesmen from among phase one faculty. Younger social scientists form the first elite subgroup. They were likely to have represented the more progressively inclined among the phase one group in the period just preceding the return of the natural scientists and their absorption into state and Academy of Sciences positions. In the 1956–57 period, this second subgroup of natural scientists was incorporated into CCP ranks. The reversal of 1958–60 reflects the Party's decision to exert its direct control over the third elite subgroup of social scientists whose errant behavior in the Hundred Flowers campaign defined the need for Party control. The final reversal in the sixth period reflects the Party's commitment to scientific and technological advancement just before the

GPCR caught up with its academic planners—the fourth elite sub-group among the academic spokesmen to the CCP.

Beta coefficients in the one attempt to apply step-wise multiple regression to the subsample label the best predictors of high CCP status: high rank in mass organizations in time periods 1 and 2, membership in academic associations serving the theoretical natural sciences in time period 3, membership in academic associations serving the social sciences in time period 4. These findings confirm those drawn from multiple correlations. To the three elite subgroups whose power derived primarily from positions held within the university, we now add five more: one representing academic spokesmen to command elites in the state apparatus and four representing academic spokesmen to command elites in the CCP.

Conclusions

Our findings, as they have been presented in the preceding pages, are restricted to a limited subsample drawn from a much larger group: a subsample of faculty elites composed of Peking University teachers in two graduation cohorts entering teaching positions at Peita during its first phase of faculty growth. The full significance of the data based upon this limited subsample must await an application of the same methods applied here to groups spanning all four phases of faculty entry into Peita. Yet some points of interest have emerged from even this limited selection.

First, faculty membership is in itself an elite status if viewed in terms of faculty relations with nonelite students. But knowledge of the differences within the faculty elite provides us with a much more precise definition of what it is that constitutes the difference between elites and nonelites. Furthermore, by focusing on the composition and changing distributions of statuses within status sets, we obtain both a spatial and a temporal perspective on the meaning of elite status. We have some basis for determining how much distance there is between those on the boundary line between elites and nonelites and those who are likely to have access to power resources from command elites at different times and for varying situations.

The changing distribution of statuses within faculty status sets highlights the fact that positions underlying elite power are subject to sharp, irregular fluctuations caused by events taking place both inside and outside Chinese society. Among such events, the reorganization of

1952, the return of the natural scientists following the Korean War and the McCarthy period, the twelve-year plan for scientific development, and recurrent campaigns have had a marked impact on our subsample. Especially important were the sharp decline in state representation and the "academization" of status sets for the phase one group after 1959.

Our examination of faculty elite structure through the use of multiple correlations disclosed a number of subelites—those straddling the boundary line between Peita as an organizational subsystem and the command elites in the state and Party apparatus. We labeled those subelites "academic spokesmen" to indicate both their access to command elites and their availability.[30] Eight groups of academic spokesmen emerged from the correlational analysis. They differed both in terms of the channels through which their influence upon command elites was likely to have been conveyed, the types of supporting statuses they held, and their sensitivity to those same events that influenced the composition of the same as a whole. If we reorganize these eight groups according to their channels of influence, four major elites within an elite take substance: (1) academic spokesmen who confronted command elites principally from university platforms; (2) academic spokesmen whose channels to command elites incorporated both the university and the state apparatus; (3) academic spokesmen whose high rank in state or Party centers of command proffered opportunities for influence; and (4) academic spokesmen whose influence may have stemmed from occupancy of high-ranking positions independent of the university and outside the state and Party apparatus proper.

In our subsample, the first group played an important role in two periods of moderate campaign activity, 1956–57 and 1961–64. The second emerged briefly before the reorganization of higher education in 1952. The third group appeared after 1952, but its composition, particularly for those who held high-ranking Party positions, altered significantly in each of the campaign periods following reorganization. The fourth remains unknown, for we have not yet applied the same

---

30 The terms "access" and "availability" are drawn from William Kornhauser's *The Politics of Mass Society* (Glencoe, Ill.: Free Press, 1959), pp. 30–39. Although Kornhauser uses these terms to describe the reciprocal relationship between elites and masses, they are equally applicable to the relationship between command elites and subsystem elites. Academic spokesmen are "available" to superordinate command elites for mobilization on behalf of command elite goals. They also have "access" to higher elites for the expression of subsystem demands. This paper does not attempt to measure accessibility and availability, but rather to locate the structural points at which both are generated.

tests to high status occupancy in mass organizations, publications, international organizations, academic associations, and the Academy of Sciences. For a limited subsample, we have identified and characterized important elite subgroups and the locations from which their power is likely to have stemmed.

The methods we have applied here require considerable refinement and revision, and we have attempted to indicate where such refinements are already underway. The application of multiple regression to a larger sampling of dependent variables comes first in importance, and the development of both position and campaign scores will certainly strengthen our design and the weight of our findings. The indirect approach to campaign behavior, collapsing political movements into six campaign periods, will also be refined, but it does succeed in registering, if not measuring, the dynamism of a society undergoing rapid change.

In the course of this report, we have laid especially heavy emphasis on structural analysis. Obviously, we consider it important. But we do not presume that it is the only key to elite analysis. Data derived from interviews, documentary analysis, and content analyses are crucial parts of the larger research of which this report constitutes but one part. Results from that research have been arbitrarily excluded here to point up the value of structural aspects of elite behavior.

PART V

Elites under Stress

PARRIS H. CHANG

Provincial Party Leaders' Strategies for Survival during the Cultural Revolution*

"The gradual deepening of the socialist revolution and of the socialist education movement inevitably brings the question of the proletarian cultural revolution to the fore. Whether or not you are genuinely in favor of the socialist revolution or whether you are even against it is bound to manifest itself in your attitude toward the proletarian cultural revolution. This is a vital question that touches people to their very souls. . . ."

Editorial, *JMJP*, June 2, 1966

For many CCP cadres in the provinces (and in the center), the Great Proletarian Cultural Revolution (GPCR) was not merely a vital question that touched their souls; it was the most serious and damaging political storm they had ever experienced. Indeed, most of the provincial leaders (and the leaders in the central apparatus as well) failed to navigate its treacherous course and became its casualties. Out of the twenty-eight first secretaries who headed the Party committee in China's twenty-eight provincial-level units in 1966, only eight remained in good standing when the Ninth Party Congress was held in April, 1969. The others, twenty provincial Party first secretaries, lost their positions. Most of them were dragged out, struggled by the revolutionaries in public meetings, and denounced in the official media as "three anti" elements (anti-Party, antisocialist, and anti-Mao Tsetung). Below the first secretaries, other provincial Party leaders also

* The author wishes to acknowledge the support of the Center for Chinese Studies, University of Michigan, during 1969–70 which made this study possible.

fared poorly in the GPCR purges. Of 247 provincial leaders, 186 among those holding the ranks of alternate secretary, secretary, second secretary, and first secretary were ousted.[1]

Realizing that their political survival was at stake, the incumbent provincial power-holders did not wait for their political demise with folded arms. On the contrary, many of them used all of the leverage provided by their positions and resorted to various ingenious devices for self-preservation. Although an overwhelming majority of them met their downfall in the course of the GPCR, the circumstances under which they were finally brought down attested to the tenacity of their resistance and the remarkable effectiveness of their survival strategies. Of equal importance, it exposed the failures and inability of Maoist leadership to secure compliance through the existing system of central control.

In this study, I will first examine the provincial leaders' perception of the events in China from the spring to the fall of 1966. Then I will analyze the strategies which they devised to protect themselves. In the concluding section, I will explore the provincial leaders' sources of

---

[1] Among the 186 purgees, 20 were first secretaries, 10 were second secretaries, 124 were secretaries, and the remaining 32 were alternate or deputy secretaries, while the 61 survivors consisted of 8 first secretaries, 4 second secretaries, 37 secretaries, and 12 alternate or deputy secretaries. Judgment on the political status of these 247 provincial Party leaders is based on information available as of the summer of 1970 and has not taken into account subsequent political developments. Since that time, a few of the 61 survivors, such as P'an Fu-sheng of Heilungkiang, have been purged and, on the other hand, several previously purged officials, such as Chao Tzu-yang of Kwangtung and Chang P'ing-hua of Hunan, have been rehabilitated and transferred to other provinces in positions of somewhat less importance.

It should be noted that, of the 186 purgees, approximately 55 had rather detailed and specific accusations of "crime" leveled against them in official (central and provincial) and Red Guard media; another 60 were under only vague and general indictments; and the remaining 71 have not been publicly attacked in the official or Red Guard media. I have included the last group in the category of the purgees inasmuch as they have lost their former leadership positions and have not been rehabilitated as of the summer of 1970, long after the provincial revolutionary committees have been set up and the new provincial leadership installed.

My survey of the purgees and the survivors reveals no objective, explicit criteria whereby a provincial official was judged to be a "revolutionary leading cadre" or a "three anti element." His fate appears to have hinged on a host of variables in addition to what he actually was or did. Some of the survivors undoubtedly had been Mao's supporters (such as Chang Ch'un-ch'iao of Shanghai). The majority, like the purgees, had actually committed "errors" of one kind or another, but they had jumped on Mao's "revolutionary bandwagon" in the initial stages (as did Liu Chien-hsün of Honan and Wu Teh of Peking), or had good connections with powerful leaders in Peking who "vouched" for them (for example, Li Ta-chang of Szechwan was Madame Mao's sponsor when she applied to join the Chinese Communist Party in the late 1930's), and thus they were allowed to "pass the test."

power and their vulnerability, also commenting on the pattern of compliance and the structure of authority in China's political system.

PROVINCIAL LEADERS' PERCEPTIONS OF
THE CULTURAL REVOLUTION

As was evident from the mainland press in the spring of 1966, China was entering a new phase of politico-ideological campaigning and mobilization. On April 18, *Chieh-fang-chün pao* (Liberation Army News), organ of the People's Liberation Army (PLA), had editorially launched a fierce campaign against an "anti-Party and antisocialist black line" in the cultural front and called for a "great socialist cultural revolution" in China. Three weeks later, on May 8, the same paper directed its spear of attack toward the "Three Family Village" of Teng T'o, Wu Han, and Liao Mo-sha, aides in the Peking Party-government organization; by implication it also involved P'eng Chen, first Party secretary and mayor of Peking.

The PLA organ's attack upon P'eng Chen and his Peking group as well as upon key cadres in China's cultural "establishment" posed a difficult problem for the provincial leaders. P'eng was a member of the Politburo and the Central Committee (CC) Secretariat. Only recently he had been described as Chairman Mao's "close comrade-in-arms," [2] and in 1964 he had been appointed by Mao to head a CC "Cultural Revolution Group" (CRG) given authority over rectification in the cultural and ideological sphere. Was the attack on P'eng authorized by Mao himself? If so, provincial leaders would be obliged to follow Mao's dictate, and the sooner the better; but if not, attacking such a powerful figure would be tantamount to committing political suicide. Provincial officials, moreover, were perplexed by an unusual aspect of this campaign, namely, that the assault was launched by the organ of the PLA, not by the most authoritative organ of the Party, *Jen-min jih-pao*.[3]

To survive and thrive in a political system like that of the People's Republic of China, the provincial leaders had previously had to learn how to read the line from the center correctly and then how to respond to its various shifts expeditiously. Any confusion in communications

---

[2] NCNA, Peking, September 12, 1964.

[3] Throughout May, 1966, *JMJP* maintained a puzzling silence on the important matter of the Cultural Revolution, which had first been raised by *Chieh-fang-chün pao* on April 18. Although it reproduced articles attacking the "Three Family Village" group from other newspapers from May 9 onward, it did not take the initiative at the beginning.

was thus hazardous from the perspective of these leaders. For them, the spring of 1966 was a period of political uncertainty and anxiety. Theirs was a search for clues to the political puzzle so that they could respond properly.

By the end of May, 1966, the political picture had become somewhat clearer, but considerable uncertainty still remained. The Politburo Standing Committee which met in an enlarged session from May 4 to 18 had officially sealed the fate of P'eng Chen, Lu Ting-yi (an alternate member of the Politburo and a secretary of the CC Secretariat), and Lo Jui-ch'ing (a secretary of the CC Secretariat and chief of staff of the PLA). Further, it had issued the "May 16 Circular," a document revoking the "February Outline Report," which was the guideline for the Cultural Revolution produced the previous February by the CRG under P'eng Chen's leadership.[4] As the enlarged Politburo Standing Committee session was usually attended by first secretaries of the Party's regional bureaus or of all provincial committees,[5] and the "May 16 Circular" was disseminated to lower Party organizations via intra-Party communications channels on May 18, it is reasonable to assume that during or soon after the top-level Party meeting all provincial leaders became aware of the identity of some of Mao's purge targets and knew at least some of the issues under contention.

With the unfolding of this conflict at the top level of leadership toward the end of May, the provincial leaders' feelings of uncertainty and anxiety gave way to those of apprehension, since in the "May 16 Circular" they now perceived the threat of a new purge. The Party directive, said to have been drafted under Mao's personal guidance, called for the whole Party to "criticize and repudiate *those representatives of the bourgeoisie who have sneaked into the Party, the government, the army, and all spheres of culture, to clear them out or transfer some of them to other positions. . . . Some of them we have already seen through, others we have not. Some are still trusted by us and are being trained as our successors, persons like Khrushchev, for example, who are still nesting beside us*" (emphasis added).

This sharp, polemic language indicated in unambiguous fashion the approach of a dangerous political storm which was likely to encompass Party officials in *all* fields. Although few provincial leaders at this stage appeared to see the purge as being directed against them (their posi-

---

[4] The full text of the "May 16 Circular" is in *Peking Review,* No. 21 (May 19, 1967), pp. 6–9.

[5] For this point, see Parris H. Chang, "Research Notes on the Changing Loci of Decision in the CCP," *CQ,* No. 44 (October–December, 1970), pp. 170–71.

tion in the Party hierarchy was not high enough to fit the description of the purge targets given in the circular), they were nevertheless nervous and apprehensive. They knew too well from the experiences of past campaigns that they could be adversely affected by actual or potential "guilt by association" with the subsequent purge victims. Thus, at the end of May, 1966, even though the lines of political conflict were not clearly drawn and few provincial leaders seemed certain of Mao's goals, they apparently realized that they were facing a new political crisis in which their loyalty to the Party and the chairman would be tested severely.

The crisis was not long in coming, although its first manifestations were difficult to interpret. On May 25, 1966, Nieh Yuan-tzu, a teaching assistant of the department of philosophy at the Peking University, and her six followers posted a big-character poster on a university notice-board denouncing Lu P'ing, president and Party secretary of the university, for having obstructed and undermined the Cultural Revolution there. As a result of Mao's personal intervention, the text of the poster was broadcast throughout the nation by Radio Peking on June 1 and reproduced in *Jen-min jih-pao,* accompanied by an affirmative commentary, the following day. The publicity and approval accorded to Nieh's action by Radio Peking and *Jen-min jih-pao* emboldened "revolutionary" students in Peking and elsewhere to emulate Nieh in launching attacks against their school authorities who had, thus far, executed the line of P'eng Chen which had been denounced in the "May 16 Circular."

The activities at Shensi's Chiaotung University and Kansu's Lanchow University were typical of the situation in educational institutions throughout China in early June, 1966. Radio Sian broadcasted this report on August 29:

Since the publication of the June 1 *Jen-min jih-pao* editorial and the big-character poster of Peking University, the suppressed revolutionary emotion of the revolutionary teachers and students of Sian Chiaotung University has burst forth like a volcano. Within one day, they posted some 10,000 big-character posters exposing the anti-Party, antisocialist, and anti-Mao Tse-tung thought criminal deeds of P'eng Kang, the secretary of the University Party Committee and president of the university, and his counterrevolutionary activities to sabotage the Great Proletarian Cultural Revolution.

A similar account told of actions taken at Lanchow University.

On June 1, 1966, after Chairman Mao had personally ordered the broadcast of the first Marxist-Leninist big-character poster in the entire nation, a new high tide of the Cultural Revolution in Lanchow University immediately rose, and a vast number of revolutionary teachers, students, and revolutionary cadres pointed the spearhead of struggle directly at the capitalist power-holders in the Party and reactionary academic "authorities." [6]

Now the provincial Party officials faced a serious dilemma. They could not openly oppose the "revolutionary" activities of the students, who clearly had the blessings of Chairman Mao; on the other hand, however, they were genuinely worried that the student agitation and protest might spread to the entire society and get out of control. The students' unrestrained criticism of school administrators, who were under the jurisdiction of provincial Party-government authorities, could escalate and subsequently undermine their own position.

Seized with such sentiments, provincial leaders were momentarily relieved when they learned of the actions being taken by the central Party leadership in Peking. In early June, Liu Shao-ch'i and Teng Hsiao-p'ing who were then in charge of Party affairs in Mao's absence from Peking, authorized the Peking Party Committee to dispatch "work teams" to various Peking schools to "lead" the GPCR and put forward a GPCR guideline, known as the "Eight Articles of the Central Committee," designed to guide the GPCR in educational institutions and to keep the activities of students within bounds.[7] In accordance with the current central policy, and following the example of the Peking municipal authorities, various provincial authorities soon dispatched work teams to schools to provide similar leadership. Initially the work teams appear to have been welcomed by most students and to have established their "revolutionary credentials." In the name of the respective provincial authorities, they quickly removed the top officials in the school administration and organized students to wage a struggle against the deposed school administrators, blaming them for having suppressed and undermined the GPCR.[8]

---

[6] *Wen-ko t'ung-hsün* (Cultural Revolution Bulletin), No. 27 (May 11, 1967) (Lanchow: Wen-ko T'ung-hsün Publishing House, Lanchow University).

[7] Liu Shao-ch'i, "Confession," *Mainichi shimbun* (Tokyo), January 28–29, 1967. The full contents of this eight-article directive remain unknown. According to one Red Guard source, it contained provisions such as "differentiating the inside from the outside," "guarding against the leakage of secrets," and "firmly holding the fort." See "Down with Liu Shao-ch'i: Life of Counter-revolutionary Liu Shao-ch'i," in *CB*, No. 834 (August 17, 1967), p. 27. It is reasonable to infer that the directive tried to limit the students' scope of activities, confining them to their schools.

[8] An incomplete tabulation shows that thirteen such officials in eleven universities were dismissed and publicly humiliated during June and July of 1966. The more notable ones included Lu P'ing, the victim of Nieh Yuan-tzu's big-character poster campaign; K'uang Ya-ming, president and Party secretary of Nanking University; Li Ta, president of Wuhan University and a founder of the CCP in 1921; Ho Lu-ting, president of Shanghai

Soon, however, leftist students discovered that the work teams, by assuming the power of university authorities, were stepping into the old shoes of their former suppressors and that the repeated struggle sessions organized by the work teams against the school administrators and alleged rightist professors and students represented a cunning attempt to confine the GPCR within schools and to shift the targets of attack away from "capitalist power-holders" in the provincial Party apparatus. Therefore, at least if later Maoist reports are to be credited, opposition against the work teams gradually rose and subsequently became widespread. But the work teams hit back hard at their critics. They were able to manipulate the slogan "To oppose the work teams is to oppose the Party" to maximum advantage and in most instances won support from the majority of students.[9]

If we are to believe later reports—most of them emanating from Maoist sources—the work teams were extremely harsh toward the "revolutionary masses." In many cases, the work teams struck at those who had the audacity to oppose their leadership, calling them "counter-revolutionaries," "fake leftists," "conspirators," and so forth, and organized their supporters to struggle and persecute the dissidents. In Peking's Tsinghua University, for example, when a student leader, K'uai Ta-fu, and his followers posted a big-character poster attacking the work team, Wang Kuang-mei (Madame Liu Shao-ch'i) and other members of the Tsinghua work team allegedly instigated the "hood-winked masses" to struggle against K'uai, branding him and more than 800 "revolutionary teachers and students" as "counterrevolutionaries" and "pseudo-leftists but actual rightists" and spreading "white terror" that caused the death of one person and impelled many persons to commit suicide.[10]

There are indications that student opposition to the work teams was either directed and manipulated behind the scenes by Mao's top aides in the CRG or at least had their blessing. When the case of K'uai was brought up in a high-level Party meeting in early July,

---

Musical College and composer of the current national anthem, "East Is Red"; and K'o Lin, president and the Party secretary of Chungshan Medical College in Canton.

[9] Liu Shao-ch'i and Teng Hsiao-p'ing reportedly assured members of the work teams that "dispatching the work teams embodies the leadership of the Party. You are sent by us; to oppose you is to oppose us." "Excerpts of Teng Hsiao-ping's Self-criticism," carried in a Canton Red Guard publication and reproduced in *Ming pao* (Hong Kong), May 20, 1968. The "Sixteen-Point Decision" on the GPCR also criticized those who equated opposition to work teams with opposition to the Party center. See *JMJP*, August 9, 1966 (also *Peking Review*, No. 33 [August 12, 1966]).

[10] "Down with Liu Shao-ch'i," p. 27.

K'ang Sheng came out to defend K'uai. Allegedly, Liu Shao-ch'i denounced K'ang for "failure to understand the situation," and K'ang pointed out that "forbidding K'uai Ta-fu to bring his complaint to the Central Committee at least is not in accord with state law and is in contravention of Party regulations." Reportedly, Ch'en Po-ta supported K'ang's viewpoint and sent two CRG members, Kuan Feng and Wang Li, to Tsinghua to pay a visit to K'uai who was under custody.[11]

Presumably, Mao quickly learned of the Liu-Teng efforts to counterbalance and "subvert" his opening moves, and there followed a massive and decisive Maoist attack. In the Eleventh CC Plenum held during the first half of August, 1966, Mao and his supporters, under circumstances which still remain mysterious to outsiders, managed to discredit the leadership of Liu and Teng and censured them for having produced and enforced an erroneous "bourgeois reactionary line." [12] The plenum also reshuffled the Politburo, elected Lin Piao as the sole vice-chairman of the Party and as Mao's successor, and formally approved Mao's blueprint for the GPCR—the now celebrated "Sixteen-Point Decision," which, among other things, endorsed Mao's call to purge "those power-holders within the Party who take the capitalist road." [13]

The censure of Liu and Teng and the attack upon their policies in the plenum suddenly put the provincial leaders in a highly vulnerable political position. It had now been demonstrated that Mao possessed the power to redefine issues, and he had ruled the policies of Liu and Teng both politically and ideologically erroneous. Thus the provincial leaders, to their dismay and horror, found themselves the executors of a policy line denounced by none other than Mao himself as having "enforced a bourgeois dictatorship and struck down the surging movement of the great cultural revolution of the proletariat." [14] Needless

11 *Ibid.*

12 The Eleventh Plenum deviated from previous practices in several respects. In addition to the presence of large numbers of "revolutionary teachers and students," no mention was made in the Plenum communiqué of the number of CC members and alternate members who attended the plenum. A Japanese source reported that only forty-six members and thirty-three alternate members of the CC, or approximately 46 per cent of the total membership, actually attended; see *Seikai shuho* (World Weekly) (Tokyo), No. 37 (September 13, 1966).

13 The text of the "Sixteen-Point Decision" on the GPCR is in *JMJP*, August 9, 1966. An English text is in *Peking Review*, No. 33 (August 12, 1966).

14 Mao Tse-tung, "My First Big-Character Poster" (August 5, 1966), *JMJP*, July 31, 1967; also in *Peking Review*, No. 33 (August 11, 1967).

to say, few provincial leaders had had any intention of opposing Mao. Indeed, all of them had been at great pains to display their loyalty to Mao by carrying out the policies laid down by Liu and Teng in the name of the central leadership, policies which they undoubtedly believed had Mao's endorsement. Yet now, in the midst of rapidly changing events, they found themselves opposing Mao and directly involved in a furious political conflict. Consequently, they had good reasons to fear and suspect that they would become primary targets in the purge projected in the plenum's "Sixteen-Point Decision."

The Maoist leadership did nothing to allay their misgivings. On the contrary, it added fuel to the provincial leaders' fears and suspicions by both words and deeds. Rightly or wrongly, a rapid succession of developments were interpreted by them as unmistakable signs that a sweeping purge by Mao was imminent: Lin Piao's speeches at the Peking Red Guard rallies on August 18 and 31; the simultaneous press campaign which enthusiastically acclaimed the "rebellion" of the Red Guards and "revolutionary rebels," and encouraged them to go to provinces to storm the "bourgeois headquarters" and to drag out the capitalist power-holders; and the subsequent activities of the Red Guards and rebels in response to these orders. Under the prevailing conditions, the provincial leaders felt they could not take a chance, so they devised a number of strategies for self-preservation. Their efforts in this regard in turn provoked the Maoist leadership to press harder. As a result, the conflict escalated rapidly and continuously on both sides up to the end of 1966 when the Rubicon was finally crossed.

Had Mao already intended from the outset to oust as many provincial Party leaders as were subsequently purged? Or, as has been suggested, did he initially want merely to subject most of them to a "test," but under the conditions that developed, found himself forced to remove most of them when they were found deficient in loyalty and/or intransigent? These are intriguing questions, but they cannot be easily answered. At times, Mao and his close associates did speak of the GPCR as entailing a test of the Party officials' ideological outlook; to "pass the test," provincial officials were told that they must confess and amend past errors, "lay down their packs," return to the side of Chairman Mao's proletarian revolutionary line, and submit themselves to the judgment of the revolutionary masses.[15] Good revolutionaries

---

[15] See Article Three of the "Sixteen-Point Decision" in *JMJP,* August 9, 1966, and editorials in *Hung-ch'i* (Red Flag), Nos. 13 and 14 (October 1 and November 1, 1966).

though they might consider themselves, these Party officials were also human beings with ordinary human feelings. The demands of the Maoist leadership that all Party officials would have to confess their shortcomings and mistakes, and submit themselves to the criticisms and judgment of the masses whom they had not infrequently regarded as "docile tools," were probably too much for the thin-skinned and proud Chinese officialdom.

Face and pride, however, were not the only issues involved in such a submission. Obviously, political power and even physical survival were also at stake. The examples of Wan Hsiao-t'ang, first secretary of the Tientsin Municipal Party Committee, and several others who submitted themselves to the criticism of the masses and died as a result of the harsh treatment they received in the mass struggle meetings were frightening, to say the least.[16] Thus, even though Mao personally might have wanted merely to subject provincial Party officials to a "test" without any intention of ousting them, those being subjected to this test, mindful of the ordeal experienced by Wan and others, apparently viewed the entire matter from an entirely different perspective. With the price of "submission to the judgment of the masses" possibly political and even physical demise, most provincial officials refused to cave in.

Several other factors may have also led provincial officials to hold out and take a "wait and see" attitude. First, the continuing division of opinions within the central leadership, as reflected in the speeches of Lin Piao and Chou En-lai, pointed to the possibility of further changes in policy which might in turn set new rules for the game.[17] Secondly, Liu Shao-ch'i and Teng Hsiao-p'ing, who were blamed for producing a "bourgeois reactionary line" in opposition to Mao's GPCR, were not totally removed from the political scene at this point, though they had been demoted. They were present and in the company of Mao, for example, at each of the eight big Peking Red Guard rallies from August 18 to November 25. Most Party officials in the province as well as in the center (except those in Mao's inner circle) may have thought that Liu and Teng were still in reasonably good standing and were continuing to exercise power within Party councils—a belief

[16] Even P'an Fu-sheng, first Party secretary of Heilungkiang, who confessed errors and pledged to Mao immediately after the Eleventh Plenum, was violently struggled by the Red Guards, and had to be rushed to a hospital after being kept from eating and sleeping for four days. See his own account in *Hung-ch'i*, No. 6 (May 8, 1967), p. 35.

[17] Compare the speeches by Lin and Chou on August 18 and September 15, 1966, as reported in *JMJP*, August 19 and September 16, 1966.

which could have had the effect of stiffening Party officials' resistance to the Red Guard challenge.[18]

STRATEGIES FOR SURVIVAL

Although the GPCR had been fathered by Mao, it developed a logic and momentum of its own, taking many dramatic twists and turns. The provincial power-holders, motivated by their primary concern for self-preservation, thus had to adjust their strategies to cope with the shifting goals of the GPCR and with changes in both the actors in and the scope of the conflict.

The following analysis is based, in large part, upon Red Guard materials and on facts that have come to light as a result of later retrospective accounts provided by the official Chinese media, often in the form of specific denunciations of some given individual or propaganda appeals. These sources, undoubtedly, contain biases and distortions. By carefully comparing them with other sources, however, and with circumstantial evidence available to us, we can possibly piece together and draw the main outline of the true picture.

"SACRIFICING THE KNIGHTS TO SAVE THE KING": THE STRATEGY OF EVASION AND DIVERSION

From June, 1966, onward, after the "May 16 Circular" had been disseminated, the provincial leaders, trying to display their conformity with the new Party directive, began to dismiss various subordinates in the provincial propaganda apparatus.[19] Convenient charges were publicized. The victims were denounced as representatives of the bourgeoisie who had sneaked into the Party; followers of Chou Yang, the already deposed "cultural tsar" in China; or "fellow travelers" of the Teng T'o "Three Family Village" group.

Naturally, top provincial leaders made every effort to disassociate

---

[18] As late as October, 1966, Mao still had some kind words for Liu and Teng, saying they were not to be blamed for all the mistakes they had committed. See Mao's speeches on October 24 and 25 to the CC Work Conference in *Mao Tse-tung szu-hsiang wan-sui* (Long Live the Thought of Mao Tse-tung) (n.p., April, 1967). Even though Mao was merely making a gesture here, his remarks seem to have been construed differently. Thus, an official as high as T'an Chen-lin, a Politburo member, could claim that Liu's mistakes belonged to the category of "contradictions among the people" and that "Chairman Mao was still very polite" to Liu; see *P'i-Tan chan-pao* (Criticize T'an Chen-lin Combat News), No. 1 (June 1, 1967) (Peking: The Capital Agriculture System Revolutionary Rebel Liaison Center), p. 3.

[19] For a list of the provincial officials thus denounced or purged, see *China News Summary* (Hong Kong), Nos. 141, 142, 146, 147, and 151 (October 13, October 20, November 17, November 24, and December 22, 1966).

themselves from the accused and thereby to exonerate themselves from the affiliations and acts that might ruin them. After students rose to attack the school authorities in early June, moreover, the provincial leaders dispatched work teams and ousted many school administrators, holding them responsible for having suppressed the GPCR in order to placate the students and keep the student protest within bounds. When the work teams were challenged and student revolts threatened to get out of hand, the provincial leaders hit hard on their challengers. Following the Eleventh CC Plenum, as a concession to the supposed demand of the masses for the purging of the "capitalist power-holders" in the provincial government and as a measure of self-protection, the provincial leaders arranged for a few scapegoats to be dragged out for public repudiation. These victims were described as "those in the Party who are taking the capitalist road." They were denounced for having struck down the revolutionary students, undermined the GPCR, and a host of other earlier anti-Party, antisocialist crimes. Obviously, the provincial leaders were trying to channel the attack of the revolutionary masses to a handful of scapegoats who, they hoped, would serve as an outlet for the accumulated hostility whipped up by Maoist propaganda, and thereby to avoid becoming the target of mass action themselves.

"NEWS MANAGEMENT": THE STRATEGY OF DECEPTION

Invariably, the provincial leaders tried to manipulate the flow of information from their areas to ensure that they would be portrayed as resolute supporters of the GPCR. A vivid revelation of this was provided by Li Pao-hua, first secretary of Anhwei, who, in the name of the provincial Party committee, convened a Congress of Proletarian Cultural Revolution Activists on July 14. To an assembly of more than 10,000 activists in Hofei, the provincial capital, Li delivered a seventy-five-minute speech in which he stated that the GPCR campaign in Anhwei had already exposed a number of anti-Party and antisocialist representatives of the bourgeoisie who had managed to sneak into the Party and that activists in Anhwei province were now being mobilized to expose and criticize "all freaks and monsters" in their localities and units.[20]

To show where he stood, Li adhered closely to the line propagated by the PLA organ, *Chieh-fang-chün pao*. His speech was liberally interlarded with slogans and passages taken directly from its editorials

[20] Radio Hofei, July 16, 1966.

of April 18 and May 4, 1966. Li's estimation of the importance of his speech was revealed by the fact that it was broadcast in full several times over the Anhwei Provincial Broadcasting Station on July 16 and 17. Provincial leaders in many other provinces also put on similar "shows."

After the Eleventh Plenum, provincial authorities repeatedly held mass rallies in provincial capitals to display their support for the GPCR. As Maoist political pressure was intensified in the provinces, moreover, top provincial leaders made numerous public appearances to applaud the formation of Red Guard organizations, to welcome Red Guards from Peking and other provinces, and to mingle "freely" with the "masses," seeking to convey the impression that they basked in the warm light of mass support. Despite their probable uneasiness at this point, as evidence mounted that they themselves were the objects of the GPCR, the provincial leaders purposely coopted the slogans of the Maoist leadership in their speeches at the rallies, denouncing the "handful of power-holders taking the capitalist road" in the Party and calling upon the masses to bombard the "bourgeois command headquarters."

Purporting to encourage "the masses" to criticize the shortcomings and mistakes in their work, as stipulated in Article Three of the "Sixteen-Point Decision," the provincial leaders sponsored public "debates" among the masses to determine "whether or not the provincial Party committee is revolutionary." The result of these "debates" in different provinces was predictably the same: the masses affirmed that the leadership of the "provincial Party committee is revolutionary." By this ploy, the provincial leaders sought to move public opinion in their provinces behind them and to present a good image of themselves in the eyes of national Party leaders. To obstruct antagonistic Red Guards and rebels from putting up wall posters, which were apparently a very effective channel of communication and the only powerful weapon available against the Establishment, Party officials in various places, on the pretext of "writing quotations of Chairman Mao" and "beautifying the appearance of the city," had ordered the walls and front doors of public buildings to be painted red and inscribed with Maoist quotations in an attempt to deny space to the masses.[21]

---

[21] See "Circular of the CCP Central Committee and the State Council on Prohibiting the Extensive Promotion of the So-called 'Red Ocean' " (December 28, 1966), in *CB*, No. 852 (May 8, 1968), p. 33.

ORGANIZING THE "ROYALIST" MASS ORGANIZATIONS

Immediately following the Eleventh Plenum, Mao, as is well known, invoked the aid of important extra-Party forces—the Red Guards and the "revolutionary rebels"—in his GPCR crusade. He was fully aware that his supporters within Party councils were in the minority. Thus, to project his will, he had no alternative but to enlarge the scope of the conflict and to draw more political actors into the scene in order to redress the political balance of power.[22]

Confronted with this new situation, the provincial leaders followed much the same course of action. They created their own Red Guard and "rebel" groups, and used them to fight against Mao's supporters. Li Ching-ch'üan, first secretary of the Party's Southwest China Bureau and the boss of Szechwan as well as the southwest region prior to his downfall in 1967, was specifically accused by his critics of having telephoned the officials in the Kweichow Provincial Party Committee in late August to tell them that if the Red Guards mobilized ten thousand supporters to surround Party headquarters, the Party committee should arrange for twenty thousand of their followers to come and surround the others. Moreover, if the Red Guards claimed they were obeying Chairman Mao's instructions, said Li, the Party committee and its mass followers should make the same claim.[23]

Clearly, it is no accident that the Red Guards in each province had at least two major factions fighting against each other, one opposing the provincial establishment and the other defending it, with both loudly proclaiming that they were loyal followers of Chairman Mao and resolute supporters of the GPCR. Each accused the other of being the stooge of "the capitalist power-holders in the Party," much to the confusion of outside observers and even to the Chinese Communists themselves.

Those Red Guard groups which supported the Establishment were largely children of the so-called five Red categories (workers, middle-lower and poor peasants, soldiers, cadres, and martyrs). In many cases, the "children of high-level cadres" (kao-kan tzu-ti) were leaders of these Red Guard organizations. On the other hand, Red Guards who came from politically less favorable or underprivileged

22 Cf. Richard Baum's treatment of this point in his "Elite Behavior under Conditions of Stress: The Lesson of the 'Tang-ch'uan P'ai' in the Cultural Revolution" in this volume.
23 Radio Kweiyang, Jung 25, 1967.

social classes or strata were, for obvious reasons, more militant and anti-Establishmentarian.

In the fall of 1966, the power-holders in the provinces (and in Peking as well) apparently exploited critical social divisions in Chinese society in instigating the Red Guards composed of the five Red categories to fight against the more militant Red Guards upon whom the Maoist leadership was relying to topple the provincial authorities. For instance, Chia Ch'i-yun, first Party secretary of Kweichow, was quoted by Radio Kweiyang (June 10, 1967) as having said to a forum of Red Guards in early September, 1966:

You are all sons and daughters of the five Red categories; the regime relies on you for protection. . . . Many of those in the liaison teams [from Peking and other provinces that came to Kweichow] have bad backgrounds. Before, we struggled against their parents and established our regime. Today, obviously, their parents are not reconciled to this and are using their children to struggle against us. You must battle against them.

Slogans such as "A hero's son is a real man! A reactionary's son is no damn good!" and "A dragon begets a dragon, a phoenix begets a phoenix, and those begotten by rats are good at digging holes" were advanced to castigate and discredit Red Guards of a less favorable background politically and, in the words of Maoist propagandists, "to create antagonism among revolutionary students." As we shall have occasion to note later, provincial authorities, according to Maoist sources, also organized "royalist" factions among the "established" workers, using them to fight Maoist Red Guards and the less privileged workers like temporary and contract workers.

Caution must be observed in accepting later Maoist charges carte blanche. "Mass factionalism," the striking political phenomenon which, having been brought to the surface by the GPCR, had spread to epidemic proportions during 1966–68, was certainly not created entirely by the so-called provincial power-holders and class enemies, as the Maoist propagandists have repeatedly asserted. The sources of mass factionalism were many. Numerous issues—personal, organizational, and political—divided the various new mass organizations against one another. Not that this division should be surprising: individual students, workers, and cadres had joined them out of a wide range of motives.[24] Nevertheless, the power-holders' machinations and manipu-

[24] For an informative and interesting discussion of these problems, see "Mass Factionalism in Communist China," *Current Scene* (Hong Kong), VI, No. 8 (May 15, 1968), 1–13.

lations behind the scenes undoubtedly caused further splits and intensified the rivalry among such organizations. And one result was to divert and dilute Mao's attack upon them.

DETERRENCE AND REPRESSION

When necessary, the provincial power-holders did not hesitate to use various devices for suppressing the Red Guards and revolutionary rebels who challenged their authority and threatened their survival. In addition to deploying agents to maintain surveillance and gather "black materials" on the leaders of the hostile mass organizations, the provincial power-holders also used instruments of coercion to suppress the revolutionary rebels. Although the command relationship between the Party organizations and the regime's coercive system is not wholly clear, the public security forces, the procuratorate, and justice organs, were more inclined to oppose those who challenged the status quo because of their responsibilities for the maintenance of law and order. The available evidence shows that the provincial leaders were able to make use of those "organs of dictatorship" to arrest and persecute the so-called revolutionaries. For example, in Szechwan alone, 30,000 "Maoist rebels" were arrested. Because the organs of coercion stood on the side of the provincial power-holders, Mao had to urge his supporters repeatedly to "thoroughly smash the public security, procuratorate, and justice organs." [25]

Furthermore, capitalizing on popular resentment against the unruly disruptive activities of the Red Guards and the almost unlimited licenses taken by them as well as upon the strong provincialism of local residents which could be directed against outside "troublemakers," the provincial leaders were able to play off local Red Guard groups against outside groups, and to mobilize peasants and workers to fight the "revolutionary students." This was confirmed by an editorial in *Jen-min jih-pao* on September 11 which stated:

The Sixteen-Point Decision has explicitly and definitely pointed out: "To prevent the struggle from being diverted from its main target, it is impermissible to use any pretext to instigate the masses to struggle against the masses or students to struggle against students." However, responsible persons in some places and in some units have directly disobeyed this decision of the Party center. They have

[25] *Chiu p'eng-lo chan-pao* (Expose P'eng [Chen]-Lo [Jui-ch'ing] Combat News) (Canton), No. 3 (February, 1968), in *SCMP*, No. 4139 (March 15, 1968), pp. 6 and 7. According to Vice-Premier Hsieh Fu-chih, there was not a single major city where the public security forces supported the "proletarian revolutionaries."

found various pretexts to suppress the mass movement. They have even incited a section of the workers and peasants who do not know the true situation into opposing the revolutionary students and into standing in confrontation against the revolutionary students. This is . . . an error in direction and in line. *We shall never allow anyone to make use of the workers' and peasants' profound class feelings for the Party in order to sow dissension and to manufacture opposition between the workers, peasants, and revolutionary students* [emphasis added].

The interesting point in this last sentence is its revelation that provincial Party officials were able to "make use of the workers' and peasants' profound class feelings for the Party" to fight revolutionary students. This statement also reflects the predicament encountered by Mao in attacking Party organizations whose authority had hitherto been accepted without question. In the eyes of the average Chinese, Party officials personified the Party, and to oppose the provincial Party authorities was to oppose the Party "center." Undoubtedly, the power-holders were aware of their "position of strength" and thus they were consciously manipulating the sacred aura of Party authority in a desperate effort to defend themselves against Chairman Mao's initiatives.

FORMING CIVILIAN-MILITARY ALLIANCES

In the course of the tug of war between provincial authorities and their Red Guard challengers, the provincial leaders had sought and secured the support of local PLA commanders. Since the local PLA units, like the security organs, had had the responsibility to assist in maintaining law and order, their leaders probably viewed those attacking the status quo with suspicion and resentment and were more inclined to align themselves with the provincial Party leaders. Personal and organizational ties between PLA and Party leaders were also close. In many provinces, children of the local PLA leaders and of local Party leaders had worked together to organize the initial Red Guard groups, an action possibly initiated by the parents and in any case quite likely to affect parental attitudes. Moreover, since senior regional-provincial Party secretaries often served concurrently as first political commissars of military regions or districts, and the PLA commanders also served in the Party's regional bureaus or provincial committees, close ties tended to be forged between civilian Party leaders and PLA officials.

The reported "confession" of Ch'en Tsai-tao, the commander of the Wuhan Military Region until July, 1967, shed some light on the nature of the civilian-military alliance, and deserves to be quoted in length:

After recuperating for over a year, I returned to Wuhan in September last year [1966]. As a Standing Committee Member of the Hupeh Provincial Party Committee, I attended sessions of the Standing Committee after my return to Wuhan; I listened to the opinions of Chang T'i-hsueh [acting first secretary] and sided with him. . . . I followed Chang T'i-hsueh and promptly answered his call whenever he wanted me. He asked me to preside over four general meetings convened by the conservatives.

In all of the rallies that I had attended I sided with the provincial Party committee and the conservatives, supporting the conservatives and suppressing the rebels, embellishing the provincial Party Committee, and advancing the cause of Chang T'i-hsueh. . . . In shielding Chang T'i-hsueh, I accommodated him in a rented house and provided his staff with office premises. I was even prepared to provide them with an office building. What for? I did so to hide, and provide cover for, the members of this black provincial Party committee and to support their reactionary line.[26]

In many provinces, the Party leaders deposited the "black materials" which they had collected in the PLA headquarters to prevent them from falling into the hands of the Red Guards, or persuaded the local PLA leaders to deploy troops to guard the premises of the Party against a possible invasion by rebels. Some civilian Party leaders allegedly also put on PLA uniforms, rode in cars carrying military license plates, and worked in the office of the local PLA headquarters, using those quarters as their "shelter."[27]

Cooperation was not forthcoming in all cases. The provincial power-holders in Shansi, for example, tried but failed to secure the cooperation and assistance of the local PLA units.[28] Shansi, in fact, was one of the four provinces where the PLA had positively responded to the appeal of Maoist leadership in January, 1967, to support the left and wrest power from the provincial authorities. The other provinces were Heilungkiang, Kweichow, and Shantung. The success or failure of the provincial authorities in obtaining local PLA support against the Maoist rebels, or, to put it in a different way, the responses of the local

[26] "Ch'en Tsai-tao's Examination" (transcribed and edited from a recording on December 1, 1967), Na-han chan-pao (Outcry Combat News), No. 4 (April, 1968) (Canton: Suburban Cultural-Educational Revolutionary Rebel H.Q. of Red H.Q. of Municipal Organs), also translated in SCMP, No. 4167 (April 30, 1968), pp. 3-4. The quoted passages are based on the SCMP translation with minor corrections in English.

[27] Ta p'i-p'an t'ung-hsun (Mass Criticism and Repudiation Report) (Canton: Canton News Service of Shanghai T'ung-chi University Tung-fang Hung Corps), October 5, 1967.

[28] See Chang Jih-ch'ing's article in JMJP, February 28, 1967. Chang was then second political commissar of the Shansi Military District.

PLA toward the order of "supporting the left," was one of the important variables in determining the ability of the provincial authorities to withstand the Maoists' onslaught; it also figured in determining the speed with which the revolutionary committees—the new organs of provincial power—were established in the different provinces.

LOBBYING IN PEKING

To survive and to thrive in a political system like that of the People's Republic of China, provincial leaders had learned early to keep a watchful eye constantly on Peking so as to detect any shifts in the power relations of the top leaders or in policies. Various provinces appeared to have maintained a liaison office in Peking partly for the purpose of gathering information on central politics. Li Ching-ch'üan and T'ao Chu allegedly even operated Szechwanese and Cantonese restaurants, respectively, in the nation's capital for public relations and intelligence-gathering purposes. In addition, the provincial leaders also maintained close ties with, or found protectors in, certain central leaders who could represent their interests and argue their case at critical moments in higher Party councils. The case of Li Ching-ch'üan, who allegedly had close relations with high Party figures like Teng Hsiao-p'ing, P'eng Chen, Ho Lung, and Yang Shang-k'un (if his critics may be believed),[29] was not a unique one. Most, if not all, of the provincial leaders continued to keep contacts with their former superiors in the army or in the Party after the latter moved to Peking.

During the GPCR, when their political survival was endangered, the provincial leaders naturally sought to use their contacts and protectors in Peking to "pass the test" (*kuo-kuan*). T'an Chen-lin allegedly "vouched" for Chiang Hua and Chiang Wei-ch'ing, first Party secretaries of Chekiang and Kiangsu, respectively, in a Party meeting of February, 1967, when they were in trouble. It was charged later that because of this, the "lid" of class struggle in these two provinces was not lifted for a long time.[30]

When the Honan Party Committee, headed by Wen Min-sheng, acting first secretary, submitted a "self-criticism" report to the CC in October, 1966, its former first secretary, Liu Chien-hsün, who had been transferred to Peking to serve in the reorganized Peking Munici-

[29] Radio Kweiyang, June 4, 1967.
[30] See *Hsin-hua jih-pao* (New China Daily) (Nanking), June 23, 1968, and K'ang Sheng's speech in *Chung-ta hung-ch'i* (Chungshan University Red Flag) (Canton: Chungshan University Red Headquarters of the Canton Red Guard Congress), April 4, 1968; also in *SCMP,* No. 4166 (April 29, 1968), pp. 2–3.

pal Party Committee, checked and revised the report himself and reportedly used his influence to protect the position of his former associates in Honan and to get the Honan Party Committee absolved for whatever "mistakes" it had earlier committed.[31]

Chao Tzu-yang, first Party secretary of Kwangtung, is also alleged to have been in touch constantly with T'ao Chu by telephone after the latter moved to Peking. On several occasions, T'ao was said to have informed Chao in advance of the new moves of the central leadership and "coached" Chao on strategies for dealing with the revolutionaries.[32]

In addition to working through their former superiors and protectors, the provincial leaders may have sought to "lobby" those central leaders more inclined to listen to their views. One of these leaders was T'ao Chu, the rising political star in the summer of 1966 who, after the Eleventh Plenum, occupied the number four spot in the Politburo line-up and was adviser to the Cultural Revolution Group. There are signs that he, together with Wang Jen-chung, tried to protect the provincial authorities in the Central-South China area, and took a generally sympathetic stand toward all provincial authorities—a stand which eventually led him to clash with the radical, iconoclastic Maoist Red Guards and their political mentors in the CRG, Ch'en Po-ta and Chiang Ch'ing.[33]

For instance, T'ao defended the provincial officials who were accused of executing the "bourgeois reactionary line" by saying that "whatever mistakes were committed, they have an organizational basis, because the lower level has to obey the higher authorities and central directives must be carried out." [34] When Maoist rebels in the provinces came to Peking to make accusations against the provincial leaders, T'ao, in most cases, supposedly exculpated or played down the offenses of the provincial leaders. For example, he was accused of

31 "A Brief Report on the Situation of Honan's Great Proletarian Cultural Revolution to the Revolutionary People of the National Capital," a pamphlet published by the Honan Provincial Revolutionary Rebel General Command, March 8, 1967. A copy of this pamphlet is in the author's possession.

32 "See How T'ao Chu Tries to Strangle the Great Cultural Revolution in Kwangtung through Chao Tzu-yang," *Hung-se pao-tung* (Red Riot), No. 2 (February 27, 1967) (Canton: Red Rebels, South-Central Forestry Institute), in *SCMP*, No. 3935 (May 9, 1967), pp. 12–14.

33 "Remarks by the Central Leaders on T'ao Chu," *Chin sung* (Sturdy Pine) (Shanghai Liaison Center of the Mao Tse-tung Thought, Red Guard, and the Wuhan Revolutionary Rebel Headquarters), February 7, 1967.

34 "The Records of the Words and Deeds of T'ao Chu in Undermining the Great Cultural Revolution," *ibid.*

"bailing out" provincial Party leaders politically by asserting on November 16, 1966: "In the nation's twenty-eight provinces and municipalities, all but two provincial officials should have their problems handled as nonantagonistic; the two exceptions are Li Fan-wu of Heilungkiang and Wang Feng of Kansu." [35] Thus, a remark attributed to Chao Tzu-yang that T'ao Chu tended to listen to the views of provincial officials, while other CRG leaders tended to listen to the opinions of Red Guard students, has a certain ring of truth.[36]

In the fall and winter of 1966, many provincial leaders had complained that the Red Guard and GPCR activities were having adverse effects on economic production. They warned the central leadership that they might not be able to fulfill production plans. Their concern with the economy, whether or not it was merely a pretext to suppress the GPCR and to protect their power, as alleged by *Jen-min jih-pao* (January 1, 1967), was apparently shared by Premier Chou. In the first Peking Red Guard rally on August 18, 1966, he stressed that the principal task for both "revolutionary teachers and students" from Peking and other provinces was to carry out well the cultural revolution in "their own units." This point seems to suggest Chou's reservations concerning the Red Guards' massive "exchange of revolutionary experience" which ended up by clogging rails and roads and adversely affecting the economy.[37] Significantly, perhaps, it was not a point mentioned by Lin Piao, speaking on the same occasion.

Possible differences between Chou and Lin became more explicit when both of them spoke again on September 15.[38] While Lin actively encouraged Red Guard fighters and revolutionary students to "bombard the handful of power-holders in the Party who are taking the capitalist road," Chou chanted a different tune, devoting most of his speech to the economy. He told the Red Guards that to carry out industrial and agricultural production well would have great effect "upon our socialist construction, upon the third five-year plan, upon the people's livelihood in the town and country, and upon the Great Proletarian Cultural Revolution" as well as upon "our support to the Vietnamese people in their anti-U.S. struggle and upon the revolutionary struggle of the oppressed peoples of the world." He also declared

---

[35] *Ibid.*

[36] "A Bundle of Poisoned Arrows Shot by Chao Tzu-yang at the Central Cultural Revolution Group," *Hung-ch'i ju-hua* (Red Flag as a Picture) (Canton), No. 1 (January, 1968), in *SCMP*, No. 4112, pp. 4–5.

[37] See the speeches by Chou and Lin in *JMJP*, August 19, 1966.

[38] *Ibid.*, September 16, 1966.

that "in order to facilitate the normal operation of industrial and agricultural production," Red Guards "should not at the present time go to factories, enterprises, offices below the county level, and rural communes to establish revolutionary ties there."

There is no concrete evidence that the provincial officials imparted their concern over the disruptive effects of the GPCR upon the economy to Chou, who then worked to place restraints on Red Guards. That action was probably unnecessary because Chou, as premier, was the man who had the major responsibility for running the nation's economy and thus he had a strong vested interest in ensuring the normal operation of economic production. Consequently, provincial leaders and Premier Chou logically could find common ground here. It probably required no active "lobbying" by the former to get Chou to argue against extending the GPCR to factories and communes.

In any case, since the Chinese leadership in Peking did place increased emphasis on economic tasks in the fall of 1966, and imposed certain restrictions on the Red Guards, it appears that Chou and other leaders who held similar views had temporarily prevailed in national Party councils.[39] Provincial leaders apparently were able to use the theme of "promoting production" to restrict the scope of Red Guard activities and ward off their assaults.[40] In the second half of December, 1966, however, the leftist elements within the national leadership seemingly gained the upper hand, and the previous policy of moderation was abruptly reversed. On December 26, *Jen-min jih-pao* announced editorially that the GPCR would be extended to farms and factories, and "Maoists" throughout China intensified their attack upon "capitalist power-holders" both in Peking and in the provinces.

"SUGAR-COATED BULLETS": THE STRATEGY OF COOPTATION

In light of the fact that the provincial power-holders were able to enlist the support of workers and peasants to fight revolutionary students, it is not surprising that the Maoist leadership felt compelled to expand the scope of the political conflict further by extending the GPCR to factories, mines, and rural areas. In the words of *Jen-min jih-pao* (January 1, 1967), this action was taken to "enable the

[39] For restrictions placed on the Red Guards, see the editorial, "Grasping Revolution and Stimulating Production," *JMJP*, September 7, 1966; and CC "Provisions concerning the Great Cultural Revolution in Rural Districts below the *Hsien* Level" (September 14, 1966), in *CB*, No. 852 (May 6, 1968), p. 17.

[40] Editorial, *JMJP*, January 1, 1967.

thought of Mao Tse-tung to occupy all fronts." The "capitalist power-holders" in turn were accused of "persecuting" workers who appeared to be supporting Mao's cause. At least, so the *Jen-min jih-pao* editorial of December 26 charged when it enjoined officials from persecuting and intimidating workers, and ordered that back wages be paid to workers who had been laid off for taking part in the GPCR.

In a desperate attempt to oust the provincial authorities who apparently enjoyed the support of most "established"—that is, permanently employed—workers, the Maoist leadership now actively courted the support of temporary and contract workers who, under the prevailing labor system in China, were the underprivileged labor group. Receiving lower wages and getting poorer welfare benefits than the regular workers, they were potentially the most revolutionary, inasmuch as they had more to gain from changing the status quo.[41] (Admittedly this is a hazardous assumption, as data drawn from many political struggles indicate.)

According to reports in several Red Guard publications, Chiang Ch'ing and other CRG leaders had received a delegation of temporary and contract workers on December 26, 1966, and blamed Liu Shao-ch'i for instituting the "exploitative" temporary-contract worker system.[42] Reportedly, Chiang Ch'ing demanded restitution for the temporary-contract workers, and they were subsequently reinstated and received back wages from their employers. Such action would have been in agreement with the policies set forth in the December 26 *Jen-min jih-pao* editorial cited above. However, the use of material rewards to secure political support soon proved to be a double-edged sword for the Maoist leadership and produced serious, undesired, and unanticipated consequences.

The temporary and contract workers were not the only group that harbored disaffection and grievances against the regime. Serious discontent also existed among the demobilized and transferred soldiers who were unreconciled to the rigors involved in reclaiming land in Heilungkiang and other border provinces, and among the youth from cities and populated areas who had been sent to rugged frontier or

[41] See "Sources of Labor Discontent in China: The Worker-Peasant System," *Current Scene*, VI, No. 5 (March 15, 1968), 1–28.

[42] "Smash the Liu-Teng Reactionary System and Thoroughly Liberate the Temporary-Contract Workers," *Shou-tu hung-wei-p'ing* (Capital Red Guard), No. 1 (January 10, 1967) (Peking: Propaganda Department of the Revolutionary Rebel Headquarters of Red Guards from Capital University and Colleges).

mountainous regions to engage in agricultural or construction labor. And still other groups, such as the underpaid apprentice workers and a vast number of unemployed citizens, were deeply unhappy.

During the GPCR, elements from these various groups formed their own rebel organizations to "bombard" the "capitalist power-holders" in the Party and "make rebellion" against the "unreasonable system." They pressed a wide range of demands in an effort to better their lot and redress their practical, nonideological socioeconomic grievances, although the demands were invariably stated in proper orthodox fashion, replete with Maoist phrases and slogans. Thus, taking advantage of the disruptions during the GPCR, and in the name of "making rebellion," peasants trekked into provincial capitals to advance their own demands for economic betterment, while within the towns and cities workers were pressing for improved working conditions and a better wage system.[43]

The provincial authorities apparently yielded to some of the demands of these groups as a way of building local support. For example, they reinstated the dismissed workers and paid them back wages, authorized wage increases for other workers, promised greater welfare benefits, and rehired workers who had been previously sent to rural areas to "support agriculture."[44] Groups whose demands were not met resorted to protest strikes to enforce those demands.

In some cases, the provincial authorities were, or they claimed they were, unable to accommodate the demands of a given "rebel" group on account of state regulations. Unwilling to alienate these groups, they merely "passed the buck" by paying for the expenses involved in taking their cases to Peking. As a result, work in many factories, mines, and shipyards came to a halt. Hundreds of thousands of workers clogged the rails and roads winding their way to Peking to "make complaints" or to exchange revolutionary experiences. Transportation was paralyzed.

The crisis became widespread throughout China in the second half of December, 1966, and in January, 1967, with particularly serious impacts upon such major industrial centers as Shanghai and Harbin. By this time, attacks on Party and government authorities, launched

---

[43] See Evelyn Anderson, "Shanghai: The Masses Unleashed," *Problems of Communism*, XVII, No. 1 (January-February, 1968), 13–16; and Parris H. Chang, "The Revolutionary Committee in China: Two Case Studies: Heilungkiang and Honan," *Current Scene*, VI, No. 9 (June 1, 1968), 3–5.

[44] See reports in *JMJP*, January 16, 1967, and "Proletarian Revolutionaries, Unite!" *Hung-ch'i*, No. 2 (January 16, 1967).

in the name of the GPCR, had considerably weakened the regime's grip on the population, thereby opening the floodgates to spontaneous demands by workers, peasants, and other underprivileged segments of the society for social and economic betterment. The Maoist leadership, however, persisted in blaming "a handful of capitalist power-holders in the Party" who, they claimed, were inciting the workers to leave their work posts so as to "sabotage production, communications, and the whole national economy" and "to put pressure on the Cultural Revolution groups." Unable to meet these socioeconomic demands, the Maoist leadership also charged the "handful" with employing "economism to divert the general direction of the struggle, in an effort to lead a dignified political struggle onto the evil road of economic struggle, and at the same time to corrupt the revolutionary will of the masses with material benefits." [45]

Certainly, the Maoist charges against the provincial power-holders were distorted and exaggerated. They were not totally groundless, however. There is no doubt that the provincial leaders had exploited existing sources of popular discontent and labor unrest (as did the Maoist leadership itself) to compete with the Maoists for the support of those rebel groups still uncommitted politically. In the face of the Maoists' attempt to bring them down, many provincial leaders, understandably, did not wish to weaken further their own positions or to create more enemies than necessary. Thus they were probably much more responsive to the economic demands of the rebel groups than they might normally have been. When the Maoist leadership attempted to seek support from certain segments of labor by authorizing workers to establish revolutionary ties and exchange revolutionary experiences elsewhere, and approving the payment of back wages to dismissed workers, the provincial authorities quickly tried to coopt these same elements. Consequently, they pushed those measures to the ultimate extreme, forcing the Maoists' hands and producing social and economic chaos, thereby leading to the failure of the new Maoist maneuver.

"SHAM" SEIZURES OF POWER: THE STRATEGY OF PRE-EMPTION

By the beginning of 1967, it must have become clear to Mao and his top aides that the GPCR had failed to make the desired headway. Provincial authorities, using the full range of the powers granted them,

---

[45] *JMJP*, January 22, 1967; also see "Oppose Economics and Smash Bourgeois Reactionary Line," editorial, *JMJP*, January 12, 1969.

had been able to stem the assaults of the "Maoist rebels." The "black wind of economism" had also generated chaos, presenting the central leadership with the threat of a disastrous economic breakdown. In the face of this, the Maoist leadership decided not to retreat, but to take the most extreme measures yet. They now mounted an all-out attack on "the power structure," trying in a curious fashion to emulate the 1871 Paris Commune effort.

In early January, Maoists in Shanghai physically seized control of the city's two major newspapers, the *Wen-hui pao* (Cultural Exchange Daily) and *Chieh-fang jih-pao,* and on January 17 they took over Shanghai's radio and television stations from the city's Party officials. Subsequently, on February 5, Maoist rebels in Shanghai under the direction of Chang Ch'un-ch'iao and Yao Wen-yuan set up the Shanghai People's Commune and proclaimed that they had succeeded in eliminating the authority of officials in the Shanghai Party and government organizations.[46] When the rebels seized the Shanghai newspapers, the Maoist leadership in Peking immediately acclaimed their revolutionary action and, on January 12, they openly encouraged rebels throughout China to follow the example of Shanghai.[47] The exhortation was turned into an official directive on January 22, when *Jen-min jih-pao* editorially instructed proletarian revolutionaries to form a great alliance in order to seize all power from those in authority who are taking the capitalist road.

The editorial made it clear that "the basic question of revolution is political power" and that "from the very beginning, the Great Proletarian Cultural Revolution has been a struggle for the seizure of power." The Maoist leadership candidly admitted that "reversals and twists and turns" had occurred, and asserted that "the reason why the revolution has suffered setbacks" is "due precisely to the fact that they [the rebels] did not take the seal of power into their own hands." The editorial went on to say:

Of all the ways in which the revolutionary masses can take their destiny into their own hands, in the final analysis, the only way is to seize power! He who has power has everything; he who is without power has nothing. . . . All the Party power, political power, and financial power usurped by the counterrevolutionary revisionists and the bourgeois reactionary line die-hards must be recaptured!

[46] *Wen-hui pao* (Shanghai), February 6, 1967.
[47] "Oppose Economism: Smash the New Counteroffensive of the Bourgeois Reactionary Line," editorial, *JMJP,* January 12, 1967.

To ensure the success of this seizure of power, the Maoist leadership now ordered the PLA to "support the left"—in other words, to intervene on the side of the Maoists.[48] While the PLA or segments of the PLA had earlier supported Mao to help defeat such top Party figures as P'eng Chen, Teng Hsiao-p'ing, and Liu Shao-ch'i in the spring and summer of 1966, PLA commanders do not appear to have been actively involved in the Maoist attacks on provincial authorities in the fall of 1966. Apparently, certain PLA leaders had succeeded in arguing against involvement and in advocating a neutral role for the PLA.[49]

As pointed out earlier, some provincial authorities were able to obtain the support or cooperation of local PLA units in their fight against Red Guards. Therefore, certain units of the PLA had actually been politically involved already. This was precisely Mao's argument. He was quoted as having said:

The so-called noninvolvement is false, for the army was already involved long ago. The question, therefore, is not one of involvement or noninvolvement. It is one of whose side we should stand on and whether we should support the revolutionaries or the conservatives or even the rightists. The PLA should actively support the revolutionary leftists.[50]

Although the Maoist leadership succeeded in pushing the PLA into support of the "revolutionary leftist," it was well aware that at least some PLA leaders, both in Peking and in provinces, were opposed to using the PLA to crush opposition from within the Party.[51] Therefore, the Maoists reactivated the aged and semiretired Marshal Hsu Hsiang-ch'ien to head the All-PLA Cultural Revolution Group, and promoted Hsu and Marshal Ch'en Yi to the posts of vice-chairmen

---

[48] See "Decision of the CCP Central Committee, the State Council, the Military Affairs Commission and the Cultural Revolution Group on Resolute Support for the Revolutionary Masses of the Left" (January 23, 1967), in *CB*, No. 852 (May 6, 1958), pp. 49–50.

[49] *Ibid.*

[50] *Ibid.*

[51] See "The PLA Resolutely Supports the Proletarian Revolutionary Faction," editorial, *Chieh-fang-chün pao,* January 25, 1967. In late December, 1966, and early January, 1967, preceding the formal involvement of the PLA in the GPCR, several top PLA figures were purged, including Ho Lung, vice-chairman of the Military Affairs Commission; Yang Yung and Liao Han-sheng, commander and political commissar, respectively, of the Peking Military Region; Wang Shan-jung and Lei Ying-fu, director and deputy director of the PLA General Staff Department of Operations; and Liang Pi-yeh, deputy director of the PLA General Political Department. They may have been the high-level examples of "capitalist power-holders in the army" who opposed the GPCR and who were denounced in the editorials of *Chieh-fang-chün pao.* See *ibid.,* January 12 and 14, 1967.

of the Party's Military Affairs Commission (MAC), in an apparent maneuver to commit them to Mao's cause so that they would use their influence to win over their followers and former associates in the PLA to Mao's side.

The Maoist leadership's plans did not completely materialize, however. During the seven months that followed the January 23 directive ordering the PLA to intervene on the side of the revolutionary leftists, PLA units supported Maoist rebels in their efforts to seize power from provincial authorities only in Heilungkiang, Kweichow, Shanghai, Shansi, Shantung, and Tsinghai. In the remaining twenty provinces (excluding Peking) the responses of the local PLA leaders were equivocal.[52] In some provinces, the PLA actually intervened, knowingly or unknowingly, against the Maoist rebels, and in other provinces different PLA leaders supported opposing rebel groups. Consequently, at a later point, PLA leaders in many provinces were purged for errors committed in "supporting the left." [53]

The reasons why so many local PLA leaders had committed "errors" were varied and complicated. Some, undoubtedly, were strongly opposed to the GPCR and consciously collaborated with local Party officials to suppress the Maoists. Others were resentful of the Red Guards and other rebels who disrupted law and order and sought to overthrow the Establishment of which they were a part. The most

[52] For the accounts of the PLA's support of "seizure of power by Maoists in Shansi, Heilungkiang, Shantung, and Kweichow, see editorials in *JMJP*, January 25, February 2, March 2, 1967, and in NCNA (Kweiyang), February 22, 1967. The case of Shanghai was more complicated. Maoist youth and workers did play a significant role, but Chang Ch'un-ch'iao also admitted that PLA units in Shanghai had lent a hand (*JMJP*, February 28, 1967). In Tsinghai, Liu Hsien-ch'uan and Chao Yung-fu, commander and deputy commander of the military district, respectively, appear to have helped opposing rebel groups to seize power, and the Maoist leadership had to dispatch troops from the Lanchow Military Region to Tsinghai to suppress Chao, who was then accused of engineering a "counterrevolutionary coup"; see "Decision concerning the Question of Tsinghai" (March 24, 1967), in *CB*, No. 852 (May 6, 1968), p. 109.

In Peking, since it was under the direct control of the Maoist leadership, the PLA units do not appear to have taken part in the Maoist "seizure of power." According to Hsieh Fu-chih who was appointed chairman of the revolutionary committee of Peking in April, 1967, the PLA joined the "three-way alliance" only during the process of planning and organizing the Peking municipal revolutionary committee. *JMJP*, April 21, 1967.

[53] In a separate study on PLA intervention in the GPCR which is in progress, I will examine in detail the patterns of PLA response in different provinces to Mao's call for "supporting the left." Suffice it to say here that the PLA, as a whole, failed to support Mao's crusade against the provincial power-holders.

According to my tabulation, during 1967–68, the leadership personnel in eight out of thirteen military regions and in fourteen out of twenty-seven provincial-level military districts was reshuffled, involving, in most cases, the dismissals of commanders, deputy commanders, and/or political commissars.

frequent reason, however, was the "factionalism of the masses" which inevitably trapped many PLA leaders into supporting one faction against another—a conservative against a radical faction, or one radical group against another radical group.

When the Maoist leadership called for the "revolutionary masses" to seize power from the provincial authorities in January, 1967, individual rebel groups immediately jockeyed for position in competition with one another. They seized different units of the same provincial Party committee and, in some cases, seized the units already taken over by other rebel groups. The factional fighting was so serious that the Peking leadership had to urge the "revolutionary masses" repeatedly to form a "great alliance." [54] But Peking apparently failed to impose tight control from above.

Taking advantage of these circumstances, the provincial leaders put forward a device which the Maoists described as a "sham seizure of power." Trying to pre-empt the seizure by the Maoists, astute Chinese officials in many provinces handed "power" over to the rebel groups they controlled and thereby managed to exercise control continuously behind the scenes. A typical example was provided by a coalition of Red Guard and rebel organizations in Szechwan, called the "United Revolutionary Association," who claimed to have wrested power from Szechwan's provincial Party authorities on February 8, 1967, and then paraded Li Chiang-ch'üan, first secretary of the CCP Southwest China Bureau, Liao Chih-kao, first secretary of Szechwan, and other top local officials through the streets of Chengtu the following day.[55] According to the Maoist rebels, however, these events were nothing more than a scene from a political Chinese opera, carefully staged by Li and his cohorts, who had handed power over to the "royalist" United Revolutionary Association and used the revolutionary smoke screen of seizure of power to preserve their influence.[56] Subsequently, Peking refused to endorse the February 8 "seizure of power" in Szechwan.

Judging from Chinese provincial radio broadcasts and Red Guard

[54] See, for example, "Proletarian Revolutionaries, Unite!"; "Proletarian Revolutionaries Form a Great Alliance to Seize Power from the Capitalist Power-holders," editorial, *JMJP,* January 22, 1967; and "The Key Is to Form a Great Alliance," editorial, *JMJP,* January 30, 1967.

[55] Red Guard sources quoted in "Stalemate in Szechuan," *Current Scene,* VI, No. 11 (July 1, 1968), 6.

[56] *Ibid.*

sources, the so-called sham seizure of power took place at least in Anhwei, Kiangsi, Shensi, Kwangsi, Honan, and Kwangtung, in addition to Szechwan.[57] It was also reportedly attempted in Shantung, but failed because the Maoists, with the help of local PLA units, recaptured power.[58] The Peking leadership was silent on the seizure of power in these provinces because, in most cases, power was not seized by groups whom it considered to be truly revolutionary. Although the central leadership did not recognize the seizures of power in these provinces, the local PLA authorities, with the exception of those in Honan and Kwangtung (where, ironically, power was actually seized by Maoist groups), apparently did.[59]

Such PLA approval alienated and enraged other rebel groups, namely, those who did not take part in the seizure of power and were left out of the "new Establishment." [60] In many other provinces, the PLA refused to take sides in the factional struggle of rebel groups who were competing to seize power from the provincial authorities, but intervened only to maintain order when violence broke out. The neutrality of the PLA in effect obstructed the seizure of power and lent a helping hand to the power-holders. Thus, from February, 1967, on, those disaffected rebel groups began to point their "spearhead of struggle" at the local PLA authorities. They denounced local PLA leaders for protecting the "capitalist power-holders in the Party" and executing the "bourgeois reactionary line," and in some cases they actually raided PLA headquarters.

In response, the PLA authorities, using the pretext of "supporting the revolutionary leftists" who had seized power, or in the name of suppressing "counterrevolutionary elements" according to the eight-article order of the MAC issued on January 28, 1967, persecuted the trouble-making rebels, labeled their groups "reactionary" or "counterrevolutionary," banned their organizations, and arrested their lead-

---

[57] Radio Hofei, January 26, 1969; Radio Nanchang, January 26, 1967; Radio Sian, January 26, 1967; Radio Nanning, January 27, 1967; Radio Kweiyang, June 4, 1967; Radio Chengchow, March 8, 1967; and *Kuang-chou hung-wei-p'ing* (Canton Red Guards), No. 14 (February 10, 1967) (Canton: Canton College and Universities Red Guard Revolutionary Rebel Headquarters).

[58] Editorial, *JMJP*, March 2, 1967.

[59] In the case of Anhwei, for example, the central leadership claimed that the January 26 power seizure failed to bring about a proletarian revolutionary alliance, to point the spearhead at the small handful of capitalist power-holders in the provincial Party committee, or to practice a revolutionary "three-way alliance." "Decision of the CCP Central Committee on the Question of Anhwei" (March 27, 1967), in *CB*, No. 852 (May 6, 1968), pp. 113–14.

[60] In Honan and Kwangtung, conversely, the failure of the PLA to endorse the seizure of power antagonized the "in" groups.

ers.[61] Through the sham seizure of power and/or the suppression of the Maoist rebels by the PLA, Party leaders in many provinces were able to manipulate events behind the scenes and, once again, thwart the assaults of the Maoists.

JOINING THE "THREE-WAY ALLIANCE"

These developments in provinces were subsequently described by the Maoists as the "February adverse current." In Peking this "adverse current" allegedly found expression in a drive to "reverse the verdict" for Liu Shao-ch'i, Teng Hsiao-p'ing, and other "capitalist-roaders" in the top Party leadership. According to Chiang Ch'ing, Vice-premier T'an Chen-lin, a Politburo member in charge of the regime's overall rural policies, was in the vanguard of this movement.[62] It is doubtful that T'an would have sought to rehabilitate Liu and Teng directly. Very likely, what actually occurred in the first quarter of 1967 was that T'an and other moderate elements of the Chinese leadership in Peking, apprehensive of the rebels' excesses and worried about the harmful effect of the GPCR, plucked up the courage to assert themselves and sought to curb the activities of the rebels, particularly their indiscriminate attacks on Party officials at all levels. Red Guard sources reveal that T'an stood up in a high-level Party meeting on February 19 "to speak for all the old revolutionaries": he made such remarks as, "Veteran cadres have been struck down and persecuted severely," and "I firmly disagree with the striking down of so many veteran cadres, even if it causes my head to be chopped off and my Party membership canceled." [63]

Such statements would be in line with the interpretation we have offered above. In any case, the moderate elements in Peking appear to have prevailed temporarily, for a campaign to show tolerance and leniency toward cadres who had made mistakes was launched at the end of January, and was intensified in February and March, 1967.[64] Some people, interestingly enough, even accused the Maoist rebels and their mentors of carrying out a bourgeois reactionary line on cadre

---

[61] PLA suppression of mass organizations because they "trespassed against or criticized a military district command, or voiced disagreement over the power seizure" was also disclosed by a CC document marked *"Chung-fa 117 (67)"* on April 1 and by an order of the MAC on April 6. See *CB*, No. 852 (May 6, 1968), pp. 111–12, 115–16.

[62] *Chung-ta hung-ch'i*, April 4, 1968.

[63] *Ibid.*

[64] See "Cadres Must Be Treated Correctly," editorial, *Hung-ch'i*, No. 4 (February 23, 1967); and "Resolutely Defend the Correct Principle of a 'Three-way Alliance,'" editorial, *JMJP*, February 17, 1967.

policy by erroneously hitting hard at the cadres—an accusation which *Jen-min jih-pao* (April 24, 1967) editorially rejected as "nonsense."

Meanwhile, the Maoist leadership apparently realized that in order to seize power and then to maintain that power, cooperation of former Party cadres would be indispensable. It made this point first by appointing the former first secretary of Heilungkiang, P'an Fu-sheng, as chairman of the revolutionary committee in that province after the Maoists had seized power from the provincial authorities there in January, 1967. It also called for rebels in other provinces to emulate the Heilungkiang example whereby revolutionary rebels allegedly united with those leaders in the provincial Party committee who had executed Chairman Mao's correct line, *and* with the leaders of the PLA to seize power jointly.[65]

Thus, in February and March, official propaganda repeatedly emphasized the necessity of forming a "three-way alliance" among rebels, revolutionary cadres, and the PLA representatives. Only by the three-way alliance, stated the *Jen-min jih-pao* editorial of February 10, 1967, "can we truly seize Party, political, financial, and cultural power from the handful of capitalist power-holders in the Party, can we consolidate political power and win thorough victory in the struggle to seize power."

The emphasis placed upon the three-way alliance and upon the functions of former Party officials (now transformed in title into "revolutionary leading cadres") resulted from several political considerations. It was, on the one hand, an enticing carrot calculated to break up leadership solidarity in most provinces, to divide the opposition, and to weaken their resistance by offering a way out for those who might wish to ride on Mao's "revolutionary band wagon," or in Chinese Communist jargon, to "stand out" (*liang-hsiang*, literally, "making appearances"). On the other hand, it was a camouflaged retreat, or at least a change of tactic from the previous radical policy of denouncing and attacking all power-holders. Now the "revolutionary leading cadres" were, in the words of a *Hung-ch'i* (Red Flag) editorial, "the Party's valuable treasure," "rich in struggle experience, politically mature, and with stronger organizational ability," and as such, indispensable to Mao's struggle to seize power and to operate a viable administration. Finally, the new approach was also a conces-

---

[65] See Parris H. Chang, "The Revolutionary Committee in China," pp. 8–9.

sion to the moderate elements in the leadership who still exercised influence at that time.

In any case, the stress on the three-way alliance and on the correct treatment of cadres provided the power-holders with yet another opportunity to play political games. Professing themselves to be "revolutionary leading cadres," provincial leaders in various provinces "stood out" to "make rebellion," and manipulated their "royalist" rebel groups so as to have themselves included in the three-way alliance. This practice was evidently sufficiently widespread so that the central leadership's organ, *Hung-ch'i*, editorially denounced those who had "distorted the principle of revolutionary three-way alliance and, under the pretense of a 'three-way alliance,' carried out eclecticism, conciliationism, and the combination of two into one, and furthermore, in a hundred and one ways, pulled into the Party persons in authority taking the capitalist road." [66]

By this time, however, both the nature and rules of political conflict had undergone significant qualitative changes. At first Mao had thought that only "a small minority" of Party cadres would oppose the GPCR and he had therefore operated more or less within the confines of the power structure to force the provincial officials into submission. But they, buttressed by their control over the Party machinery in the province, were able to use their positions of strength and manipulate the legitimate political symbols of the system to obstruct and frustrate his goals. Since January, 1967, therefore, Mao, instead of working within the system, had launched an all-out assault against the power structure by calling upon the "revolutionary masses" to "seize power from below." The new Maoist offensive strategy proved to be a *coup de grâce,* because it deprived the provincial leaders of their organizational base of power by means of the creation of revolutionary committees in Heilungkiang and four other provinces in the first quarter of 1967. This new organ of power supplanted the former Party-government organizations in these areas and effectively suppressed all of those designated as Mao's antagonists.

In other provinces where a revolutionary committee or its preparatory group was not set up, the Maoist leadership now resorted to the direct use of military force to remove power from the hands of the provincial authorities. The Maoist leadership set up a military control

[66] "On the Revolutionary 'Three-way Alliance,'" editorial, *Hung-ch'i*, No. 5 (March 10, 1967).

committee in each province and authorized it to enforce direct military rule, thereby rescinding the powers of the provincial Party and government organs.[67] Judging from available information, military control committees were set up first in Tsinghai and Anhwei in late March.[68] By the end of June, they had been set up in most provinces where a revolutionary committee or its preparatory group had not been formed. This Maoist measure had the effect of *organizationally* disarming the provincial leaders, for they thereby lost their organizational base of power. No longer could they invoke the powers and authority vested in the former Party and government organizations which they had controlled in order to enforce their will.

Thus, by the summer of 1967, most provincial leaders had lost out as power in their provinces devolved into the hands of local PLA authorities, even though "seizure of power" in these provinces had not been formally proclaimed and the new organ of power, the revolutionary committee, had not been established yet.[69] The exceptions were Sinkiang and Kwangsi, where Wang En-mao (Sinkiang's first Party secretary and commander as well as first political commissar of the Sinkiang Military Region) and Wei Kuo-ch'ing (first Party secretary of Kwangsi and first political commissar of the Kwangsi Military District) were in control of at least some local PLA units. They were apparently able to use their military power to fight back the repeated assaults of Maoist rebels and to resist the policies of Peking well into 1968. Partly because of their strength, and partly because of the strategic location of these provinces, Peking found it necessary to come to terms with them.[70]

[67] By the end of June, 1967, if not earlier, central directives were no longer addressed to the regional Party bureaus and provincial Party committees. In so doing, the central leadership officially denied the existence and authority of these Party organizations. For an example of such documents, see *CCP Documents of the Great Proletarian Cultural Revolution, 1966–1967* (Hong Kong: URI, 1968), pp. 466, 475.

[68] *Ibid.*, pp. 387, 392.

[69] As of then, only Heilungkiang, Shansi, Shanghai, Kweichow, Shantung, and Peking had set up their respective revolutionary committees, and only one province, Szechwan, had its revolutionary committee preparatory committee.

[70] An MAC directive dated January 28, 1967, ordered PLA officials in Sinkiang Military Region, Canton Military Region (which has Kwangsi under its jurisdiction), and in several other strategically located military regions to postpone the Cultural Revolution activities for the time being; see *CB*, No. 852 (May 6, 1968), p. 56. This directive, aimed at "stabilizing" military regions "on the first line of defense against imperialism and revisionism," appeared to have strengthened the hands of the power-holders in these areas who, on the pretext of "war preparations," used strong measures to suppress Maoist Red Guards subsequently.

In addition, Wei Kuo-ch'ing seemed to have been saved from his downfall partly by his good relations with leaders in Hanoi. The following two items of information

Consequently, Wei emerged from the GPCR unscathed and was appointed chairman of the Kwangsi Chuang Autonomous Region Revolutionary Committee when it was set up in July, 1968. In the case of Sinkiang, the central leadership had to move in outside troops and remove Wang from the post of commander of the Sinkiang Military Region. Although he was appointed vice-chairman of the Sinkiang Revolutionary Committee when it was finally set up in September, 1968, and later received an alternate membership on the Ninth Central Committee, it seems clear that he, like many other provincial power-holders before him, has basically lost his old role.

CONCLUDING REMARKS

In the preceding pages, I have shown that the provincial leaders' perception of events and their strategies for survival changed extensively over the months as more political actors became involved and the scope of conflict expanded in the course of the GPCR. In abbreviated form, we can correlate external events with provincial leaders' perceptions of those events and their resulting strategies in the following terms. In the spring of 1966 and before the results of the top-level Party meeting were known in mid-May, the provincial Party leaders became sensitized to a new politico-ideological campaign waged by the *Chieh-fang-chün pao* and other newspapers against P'eng Chen, his Peking group, and the officials in the Party's cultural-ideological apparatus, but they were puzzled by the silence of *Jen-min jih-pao*, the organ of the Party's CC. Generally speaking, therefore, they took a noncommittal stand and attempted to find out what the "rules of the game" were.

In the second half of May and prior to the Eleventh Plenum in August, 1966, the provincial leaders appeared to see the GPCR as being directed primarily against P'eng Chen, Lu Ting-yi, and other top-level Party officials; but they also perceived the possibility of a sweeping, new purge after the "May 16 Circular" and they felt insecure and apprehensive. Their strategies at this stage were those of evasion, diversion, deception, and containment. At pains to display

---

are highly suggestive. An unnamed official in Peking was quoted by a handbill, distributed on June 27, 1968, by the "Breakthrough Appeal Group" of the Kwangsi April 22nd Rebels Headquarters (a copy is in my possession), to have said: "Wei Kuo-ch'ing is not a good comrade, but he is difficult to handle; we have to treat him very cautiously, [*the treatment*] *must be convincing to the* [*North*] *Vietnamese people*" (emphasis added); and second, Wei was the only provincial figure in the Chinese delegation led by Chou En-lai to attend Ho Chi Minh's funeral in Hanoi in September, 1969.

their loyalty to the central leadership, they quickly purged the "rightist" provincial officials, real or imagined, in the cultural and ideological apparatus, and used them as scapegoats in an effort to shift the attack from themselves. When student unrest became widespread, moreover, they operated through work teams to contain the scope of the conflict and guide the students' protest activities into prescribed channels.

The defeat of Liu Shao-ch'i and Teng Hsiao-p'ing and the censure of their policy at the Eleventh Plenum adversely affected the position of the provincial leaders because they had dutifully carried out the Liu-Teng "bourgeois reactionary line" in their provinces. They could only interpret the subsequent inauguration of the Red Guards and the call for "bombarding the headquarters" by the Maoist leadership as Mao's attempt to purge them, and the death of some provincial officials as a result of being struggled against by Red Guards only heightened the decision of most provincial leaders to fight for their personal and political survival.

Once this basic decision was reached, they devised an ingenious series of tactics to defend themselves against the assault of the Red Guards and Maoist rebels. When the Maoist leadership enlarged the scope of political conflict to redress the existing balance of power by invoking assistance of such elements, the provincial leaders followed suit. They recruited and organized their own "royalist" groups, and incited the workers and peasants to fight against those proclaiming themselves Maoists. When necessary, they did not hesitate to use coercion to persecute the Maoists and fend off their challenge. When the Maoist leadership tried to cultivate the support of underprivileged workers, the provincial power-holders countered with a strategy of cooptation, using material incentives and economic rewards to woo workers, or at least to neutralize them. When in January, 1967, the Maoist leadership, in an all-out assault against the power structure, ordered the Red Guards and rebels to seize power from the provincial power-holders, the latter tried to pre-empt this new initiative either by handing "power" over to the "royalist" groups (in what was called a "sham seizure of power") or by taking part in the "three-way alliances" in the capacity of "revolutionary cadres."

While the provincial leaders were trying desperately to push back the sustained attack by the Red Guards and rebels and to insure their personal and political survival, they continuously maintained loudly that they were loyal Maoists and ardent supporters of Mao's GPCR.

And as long as Mao operated within the confines of the power structure, the provincial leaders were able to use their positions of strength, manipulating orthodox political symbols to "wave red flags to oppose the Red Flag." Ultimately, Mao was compelled to change the "rules of the game" and to launch a frontal attack on their organizational base of power. And this required the use of the PLA.

The fact that it was the use of military forces that finally brought down the recalcitrant, well-entrenched provincial Party leaders attests to the remarkable effectiveness of their survival strategies. Undoubtedly, their ingenuity, political astuteness, and experience in political manipulation helped. They had skillfully made use of the slogans and policies put forward by Mao and his supporters, "waving the red flags to oppose the Red Flag." These slogans and policies were coopted, and the effort was made to turn them against Mao and his followers.

The remarkable cohesiveness of the provincial leadership was another source of strength. Despite repeated cajoling and appeals by the Maoist leadership to "stand out," few leaders broke with their immediate colleagues and joined the Maoists. On the other hand, one major factor that enabled the rebels to succeed in seizing power in Heilungkiang, Shansi, Kweichow, and Shanghai in January and February, 1967, was that in each of the four provinces one or more Party secretaries supported the rebels and took part in the power seizure.

In addition, provincial leaders' control and skill in the manipulation of the media enabled them to "confuse right and wrong," "juggle black and white," "manage" news, and create public opinion in their favor. The fact that the Maoists invariably took over the propaganda agencies and mass media before they attempted to seize power from the provincial Party committees attested to the importance of control over information.

However, the most important source of power for the provincial Party leaders undoubtedly came from the positions of leadership which they occupied in the Party and state hierarchies. Because of these positions, they had the authority to command the organs of power. They could use all of the political and military power at the joint command of Party and state including the public security apparatus and all of the material resources in their sphere of authority. Thus they could recruit and reward supporters as well as intimidate and punish the opposition.

The fact that the provincial power-holders were able to use their positions of strength within the system and effectively thwart the Maoists' assault for a considerable period of time sheds much light on the pattern of compliance and the structure of authority in China's political system. Obviously, obedience to the command of the Party had become habitual in the society. Therefore, provincial leaders were able to describe themselves as the "personification of the Party," and their words and actions were treated as the unchallengeable expression of Party leadership. In this fashion, these leaders were able—in the words of their opponents—to make use of the "high prestige enjoyed by Chairman Mao and the Party among the masses" to carry out activities "in opposition to Chairman Mao." In other words, as one writer has correctly pointed out, the ability of the provincial leaders to gain ready acceptance of their command indicated conclusively that the Party's authority was accepted as legitimate in the society.[71] (Legitimacy, of course, must often be measured against the risks involved in any challenge.) Furthermore, since the structure of power in China had become highly bureaucratized, and since the top leadership that dominated the peak of the centralized edifice had to delegate powers to, and depend upon, subordinate bureaucratic instrumentalities to project its will, the provincial leaders were thus in a position to control the system at provincial and lower levels, and to manipulate the powers vested in their organizations on behalf of themselves.

However, it is notable how little of their resistance took the form of *open* opposition to Mao and his policies. As the thought of Mao had increasingly become "a new standard of legitimacy and correction" in China in the 1960's, the provincial Party leaders (and leaders at the center as well) could only exercise power and justify their right to rule by claiming their loyalty to Mao and averring conformity with his thought.[72] Thus, the unique position of Mao in the system constrained the strategies which the provincial leaders could adopt and the means available to them. They were deprived of the capacity to attack Mao and his policies openly (even when they were actually acting against them), and they were forced to hide under a Maoist smoke screen and defend themselves "under the major premises and rules of game laid down by Mao." [73] As the top ideologue and the fountainhead of legitimacy in the system, Mao was in a position to

[71] Tang Tsou, "The Cultural Revolution and the Chinese Political System," *CQ*, No. 38 (April–June, 1969), pp. 83–84.

[72] Quotation from *ibid.*, p. 79.

[73] *Ibid.*, p. 84; also Richard M. Pfeffer, "The Pursuit of Purity: Mao's Cultural Revolution," *Problems of Communism*, XVIII, No. 6 (November–December, 1969), 19–20.

define both the parameters and the issues of political conflict. He could change the "rules of the game," as well as involve more political actors in the conflict in order to change the balance of power. In the final analysis, therefore, the provincial leaders could only be on the defensive strategically. Here lay their greatest vulnerability, and the source of their ultimate defeat.

RICHARD BAUM

Elite Behavior under Conditions of Stress: The Lesson of the "Tang-ch'üan P'ai" in the Cultural Revolution

Throughout the Great Proletarian Cultural Revolution (GPCR), "power-holders" (*tang-ch'üan p'ai*) at all levels of the Chinese Communist Party (CCP) hierarchy were on the strategic defensive. For the first time in the history of a ruling Communist regime, non-Party elements (the "revolutionary masses") had been given virtually unlimited license to seek out, denounce, and ultimately seize power from "hidden enemies" within the Party apparatus. Under officially sanctioned political attack from Red Guards, "revolutionary rebels," and various other dissident groups in Chinese society, the power-holders sought to cushion themselves against the impact, marshaling their resources and improvising various strategies of action designed to minimize political risks and maximize self-protection.

In previous Party rectification campaigns the CCP had taken care of its own, shielding its leadership cadres at all levels against "excessive" or "unprincipled" criticism at the hands of the non-Party masses. Now, however, with the very legitimacy of the Party establishment having been called into question by the supreme leader himself, Party membership and position offered no refuge. No exemptions were granted to those veteran cadres with long records of faithful Party service. No precedents were available to help the cadres, veteran and novice alike, accommodate to only dimly perceived "rules of the game" in the new revolutionary movement. All bets were off as the cadres, stripped of their organizational and reputational defenses, were faced with the necessity of fighting for their political lives.

This study traces the development of the cadres' struggle for survival during the GPCR. More specifically, it examines the political behavior of middle- and lower-echelon rural Party cadres during the height of revolutionary upheaval in China, from August, 1966, to April, 1967.[1] Our primary concern is with the strategy and tactics of survival, or how the cadres responded to the challenge of officially legitimated mass political insurgency. Secondarily, we are examining the particular environmental conditions, the situational constraints or parameters of action, under which the cadres operated in the period in question. A third and related concern is the question of who supported and who opposed the power-holders, and why, which indicates the social bases of political conflict.

Any study which purports to "explain" the behavior of China's political elites during the GPCR must also address itself to motivational questions: Why did the cadres behave in certain ways at certain times and under certain conditions? How was their overt behavior influenced by their values, beliefs, attitudes, and cognitions? Unfortunately, reliable data on the motivational bases of political behavior in China are virtually nonexistent. For this reason great caution must be exercised in attributing or inferring the motives of any individual actor or group of actors.

The nature of this problem is well illustrated by the production brigade leader who attempted to seize power from his immediate

[1] Although the GPCR was primarily an urban phenomenon, there was a significant amount of spillover into the countryside. Most heavily affected by Red Guard agitation, "power seizures," and internecine political struggles were those rural areas that lie in close proximity either to China's 125 or so large and medium-sized municipalities or to the major transportation networks which serve to link these municipalities. Such areas comprise a rather small but statistically significant minority of China's 74,000 rural communes—perhaps on the order of 20 per cent. These proximate communes have provided the overwhelming bulk of data for the present study; and the reader is forewarned of the hazards involved in attempting to generalize about political conditions in rural China as a whole on the basis of an admittedly narrow—and in many ways atypical—geographical data base.

For a detailed analysis of the urban-rural nexus in GPCR politics, and of the ecological patterns of conflict diffusion in the countryside, see Richard Baum, "The Cultural Revolution in the Countryside: Anatomy of a Limited Rebellion," in Thomas W. Robinson (ed.), *The Cultural Revolution in China* (Berkeley and Los Angeles: University of California Press, 1971).

superior, the brigade Party branch secretary.[2] The motivational possibilities in this situation were manifold: (1) the Party branch
chairman was a "bourgeois revisionist" and hence the brigade leader
sought his removal out of the purest of ideological motives; (2) the
brigade leader himself was a "bourgeois revisionist" who feared exposure by the Party branch secretary and hence took pre-emptive
action against him; (3) the brigade leader was a political opportunist
who saw in the GPCR the chance for a rapid promotion by informing
on his superior; and (4) the brigade leader held a personal (nonpolitical) grudge against the Party branch secretary and hence took
advantage of the revolutionary climate to settle a private score. The
possible permutations of motivational alternatives in the above example are virtually limitless. The point is simply that, lacking intensive case study material or extensive survey research data, there is no
way to resolve the problem satisfactorily.

There has been an unfortunate tendency in much of the Western
literature on the GPCR to explain the behavior of individual and
collective actors in situations of political conflict either in terms of
Manichaean ideological struggles (for example, Reds versus experts,
Maoists versus "revisionists") or in terms of Machiavellian power
struggles (political man's instinctual drive for self-aggrandizement).
Without denying the possible relevance of either of these factors, it
would seem that a more open-ended, less rigidly reductionist approach
to the question of motivation is required. Such an approach is provided by the twin concepts of "interests" and "interest groups."
Throughout this study we have attempted wherever possible to isolate
the probable motives of individual and collective actors in terms of
the following set of questions: What did they have to gain? What did
they have to lose? With whom did they ally and for what purposes?
In short, what interests (latent or manifest) were served by their
actions? By focusing on the concept of situationally defined interests,
we may hope to avoid becoming impaled on the horns of the reductionist dilemma. Neither Manes nor Machiavelli holds the key to
understanding the behavior of China's elites in the GPCR.

THE RED GUARDS REBEL: AUGUST–SEPTEMBER, 1966

The activation of the Red Guards in the last half of August, 1966,
marked a watershed in the GPCR. Mao's "little generals" had been

---

[2] This illustration is drawn from an actual incident. See Richard Baum, "A Parting
of Paupers," *Far Eastern Economic Review,* LIX, No. 1 (January 4, 1968), 17–19.

instructed to "destroy the four olds," and they went at their work with an enthusiasm seldom seen in modern China.[3] When they left their urban staging areas at the end of August to "link up" and "exchange revolutionary experiences" with their counterparts from other regions and districts, the results were predictably unsettling.

Party authorities at the provincial, subprovincial, and basic levels clearly resented the intrusion of the young agitators into their local bailiwicks. One report from Szechwan province told of a provincial Party power-holder who, when informed in late August that Red Guards from Peking were on their way to the southwest to link up with local workers and peasants, hastily set up a number of "special investigatory organs" to harass and confine the itinerant students. In Anhwei province it was similarly reported that local cadres had initially tried to prevent revolutionary students from going to the countryside by setting up "layers and layers of defense lines." When such preventive measures failed, the local authorities reportedly reacted by "labeling as counterrevolutionary all peasants who rose to support the students." And in Kiangsu province the entire militia squadron of a suburban production brigade was allegedly detained and placed under surveillance by the local Party committee in late August for having dared to support the Red Guards.[4]

As measured by the response of the power-holders, a great deal more was at stake than the mere eradication of feudal customs and superstitions. Although the "big blooming and contending" of Red Guards was largely confined at this early stage to exposing and criticizing the "counterrevolutionary crimes" of a relatively small number of leading officials in provincial and municipal-level Party and governmental organs, the very physical presence and officially sanctioned freedom of action of the migratory "little generals" posed an implicit threat to local power-holders throughout China. The power-holders in many cases clearly recognized the nature of this threat and acted accordingly.

Apprehensive at the prospect of antiestablishmentarian "blooming and contending" in their local bailiwicks, basic-level Party and administrative functionaries in those rural districts where Red Guard units were active began to take defensive measures. Fighting fire with fire (or, as it was later described, "waving red flags to oppose the red

---

[3] The "four olds" were old thinking, old culture, old customs, and old habits.

[4] Radio Chengtu (Szechwan), April 10, 1968. The power-holder in question was Liao Chih-kao, who was subsequently purged as a "three anti" element. Radio Hofei (Anhwei), February 2, 1967. *JMJP*, February 20, 1967.

flag"), local power-holders in some areas quickly recruited their own supporters and set up rival "revolutionary" mass organizations to act as a counterforce to the Red Guard insurgents. The following report from a suburban Peking production brigade, though admittedly partisan in nature, is typical of the many available descriptions of such pre-emptive tactics:

In August, when Chairman Mao openly signified his support for Red Guards . . . several poor and lower-middle peasant youths took the lead in organizing the "Poor and Lower-Middle Peasant Red Guards." They vigorously destroyed the "four olds" and struggled against the bourgeois power-holders. . . . Frightened, [Brigade Party Branch Secretary] Li Ch'un-ch'ang and his gang immediately called a meeting of the Party branch and decided to organize the "Red Guards of the Thought of Mao Tse-tung." . . . Everyone except the "five category elements" was eligible for admission into this organization. Overnight it enrolled more than ninety members, many of whom were children of cadres and "relatives of the emperor." There were several leading cadres in the organization. . . . They were in reality the Royalist Guards of Li Ch'un-ch'ang and his gang. . . .[5]

In addition to organizing proestablishment Royalist Guards to counteract antiestablishment Red Guards, local power-holders in several suburban communes reportedly adopted a series of other hastily contrived measures to ward off the militant youths. In suburban Shanghai, local cadres attempted to forestall mass participation in the GPCR by reducing the work points of all peasants who joined in revolutionary criticisms.[6] From rural communes in Kweichow, Szechwan, and Anhwei provinces came allegations that local power-holders had sought to finesse the Red Guards by distorting and "making surreptitious changes" in Party regulations which called for limiting revolutionary activity to "slack periods" in production.[7] In suburban Yangchow, Kiangsu, a local Party committee sought to brand as counterrevolutionary all peasants who had written big-character posters against the committee members or maintained contacts with urban Red Guards.[8] And in Shanghai, finally, an "ordinary" cadre in a suburban commune alleged that a handful of "capitalist roaders" in the commune Party committee had sought to save their own political

[5] *Nung-min yün-tung* (Peasant Movement) (Peking), No. 3 (February 22, 1967), in *SCMP*, No. 3910, pp. 9–10.

[6] NCNA, Peking, February 9, 1967.

[7] See Radio Kweiyang (Kweichow), December 19, 1967; Radio Chengtu, April 10, 1968; and Radio Hofei, February 2, 1967. In all three of the provinces cited, local cadres had reportedly argued that "the Cultural Revolution will adversely affect agricultural production . . . and thus is to be temporarily halted."

[8] *JMJP*, February 20, 1967.

skins by "pushing me to the 'first line' and ordering me to go and represent the commune Party committee at criticism meetings convened by various units. By this evil scheme they hoped to enable themselves to 'slip through the net.' " [9]

In the above examples, we see evidence of three distinct tactical approaches adopted by members of the local establishment in suburban communes and production brigades to minimize the disruptive effects of revolutionary agitation. These approaches may be broadly characterized as evasion, suppression, and pre-emption. In some areas local power-holders adopted yet a fourth approach to the problem of mitigating the effects of revolutionary "great debates." This method can be labeled cooptation.

In suburban Canton, Kwangtung, local cadres attempted to disarm the rebellious Red Guards by praising the activism of those revolutionary students who wrote big-character posters against the local Party branch committee.[10] And in suburban Yangchow, Kiangsu, it was reported that a production brigade cadre turned to "sugar-coated bullets" when his repressive tactics failed to deter the movement of revolutionary criticism by Red Guards: "When the brigade Party branch secretary saw that his hard-line approach would not work, he changed his tactics. . . . He said, 'In the past you did such a good job of leading the study of Mao's works in your production team. How would you like to be selected to go to the commune headquarters to lead a study meeting? I'll even lend you a bicycle.' " [11] The use of "sugar-coated bullets" to coopt rebellious youngsters in rural China was by no means an isolated or temporary phenomenon. A few months later, during the storm of the January Revolution, such tactics (known generically as "counterrevolutionary economism") were to be widely used by local power-holders in an attempt to gain the support of peasants and forestall power seizures by revolutionary rebel organizations throughout China.

By the time the crucial autumn harvest season arrived in rural China in mid-September, 1966, there was evidently considerable concern at the Party center that the spread of the GPCR to the countryside might interfere with the normal seasonal processes of production. Such concern was not without foundation, for the newly mobilized

[9] *Ibid.*, March 10, 1967.
[10] *Hung-se pao-tung* (Red Riot) (Canton), No. 12–13 (July 8, 1967), in *SCMP*, No. 4030, p. 15.
[11] *JMJP*, February 20, 1967.

Red Guards had indeed created a considerable amount of upheaval, despite the fact that "great debates," "linking up," and "exchanging revolutionary experiences" had occurred in only a limited number of communes.

On September 7 the Party center called for the temporary suspension of all political mobilization activities in rural China in order that "all efforts can be concentrated on making a good job of this year's autumn harvest." [12] One week later, the Central Committee issued a formal five-point directive entitled, "Regulations concerning the Great Cultural Revolution in Rural Districts below the County Level." [13] While ostensibly reinforcing the moratorium of September 7, the new directive embodied a number of subtle shifts of emphasis.

In the first place, the September 7 statement had declared that urban Red Guards would not be sent to, and the GPCR would not be launched in, those rural units where "existing arrangements" were considered "appropriate" by the masses. The new Central Committee directive, however, explicitly took the power of such determination away from the masses and put it squarely into the hands of Party committees at the provincial and subprovincial levels: "Except for separate arrangements made by Provincial and district Party committees, students and Red Guards from Peking and other localities shall not go to rural organs below the county level, communes or production brigades to exchange revolutionary experiences or take part in debates. . . ." [14] The distinction here, though ostensibly slight, was later to prove extremely significant. For, by granting to entrenched Party officials full discretionary power to dispatch "outside investigators" to the countryside, the September 14 directive indirectly opened the door to a host of defensive tactics employed by apprehensive Party power-holders in the provinces either to suppress, pre-empt, or redirect the "spearhead" of GPCR struggle.

Party officials in some areas took advantage of the discretionary powers granted them under the terms of the September 14 directive to dispatch any number of investigatory "work teams" to those rural units where rebel activities were threatening to get out of hand. These work teams, being the creatures of entrenched Party interests, were understandably oriented toward the maintenance of the political *status*

---

[12] *Ibid.*, September 7, 1966.

[13] The text of this directive, dated September 14, 1966, appears in *CCP Documents of the Great Proletarian Cultural Revolution, 1966–1967* (hereafter *CCP Documents*) (Hong Kong: URI, 1968), pp. 77–80.

[14] *Ibid.*, Article I.

quo.[15] A report from rural Kweichow described the "counterrevolutionary machinations" of a provincial-level work team:

Towards the end of 1966 . . . a work team directly controlled by the handful of capitalist roaders in the provincial Party committee was sent to [our] brigade in the hope of . . . organizing the members of the brigade to protect the capitalist roaders. They thought that because [Brigade Party Branch Secretary] Wang Chung-chan had been admitted to the Party with their approval she would undoubtedly support them. The work team tried to deceive the masses by spreading rumors, turning things upside down and doing all they could to confuse the distinction between revolution and counter-revolution. . . .[16]

In Lankao county (*hsien*), Honan (home district of the martyred Party cadre, Chiao Yü-lu), it was similarly reported that a work team had been sent to a local production team by "agents of China's Khrushchev," Liu Shao-ch'i, in the county Party committee to suppress local Red Guards who had risen to defend the late Chiao Yü-lu and his supporters against the deprecations of "class enemies" and "bourgeois power-holders" in the area.[17]

Although the stereotyped ideologism of the above-cited reports is undoubtedly misleading, there is little reason to question the veracity of the events described therein. Certainly, large numbers of work teams were dispatched to conflict-ridden rural and urban units in the autumn of 1966. And judging from subsequent attempts by revolutionary rebel organizations to "reverse the verdicts" imposed by these work teams, the main thrust of work team intervention had been to defend entrenched Party interests against all manner of rebel insurgency, whether from above or from below.

In addition to delegating the power to dispatch rural investigatory personnel to Party committees at the provincial and subprovincial levels, the Central Committee directive of September 14 also stipulated that "cadres below the county level . . . who have been appointed by higher-level Party committees or governmental organs should not be directly 'removed from office' by the masses." [18] What this meant, in effect, was that the "principal" Party cadres at the commune and production brigade levels (including Party committee and branch secretaries, commune and brigade chairmen, militia commanders, chief

---

[15] This conclusion is fully consistent with what is known of the activities of Party-led work teams in China's urban educational and cultural institutions in the early summer of 1966, when work team personnel generally opted for the "conservative" course of supporting incumbent cadres against their student critics.

[16] NCNA, February 25, 1968; see also *Peking Review*, No. 27 (July 5, 1968), pp. 14–16.

[17] *Peking Review*, No. 9 (March 1, 1968), pp. 7–10.

[18] *CCP Documents*, Article IV, p. 80.

accountants, and Women's Federation and Youth League directors) were to be exempted from mass struggle and criticism during the busy autumn harvest season, when their specialized leadership skills were needed to ensure smooth harmony and coordination of the productive process.

A third (and closely related) area of official concern was the question of how to "restore and strengthen the leading force" in those rural communes and production brigades where leadership had become paralyzed as a result of the initial wave of "blooming and contending" in the late summer of 1966. The problem of leadership paralysis was particularly acute in those areas which had experienced Red Guard activism; and reports of cadre demoralization and unwillingness to assume active responsibility over production (for fear of inviting criticism and thus losing face) were numerous in this period. As one disillusioned and dispirited young cadre reportedly put it, "Of all possible mistakes, the worst mistake is to hold power." [19] In order to combat the problem of incipient leadership paralysis, rural Party organs were instructed to "immediately readjust the cadres"—that is, to transfer administrative personnel to those areas most severely affected by cadre demoralization.[20]

With revolutionary "great debates" officially suspended for the duration of the autumn harvest season, new policy guidelines were promulgated concerning the question of how the twin tasks of "grasping revolution" and "promoting production" were to be coordinated and carried out simultaneously in the countryside. A *Hung-ch'i* (Red Flag) editorial of September 17 called for the establishment of a "suitable division of labor" between the two aspects, with different "leading groups" assigned to take charge of each.[21] Clarification on the question of how this division of labor was to be properly coordinated was provided when the experiences of a production brigade in Hopeh province were given nationwide publicity in early October:

To grasp revolution and promote production, and to guarantee their double victory, we have made a proper division of labor and suitable arrangement of the leadership force. From the production brigade to the production team levels, two groups are organized in each unit, under the unified guidance of the Party branch. One group mainly . . . promotes the [GPCR]. The other mainly devotes itself to pro-

---

19 *JMJP*, March 10, 1967. The original Chinese version of this lamentation, which unfortunately loses a great deal of its poignancy in translation, is: *"Ch'ien ts'o wan ts'o, chiu ts'o tsai 'tang-ch'üan' liang-ko tzu shang."*

20 *CCP Documents*, Article V, p. 80.

21 *Hung-ch'i* (Red Flag), No. 12 (September 17, 1966), pp. 13–14.

duction and construction. Thus, the high morale of the people brought out in the revolution is channeled to the production struggle. . . .[22]

Although the official policy of the period was one which ostensibly gave equal emphasis to revolution and production, the above-quoted statement, when viewed in the context of the time, could only be interpreted to mean that top priority was to be given to production, with the main purpose of "grasping revolution" being to mobilize the peasantry to take a more active role in productive tasks. Thus, the slogan "grasp revolution, promote production" was interpreted to mean, in effect, "grasp revolution *in order to* promote production." Moreover, the fact that overall coordination of both aspects was to be carried out "under the unified guidance of the Party branch" could only serve to reinforce the supremacy of incumbent power-holders in the villages. And as long as local Party officials continued to exercise ultimate authority over both revolutionary and productive enterprises, it could be safely assumed that the former would be de-emphasized in the name of the latter.

With Red Guard "great debates," destruction of the "four olds," and all other (actual or potential) sources of political turmoil uniformly suspended by official decree, it appeared for a short time in the latter part of September that the situation in rural China might return to normal. But social order and discipline were more easily restored on paper than in practice; for once the Red Guard genie had been let out of the jar, it proved most difficult to coax him back inside.

THE STRUGGLE INTENSIFIES: OCTOBER–DECEMBER, 1966

Residual manifestations of both intramural (localized) and extramural (rural-urban) conflict continued to find expression in a number of villages throughout the autumn harvest season. Although the regime's mid-September drive to curtail revolutionary activity in the countryside apparently succeeded in preserving political tranquillity in those communes and production brigades which had not experienced significant turbulence in the previous period, the political pot continued to simmer—and on occasion to boil over—in those relatively few rural districts which had been directly affected by the first wave of Red Guard "great debates." In such areas an initial polarization of forces had already occurred, and preliminary battle lines had been drawn.

---

[22] *Ibid.*, No. 13 (October 1, 1966), pp. 13–15.

The October–December stage of the GPCR witnessed the attempt by urban power-holders and mass organizations to expand their respective power bases by enlisting the active, partisan support of suburban cadres and peasants.[23] In the struggle to dislodge (or defend) incumbent Party office-holders, one key to success was the ability of the various contestants to gain constituency support at the grass-roots level.

A number of reports concerning the formation of municipal-rural, county-rural, and provincial-rural protocoalitions (or tactical alliances) serve to shed light on the methods adopted by rival groups and factions to expand and consolidate their political support. In Szechwan, for example, alleged "bourgeois power-holders" in the provincial Party committee (located in Chengtu) attempted to recruit large numbers of suburban peasants to "encircle the city from the countryside" and hold counterdemonstrations against those Red Guards and revolutionary rebels who were currently besieging the Party headquarters. In Changkang township (*chen*), Kiangsi (an old revolutionary base area), more than 400 peasants from a local production brigade reportedly were recruited to march on the county Party committee headquarters to struggle against a handful of power-holders. And in suburban Hofei, Anhwei, it was claimed that certain "mandarins" (of unspecified organizational affiliation) had "incited large numbers of misled commune members to parade and demonstrate in the city to protect the provincial and municipal Party committees." [24]

What these and other similar incidents suggest is that embattled Party officials in China's provincial capitals, municipalities, and county towns, in order to bring countervailing power to bear on insurgent rebel organizations, hastily recruited large numbers of sympathetic and/or mercenary supporters in suburban communes and production brigades to help turn the tide of battle. And the rebels, in turn, finding themselves subjected to organized counterattacks, adopted similar recruiting tactics to bolster their own forces. Thus did an essentially urban-centered series of political confrontations become enlarged to encompass significant numbers of suburban peasants, cadres, and militiamen. This process of progressive conflict diffusion may be described in the form of a general hypothesis: *Those actors*

[23] In the following discussion, the term "urban power-holders" refers not only to municipal-level Party personnel, but to provincial and county-level officials as well, since they were also headquartered in the cities.

[24] Radio Chengtu, April 10, 1968. NCNA, October 31, 1968. Radio Hofei, February 2, 1967.

who perceive themselves to be in imminent danger of defeat in what are essentially struggles for political survival are compelled sequentially to enlarge the scope of conflict in order to avert defeat and secure a more favorable balance of forces.[25]

If the desire to enlarge the scope of conflict, and thereby alter the balance of forces, constituted (in the Aristotelian sense) the "final cause" of the urban-to-rural conflict diffusion process in the autumn of 1966, then the "sufficient cause" of that process lay in the potential mobilizational capacities of Party power-holders and their rebel antagonists, respectively. (The "formal cause," of course, lay in the Party center's August, 1966, call to "bombard the headquarters.")

One obvious advantage which the power-holders enjoyed over their opponents from the outset was the built-in advantage of official patronage, both political and economic. Party officials at the provincial, municipal, and county levels in China, like their counterparts in any hierarchical organization, exercised considerable discretionary power over the recruitment, job assignments, and promotions of their subordinates.[26] It is hardly surprising to find that urban power-holders utilized such discretionary powers to expand and consolidate their support among basic-level Party cadres in municipally administered suburban communes and production brigades (and, by direct extension, among the peasants who were subject to the authority of these suburban cadres). We thus find numerous reports in the autumn of 1966 describing the attempts of provincial, county, and municipal Party officials either to remind suburban cadres (many of whom owed their Party membership and/or official appointments to higher-

[25] This hypothesis was adapted by the author from the concept of the "socialization of conflict" formulated by Professor E. E. Schattschneider in his provocative essay, *The Semi-Sovereign People* (New York: Holt, Rinehart and Winston, 1960), pp. 36–43. Although this concept was articulated on the basis of Schattschneider's observation of pressure group politics in the American political system, the concept is, *mutatis mutandis,* apposite to widely differing situations of political conflict. In its original form, the "socialization of conflict" hypothesis holds that "it is the weak, not the strong, who appeal to [the] public for relief. It is the weak who want to socialize conflict, i.e., to involve more and more people in the conflict until the balance of forces is changed . . ." (*ibid.,* pp. 40–41).

[26] Michel Oksenberg has described the vulnerability of lower-level rural cadres to manipulation by their superiors at the county level in terms which are suggestive of the range of resources potentially available to embattled urban power-holders in their effort to mobilize active support among their rural subalterns. While such vulnerability is by no means one-sided, the initial advantages of the power to command, persuade, and reward compliant behavior undoubtedly accrued to higher-level power-holders vis-à-vis their lower-level subordinates. See "The Institutionalization of the Chinese Communist Revolution: The Ladder of Success on the Eve of the Cultural Revolution," *CQ,* No. 36 (October–December, 1968), pp. 82–84.

level sponsorship) of the existence of old political debts; or, alternatively, to create new obligatory bonds by offering promises of rapid vertical mobility or other such "sugar-coated bullets" in exchange for pledges of active support.[27] In addition, there is evidence that by November, 1966, urban power-holders began appealing directly to the material aspirations of suburban peasants. Authorizing the allocation and distribution of relatively large sums of "linking-up money" (*ch'üan-lien fei*), Party officials in many areas encouraged (perhaps "bribed" is a better word) peasants to leave their production posts to stage counterdemonstrations against militant Red Guards and revolutionary rebels in the cities.[28]

For their part, antiestablishment Red Guards and revolutionary rebel organizations responded in kind to the initial efforts at conflict socialization on the part of their power-holding opponents. Although lacking the political and economic resource base of their opponents, the rebels were able to capitalize on the one major asset which worked almost exclusively to their advantage: latent rural discontent with the *status quo*.

The sources of such discontent were manifold; moreover, they cut across the entire spectrum of socioeconomic and political classes and strata. In suburban communes, by virtue of their proximity to and direct administration by municipal Party authorities, a major focal point of local disaffection centered around the so-called worker-peasant system—the system of temporary contract labor under which large numbers of peasants were periodically and in rotation recruited to perform urban-industrial jobs at substandard wages and under poor living conditions during slack agricultural seasons. Permanent industrial workers thus displaced were assigned to work as agricultural laborers in rural communes, with the burden of their wage payments, medical care, and welfare benefits being assumed by the communes, rather than by the state as before. Understandably, the net effect of this system was to alienate both the displaced industrial workers and their underpaid peasant surrogates. Thus, opposition to

---

[27] See, for example, *Hung-se pao-tung*, No. 12–13 (July 8, 1967); also *JMJP*, February 20, 1967; NCNA, February 25, 1968; and *Peking Review*, No. 9 (March 1, 1968), pp. 7–10. While empirical research on the nature and durability of vertical (hierarchical) ties of personal and/or organizational loyalty in Chinese bureaucratic politics is regrettably sparse, it is nevertheless virtually certain that such ties do exist, and that they tend over time to create bonds of mutual interdependence between superior and subordinate.

[28] See, for example, NCNA, February 9, 1967, and October 14 and 31, 1968.

the worker-peasant system became a major rallying point for anti-establishmentarian agitation in China's rural suburbs.[29]

Another source of rural resentment against urban power-holders which was potentially exploitable by coalition-minded urban revolutionary organizations was the alienation experienced by those "intellectual youths" (middle-school and college students) who had been sent down to the countryside to be employed as agricultural laborers in the massive *hsia-hsiang* ("down to the village") movement of the early and mid-1960's. By the Party's own estimate, there were approximately forty million such intellectual youths working in the Chinese countryside on the eve of the GPCR.[30] The frustrations and disillusionment experienced by these cultured youngsters when confronted with the prospect of having to spend the rest of their lives performing burdensome and distasteful farm labor had been a cause of serious concern to the Maoist regime for several years. With the initiation of the GPCR, such frustration and disillusionment were readily politicized and channeled into opposition to the urban *status quo,* since municipal and county Party committees had been directly responsible for assigning the intellectual youths to the countryside in the first place.[31]

A third source of latent rural discontent was the movement toward imposing new restrictions on the cultivation of private plots which had been officially (though not uniformly) underway since the late summer of 1966.[32] Red Guards in some areas were quick to foresee the alienative potential of such a movement and therefore attempted in some instances to place the onus for such new restrictions squarely on the shoulders of local power-holders. For example, Red Guards in one suburban Peking production brigade charged that a local Party secretary, instigated and protected by "counterrevolutionary revisionists" in the municipal Party committee, had issued an order to "return

[29] For a detailed examination of the operation of this system, and the discontent engendered thereby, see "Sources of Labor Discontent in China: The Worker-Peasant System," *Current Scene,* VI, No. 5 (March 15, 1968), 1–13.

[30] *JMJP,* December 9, 1965.

[31] On the nature and manifestations of discontent engendered among intellectual youths by the *hsia-hsiang* system, see, *inter alia,* Radio Shanghai, February 8, 1967; *JMJP,* February 20, 1967; *Hsing-tao jih-pao* (Singtao Daily) (Hong Kong), December 14, 1967, and March 5, 1968. On the use of repressive or diversionary measures by local power-holders to prevent intellectual youths from participating in GPCR demonstrations and "great debates," see *Ko-ming ch'ing-nien* (Revolutionary Youth) (Canton), November 10, 1967, in *SCMP,* No. 4102, pp. 6–8.

[32] See NCNA, September 14, 1966.

all private plots to the production teams." Having made this accusation, the Red Guards then bitterly denounced the order (and its alleged sponsors) for having "turned the spearhead of struggle against the masses," whereupon the young rebels set out to mobilize the hostility of the peasants and direct it against both the local Party secretary and his municipal overlords.[33]

An additional source of suburban opposition to urban power-holders was the desire for political restitution or revenge on the part of those "five category elements" and former basic-level rural cadres who had been "labeled," struggled against, dismissed from office, or otherwise punished in previous rectification campaigns. Municipal Party committees generally supervised the investigative and disciplinary phases of rectification campaigns in suburban counties and communes under their administrative jurisdiction. Since those cadres and peasants who had suffered political and/or economic sanctions in the course of earlier campaigns had an understandable desire to see a "reversal of verdicts" in their own cases, they too were potential allies of urban-centered rebel organizations.[34]

A final source of latent opposition to urban power-holders in China's rural suburbs in the autumn of 1966 lay in the opportunism and personal ambition of those low-ranking basic-level cadres (and other would-be power-holders) who cherished hopes of attaining rapid upward political mobility by riding the winds of revolutionary change. Political purges in authoritarian societies provide unparalleled opportunities for career advancement to those who are adept at gauging the velocity and direction of such winds. Thus, the desire to participate in the postrevolutionary division of political spoils undoubtedly provided a prime incentive for at least some rural cadres and peasants to join with urban rebels in "bombarding the headquarters." [35]

[33] In a similar case, also reported from suburban Peking, "capitalist roaders" and "five category elements" were charged by Red Guards with the crime of having advocated "egalitarianism" in land distribution. *JMJP*, March 8, 1967.

[34] See, for example, *JMJP*, March 8, 1967. The movement for "reversal of verdicts" (*fan-an*) became so widespread and acute by January, 1967, that the Party center was forced to issue a directive expressly prohibiting all such agitation.

[35] While it is extremely difficult to isolate and assess the importance of the factor of opportunism in the composite mixture of motivations which contributed to the formation of both pro- and antiestablishment coalitions in China in this (or any other) period of the GPCR, there can be little doubt that opportunistic considerations did weigh heavily in the selection or rejection of alternative strategies of action by peripheral (or secondary) participants in the conflict. Consider, for example, the case of a deputy commune leader (*fu she-chang*) in suburban Canton, as related to the author by a young intellectual who escaped from the commune in question to Hong Kong in January, 1967: "[The deputy commune leader] was a former high-ranking colleague of Canton Mayor Tseng

All of the above-mentioned factors combined to facilitate the more or less rapid diffusion of urban-centered political disputes to the surrounding countryside in the early autumn of 1966.[36] Alarmed by the potentiality for chaos inherent in the untrammeled process of suburban conflict diffusion, Peking attempted in mid-November to further clarify and define the acceptable limits of "grasping revolution." Breaking a long period of official silence on the subject, *Jen-min jih-pao* (People's Daily) on November 10 published an editorial ordering rural peasants and cadres to stay at their production posts, observe labor discipline, and not go to other (urban) localities to "exchange revolutionary experiences." Urban Red Guards were similarly told to refrain from intervening in the internal affairs of communes and production brigades. "Any action which affects production," warned the editorial, "may bring about grave consequences."

The November 10 editorial officially confirmed for the first time (albeit in circumlocutory fashion) the existence of serious unintended consequences of GPCR "spillover" into the countryside. The editorial thus spoke disparagingly of such adverse phenomena as "obstructionism," "suppression of the masses," "actions of assault and revenge," "abdication of production leadership," and "counterposing the Cultural Revolution against the development of production." As might be expected, all such phenomena were attributed to the "evil influence of the bourgeois reactionary line" as promoted by the ever-present, ever-malignant "handful of Party persons in authority taking the capitalist road."

Most significant of all, the November 10 editorial did not repeat earlier, conditional injunctions against launching the GPCR intra-

---

Sheng in the Canton Municipal Party Committee. In 1960 he was sent down to my commune. Ever since that time he has cherished the ambition to return to his urban post. When Tseng Sheng and the Canton Municipal Party Committee came under Red Guard attack last fall, he saw his opportunity to be reinstated. He quickly allied himself (and his village subordinates) with the ——— Red Guards in Canton who were then 'bombarding the headquarters.' "

The tendency for self-interested, career-minded subordinates to denounce their superiors in the hope of gaining promotion was also a major unintended consequence of the Stalinist Great Purge of 1936–38. As one cynical young Soviet refugee reportedly remarked, "The best way to get ahead is to inform on your superior. If he makes a mistake a political reason must be found for it. . . . Your superior will be arrested and there is a place open. Who is to fill it? I, of course . . ." (quoted in Zbigniew K. Brzezinski, *The Permanent Purge* [Cambridge, Mass.: Harvard University Press, 1956], p. 89).

[36] It should be noted that the various sources of alienation discussed above bear only a very loose relationship to the existence of pro- and anti-Maoist ideological cleavages within the CCP. Ideology and self-interest are not inherently either mutually congruent or incongruent.

murally in the countryside during the autumn harvest season. On the contrary, it was now stated (for the first time) that "the Great Proletarian Cultural Revolution should be carried out in both urban and rural areas actively and step by step." To be sure, revolution was to be grasped by the peasantry "off duty and in their spare time"; but even this caveat betrayed a significant retreat from the near-total moratorium on revolutionary agitation which had been in effect since mid-September.

The most likely explanation for this partial about-face lay in the previously noted fact that under the terms of the earlier September 14 Central Committee directive, entrenched Party power-holders at the provincial and subprovincial levels had been granted sole discretionary powers to make "special arrangements" for dispatching outside personnel (that is, work teams) to the countryside to launch, investigate, and direct the GPCR in certain selected rural communes and production brigades. But with their own vital interests at stake in preserving the *status quo*, these Party power-holders (and the work teams at their disposal) more often than not utilized such discretionary powers to suppress, or launch counterattacks against, local Red Guards and revolutionary rebels. Since the power to suppress antiestablishment criticism constituted, in effect, the power to suppress the GPCR itself, the Maoist leadership in Peking probably felt constrained to remove such power from the hands of entrenched Party officials. Hence the November 10 decision decreed that the GPCR in the countryside would henceforth be carried out "actively and step by step." For the first time since early September, "grasping revolution" and "promoting production" were placed on relatively equal footing. Although this "swing to the left" was accompanied by renewed injunctions against the use of violent, coercive tactics by Red Guards and revolutionary rebels, Mao's "little generals" and their worker and peasant allies were now to be permitted to resume the task of "bombarding the [local] headquarters." [37]

The period from mid-September to early November had witnessed the diffusion of extramural, urban-centered political conflicts to a certain (indeterminate) number of municipally administered suburban communes and production brigades. Now the lifting of existing restraints on intramural "great debates" led to emergence and/or inten-

---

[37] For a general review of the main trends of this period see Philip Bridgham, "Mao's 'Cultural Revolution': Origins and Development," *CQ*, No. 29 (January–March, 1967), pp. 32–34.

sification of localized, intravillage disputes and factional conflicts. For the first time, *local* power-holders found themselves the prime targets of revolutionary criticism. This change of emphasis is clearly reflected in the following passage from a Red Guard newspaper published in suburban Canton:

> In the first stage, from July to October 1966 . . . the main tasks were the destruction of the "four olds" and the controlling of "five category elements." *The power-holders were not yet panicked by these activities.* . . . In the second stage, from November [1966] to February [1967], the [revolutionary peasants] . . . precipitated an unprecedented major revolution in the rural areas within a relatively short period. *Power-holders within the Party now abhorred these revolutionary peasants, and secretly planned a "post-autumn reckoning" with them.* . . .[38]

In line with the new policy of extending the GPCR to the countryside, the period November–December, 1966, witnessed the proliferation and numerical expansion of indigenous revolutionary (and quasi-revolutionary) mass organizations in China's rural communes and production brigades. In one rural county alone (Lankao), no less than sixty-six such organizations were formed in this period.[39] In suburban Canton, mass organizations with such exotic titles as "After the British Quellers of San-yüan Li," "Red Guard Force of Sha-ho," and "Red Peasants' Friends of Hsiao-p'ing" were similarly set up, with a combined peasant membership reportedly numbering in the tens of thousands.[40] And in suburban Hofei, a "Revolutionary Rebel Squadron" which had started with an initial membership of ten in late August expanded its organizational base to include over three thousand peasants by the end of the year.[41]

Unlike the September–October "high tide" of extramural conflict diffusion, intravillage political activities in the November–December period tended to involve primarily localized issues and cleavages. Although ostensibly polarized around the universalistic political criterion of struggle between "proletarian revolutionaries" and "bourgeois power-holders," in actual practice rural mass organizations frequently tended to promote narrow, particularistic interests.

The range of local interests (both latent and manifest) which sought—and found—organized expression in the countryside in this period was understandably broad. More important, such interests tended to cut across (and thereby obscure), rather than reinforce, the

[38] *Hung-se pao-tung,* No. 12–13 (July 8, 1967) (emphasis added).
[39] NCNA, February 2, 1968.
[40] *Hung-se pao-tung,* No. 12–13 (July 8, 1967).
[41] Radio Hofei, February 2, 1967.

major lines of doctrinal cleavage in the "struggle between two roads and two lines." So long as all such interests routinely and of necessity "waved the red flag," however, it was extremely difficult to determine which red flags were genuine and which counterfeit.

As an illustration of the aggregation and articulation of particularistic rural interests in the late autumn of 1966, the following firsthand report from a suburban Shanghai commune is highly revealing:

> A host of fairly small organizations, all claiming to be genuine revolutionary groups, and all representing quite specific social elements, suddenly sprang up during November and December. Instead of broad mass organizations representing the peasants' political interests as a whole, there appeared organizations of temporary and contractual rural workers, former Shanghai residents now employed in the commune, army veterans, and so on, all pressing the local Party committee for some improvement in their economic position. . . .[42]

Other descriptions of incipient rural "pluralism" and special interest promotion shed further light on the nature of extant socioeconomic and political cleavages in the countryside. We have already examined the case of the brigade Party branch chairman in suburban Peking who attempted to bring countervailing power to bear on his Red Guard critics by creating his own organization of Royalist Guards. Also from suburban Peking came the revelation that local victims of the earlier Socialist Education Movement in a certain production brigade had banded together in the autumn of 1966 to form a "Red Flag Struggle Brigade" for the purpose of agitating for a "reversal of verdicts." The leaders of this alliance reportedly attempted to gain the active support of local peasants by advocating the distribution of all collectively owned lands in the brigade to individual commune members.[43] Other reports of organized attempts on the part of various and diverse interest groups, donning the guise of proletarian revolutionaries, to promote their own particular ends in this period came from rural communes in Tsinghai, Kiangsi, Kiangsu, Liaoning, Anhwei, Kweichow, and Kwangtung provinces.[44]

Among the various tactics adopted by local interest groups, the most favored were those involving appeals to the material interests of

---

[42] Ray Wylie, "Red Guards Rebound," *Far Eastern Economic Review*, LVII, No. 10 (September 7, 1967), 462–63.

[43] *JMJP*, March 8, 1967.

[44] See Radio Sining (Tsinghai), March 23, 1967; NCNA, October 14, 1968; *Nung-ts'un ch'ing-nien* (Rural Youth), No. 18 (September 25, 1967), in URS, XLIX, No. 10 (November 3, 1967), 133; NCNA, September 28, 1968; Radio Hofei, February 2, 1967; *Peking Review*, No. 27 (July 5, 1968), pp. 15–16; and *Hung-se pao-tung*, No. 12–13 (July 8, 1967).

local peasants. In a process not unlike machine politics in the United States, various localized revolutionary groups and factions in the countryside strove to gain constituency support by bribing, cajoling, or otherwise bargaining with the local "electorate." In a pastoral production brigade in Tsinghai, for example, leaders of a so-called August 18 Red Guard Combat Detachment allegedly sought mass support by dividing among their sheepherding followers more than 4,000 catties (3,600 pounds) of animal fodder.[45] In a suburban Shanghai commune, besieged power-holders reportedly distributed over ￥10,000 ($4,200) to various groups of local dissident elements to buy off their opposition and, in addition, released "large sums of money . . . to the peasants in the form of extra-generous year-end bonuses." [46] And in Lotien county, Kweichow, a "Red Rebel Squad" allegedly incited local peasants to divide up public accumulation funds and grain reserves and hand over collectively raised pigs to individual commune members.[47]

The calculative motive of self-aggrandizement thus combined with the more basic motive of self-preservation to distort significantly the main lines of struggle between "proletarian revolutionaries" and "bourgeois power-holders" in the Chinese countryside. And when, as in many cases, the mobilization of particularistic intramural interests overlapped with the process of extramural conflict diffusion, the resulting configuration of forces was extremely complex and anamorphic.

Thus, by December, 1966, the ranks of the revolutionary rebels had swelled to include dissident elements of all political (and apolitical) hues and persuasions, as diverse rural interests were mobilized and drawn into the struggle either to overturn or make increasingly bold demands on local representatives of the existing power structure. And in some cases a virtual "united front" was created between genuine radical antiestablishment elements on the one hand, and a variety of self-interested, red flag-waving, "not so revolutionary rebels" on the other.[48]

[45] Radio Sining, March 23, 1967.

[46] Wylie, "Red Guards Rebound," p. 463.

[47] Radio Kweiyang, December 19, 1967.

[48] This latter category would include such previously mentioned groups and strata as retribution-minded former cadres and "five category elements" who had been purged or otherwise punished during the Socialist Education Movement; ambitious and opportunistic subaltern officials (or would-be officials) who cherished hopes of political mobility; temporary and/or contract laborers who wished to repeal the noxious worker-peasant system; intellectual youths who had a profound distaste for agricultural labor; and ordinary peasants who harbored personal or familial antipathies of one sort or another against local power-holders.

At the other end of the rural political spectrum was arrayed a variety of groups and strata whose sole common interest ostensibly lay in defending the political *status quo*, or selected components thereof. These "conservative" forces included, for obvious reasons, the majority of the "principal" rural power-holders (such as commune- and brigade-level Party secretaries and chief administrative officers) and their families; subordinate officials whose primary loyalties lay with their superiors (whether for reasons of political obligation or personal empathy); ordinary peasants who had ties of kinship or other solidary relationships (again, of either an obligatory or empathetic nature) with village leaders; and those more affluent or tradition-bound peasants who either possessed an economic stake in the *status quo* or had been alienated by the provocative (and in some cases, violent) actions of the militant young Red Guards in the initial campaign to destroy the "four olds." [49]

Elsewhere, I have attempted to describe the origins and early manifestations of factional conflict in rural China during the GPCR in terms of the cathartic release of pent-up personal (or group) frustrations, ambitions, and antipathies, wherein private motives were rationalized, articulated, and acted out upon public objects—all in the name of officially sanctioned political and ideological principles.[50] If there is any validity to this notion, then some of the apparent anomalies of GPCR politics in this early period become somewhat less confusing and enigmatic. The fact that the Maoist leadership in Peking sought to apply simplistic analytical formulae to cope with highly complex motivational bases of intergroup conflict (including calculative and instinctual, as well as politico-ideological factors) was perhaps the greatest single flaw of the entire GPCR endeavor. The implications of this flaw were to be fully revealed a short time later, at the time of the ill-fated January Revolution of 1967.

[49] Assuming that the motivations and priorities of the various participants in GPCR conflict are knowable on the basis of their respective socioeconomic and political interests, it then becomes possible at least in theory to replicate the dynamics of the process of (proto-) coalition formation and bargaining. All that is further required for such replication is knowledge of the situational parameters—or environmental constraints—that bound the various participants to a certain set (or sets) or "rules of the game" in any given political context.

[50] See Baum, "Revolution and Reaction in the Chinese Countryside," *CQ*, No. 38 (April–June, 1969), pp. 99–100.

THE JANUARY REVOLUTION

By mid-December, 1966, with the completion of what was officially described as an "unprecedented bumper harvest" in rural China, there was an obvious need for further clarification of policy.[51] In September the Chinese peasantry had been told unequivocally to postpone all nonproduction-related political activities "until the slack season at a later date." Subsequently, in mid-November, Maoists at the Party center had modified this blanket injunction by calling for the active, step-by-step implementation of the GPCR in the countryside on a spare-time, after-hours basis. Now, in December, the autumn harvest was over and the slack winter season had arrived. With peasant spare time in relatively great abundance, the opportune moment for "grasping revolution" was at hand. But one important question still remained unanswered: What kind of revolution, against whom, and for what?

The first systematic attempt to answer this question was made by the Party Central Committee on December 15, 1966, in the form of a ten-point "[Draft] Directive of the Central Committee of the Chinese Communist Party on the Great Proletarian Cultural Revolution in the Countryside." [52] The overall thrust of the new directive was unmistakable: rural China was to undergo a thorough, mass-oriented political revolution. Peasants (and particularly the poor and lower-middle peasants) were to establish their credentials as "masters of their own house" (*tang chia tso-chu*) by "educating themselves, liberating themselves and rising to make revolution for themselves." [53] No interference was to be brooked in the process of "grasping revolution." The "four bigs" were henceforth to be introduced universally in communes and production brigades, and rural power-holders were expressly prohibited from attacking, retaliating against, or reducing the work points of those peasants who voiced criticism or wrote big-character posters against them.[54] In a similar vein, Party organs were now expressly prohibited from sending out supervisory work teams to guide (that is, suppress) the "blooming and contending" of the "revolutionary masses." [55]

---

[51] NCNA (Peking), January 1, 1967. Available evidence tends to support the conclusion that the 1966 grain harvest was better than average.

[52] *CCP Documents*, pp. 137–42.

[53] *Ibid.*, Article II.

[54] *CCP Documents*, Articles VII and VIII, pp. 140–41. The "four bigs" were big blooming and contending, big debates, big-character posters, and big democracy.

[55] *Ibid.*, Article II.

The most striking feature of the December 15 directive, however, was the total absence of any references to the leadership functions of existing Party organs and management committees in the countryside. Earlier, it will be recalled, the twin tasks of "grasping revolution" and "promoting production" in the rural areas had been undertaken under the "unified leadership" of Party committees in the communes and production brigades. Now, existing Party organs were to be bypassed and supplanted by a new instrument of revolutionary political power— the "cultural revolution committees": "The authoritative organs leading the Cultural Revolution in the rural areas shall be the cultural revolution committees of poor and lower-middle peasants, which are democratically elected by poor and lower-middle peasant congresses. . . ."[56] The main significance of the Central Committee directive of December 15 was the fact that previous restraints on mass political agitation in the villages were now clearly and unequivocally removed. Unlike all previous rectification campaigns, which had been tightly controlled "revolutions from above" (that is, organized and led by the Party apparatus), the GPCR in the countryside now became a populistic "revolution from below," directed, as was soon to become apparent, against major segments of the rural Party apparatus itself.

The December 15 Central Committee directive constituted a direct, militant call to organized political action in the countryside. By early January, 1967, the first convulsive effects of the new revolutionary edict were clearly in evidence, as an unprecedented wave of "Red terror" swept through a large number of hitherto tranquil rural communes. Freed from the (often repressive) political domination of local Party organs and work teams, and spurred on by the official call to "seize power" (to-ch'üan) issued by the Maoists shortly after the New Year, various dissident elements and "interest groups" in the countryside launched a series of attacks against rural power-holders of all kinds and at all levels in January and February, 1967. With the example of the "Shanghai storm" available as an officially sanctioned prototype of revolutionary power seizure, these dissident elements and "interest groups," acting out of a variety of motives, which all stemmed from opposition to the *status quo,* soon raised the battle cry "suspect all, overthrow all."

In a production brigade in Tsenkung county, Kweichow, it was reported that "of the 182 brigade and production team level cadres, 98

[56] *Ibid.,* Article V.

were submitted to cruel struggles. Even those not so persecuted were forced to stand aside without exception. . . ." From Fuch'uan county, also in Kweichow, came the allegation that 90 per cent of the production team cadres and all the Party branch secretaries in a local production brigade had been struggled against and dismissed in this period. In Kiangsi it was similarly reported in mid-February that "production team cadres are being indiscriminately attacked and struggled against." And in Enp'ing county, Kwangtung, undisciplined, overzealous "rebel" elements were reportedly spreading rumors to the effect that "cadres at the production team level and above are all power-holders. This campaign means struggling against all county, commune, brigade, and production team cadres. Everyone has to go through the ordeal. . . ." [57]

One consequence of the uncontrolled tendency to "suspect all, overthrow all" was that beleaguered rural cadres in a number of communes simply lay down on the job and refused to carry on their work. As a result, a condition verging on anarchy prevailed in certain localities. From a production brigade in suburban Peking, for example, came the following acknowledgment:

After the launching of the revolutionary movement, all organizations and offices in the brigade were in a state of complete paralysis. Some of the responsible persons voluntarily quit their jobs and refused to resume work; or, under the pretext of "grasping revolution," spent all of their time [trying] . . . to evade the trial of the Cultural Revolution. . . . They appeared to pay attention to production and manage it, but in reality did nothing of the sort. They did not actively provide leadership over production . . . or make proper arrangements for the livelihood of members of the brigade. As a result, some production team members have very little enthusiasm for production. . . .[58]

In addition to precipitating a situation of rural leadership paralysis, the January, 1967, call to "seize power" ushered in a period of "pure conflict" in some rural areas and thereby altered the basic parameters of intramural politics. Rural "great debates" between rebel organizations ("revolutionary" or otherwise) and local power-holders ("bourgeois" or otherwise) were no longer confined to the promotion and defense of their respective special interests and prerogatives, but were now restructured along the lines of overt, all-out struggles for political

[57] Radio Kweiyang, April 1, 1969. *Ibid.*, September 1, 1967. Radio Nanchang (Kiangsi), February 15, 1967. Radio Canton (Kwangtung), May 1, 1967.
[58] *Nung-min yün-tung,* No. 3 (February 22, 1967), p. 14.

power itself.[59] With the stakes of conflict significantly raised, the burning question in rural China was no longer "revolution for what?" but "power for whom?"

In a situation of intramural "pure conflict," local power-holders and their allies proved extremely adept at devising ways of protecting themselves from the onslaught of the "revolutionary masses." And rebel insurgents, for their part, proved equally adept at manipulating the issues of conflict to their own advantage. With everyone, power-holders and rebels alike, waving the "red flag" of revolution, the political situation in some areas was predictably chaotic.

Although official media reports and Red Guard newspaper descriptions of the events of January–March, 1967, are highly polemical and ideologically stereotyped in nature, they nevertheless tell us a great deal about the manifold concomitants and consequences of rural power seizure struggles during the period of the January Revolution. In Anhwei province, for example, it was reported in early February that "bourgeois power-holders" and other class enemies in various rural communes were taking advantage of parochial "clan mentality" among the peasants to "disrupt the revolutionary ranks, shift the target of struggle, and undermine the great alliance [of proletarian revolutionaries]," thereby turning the power seizure movement from a "class struggle" to a "clan struggle." [60] From suburban Peking came the allegation that "when the storm of Shanghai's January Revolution spread across China . . . those capitalist roaders and 'five category elements' who had been overthrown during the Socialist Education Movement launched a fierce counterattack and seized power from the proletarian revolutionaries. They cruelly beat up the brigade cadres and carried out white terror. . ." [61] In a similar vein, it was reported in Heilungkiang province that former cadres and "five category elements" who had been purged during the Socialist Education Movement were now waving the banner, "we are the masses; we want to make revolution," in order to "reverse verdicts" and bring about a "counterrevolutionary restoration." [62]

One of the more interesting phenomena to arise in this period was

[59] In the somewhat oversimplified vocabulary of game theory, this change can be described as the conversion of a non zero-sum game into a zero-sum game. See William H. Riker, *The Theory of Political Coalitions* (New Haven and London: Yale University Press, 1962), pp. 28–31.

[60] Radio Hofei, February 2 and 18, 1967. For a similar description of the revival of clan feuds in this period, see Radio Canton, July 29, 1968.

[61] *JMJP*, March 8, 1967.

[62] Radio Harbin (Heilungkiang), March 16, 1967.

that of overt conflict between elite "factions" led by higher- and lower-level rural cadres within a single commune or production brigade. In Kweichow province, for example, a "revolutionary" production team leader described how a "bourgeois power-holder" in his production brigade had attempted to seize power from his lower-level subordinates in order to "divert the spearhead of struggle" away from himself. The following report is noteworthy for the light it sheds on the ways in which rival leadership factions made use of pre-emptive, evasive, and dissimulative tactics to promote their respective political ends during the January Revolution.

On January 5, I went to the county town to attend a cadre meeting. Yang XX [the "bourgeois power-holder" in the brigade] seized this opportunity to write 10 big-character posters against me . . . and incited the masses to struggle against me. . . . How was I going to strike down this scoundrel? . . . Our Red Rebel Squad on the one hand opened fire on Yang XX, and on the other hand launched the . . . poor and lower-middle peasants to study seriously Mao's quotations on class struggle. . . .

Yang XX then hatched a new plot. He set up a phoney cultural revolution committee. From the day it was set up, this committee directed the spearhead at . . . revolutionary leading cadres in the commune, savagely struggling against them. . . . But it neither criticized nor struggled against Yang XX, not even putting up a single big-character poster against him.

[The committee] also spread it around that "production team cadres of the rank of accountant and above and representatives of the poor and lower-middle peasants associations are all power-holders and must all be set aside. . . ."

We then raised the slogan, "Smash the cultural revolution committee; make total revolution," and waged a tit-for-tat struggle against them. . . . Many cadres and masses saw that the aim of the cultural revolution committee . . . was to protect Yang XX and other capitalist roaders. This aroused the ire of the masses. Yang XX was exposed, together with his backstage bosses, the handful of capitalist roaders in the old district [*ch'ü*] Party committee . . . all of whom were brought to the production brigade for struggle. . . .

In the course of this struggle, we thoroughly exposed the problems of the old cultural revolution committee . . . and set up a new one. . . . Yang XX, seeing that his royalist army had collapsed, went all out to attack the new committee. . . . He also instructed his faithful lackeys to go to the county seat to accuse us of crimes. However, the moment they left, their master [Yang XX] stood alone, like a rat crossing the street, with everyone shouting, "Kill it," so they came scuttling back. . . .

After the new cultural revolution committee had been set up, we convened six meetings of peasants to struggle against Yang XX, and also dragged him around to all the production teams to be repudiated and struggled against. . . .[63]

[63] Radio Kweiyang, December 19, 1967.

As revealed in this and other similar descriptions of the rural impact
of the January Revolution, under conditions of "pure conflict" engendered by the Maoist call to seize power, it was largely a case of
every man for himself and the devil take the hindmost. And in such a
situation there quickly arose a number of so-called adverse currents,
or unintended (and from the Maoist point of view, unfavorable)
consequences of political conflict.

When stripped of their rigidly stereotyped (and highly misleading)
ideological content, widespread reports in this period of the prevalence
of such adverse currents as "suspecting all, overthrowing all," "sham
power seizures" (or counterseizures), "White terror," "rightist reversal
of verdicts," "counterrevolutionary economism," and so on, all tend
to point to the emergence of survival, self-interest, and self-aggrandizement as primary motivational forces in the January Revolution.

Of all the various adverse currents of this period, "counterrevolutionary economism" was by far the most prevalent. The variant forms
and manifestations of economism were manifold, but all contained the
common denominator of appeals made by various contending groups
and leadership factions to the material interests and aspirations of
their actual or potential supporters. From such widely separated cities
as Shanghai and Nanchang, for example, came allegations that local
power-holders in suburban communes had instigated large numbers
of local peasants and contract laborers to leave their rural production
posts and go to the city, there to demand and demonstrate in support
of various "unreasonable" economic and welfare benefits.[64] In Shansi
province class enemies allegedly joined with capitalist roaders and
"five category elements" in a plot to curry favor with local peasants
by dividing, slaughtering, or selling draft animals, and distributing
all collective sideline products to individual commune members, rather
than selling them (at artificially low prices) to state-run supply and
marketing cooperatives.[65] In Kwangtung and Kiangsu, it was similarly
reported that collectively owned pigs and animal fodder were being
freely distributed to individual peasants.[66] And in some cases it was
claimed that bourgeois power-holders were arbitrarily subdividing
production teams into smaller, family- or clan-based units and inciting

---

[64] Wen-hui pao (Cultural Exchange Daily) (Shanghai), January 20, 1967; Radio Nanchang, January 25, 1967.

[65] Radio Peking, February 8, 1967.

[66] Radio Canton, March 14, 1967; Radio Shanghai, February 19, 1967.

peasants to "go it alone" in land reclamation and sideline production.[67] In a number of provinces, class enemies reportedly "hoodwinked" large numbers of intellectual youths who had settled in the country-side in recent years to return to the cities to seek reinstatement as students, employment in factories, or other jobs. In some cases, the intellectual youths were provided by local Party officials with "linking-up money" to cover the expenses of their movement to the cities.[68]

The prevalence of various manifestations of "counterrevolutionary economism" in the countryside (as in the cities) of China during the period of the January Revolution was as much a spontaneous reflec-tion of the generalized political chaos of the times—a sort of "enrich yourself" mentality spawned under conditions of leadership uncer-tainty and paralysis—as it was a conscious, manipulative strategy adopted by various rival groups and factions to augment their follow-ing among the rural masses. In this sense, then, economism must be regarded as a by-product, or symptom, of incipient political-institu-tional decay.[69]

The various adverse currents described and documented above were a source of serious concern to the Maoist leadership in Peking. A plethora of central Party directives was issued in the period January–March, 1967, warning against the specific dangers inherent in such adverse currents and providing broad normative guidelines for their eradication or amelioration. In order to "immediately check the ten-dency to indulge in economism," the Party center on January 11 or-dained that all ruralized intellectual youths and other *hsia-hsiang* personnel settled in the countryside "should be contented with agri-

---

[67] Radio Canton, March 16, 1967, and July 29, 1968; Radio Nanning (Kwangsi), Feb-ruary 13, 1967; Radio Changsha, November 1, 1968; Radio Kweiyang, February 16, 1967; Radio Nanchang, March 16, 1967; and *JMJP, January* 30, 1969.

[68] See, for example, Radio Nanchang, January 23, 1967; Radio Wuhan (Hupeh), September 23, 1968; and *JMJP,* January 30 and February 20, 1967. In one Red Guard newspaper a group of rural intellectual youths published an article complaining that they had been "persecuted" by commune officials and prevented from responding to "Chair-man Mao's call to . . . resume classes to make revolution." Despite the fact that this Maoist edict was meant to apply solely to itinerant Red Guards rather than to per-manently ruralized intellectual youths, the young people in question charged those local power-holders, who had acted to prevent their exodus to the cities with "suppressing the revolution." This case provides a relevant illustration of the tendency for various self-interested groups and strata to distort central policy directives for their own purposes. See *Ko-ming ch'ing-nien,* November 10, 1967, in *SCMP,* No. 4102, p. 7.

[69] For an interesting theoretical discussion of the nature and consequences of institu-tional decay, see Samuel Huntington, "Political Development and Political Decay," *World Politics,* XVII, No. 3 (April, 1965), 405–15.

cultural production work and *should take part in the Cultural Revolution in the rural areas.*" Party committees at all levels were assigned the responsibility of enforcing this injunction.[70] The Central Committee also took notice of a phenomenon previously described in our discussion of coalition building in the countryside, namely, the conscious attempt on the part of various local power-holders to evade revolutionary criticism by corrupting or otherwise coopting the masses:

> According to reports from various places, . . . a small number of Party and government leaders, for the purpose of avoiding the criticism and repudiation of the revolutionary masses, and in order to corrupt the masses, have recently deliberately provided mass organizations with large sums of money and goods. In the name of showing "concern" . . . they use money to win over the revolutionary masses who are opposed to them. Meanwhile, they also grant liberal material benefits to some mass organizations that have been hoodwinked into supporting them. . . .[71]

Taking the position that this was an "extremely erroneous method of work that must be brought under strict control," the Party center exhorted all revolutionary mass organizations to "guard strictly against extravagance and waste," and "heighten vigilance against some leaders who attempt to shift the orientation of the political struggle . . . by economic means." [72]

Another major issue confronting the Maoist leadership in Peking was the question of how to turn back the rising tide of factional political conflict in the villages. As we have seen, throughout the period of the January Revolution, rural cadres at the production brigade and team levels in many areas were overzealously and indiscriminately criticized and struggled against, with the result that the twin conditions of leadership paralysis and labor indiscipline were increasingly prevalent. During the slack winter season, December to February, such conditions could be endured with only minimally adverse effects upon the rural economy. But by the end of February, with the all-important spring planting season rapidly approaching, the phenomenon of leadership paralysis could no longer be tolerated.

---

[70] *CCP Documents*, pp. 163–66 (emphasis added). Despite the new prohibition on urban migration by ruralized youths and *hsia-hsiang* elements, large numbers of (primarily suburban) rural dwellers continued to pour into the cities of China in the first half of 1967. The inefficacy of the January 11 regulations can be traced in large measure to the fact that those "Party committees at all levels" which were supposed to enforce the new directives were themselves paralyzed by power seizures in the course of the January Revolution. On this latter point, see Charles Neuhauser, "The Impact of the Cultural Revolution on the Chinese Communist Party Machine," *Asian Survey*, VIII, No. 6 (June, 1968), 475–76.

[71] *CCP Documents*, pp. 169–70.

[72] *Ibid.*

In order to ameliorate the conditions which had given rise to this phenomenon, and to quell the anxieties of those basic-level cadres who were unwilling, whether for reasons of demoralization or fear of provoking further criticism by the "revolutionary masses," to assume active leadership over production, the Central Committee on February 20 published an "Open Letter" to the nation's poor and lower-middle peasants, calling on them actively to "support and cherish" all rural cadres who were "willing to make amends" for past mistakes and shortcomings. The Open Letter strongly emphasized the traditional Maoist affirmation that "the great majority of cadres at all levels in the rural people's communes are good or basically good." Even those former cadres removed from office during the Socialist Education Movement were now to be offered a way out by "taking an active part in labor and remolding themselves." [73]

In order to provide concrete operational guidelines for implementing the imperatives of the Open Letter, and to provide rural cadres with a much-needed sense of security against indiscriminate attacks at the hands of the "revolutionary masses," a new definition of the term "power-holders" was officially promulgated in late February. Previously, it will be recalled, this term had been widely (though not necessarily uniformly) interpreted by various groups of self-styled revolutionary rebels to apply to Party and administrative cadres at all levels in the countryside, from the production team to the county. Now, however, it was necessary to restore the shaken confidence and morale of basic-level cadres, and to halt the adverse current of "suspecting all, overthrowing all" that threatened seriously to affect production leadership. Accordingly, it was ruled that

since production team cadres are not divorced from production, they are only charged with the duties of making production arrangements, organizing labor forces and carrying out such concrete tasks as are planned by communes and production brigades. *In this sense, they are by no means "power-holders." Neither are the ordinary cadres* [i-pan kan-pu, as distinguished from chu-yao kan-pu, or "principal cadres"] *of the production brigades.* Therefore, with the exception of a very small number of "five category elements" who have wormed their way into production brigades and teams to become cadres or ordinary cadres, . . . *they should not be subjected to struggle, let alone be treated as targets of struggle.* . . .[74]

Despite such assurances, however, there was no immediately apparent decrease in either the frequency or intensity of reported inci-

[73] *Ibid.*, p. 332.
[74] *NFJP* (Canton), February 24, 1967, in *SCMP*, No. 3904, pp. 12–13 (emphasis added).

dents of political conflict in rural China.[75] And throughout the months of February and March, provincial media reports continued to cite numerous cases of rural anticadre struggles and leadership paralysis. Such reports were almost always accompanied by fresh pleas to unify and consolidate the cadre ranks, and by assurances to basic-level rural cadres that they were not the legitimate targets of revolutionary struggle. Such assurances were apparently honored in the breach as much as in the observance.[76]

By early March, with seasonal production pressures weighing more and more heavily on the countryside, concerned leaders at the Party center were compelled to take resolute action to try to preserve (or in many cases restore) social order and labor discipline in the villages. A Central Committee notice of March 7 thus stated categorically and unconditionally that there were to be no further power seizures in production brigades and teams throughout the remainder of the spring farming season.[77] At the same time, it was stated that in those production brigades and teams "where leadership has already become paralyzed" (by factional strife or cadre demoralization), "activist elements" among the poor and lower-middle peasants, militia members, and revolutionary cadres were empowered to establish three-way "provisional leading groups" (lin-shih te ling-tao pan-tzu) to "firmly grasp spring farming work."

Although the overall current situation of the GPCR in the Chinese countryside was described in the March 7 Central Committee notice as being "excellent," the veracity of this claim was at least partially belied by continuing reports of fresh outbreaks of serious rural political conflict in some provinces.[78] Moreover, to the extent that there was a certain leveling off of factional violence in some rural areas in this period, this probably reflected less on the general excellence of the

[75] One major exception to this generalization was in those areas where local units of the People's Liberation Army (PLA) were assigned to the countryside to quell factional violence and "support agriculture."

[76] A partial explanation for the lack of widespread, rapid response to central Party directions and exhortations in this period is that normal channels of mass communication (such as provincial newspapers and wired broadcasts) had been either disrupted or "captured" during the January Revolution. Moreover, a great many rural villages in China, by virtue of their remoteness, were without direct, regular contact with central or regional Party authorities.

[77] CCP Documents, pp. 347–50. Some two weeks later this official moratorium on power seizures was further strengthened when Premier Chou En-lai publicly stated that "there will be no further power seizures even in those brigades and teams where power ought to be seized" (NCNA, March 20, 1967; emphasis added).

[78] See Radio Harbin, March 5 and 16, 1967; Radio Huhehot (Inner Mongolia), March 28, 1967; and Hung-se pao-tung, No. 12–13 (July 8, 1967).

revolutionary situation in the countryside than on the fact that the Maoists in Peking, in their increasing anxiety over the spread of incipient chaos, had been compelled to call upon the PLA to restore order in the countryside. For it was only with the entry of the PLA into the twin struggles to "support the left" and "support agriculture" in the late winter and spring of 1967 that the January Revolution and its many attendant adverse currents were first tentatively brought under control in China's villages. But "control" (of overt conflict) and "excellence" (of the general political situation) were not necessarily synonymous. And within a short time, the two proved to have significantly divergent and somewhat contradictory meanings.[79]

The regime's objective in attempting to curb rural power seizures was clear. Since the phenomenon of "factionalism" had developed under conditions of pure conflict engendered by the Maoists' call to seize power, it followed that only by resolutely prohibiting such seizures could this phenomenon be controlled and the polarization of rural political forces—with its attendant consequences in terms of leadership paralysis and labor indiscipline—halted, if not reversed. By removing the incentive to carry out new power seizures, the regime hoped to alter the parameters of conflict to convert what had been essentially a zero-sum situation of direct factional confrontation into a non zero-sum situation of intercoalitional bargaining and compromise. Thus, it is not surprising to find that official prohibitions against further power seizures in the countryside were generally coupled both with strong positive exhortations for the "revolutionary peasants" to cease quarreling among themselves and bring about the rapid formation of a "great alliance" of contending factions, and with severe negative sanctions against such divisive activities as "inciting the masses to fight among themselves," "rumor-mongering," "settling [factional] accounts," and all other potentially exacerbating actions.[80]

Throughout the remainder of the GPCR (with the exception of a brief period in the spring and early summer of 1968), the official emphasis in rural politics was on narrowing, rather than enlarging, the scope and targets of mass struggle. It was continuously reasserted, for example, that the vast majority of pre-GPCR rural cadres were either "good" or "relatively good," and should therefore be retained in their posts or rehabilitated. And in order to pacify an increasingly

---

[79] For a detailed discussion of PLA involvement in rural politics in the spring of 1967, see Baum, "The Cultural Revolution in the Countryside," Section V.

[80] See, for example, *CCP Documents*, Article VI, p. 631.

apprehensive and restive peasantry it was officially reiterated that no new restrictions, either legal (that is, compulsory) or normative (voluntary), would be placed on the cultivation of private plots in the near future; similarly, it was stressed that the current three-level system of ownership in the countryside, with the production team as the basic level, would not "in general" be changed.[81]

In an effort to neutralize further the immediate causes of intramural factional conflict and peasant unrest, the Maoists initiated a rural campaign of "revolutionary criticism and repudiation" in the late spring and summer of 1967. Making use of the technique of displacement, this campaign was designed in part to redirect the hostility of the peasants and basic-level cadres away from local Party power-holders and/or factional rivals onto the "number one Party person in authority taking the capitalist road," Liu Shao-ch'i. In the course of the repudiation movement, which was launched initially in the rural suburbs of Shanghai municipality, any and all "ill winds" and "adverse currents" in the countryside were attributed either directly or indirectly to Liu and a "small handful" of his alleged agents.[82]

The significance of this massive effort to create a nationwide displacement effect lay in the fact that the vast majority of basic-level cadres and peasants who had been either individually or collectively struggled against as "capitalist roaders" or "class enemies" in the early stages of the GPCR were now to be exonerated of primary responsibility for their political errors. According to new official Party guidelines on rehabilitation (p'ing fan), most of these aberrant cadres and peasants had been unwittingly "hoodwinked" or "misled" by Liu Shao-ch'i and his agents. Others had strayed from the Maoist path because they lacked a thorough understanding of "new things" which had arisen in the course of the GPCR. So long as the people involved acknowledged their mistakes and pledged to return to the proletarian road, all such aberrations would be forgiven.[83]

Equally significant were official admissions in the summer and autumn of 1967 that large numbers of "revolutionary" cadres and peasants had been mistakenly labeled and struggled against as counter-revolutionaries by Party-controlled work teams in the autumn and

81 *Ibid.*, Articles IV and V.

82 See *JMJP*, November 23, 1967. For a collection of official reports describing the initial phases of the "criticism and repudiation" movement in rural China, see URS, XLVIII, No. 5 (July 18, 1967).

83 See *JMJP*, October 20, 1967, and February 13, 1968; also, NCNA, October 4 and December 24, 1967.

winter of 1966–67, during the high tide of revolutionary "great debates." In a series of policy statements issued through a number of provincial "reception centers" which had been established on an *ad hoc* basis under the auspices of the General Office of the Party Central Committee to deal with complaints of erroneous classification and labeling, it was held that "those comrades who were branded [by Party work teams] as counterrevolutionaries in the period after May 16 [1966] should as a rule be rehabilitated. This is an irrevocable decision." It was further stated that "in general, there should not be any dismissal of working personnel during the Great Cultural Revolution." [84]

CONCLUSION

A pronounced decrease in the frequency and intensity of reported fresh outbreaks of political conflict in the countryside in the latter half of 1967 would seem to indicate that the several palliative measures described above, taken in conjunction with the previously noted imposition of direct military control in the worst rural trouble spots, did indeed achieve their immediate objective. Yet, although both the level and scale of overt political conflict in China's rural communes apparently diminished steadily after the spring of 1967, the disintegrative by-products of the GPCR continued to impede the regime's search for a new rural political order. Whether expressed in terms of the creation or exacerbation of bitter and profound personal antagonisms within a given commune or village, the reluctance of many rural cadres to assume leadership responsibilities when confronted with mass "criticism and repudiation" by the peasants, the relatively high degree of institutional decay spawned under conditions of local leadership paralysis and intraelite competition for peasant support, or in terms of all of these factors, the obstacles to political unification were considerable.

As of this writing, China's rural elites have yet to heal fully the profound breaches which both divided them among themselves and strained their relations with the peasant masses. The politics of survival has now given way to the politics of reconciliation. But old wounds heal slowly. And one can only speculate as to the ultimate efficacy of the current consolidation effort.

Prior to the advent of the GPCR it was widely believed by the

---

[84] See the collection of documents on the question of rehabilitation in *SCMM*, No. 617 (April, 1968), pp. 8 ff.

Chinese Communists that the "self-interest" of Party cadres generally coincided with, or was at least congruent with, the "class interests" of the proletariat, and that the two merged in the concept of "public interest." Under the conditions of extreme personal and organizational insecurity generated during the early stages of the GPCR, however, the cadres' perception of their own self-interest increasingly came into conflict with the Maoist perception of the proletarian (or public) interest. The slogan, "fight self, promote the public" (*p'o ssu, li kung*) first promulgated by the Maoists in the autumn of 1966, clearly reflects this growing divergence.[85] The inability of the Maoists successfully to close the "interest gap" is perhaps the best measure of the GPCR's major weakness. For in the final analysis, the "lesson of the *tang-ch'üan p'ai*" was a lesson in the manipulation of public conflict for private ends.[86]

[85] It is interesting to note that the notion of the merging of individual and public interests was subsequently denounced by the Maoists as "bourgeois claptrap" and was attributed to arch-revisionist Liu Shao-ch'i. See, for example, *Peking Review*, No. 30 (July 26, 1968), p. 26.

[86] Samuel Huntington's conception of "political decay" comes close to capturing the essence of this phenomenon: "A society with weak political institutions lacks the ability to curb excesses of personal and parochial desires. The 'amoral familism' of Banfield's village has its counterparts in amoral clanism, amoral groupism, and amoral classism. Without strong political institutions, society lacks the means of defining and realizing its common interests. The capacity to create political institutions is the capacity to create public interests" (Huntington, "Political Development and Political Decay," p. 411). I have argued throughout this paper that it was the Maoist challenge to the authority of Party power-holders that weakened China's political institutions and thereby undermined the Party's ability to "curb excesses of personal and parochial desires."

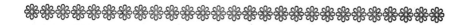

RONALD N. MONTAPERTO

From Revolutionary Successors to Revolutionaries: Chinese Students in the Early Stages of the Cultural Revolution *

Beginning in August, 1966, the Great Proletarian Cultural Revolution (GPCR) reached the most basic levels of Chinese society as millions of Chinese students took to the streets in response to the call of Mao Tse-tung and Lin Piao to destroy the "four olds." Not since the May Fourth Movement some fifty years earlier had students so completely dominated Chinese politics.

Yet, with few exceptions, the students themselves have received but scant attention in the literature of the Cultural Revolution. Little is known about the kinds of things which motivated students to join in the Cultural Revolution and which influenced and determined the broad outlines of their behavior. Similarly, we have learned but little regarding the specific impact of the Cultural Revolution upon student perceptions of Chinese society and upon individual relations within various student bodies. Such questions form the central focus of this essay.

The following pages consist of a case study of a student leader of an upper middle school in Canton during the GPCR. By examining his interpretations of some of the more significant events of the move-

* The author wishes to acknowledge and express his thanks for the support of the University of Michigan Center for Chinese Studies which made research in Hong Kong possible.

ment's early period, we hope to determine tentatively what factors were most important in motivating student behavior. An attempt will also be made to evaluate the relative potency of different factors and to suggest how they might account for different characteristics of Red Guard behavior. It is hoped that such an examination will enable us to move beyond the rather simplistic explanations of China's students as the unwitting dupes of cynical politicians, as self-seeking opportunists, as immature youngsters out for a lark, or as idealistic young warriors actively striving for union with the workers and peasants for the greater glory of the dictatorship of the proletariat.

The pool of data upon which this essay is based reflects both strengths and limitations. The informant had completed two years of the three-year curriculum of his school in the summer of 1966. The son of a worker, he had been a member of the Communist Youth League (CYL) since lower middle school days. He was also the assistant leader of his class and the officer in charge of "study" of the all-school student association. Thus he was, virtually from the day of his first enrollment, privy to information concerning most aspects of day to day student problems and an active participant in the deliberations and programs designed to resolve them. He was an activist rather than a passive observer and was in a unique position to remain attuned to the pulse of his school. Finally, like all students in China, he was required to keep a diary of daily events, one volume of which he brought to Hong Kong. Unquestionably this constituted an aid to his recollection of events and impressions.

Data are drawn from many hundreds of hours of interviews with this informant while the author was in Hong Kong from June, 1968, until July, 1969. The informant was asked for written responses to fifteen broad questions such as, "What was the relationship between your youth league branch and the work team during the period July–August, 1966?" Additional questions were then raised in supplementary interviews. Including writing time, more than one thousand hours were spent with the informant.

The basic lines of the story were checked when possible in interviews with other refugees, both student and nonstudent, and including a former cadre of the Kwangtung Provincial Grain Bureau who had also held a commission as a reserve officer in the provincial security forces. Because of the experience gained in the performance of his regular duties, his membership in the Chinese Communist Party (CCP), and because he had made several trips to Hong Kong and

Macao, this man was able to provide an element of breadth to the rather narrowly focused observations of the main student informant. Finally, data from refugee sources were checked with Red Guard publications and general news releases.[1] The degree of correspondence among all sources seemed sufficiently high to justify this first and very tentative attempt at a general analysis of the factors which motivated and influenced student participation in the Cultural Revolution.

On the other hand, it must be clearly understood that what is presented here is really a case study of how one individual perceived a complex and extremely fluid social movement. His account is inevitably one-sided and should be treated accordingly. Similarly, even if possessed of total recall and complete accuracy, we remain faced with the problem of whether the experience of one individual can be generalized to the nation as a whole. Therefore, the conclusions offered here are intended as no more than tentative propositions which we hope will stimulate other writers to raise similar questions in their own work. Final answers must await the accumulation of a vastly larger body of data.

Examination of the case study data suggests the following four general hypotheses regarding student participation in the Cultural Revolution. (1) By the time of the August 18, 1966, rally which marked the formation of the Red Guards, the Central Cultural Revolution Group had succeeded in changing the student perception of the Party from one which emphasized the Party as an institution to one which emphasized the Party as a collection of personalities engaged in a particular style of action. (2) This change in conceptualization made widespread student participation possible by providing a rubric under which students could attack primary and local Party units and at the same time justify those attacks by reference to loyalty to the Party as they had come to perceive it. (3) Loyalty to the newly conceived

---

[1] These sources are not cited here for two reasons. First, limitations of space are such that it would be impossible to do more than merely note the relevant Red Guard publication without quotation and evaluation. While this approach has the advantage of calling the reader's attention to the fact that the data have been checked, it also raises other questions which take us far from our path. Second, an ancillary purpose of this exercise is to illustrate the validity and the utility of in-depth interviews of one informant as a *supplementary* method of studying Chinese society. Readers interested in this problem are referred to the essays of Richard Baum and Parris Chang contained in this collection, and *Red Guard: The Political Biography of Dai Hsiao-ai* (New York: Doubleday and Co., 1971), by the author and Gordon A. Bennett. Even the most cursory comparison will illustrate the correspondence between the informant's perception of events and those contained in the primary sources utilized in these works.

CCP was a significant factor in motivating students to join in the GPCR. (4) This motivating force was seriously qualified and influenced by other essentially nonpolitical variables, the most important of which were: (a) student perceptions of the benefits and responsibilities which accrued from their education; (b) the officially designated social class status of the students; and (c) student grievances concerning the student power structure as represented by the school branch of the CYL.

In other words, it is first argued here that while students were engaged in opposing Party officials at all levels, they did so in the name of a higher authority, that of Mao Tse-tung and the Central Cultural Revolution Group, and that this provided justification for their actions. Local Party committees had ceased to represent the Party; to attack them had been defined as acceptable and orthodox behavior. Furthermore, it is argued that widespread student participation began only after this cue had been provided.

Yet, the shift in the student view of the Party served only to make it possible for students to engage in action aimed against it. Students were immediately confronted by the necessity of opting either for or against such action; it is in this connection that other essentially nonpolitical variables came into play as the risks and advantages of participation were weighed. Three factors seem to have been of greatest significance. First, students had a particular view of the benefits to which they were entitled by virtue of their educational experience. Similarly, they had developed a perception of responsibilities to be discharged. Both of these considerations weighed heavily in individual decisions. Second, students were officially designated as members of social classes. The sons of poor peasants viewed the GPCR differently from the sons of landlords and were subjected to different pressures. Class status, as will be shown, was a particularly potent influence upon behavior. Finally, depending upon perception of rights and benefits and also upon class status, students enjoyed varying degrees of access to centers of power. For a variety of reasons also to be discussed later, the school's CYL branch had come to be identified as the nexus of this power constellation. Thus, student attitudes toward the CYL and reactions to their treatment at the hands of league members also influenced their decisions.

Naturally, other nonpolitical factors also played an important role. Students were most certainly influenced by the actions of their friends and comrades. And pressure to join the "home town" group which resulted from the informal division of the student body along lines of common geographic origin within the province must have been significant. However, these considerations seem clearly secondary to the three listed above. Expectations of benefits and responsibilities, class status, and perception of the CYL seem to have been truly fundamental in determining behavior, while factors related to friendship and commonality of geographic origin apparently served mainly to modify impulses springing from more basic sources. For this reason, they will not be discussed here.

The school under examination offered a special three-year curriculum designed to train students for administrative positions in such state-run enterprises as banks, accounting offices, and stores. On the eve of the GPCR, the 750 students were organized into fifteen classes of approximately fifty members each. Each class was further divided into small groups of between five and seven members each. The students elected a student association with a chairman, vice-chairman, and five general members or officers who supervised the study, labor, general livelihood, culture and recreation, and physical education activities for the student body. Each class had a similar set of officers who managed these affairs for their colleagues. All were known collectively as school cadres.

Approximately half of the student body belonged to the CYL. The league's organization comprised a school-wide general branch with individual branches in each class. Each branch was, like the classes, divided into small groups of between three and seven members each. Significantly, about 95 per cent of the school cadres were members of the youth league, a fact which was to have a marked effect upon the student power structure later on.

Administratively the school was run by a principal and a vice-principal through five departments charged with responsibility for overseeing educational methods, student affairs, labor affairs, and school maintenance. With the exception of the first and the last, the members of all departments were teacher-administrators who divided their time more or less equally between their dual responsibilities.

Unity was provided by the school's general branch of the CCP whose fifteen members (one-third of the total faculty of forty-five) elected a seven-man Party committee. Significantly, the committee was composed of the principal, who served as secretary, the vice-principal, who served as vice-secretary, and the heads of the five administrative departments who functioned as general members. Party control was pervasive. School cadres and CYL officers were elected from a list of candidates approved by the Party committee. Because of such overlapping membership, administrative decisions acquired the force of Party policy which could be changed only by higher Party officials.

The informant identified three centers of power. The first consisted of the principal, the vice-principal, and one department head. These three enjoyed the longest experience as Party members and functioned as the Party fraction. It was felt that the three talked together daily about school problems and then presented conclusions and recommendations to the second center of power, the full Party committee.

The students themselves, however, in practice had little contact with these officials. Rather, school cadres would discuss certain problems together, either informally or in full session at the class or school level, and make recommendations for their resolution. These would in turn be forwarded to the Party committee, which would approve, disapprove, or ask for additional information. Thus, school cadres in effect implemented and administered decisions of the Party committee; their power to report and recommend earned for them a widespread respect.

But admission to the select circle of school cadres was contingent upon membership in the CYL. The upwardly mobile student had first to secure league membership and then to safeguard and create his reputation as an activist CYL member. Since the most highly rated students received the best work assignments after graduation, there was keen competition both for league membership and for recognized excellence in CYL-sponsored activities. Thus, from the students' point of view, the center of power which affected them most directly was located among the fifteen or so senior league members whose opinions carried weight. In effect, the CYL was the cutting edge of the Party and the link between Party and students. Because of this, students viewed it as the most proximate center of power even though it was subservient to the Party fraction and the Party committee.

The central theme of this essay holds that the Central Cultural Revolution Group was successful in changing the student perception of the Party from one which emphasized the Party as an organization to one which emphasized the Party as a group of personalities acting in a particular way. In this section, we will examine and contrast these two different views of "Party," attempt to explain how the change came about, and finally discuss its implications for student behavior.

Prior to the GPCR, Party organization confronted the students in three different forms. The Party fraction was first; the seven-man Party committee came second; and the organization of all Party members, the Party general branch, was third. More important, lines of communication and authority were perceived to run from the Party fraction, through the Party committee, the general branch, the CYL organization, and the school cadres to the students. The Party stood at the apex of the pyramid. The students were also acutely aware that the Party organization of their school was articulated with other similar Party organizations progressing upward through a hierarchy of positions and culminating in the central secretariat located in Peking.

However, they had virtually no direct knowledge of the method of operation of Party organizations at different levels. In fact, their only information was derived from the Party constitution and other documents which emphasized formal power relations. Party meetings and the details of inner Party life were conducted in relative secrecy, and the informant and his classmates could only guess in their attempts to understand this aspect of the Party. Thus, three aspects of the pre-Cultural Revolution perception of the Party are apparent: hierarchical organization, the center of authority, and secrecy. These are revealed in the following comment by the informant.

It is meaningless to talk of any relationship between students and the Party. We had no relations with the Party. Rather, we thought of it as a powerful but secret organization. I didn't even know which teachers were members, although a few were openly identified as such. I had little idea of what went on in Party meetings. It might have been different if some students had been members, but this was not the case.

Of course it was possible to get a line on what was going on within the Party. *Jen-min jih-pao* [People's Daily] and the local press were full of Party news, and these articles were usually reflected in policy announcements made by the principal. We knew there were things the principal could do only with the approval of higher Party authorities and certain things we could not do because we thought they would be vetoed by the higher levels. Whenever we made recommendations as school cadres, we had to take into account what we thought the Party reaction would be. We judged this on the basis of precedent and on what we could gather from the press about the present political climate. With few exceptions, there was no close relationship between Party members and students outside of school affairs. The distance between us was too great. They ordered and we obeyed.

There is yet another dimension to the student view of the Party immediately before the GPCR. Most students aspired to Party membership. Furthermore, they were keenly aware that eventual admission depended upon excellence in the performance of every aspect of their role as students. For most, Party membership stood at the top of the achievement scale.

> Almost every student in the school hoped to join the Party. We thought of it constantly and were always discussing our chances. Different students were motivated for different reasons. Some were idealistic and saw the Party as the best way to serve the country. Others viewed the Party as a means to fame and fortune. Still others wanted it just for its own sake. There were many reasons, but we all wanted it very badly.
>
> We also knew that our admission depended upon our records as students. Thus we tended to evaluate things as good or bad according to whether they enhanced or detracted from our reputations as revolutionaries. For example, many students volunteered for extra labor assignments while others made a point of getting up early and arranging everyone's soap, washcloths, and toothbrushes. In China, everyone knows how to be revolutionary and we acted accordingly. Our sincerity, or lack of it, was quite beside the point. We did these things because we knew we had to please certain people or else forfeit our chance to join the Party.

This statement suggests another element in the students' perception of the Party. They were aware of the existence of standards to be met and of a system of rewards and punishments. This view implies a pattern of set procedures and personnel trained in administration to oversee their implementation. In sum, it suggests that the students saw the Party as a hierarchy organized for the purpose of attaining certain desired goals in as efficient and as rational a manner as possible.

Thus, in May, 1966, the students were reasonably clear about the nature of the Party and had a basic understanding of their relationship to it. However, by mid-August, they had altered both their understanding of the Party and of their responsibilities. This change is somewhat more difficult to describe.

On the basis of the case study data, it appears that students continued to regard the Party as the center of all authority. As before, most continued to regard Party membership as the ultimate object of achievement and acted accordingly. What had changed was the students' perception of the Party as a rationally organized hierarchy. They were no longer so sensitively attuned to the fulfillment of approved patterns of communication and command. These had ceased to be relevant. Indeed, they had been defined as heterodox and as positive hindrances to the accomplishment of the larger goal of revolution. The organizational dimension of the Party as it had existed up to mid-August was judged to be dysfunctional and the students were quick to perceive that it need not concern them so directly.

Rather, they now turned their attention to those aspects of the Party which retained the mantle of orthodoxy and, in doing so, they inevitably readjusted their conception of the Party. What remained was Chairman Mao, the group of eight to ten persons in Peking who later emerged as the Central Cultural Revolution Group, and those Party members and officials who were loyal to Peking. With the exception of a few persons, the Party apparatus of Kwangtung province had fallen under a pall of suspicion and so remained outside of this category. In Kwangtung the Party had come to stand for that group of individuals who remained loyal to its original goals as restated by Peking and who demonstrated that loyalty in daily conduct. With the destruction of the canalizing influence of provincial, city, and local Party organizations, students responded directly to Peking. "Party" now referred to a group of individuals demonstrating a particular style of action. The notion of Party as organization persisted, but only as an object of struggle. Let us see how this change was brought about.

The shift in perception occurred gradually as the students viewed the responses of local and provincial leaders to initiatives from the center during the period from May to August, 1966. By mid-August, and with the aid of publicity from Peking, they had decided that local Party representatives were guilty of crimes similar to those committed by their high-ranking counterparts in the capital. Accordingly, they ceased to regard them as a legitimate leadership force.

With the dissemination of the "May 16 Circular" of the Party Central Committee and the condemnation of Lo Jui-ch'ing, the focus of the GPCR shifted away from distant problems like Wu Han and the "Three Family Village" and toward ". . . those representatives of the bourgeoisie who have sneaked into the Party, the government, the army, and all spheres of culture. . . ." Specific individuals in local units were to be criticized and repudiated.[2]

The principal immediately called the Party committee into session and targeted two teachers, one an older man who had been denounced as a rightist in 1957 and the other, a young literature teacher whose

<hr/>

[2] To the best of the author's knowledge, the "May 16 Circular" was not officially published throughout China until May, 1967, or one year after it was first approved. However, the informant reported that the principal had announced the passage of the circular and the purge of Lo Jui-ch'ing in May, 1966, almost immediately after the action had been taken. The announcement was made, he recalled, at a meeting of the school's general branch of the CYL convened especially for the purpose. The informant also reported that such inside knowledge was not infrequently "leaked" to members of the CYL, that the purge of Lo was in fact common knowledge among large numbers of Canton's students, but that it was not generally discussed until August, 1966.

"bad" family background placed her under suspicion. He identified the school's representatives of the bourgeoisie at an all-school meeting and also outlined a rigid plan of activity. Students subsequently spent the mornings making big-character posters which denounced the teachers. The teachers then read these and composed replies. Later the students discussed the self-criticisms of the teachers in their small groups and composed new denunciations which were again read by the teachers in a seemingly endless cycle. Twice each week, the students wrote essays describing how struggle against the teachers had helped their own political development. Finally, every three or four days the principal convened a "condemnation meeting" at which selected students and teachers summarized developments, evaluated the self-criticisms of the teachers, and made new accusations based upon the shortcomings of the documents. Such meetings provided a means of developing a "line" for further criticisms and denunciations. This pattern of activity persisted, the informant recalled, from about May 20 until the second week in June.

However, the June 1 *Jen-min jih-pao* editorial, "Sweep Out All Monsters and Ghosts," the June 2 publication of Nieh Yuan-tzu's big-character poster attacking Sung Shih, Lu P'ing, and P'eng P'ei-yun, and the June 4 announcement of the purge of P'eng Chen and the reorganization of the Peking Party Committee soon forced the principal into an action which resulted in his downfall. He immediately targeted seven more teachers, three as "rightists" and four as "bad elements," and continued the program of struggle as before.

The informant reported that many students were mystified by the new denunciations. All seven of the teachers were highly regarded and enjoyed reputations for dedication, commitment to the revolution, and fairness. That they should suddenly emerge as "monsters and ghosts" strained the students' heretofore willing acceptance of the Party's omniscience. Their doubts were reinforced from another quarter. Students who on weekly visits home had managed to keep abreast of events in other schools reported evidence of widespread student participation in both the selection of targets and in planning the program of activities. The informant and a group of about twenty of his friends discussed this new development and contrasted it with the rigid control exercised over their actions by their principal. Their doubts increased. They noted that even the "line" of criticism was controlled by the Party committee, for the teachers and students selected to speak were all either members of the committee or known to be closely linked to that power center by their leading positions in the CYL.

Ultimately, the group of twenty concluded that the Party leadership and a clique of about twelve favored teachers were dominating the movement to protect themselves from being denounced as "monsters and ghosts." These students were also quick to perceive similarity between the actions of their local Party leaders and those of the high-ranking officials who had been purged in Peking. If, as *Jen-min jih-pao* implied, Sung Shih and P'eng Chen were guilty of inhibiting the development of mass criticism, so was their own principal. The center had provided an example of heterodox behavior and a clear demonstration of how such behavior was to be punished.

> All of us had been raised to accept the leadership of the Party. Naturally, we all knew that in a movement strong Party leadership was even more essential. That is why we were not at all concerned in the beginning when the first two teachers were attacked.
>
> But, after the first week in June, our ideas began to change. We knew that the Cultural Revolution was no ordinary movement, for high-ranking Party officers had been purged. The charges against them were really the same kinds of things that our school's Party leaders had been doing. It seemed to us that if the national leaders were guilty of mistakes and crimes, their counterparts in our own school were equally guilty. What we previously regarded as the prerogative of strong leadership now became in our minds pure domination for selfish purposes. It was the information from Peking about the mistakes of national Party leaders that enabled us to see this.

The school Party apparatus had ceased to have any meaning for the students as a force of effective leadership.

As the informant discussed the problem with his friends, they became aware of one course of action which might rectify the situation: an appeal to the Kwangtung Provincial Party Committee to send a work team to the school. The idea, the informant recalled, occurred to them after reading accounts in *Jen-min jih-pao* to the effect that provincial authorities elsewhere had adopted this course in response to similar complaints from other units. When the work team arrived during the first week in July, it put the seal on the collapse of the school Party authorities. But it also sowed the seeds of its own destruction for the same reason: students felt that provincial leaders were using the work teams to direct the course of the movement to protect their own positions.

The sixteen-member work team immediately set up its headquarters in a vacant classroom and set about interviewing the members of the school Party committee. Simultaneously, other team members were assigned to each class to practice the "three togethers" (living, eating, and studying together) and to gather information on the student point of view. After three days of investigation, the team leader called an all-school "mobilization meeting" where he "rehabilitated" the nine teachers and announced that henceforth criticism would center upon the "former power-holders." The informant recalled that the team leader cited as his authority the instructions of Provincial Party Secretary Chao Tzu-yang given at a recent conference of work-team leaders.

Thus began nearly a month of activity in which the principal and other power-holders were mercilessly criticized by students and teachers alike. The plan of action was identical to that followed before the advent of the work team, with the members of the Party committee writing self-criticisms and the students making countercharges in big-character posters and in condemnation meetings.

However, the informant recalled that by the third week of July the pace of activity cooled. Criticism of the principal had been overdone; the list of charges and countercharges was growing repetitious. Everyone had in fact run out of things to say. A group of students attempted to revive enthusiasm by calling for an all-school "struggle meeting" to "completely smash the local power-holders," but this attempt to dismiss formally the principal was turned down by the team leader on grounds of insufficient evidence. In the student view, the movement had once again degenerated into a kind of stage play designed to prevent the dismissal of the school's Party authorities from their posts. Gradually, the work team came to be regarded with the same suspicion as the former school officials.

This feeling was reinforced by news from Peking where the work teams had been the subject of dispute for some time. In the capital many students had overtly condemned the teams as devices by which Party officials blunted the development of thoroughgoing mass criticism. As a result, Peking's campuses were divided into pro– and anti–work team factions. The tension was reported to be most acute at Tsinghua University where the work team had been led by the deputy chairman of the State Economic Commission, Yeh Lin, and "advised" by the wife of Liu Shao-ch'i, Wang Kuang-mei. In an attempt to end the strife, Yeh and Mrs. Liu had labeled the leader of the anti–work team faction, K'uai Ta-fu, as a counterrevolutionary. To call attention to what he regarded as suppression of Tsinghua's anti–work team students, K'uai resolved to fast to the death. Eventually, the Central Cultural Revolution Group dispatched Ch'i Pen-yü, one of its newest members, to investigate. Ch'i reported in favor of the anti–work team students, and Yeh Lin and Wang Kuang-mei were criticized.

The informant recalled that news of this incident brought to Canton by Peking students in late July and early August caused student opinion to tip against the work team still further because it supported the already strong suspicion regarding work team methods. Also, students began to feel, apparently for the first time, that the provincial Party committee itself was implicated in the situation.

> Until we heard the news of K'uai Ta-fu, we were, despite our growing doubts, reasonably certain that the work team policy was in accord with the central leadership. Now, however, it was apparent that the work teams were at the very least under suspicion at the center. This meant that the provincial authorities who had dispatched them were also suspect. Our confidence in them suffered accordingly. It seemed that our work team had done the same thing as Tsinghua's and should have been criticized in the same way. But Canton was a long way from Peking and we had no way of contacting the Central Cultural Revolution Group. We could only make allowances for our suspicions and follow along in the hope that events would permit us to take some action of our own.

The Eleventh Plenum of the Party Central Committee provided the students with the opportunity they sought. On about August 8, while the plenum was still in session, representatives of Canton's middle schools were called to the Sun Yat-sen Memorial Hall and to the municipal stadium to hear recordings of speeches made at the plenum by Liu Shao-ch'i, Teng Hsiao-p'ing, and Chou En-lai. In these speeches it was admitted that the work teams had made mistakes and they were instructed to withdraw. Later, the August 8 "Sixteen-Point Decision" and articles in *Hung-ch'i* (Red Flag) elaborated upon the instructions and registered specific criticisms. The work team left the school immediately, leaving behind one "liaison member" who linked the school with external Party organization.

The explicit criticism of the work teams and their withdrawal set majority student opinion squarely against provincial Party authorities. It now appeared to the student body that these officials had attempted the same course as the school Party committee before them: to channel and direct student action in such a way as to insulate themselves from direct criticism.

We came to view the provincial Party committee with deeply mixed feelings. We knew that it must contain elements who were out to block student activism. But, we didn't know who they were. Thus, we were in the position of having to evaluate each member individually—an impossible task. As a result, the whole organization lost effectiveness in our eyes. Individual members might continue to wield influence, but we were resigned to the fact that we would have to evaluate their actions in light of the response of the Central Cultural Revolution Group in Peking.

Accordingly, we no longer trusted any information which came from provincial Party headquarters. I would say that by mid-August, the provincial Party apparatus had lost at least 80 per cent of its effectiveness. When we wanted information, we turned to the newspapers. Anything which came from the province headquarters was immediately examined in terms of what we heard from *Jen-min jih-pao* and other national sources. For the bulk of my classmates, the provincial apparatus existed only as the object of suspicion, just as the school's Party committee existed only as an object of criticism and attack. We weren't prepared to attack in this instance, however, because we weren't 100 per cent certain.

Thus, by mid-August the informant and most of his fellow students had come to view the local provincial Party apparatus as standing outside the circle of orthodoxy. The school's Party organization had been physically destroyed, while the provincial Party authorities had ceased to have any real function as a vehicle of organization, communication, and discipline. Indeed, students felt that Party officials had used their control of these means of leadership to subvert the larger goal of making revolution. Accordingly, they lost their authority. Loyalty was now directed toward those remaining members who had remained faithful to revolutionary values, Mao Tse-tung and the emergent Central Cultural Revolution Group. "Party" referred to this group of personalities and to their style of action. Students related directly to Peking without the canalizing influence of the intermediate Party organization.[3]

---

[3] This in turn raises another interesting question. It should be apparent from what has been said thus far that, despite their now direct relation to the authorities in Peking, students remained confused regarding the dynamics of power relations at the center. Indeed, students had always evinced confusion regarding this important question, and the new relationship served to compound this condition. Why, then, did this not influence student behavior, or if it did, in what ways did it do so?

From an examination of the data in an attempt to resolve this question, one plausible, but not entirely satisfying, theme emerges. In fact, student confusion regarding the nature of power relations at the center and the demands of the center did influence student behavior. But this influence did not assume major significance until much later, when the movement reached the "seize power" stage in the period January–April, 1967. By that time, students had been acting in accord with the new orthodoxy for several months and at considerable risk to their own safety. Only after this point had been reached did the nebulous quality of instructions from Peking qualify student behavior by influencing them to withdraw, or at least to scale down their participation. That the students were willing to struggle along under conditions of imperfect information for such

This change in their conception of the Party and their relationship to it had marked consequences for student behavior. After the Eleventh Plenum, students were partly freed from a wide range of constraints upon their actions. They no longer found it necessary to evaluate their conduct in light of the possible adverse reaction of local Party authorities; these individuals had, at least for the present, been rendered ineligible to serve as arbiters of student conduct. More important, students were also freed from constraints springing from internalized patterns of socialization. In the past they would not have dared to criticize Party members so vehemently; but now such action was posited as the most admirable form of orthodoxy.

As a result of the events of the summer of 1966, China's students were prepared for conducting a new style of political action which carried the approval and the encouragement of the highest authority in the land. But not all students elected to act, and some who did opt for activism were more involved than others. Let us now examine the factors which influenced their participation.

The informant was one of 750 students in a special school run by the provincial government for the training of administrative cadres. The degree was terminal, which meant that students were not prepared to sit for the college and university entrance examinations. However, this disadvantage was compensated for by the certainty of a significant job appointment after graduation and the possibility of being sent to one of the numerous training institutes run by various ministries for advanced study. The students were thus members of a select circle whose future was assured as long as they maintained minimum standards of technical expertise and, most important of all, a highly intense political involvement.

In line with this emphasis upon practical things, the informant thought the student body to be quite different from that of most other schools. For the most part, students were interested in practical affairs and very much oriented toward the nontheoretical aspects of nation-building. All sought active assignments as cadres so that they could concern themselves with the process of "making the country go." The informant identified the source of this motivation as an intense commitment to the goals of the Chinese revolution and not simply as the result of a desire for personal comfort and advancement.

---

a long period is probably the result of the overwhelming loyalty to Mao Tse-tung developed over years of education and practical political participation. That is, the students were apparently willing to act on the basis of Mao's word.

He was quick to point out the high degree of politicization of the student body and to contrast it with that of students in other, more academically oriented schools. For him and his friends, he said, politics went beyond the mere study of theory and practice and was constantly related to concrete and practical problems. Thus, he felt that he and his fellows spent more time discussing the specifics of national domestic policies than did other students and that they were generally more interested in questions of this kind.

In fact, his comments reveal that the students sensed the existence of a covenant between themselves and the leaders of the country. The students thought of themselves as an elite who, because of their superior commitment and demonstrated talent, had been selected for a particular kind of training which enabled them to do what they wanted to do. In return for these benefits, the students felt a responsibility to serve the nation and the Party to their last measure of devotion. They found strength and support in perceiving themselves as being unique among China's young people.

It wasn't only the special program that made us different from nearly every other school in Canton. Our uniqueness came from within. It made us possibly the most revolutionary and politically aware student body in all of Canton.

First, even to consider applying for admission, one had to have a strong desire to engage in practical work. None of us were theoreticians. All we cared about was implementation and results.

Second, we were all deeply committed to building the country and to completing the revolution as quickly as possible. Maybe it was the result of all the political indoctrination we received. Naturally, other students had it too, but they went to college where they almost always seemed to become flabby and somehow to lose their resolution.

The school gave us our chance. We were doing exactly what we wanted to do and at the expense of the nation. On the one hand, this made us grateful, while on the other, it caused us to develop a sense of obligation. Ultimately, it had the effect of re-enforcing our dedication and caused us to work even harder. We thought of ourselves as the ones who would actually keep China moving.

Because we were thankful for our opportunities, including the material comfort, we felt a greater sense of responsibility. We always strove to set the best example possible. Students from other schools noticed this and usually treated us with a certain respect. When we sensed it, it inspired us to new heights of enthusiasm. Just before the Cultural Revolution, I felt there was nothing we could not accomplish if we tried. We all felt this way. We were ready for anything.

Thus the students had internalized the values of the system, and all or nearly all of them had a great emotional and material stake in its continuing development. How did this perception of benefits and responsibilities affect participation in the Cultural Revolution?

As might be expected, the generalized pattern of benefits and responsibilities served as a double-edged sword. On the one hand, the students' high degree of politicization produced intense involvement as local and provincial leaders responded to central initiatives. Yet, this involvement was seriously qualified by the students' relatively high level of sophistication and by their perception of their own stake in the system. They were unwilling to rush headlong into what they were inclined to feel was mindless criticism and opposition. Rather, many preferred to make "getting to the truth of the matter and then participating" their goal. Finally, as they sought the "truth," they were more susceptible to being persuaded to accept and become involved with the alternative views of orthodoxy which were being presented by Peking and at the local level. As a result, the student body rapidly polarized along different lines.

Examination of student behavior in criticizing the school Party committee seems to support this thesis. The cue for attacking local Party officials, it will be recalled, was the publication of the June 1 editorial, "Sweep Out All Monsters and Ghosts," and the June 2 reportage of Nieh Yuan-tzu's big-character poster attacking the Party leadership of Peking University. By citing this as a revolutionary act, Mao let it be known that such action was orthodox and that it should be emulated elsewhere. However, the informant reported that the students did not all immediately move to condemn the local Party officials.

On the contrary, many began an immediate analysis of the actions of the school's Party leaders in an attempt to determine whether or not they in fact fitted the definition of "monsters and ghosts." Since the initiatives from the center did not include definitive criteria, there was room for doubt. Accordingly, some students (nearly a majority, the informant recalled) chose not to attack. They became known as "conservatives," while their opponents assumed the designation of "rebels." It was not until the advent of the work team that the rebels prevailed over the conservatives. By then, however, it was readily apparent from statements in the press that the new orthodoxy demanded criticism of local Party leaders. It was only then that the overwhelming majority of students began to participate in attacks upon the principal and his associates.

The pattern was repeated during the debate over the work teams. The informant recalled that there was intense argument within the school over the actions of K'uai Ta-fu. Again, nearly a majority—but not so many as before—were not satisfied that the actions of their work team were identical to those of the team headed by Yeh Lin at Tsinghua University. The report issued by Ch'i Pen-yü did not provide students in Canton with information they considered necessary to make such a judgment. As a result, the rebel-conservative split emerged anew and with greater intensity than before. It was not until the Eleventh Plenum's decision on the work teams had been announced and publicized that the debate was resolved in favor of the so-called rebels.

Interestingly enough, there was virtually no hesitation about participating in the Red Guards. By August 18, local and provincial Party authorities had fallen into such disrepute that an immediate response to Lin Piao's call was perhaps inevitable. The informant recalled that, given their new view of the Party, all students rapidly, albeit temporarily, put factional differences aside and for a short period the rebel-conservative split ceased to be a problem.

The intensity with which students adhered to their respective positions was a function of their deep involvement in politics. That they did not respond automatically or even spontaneously was in part the result of their commitment to the system. "Careerism" was apparently an important factor.

> The situation was very complicated. All of us were deeply involved in the Cultural Revolution. We all wanted to do the right thing. But we didn't always feel that we had all of the necessary facts.
>
> We felt that we had to have a firm basis for our actions before moving ahead. We wanted to be absolutely certain that we were in harmony with the changes we saw taking place in the Party. There were two reasons for this. First, we felt that we should take steps to find out just because it was the right thing to do. All of our training and experience, little though it was, indicated this. Also, many of us were frankly afraid of what might happen if we moved too soon. We had never participated in a movement before and as we related our impressions to our teachers who had been through events of this type, they were quick to caution us. They told us how after the Antirightist Campaign of 1957 many who had spoken out became targets of revenge when the movement came to an end. None of us wanted to jeopardize our future by moving too quickly. Many of my fellow students lost this fear eventually but, especially in May and June, it affected everybody.
>
> The trouble was that we never knew exactly how to apply the experience of Peking to our local situation. *Jen-min jih-pao* told us to "repudiate all monsters and ghosts," but it never really helped us to define "monster" or "ghost." This left

room for different interpretations and caused factionalism to develop. It was fear of a negative effect upon our careers that caused this.

Because we were all so deeply involved, the debate became very intense. On occasion there was name-calling and even a fistfight or two. It was only after we got the signal that Sung Shih had actually been purged that we felt it safe to criticize the principal. Afterward, those who had been first to criticize him attained a new status. Later on, the same thing happened with the work teams. Everybody at first held back for fear of making too early a commitment. But the announcement of the events of the Eleventh Plenum also ended that conflict. We knew then that criticizing the work teams was a revolutionary act.

Examination of the effect of students' expectations of their educational experience upon their participation in the GPCR suggests a number of themes which bear upon broader interpretations of the movement. First, it is apparent that the students did for the most part regard the GPCR as an important event, both for the nation as a whole and also because of its possible effect upon their own positions within the system. While large numbers of students may have lapsed from time to time into a pattern of participating for fun, on the whole most of them were basically sincere and intensely serious about their activities. At the core, the students saw themselves as active participants in an important debate; thus, they tried to relate all of their training and experience to the problems at hand in a concrete way.

However, the seriousness with which the students viewed the situation also served to complicate the process of deciding for or against participation. Student response to central initiatives was neither automatic nor unthinking. On the contrary, the data suggest that individual decisions were the result of serious searching and evaluation. Furthermore, behavior was mixed and characterized by not a little vacillation.

The data also suggest two tentative explanations for this phenomenon. On the one hand, the students were deeply committed to fulfillment of their career goals. Some may have been motivated more altruistically than others, but all were at least eagerly anticipating enjoyment of the relatively privileged life styles of highly trained administrative cadres. Accordingly, because they were loath to risk that status, many students evidenced hesitation when confronted with the necessity of choosing a path of action. As was noted earlier, careerism was most definitely a factor in influencing individual decisions. On the other hand, assuming the veracity of the informant, it is difficult to accept that so highly politicized and so deeply committed a group of young people could be so easily influenced by prospects of future reward.

Rather, it is suggested here that students were subjected to a set of cross pressures which made rapid and unqualified response difficult, if not impossible. Students were first asked to attack socially distant personages such as Wu Han and other literary figures. Later they were asked to repudiate high-ranking Party officials located in Peking. These tasks were relatively clear-cut and did not affect them directly. However, attacking persons whom they knew personally and whom they had perceived as models for their own achievement patterns proved to be a vastly different chore which raised a host of problems quite unrelated to any considerations of career fulfillment. It could not have been easy to repudiate actively the principal-Party secretary who had previously been such a potent force in their lives. Indeed, it was only after the mounting of such attacks had been justified essentially on ideological grounds that students were willing to undertake more than tentative efforts in that direction.

Finally, the problem was intensified because the students felt that they lacked definite information regarding the nature of their new tasks. Although they now related directly to Peking, the demands of Mao and of those around him were still unclear to them. At no point, except for a brief period around the time of the August 18 rally when the Red Guards were formed, did the students feel secure in their own knowledge of the development of national trends. In sum, the informant and his fellow students were being asked to attack their former leaders, a task which produced significant emotional stress. At the same time, given their but sketchy grasp of the new standards, they also felt the lack of a clear mandate to engage in such actions, and this condition compounded their emotional dilemma. The result was temporary paralysis.

A final point to be amplified here concerns the factionalism which characterized the entire Red Guard movement. Apart from factors such as friendship and commonality of linguistic background, it appears that student expectations regarding benefits and obligations arising from the educational experience may provide a variable of some explanatory value in evaluating the sources of student factionalism. In the early stages of the movement, the student body rapidly polarized over the issues of who should be attacked and in what ways. It has already been suggested that the high sense of responsibility, concern for career development, and psychic dislocation—all engendered by perception of benefits and responsibilities relative to the educational process—were responsible for this. However, the question of why these differences were never wholly resolved remains. It is suggested simply that high involvement and a deep stake in the system produced a concomitantly high intensity of attachment to and identification with different points of view. These in turn rapidly came to be embodied in relatively well-defined factional groupings. When students did unite during the Red Guard phase of the movement, they did so within the framework of groupings which already existed and thereby carried factional alliances into the new form of organization. Later, when new pressures challenged the students and broke the façade of Red Guard unity, individual students related most directly to those who had shared their point of view since the beginning challenge in June. Moreover, differences in viewpoint were re-enforced by months of shared experiences and joint participation in activities. The result was the creation of a pattern of factional conflict which was difficult for the students to resolve.

Two other factors remain to be considered: class status and relationship to the school's CYL organization. The data suggest a strong relationship between the actions of individual students and their social class status. There is also a relationship between student participation and perception of the student power structure. Since class status largely determined this perception, as will be seen, it is appropriate to discuss these variables together.

Students identified three broad groups of classes. The first, called the "revolutionary classes," consisted of children of workers, poor peasants, lower-middle peasants, revolutionary martyrs, revolutionary cadres, and revolutionary soldiers. The second, representing the opposite end of the continuum, was referred to as the "backward classes." These were the children of landlords, rich peasants, capitalists, rightists, and "bad elements" (criminals, petty thieves, former convicts, unemployed loafers, former Kuomintang officials). The third group belonged to a middle range of classes, called the "free professions," whom the leadership judged to have revolutionary potential because they accepted the leadership and program of the Party. Neither "revolutionary" nor "backward," these were children of doctors, shop clerks, teachers, technicians, and middle peasants. The informant recalled that about 30 per cent of the school's 750 students were drawn from the revolutionary group, about 10 per cent from the backward classes, and the remaining 60 per cent represented the free professions.

However, this threefold classification does not provide an adequate tool of analysis for the examination of student behavior. Rather, it must be interpreted in relation to the organization and operation of student politics. It will be recalled that the student body identified the most proximate source of power and authority as residing with the leading members of the school's CYL organization. League membership was a virtual prerequisite to election as a school cadre. The CYL also played a leading role in mobilizing students for the required one month of labor participation each year. At the same time, league members who were in charge of individual labor brigades reported upon the performance of individual students, and these reports were entered into the permanent record. Finally, during the year, CYL members engaged in "heart-to-heart talks" with nonmembers which also became a part of the student files. Because of this power of recommendation, administration, and reporting, the CYL was a strong force in the pattern of student life.

As with the Party, nearly everybody wanted to join the CYL. In fact, it was regarded as a necessary first step in attaining Party membership. Even though the CYL itself was completely subservient to the Party, it had a measure of real influence. We league members were also school cadres and could make or break a student by denying him league membership, by writing a bad report on his performance in labor or study, or by giving him a less desirable work assignment. Since the Party committee nearly always backed us, we really exerted a great deal of influence.

The informant recalled that class status was a crucial element in determining who gained access to the center of student power and that each class was treated differently.

Beginning in 1964 there was a marked change in the content of our political study. We began work in what was called class education. This was tied in with a campaign to emulate the People's Liberation Army and eventually with the Socialist Education Movement. We spent a great deal of time studying the origins and distinguishing characteristics of different social classes.

As a result, the concept of class was very much in our minds. Everybody was evaluated in terms of his social class background. This didn't mean that we had outright conflict within the school; actually, everybody continued to get along well enough. It was just that we began to grow more aware of an individual's class background and there was a tendency to explain his conduct in terms of this factor.

When the informant had first enrolled in 1964 (transferring his CYL membership from lower middle school), each of the school's fifteen classes had about ten CYL members. In 1966, however, that number had increased to the point where each class had between twenty and twenty-five members. He pointed out that in 1964 more than 75 per cent of the school's league members had been drawn from the revolutionary classes. However, by 1966 that percentage had dropped to less than half. The overwhelming majority of new members had been recruited from among the free professions.

There were, he recalled, two reasons for this. First, after the Ninth National Congress of the CYL in June, 1964, it was decided that the league should increase its efforts to train members of the middle range of classes as "revolutionary successors." Thus, the CYL policy of the school was in accord with national policy. However, the second reason is less orthodox. The informant felt that the basic leadership core of the CYL in his school, all of whom were drawn from the revolutionary classes, deliberately kept out other members of the revolutionary stratum in order to preserve their own positions of leadership. In effect, membership in the CYL had become subject to blackball.

The years 1964–66 were strange ones for the league in our school. Of course, everyone wanted to join, but it seemed that we only recruited from the middle range of classes. It was as though the local CYL and Party leaders had forgotten that students from the revolutionary classes were also to be recruited and used as examples in training revolutionary successors. That seemed to some of us to be the main idea of Hu Yao-pang's "Report" to the Ninth CYL Congress. Eventually it got to the point where students were admitted to membership just because they had good academic records. The theory was that they would be trained once they entered the organization. This sounded good, but the training wasn't all it should have been. In any case, we should have drawn more from the revolutionary classes. Because we didn't, we offended many people, including even students from the backward classes who felt that they too should be given a chance to demonstrate their revolutionary spirit. The result was to leave the CYL open to charges of "exclusivism" and "elitism." The charges were probably accurate!

I must also admit that we discriminated against nonleague members. For example, CYL members automatically received good reports for labor performance. Nonmembers, however, were subjected to careful scrutiny and judged fairly rigorously. Again, this offended many students and contributed to the gap which separated us from the student body as a whole.

The effect of these policies was enormous. Students tended to view their relationship to the CYL as being determined by their class status. In examining the class composition of the student body in relation to that of the student power structure, five major categories rather than three emerge: (1) students of revolutionary class background who were members of the CYL-student elite; (2) students from the middle range of classes who were members of the CYL-student elite; (3) students of revolutionary class background who had been denied access; (4) students of the middle range of classes who had been denied access; and (5) students from the nonrevolutionary classes who had been denied access. With this refined version of the school's class structure, its influence and that of the student power center are more readily apparent.

Several different patterns are observable. The informant identified students of revolutionary class background and students from the middle range of classes who were members of the CYL-student elite (categories 1 and 2) as those who were least active during the period of criticism of the school Party authorities and the work team, but most active during the early period in May when criticism centered upon Wu Han and the "Three Family Village." At that time, it will be recalled, activities were firmly under the control of the school authorities and conducted through the regular network of academic classes and small groups. Thus, these students played a leading role in directing activities and were most frequently called upon to speak out during condemnation meetings.

Later on, in June, as the notion of orthodoxy changed, this group was judged by the informant to be the most cautious in speaking and the first to point out gaps in communication from the center which might lead to mistakes at the local level. Further, the informant estimated that virtually all of those students who were identified as conservatives were of revolutionary class origin and recognized members of the student power structure. Finally, when the GPCR entered the Red Guard phase after August 18, these students eagerly participated, but also adamantly insisted that the Red Guard organization should follow the school's administrative structure. They even suggested the formation of an all-school committee to coordinate Red Guard activity. It is not surprising that the informant reported that these students eventually drifted into the East Wind faction of Canton's Red Guards, which was generally regarded as being most closely identified with former Party officials. In sum, the data suggest that those students who were closest to the center of student power within the school eagerly participated in the GPCR, but also that they were naturally less inclined to undertake activities which might threaten their own positions of leadership. Thus, they tended to hold back until they were certain their participation had official sanction.

Students from the revolutionary classes and the middle range who were CYL members acquitted themselves less well than others during the Cultural Revolution. They were always sounding warnings about how we should be very sure of our ground before doing anything. The rest of us thought they were out to protect their positions, but we were a minority within the CYL. They tried to control the

Red Guards by insisting that those with the greatest experience should exercise leadership. Later on, they were the first to participate in the "great alliances" proposed in the summer and fall of 1967. They were also the first to suggest the end of the Red Guards and a return to the Communist Youth League as the proper form of student organization for constructing great alliances.

On the other hand, students from the revolutionary classes and those from the middle range who had been denied access to the school's power center (categories 3 and 4) were far and away the most active in challenging the authority of Party officials. In this case, class status and perception of the student power structure produced a higher degree of activism. The informant reported that these students were the first to express dissatisfaction with the course of the movement in its earliest stages and also the first to point out the similarity between the actions of purged Party officials in Peking and those of the school officials. Also, more than half of the group of twenty who first petitioned the Kwangtung Provincial Party Committee to send a work team to the school were students from these two categories. This group of students also led the attack against the work team and worked hardest to publicize the case of K'uai Ta-fu, the report of Ch'i Pen-yü, and the criticism of Yeh Lin and Wang Kuang-mei. Finally, the idea of the all-school struggle meeting to formally purge the members of the Party committee from office originated and received greatest support from these two categories of students.

After August 18, these students emerged as the most active of all of the school's Red Guards. They appear to have viewed the Red Guard phenomenon as a means of securing themselves access to positions of leadership which had been denied them in the past. Thus, according to the informant's comments, they took the lead in searching out the "four olds" and destroying them in full view. He also reported that when the Red Guards returned to the school in the evening after a day in the streets, these students were most vocal in the meetings held to discuss and evaluate the progress of the movement. Their most frequent comments indicated dissatisfaction regarding the leniency with which "some people" treated class enemies. By demonstrating superior commitment and capacity for action, they aimed to place themselves within the leadership structure.

As the movement gained momentum, a group of real activists emerged. Most of them were students of revolutionary class background who had not been admitted to the CYL. There were also quite a number from the free professions.

The CYL leadership was O.K. as long as we were criticizing figures like Wu Han, but when the principal fell under suspicion, this group quieted down rapidly. As they did, a new group arose to take their places, at least informally. These were the teachers who had suffered at the hands of the Party committee and the students who had been kept out of things.

Even at the time it seemed natural enough. These students had been deprived of a chance to demonstrate their abilities, and many of them were really very talented. Now they saw a chance and took it. I sympathized with them and was encouraged as they gradually displaced the older leaders.

By November, 1966, things had changed in our school. Few of the old student leaders had much influence at all. The CYL had long ceased to function, and its former leaders were mostly discredited. The new leadership had its core among those students who had emerged during the early stages of the Red Guard movement. In fact, there was a kind of unspoken alliance between revolutionary students who had been kept out, those of the free professions who had been kept out, and a few of the old leaders like myself who had always agreed with their complaints.

Last to be discussed are the students whose origin among the "backward classes" (former landlords, rich peasants, counterrevolutionaries, rightists, and bad elements) had caused them to be denied access to the CYL-student elite (category 5). The informant reported that this group of students, like those from the revolutionary and middle ranks who had been denied access to the student power center (categories 3 and 4), also tried to effect a change in their status by demonstrating their higher commitment and activism. That is, their response was identical to that manifested by other categories of students who had been denied the chance to vie for positions of power. However, the number who tried was small and the attempt was doomed to failure. It is for this reason that this group is discussed separately here.

Before the GPCR, students from the backward classes had existed on the periphery of school affairs. While not persecuted, they were subjected to a subtle discrimination.

We never had any trouble with students from the backward classes. In theory they were equal to any of us and eligible for all offices and positions. However, whenever they applied for anything, they were subjected to such careful examination that they were never admitted to any office. As a result, most of them kept out of activities entirely and never applied for anything. They tended to concentrate on their studies. Many of us felt it our duty to educate them, but we could not accept them as friends. They were definitely outsiders.

The informant recalled that when criticism of the school Party committee was begun, a group of about ten of these students attempted to join in. However, it was not to be, for they themselves were considered to be similar, at least because of their origins if not their actions, to the very targets of the movement. In the circumstances, participation was impossible. Under the aegis of the work team, these students were specifically prohibited from criticizing the former power-holders, although they were permitted to observe as an inducement to "mend their ways." They were similarly barred from criticizing the work teams and from joining the Red Guards.

However, it is significant that they attempted to do so. The informant thought that they saw in the movement a chance to redeem themselves and thereby gain at least a measure of respectability.

I have little doubt that these students wanted to join in the movement. In fact, a group of about ten once requested permission to do so. We thought about it, but came down against the idea. Once there was even a suggestion to allow them to participate as probationary Red Guards to see what they could do. But since some students from the middle range of classes had already been admitted to the Red Guards on that basis, we thought it unwise. Frankly, the backward classes were in one sense the targets of the movement. How could we allow them to participate even if we had wanted to?

It seems apparent that the two variables of class status and positive or negative attitude toward the student power structure were significant factors in motivating student behavior at all stages of the GPCR.

Class status in fact determined who gained access to the power center and therefore was the crucial element in determining the power structure itself. In this sense, it cannot be ignored in our discussion of GPCR. Class status is also important in that it served to influence the attitudes of students toward the power structure in a positive or negative way. Students who felt their class status entitled them to positions within the system but who had been denied access to the system by those who dominated it were motivated to participate in GPCR activities in an attempt to improve their own positions. Those who were in and of the power structure also opted for participation, but only after a cautious appraisal of the possible impact of activities upon their relatively privileged positions. Finally, those students whose class status denied them access to positions of influence also tended to view the operation of the CYL-student elite in a negative way. Like others who had been denied access and viewed the system in negative terms, they opted for participation in order to improve their positions, but were denied the opportunity.

With the reminder that the pool of data considered consists mainly of one individual's perception of a complex and fluid social movement, it is possible to suggest several themes which later might be reformulated as hypotheses for further study of the GPCR. The data strongly support the notion that a small segment of the CCP which later emerged as the Central Cultural Revolution Group successfully changed the concept of the Party held by a significant number of Chinese students. It is also suggested that widespread student attacks upon Party officials began only after the change had been effected. In other words, China's students were not engaged in attacks upon the CCP, but rather upon individual Party members who did not meet the new standards of orthodoxy and on the authority of personalities who had come to represent its apotheosis. Thus, their activities were sanctioned by the highest authorities of the land.

A second theme suggested by the data concerns the educative and socializing functions of the GPCR. By producing a change in the students' conception of the Party, the Maoist leadership in effect prepared China's young people for a new style of political action. This occurred in several ways. First, by branding the Party apparatus at the provincial and local levels as heterodox and by offering an alternative example of orthodoxy in their own conduct and behavior, the central leadership loyal to Mao Tse-tung made it possible for China's students to relate to Peking directly. Despite their frequent confusion regarding Maoist demands, students no longer found it necessary to consider actively their relations with the intermediate levels of the Party hierarchy, although, to be sure, they did consider it as it might affect them in a negative way later on. Because of this, students were partly freed from basic institutional constraints upon their behavior which had been enforced by the Party. Also, by illustrating and expressing the new orthodoxy in terms of attacks upon local Party officials, the Maoist center also succeeded in freeing students from certain constraints which were the product of years of socialization. In effect, students were told that criticizing their superiors was not only legitimate behavior, but also that it was to be admired as a high expression of commitment to new orthodox political values. Thus, changing the conception of the CCP from an institution to a group of personalities engaged in a particular style of action had the effect of transforming the nature of political life for a large number of students. No longer passive beings who related theory to practice in the relatively controlled environment of labor participation or visits with units of the People's Liberation Army, China's students now felt themselves to be relating theory to practice by direct participation in the important affairs of state. They felt their involvement in politics to be more direct and less constrained because of the heightened sense of identification with the emergent Maoist power center in Peking.

Third, it should be noted that the response to the signals emanating from Peking was basically positive. The data suggest that China's students were keenly aware of the existence of an important problem and that large numbers of them marshaled and applied their full capacities in the quest for finding solutions. The students apparently had internalized the values of the system in a thoroughgoing way; accordingly, they devoted themselves to responding in ways which were themselves determined by the system. For example, many were concerned with making absolutely sure of their ground before proceeding. This was in accord with the major thrust of their previous training. In other words, China's students basically accepted the legitimacy of central initiatives and strove to act as they thought they should.

However, despite their sincere acceptance of the legitimacy of central directives, the students did not respond automatically. On the contrary, the decision to participate or not seems to have been the product of a reasoned calculus involving at least four elements: (1) their own perception of the reliability of available information; (2) the extent to which the targets of the movement were previously regarded as the embodiment of authority; (3) considerations of benefits and responsibilities accruing from their education; and (4) student perceptions of the reality of their lives as indicated by their treatment at the hands of the leaders of the student power system.

The data reveal that the spread of the new orthodoxy was uneven, both in terms of the breadth of its dissemination and also in terms of the depth of its penetration. Some students perceived changes more rapidly than others, while still others accepted them more readily than their classmates. Similarly, the content of the new orthodoxy was not clearly stated and therefore subject to different interpretations. Because their prior training called upon students to make sure of their ground before acting, many of them quite reasonably eschewed immediate participation in favor of first conducting an analysis of relevant factors and conditions. However, because they lacked clear guidelines, the process was difficult and ultimately engendered much divisiveness and factional discord.

Second, it appears that student willingness to participate in attacks grew less spontaneous as the targets came to include local personalities whose authority had been greatest. Virtually all of the informant's schoolmates participated in the May attacks upon Wu Han and the "Three Family Village." Similarly, in June most of them joined in attacks upon the first teachers selected by the principal, although a few expressed initial doubts. Later in June, when the principal targeted additional teachers, students became less willing to participate. Still later, in July, when the principal and the school Party committee became involved, the number of students expressing opposition to attacks grew. Finally, in July and August, when the provincial Party committee emerged as an object of attack through the work team, divisions among the student body reached a peak. Thus, as the targets came to include persons whose authority relative to the students had been greatest, the question of participation in the attacks became increasingly subject to deliberation. Furthermore, as the deliberation proceeded, many students fell prey to a virtual paralysis engendered by the cross pressures attached to confronting those who had so recently functioned as their superiors and models. Despite the change in conception of the Party, internalized patterns of socialization persisted and served to qualify student behavior.

Third, the decision regarding participation was further complicated by factors related to student perceptions of the benefits and duties accruing from their educational experience. There can be no doubt that the students considered here felt they owed a real debt to the Party and to the nation which sustained them. Accordingly, their immediate impulse was toward full-scale participation in accord with their perception of the new orthodoxy. In short, political participation was motivated by political idealism and a sense of duty. Yet the form of their participation as well as its intensity was affected by their perception of what the system owed them. To the extent that the informant and his fellow students thought participation would endanger their chances for appointments as administrative cadres and other benefits of the system, a significant number were induced to hold back. The relative influence of this factor in motivating behavior seemed to grow as attacks spread to such local power-holders as the principal and the provincial Party committee. As students were called upon to attack those who might in more normal times be responsible for their work-post assignments, the perception of risk increased in intensity and careerism became a more vital factor in causing students to defer participation.

Finally, and related to this, is the conclusion that student perceptions of the reality of their lives as indicated by their treatment at the hands of the leaders of the student power system influenced student behavior. Those who enjoyed positions of relative privilege were loath to risk them by engaging in precipitate behavior. It will be recalled that members of the CYL-school cadre elite led the movement and participated most actively in the early stages when attacks centered upon distant literary bureaucrats and Party officials. However, as the movement devolved into the school itself, this group of students tended to hold back and seek reasons for not participating in attacks upon the principal and the school Party committee. Simultaneously, students who had been defined out of the CYL-school cadre elite, but who thought they were entitled to membership, seized what they perceived to be an opportunity to enhance their own positions and demanded increased activism as the targets of the movement became more encompassing and inclusive. Those who had been defined out of the system found in the new orthodoxy and in the new style of political action an efficient means of justifying actions undertaken at least in part for reasons of personal advancement. Ultimately, because of the high involvement of all students in matters of politics, factions formed and each factional point of view was adhered to with great intensity. The result was the destruction of student organization as it had existed previously and the creation of a new student elite which based its claim to legitimacy upon its embodiment of new principles of leadership and political action. In sum, student participation in the GPCR was the product of both high political idealism and self-serving ambition.

PART VI

Source Materials

DONALD W. KLEIN

Sources for Elite Studies and Biographical Materials on China*

The following outline has been provided to facilitate usage of the material in this chapter.

* The author wishes to give special thanks to Susan Horsey, who helped in many ways in the preparation of this paper.

Introduction

What do we know of the men who have run the Chinese People's Republic (CPR) for two decades, and how amenable is the source material to elite analysis? There are no easy answers to these questions, but in this paper I have attempted to devise a general framework for the prime purpose of describing the quality and quantity of the data and for the secondary purpose of suggesting avenues for further research and/or the dead ends.

This essay does not focus on individual biographies, nor even on analyses of relatively small groups, such as a twenty-five-member Politburo. Rather, it concentrates on large-scale aggregate analyses which deal with hundreds or even thousands of persons. The data necessary for elite studies can be subdivided in various ways, including: (1) *social background* information, such as age, place of origin, and family status; and (2) *career* information, which would include affiliations with hierarchies, systems, and interest groups.

By way of a preliminary explanation for this paper's emphasis on the availability of career data and a relative de-emphasis on social background information, we might begin with general comments on the state of the art as it has evolved since 1949. When the CPR was established in that year, information on Chinese leaders was woefully marginal. The journalistic writings of Edgar Snow, Nym Wales, Harrison Forman, and others served as an invaluable stopgap; but, understandably, these sources provided only fragmentary data on the hundred or so men who stood at the pinnacle of power. In later years such scholars as Benjamin Schwartz and Stuart Schram threw some light on the subject of social backgrounds, but this is little more than a pencil-thin beam in terms of large-scale aggregate elite studies concerning the post-1949 era. In the past two decades the Chinese Communists have published many reminiscences of revolutionary martyrs (as they call them), but the overwhelming majority of these deal with men who perished in the 1920's.[1] Within the perspective of Chinese Communist Party (CCP) history, these reminiscences deal mainly with luminaries from the period before the late 1920's, when the Party was almost exclusively urban-based. In other words, social background data on CCP leaders recruited *after* the Party turned to the countryside is sorely lacking; and, as demonstrated below, the Communists have released little data of this sort for the leaders who emerged during or after the Sino-Japanese War.

Another state-of-the-art question deals with the compilations (such as who's whos and personnel directories) so necessary to elite studies. Because of the time and expense involved, the task has fallen mainly to governments or research institutions. Such organizations, located primarily in the United States, Japan, Hong Kong, and Taiwan, eventually produced an impressive number of volumes, but they were generally slow in performing this work and many of the efforts were (and are) uncoordinated. In fact, it was not until the 1960's that data were sufficiently collated to allow for in-depth elite studies. Finally, the number of scholars studying China during the first decade

---

[1] Many of these accounts are in the bibliography of Donald W. Klein and Anne B. Clark, *Biographic Dictionary of Chinese Communism, 1921–1965* (Cambridge, Mass.: Harvard University Press, 1971). The best of these is the *Hung-ch'i p'iao-p'iao* series; see Robert Rinden and Roxane Witke, *The Red Flag Waves: A Guide to the Hung-ch'i p'iao-p'iao Collection* ("China Research Monographs" [Berkeley, Calif.: Center for Chinese Studies, University of California, 1968]).

of the CPR was at a premium. Most of them were generalists who, not surprisingly, gave scant attention to elite studies. Parenthetically, this coincided with the period when elite studies were still a relatively minor subdiscipline of political science.

AN APPROACH TO SOURCES FOR ELITE STUDIES ON CHINA

The structural approach to political institutions is in mild disrepute these days, and many students of comparative politics regard it as passé and unsophisticated. Nevertheless, it provides a useful entree to Chinese elite studies simply because the CPR has released biographic information on the basis of institutions. Consequently, compilers of who's whos and personnel directories have been forced to follow this approach. The structural approach divides the administrative apparatus into five *hierarchies:*

CCP
Government
People's Liberation Army (PLA)
Mass organizations
Universities

These hierarchies are then each divided into three geographic *levels:* [2]

National
Regional
Provincial-municipal

Lastly, within each level of each hierarchy there are also internal *echelons:*

First echelon
Second echelon
Third echelon, etc.

The hierarchies and geographic levels are self-explanatory, but the echelons require some elaboration. The following outline should help clarify the matter:

Ministry of Foreign Affairs
    Minister—first echelon
    Vice-ministers—second echelon
    Director, Information Department—third echelon
    Deputy directors, Information Department—fourth echelon

[2] As explained below, universities are treated only at the national level. Concerning the provincial-municipal level, I have not attempted to give a strict definition for cities; in general, I have in mind Peking, Shanghai, and the more important provincial capitals.

However, this four-echelon example should not be regarded rigidly, nor as "official" CPR practice.[3]

Because the five hierarchies and their subordinate levels and echelons are so central to our discussion, it would be best at this juncture to put them in table form, even if all the details are not immediately clear. The tables are suggestive, not exhaustive,[4] and any researcher plunging into a detailed study doubtlessly would create his own more refined "models."

TABLE 54

GOVERNMENT HIERARCHY

Echelon	National Level	Regional Level	Provincial-Municipal Level
First echelon	Premier; vice-premiers; ministers; secretary-general	Chairman	Governor/mayor
Second echelon	Vice-ministers; assistant ministers	Vice-chairmen; secretary generals	Vice-governors/vice-mayors; secretary-generals
Third echelon	Ministry department directors	Committee members; * department directors and deputy directors	Council members
Fourth echelon	Ministry department deputy directors	Committee members †	Department directors and deputy directors; committee members

* A committee member in this instance refers to a member of the entire regional administrative committee, for example, a member of the East China Military and Administrative Committee.

† A committee member in this instance refers to membership on one of the subordinate, functional committees under the larger regional committee. For example, a man might be a member of the Finance and Economics Committee of the East China Military and Administrative Committee.

[3] In terms of our immediate problem—a framework for biographic and organizational data—a breakdown of about four echelons is probably fairly accurate. However, if one were engaged in a highly detailed elite study of a single institution, and assuming further the availability of an unusual source or detailed interviews of a former cadre of the institution, one would doubtless want to create echelons which might easily total a dozen or more. In the final analysis, echelons are simply one means of "weighting" the importance of the man or the post, and should be treated accordingly. For example, in many organizations the secretary-generalship is the key operative post, whereas in others it is more administrative in nature.

[4] For example, under the government hierarchy I have not included the legislature, the court system, or the procuracy.

TABLE 55

CCP Hierarchy

Echelon	National Level	Regional Level	Provincial-Municipal Level
First echelon	Full and alternate Politburo members; Secretariat members; Control Commission secretary	First secretary	First secretary
Second echelon	Alternate Secretariat members; Control Commission secretaries; Central Committee department directors	Second, third, and fourth secretaries	Second, third, and fourth secretaries
Third echelon	Central Committee department deputy directors; Control Commission members	Department directors; lesser secretaries; deputy secretaries	Department directors; lesser secretaries; deputy secretaries
Fourth echelon	Control Commission alternate members; deputy editors of *JMJP, Hung-ch'i*	Department deputy directors	Department deputy directors

TABLE 56

PLA Hierarchy

Echelon	National Level	Regional Level	Provincial-Municipal Level
First echelon	Commander in chief; chief of staff; deputy chief of staff; director, General Political Department; director, General Rear Services Department; service arm commanders and political commissars	Commanders and (first) political commissars	Commanders and political commissars
Second echelon	Deputy director, General Political Department; deputy director, General Rear Services Department; service arm deputy commanders and deputy political commissars	Deputy commanders and deputy political commissars; chief of staff	Deputy commanders and deputy political commissars; chief of staff

Echelon	National Level	Regional Level	Provincial-Municipal Level
Third echelon	Senior officers of military academies; directors of subdepartments	Deputy chief of staff; department directors; service arm commanders and political commissars	Deputy chief of staff; department directors; service arm commanders and political commissars
Fourth echelon	Deputy directors of subdepartments	Department deputy directors; service arm deputy commanders and deputy political commissars	Department deputy directors; service arm deputy commanders and deputy political commissars

TABLE 57

MASS ORGANIZATION HIERARCHY

Echelon	National Level	Regional Level	Provincial-Municipal Level
First echelon	Chairman (sometimes secretary-general)	Chairman	Chairman
Second echelon	Vice-chairman; secretary-general	Vice-chairman; secretary-general	Vice-chairman; secretary-general
Third echelon	National committee members; department directors	Members; department directors	Members; department directors
Fourth echelon	Department deputy directors	Department deputy directors	Department deputy directors

TABLE 58

UNIVERSITY HIERARCHY

Echelon	National Level	Regional Level	Provincial-Municipal Level
First echelon	President	————	————
Second echelon	Vice-president	————	————
Third echelon	Deans	————	————
Fourth echelon	Outstanding academicians	————	————

These oversimplified tables could suggest some seemingly easy research topics. For example, could a comparative study be made of first-*echelon* personnel among two or more *hierarchies* at the national *level?* In some cases, probably yes; in others, emphatically no. In some time periods, yes; in others, no. In short, comparisons not based upon a knowledge of the institutions and the functional allocation within them, the general political process, and the time periods are bound to yield misleading if not downright foolish results.[5] The point, in any case, is that the tables were *not* devised to indicate tidy comparability, but rather to amplify upon the quality and quantity of information available within each hierarchy, each level, and each echelon. To cite two examples (before dealing with the problem in more detail), there is rich source material for the first echelon in the national government hierarchy (for example, the cabinet ministers), but the data base is markedly weaker in the fourth echelon under the PLA provincial structure (such as for deputy directors of the political departments in the provincial military districts).

The Quantity and Quality of Data

Having suggested one framework within which to organize aggregate data and undertake certain comparisons, I can turn to the more detailed description of the data themselves. First, to hazard a rough estimate, there is information on some 40,000 to 50,000 Chinese Communist leaders or members of the elite. Not surprisingly, the quality of information varies enormously. Granting this variation, how much of this enormous vein of raw data is collated in some usable form? The response to this question is complex, but in the first instance it can be reduced to two broad categories: who's whos (and biographical dictionaries) and personnel directories arranged by institutions and organizations. Both types of works, of course, are heavily dependent upon the way in which the CPR has chosen to release information.

who's whos

Any competent who's who dealing with the CPR should cover personal data (date and place of birth, social origins, education, family information), early revolutionary activity, positions held within

---

[5] For example, in the Party hierarchy at the national level, Mao Tse-tung and Chou En-lai would be first-echelon personnel; they surely could not be compared (in most cases) with Fu Tso-i (an ex-Kuomintang general) and Chu Hsueh-fan (a non-Communist labor leader), who would be first-echelon personnel at the national level in the government hierarchy.

hierarchies (which often implicitly carry information about the "system" in which a man has worked, or the interest group which he potentially represents),[6] travel within China and abroad, published works, and participation in important meetings (which often takes the form of speeches given at these conferences). In some cases individual items in a who's who will contain an implicit suggestion of its importance, but by and large who's whos list quantifiable items with little regard to their qualitative importance.

CPR-produced Who's Whos

The CPR has yet to produce a standard who's who, although in the takeover period a few yearbooks and dictionaries contained appendixes with a who's who format (for example, Appendix B, items 1, 15). These need not concern us, because the information was marginal and because it has been incorporated virtually *in toto* into the various who's whos and biographical dictionaries published outside of China.

Non-CPR Who's Whos

Some major who's whos have been compiled outside of China, principally by the Union Research Institute (URI) in Hong Kong (Appendix A, item 1), the Japanese government (Appendix A, item 2), and the Chinese Nationalist government. Appendix A deals with these bibliographically, but some general remarks are necessary here. Assuming the accuracy of my estimate that information exists on some 40,000 to 50,000 Chinese Communists, how many of them are covered in who's whos? I would estimate the figure to be about one-third, but certainly not more than half. This is not really a discouragingly low level of "control" over biographic information, because the data are extremely fragmentary on the thousands of persons *not* listed in who's whos. In addition, there is a means of finding data on most of these "marginal" people (see below in the section entitled "American Consulate-General Biographic Files").

Of an estimated 15,000 names found in the various who's whos, how amenable is the information to elite studies? Using the "ideal"

---

[6] For a description of "systems," see A. Doak Barnett, *Cadres, Bureaucracy, and Political Power in Communist China* (New York: Columbia University Press, 1967), especially pp. 6–9 and 456–57. This is not the place for a discussion of the controversial term "interest group," so I will simply offer the Almond-Powell definition. "By 'interest group' we mean a group of individuals who are linked by particular bonds of concern or advantage, and who have some awareness of these bonds." Gabriel A. Almond and G. Bingham Powell, Jr., *Comparative Politics: A Developmental Approach* (Boston: Little, Brown, 1966), p. 22.

who's who described above, we might examine two of the better known works to test some possible approaches to elite studies. The 1966 Japanese who's who has about 10,000 entries; [7] the 1969 URI who's who has over 2,800. A sampling of the URI volume indicates that only 25 per cent of the entries contain information on such prosaic categories as date and place of birth, and only 15 per cent have data on education. Moreover, a closer check reveals that these percentages are skewed in favor of those older Party veterans for whom information is relatively easily obtained. Much the same results are indicated even when the URI volume is compared with the much larger Japanese work. The following table was drawn up from an examination of randomly selected entries in both who's whos; the only item of information sought was the place of birth of men elected to the First, Second, and Third National People's Congresses (NPC) (1954, 1959, and 1964). Using cohort analysis, I selected from each who's who a sample of persons based upon their *first* election to each of the congresses, assuming that there would be fairly good information for the First NPC, but that the information would thin out as presumably newer and younger men were advanced to assume seats in the second and third congresses.

TABLE 59

COMPARISON OF URI AND JAPANESE WHO'S WHOS

NPC	No Entry		Entry, but Native Province Not Listed		Entry, with Native Province Listed	
	URI	Japanese	URI	Japanese	URI	Japanese
First NPC	53	18	9	43	38	39
Second NPC	67	7	15	80	18	13
Third NPC	90	0	6	96	4	4

Particularly striking are the 96 entries in the Japanese who's who which do *not* list a native province; in 61 of the 96 cases the *only* item of information was the person's election to the Third NPC. Thus, amplifying upon earlier remarks and setting aside elite analysis which concentrates on relatively few senior leaders (such as the pre-Cultural Revolution CCP Central Committee), one is led to the inexorable

---

[7] The Japanese who's who contains 12,000 entries, but some are Chinese Nationalists; the 10,000 figure is only a calculated guess. This who's who, incidentally, is very thorough after about 1953, but it is notoriously weak for the early years of the CPR, especially at subnational levels.

conclusion that studies cannot be done which seek to analyze the socioeconomic status (SES) of the elite or to correlate SES data with other variables. The data are too fragmentary.

In a more positive vein, the URI and Japanese who's whos are typical of most such works in stressing post-1949 career data, especially positions held within hierarchies, trips abroad, and (where appropriate) agreements signed with other nations. There is in fact a superabundance of data on organizational or institutional affiliations, which in turn suggests that the study of recruitment patterns, interest groups, and elite mobility is a fertile field. Whitson's study of field army affiliations is one of the best examples of this sort.[8] But if one wishes to refine such studies—to determine, for example, the ability of a particular group to articulate its interests—then he is faced with new problems. One useful way to examine interest articulation is to analyze the speeches and writings of the members of any given interest group. No who's who has adequately listed such speeches and writings, but some notable efforts in this direction have been undertaken in selected cases.[9]

Biographical Dictionaries

As in the case of who's whos, the CPR has not published a biographical dictionary. Outside of China two have been produced, one by Howard L. Boorman and the other by the present author in collaboration with Anne B. Clark. In terms of aggregate elite analysis, a major advantage of dictionaries over who's whos is that the former frequently "weight" data by stressing key posts while indicating the nominality of others.[10] Dictionaries will often relate one man's work to another man's, something rarely found in who's whos.[11] And dictionaries also pay much closer attention to speeches and writings. On the other hand, they inevitably have far fewer entries (Boorman, about

---

[8] William Whitson, "The Field Army in Chinese Communist Military Politics," *CQ,* No. 37 (January–March, 1969), pp. 1–30.

[9] Michel Oksenberg and Patrick Maddox of Columbia University are preparing a bibliography of speeches and writings from selected periodicals of all provincial first secretaries from 1949 to 1966. There is a highly useful title-author index to the important journal *Hung-ch'i* (Red Flag) ; see James Chu-yul Soong (comp.), *The Red Flag (Hung Ch'i), 1958–1968: A Research Guide* (Washington, D.C.: Center for Chinese Research Materials, 1969).

[10] The question of nominality is important, but rather than interrupt the text here I have discussed it at length under the section entitled "Miscellaneous."

[11] Huang's who's who of military leaders is a happy exception (see Appendix A, item 4) ; in listing a division deputy commander, for example, Huang will usually indicate the commander in parentheses.

100 Communist entries; Klein-Clark, 433), and thus aggregate studies which deal with large numbers of persons can utilize biographical dictionaries only marginally.

American Consulate-General Biographic Files

Even the best who's whos are skeletal in nature, giving little sense of the pace and variety of activities of the man holding "X" post. For example, the URI biography of Ch'en Yün notes that he was minister of heavy industry from October, 1949, to April, 1950, and then records two inconsequential facts before mentioning Ch'en's trip to Moscow in 1952 in the company of Chou En-lai. Such a presentation gives almost no indication that Ch'en was the predominant economic figure in China and that he was deeply involved in scores of vitally important activities.

The problem of tracing the pace and variety of activities of individual leaders has been greatly alleviated by the availability of the biographic files of the American consulate-general (ACG) in Hong Kong. These files contain approximately one-third of a million separate and sourced items on some 30,000 to 40,000 Chinese Communists. In general, the files are of marginal use until about 1951–52, after which they are probably unexcelled anywhere outside China. The major national newspapers (such as *JMJP* and *Kuang-ming jih-pao* [Bright Daily]) are particularly well scanned for biographic information, but the coverage of regional and provincial newspapers is less thorough (and, of course, this process was sharply curtailed in the 1960's because of the unavailability of most regional-provincial papers). Some radio broadcast material has also been incorporated into this massive file, as well as data from some major journals, such as *Hung-ch'i* (Red Flag). On the other hand, specialized journals dealing with subjects such as medicine and architecture are apparently only scanned sporadically. Finally, and perhaps most important, the New China News Agency daily wire service is scanned for pertinent data.

In the section above dealing with non-CPR who's whos, it was noted that there is one means of uncovering biographical data on "marginal" members of the elite who may number about 20,000 to 25,000 persons. The means is simply the exploitation of the ACG files.[12] The ACG collection also includes an organizational file. For example, the *bio-*

---

[12] The ACG files are available at several American East Asian research centers, including Columbia, Harvard, California (Berkeley), Michigan, Chicago, Stanford, and the University of Washington.

graphic file item noting Ch'en I's appointment as foreign minister in February, 1958, is, in theory, duplicated as a position entry under the State Council in the *organizational* file. Unfortunately, this cross referencing has been poorly maintained, and it can be quite misleading if one assumes he is examining a "complete" organizational file.[13]

PERSONNEL DIRECTORIES

The researcher armed with an array of first-rate who's whos, as well as the ACG files, is still only half-equipped to begin aggregate elite analysis. The oft-neglected half of the formula rests upon the availability of personnel directories (or, if one prefers, tables of organizations and names). Because no directory is any better than the data available, and because we depend so heavily on Chinese Communist printed sources, it is necessary to note that the CPR has published two types of information: systematic and random. "Systematic" refers to official appointment/dismissal lists (such as ministers) or the results of elections (such as to the CCP Politburo). As explained below in detail, systematic information has changed over time within the various hierarchies.

The term "random" applies to information not released systematically. For example, prior to 1956 the CCP did not publish the names of its Politburo members (that is, it was not "systematic" information). Therefore, when P'eng Teh-huai was identified in 1954 as a Politburo member, this identification was "random." The failure to publish information "systematically" has thrust upon scholars and government researchers the staggering task of an endless scanning of the media to "identify" which person holds what post. All in all, this work has been performed well, and countless lower-echelon personnel are listed in the directories mentioned below and in the appendix. Nonetheless, any research model which stresses "earliest-date-holding-a-post" must recognize the fact that the "earliest identification" date in the various directories may be months or even years off the mark. Obviously, therefore, much time and effort can be saved by knowing which information has been compiled "systematically" and which "randomly" within any given hierarchy, level, echelon, and time span.[14]

---

[13] For example, working with a colleague, I recently tried to track down every first- and second-echelon figure in the public security network, the court system, and the procuracy, at national, regional, and provincial levels, from 1949 to 1966. The ACG organizational file proved to be about 90 per cent deficient.

[14] Because the "earliest/latest" identifications can be troublesome, the following remarks may be useful. United States government directories consistently and erroneously equate

These remarks also apply to the problem of "latest identification." It has often happened, for example, that a man received a government hierarchy, national level, third-echelon post when such data were being issued "systematically," but by the time he was removed from the post the fact of his removal had to be ascertained on the basis of "random" information.

CPR Personnel Directories

As in the case of who's whos and biographical dictionaries, the CPR has never issued a complete personnel directory—or at least not in terms of the five hierarchies under discussion. There are some important halfway houses, the best known being the *Jen-min shou-ts'e* (People's Handbook) series (see Appendix B), issued annually from 1949 to 1965 (excepting only 1954). However, even using the handbooks, one can make the following generalization: they *do* contain many of the "systematic" appointments/elections, but they do *not* list "random" identifications. Refining this assertion in terms of our five hierarchies, the handbooks can be described as very useful for the government and mass organization hierarchies, but virtually useless for the CCP, the PLA, and the universities. For example, the 1951 handbook follows our four-*echelon* breakdown in the government *hierarchy* at the national *level*. In other words, one can find listings of all personnel down to the deputy directors of the ministerial departments. In sharp contrast, however, at the provincial level the same edition lists only the governors and vice-governors. Translated into research problems, this means that anyone dealing with third- and fourth-echelon personnel in the provinces (assuming he is relying on the people's handbooks) "loses" several thousand names.

"first identification" and "appointment date," or, to put it in the terms I have used, they do not reflect "systematic" and "random" information. On the other hand, these directories do list both "earliest" and "latest" information dates. The Japanese have adopted a somewhat confusing system. When dealing with "systematic" information, they use the character *nin* (or, in the Chinese rendering, *jen*), to indicate an appointment, and they also give the exact date. On the other hand, when dealing with "random" information, the Japanese usually list only the last date when the person in question has been identified in the post. The Japanese also include the source of their information (something not found in United States government directories).

This is an appropriate place to mention that Japanese who's whos are generally the only ones which clearly distinguish between appointments and identifications. For appointments they list the month and year, and for identifications they use the month and year plus what in Chinese would be rendered *tang-shih* (which in this case is best translated "as of that time").

Non-CPR Personnel Directories

Has this important research "loss" been compensated for in some fashion? The answer is a carefully qualified yes, if the researcher turns to non-CPR sources. As already indicated, CPR directories generally list only "systematic" appointments/elections. The major and vital difference between CPR and non-CPR directories is that the latter carry both "systematic" appointments/elections and those names identified on a "random" basis in Chinese media. Lest anyone assume these "random" identifications represent an increment of, say, 10 per cent, he should understand that the figure is probably closer to 300 to 400 per cent. In short, non-CPR directories must be consulted; the sole reliance on CPR directories alone would lead to wildly distorted results for most elite studies.

Unhappily, the first thorough directory was not compiled until mid-1953, when one was issued by the United States government (see Appendix B, item 21).[15] This is especially useful for three hierarchies (CCP, government, and mass organizations) and marginal for one (PLA); it contains no information on the fifth (universities). Beginning in 1957 the Japanese government began issuing a series of solid personnel directories (see Appendix B, item 33). By taking this series in conjunction with various other United States government directories of the 1960's (Appendix B, items 40, 48, 59), it is possible to put together a reasonably good directory spanning the period from the middle 1950's to the middle 1960's.

Special Problems with Non-CPR Personnel Directories

Cumulative directories. No organization has yet produced a cumulative directory of CPR officialdom, one which would list sequentially all ministers, all governors, and so forth over time.[16] For some elite studies this is a marginal problem, but for others (for example, mobility studies) it is vital. In any event, given the present state of our research tools, some topics call for the painstaking task of piecing together cumulative listings. (The potential completeness of any such

---

[15] This and subsequent United States government directories are based for the most part on the ACG files described above.

[16] Appendixes 50 through 69 in Klein and Clark, *Biographic Dictionary,* contain a number of cumulative listings pertaining to the CCP, government, PLA, and mass organization hierarchies. In general, however, these emphasize the national level and contain mainly "first-echelon" personnel.

endeavor is dealt with in greater detail in the discussion below of the five hierarchies.)

Geographic biases. Another special problem is geographic in nature. Considering the period from 1949 to 1966, the most complete data have been compiled about persons working in Peking and the major coastal cities. And, in particular, because Kwangtung adjoins Hong Kong, the information from there is superior to that for any other province. In addition, some severe research problems arose in the post-Great Leap Forward period when access to provincial newspapers was sharply curtailed. This is obviously a serious drawback for any elite study which purports to analyze provincial-level personnel over time.[17] The situation has been partially alleviated by the use of radio broadcast materials, but because of technical problems in monitoring, not all areas of China have been covered equally. Moreover, although a text of a provincial radio editorial can be easily transcribed, there are often doubts about names because they are monitored phonetically (without the availability of the exact Chinese characters).

Periodization. Implicit in many remarks above is the problem of periodization. No institution or its personnel remains constant over time, and many elite studies must take this into account. Further, and of special concern in this paper, there must be an awareness of the data base over time. For reasons which will soon be clear, the most convenient periodization falls into two time spans: 1949–54 and 1954–66. As in the case of using institutional hierarchies as a research technique, I would not necessarily argue that these are the best periods for analysis. Rather, once again, they reflect the changes in the quality of raw information—particularly that required to compile accurate personnel directories. Secondarily, and perhaps coincidentally, the two time spans coincide roughly with key institutional changes after 1949. The nature of this data and the institutional changes are tedious to describe, but they are nonetheless fundamental to any elite study undertaken within the framework of our five hierarchies.

HIERARCHIES

In discussing the five hierarchies below, I begin with, and pay the greatest attention to, the government hierarchy. Hopefully, this will clarify the basic issues and problems, and thus avoid undue repetition

---

[17] Anyone engaged in a provincial-level study—especially for the post-1960 period—should consult listings of newspaper holdings issued by the Library of Congress, URI, and other major centers of China studies.

in describing the four other hierarchies. Special stress is placed on the quantity and quality of biographic information about the men in each hierarchy, but the reader will realize that these assessments are based on my own research experience and thus are often no more than educated guesses. Less emphasis is given to personnel directory-type information because, in contrast to biographic data, it is more feasible to put this in table form. These sources are in Appendix C, which is coordinated with the paragraphs that follow.

GOVERNMENT HIERARCHY

In general, biographic data and personnel directory-type information are more complete for the government hierarchy than any other for *all* levels, *all* echelons, and *all* time periods from 1949 to 1966. Not only are they most complete, but in terms of the number of men involved they also comprise the largest, by a wide margin. A major reason for the completeness is that within this hierarchy the CPR has most "systematically" issued appointment/dismissal lists (especially when compared to the Party and PLA hierarchies). These lists are also the most readily available, having been published in such key periodicals as *JMJP, Kuang-ming jih-pao, Hsin-hua yueh-pao* (New China Monthly), *Hsin-hua pan-yueh-k'an* (New China Bimonthly), and the *Survey of the China Mainland Press* (*SCMP*) (after its establishment in late 1950). As already noted, many of these name lists have been aggregated in the *Jen-min shou-ts'e* and, more important, in the various personnel directories described above. As a consequence, any multihierarchical elite study involving the governmental hierarchy might well begin with this one, particularly if the researcher wishes to run a feasibility check on his data.

There have been many changes in the government structure in the period from 1949 to 1966. Although complex in detail, they are simple in essence and are not an impediment to elite research. The essential changes are found in Klein and Clark, *Biographic Dictionary*, Appendixes 58 through 67.

National, Regional, and Provincial-Municipal
Levels, from 1949 to September, 1954

Appointment/dismissal lists were issued between 1949 and 1954 at the majority of the thirty-four meetings of the Central People's Government Council (chaired by Mao Tse-tung) and the 224 meetings of the Government Administration Council (chaired by Chou En-lai).[18] These lists contain appointments for four or five echelons at all three geographic levels. For example, a typical list might announce the appointment of a minister, three vice-ministers, three ministerial department directors, and six ministerial department deputy directors. Moreover, most of the name lists were annotated to include one or more of the following items: Party membership, sex, native province, nationality (where appropriate), and previous or present posts.[19] Party membership and native province are often omitted, but an examination of scores of these lists does not suggest any particular reason for their inclusion on one occasion and omission on another.

These annotations were of enormous use, and very often provided the earliest biographic data about the person in question. They were also suggestive of topics for further study. For example, when the

[18] We have not stressed the official dismissal lists, but we might make some observations for those not familiar with CPR practices. Prior to the Cultural Revolution, the appearance of a man's name on a dismissal list generally signaled a promotion or a transfer—not a purge. Even when we know retrospectively that a man was purged, he was normally "dismissed" without comment within the government hierarchy.

Peking's normal practice is to "dismiss" a man from a post even though the same appointment/dismissal list indicates that, in fact, he has been "appointed" (that is, promoted) to a higher post. For example, Chang Chang will be "dismissed" as assistant minister of railways, but the same name list will carry the fact that he was "appointed" to the higher-level post of vice-minister. On occasions, however, a man will simply be appointed a vice-minister, but not "dismissed" as an assistant minister. This seems to be a contradiction in terms, and eventually the CPR gets around to "dismissing" the man from his lesser post—sometimes many months later. I have never discovered any political significance in such instances.

[19] Party membership in this case means both CCP members and members of the various non-Communist (or "democratic") parties, such as the China Democratic League. The importance of the previous or present post annotations merits further explanation because there are several types. The use of *hsien* ("presently") before the post name simply means that it is a concurrently held post, usually in another hierarchy. However, *hsien* is sometimes omitted. If the post is preceded by *ts'eng* or *ch'ien* ("previously"), it indicates a post which the appointee has already relinquished at some time in the past. Confusion arises when the post is preceded by *yuan*: this sometimes indicates a previously held post, but it can also mean, in effect, that the man in question has merely been reappointed to the position. Unfortunately, NCNA has variously translated *yuan* as "originally," "previously," or "formerly." Because this can be particularly confusing, an example might help. An appointment list of two seemingly "new" Shanghai vice-mayors might read:

Wang Wang-wang (*yuan*, vice-mayor of Shanghai)

Lin Lin-lin (*yuan*, vice-mayor of Canton)

Obviously, it would be more useful if Wang's annotation read "re-elected," and Lin's annotation, "transferred from post of vice-mayor of Canton."

Finally, some names will be followed by *chien* ("concurrent"), but no other information. This means that the person in question was previously appointed to some post within the same organization. For example, P'eng Teh-huai was already chairman of the Northwest Military and Administrative Committee when he was additionally appointed to head the subordinate Finance and Economics Committee; upon receiving the initial appointment, there was an annotation, but only *chien* appeared when he received the second post.

Communists captured a province in the takeover period, they customarily appointed a provincial council of thirty to forty members. Let us suppose that the annotations to the names of forty council members revealed that thirty seats were given to military men, and that twenty-five of these thirty men had occupied political (as opposed to command or staff) posts within the PLA. This bit of "instant analysis" would suggest the Communists were turning to their political commissars, and not their commanders, to assume newly created civil posts. In other words, a researcher might be alerted to the rise of a potentially new bureaucratic cluster, and move from there to make parallel examinations of the data for other provinces. Similarly, the annotation listing native province would be useful to anyone interested in historical perspectives (such as continuities and discontinuities); he could see instantly from the same council name list the degree to which the CPR adhered to the historic "law of avoidance" in making provincial-level appointments. Or, a researcher interested in cooptation could quickly compile the percentages of council seats allotted to non-Communists.

We have already given some notion of the size of the overall elite. But as we begin to examine the hierarchies in detail, it may be useful to mention again the sheer magnitude—and thus the research potential —of the persons presently under discussion, keeping in mind that the following example is drawn *solely* from the government hierarchy. In the takeover years, the CPR constantly issued appointment lists as it staffed its numerous administrative offices. Two such name lists were published in the *JMJP*, July 6, 1950. Aside from two national-level appointments and two university appointments, these lists contained no less than 670 appointments at the regional and provincial-municipal level. Moreover, the overwhelming majority pertained only to three provinces, two cities, and one of the six regional-level governments. Extrapolating from these lists (and without pretending to provide a precise figure), one can assume that during the takeover period alone some 12,000 to 15,000 appointments were made simply to staff two of the three geographic levels (the regions and provinces-cities) at the four echelons described above.

Mention of a 12,000 to 15,000 potential data base at the regional and provincial-municipal levels raises the question: Is this base readily retrievable? It is a question worth examining because it serves as a means of recapitulating many of the complex points we have been discussing and because it represents an exciting research potential. To reiterate, the necessary data were poorly collated in the crucial takeover years. In support of this statement we noted that the first reasonably thorough personnel directory was not compiled until mid-1953. A check of the regional and provincial-municipal levels in this directory suggests it is about 25 per cent out of date if, for example, one wished to trace personnel turnover from 1949–50 to mid-1953. Now, to answer the question at hand, regional and provincial-municipal personnel data are not too readily retrievable. However, there is one feasible means. By using the index to the *JMJP* (*Jen-min jih-pao so-yin*), it is possible to locate quite rapidly the pertinent appointment/dismissal name lists. After getting the actual texts of the name lists, one can then create his own cumulative lists, remembering in advance that he can "build" on the above-mentioned 1953 United States government directory. Anyone venturing into such a project should take special note of the biographic annotations to the appointment lists because, as noted earlier, the quality and depth of biographic data in all of the who's whos and the ACG files are extremely poor for 1949–50.

For the 1949–54 period in the government hierarchy, we should pinpoint the unusual potential for an elite study at the regional level. First, this level has both beginning and terminal dates (1949 to 1954). Second, considering all four echelons, there is no other category, over time, for which basic name lists are so excellent. Finally, because the regional-level personnel were so important, there is relatively rich biographic information about the hundreds of men who held regional posts during the five years this administrative level existed. There are, of course, scores of approaches that might be used in a regional elite study. In another context Michel Oksenberg has drawn attention to the research potential found in hypotheses advanced in Chi Ch'ao-ting's landmark *Key Economic Areas in Chinese History*. A regional elite study relating to Chi's work might yield interesting results.[20]

National Level Only, September, 1954, to Spring, 1966

After the inauguration of the constitutional government at the first session of the First National People's Congress in September, 1954, the CPR continued to issue national-level name lists through the spring of 1966. However, there were two fundamental differences: (1) the name lists no longer carried annotations (such as previous or

---

[20] Michel C. Oksenberg, *A Bibliography of Secondary English Language Literature on Contemporary Chinese Politics* (New York: East Asian Institute, Columbia University, 1970), pp. xxvii–xxix. Obviously, I would not rule out the possibility of using data on elites in the other hierarchies having regional levels; these are discussed in later portions of this paper.

present post); and (2) the CPR only issued name lists through two echelons (covering ministers, vice-ministers, and assistant ministers).[21]

At first glance it might seem that this lack of annotations and the "loss" of "systematic" appointments for two echelons were critical. Happily, as we know from empirical tests, the lack of annotations at the national level was not generally a serious problem; there was such great continuity of assignments prior to the Cultural Revolution that only rarely did a totally new face turn up in top government echelons after 1954. Or, to put it another way, we almost always knew from some previous lower-level appointment the man's Party affiliation, his previous post, and so forth. Moreover, as common sense would suggest in regard to the third- and fourth-echelon personnel, most of the men holding these posts continued in them after 1954. Finally, there was a relative openness in the media in the mid-1950's, which meant that many third- and fourth-echelon men were frequently in the news.

Regional and Provincial-Municipal Levels, 1954–66

Regional. The regional level is quickly disposed of simply because it was abolished in 1954 when the constitutional government was inaugurated. However, it is worth mentioning if only as a reminder that the PLA regional-level hierarchy continued after 1954 (see below), whereas the CCP regional-level hierarchy was discontinued (although reconstituted in 1961—see below), and the mass organization regional-level hierarchy was dissolved. Thus, any "horizontal" hierarchical elite study must be adjusted to these circumstances if it is carried beyond 1954.

Provincial-municipal. Beginning in 1954, provincial governors and municipal mayors (as well as the subordinate officials) were no longer appointed by the national government. Rather, they were elected at provincial (or municipal) congresses. The results of the elections (in effect, name lists) were "systematically" reported in the national press, and they have been carefully translated and indexed in the *SCMP*.[22] Setting aside the superficial distinction between "appointments" and "elections," the prime differences with the pre-1954 period are: (1) the name lists no longer carried annotations and (2) the CPR regularly

---

[21] The post of assistant minister (*pu-chang chu-li*) was created in 1954. For the purposes of this paper I have placed it at the same echelon as the vice-ministers. The CPR has continued to identify women and, where appropriate, the nationality of the appointee.

[22] The provincial press also carried this information in the 1960's, but because of the above-mentioned lack of access to provincial newspapers in the 1960's, it is not possible to know if this practice continued.

issued name lists through two echelons (governors/mayors and vice-governors/vice-mayors), but name lists of the third echelon (members of the provincial people's council) are only available to the 1958–59 period. To put the second point in negative terms, after 1954 the names of fourth-echelon personnel (directors and deputy directors of provincial departments, which might be likened to a cabinet structure) were no longer "systematically" reported.

An elite study of governors would probably be fruitful. The biographic data are generally very good, and a cumulative list has been compiled.[23] Moreover, it is not difficult to compile a near-perfect list of all vice-governors, but the biographic data are clearly less in quality and quantity than those for governors.[24]

One of the research problems at the provincial-municipal level of the government hierarchy is related to the growth of the national level in the mid-1950's. During this period, scores of men were recruited into the national level from the provinces. To illustrate the point (and recalling that even third- and fourth-echelon personnel appeared on annotated name lists prior to 1954), we might take the hypothetical Ma Ti-lan. In December, 1949, Ma was appointed a deputy director of the Animal Husbandry Department in Kansu, at which time he was identified as a CCP member, a Hui from Kansu, and as the former commander of a cavalry brigade in the First Field Army. From a March, 1952, appointment list we learn that he was promoted to director of animal husbandry in Kansu, and then in January, 1955, he was transferred to Peking to become an assistant minister of agriculture. We are thus armed with fairly good biographical data about one more man at the national level.

But what of Ma's successor in the Kansu post? We might hypothesize that he was recruited from an echelon below our four-echelon scheme in the Kansu Animal Husbandry Department, or from one of the special districts or *hsien* in Kansu, or even from a low-echelon post in the Ministry of Agriculture in Peking. However, there is a striking paucity of biographic data about personnel at those levels, not to mention detailed personnel directory-type information.[25] In short, we

---

[23] See Appendix 66 in Klein and Clark, *Biographic Dictionary.*

[24] Because of the Chinese practice of multiple vice-governorships, the total number of vice-governors is much larger than governors. Frederick C. Teiwes, *Provincial Party Personnel in Mainland China, 1956–1966* ("Occasional Papers of the East Asian Institute" [New York: Columbia University, 1967]), p. 5, notes the growth in the number of vice-governors from 128 in 1956 to 237 in 1965.

[25] For one of the few sources with organized lists of *hsien* government officials, see *Chūka jinmin kyōwakoku chihōbetsu soshiki jinmei hyō* (Directory of Local Organizations

are unlikely to know much about Ma's successor and, given the lack of systematic appointment lists at this level after 1954, we might not even know the man's name for a year or two after Ma's departure for Peking.

Implicit in this "problem," however, is the more favorable potential for a study of (presumed) upward mobility of provincial-level specialists—such as officials in provincial departments of industry, communications, and agriculture—to counterpart ministries in Peking. Bearing in mind again the dearth of information on such factors as education, which we might presume would help "qualify" a man for a ministerial post, one of the few variables we can test with some accuracy is the experience a man has gained in some specialized field at the provincial level. Such a study might shed useful light on the familiar "Red and expert" issue.

Assuming a different set of circumstances—such as a high degree of carry-over in the provinces from the 1949–54 period into the post-1954 period—we must still revert to a point mentioned earlier. Namely, in the post-Great Leap Forward period (around 1960 and later) there is a drying up of source material for most provinces because of the unavailability of many provincial newspapers. In short, there are severe handicaps to elite studies for the post-1954 period which seek to delve into the lower echelons of provincial-municipal governments.

THE UNIVERSITY HIERARCHY

The university hierarchy is rather simply described and, in terms of sources, is broadly similar to the government hierarchy. The chief difference is that geographic levels utilized above (national, regional, and provincial) can be ignored. In a nontechnical sense, all universities are "national" in that the name lists all derive from the national government through all periods, and the echelons are fewer in that official name lists have consisted only of university presidents and vice-presidents. As in the case of the government hierarchy, university name lists were annotated with biographic data about the appointees until 1954, but not thereafter.

Unfortunately, no personnel directories listed university officials until one was published by the Japanese in 1957. The problem is compounded by the fact that there is not available even a complete list of universities. The most extensive list of schools, but one which does

in the People's Republic of China) (Tokyo: Ajia Kenkyujō [Asian Research Institute], 1963). While useful, even this source is far from complete.

not contain any names, was published by the CPR in 1957, and subsequently printed in *Current Background,* No. 462 (July 1, 1957), and reproduced in Leon A. Orleans' *Professional Manpower and Education in Communist China.*[26]

One might logically ask why universities should be regarded as a separate hierarchy, especially since doing so tends to equate them with the obviously more important government, CCP, PLA, and mass organization hierarchies. In political terms, I would not consider the university hierarchy on a par with the others. However, we can note that the CPR has seen fit to give it "equal treatment," at least by including the appointments and dismissals of top university officials on the same name lists that carry the appointments and dismissals of government officials. In any case, this is a fact worth keeping in mind if we are attempting to view the CPR through Chinese eyes.

It might appear that university officials would be no more than an important subgroup of the propaganda and education "system," and obviously this is often true. On the other hand, a check of the more specialized institutes of higher learning reveals that the careers of their senior officials are frequently oriented toward other systems. For example, officials who have headed the Anhwei Agricultural Institute are more likely to have worked in the agricultural and forestry system both before and after their association with the Anhwei school than they are to have worked in the propaganda and education system. In short, the university hierarchy cuts across systems, though not so markedly as the government hierarchy.

CCP HIERARCHY

Prior to the Cultural Revolution it was customary to describe the CCP as the organization in which relatively few men set basic policies, and the government as the one staffed by large numbers of men who

---

[26] Orleans' study (Washington, D. C.: National Science Foundation, 1960) provides a good introduction to China's scientific establishment, which is an important part of the several hierarchies discussed in this paper. For further information on this subject, see Chu-yuan Cheng, *Scientific and Engineering Manpower in Communist China, 1949–1963* (Washington, D. C.: National Science Foundation, 1965); Chi Wang (comp.), *Mainland China Organizations of Higher Learning in Science and Technology and Their Publications* (Washington, D. C.: Library of Congress, 1961); Amy C. Lee and D. C. Dju Chang (comps.), *A Bibliography of Translations from Mainland Chinese Periodicals in Chemistry, General Science and Technology* (Washington, D. C.: National Academy of Sciences, 1968); John M. H. Lindbeck, "The Organisation and Development of Science," *CQ,* No. 6 (April–June, 1961), pp. 98–132. The Lindbeck article was reprinted in Roderick MacFarquhar (ed.), *China under Mao* (Cambridge, Mass.: M.I.T. Press, 1966). Information on the Academies of Sciences, Agricultural Sciences, and Medical Sciences can be found in most of the personnel directories cited in Appendix B.

implemented these policies. Reflecting this situation, the CCP hierarchy comprises a much smaller number of men working in the
echelons employed in this paper, but the intrinsic importance of the
Party has meant that its personnel have been frequently in the news.
This "high visibility" factor means there is often better biographic
data over time for the CCP man than for his government hierarchy
counterpart(s), and this in turn frequently outweighs the negative
factor of not having the precise appointment lists so often available in
the government hierarchy. After all, it is not very enlightening to have
a man's appointment date if we know little about him over the next
decade. In sum, we know the names and posts of far fewer CCP
personnel than government bureaucrats, but we often know far more
about the activities of the Party man.

As with the government hierarchy, there have been numerous
structural changes in the Party since 1949, but none is a serious
impediment to elite research. The salient changes are found in Klein
and Clark, *Biographic Dictionary*, Appendixes 15, 17, and 52 to 57.

National Level, 1949–56

It is necessary to alter somewhat the periodization scheme to high-
light the Eighth Party Congress, held in September, 1956. Prior to that
time it was not normal practice for the CCP to announce officially its
appointments or elections.[27] To emphasize the paucity of data before
1956, there was not even an "official" listing of the Politburo or
Central Secretariat.[28] Nevertheless, even though the number of names
at the echelons which concern us is not so plentiful before 1956, the
biographic information for the persons involved is excellent. Moreover, unlike so many other levels and echelons, even social background
information is of generally high quality.

National Level, 1956–66

After the Eighth Party Congress in 1956, complete ("systematic")
lists became available for the top echelons of the CCP, namely: (1)
the chairman, vice-chairmen, and general secretary of the Central

[27] We do, of course, have an exact list of the Seventh Central Committee, elected in
June, 1945. However, as the reader may have noticed from Table 55, I have not included
CC membership in any echelon. This is because I do not regard CC membership *per se*
as being important in a functional sense. To put it in another way, a person is elected to
the CC because he is first secretary of a province, not vice versa.

[28] The pre- and post-1956 secretariats should not be confused. The former, headed by
Mao, was a kind of "inner Politburo" and is best likened to the post-1956 Politburo
Standing Committee.

Committee (CC) (who, collectively, form the Politburo Standing Committee); (2) other Politburo members and alternates; (3) secretaries and alternate secretaries of the Central Secretariat; and (4) the secretary, deputy secretaries, and members and alternate members of the Central Control Commission. All of the above have been regularly listed in the *Jen-min shou-ts'e* series and many other sources.

In terms of the Politburo and the Secretariat, the quality of biographic information is about the same as before 1956—excellent. The quality declines somewhat regarding the Control Commission elected in 1956, and it falls off quite sharply when the size of the commission was tripled in 1962.[29]

Names have not been "systematically" released regarding the key officials of the important CC departments, a situation that prevailed both before and after 1956. Nevertheless, the press exposure of these officials has been high, and many of them are well-known figures for whom there is much biographic data. This was particularly true through the 1950's, but by the 1960's the expanding size of the Party bureaucracy brought about the introduction of some relatively lesser known officials, especially among the department deputy directors.

Regional Level, 1949–55 and 1961–66

When the Communists took power in 1949, they already had intact a regional Party apparatus. The most senior regional bureau officials (for example, Lin Piao and Kao Kang) were clearly "national" in importance despite the fact that they were posted away from Peking. Presumably because of their national importance, many of them were already working much of the time in Peking by 1952–53, even though they usually retained their official Party bureau titles until the bureaus were dissolved in 1954–55. Another consistent pattern among the senior regional Party figures is that they uniformly held a multiplicity of concurrent posts spanning the Party, government, PLA, and mass organization hierarchies.

As the lines above suggest, there are high-quality biographic data about the regional Party officials during the 1949–55 period. However, an elite study on this topic must take into consideration the frequent (and sometimes total) absence of the officials in question, especially

---

[29] For a study of this organization see Paul Cocks, "The Role of the Party Control Committee in Communist China," *Papers on China* (Cambridge, Mass.: East Asian Research Center, Harvard University, 1969), pp. 49–96.

among the first two echelons of leadership, from the regions where they nominally served. Similarly, any such study would probably need built-in checks to determine whether the men in the sample were actually functioning in their Party post, or whether they devoted most of their energies to one or more of their concurrent positions in a different hierarchy. This line of thought suggests that the aggregation of data by systems rather than hierarchies may be the best approach at the regional level through 1955.

A special word of caution may be useful regarding the North China Bureau. Probably because of the locale of the bureau headquarters in Peking, one gets the impression that it never reached the importance of the other five regional bureaus. (Much the same impression is gained from an examination of the government hierarchy for North China.) Secondly, the concurrent posts held by the senior North China Bureau officials were often in critically important *national* government posts. For example, Po I-po, the senior secretary, was concurrently minister of finance from 1949 to 1953. In short, it can probably be argued that an elite study of the Party bureaus from 1949 to 1955 would do well to omit the North China Bureau, or that such a study needs special mechanisms to deal with the somewhat maverick nature of this bureau.

In early 1961 the Party re-established the six Party regional bureaus.[30] In general, the remarks above about the 1949–55 period also apply to the post-1961 years, but in the latter period the quality of biographic data is somewhat less thorough.

Provincial-Municipal Level, 1949–66

Biographic data on provincial-municipal first secretaries are quite good, with a few exceptions, but below this echelon there is usually a sharp deterioration of information. Frederick Teiwes has already demonstrated most of the strengths of a provincial elite study, and he has also carefully charted many of the dead ends. (Within the framework of this paper, the Teiwes study covers the first two and a portion of the third echelon of the CCP provincial hierarchy.) However, a study remains to be done from the interesting takeover years to the mid-1950's.

[30] The provinces subordinate to the bureaus were the same as during the 1949–55 period, with one exception: Kiangsi had been under the Central-South China Bureau in the earlier period, but after 1961 it was subordinate to the East China Bureau.

PLA HIERARCHY

Of the critical hierarchies, none is more difficult to handle than the military establishment. In some ways, it is not readily adaptable to the concept of hierarchy used in this paper. For example, in the 1949–54 period such important organs as the General Political Department and such key service arms as the air force were, in the technical sense, subordinate to the government hierarchy; the same applies to the Ministry of National Defense, established in 1954. Similarly, no serious research could be done on the PLA in the 1960's without considering the Military Affairs Committee, a Party hierarchy organ. In this sense, the institutional framework of this paper approximates the military affairs "system" employed by Barnett.

National Level, 1949–66

From the establishment of the CPR to the Cultural Revolution, the PLA headquarters in Peking was dominated by the towering figures of Red Army history—Chu Teh, P'eng Teh-huai, and many others. Many of these men, of course, are of Politburo or near-Politburo status, and consequently there are extremely good biographic data. For the 1954–66 period, John Gittings has aggregated most of the key first- and second-echelon personnel at the national level; moreover, his text contains what is probably the best explanation of the complexities of the PLA hierarchy for the entire period since 1949.[31]

Regional Level, 1949–54

From 1949 to 1954 the PLA regional structure was territorially contiguous with both the CCP and the government hierarchies, that is, there was an East China Military Region, a Northeast China Military Region, and so forth. Moreover, in four of the six regions there were numbered field armies.[32] As already indicated, most of the senior commanders and commissars concurrently held the top posts in the other hierarchies. Many of them, such as Liu Po-ch'eng and Ch'en I, had as much prestige in the Red Army as their military colleagues in Peking. In short, there are very good biographic data on the first two echelons and the quality remains quite high through the third and fourth echelons.

[31] For the aggregations see the appendixes in John Gittings, *The Role of the Chinese Army* (London and New York: Oxford University Press, 1967).

[32] The First Field Army was in the northwest, the second in the southwest, the third in East China, and the fourth in Central-South China.

Regional Level, 1954–66

In the post-1954 period the earlier six military regions were reorganized into thirteen regions. This meant, of course, that the new regions had smaller areas under their jurisdiction, and also that most of the famous regional PLA leaders from the pre-1954 period had gone to Peking. As a consequence, lesser military figures moved into the top echelons of the "new" regional PLA structure, and as a further consequence the biographic data about these men are of a lower quality than those of the pre-1954 period. For the 1954–66 period, cumulative lists exist for the first-echelon commanders and political commissars (see Appendix C). Unfortunately, the same is not true for the second, third, and fourth echelons; no personnel directories reaching to these echelons were prepared until the late 1950's, and it was not long afterward that the lack of access to provincial newspapers precluded good compilations for the regional level. In any event, the biographic data are marginal for the second- through the fourth-echelon leaders.

Provincial-Municipal Level, 1949–54

Military districts (coterminous with provinces) have existed since 1949, but there are marked differences in the types of personnel holding the key posts in the pre- and post-1954 periods. As in the case of the larger regions, the first-echelon provincial commanders and political commissars were very well-known figures who almost always held the key (concurrent) posts in the provincial CCP and government hierarchies, and thus the biographic information is very good. Information is somewhat less adequate for the second-echelon deputy commanders and deputy political commissars, but then it drops off sharply in quality for the third- and fourth-echelon men. Given the present state of our research tools, a 1949–54 PLA provincial-level study would be extremely difficult to undertake because, as demonstrated in Appendix C, there are no directories listing personnel for this period.

Provincial-Municipal Level, 1954–66

With the growth of military professionalism in the mid-1950's, few district commanders held concurrent posts in other hierarchies, and the biographic data about these men are of a lower quality than for the pre-1954 period. On the other hand, there was a strong tendency throughout this period for district political commissars to hold the concurrent post of provincial Party first secretary. As a consequence, biographic data are substantially superior for commissars as compared with commanders. For the lower echelons, however, this period witnessed the influx of many new personnel, with a resulting loss of good biographic data. Moreover, to repeat one comment made about the regional level in an even more forceful manner: no personnel directories for *any* provincial (district) echelons were prepared until the late 1950's, and it was not long afterward that the lack of access to provincial newspapers precluded good compilations for the 1960's.

There are some technical problems in dealing with the PLA. Prior to 1954 one could usually tell with certainty which men were *the* commanders at the regional and provincial (or district) levels. However, since the mid-1950's any of the senior regional or provincial officials may be referred to as "a" commander or as "commanding officers." Compilers of personnel directories have usually unsorted these generic usages, but it often has taken months or years. (The task of singling out the key officials was greatly assisted by the knowledge of the man's military rank, but the task became more complex after ranks were abolished in 1965.) The situation is somewhat better regarding the political commissars, owing in part to the fact that in the late 1950's and early 1960's the Communists frequently designated "first" and "second" political commissars.

Another problem within the PLA hierarchy at all levels is that of determining whether the commander or the political commissar is *the* key official. During the takeover years this was often a moot point, because the commander frequently doubled as the political commissar. From the mid-1950's to the mid-1960's the evidence points to the political commissar as the single most important official, but since the advent of the Cultural Revolution the question has been reopened. The same question, of course, arises when considering the deputy commanders and the deputy political commissars. A commander/political commissar mobility study would be useful.

MASS ORGANIZATION HIERARCHY

National Level, 1949–66

In other hierarchies, there are often specific dates when they underwent a major reorganization—such as the government hierarchy at the inaugural session of the First National People's Congress in September,

1954—but there are no specific benchmarks regarding the mass organizations. Each one was established separately, and each held national congresses (when new officials were elected) at varying dates. Fortunately, most of this information is readily available. Brief organizational histories of most mass organizations are included in the 1950 through the 1957 editions of the *Jen-min shou-ts'e*. Moreover, after 1951 the important meetings of mass organizations are competently covered in the *SCMP* and *Current Background* series.

The complexities of the mass organization hierarchy call for some preliminary observations before assessing the quality of biographic and personnel directory-type information. First, "mass organization" has a twofold meaning. Some of them are more genuinely "mass" or "people's" associations which claim a membership numbering into the millions, of which the All-China Federation of Trade Unions is an example. Others, such as the China Scientific and Technical Association, are more appropriately thought of as professional groups, with highly restricted membership.

The proliferation of mass organizations from 1949 to 1966 is another point to recognize. The growth initially suggests an increasing importance over time for this hierarchy, but closer scrutiny reveals a different picture. The earliest and most important mass organizations flourished during the first decade of the CPR, but they have generally languished since then. For example, the two major youth organizations, the labor federation, and the women's federation were exceptionally active until 1957–58. All four organizations held three national conferences in the 1949–58 period, and on each occasion there was massive press coverage, including complete name lists of the chairmen, vice-chairmen, national committee members, secretaries-general, and so forth. But, to emphasize the point, in the dozen years since 1957–58, neither the labor nor the women's federation has held a single congress, and the few convened by the youth organizations received only marginal press attention.

The proliferation of mass organizations must also be viewed in terms of their functions. As the above examples suggest, most of those established in the early CPR years were *domestically* oriented, and most of them were apparently more important in the 1950's than in the 1960's. Beginning in the middle and late fifties, a number of new mass organizations were created, and more often than not they were oriented toward *foreign* affairs. On a single day in September, 1958, for example, "friendship associations" vis-à-vis no less than ten countries were established. Some of these foreign-oriented organizations have been quite active, but others have been virtually moribund and detailed data are nearly nonexistent.[33]

Another factor to consider is the extraordinary unevenness in importance among the various mass organizations. If a scale of importance were devised for government ministries, a range of one to five would probably suffice, but a one-to-twenty range might be necessary for the sundry mass organizations. Consider the difference between the China Committee for the Promotion of International Trade (virtually an adjunct of the Foreign Trade Ministry) and the Sino-Bulgarian Friendship Association. Similarly, the study of mass organization data must take account of the time factor. For example, the Sino-Soviet Friendship Association was extremely active in the 1950's but virtually dormant afterward.

In general, there is good personnel directory-type information available through the 1950's, and the biographic data are also good. To a considerable degree the quality of data results from the fact that so many mass organization leaders held top posts in other hierarchies. Indeed, in some instances the leading bodies read like a slightly altered version of the CCP Central Committee. A case in point is the Executive Committee of the Sino-Soviet Friendship Association elected in 1949. Because of this situation, an elite study of the mass organization hierarchy in the 1950's is likely to yield slanted or even absurd results if organizational charts are blindly pursued. However, the specialization that has affected the other hierarchies is also a characteristic of the mass organizations, and thus by the 1960's many lesser known figures assumed key posts. As a consequence, the biographic data are of a lower quality than those for the 1950's. Moreover, the decreasing importance of mass organizations in the 1960's (or at least a lessening of press attention) has meant that we have fewer personnel rosters running down through the four echelons. But regardless of these and other factors, no other hierarchy is characterized by such a rich variety of political and social endeavors.

Regional and Provincial-Municipal Levels, 1949–66

Most mass organizations have had regional and provincial-municipal branches. (Following the government hierarchy, regional-level branches

---

[33] The *1965 Jen-min shou-ts'e* lists 57 mass organizations, or triple the number existing in the early years of the CPR. Of these 57 organizations, 33 are oriented toward foreign affairs and 24 toward domestic affairs. However, if the 26 "friendship" associations are deducted, the domestic:foreign ratio becomes 24:7.

of mass organizations were abolished in 1954.) However, at both levels the data readily available are quite scarce. For the most part, one would be forced to undertake the staggering task of consulting the local press to reconstruct the organizational structure and personnel at regional and provincial levels. In brief, given the available collated materials, the researcher is virtually forced to concentrate on the national level for elite studies.

MISCELLANEOUS

Pen Names, Aliases, and Pseudonyms

Pen names, aliases, pseudonyms, and nicknames, which can be the scourge of any pre-1949 study of Chinese personalities, are not a serious problem for the post-1949 period. The long-time Minister of Culture Shen Yen-ping will often be cited by his pen name (Mao Tun), and Teng Ying-ch'ao may occasionally be mentioned as Madame Chou En-lai. But these are the exceptions, and they are usually solved with ease by referring to a who's who.[34] Perhaps the one important exception would be an elite study of the Union of Chinese Writers, but even then no problem would arise unless the researcher attempted to tabulate the writers' pre-1949 works.

Identical Names

It is often assumed there are many identical names. In English transliteration, of course, many "identical" names do appear; but a check of the characters usually reduces this number to a minute fraction, and common sense almost always reduces this fraction to zero. For example, the Wang Li-kuang who is the commercial counselor of the embassy in Warsaw most assuredly will not be the Wang Li-kuang who is director of the Kiangsu Agricultural Department.

Standard Telegraphic Code Numbers

In printed versions of monitored radio broadcasts, and in indexes to English-language personnel directories, personal names are often followed by four-digit numbers. For example, the number for the family name "Wang" is 3769. These are Standard Telegraphic Code (STC) numbers which, as the name suggests, were created to send telegrams by using a number to represent a character.[35]

---

[34] The glossary-index to Klein and Clark, *Biographic Dictionary*, contains the alternate names of many of the major CCP leaders since the founding of the Party in 1921.

[35] STC handbooks are available in Hong Kong and Japan for a few cents. Surprisingly,

"Reading" Japanese

Implicit throughout these pages is the assumption that those who can read Chinese can also "read" the oft-cited Japanese who's whos and personnel directories. Fortunately, with the rare exceptions, the Japanese have followed Chinese institutional terminology, and thus one can "read" Japanese personnel directories virtually to the 100 per cent mark. In terms of the who's whos, there are minor problems, but anyone who reads Chinese can still usually reach the 90 per cent or above mark. Even this can be improved upon by learning a few of the Japanese *hiragana* (for example, the Japanese *"no"* indicates the possessive). The one real difficulty would arise for an elite study with a high input of foreign affairs information. The Japanese write most foreign proper and place names with *katakana*, which one would have to master in order to read them. (As a stopgap, one can consult a table of *katakana* which is available in any good Japanese-English dictionary.)

Ranking by Political Importance and Number of Strokes

Most lists of Chinese Communist personalities are ranked by political importance or by the number of strokes in the name (the latter being the Chinese version of alphabetical order). In general, political ranking is reserved for the highest CCP, government, and PLA personalities. Prior to the Cultural Revolution, for example, the Politburo was listed in this way. However, if the occasion is fitting, changes will be made. For example, if a foreign parliamentary delegation visits China, Politburo members might be listed below other men—including even non-CCP persons—if the Politburo member ostensibly holds a lower post in the NPC. Thus, NPC Standing Committee Vice-Chairman Chang Chih-chung would precede Politburo member Liu Po-ch'eng, who is only a member of the NPC Standing Committee.

The Chinese almost always indicate with a parenthetical note when they list names according to the number of strokes. This is done, for example, in the *Jen-min shou-ts'e*. A word of caution for comparisons of roughly similar pre- and post-1956 name lists: in 1956 the CPR

---

they are not easily available in standard reference works in the United States. However, there is an STC list in the first volume of *Modern Chinese-English Technical and General Dictionary* (New York: McGraw-Hill, 1963).

began to use simplified characters, and thus a man who appeared in the fiftieth slot in a 1954 list might be in twelfth place on a 1958 list.

Multiplicity of Deputy Heads of Organizations

Virtually all Chinese organizations have more than one deputy head (for example, vice-ministers, deputy directors, deputy commanders, and deputy leaders of delegations). The problem is compounded because Chinese does not have indefinite or definite articles, and thus one cannot be certain if he is reading about "the" or "a" vice-minister. Moreover, who's whos do not distinguish between "the" or "a." Within the framework of this paper, the multiplicity of deputy heads is no problem in those instances where "systematic" information is available (such as lists of vice-ministers), but it can be a problem where the data were assembled in "random" fashion (as deputy secretaries of provincial CCP committees). Obviously, there can be no absolute rules to govern this situation, but—to repeat—the supposition should always be that there is more than one deputy head.

Obituaries

Prior to the Cultural Revolution, the CPR faithfully recorded the deaths of its elite, with the obituary normally appearing in the press a day or two after the death. Unfortunately, these have seldom revealed new information. Of interest, however, is the fact that those persons out of political favor will usually receive a "normal" obituary. For example, an obituary was published for ex-Yunnan warlord Lung Yun, even though he had been named as a "rightist." Parenthetically, where "systematic" name lists exist and are published in the *Jen-min shou-ts'e,* the names of those who have died are underlined with a heavy rule (for example, Politburo members Lin Po-ch'ü and Lo Jung-huan). Also, obituaries are an integral part of the ACG file.

Specialized Periodicals

There are hundreds of specialized periodicals which can often aid elite studies. For example, *Cheng-fa yen-chiu* (Political and Legal Research) might be useful for a study pertaining to political science and law. Many journals which are the specific organs of mass organizations are listed in the descriptions of the mass organizations in the *Jen-min shou-ts'e* (especially the editions for the mid-1950's).

The Library of Congress, URI, and many major Asian study centers in the United States have published listings of their periodical and newspaper holdings. *Current Background*, No. 436 (January 30, 1957) and No. 478 (October 28, 1957), respectively, contain lists of periodicals and newspapers published in China, but this does not mean they are necessarily available outside of the mainland.

Nominality

The subject of nominality has been referred to above in several places, especially in regard to the mass organization hierarchy. There is obviously no sure-fire way to be certain that a given post or activity is "nominal" and that another is "real," and therefore the following can only be viewed as general observations.

Nominality by hierarchies. Nominality differs from hierarchy to hierarchy. As a general proposition, nominality virtually never occurs within the CCP. The one exception might be the retention of a few extremely elderly Party veterans as CC members. There has been some degree of nominality in both the government and PLA hierarchies, particularly in the early CPR years when the Communists emphasized the "united front" aspect of their rule. In the government, most nominal position-holders were politicians who, though not Communists, had in some fashion displayed their dislike of Kuomintang (KMT) rule. Most nominal position-holders in the PLA are ex-Nationalist generals who "rose up" against the KMT at the eleventh hour in 1949. There appears to have been some degree of nominality among top university officials, but the question has not been studied in detail. Finally, to repeat, there has been considerable nominality in position-holding in the mass organization hierarchy.

Nominality because of multiple offices. Particularly in the early CPR years, many senior figures held concurrent posts in many organizations. Ch'en Yün, for example, was the top Party and government economic expert and concurrently the chairman of the All-China Federation of Labor. The available record suggests that Ch'en's labor post was largely nominal. Nominality by position most generally occurs in connection with the very top figures, and is especially marked within the mass organization hierarchy. (In such instances, the "real" leader will often be one of the vice-chairmen or the secretary-general.) Increasing specialization has tended to erode multiple office-holding.

Nominality because of Non-CCP Status. It is generally accepted that the many positions held by non-Communists are often—but by no means always—nominal. Since the establishment of the CPR, for example, many non-Communists have held ministerial posts. In such cases there will invariably be a vice-minister who is a Party member of long standing. It would seem reasonable that the degree of nominality may be in proportion to the skills which the non-Communist brings to his office. Li Szu-kuang, for example, has perhaps more "real" authority as minister of geology, because of his training in this field, than the now-purged Minister of Timber Industry Lo Lung-chi, who had no experience in this work.

Nominality through time. To re-emphasize a point implicit in the above three subsections: nominality has diminished over time since 1949, principally because of the decline of the united front and the growth of specialization. The reverse situation can occur if a position was held in a relatively inactive organization which *later* became very active. An example of this is the Sino-Albanian Friendship Association, which seemed ephemeral when established in 1958, but which became quite active in the 1960's with increasing Sino-Albanian contacts.

Nominality through absence from post. In a number of instances, especially in the 1952–54 period, key leaders held posts in the regions or provinces but in fact spent most of their time in Peking. This situation rarely occurs at the national level.

Nominality as delegation leader. The Chinese have sent thousands of delegations abroad since 1949. The nature of many such groups will call for a leader who, in the Chinese Communist political milieu, can probably be regarded as a nominal leader. For example, the novelist Mao Tun, who heads the Union of Chinese Writers, has led writers' groups abroad, but he has always been accompanied by a senior Party figure who works in cultural affairs.

Historical nominality. One of the less debatable forms of nominal posts are those associated with historical occasions. Membership on an *ad hoc* committee to celebrate the 1911 revolution is an example. Such committees are set up to give a sense of continuity with pre-Communist revolutionary events, and the members of such committees will often be very elderly men no longer active in political life, or sometimes the membership will include the wives of men associated with the event in question. The fact that Madame Sun Yat-sen is one of the two vice-chairmen of the CPR is another example of historic nominality.

Bias toward Foreign Affairs

Who's whos on China generally have a bias toward foreign affairs. For example, a who's who will exhaustively list all trips abroad for the man in question, but will often ignore travels within China to inspect an industrial enterprise or a model commune. NCNA is in part responsible for this bias because it covers with meticulous detail the endless comings and goings of visitors to China, most of whom are feted in one fashion or another by senior Chinese leaders.

APPENDIX A

WHO'S WHOS

The following list of who's whos includes the better works and omits the marginal ones and those which are out of date. For a more inclusive list, see Peter Berton and Eugene Wu, *Contemporary China: A Research Guide* (Stanford, Calif.: The Hoover Institution, 1967), pp. 160 ff.

1. *Who's Who in Communist China*. Hong Kong: URI, 1966. Revised edition, Volume I (1969) and Volume II (1970). The 1966 edition contains 1,200 biographies; the revised edition contains 2,837. This is the most convenient English-language who's who available. The pre-1949 material is often marginal, but at least a serious effort was made to exploit important collections of reminiscences published in China since 1949 which deal with the early history of the CCP. Like many who's whos, the takeover period (1949–50) is given only scanty treatment, but from the early 1950's to the late 1960's there is an abundance of information. The 1966 edition contained scores of factual errors, but many of them were corrected in the revised edition.

2. *Gendai chūgoku jinmei jiten* (Who's Who of Contemporary China[36]). Tokyo: Kazan Kai, 1966. From 7,000 entries in the 1957 edition, this book has gone to 12,000 in the 1966 edition. In many respects this is the best available who's who. The material is drawn from the files of the Japanese Foreign Ministry, but it is clear that archival materials in Japan on early CCP history have been largely neglected. Thus, like the URI who's who, it is weak in terms of pre-1949 information. Similarly, it is of marginal use for the takeover

[36] Translated elsewhere in this volume as "A Biographical Dictionary of Contemporary Chinese."—ED.

period. On the other hand, it is reliable and comprehensive from the early 1950's to the mid-1960's.

3. Kuo Hua-lun (ed.), *Chung-kung jen-ming lu* (Who's Who of Chinese Communists [37]). Taipei: Institute of International Relations, 1967. Comprising 2,013 entries and a supplement of 89 entries, this volume is very useful, but it also contains a lot of unsupported gossip. Under the title *Chinese Communist Who's Who,* an English translation of this work was published in 1970–71.

4. Huang Chen-hsia (ed.), *Chung-kung chün-jen chih* (Who's Who of Chinese Communist Military Figures). Hong Kong: Research Institute of Contemporary History, 1968. This volume, containing 726 entries, uses *Mao's Generals* as the translation of the title. Reviews of this work appear in *CQ,* No. 40 (October–December, 1969), pp. 164–66, and *Issues and Studies,* VII, No. 2 (November, 1970), 80–90.

5. Chu-yuan Cheng, *Scientific and Engineering Manpower in Communist China, 1949–1963* (Washington, D.C.: National Science Foundation, 1965). Appendix IV in this volume contains information on 1,200 scientists and engineers. It is especially useful for education and career specialization, but marginal otherwise.

APPENDIX B

Personnel Directories and Related Items

1. *1950 Jen-min nien-chien* (People's Yearbook, 1950). Hong Kong: Ta-kung shu-chü, January, 1950. This also contains a who's who section.

2. *1950 Jen-min shou-ts'e* (*JMST*) (People's Handbook, 1950). Shanghai: Ta-kung pao, January, 1950.

3. *Tu-pao shou-ts'e* (Newspaper Readers' Handbook). Hankow: Ch'iang-chiang jih-pao, August, 1950.

4. "Regional Organization of China, December 1950," *CB,* No. 37 (December 7, 1950).

5. "Chinese Communist Party Regional Bureaus, January 1951," *CB,* No. 48 (January 2, 1951).

6. *1951 JMST.* Shanghai: Ta-kung pao, February, 1951.

7. "Chinese Communist Military Leaders," *CB,* No. 111 (August 29, 1951).

[37] Translated elsewhere in this volume as "Biographical Dictionary of Chinese Communists."—ED.

8. "The Central Organization of the Communist Party of China (November 1951)," *CB*, No. 137 (November 15, 1951).

9. "The Evolution of the North China Region (1948–1952)," *CB*, No. 161 (February 20, 1952).

10. *A Guide to New China*. 2nd rev. ed.; Peking: Foreign Languages Press, March, 1952.

11. "Pattern of Control: The Regional Organization of Communist China (April 1952)," *CB*, No. 170 (April 8, 1952).

12. "The Inner Mongolia Autonomous Region (1949–1952)," *CB*, No. 190 (July 22, 1952).

13. "The Central Organization of the Communist Party in China (July 1952)," *CB*, No. 192 (July 24, 1952).

14. *1952 JMST*. Shanghai: Ta-kung pao, August, 1952.

15. *Hsin ming-tz'u tz'u-tien* (New Terminology Dictionary). Shanghai: Ch'un-ming ch'u-pan she, August, 1952.

16. "Leading Officials of CPG Government Administration Council," *SCMP*, No. 468 (December 9, 1952). Corrections and additions to this source are in *SCMP*, No. 479 (December 24, 1952).

17. "List of Chairmen and Mayors of Provincial and Municipal People's Governments," *SCMP*, No. 474 (December 17, 1952).

18. *A Guide to New China*. 3rd ed.; Peking: Foreign Languages Press, May, 1953.

19. "Regional Administration in Communist China (May 1953)," *CB*, No. 245 (May 25, 1953).

20. *1953 JMST*. Tientsin: Ta-kung pao, August, 1953.

21. U.S. State Department, *Directory of Party and Government Officials in Communist China*. Biographic Directory No. 234. Washington, D. C., August 1, 1953.

22. "Government Directory of Top National Positions, People's Republic of China (October 1, 1953)," *CB*, No. 263 (October 1, 1953).

23. John Gittings, *The Role of the Chinese Army*. London and New York: Oxford University Press, 1967. See the appendixes.

24. *1955 JMST*. Tientsin: Ta-kung pao, January, 1955.

25. "Directory of Top National Positions in Chinese Communist Party, Government, and Armed Forces (March 1, 1955)," *CB*, No. 316 (March 7, 1955).

26. "Chinese Communist Military Honors," *CB*, No. 368 (November 15, 1955).

27. *1956 JMST*. Tientsin: Ta-kung pao, May, 1956.

28. "Directory of Top National Positions in the Government and Armed Forces of Communist China (July 1956)," *CB*, No. 404 (July 26, 1956).

29. "CCP Eighth National Congress: XVII—Conclusion," *CB*, No. 426 (September 9, 1956).

30. *1957 JMST*. Peking: Ta-kung pao, April, 1957.

31. *Handbook on People's China*. Peking: Foreign Languages Press, April, 1957.

32. "Position Directory of Ranking Personnel in the Government and Armed Forces of Communist China (June 1957)," *CB*, No. 461 (June 29, 1957).

33. *Chūka jinmin kyōwakoku soshikibetsu jinmei hyō* (Organizational Directory of the People's Republic of China). Tokyo: Naikaku Chosashitsu (Cabinet Research Council), 1957.

34. *1958 JMST*. Peking: Ta-kung pao, May, 1958.

35. "Directory of Top National Positions in Chinese Communist Party, Government, and Armed Forces," *CB*, No. 513 (July 16, 1958). This has a name index.

36. *Chūka jinmin kyōwakoku soshikibetsu jinmei hyō*. Tokyo: Naikaku Chosashitsu, 1959.

37. "Leading Personnel of the Chinese Communist Regime: Before and after the 1st Session of the 2nd National People's Congress, April 1959," *CB*, No. 578 (May 15, 1959).

38. *1959 JMST*. Peking: Ta-kung pao, September, 1959.

39. "Leading Personnel of the State Council in Communist China," *CB*, No. 597 (October 8, 1959).

40. U.S. State Department, *Directory of Party and Government Officials of Communist China*. Biographic Directory No. 271. Washington, D. C., July 20, 1960.

41. *1960 JMST*. Peking: Ta-kung pao, September, 1960.

42. "Directory of Chinese Communist Leadership," *Biographic Information*, Report No. 1, November 29, 1960. Hong Kong: U.S. Consulate-General. This is updated in *Biographic Information*, Report No. 1-a, May 1, 1961.

43. *1961 JMST*. Peking: Ta-kung pao, December, 1961.

44. *Chūka jinmin kyōwakoku soshikibetsu jinmei hyō*. Tokyo: Naikaku Chosashitsu, 1962.

45. "Directory of Chinese Communist Leadership," *Biographic In-*

formation, Report No. 2, May 9, 1962. Hong Kong: U.S. Consulate-General.

46. "The Reshuffle of Chinese Communist Party Personnel in 1961," URS, XXVII, No. 21 (June 12, 1962).

47. *1962 JMST.* Peking: Ta-kung pao, August, 1962.

48. *Directory of Chinese Communist Officials,* No. BA 63–7, May, 1963 (U.S. government publication).

49. "Latest Information on Party and Government Personnel in Kwangtung Province," *Biographic Information,* Report No. 3, May 23, 1963. Hong Kong: U.S. Consulate-General.

50. "Latest Information on Party and Government Personnel in Canton Municipality," *Biographic Information,* Report No. 4, May 24, 1963. Hong Kong: U.S. Consulate-General.

51. *1963 JMST.* Peking: Ta-kung pao, October, 1963.

52. *Chūka jinmin kyōwakoku chihōbetsu soshiki jinmei hyō* (Directory of Local Organizations in the People's Republic of China). Tokyo: Ajia Kenkyujō (Asian Research Institute), 1963.

53. *Chūka jinmin kyōwakoku soshikibetsu jinmei hyō.* Tokyo: Naikaku Chosashitsu, 1964.

54. "Changes in Chinese Communist Personnel," URS, XXXV, Nos. 6, 8, 9 (April–May, 1964).

55. *1964 JMST.* Peking: Ta-kung pao, October, 1964.

56. "Leading Personnel of the Chinese Communist Regime: Before and after the First Session of the Third National People's Congress, December 21, 1964–January 4, 1965," *CB,* No. 752 (February 1, 1965).

57. Michel Oksenberg, "Paths to Leadership in Communist China: A Comparison of Second Echelon Positions in 1955 and 1965," *Current Scene,* III, No. 24 (August 1, 1965).

58. *1965 JMST.* Peking: Ta-kung pao, October, 1965.

59. *Directory of Chinese Communist Officials,* No. A 66–8, March, 1966 (U.S. government publication).

60. *Who's Who in Communist China.* Hong Kong: URI, 1966. See the appendixes.

61. "Who's Who in Peking? Leadership and Organization in the Chinese Party, Government and Army," *Current Scene,* IV, No. 15 (August 8, 1966).

62. *Chūka jinmin kyōwakoku soshikibetsu jinmei hyō.* Tokyo: Naikaku Chosashitsu, 1966.

APPENDIX C

SOURCES BY HIERARCHIES

TABLE 60

GOVERNMENT HIERARCHY

Level	1949–September, 1954	September, 1954–Spring, 1966
National First echelon	1, 2, 3, 6, 10, 14, 16, 18, 20, 21, 22	24, 25, 27, 28, 30, 31, 32, 33, 34, 35, 36, 37, 38, 39, 40, 41, 42, 43, 44, 45, 47, 48, 51, 53, 54, 55, 56, 58, 59, 60, 61, 62
Second echelon	1, 2, 3, 6, 10, 14, 16, 18, 20, 21, 22	24, 25, 27, 28, 30, 31, 32, 33, 34, 35, 36, 37, 39, 40, 41, 42, 43, 44, 45, 47, 48, 51, 53, 54, 55, 56, 58, 59, 60, 62
Third echelon	1, 6, 10, 14, 18, 20, 21	33, 36, 40, 44, 48, 53, 59, 62
Fourth echelon	1, 6, 10, 14, 18, 20, 21	33, 36, 40, 44, 48, 53, 59, 62
Regional First echelon	1, 2, 3, 4, 6, 9, 10, 11, 14, 18, 19, 20, 21	
Second echelon	1, 2, 3, 4, 6, 9, 10, 11, 14, 18, 19, 20, 21	
Third echelon	1, 2, 3, 4, 6, 9, 11, 14, 19, 20, 21	
Fourth echelon	3, 6, 14, 21	
Provincial-Municipal First echelon	1, 2, 3, 6, 9, 12, 14, 15, 17, 19, 20, 21	24, 27, 30, 33, 34, 36, 38, 40, 41, 42, 43, 44, 45, 47, 48, 49, 50, 51, 52, 53, 54, 55, 58, 59, 60, 62

TABLE 60 (*Continued*)

Level	1949–September, 1954	September, 1954–Spring, 1966
Second echelon	1, 2, 3, 6, 9, 12, 14, 15, 17, 19, 20, 21	24, 27, 30, 33, 34, 36, 38, 40, 41, 42, 43, 44, 45, 47, 48, 49, 50, 51, 52, 53, 54, 55, 58, 59, 60, 62
Third echelon	1, 3, 12, 19, 21	40, 48, 49, 50, 52, 59
Fourth echelon	1, 3, 12, 21	40, 48, 49, 50, 52, 59

TABLE 61

CCP HIERARCHY

National	1949–56	1956–66
First echelon	2, 8, 13, 18, 21, 25	29, 30, 31, 33, 34, 35, 36, 38, 40, 41, 42, 43, 44, 45, 47, 48, 51, 53, 54, 55, 58, 59, 60, 61, 62
Second echelon	2, 8, 13, 21, 25	29, 30, 31, 33, 34, 35, 36, 38, 40, 41, 42, 43, 44, 45, 47, 48, 51, 53, 54, 55, 58, 59, 60, 61, 62
Third echelon	2, 8, 13, 21, 25	29, 30, 31, 33, 34, 35, 36, 38, 40, 41, 42, 43, 44, 45, 46, 47, 48, 51, 53, 54, 55, 58, 59, 60, 62
Fourth echelon		29, 30, 31, 33, 34, 35, 36, 38, 40, 41, 42, 43, 44, 45, 47, 48, 51, 53, 54, 55, 58, 59, 60, 62

Regional	1949–55	1961–66
First echelon	5, 8, 9, 11, 13, 21	44, 45, 46, 48, 53, 54, 57, 59, 60, 61, 62
Second echelon	5, 8, 9, 11, 13, 21	44, 45, 46, 48, 53, 54, 57, 59, 60, 62
Third echelon	9, 11, 21	44, 46, 48, 53, 54, 57, 59, 60, 62

Regional	1949–55	1961–66
Fourth echelon	21	48, 53, 54, 59, 62

Provincial-Municipal		1949–66
First echelon	8, 9, 12, 13, 21, 33, 36, 40, 42, 44, 45, 46, 48, 49, 50, 52, 53, 54, 59, 60, 62	
Second echelon	9, 12, 21, 33, 36, 40, 44, 46, 48, 49, 50, 52, 53, 54, 59, 60, 62	
Third echelon	12, 21, 33, 36, 40, 44, 46, 48, 49, 50, 52, 53, 54, 59, 60, 62	
Fourth echelon	21, 33, 36, 40, 44, 48, 49, 50, 52, 53, 59, 62	

TABLE 62

PLA HIERARCHY

National	1949–66
First echelon	1, 2, 3, 6, 7, 14, 18, 20, 21, 23, 25, 26, 28, 32, 33, 35, 36, 40, 42, 44, 45, 48, 53, 59, 60, 61, 62
Second echelon	7, 21, 23, 25, 26, 28, 32, 33, 35, 36, 40, 42, 44, 45, 48, 53, 59, 60, 62
Third echelon	23, 33, 36, 40, 44, 48, 53, 62
Fourth echelon	33, 36, 40, 44, 48, 53, 62

Regional	1949–54	1954–66
First echelon	1, 3, 7, 9, 11, 21, 23	23, 26, 36, 40, 42, 44, 45, 48, 53, 59, 60, 61, 62
Second echelon	3, 11	36, 40, 44, 48, 53, 59, 60, 62
Third echelon	3	36, 40, 44, 48, 53, 59, 62

TABLE 62 (*Continued*)

Regional	1949–54	1954–66
Fourth echelon	3	40, 44, 48, 53, 59, 62

Provincial-Municipal	1949–54	1954–66
First echelon	1, 9, 12	26, 33, 36, 40, 44, 48, 52, 53, 59, 62
Second echelon	12	26, 33, 36, 40, 44, 48, 52, 53, 59, 62
Third echelon	12	36, 40, 44, 48, 52, 53, 59, 62
Fourth echelon		36, 40, 44, 48, 52, 53, 59, 62

TABLE 63

Mass Organization Hierarchy

National	1949–66
First echelon	1, 2, 3, 6, 10, 14, 18, 20, 21, 24, 27, 30, 31, 33, 34, 36, 38, 40, 41, 42, 43, 44, 45, 47, 48, 51, 53, 55, 58, 59, 61, 62
Second echelon	1, 2, 3, 6, 10, 14, 18, 20, 21, 24, 27, 30, 31, 33, 34, 36, 38, 40, 41, 42, 43, 44, 45, 47, 48, 51, 53, 55, 58, 59, 62
Third echelon	1, 2, 3, 6, 14, 20, 21, 24, 27, 30, 33, 36, 38, 40, 41, 44, 47, 48, 51, 53, 55, 58, 59, 62
Fourth echelon	1, 2, 3, 6, 14, 20, 21, 24, 27, 30, 33, 36, 40, 44, 47, 48, 51, 53, 55, 59, 62

Regional	1949–54
First echelon	14, 21
Second echelon	21

Regional	1949–54			
Third echelon				
Fourth echelon				

Provincial-Municipal	1949–66			
First echelon	20, 27, 52, 59			
Second echelon	52, 59			
Third echelon	52			
Fourth echelon				

TABLE 64

UNIVERSITY HIERARCHY

Level	1949–66			
National				
First echelon	2, 6, 10, 18, 33, 36, 40, 48, 59, 62			
Second echelon	6, 33, 36, 40, 48, 59, 62			
Third echelon				
Fourth echelon				
Regional				
First echelon				
Second echelon				

TABLE 64 (*Continued*)

Regional		
Third echelon		
Fourth echelon		
Provincial-Municipal		
First echelon		
Second echelon		
Third echelon		
Fourth echelon		

Index

CONTRIBUTORS

ROBERT A. SCALAPINO. Born in the United States. Professor of political science at the University of California, Berkeley. Member of the Joint Committee for Contemporary China of the American Council of Learned Societies and the Social Science Research Council; chairman of the Subcommittee on Chinese Politics. Has also served on the Advisory Panel on China to the United States Department of State; first chairman of the National Committee on U.S.–China Relations. Editor of *Asian Survey* and author of numerous articles and books on China and other political societies of East Asia.

RICHARD BAUM. Born in the United States. Associate professor of political science at the University of California, Los Angeles, and resident consultant for the Rand Corporation. Coauthor of *Ssu-ch'ing: The Socialist Education Movement of 1962–1966* (1968); editor of *China in Ferment: Perspectives on the Cultural Revolution* (1971); and contributor to *The Cultural Revolution in China* (1971).

GORDON A. BENNETT. Born in the United States. Assistant professor of government at the University of Texas. Coauthor of *Red Guard: The Political Biography of Dai Hsiao-ai* (1971).

HEATH B. CHAMBERLAIN. Born in the United States. Assistant professor of political science at the University of British Columbia.

PARRIS H. CHANG. Born in Taiwan. Assistant professor of political science at Pennsylvania State University. Author of a number of articles in *Problems of Communism, The China Quarterly, Orbis, Current Scene,* and other journals.

JUNE DREYER. Born in the United States. Assistant professor of political science at Miami University, Oxford, Ohio. Studied in Hong Kong as a Kendall Fellow of Radcliffe College and in Japan under a Harvard Travelling Fellowship. Author of articles in *The China Quarterly, Current Scene, Pacific Affairs,* and *Far Eastern Economic Review.*

VICTOR C. FALKENHEIM. Born in the United States. Member of the Department of Political Economy, Scarborough College, University of Toronto. Field research in Taiwan and Hong Kong, 1967–69.

Sidney Leonard Greenblatt. Born in the United States. Member of the Department of Sociology, Drew University. Editor of the quarterly journal, *Chinese Sociology and Anthropology*.

Donald W. Klein. Born in the United States. Research associate and lecturer in government in the East Asian Institute, Columbia University. Coauthor of *Biographic Dictionary of Chinese Communism, 1921–1965* (1971); author of a number of articles for *The China Quarterly* and other periodicals.

Ronald N. Montaperto. Born in the United States. Assistant professor of political science, Indiana University. Field research in Taiwan, 1966–68, and in Hong Kong, 1968–69. Coauthor of *Red Guard: The Political Biography of Dai Hsiao-ai* (1971).

Thomas W. Robinson. Born in the United States. Visiting fellow at the Council on Foreign Relations. For six years a member of the research staff of the Social Science Department at the Rand Corporation. Editor of *The Cultural Revolution in China* (1971); author of *Lin Piao: A Political Biography* (forthcoming).

Derek J. Waller. Born in the United Kingdom. Assistant professor of political science, Vanderbilt University. Author of *The Government and Politics of Communist China* (1971); coauthor of *Stasis and Change in Revolutionary Elites: A Comparative Analysis of the 1956 Party Central Committees in China and the USSR* (1970).

Lynn T. White III. Graduate student in the Department of Political Science and member of the Center for Chinese Studies at the University of California, Berkeley. Field research in Hong Kong and Japan. Contributor to *The City in Communist China* (1971).

William W. Whitson. Born in the United States. Senior social scientist on China at the Rand Corporation. Formerly, political analyst of Mainland China and Far Eastern affairs in the American Consulate-General, Hong Kong, and member of policy planning staff and the systems analysis staff in the Office of the Secretary of Defense. Author of *The Chinese Communist High Command, 1927–71: A History of Communist Military-Politics* (1972), and of articles in *Asian Survey* and *The China Quarterly*.

ELITES IN THE PEOPLE'S REPUBLIC OF CHINA
Edited with an Introduction by ROBERT A. SCALAPINO

Fourteen prominent scholars examine power in Mainland China: who holds it at national and local levels, how it is allocated and exercised, and what the results are in terms of policies, programs, and goals. More specifically, this is a study of elites—political, military, and intellectual—groups within Communist Chinese society distinguished by the authority they command and the power they can wield in the decision-making and enforcing process.

In the opening essay, Gordon A. Bennett summarizes the current state of elite studies, their main trends and yet unsolved problems. Specific studies begin with elites on the national level. Derek Waller analyzes the character of the national Party elite from the Kiangsi Soviet period to 1956, and Robert Scalapino continues this examination from 1956 to 1969. Thomas W. Robinson completes the section with a timely study of the enigmatic Lin Piao.

From the national level the studies turn to subnational elites. Victor C. Falkenheim's essay on the Fukien provincial leadership is followed by Heath B. Chamberlain's examination of the corresponding elements in Tientsin, Shanghai, and Canton in the years 1949-53. Lynn T. White III contributes a similar study of the leadership in Shanghai, 1954-69.

In pointing up more specific elite groups, William W. Whitson, June Dreyer, and Sidney L. Greenblatt focus respectively on the military elite, elites involved in minority work, and the intellectual elite at Peking University.

Elite behavior under stress can reveal important characteristics of such groups. Therefore, actions of provincial Party leaders in response to the Cultural Revolution are examined by Parris H. Chang, while Richard Baum limits the same subject to the period of the most intensive Red Guard assault, 1966-67. Ronald N. Montaperto presents a single student leader's account of events during the early period of the Cultural Revolution and his reactions to them. Donald W. Klein concludes the volume with a critical analysis of the sources for elite studies and biographical materials on China.

ROBERT A. SCALAPINO is professor of political science at the University of California, Berkeley.

Studies in Chinese Government and Politics III
First paperback edition, 1972
Also available in cloth, $15.00

UNIVERSITY OF WASHINGTON PRESS
Seattle and London